Fundamentals of Financial Planning

Huebner School Series

Gary K. Stone, Editor

Group Health Insurance
Burton T. Beam, Jr.

Readings in Financial Planning
David M. Cordell (ed.)

Fundamentals of Financial Planning
David M. Cordell (ed.)

Readings in Income Taxation
James F. Ivers III (ed.)

McGill's Life Insurance
Edward E. Graves (ed.)

McGill's Legal Aspects of Life Insurance
Edward E. Graves and Burke A. Christensen (eds.)

Group Benefits: Basic Concepts and Alternatives
Burton T. Beam, Jr.

Planning for Retirement Needs
Kenn Beam Tacchino and David A. Littell

Readings in Wealth Accumulation Planning
The American College Faculty (eds.)

Fundamentals of Estate Planning
Constance J. Fontaine (ed.)

Estate Planning Applications
Ted Kurlowicz (ed.)

Planning for Business Owners and Professionals
Ted Kurlowicz, James F. Ivers III, and John J. McFadden

Financial Planning Applications
William J. Ruckstuhl and Thomas P. Langdon

The Impact of the Political and Regulatory Process on Life Insurance
Jon S. Hanson

Financial Decision Making at Retirement
David A. Littell, Kenn Beam Tacchino, and David M. Cordell

The Practitioner's Guide to Advanced Pension Topics
David A. Littell and Kenn Beam Tacchino

Executive Compensation
John J. McFadden (ed.)

Huebner School Series

Fundamentals of Financial Planning

Fourth Edition

David M. Cordell, Editor

The American College/***Bryn Mawr, Pennsylvania***

This publication is designed to provide accurate and authoritative information about the subject covered. While every precaution has been taken in the preparation of this material, the editor and The American College assume no liability for damages resulting from the use of the information contained in this publication. The American College is not engaged in rendering legal, accounting, or other professional advice. If legal or other expert advice is required, the services of an appropriate professional should be sought.

Library of Congress Catalog Card Number 98-74662
ISBN 1-57996-013-8

Printed in the United States of America

To my beloved wife, Martha Elizabeth Salter Cordell

Contents

Preface

Financial planning is a rapidly evolving, multidisciplinary profession. This book introduces the process, tools, and basic concepts of the profession.

The first three chapters describe the financial planning environment. Chapter one explains that financial planning is a six-step process and reveals the components of a comprehensive plan. It also traces the evolution of the profession and discusses opportunities for financial planners and consumer needs for financial planning.

Chapter 2 discusses important federal regulations that affect financial planners, especially the Investment Advisers Act of 1940. Chapter 3 presents ethics and professionalism for financial planners with particular attention to the codes of ethics of The American College, the Society of Financial Service Professionals (formerly the American Society of CLU & ChFC), the International Association for Financial Planning, and the Certified Financial Planner Board of Standards.

The next five chapters present tools used in financial planning. Chapter 4 shows how planners can serve clients better by learning to communicate more effectively with them. In chapter 5 the reader learns how to evaluate client risk tolerance, which is critical in determining investment suitability. Chapters 6 and 7 present basic and advanced time value of money concepts that are used in many aspects of financial planning. Chapter 8 explores the constantly changing concept of information technology as it relates to the computer hardware and software needs of financial planners.

Chapters 9 through 14 introduce readers to important subdisciplines within financial planning. In chapter 9, basic concepts of income taxation are presented with an emphasis on tax planning. Chapters 10 and 11 discuss insurance planning, including the risk management process and insurance coverages. In chapter 12 an introduction to investment planning describes categories of investments and basic risk/return concepts. Chapter 13 is an overview of estate planning basics with an emphasis on preserving the client's wealth. In chapter 14 retirement planning concepts are addressed, including calculation of retirement needs, types of tax-qualified plans, and social security and medicare programs.

Chapter 15 is a sample financial planning case that provides a narrative fact pattern and actual output from commercial software.

Readers with limited knowledge of personal financial statements will benefit from appendix A, which describes the basics of the personal balance sheet and budget, including an introduction to cash management.

As this preface and the book's title suggest, this material represents a beginning. Several of the chapters address topics that are covered in much greater detail in other books in the Huebner School Series and in courses by The American College. I encourage readers to master financial planning basics by studying the material judiciously and to keep this book for future reference. Remember, though, that it is only one step on the career path of a financial services professional. The need to pursue more knowledge never ends.

Acknowledgments

Publication of this book required the collaborative efforts of the authors as well as many other individuals. I especially thank Susan Doherty, who typed the manuscript, and Elizabeth B. Fahrig, who edited the manuscript. I also thank Keith de Pinho for preparing a glossary, Jane R. Hassinger for helping to format the mathematical and other appendixes, and Suzanne Walsh Rettew for providing editorial support. Many other members of the faculty and staff of The American College contributed in countless ways, and I offer my appreciation to all of them.

David M. Cordell, PhD, CFA, CFP, CLU
Associate Professor of Finance
The American College

About the Editor

David M. Cordell, PhD, CFA, CFP, CLU, is associate professor of finance at The American College in Bryn Mawr, Pennsylvania. Cordell has written numerous articles in finance and investments for both academic and practitioner publications. He is a frequent speaker on financial planning topics and is author, editor, or contributing author of the following books: *Financial Decision Making at Retirement, The Financial Services Professional's Guide to The State of the Art, Financial Planning Applications, Tax Companion 1995, Solutions Handbook for Financial Planning,* and *Readings in Financial Planning.* Cordell earned MBA and PhD degrees in finance from The University of Texas at Austin and holds three professional designations: Chartered Financial Analyst, Certified Financial Planner, and Chartered Life Underwriter.

Fundamentals of Financial Planning

1

Meeting Client Needs through Financial Planning

Robert M. Crowe and David M. Cordell

Chapter Outline

Although providing financial planning advice and services to clients is a relatively new and still-emerging field of professional endeavor, very affluent individuals have had access to such help for many years. Moreover, some financial services professionals, such as accountants and life insurance agents, argue that they have been financial planners all their lives. Perhaps they are correct. However, it is generally recognized that financial planning services that cover a *spectrum* of client concerns have become available to most Americans in the middle- and upper-middle-income brackets only in about the past 25 to 30 years.

Financial services practitioners claiming to be financial planners first appeared in numbers in the late 1960s, a period of rising inflation and interest rates. The financial planning movement grew rapidly during the 1970s as the general trend of prices continued upward. By the late 1970s and into the early 1980s, inflation and interest rates were virtually out of control. Confronted with very high income tax rates along with these inflation and interest rates, American consumers clamored for help. The growth of the financial planning movement was explosive. Often, however, what practitioners labeled as financial planning service consisted mostly of selling "get rich quick" products and elaborate income tax dodges, usually accompanied by an abundance of "hype." A few practitioners, sometimes with near-messianic zeal, preached the message of *comprehensive* financial planning as the financial salvation of the American household.

By the mid-1980s, much of the turbulence in economic conditions began to settle down. In addition, when income tax reform eliminated the most extreme types of tax shelters from the marketplace, many so-called financial planners disappeared from the scene. Many advocates of the comprehensive approach to financial planning, at least when provided solely on a fee-for-service basis, came to realize that this type of financial planning is practical for only a small, affluent clientele.

In the 1990s the financial planning profession gained some stability and maturity. Now it is possible to describe more realistically what financial planning is and what client needs it can fulfill.

This chapter explains financial planning and describes it as a process. It discusses what financial planners actually do and summarizes the recommended content of a *comprehensive* financial plan. Further, the chapter reviews some of the key events in the historical development of financial planning as a profession during the past 30 years. Finally, the chapter discusses the basic conditions in the marketplace that provide opportunities for professional financial planners to serve clients, and it identifies some of the obstacles that planners must help clients overcome if financial goals are to be achieved.

WHAT IS FINANCIAL PLANNING?

One factor that has hampered the development of financial planning as a discipline and as a profession is the fact that there has been and continues to be very little agreement among practitioners as to what exactly financial planning is. Indeed, it sometimes seems that there are as many definitions of financial planning as there are people who call themselves financial planners. Complicating the issue is the fact that federal and state governmental regulators have their own definitions of what a financial planner is. (Chapter 2 discusses regulatory aspects of financial planning.) From a conceptual view, though, defining financial planning can concentrate on breadth of services provided: single purpose, multiple purpose, and comprehensive focus.

Single-Purpose View

Some practitioners take the position that the simple selling of a single financial product or service to a client in order to solve a single financial problem constitutes financial planning. According to this *single-purpose* or *specialist view,* all the following individuals would be examples of financial planners:

- a stockbroker who advises a customer to buy shares of common stock of a particular company
- a salesperson who sells to a client shares in a real estate limited partnership
- a preparer of income tax returns who suggests that a client establish a Keogh plan
- a banker who opens a trust account for the benefit of a customer's handicapped child
- a life insurance agent who sells key person life insurance to the owner of a small business
- a personal finance counselor who shows a client how to set up and live within a budget

Multiple-Purpose View

Other practitioners might argue that none or only some of the preceding persons are really financial planners. These practitioners would argue that real financial planning must embrace more than just solving a single financial problem of a client and must extend beyond the selling of a single financial product or service. Practitioners adhering to the *multiple-purpose view* might emphasize that there are three basic categories of client financial needs and financial products and services: insurance planning, tax planning, and investment planning. From their perspective, true financial planning should deal with at least a large part of one of these categories, and perhaps some aspects of a second category. They might even specify that true financial planning must always include at least some investment planning activity. According to the multiple-purpose view, the following individuals would probably qualify as financial planners:

- an insurance agent who sells all lines of life, health, property, and liability insurance
- a tax attorney who assists clients with their income, estate, and gift tax planning
- an investment adviser who is registered as such with the Securities and Exchange Commission

- a life insurance agent who also sells a family of mutual funds to meet both the protection and wealth accumulation needs of clients

Comprehensive View

Still other practitioners would say that financial planning means and is synonymous with comprehensive financial planning. According to this *comprehensive view,* financial planning must consider all aspects of the client's financial position, which includes all the client's financial needs and objectives, and must utilize several integrated and coordinated planning strategies for fulfilling those needs and objectives. The two key characteristics of comprehensive financial planning are

- that it encompasses all the personal and financial situations of clients to the extent that these can be uncovered, clarified, and addressed through information gathering and counseling
- that it integrates into its methodology all the techniques and expertise utilized in more narrowly focused approaches to client financial problem solving

Because of the wide range of expertise required to engage in comprehensive financial planning, effective performance commonly requires a team of specialists. The comprehensive planner's tasks are to coordinate the efforts of the team and to contribute expertise in his or her field of specialization.

In its purest form, comprehensive financial planning is a service provided by the planner on a fee-only basis. No part of the planner's compensation comes from the sale of financial products, thus helping to ensure complete objectivity in all aspects of the plan. Some team specialists also are compensated through fees, while others might receive commissions from the sale of products. In its less pure but often more practical form, comprehensive financial planning provides the planner with compensation consisting of some combination of fees for service and commissions from the sale of some of the financial products. Again, members of the team of specialists might receive fees or commissions.

Furthermore, in its purest form, comprehensive financial planning is performed for a client all at once. A single planning engagement by the planner and his or her team of specialists creates the one plan that addresses all the clients concerns and utilizes all the needed financial strategies. This plan is then updated with the client periodically and modified as appropriate. In its less pure form, comprehensive financial planning is performed incrementally during the course of several engagements with the client. For example, the planner in one year might prepare a plan to treat some of the client's tax concerns and insurance planning problems. In another year the planner might focus on the client's investment concerns and then dovetail the strategies for dealing with them with the previously developed tax and insurance strategies. In a third engagement the planner might address the remaining issues in the tax, insurance, and investment planning areas and coordinate all the recommended strategies and previously developed plans. Again, each incremental part, as well as the overall plan, is reviewed periodically and revised as appropriate.

FINANCIAL PLANNING AS A PROCESS

What, then, is financial planning? Can the financial services professional whose focus is on only a single type of financial problem and financial product for clients legitimately be called a financial planner? What if the professional's focus is broader than this but less than comprehensive? Is the comprehensive approach the only true form of financial planning? The debate goes on among financial services professionals even now. Moreover, this debate is not merely an exercise in semantics; it becomes intensely practical when questions are raised about such issues as who shall regulate financial planners, who shall set standards for the financial planning profession, what sort of education financial planners should have, or which financial services practitioners may hold themselves out to the public as financial planners.

Financial planning is a *process,* a methodology that is valid for both practitioners and self-planning individuals. There are six steps to the financial planning process: (1) establish financial goals, (2) gather relevant data, (3) analyze the data, (4) develop a plan for achieving goals, (5) implement the plan, and (6) monitor the plan. (Many professionals will reverse steps 1 and 2. The Certified Financial Planner Board of Standards essentially combines steps one and two and adds a new step 1—establish client-planner relationships.)

Six Steps of Financial Planning
1. Establish financial goals. 2. Gather relevant data. 3. Analyze the data. 4. Develop a plan for achieving goals. 5. Implement the plan. 6. Monitor the plan.

Steps in Financial Planning

For practitioners this process for helping clients achieve their financial goals can be applied to the full range of client goals on a comprehensive basis. The process can also be applied on a more narrow basis to only a subset of those goals or even to only a single financial goal of a client. It is not the range of client concerns addressed that makes a practitioner a financial planner. Rather, it is the process that is used by the practitioner in addressing client concerns that makes a practitioner a financial planner. The following pages present a brief discussion of the six steps in the financial planning process.

Step 1: Establish Financial Goals

Few people begin a vacation without having a specific destination in mind. In contrast, millions of people make significant financial decisions without having a specific financial destination.

Goal setting is critical to creating a successful financial plan, but few people actually set clearly defined goals. By leading the client through the goal-setting exercise, the financial professional not only helps establish reasonable, achievable goals, but also sets the tone for the entire financial planning process.

Clients typically express concern about such topics as retirement income, education funding, premature death, disability, taxation, qualified plan distribution, and a myriad of others. Sometimes clients enumerate specific, prioritized goals, but they are more likely to present a vague list of worries that suggest anxiety and frustration rather than direction. The planner's responsibility is to help the client transform these feelings into goals.

Practitioners should query clients to learn what they are trying to accomplish. Usually the response is couched in general terms, such as "Well, we want to have a comfortable standard of living when we retire." At first glance this seems to be a reasonable goal, but a closer evaluation reveals that this goal is far too vague. When do they want to retire? What is meant by "comfortable"? Do they want to consider inflation? Do they want to retire on "interest only" or draw down their accumulated portfolio over their expected lives?

Skillful questioning may reveal a more precise goal, such as "We want to retire in 20 years with an after-tax income of $60,000 per year in current dollars, and we want the income to continue as long as we live without depleting the principle." Helping the client quantify goals is among the most valuable services a financial practitioner can provide.

Another important service of the practitioner is goal prioritization. Clients usually mention competing goals, such as saving for retirement and saving for education. Practitioners help clients rank these competing goals.

Step 2: Gather Relevant Data

Because there are many client concerns that a financial planner may need to address, the planner will have to gather considerable information from the client. Defining the client's current situation, determining what the client's desired future situation is and when it is to be achieved, and establishing what the client is willing and able to do in order to get there require information. This information must be accurate, complete, up-to-date, relevant to the client's goals, and well organized. Otherwise, financial plans based on the information will be deficient—perhaps erroneous, inappropriate, inconsistent with the client's other goals, or dangerous to the client's financial well-being.

After a client expresses goals, objectives, and concerns, the planner gathers all the information about the client that is relevant to the problem(s) to be solved and/or to the type of plan to be prepared. The more complex the client's situation and the more varied the number of his or her goals, the greater the information-gathering task.

Two broad types of information will need to be gathered: objective and subjective. A few examples of objective (factual) information that might be needed from the client include a list of securities holdings, inventory of assets and liabilities, a description of the present arrangement for distribution of the client's (and spouse's) assets at death, a list of annual income and expenditures, and a summary of present insurance coverages. Of at least equal importance is the subjective information about the client. The financial planner often will need to gather information about the hopes, fears, values, preferences, attitudes, and nonfinancial goals of the client (and spouse).

One piece of information worthy of special attention is client risk tolerance, which chapter 5 addresses in detail. Practitioners must determine the client's (and spouse's) attitude toward risk before making recommendations, preferably through use of a scientific, third-party evaluation. The American College's *Survey of Risk Tolerance*[1] provides the type of analysis that helps the practitioner suggest alternatives that are truly appropriate for the client. Such information offers the additional benefit of helping avoid (or at least defend) lawsuits from a dissatisfied client.

Before the financial planner begins the information-gathering process, he or she should *give* certain information to the client. First, the client should be made aware that he or she will have to invest time, perhaps a significant amount of time, in the information-gathering stage of financial planning. Even though part of the financial planner's responsibility is to avoid consuming the client's time unnecessarily, this commitment of time by the client is essential. The magnitude of the needed time commitment will depend on the scope and complexity of the client's needs and circumstances, but the proper development of even a narrowly focused and fairly uncomplicated plan requires information that only the client can furnish.

Second, the client should be made aware that he or she probably will have to provide the planner with some information that is highly confidential, perhaps even sensitive or painful, for the client to reveal. Again, the scope and complexity of the client's needs will influence this matter. The creation of even rather straightforward plans, however, may require clients to disclose such things as their income and spending patterns, their attitudes toward other family members, or their opinions as to the extent of their own financial responsibilities to others. Another prerequisite for the effective gathering of client information is a systematic approach to the task. Although there are many possible ways to systematize the gathering of information, one way that has been found useful by many financial planners is to use a structured fact finder form. Some fact finders are only a few pages long and ask for basic information, while others are thick booklets that seek very detailed data on each asset and amount. Most fact finders are designed for specific financial planning software to simplify data entry. For many client situations, a formal fact finder elicits considerably more information than needed. The sections that should be completed depend on the particular areas of concern to be addressed in each client's financial plan.

Obviously, information gathering is far more than asking the client a series of questions or filling out a form. Certainly that is required, but usually information gathering also requires examination and analysis of documents—such as wills, tax returns, and insurance policies—supplied by the client or the client's other financial advisers. It also requires advising, counseling, and listening during face-to-face meetings with the client and spouse. These skills are especially important because the planner needs to help the client and spouse identify and articulate clearly what they really want to accomplish and what risks they are willing to take in order to do so.

Step 3: Analyze the Data

Once the relevant information about the client has been gathered, organized, and checked for accuracy, consistency, and completeness, the financial planner's next task is to analyze the client's present financial condition. The objective here is to determine where the client is now *in relationship to the goals that were established by the client in step one.*

This analysis may reveal certain strengths in the client's present position relative to those goals. For example, the client may be living well within his or her means, and thus resources are available with which to meet some wealth accumulation goals within a reasonable time period. Maybe the client has a liberal set of health insurance coverages through his or her employer, thereby adequately covering the risks associated with serious disability. Perhaps the client's will has been reviewed recently by his or her attorney and brought up-to-date to reflect the client's desired estate plan.

More than likely, however, the financial planner's analysis of the client's present financial position will disclose a number of weaknesses or conditions that are hindering achievement of the client's goals. For example, the client may be paying unnecessarily high federal income taxes or using debt unwisely. The client's portfolio of investments may be inconsistent with his or her risk-taking tolerance. Maybe the client's business interest is not being used efficiently to achieve his or her personal insurance protection goals, or important loss-causing possibilities have been overlooked, such as the client's exposure to huge lawsuits arising out of the possible negligent use of an automobile by someone other than the client.

One conclusion from the planner's analysis may be that the client cannot attain the goals established in step one. For example, the client's resources and investment returns may preclude reaching a specified retirement income goal. In this case the practitioner helps the client to lower the goal or shows what changes the client must make to achieve the goal. Postponing retirement, saving more money, seeking higher returns, and deciding to deplete principal during retirement are four ways to help achieve the goal. Presented with alternatives, the client can restate the original goal by either lowering it or revising restrictive criteria to make it achievable.

Step 4: Develop a Plan for Achieving Goals

After the information about the client has been analyzed and, if necessary, the objectives to be achieved have been refined, the planner's next job is to devise a realistic plan for bringing the client from his or her present financial position to the attainment of those objectives. Since no two clients are alike, a well-drawn financial plan must be tailored to the individual, with all the planner's recommended strategies designed for each particular client's needs, abilities, and goals. The plan must be the *client's* plan, not the *planner's* plan.

It is unlikely that any individual planner can maintain an up-to-date familiarity with all the strategies that might be appropriate for his or her clients. Based on his or her education and professional specialization, the planner is likely to rely on a limited number of "tried and true" strategies for treating the most frequently encountered planning problems. When additional expertise is needed, the planner should always consult with an adviser who is a specialist in the field in question to help the planner design the client's overall plan.

Also there is usually more than one way for a client's financial goals to be achieved. When this is the case, the planner should present alternative strategies for the client to consider and should explain the advantages and disadvantages of each strategy. Strategies that will help achieve multiple objectives should be highlighted.

The financial plan that is developed should be specific. It should detail who is to do what, when, and with what resources.

Implicit in plan development is the importance of obtaining client approval. It follows that the plan must not only be reasonable, it must also be acceptable to the client. Usually interaction between practitioner and client continues during plan development, providing constant feedback to increase the likelihood that the client will approve the plan.

Normally, the report describing the plan should be in writing. Since the objective of the financial planning report is to communicate, its format should be such that the client can easily understand and evaluate what is being proposed. Some financial planners take pride in the length of their reports, although lengthy reports are often made up primarily of standardized or "boilerplate" passages. In general, the simpler the report, the easier it will be for the client to understand and adopt. Careful use of graphs, diagrams, and other visual aids in the report can also help in this regard.

After the plan has been presented and reviewed with the client, the moment of truth arrives. At this time the planner must ask the client to approve the plan (or some variation thereof). As part of this request, the planner must ask the client to allocate money for the plan's implementation. Keep in mind the warning of one college professor of financial planning who admitted that he never dared to use the "S word" in class—financial planning does involve *selling.* Even financial planners who are compensated entirely on a fee-for-service basis must *sell* the client on the need to work with the planner to develop and implement a plan.

Step 5: Implement the Plan

The mere giving of financial advice, no matter how solid the foundation on which it is based, does not constitute financial planning. A financial plan is useful to the client *only if it is put into action.* Therefore part of the planner's responsibility is to see that plan implementation is carried out properly according to the schedule agreed upon with the client.

Financial plans that are of limited scope and limited complexity may be implemented for the client entirely by the planner. For other plans, however, additional specialized professional expertise will be needed. For example, such legal instruments as wills and trust documents may have to be drawn up, insurance policies may have to be purchased, or investment securities may have to be acquired. Part of the planner's responsibility is to *motivate* and *assist* the client in completing each of the steps necessary for full plan implementation.

Step 6: Monitor the Plan

The relationship between the financial planner and the client should be an ongoing one. Therefore the sixth and final step in the financial planning process is to monitor the client's plan. Normally the planner meets with the client at least once each year to review the plan, or more frequently if changing circumstances warrant it. The first part of this review process should involve measuring the performance of the implementation vehicles. Second, updates should be obtained concerning changes in the client's personal and financial situation. Third, changes that have occurred in the economic, tax, or financial environment should be reviewed with the client.

If this periodic review of the plan indicates satisfactory performance in light of the client's current objectives and circumstances, no action needs to be taken. However, if performance is not acceptable or if there is a significant change in the client's personal or financial circumstances or objectives, the planner and client should revise the plan to fit the new environment. This revision process should follow the same six steps used to develop the original plan, though the time and effort needed will probably be less than in the original process.

Summary

The financial planning process described above is depicted schematically in figure 1-1. The blocks on the left represent the six steps in the process, while the blocks on the right indicate the main substantive activities that should occur in each step.

FIGURE 1-1
The Financial Planning Process

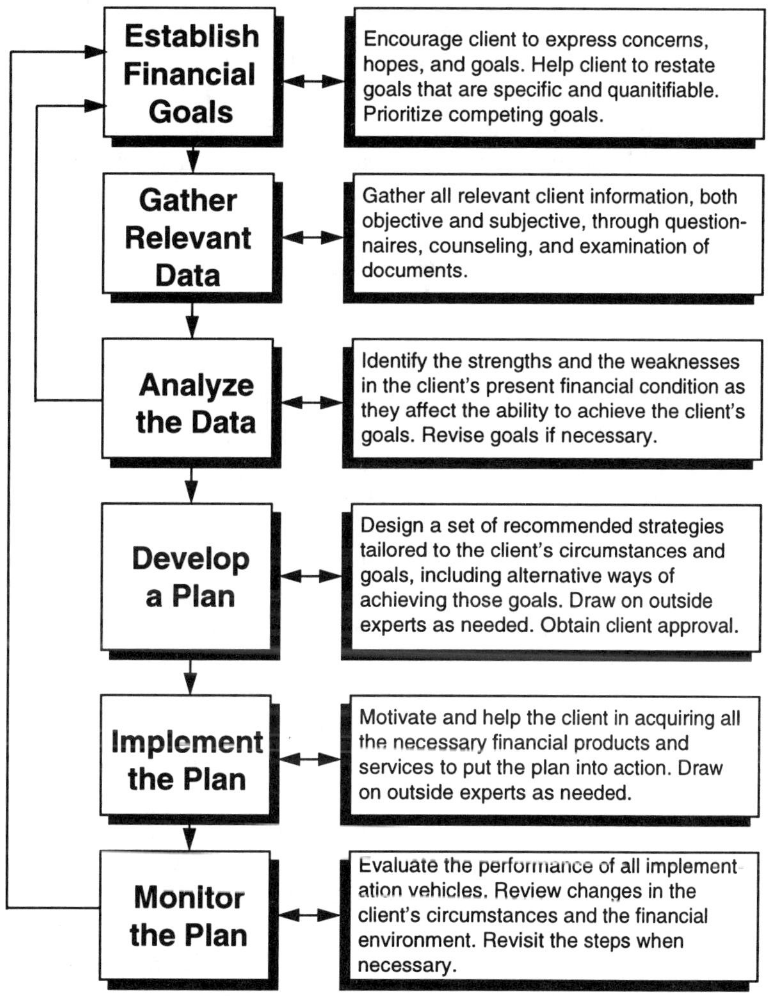

Individuals who intend to take the Certified Financial Planner certification examination should review the steps in the financial planning process as listed in appendix 1B, *Job Knowledge Requirements of the Certified Financial Planner*

Licensee: Topics, Importance Values, and Target Cognitive Level. The financial planning process in appendix 1B essentially combines steps 1 and 2 and inserts a new first step called "Establishing Client-Planner Relationships."

WHAT FINANCIAL PLANNERS ACTUALLY DO

In addition to the preceding description of the financial planning process, identifying the kinds of professional activities in which financial planners actually engage is another way to understand what financial planning is. One study sheds considerable light on this question.[2] This study surveyed a random sample of individuals who claimed to be financial planners, most of them holders of CFP, CLU, and/or ChFC professional designations, who had been active in the field for several years.

The study showed that the job activities of these practicing financial planners fall into six main categories. The principal specific activities within each category are described below.

- *marketing financial planning services*—Although these planners use a variety of techniques for obtaining and serving clients, they rely heavily on published media, such as writing articles and newsletters, as well as advertising. They frequently make personal presentations, such as lectures and seminars, and also obtain referrals from other professionals and from present clients.
- *evaluating client needs*—This category of activity centers on meeting with clients in order to collect information about them. The specific tasks considered most important to the survey respondents were interviewing and using questionnaires to explore the background, attitudes, financial resources, and obligations of clients that affect clients' financial goals and needs.
- *explaining financial planning concepts and clarifying client goals*—This set of tasks entails explaining issues and concepts related to such topics as estate plans, income taxes, insurance, investments, retirement-income plans, asset management, and budgeting. Also included is a discussion with the client of incompatibilities between the client's goals and the resources available for achieving them.
- *analyzing client circumstances and preparing financial plans*—Tasks in this category include an analysis of the client's financial records and documents, such as tax returns, insurance policies, and investment records. Other important tasks are the formulation of recommendations for meeting client goals in such areas as retirement, risk management, taxes, and investments.
- *implementing financial plans*—This task includes the preparation of the written document incorporating the recommended financial strategies and tactics, which are all tailored to meet the needs of the particular client. It also involves explaining the planner's fee structure, the

fiduciary responsibilities of the planner to the client, and full and fair disclosure to the client of material facts and opinions about recommended products and services. (Of course, some of this explanation may also take place as part of the marketing activities of the financial planner.) The implementation activities also include selecting and offering alternative financial products to the client and may entail carrying out client requests to purchase or sell them.

- *monitoring financial plans*—A planner's activities in this category reflect the continuing nature of the desired relationship with clients. Planners review and evaluate changes in their clients' personal circumstances (births, deaths, divorces, and so on), changes in laws and economic conditions, and the performance of the plan that has been implemented. Changes in financial plans are recommended to clients as needed.

The reader will undoubtedly recognize the similarity between this set of activities in which financial planners say they actually engage and the six steps in the financial planning process discussed earlier in this chapter.

The International Association for Financial Planning (IAFP) provides information on the kinds of services most frequently provided by financial planners to clients. Retirement planning is the most frequently offered service, followed by estate planning, education planning, tax planning, and risk management. Other services offered by many financial planners included long-term-care planning and asset management.

CONTENT OF A COMPREHENSIVE FINANCIAL PLAN

As noted earlier, comprehensive financial planning is only one type of financial planning. In practice, it is the least frequently encountered type for most planners for several reasons. First, not many clients are willing to invest as much of their own time in the undertaking as comprehensive financial planning requires. Second, usually only affluent clients are willing and able to pay for all the time of the planner and his or her staff that is needed in developing a comprehensive financial plan. Third, not many clients can easily deal with the totality of their financial goals, capabilities, and difficulties all at one time. Instead, most prefer to concentrate on only one or a few related issues at a time. (As has been mentioned, however, even clients in the last group can have a comprehensive plan developed and implemented for them in incremental stages.)

For those cases in which the planner is called upon to prepare a comprehensive financial plan for a client, whether entirely in one engagement or incrementally over a period of years, what should the plan contain? Clearly, comprehensive financial planning is such an ambitious and complex undertaking that it must cover numerous elements. The IAFP has developed and promulgated a set of guidelines in this regard. (The complete text of these guidelines for the content of a comprehensive financial plan appears as appendix 1A at the end of this chapter.)

FOCUS ON ETHICS
Beginning a Dialogue on Ethics

Each chapter contains an ethics dialogue box such as this one. Chapter 3 is devoted entirely to ethics and professionalism, but ethics is a topic that should be implicit in any discussion of financial planning and the role of the financial planner. It is appropriate that the first box address a question that many planners have asked: "Is the highly ethical financial planner financially rewarded for being ethical." The answer is that she or he may be, but there is no guarantee. There are examples to the contrary, just as there are some illustrations of the shady planner reaping significant financial gains. Disciplined ethical conduct, by itself, does not guarantee financial success.

Perhaps the question should be addressed from a different perspective. Do clients want to do business with someone who really understands financial planning but who has questionable morals? Do clients want to do business with someone whose integrity is unassailable but whose financial planning skills are marginal? The answer to both questions is no.

The skilled financial planner who is client centered and ethically well disciplined clearly has the attributes that clients desire and deserve. Again, ethical practice provides no guarantees of financial success. It is clear, however, that clients want to do business with financial planners that have earned their trust and are technically competent.

A comprehensive financial plan should address all pertinent areas relating to the client, according to these guidelines. If the planner does not personally address each of the areas in the development of the plan (and in this author's experience, not many planners have the range and depth of expertise needed to do so alone), the planner should then serve as the coordinator for the development of the other areas of the plan.

According to the guidelines at least 13 pertinent areas should be addressed in a client's comprehensive financial plan. Although the order, depth, and style in which they are discussed in the plan document may vary, these 13 areas are as follows:

- First, a comprehensive plan should include personal data about the client and the client's family, such as names, addresses, dates of birth, social security numbers, phone numbers, and so on.
- Second, the plan should include the client's stated goals and objectives, indicating the priority of each one and the time frame for achieving each one.
- Third, the plan should identify problems in the client's present position, including such things as possible catastrophic medical costs, unplanned high costs of educating children, and unnecessarily high current tax burdens.
- Fourth, any assumptions used by the planner in preparing the recommended strategies, such as assumptions about future inflation

rates and investment yields, should be explicitly spelled out in the plan document.

- Fifth, the plan should contain the client's balance sheet, showing his or her assets, liabilities, and net worth.
- Sixth, the plan should include a cash-flow management statement. This statement should identify all the client's sources and uses of cash and indicate his or her net cash flows.
- Seventh, a comprehensive financial plan should include a federal income tax statement and an analysis thereof.
- Eighth, the plan should analyze the client's financial exposure to losses of both a personal and business nature arising from mortality, morbidity, legal liability, and property damage. This section of the plan should also list and analyze the client's insurance coverages for such exposures.
- Ninth, the plan should provide a listing of the client's present investment portfolio, including an analysis of its liquidity, diversification, and risk characteristics.
- Tenth, the plan should analyze any future capital needs that the client will have for special purposes, such as retirement planning or children's education costs.
- Eleventh, a comprehensive plan should address the client's estate plan. There should be a review of the assets that will be included in the gross estate and an estimate of the estate tax burden that will be present.
- Twelfth, the plan should include a list of recommendations by the planner for dealing with the issues and problems identified earlier and for achieving the client's goals and objectives.
- Thirteenth, the plan should deal with implementation. It should contain a prioritized list of actions to be taken, including what is to be done, when, and by whom.

Elements of a Comprehensive Financial Plan*

1. Personal data
2. Client goals and objectives
3. Identification of issues and problems
4. Assumptions
5. Balance sheet/net worth
6. Cash-flow management
7. Income tax
8. Risk management/insurance
9. Investments
10. Financial independence, retirement planning, education, and other special needs
11. Estate planning
12. Recommendations
13. Implementation plan

*A comprehensive financial plan should contain at least these elements, though not necessarily in this order, according to guidelines developed by the IAFP.

THE EVOLUTION OF FINANCIAL PLANNING AS A PROFESSION

It was noted at the beginning of this chapter that financial planning is, in general, still a new and emerging profession. Its development as such has been facilitated by a number of organizations during the past 20 to 25 years.

Perhaps the earliest landmark event in the development of financial planning as a profession occurred in 1969 with the formation of the International Association of Financial Planners, later renamed the International Association for Financial Planning. The IAFP is a trade association that, among other things, promotes financial planning, conducts educational and training programs for members, sponsors market research about financial planning, and promotes ethical conduct among practitioners.

Several colleges and universities have played an important role in the development of the financial planning profession. In 1972 the College for Financial Planning, which is the educational institution that originally awarded the Certified Financial Planner (CFP) professional designation, was formed. (This function was later transferred to another organization, now called the Certified Financial Planner Board of Standards.) In 1973 holders of the CFP designation formed the Institute of Certified Financial Planners (ICFP), a membership organization to help build professionalism in the field.

A number of important developments occurred in the mid-1970s and thereafter at what was originally called The American College of Life Underwriters, further contributing to the financial planning movement. The name of the institution was changed to The American College to reflect a broadened educational mission within the financial services field. The College created a graduate-degree program, Master of Science in Financial Services, that originally included a full six-credit graduate course in financial counseling. Discussions by the College's Board of Trustees with various constituencies of the institution led eventually to a broadened array of designation-level courses. This broadening in the curriculum culminated with the creation of a new professional designation in the early 1980s—Chartered Financial Consultant (ChFC). Meanwhile the College's sister organization, the American Society of Chartered Life Underwriters, also broadened its mission, membership, and programs, accepting the new categories of graduates of the College into the Society and changing its name to the American Society of CLU & ChFC. Further emphasizing this direction, the Society changed its name again in 1998 to the Society of Financial Service Professionals.

Traditional colleges and universities also contributed to the emerging financial planning profession during the 1970s and 1980s, though on a much smaller scale than the College for Financial Planning and The American College, both of which serve a national student body. A number of schools developed curricula in financial planning at the undergraduate or master's level and began offering courses to help prepare people for the CFP and ChFC examinations.

Now several states allow attainment of either the ChFC or CFP designations to satisfy the education requirement for registration as an investment adviser.

Two other forces that have spurred the growth and professionalization of financial planning have been the American Institute of CPAs (AICPA) and the Life Underwriter Training Council (LUTC). In 1987 the AICPA developed for its members an educational program leading to the designation that is now called Personal Financial Specialist. At about the same time the LUTC created a Financial Planning Skills course as part of its designation program for life insurance agents. This course teaches life insurance agents how to integrate noninsurance financial products with their regular portfolio of life insurance products.

OPPORTUNITIES AND CHALLENGES IN THE FINANCIAL PLANNING MARKETPLACE

A number of trends having important implications for financial planning practitioners have emerged in the United States in recent years. They all point to enormous opportunities for financial planners to render valuable service to clients.

One of the most important trends is that the population is growing older. The median age of Americans has risen approximately 5 years in the past 3 decades, meaning that a larger proportion of the population has moved into the period of highest earnings. Also, as people get older, they tend to devote a smaller share of their income to current consumption and a larger share to saving and investing.

One of the causes of the rising median age of Americans is that the members of the "baby boom" generation are no longer babies. The children born from the middle 1940s to the middle 1960s now range in age from the early 30s to the early 50s and constitute about 30 percent of the U.S. population. Another cause of the rising average age is that Americans are living longer. Approximately 12.6 percent of them are now age 65 or over as compared to 9.2 percent in 1960, and this percentage will continue to rise. Government statistics indicate that the average life expectancy for 65-year-old males is now over 15 years and for 65-year-old females is almost 19 years.

The aging of the American population means that more and more consumers need retirement planning help during both their remaining years of active work and their retirement years. Also, an increasing proportion of the population needs assistance in planning for the cost of their children's college education.

A second important trend in the financial planning marketplace is that dual-income families are increasingly common. This trend results from an increasing percentage of women entering (and reentering) the labor force, even during the years when they have young children. Dual-income families typically have higher total incomes, pay higher income and social security taxes, and have less time to manage their finances. The opportunities for the financial planner to assist are obvious.

A third broad trend is the increasing volatility of financial conditions in the American economy. Three indicators of this volatility confronting and confusing American households in the past 35 years are the changes that have occurred in inflation rates, in the level of interest rates, and in common stock prices. For example, during the first half of the 1960s, annual increases in the consumer price index averaged only 1.3 percent; the prime interest rate charged by banks on short-term business loans averaged only about 4.68 percent, and the Standard & Poor's index of 500 common stock prices averaged around 72.0. Consider the dynamic patterns of these indicators since then, as shown in table 1-1.

Inflation and interest rates rose steadily in the late 1960s, and they were undoubtedly a motivating factor behind the growth in the number of financial planning practitioners. Inflation and interest rates then cooled but bounced up again sharply in the mid-1970s. After a 3-year respite, they rose very sharply in the late 1970s and into the 1980s. Throughout this entire period, stock prices rose only modestly.

Broad Trends Affecting Opportunities for Financial Planners

1. Rising median age
2. Increased impact of dual-income families
3. Volatility of financial conditions
4. Technological change

Inflation rates slowed again during the mid-1980s, as did the prime interest rate. Meanwhile the stock market rose dramatically but erratically. As the 1980s came to a close, inflation and interest rates were creeping up again and average common stock prices were gyrating sharply from day to day. Then in the early 1990s, inflation started cooling again, stock prices rose dramatically, and interest rates plummeted. The mid-1990s saw continued moderation of inflation, yet interest rates crept upward while the stock market set record highs. Inflation in 1997 dropped to 1.7 percent, its lowest level in 3 decades. In 1998 the stock market soared to unprecedented highs, but also displayed unsettling volatility. Meanwhile, interest rates dropped to their lowest levels in years.

In addition to the volatility of inflation rates, interest rates, and stock market prices, another destabilizing factor faced by American consumers has been important U.S. income tax law changes that affect all aspects of financial planning. Still another element of instability in the financial environment has been the failure rate among financial institutions, including some very large ones. In the 1980s and early 1990s failure rates among savings and loan associations, banks, and insurance companies were higher than they had been in many years.

Volatile economic conditions create greater demand for financial planning services. They also emphasize the need for financial planners to continuously monitor their clients' financial circumstances and to adjust the plans as circumstances dictate. These volatile financial conditions make it doubly important that planners thoroughly understand and abide by their clients' risk tolerances.

TABLE 1-1
Consumer Price Index Changes (Urban Consumers), the Prime Rate, and the Standard & Poor's 500 Stock Index: 1965–1997

Year	Percentage Change in CPI	Average Prime Rate %	Average S & P 500 Index
1965	1.6%	4.54%	88.2
1970	5.7	7.91	83.2
1971	4.4	5.72	98.3
1972	3.2	5.25	109.2
1973	6.2	8.03	107.4
1974	11.0	10.81	82.8
1975	9.1	7.86	87.1
1976	5.8	6.84	102.0
1977	6.5	6.82	98.2
1978	7.6	9.06	96.0
1979	11.3	12.67	102.8
1980	13.5	15.27	118.7
1981	10.3	18.87	128.0
1982	6.2	14.86	119.7
1983	3.2	10.79	160.4
1984	4.3	12.04	180.5
1985	3.6	9.93	186.8
1986	1.9	8.33	236.3
1987	3.6	8.21	268.8
1988	4.1	9.32	265.9
1989	4.8	10.87	323.1
1990	5.4	10.01	335.01
1991	4.2	8.46	376.20
1992	3.0	6.25	415.75
1993	3.0	6.00	451.63
1994	2.7	7.15	460.42
1995	2.5	8.83	541.72
1996	3.3	8.27	670.49
1997	1.7	8.44	873.43

Source: Statistical Abstract of the United States and *Federal Reserve Bulletin,* various issues.

A fourth major trend in the financial planning market is the technological revolution that has occurred in the financial services industry. This revolution has made possible the creation of many new financial products and has made it easier to tailor these products to individual client needs. Also the technology has made possible improved analysis of the performance of these products by planners with the skills to do so.

CONSUMER NEEDS FOR FINANCIAL PLANNING

A basic and inescapable principle of economics is the law of scarcity: In every society, human wants are unlimited whereas the resources available to fill those wants are limited. The available resources must be somehow rationed among the wants. This rationing problem creates the need for financial planning even in affluent societies, such as the United States, and even among the most affluent members of such societies. To put it colloquially, there is just never enough money to go around.

What are the main financial concerns of American consumers? Are they able to handle those concerns on their own or do they need professional help? If they need professional help, with what type of problems do they need help? If they need professional help, do they recognize that they need help? In short, do U.S. consumers have a significant need and effective demand for professional financial planning services in the late 1990s?

The IAFP surveys American consumers periodically to identify their major financial concerns. In 1995 the survey found that 55 percent of American adults were at least somewhat concerned about running out of money during retirement,[3] and numerous subsequent studies have corroborated this finding.[4] College funding and long-term care for parents are two other major concerns of Americans. (Most financial planners think clients would be even more worried if they fully understood financial planning concepts.)

An important part of the 1996 IAFP survey[5] concentrated on parents of children under age 18. Ironically, 83 percent of these parents said that they have a financial plan, and three-quarters expressed confidence in their long-term financial well-being. Yet only 44 percent of them indicated that they were saving for their children's education. Less that 10 percent appeared to have all the elements that experts regard as vital to a financial plan, such as investments, insurance, budgeting, savings, and estate planning.

Table 1-2 shows results of the 1990 IAFP survey[6] that emphasized "squeezed families" defined as those of the baby boom generation who have children likely to need financial support and parents likely to need long-term care. Although data for the general population imply serious financial concerns, the data for squeezed boomers are even more ominous. Retirement, college funding, and long-term care are important to everyone, but especially to squeezed boomers.

TABLE 1-2
Who's Worried about What

	Total Public (n=1058)	Squeezed Boomer Families* (n=268)
Meeting mortgage payment is biggest economic concern	18%	24%
Long-term financial goal is comfortable retirement	30%	42%
Cost of parental long-term care will impact ability to save for children's education	53%	66%
Cost of college education will impact ability to help parent	50%	65%
Very or somewhat concerned about outliving retirement savings	52%	62%
Very or somewhat concerned about meeting financial responsibilities	46%	59%
Saving or planning to save more because of concerns	62%	75%

*People in the "baby boom" generation who have children likely to need financial help and parents likely to need long-term care

Source: International Association for Financial Planning, Atlanta, GA, *1990 Americans Cope with Their Finances.*

Obstacles Confronting Consumers

The results of IAFP surveys and similar studies make it clear that many American households still have not gained control of their financial destinies. Certainly, there are many reasons why they have not developed financial plans that will enable them to do so. Three of the most important obstacles they face are the following:

- *the natural human tendency to procrastinate*—Among the reasons for putting off the task of establishing a financial plan may be a lack of time due to a hectic lifestyle, the seeming enormity of the task of getting one's finances under control, and the belief that there is still plenty of time to prepare for achieving financial goals.

- *the very common tendency for Americans to live up to or beyond their current income*—The pressure in households to overspend for current consumption is enormous, and many families have no funds left with which to implement plans for the achievement of future goals.
- *the lack of financial knowledge among consumers*—Although in recent years there has undoubtedly been some growth in the financial sophistication of Americans, there is still widespread ignorance about how to formulate financial objectives and how to identify and properly evaluate all the strategies that might be used to achieve them.

Financial Planner's Role

A basic inference that can be drawn from the results of consumer surveys is that Americans need help in managing their personal finances to achieve their financial goals. Moreover, many Americans seem to realize that they would benefit from professional help, and with better education, most others would reach the same conclusion. A major part of the financial planner's challenge is to help clients overcome obstacles by educating them and motivating them to gain control of their own finances.

NOTES

1. *Survey of Risk Tolerance,* The American College, P.O. Box 1400, Bryn Mawr, PA 19010. (610) 526-1490.
2. Larry Shurnik, "Job Analysis of the Professional Requirements of the Certified Financial Planner" (Denver: College for Financial Planning, 1987).
3. *1995 National Consumer Survey,* International Association for Financial Planning, Atlanta, GA. The telephone survey was conducted by The Wirthlin Group, which polled 500 people aged 21 and older with household incomes of at least $20,000.
4. David M. Cordell, "Personal Responsibility for Retirement Planning," *Journal of the American Society of CLU & ChFC,* November 1995, pp. 58-64.
5. *National Consumer Survey: Teaching Money Management Skills to Children.* International Association for Financial Planning, Atlanta, GA, 1996. The telephone survey was conducted by The Wirthlin Group, which polled 550 Americans who have children under age 18 living at home, who have annual household incomes of at least $30,000, and who play a major role in managing their household finances.
6. *1990 Americans Cope with Their Finances,* International Association for Financial Planning, Atlanta, GA. The telephone survey was conducted by the Gallup Organization. It polled 1,058 households representative of the United States as a whole and an additional sample of 600 households with incomes of $50,000 and up.

Appendix 1A

Guidelines for a Comprehensive Financial Plan*

THE COMPREHENSIVE FINANCIAL PLAN

While most financial planning practitioners are highly trained in one or several of many disciplines, the consumer often seeks assurance that a planner will be able to provide a well-rounded, comprehensive plan that spans all aspects of his or her financial situation

The development of "Guidelines for a Comprehensive Financial Plan" by the International Association for Financial Planning has made it possible for the consumer to receive that assurance, by providing a benchmark against which to measure the thoroughness of a plan.

These guidelines, developed in 1987, were the first formal, written elements that should be included in a truly comprehensive financial plan.

OVERVIEW OF PLAN ELEMENTS

A comprehensive financial plan should contain an analysis of all pertinent factors relating to the client. While order and style of presentation may vary, the plan should include, but not necessarily be limited to, the following elements:

1. Personal data
2. Client goals and objectives
3. Identification of issues and problems
4. Assumptions
5. Balance sheet/net worth
6. Cash-flow management
7. Income tax
8. Risk management/insurance
9. Investments
10. Financial independence, retirement planning, education, and other
11. Estate planning
12. Recommendations
13. Implementation

* Reprinted with permission of the International Association for Financial Planning, Atlanta, GA 30328.

When developing a comprehensive financial plan, the planner is responsible for all of the elements of the plan, from data gathering through analysis and presentation to the client. Those elements of the plan that the planner does not personally perform remain the responsibility of the planner to coordinate.

When technical areas (such as legal and insurance services) are not personally performed by the planner, the financial plan or supplement should include supporting documentation that these areas have been or will be coordinated by the planner.

Analysis of each element of the plan should consist of a review of pertinent facts, a consideration of the advantages and/or disadvantages of the current situation, and a determination of what, if any, further action is required. The plan should include a summary statement providing the planner's comments on the analysis, and his or her recommendations, where appropriate, for each element of the plan.

GUIDELINES FOR A COMPREHENSIVE FINANCIAL PLAN

1. Personal Data

Should include relevant personal and family data for parties covered under the plan.

Comments:

- Should include, but not be limited to, name, address, social security number, birthdate and other relevant data.

2. Client's Goals and Objectives

A reiteration of the client's stated goals and objectives, indicating their priority and including a time frame where applicable.

Comments:

- The statement of goals and objectives will form the basic framework for the development of the financial plan.
- The client's goals and objectives should be expressed in as specific and precise language as possible. For example, a statement of a goal should read "Retire at age 62 in present home and maintain a current standard of living" rather than "A comfortable retirement."

3. Identification of Issues and Problems

A plan must address relevant issues and problems identified by the client, the planner and/or other advisers.

Comments:

- List personal and financial issues and problems that affect the client such as major illness, education costs, taxes, etc. While the client may be aware of many, if not all, of the issues, the planner may discover other areas that are or could develop into problems.
- These issues and problems, when combined with the client's goals and objectives, will complete the framework and direction for the financial plan. Since style and order are not the primary consideration, the analysis of recommendation section(s) of the plan may be more appropriate for identifying issues and problems.

4. Assumptions

Identify and state material assumptions used in the plan's preparation.

Comments:

- Assumptions should include, but not be limited to, inflation, investment growth rate, mortality, etc.

5. Balance Sheet/Net Worth

A presentation and analysis to include, but not be limited to, a schedule listing assets and liabilities with a calculation of net worth and itemized schedules of liabilities and assets to be included as appropriate.

Comments:

- In addition to the schedules, footnotes should be included as appropriate.

6. Cash-Flow Management

Statements and analysis to include, but not be limited to, a statement of the client's sources and uses of funds for the current year and for all relevant years, indicating net cash flow, as well as a separate income statement, where appropriate.

Comments:

- Sources—earned income, investment income, sale proceeds, gifts, etc.
- Uses—living expenses, debt service, acquisition of assets, taxes paid, etc.
- Net cash flow—both positive and negative.

7. Income Tax

An income tax statement and analysis to include, but not be limited to, the income taxes for the current year and for all relevant years covered in the plan.

Comments:

- Projections should show the nature of the income and deductions in sufficient detail to permit calculation of the tax liability. The analysis should identify the marginal tax rate for each year and any special situations such as alternative minimum tax, passive loss limitations, etc., that affect the client's tax liability.
- The financial plan should include footnotes to let the client know which taxes (i.e., state or city) have not been addressed.

8. Risk Management/Insurance

A. Analysis of a client's financial exposure relative to mortality, morbidity, liability and property, including business as appropriate.

Comments:

- Mortality—survivor income and capital needs analysis.
- Morbidity—impact of loss of health.
- Liability—legal exposure.
- Property—loss of value.
- Business—loss due to business involvement.

B. Listing and analysis of current policies and problems to include, but not be limited to, life, disability, medical, business, property/casualty and liability.

Comments:

- Analysis of existing coverage and/or risk exposure in relationship to the client's needs, goals and objectives.
- If any area of insurance is not within the competency range of the financial planner, the planner has the responsibility to coordinate with other

professionals and document such coordination in the financial plan. Documentation of the above areas can include the insurance professional's summary, if completed, or the professional's name and time frame when such review will be completed.

9. Investments

A listing of the current investment portfolio and an analysis or discussion of the liquidity, diversification and investment risk exposure of the portfolio. In addition, the suitability of the investments in relationship to the client's needs, goals and objectives should be addressed, to include, but not be limited to, risk tolerance, risk management of investments, suitability, liquidity, diversification and personal management efforts.

Comments:

- Risk tolerance—addresses the client's willingness to accept investment risk.
- Risk management—analysis of client's exposure relative to loss of invested capital.
- Suitability—appropriateness of the investment for the client.
- Liquidity—the availability of assets that can be converted into cash at acceptable costs.
- Diversification—appropriate mix of assets to meet the client's needs, goals and objectives.
- Personal management efforts—the degree to which the client wants to manage and is capable of managing his or her assets.

10. Financial Independence, Retirement Planning, Education, and Other Special Needs

An analysis of the capital needed at some future time to provide for financial independence, retirement, education, or other special needs. The analysis should include a projection of resources expected to be available to meet these needs at that time.

Comments:

- In achieving the above, inflation, growth of assets and company benefits should be considered where applicable.
- Special sections of the above topics may require a separate heading in the financial plan. For example, company benefits may require an analysis of types available, pre- and post-tax contributions needed, tax treatment of plans and investment of benefit plan assets.

11. Estate Planning

Identification of assets that can be included in the client's estate and an analysis of the control, disposition and taxation of those assets.

Comments:

- Control—authority to manage or direct the use of assets by means of title, trusteeship, power of attorney, etc.
- Disposition—transfer of ownership by will, trust, beneficiary designation or operation of the law.
- Taxation—taxation of the client's estate and the income tax and estate tax consequences to the beneficiaries.

12. Recommendations

Written recommendations that relate to goals and objectives as well as financial issues and problems.

Comments:

- Written recommendations should specifically address the client's goals and objectives and all issues and problems identified in the plan, as well as a determination of the actions necessary to compensate for any shortfalls. Recommendations should be clearly identified and stated. They should not be conveyed by implication or inference.

13. Implementation

A prioritized list of actions required to implement the recommendations, indicating responsible parties, action required and timing.

Comments:

- Implementation should include a schedule reflecting actions to be taken as well as priority, dates and responsible parties.

Appendix 1B

Job Knowledge Requirements of the Certified Financial Planner Licensee: Topics, Importance Values, and Target Cognitive Level

The following topics are effective for CFP Certification Examinations administered by the CFP Board after December 31, 1996. The importance values (the result of the 1994 Job Analysis Update) are indicated by percentages to indicate the percentage of items in an examination that should be dedicated to that content area. A single number in the parentheses is a code for one of the four cognitive levels targeted for that content area: 1=knowledge of facts/terms, 2=comprehension/application, 3=analysis/synthesis, 4=evaluation.

Financial Planning Process

Financial Planning Process

1. Establishing client-planner relationships (2.53%, 2)
   - A. Explain issues and concepts related to the overall financial planning process, as appropriate to the client
   - B. Explain services provided, the process of planning, documentation required
   - C. Clarify client's and CFP licensee's responsibilities

2. Gathering client data and determining goals and expectations (5.98%, 2)
   - A. Obtain information from client through interview/questionnaire about financial resources and obligations
   - B. Determine client's personal and financial goals, needs and priorities
   - C. Assess client's values, attitudes, and expectations
   - D. Determine client's time horizons
   - E. Determine client's risk tolerance level
   - F. Collect applicable client records and documents

3. Determining the client's financial status by analyzing and evaluating (23.02%, 4)
   - A. General
     - 1) Current financial status (c.g., asscts, liabilitics, cash flow, dcbt management)
     - 2) Capital needs
     - 3) Attitudes and expectations
     - 4) Risk tolerance
     - 5) Risk management
     - 6) Risk exposure
   - B. Special needs
     - 1) Divorce/remarriage considerations
     - 2) Charitable planning
     - 3) Adult dependent needs
     - 4) Disabled child needs

5) Education needs
6) Terminal illness planning
7) Closely-held business planning

C. Risk management
1) Life insurance needs and current coverage
2) Disability insurance needs and current coverage
3) Health insurance needs and current coverage
4) Long-term care insurance needs and current coverage
5) Homeowners insurance needs and current coverage
6) Auto insurance needs and current coverage
7) Other liability insurance needs and current coverage (e.g., umbrella, professional, errors and omissions, directors and officers)
8) Commercial insurance needs and current coverage

D. Investments
1) Current investments
2) Current investment strategies and policies

E. Taxation
1) Tax returns
2) Current tax strategies
3) Tax compliance status (e.g., estimated tax)
4) Current tax liabilities

F. Retirement
1) Current retirement plan tax exposures (e.g., excise tax, premature distribution tax)
2) Current retirement plans
3) Social Security benefits
4) Retirement strategies

G. Employee benefits
1) Available employee benefits
2) Current participation in employee benefits

H. Estate planning
1) Estate planning documents
2) Estate planning strategies
3) Estate tax exposures

4. Developing and presenting the financial plan (23.1%, 4)

A. Developing and preparing a client-specific financial plan tailored to meet the goals and objectives of the client, commensurate with client's values, temperament, and risk tolerance, covering:
1) Financial position
   a) Current statement
   b) Projected statement
   c) Projected statement with recommendations
2) Cash flow
   a) Projection
   b) Recommendations
   c) Projection with recommendations
3) Estate tax
   a) Projections
   b) Recommendations
   c) Projections with recommendations
4) Capital needs at retirement
   a) Projections
   b) Recommendations
   c) Projections with recommendations
5) Capital needs projections at death
   a) Recommendations
   b) Projections with recommendations
6) Capital needs: disability
   a) Recommendations
   b) Projections with recommendations
7) Capital needs: special needs
   a) Recommendations

b) Projections with recommendations

8) Income tax
   a) Projections
   b) Recommendations
   c) Projections with strategy recommendations

9) Employee benefits
   a) Projections

10) Asset allocation
   a) Statement
   b) Strategy recommendations
   c) Statement with recommendations

11) Investment
   a) Recommendations
   b) Policy statement
   c) Policy recommendations
   d) Policy statement with recommendations

12) Risk
   a) Assessment
   b) Recommendations

13) List of prioritized action items

B. Presenting and reviewing the plan with the client

C. Collaborating with the client to ensure that plan meets the goals and objectives of the client, and revising as appropriate

5. Implementing the financial plan (1.62%, 4)
   A. Assist the client in implementing the recommendations
   B. Coordinate as necessary with other professionals, such as accountants, attorneys, real estate agents, investment advisers, stock brokers, and insurance agents

6. Monitoring the financial plan (3.76%, 4)
   A. Monitor and evaluate soundness of recommendations
   B. Review the progress of the plan with the client
   C. Discuss and evaluate changes in client's personal circumstances, (e.g., birth/death, age, illness, divorce, retirement)
   D. Review and evaluate changing tax laws and economic circumstances
   E. Make recommendations to accommodate new or changing circumstances

Job Knowledge Requirements

General Principles (11.62%)

7. Regulatory requirements for CFP licensees (4)
   A. Registration and licensing
   B. Sources of information

8. Ethical and professional considerations in financial planning (4)

9. Assessment of risk and client behavior (4)
   A. Client attitudes
   B. Client knowledge
   C. Client behavior

10. Financial planning for special needs (4)
   A. Options for funding education
   B. Other special needs and options (e.g., divorce, disability)

11. Economic environment and indicators (4)
   A. Inflation/deflation
   B. Interest rates/yield curves
   C. Life-cycle hypothesis
   D. Monetary and fiscal policy

   E. The business cycle
   F. Financial institutions
      1) Characteristics
      2) Safety and regulation

12. Calculate and interpret time value of money (4)
   A. Future value using single sums
   B. Present value using single sums
   C. Number of compounding periods using single sums
   D. Interest rate using single sums
   E. Inflation-adjusted interest rates
   F. Annuities

13. Asset valuation for financial planning functions (4)

14. Forms of business ownership/entity relationships (4)
   A. Sole proprietorships
   B. General partnerships
   C. Limited partnerships (including family limited partnerships)
   D. Limited liability companies
   E. C corporations
   F. S corporations
   G. Trusts
   H. Foundations/exempt organizations
   I. Professional associations/corporations
   J. Other

15. Ways of taking title to property (sole, joint, community, etc.) (4)
   A. Characteristics
   B. Implications

16. Legal aspects of financial planning (4)
   A. Contracts
   B. Negotiable instruments
   C. Torts
   D. Professional liability
   E. Fiduciary responsibility
   F. Agency law

17. Budgeting (4)
   A. Cash management
   B. Emergency fund planning
   C. Debt management/uses of debt
   D. Liquidity

18. Personal use-asset management (4)
   A. Home equity
   B. Types of mortgages
   C. Buy vs. lease
   D. Refinancing

Insurance Policies and Strategies (3.39%)

19. Principles of insurance (4)
   A. Concept of insurable risk
   B. Elements of insurance
   C. Methods to avoid, reduce, and eliminate loss

20. Identification of life, health, homeowners, auto and other property and liability risk exposures (4)
   A. Analysis of present coverage
   B. Loss of income to family
   C. Final expenses

21. Legal aspects of insurance (4)
   A. The law of agency as applied to insurance
   B. Tort liability as applied to insurance
   C. Basic components of an insurance contract
   D. Loss adjustment for various types of insurance

22. Insurance industry regulation (4)
   A. State regulation
   B. Federal regulation

23. Property and liability policy analysis (4)
   A. Homeowners insurance
   B. Personal auto insurance

C. Other liability insurance
   1) Umbrella
   2) Professional liability

24. Policy analysis (4)
   A. Pricing fundamentals
      1) Yield on assets
      2) Mortality/morbidity
      3) Lapses
      4) Expenses
   B. Factors affecting suitability of policy to client needs
   C. Contractual provisions vs. illustrations
   D. Insurance company crediting methods (i.e., new premium, interest, net investment yield crediting methods)

25. Life insurance policy analysis (4)
   A. Types of life insurance policies
   B. Life insurance policy provisions
   C. Life insurance policy riders
   D. Types, benefits, and risks of life insurance (including use of policy provisions and riders)
   E. Life insurance needs analysis
      1) Needs approach
      2) Capital needs approach
   F. Life insurance policy selection and replacement
      1) Cost and cost comparison methods
      2) Duration of coverage
      3) Guarantees
      4) Dividend histories
      5) Industry analysis reports and surveys
      6) Treatment of old policyholders
   G. Life insurance policy replacement
      1) Replacement forms
      2) Anti-churning legislation
      3) Disclosure requirements
      4) Insurability and non-contestability
   H. Methods of analyzing life insurance policy illustrations

26. Annuity policy analysis (4)
   A. Types of annuities
      1) Immediate
      2) Deferred
   B. Structured settlements

27. Health insurance policy analysis (4)
   A. Medical expense
      1) Types of coverage
      2) Determination of appropriate coverage
   B. Long-term care
      1) Long-term care policies
      2) Special life insurance benefits (i.e., viatical settlements)
   C. Disability income
      1) Characteristics
      2) Policy riders and provisions
      3) Determination of appropriate coverage

28. Taxation of insurance products (4)
   A. Income taxation of life insurance
      1) IRS definition
      2) Modified endowment contracts
         a) Material changes
         b) Pre-TEFRA contracts
         c) Excise tax and exceptions
      3) Dividends
      4) Withdrawals and loans
      5) § 1035 exchange
      6) Transfer for value and exemptions
   B. Estate taxation of life insurance
      1) Inclusion in the estate
      2) Effects of ownership and beneficiary designations

- C. Taxation of annuities
  - 1) Exclusion ratios
  - 2) Taxation of withdrawals
  - 3) Excise tax
  - 4) Taxation at death
  - 5) Current taxation in corporations
- D. Tax implications of owning individual medical and disability insurance
  - 1) Deductibility of premiums
  - 2) Taxation of benefits

29. Selecting insurance companies and agencies (4)
   - A. Financial strength
     - 1) Rating agencies
     - 2) Other considerations (i.e., risk-based capital, ratios, etc.)
   - B. Use by insurance company of sub-accounts and general accounts

Risk Management (1.69%)

30. Client assessment (4)
   - A. Financial goals: time, dollars, priorities
   - B. Risk tolerance and risk exposures
   - C. Client tax situation
   - D. Liquidity/marketability needs
   - E. Analysis and evaluation of client financial statements
   - F. Client preferences and investment understanding and experience

31. Marketability/liquidity (4)

32. Types of investment risk (4)
   - A. Business
   - B. Market
   - C. Reinvestment
   - D. Interest rate
   - E. Purchasing power
   - F. Regulation (tax audit, tax assessment, legislation)

33. Measurement of risk (4)
   - A. Volatility
   - B. Standard deviation
   - C. Beta

34. Influence of time on investment risk (4)
   - A. Effects of time
   - B. Duration

Investment Vehicles (2.41%)

35. Government regulation of securities and markets (4)

36. Investment vehicles (4)
   - A. Corporate bonds
   - B. U.S. government and agency securities
   - C. Mortgage-backed securities
   - D. Municipal bonds
   - E. Derivatives
     - 1) Options
     - 2) Futures
     - 3) Other
   - F. Insurance-based investments
   - G. Investment companies
     - 1) Unit investment trusts
     - 2) Open-end mutual funds
     - 3) Closed-end investment companies
   - H. Certificates of deposit and cash equivalents
   - I. Common stock
   - J. Real estate, investor-managed
   - K. Real estate, indirect ownership
   - L. International investments
   - M. Preferred stock
   - N. Tangible assets (collectibles)
   - O. Natural resources

37. Types and measures of investment returns (4)
   - A. Annualized return
   - B. Real (inflation-adjusted) return
   - C. Total return

D. Risk-adjusted return
E. After-tax return
F. Holding period return
G. Internal rate of return
H. Yield-to-maturity
I. Yield-to-call
J. After-tax yield
K. Realized compound yield

38. Bond and stock valuation methods (4)
    A. Capitalized earnings
    B. Dividend growth
    C. Price/earnings
    D. Intrinsic value

Investment Theory and Strategies (4.41%)

39. Portfolio performance measurement (4)
    A. Benchmark portfolios
    B. Risk-adjusted returns
    C. Modern portfolio theory
    D. Time- vs. dollar-weighted return

40. Formula investing (4)
    A. Dollar cost averaging
    B. Dividend reinvestment
    C. Other

41. "Active" and "passive" strategies (4)
    A. Market timing
    B. Securities selection
    C. Bond swaps
    D. Indexed portfolios
    E. Maturity selection
    F. Buy/hold
    G. Immunization

42. Leverage and use of borrowed funds for investing (4)

43. Hedging and option strategies (4)
    A. Options
    B. Covered calls and puts
    C. Portfolio insurance
    D. Short sales

44. Asset allocation: active and passive (4)
    A. Among classes: market timing and fixed mix
    B. Within classes: security selection and index funds

45. Pricing models (4)
    A. Capital asset pricing model (CAPM)
    B. Arbitrage pricing model (APM)
    C. Option pricing model (OPM)
    D. Other

46. Efficient market hypothesis (4)
    A. Strong form
    B. Semi-strong form
    C. Weak form
    D. Anomalies

47. Investment vehicles match to client needs (4)

48. Tax impact on time value analysis of investments (4)
    A. Net present value concepts
    B. Internal rate of return
    C. Risk

Tax Planning Considerations (1.95%)

49. Ethical considerations in tax planning (4)
    A. Privileged communications
    B. Tax evasion

50. Income tax fundamentals (4)
    A. Steps in conducting tax law research
    B. Sources of tax law authority

51. Tax compliance matters (4)
    A. Filing tax returns
    B. The audit process
    C. Judicial review

52. Taxation terminology (4)
    A. Inclusions
    B. Exclusions

Tax Computations (1.38%)

53. Tax calculations and special rules (4)
    A. Gross income
    B. Adjusted gross income
    C. Itemized deductions
    D. Taxable income
    E. Tax liability

54. Tax accounting (4)
    A. Cash method
    B. Accrual method
    C. "Hybrid" method
    D. Long-term contracts
    E. Installment sales
    F. Accounting periods

55. Tax characteristics of business forms (4)
    A. Sole proprietorship
    B. Limited and general partnerships
    C. Family limited partnerships
    D. Limited liability partnerships
    E. Limited liability companies
    F. Regular or C corporations
    G. S corporations
    H. Trusts
    I. Foundations/exempt organizations
    J. Professional associations/corporations
    K. Other

56. Basis and cost recovery concepts (4)
    A. Original basis rules (purchases, gifts, estates, etc.)
    B. Carryover basis
    C. Adjustments to basis

57. Concepts of property dispositions (4)
    A. Determination of gain or loss
    B. Characterization of gain or loss
    C. Netting rules
    D. Capital loss limitations

58. Interest expense deduction (4)
    A. Qualified residence interest
    B. Trade or business interest
    C. Investment interest
    D. Personal interest
    E. In connection with a passive activity
    F. In connection with an unpaid tax liability

Tax Planning Strategies (1.90%)

59. Tax management techniques (4)
    A. Deferral and acceleration
    B. Maximization of exclusions and credits
    C. Managing loss limitations
    D. Minimization of rates
    E. Capital asset transactions
    F. Minimizing (or re-characterizing) non-deductible expenditures
    G. Installment sales

60. Non-taxable transactions (4)
    A. Like-kind exchanges
    B. Disposition of personal residence (§ 1034)

61. Passive activity loss and credit rules (4)
    A. Taxpayers subject to § 469
    B. Definition of passive activity
    C. Computation of passive activity losses and credits
    D. Treatment of disallowed losses and credits

62. Tax implications of marriage dissolution (4)
    A. Alimony
    B. Child support
    C. Personal exemption
    D. Property settlement

63. Interest and penalty taxes and other charges (4)
    A. Failure to file tax return or to pay tax
    B. Preparer penalties
    C. Accuracy related penalties
    D. Fraud penalties

64. Tax pitfalls (4)
    A. Statutory
    B. Judicial
    C. Tax penalties

65. Miscellaneous (4)
    A. Alternative minimum tax
    B. Social Security self-employment tax
    C. Home office and vacation home rules

Government Plans (1.40%)

66. Social Security, Medicare, and Medicaid (4)
    A. Basic provisions of OASDHI
    B. Eligibility
    C. Level of benefits

Retirement Plans and Strategies (4.32%)

67. Ethical considerations in retirement planning and employee benefits (4)
    A. ERISA fiduciary obligations
    B. Prohibited transactions, parties-in-interest, disqualified parties

68. Types of retirement plans (4)
    A. Definitions
    B. Factors affecting suitability (for individuals or types of business)

69. Qualified plan characteristics (4)
    A. Feasibility of installation of a qualified plan
        1) Objectives
        2) Factors
        3) Recommendations: problem-solving, tax benefits, meeting objectives
    B. Qualified plan coverage and eligibility requirements
        1) Age/service
        2) Coverage requirement
        3) Minimum participation
    C. Qualified plan vesting schedule
        1) Types
        2) Top-heavy plans
        3) Recommendations: vesting schedule selection
    D. Integration with Social Security/disparity limits
        1) Defined benefit plans
        2) Defined contribution plans
    E. Factors affecting qualified plan contributions or benefits
        1) Tax considerations
        2) Nature of defined contribution
        3) Nature of defined benefit
        4) Comparison of defined contribution and defined benefit
        5) Definition of compensation
        6) Multiple plans
    F. Top-heavy plans
        1) Definitions
        2) Vesting
        3) Effects on contributions or benefits

70. Distributions and distribution options (4)
    A. Retirement plan distribution options
    B. Tax treatment of plan distributions
    C. Tax on excess distributions

71. Retirement needs analysis (4)
    A. Determination of financial objectives at retirement
    B. Calculation of retirement funds available to meet objectives
    C. Calculation of additional funds needed to meet objectives

72. Recommendation of the most appropriate type of retirement plan (4)
    A. Analysis of key factors affecting plan selection

73. Suitability of an investment portfolio for a qualified plan situation (4)
    A. Investment risk
    B. Investment constraints (unrelated business taxable income)
    C. Investment portfolio evaluation

Employee Benefits (1.55%)

74. Life, medical, and disability plans in employee benefit programs (4)
    A. Basic provisions
    B. Income tax implications
    C. Deductibility
    D. Imputed income
    E. Employee benefit analysis and application

75. Other employee benefits (4)
    A. Death benefits
    B. Fringe benefits
    C. Cafeteria plan
    D. Flexible spending accounts
    E. Voluntary Employees' Beneficiary Association
    F. COBRA

76. Business applications of individual life and disability insurance (4)
    A. Business continuation (buy/sell) plans
    B. Business overhead disability plan
    C. Executive/owner benefits
    D. Split dollar
    E. Key employee insurance
    F. Salary continuation plans
    G. Non-qualified deferred compensation
        1) Recognition: requirements necessary to defer recognition
        2) Types of plans and applications
        3) Tax implications
        4) Funding methods

Estate Planning Benefits and Strategies (3.61%)

77. Estate planning overview (4)
    A. The meaning of "estate planning"
    B. Situations in which individuals need estate planning and consequences of integrated planning
    C. Steps in estate planning process
    D. The financial planner's role on the estate planning team

78. Estate planning pitfalls and weaknesses (4)
    A. Weaknesses in a client's existing estate plan
    B. Common pitfalls to avoid during estate planning

79. Methods for property transfer at death (4)
    A. The probate process (wills and intestate succession)
    B. Title (operation of law)
    C. Trusts
    D. Contracts (insurance/pensions)

80. Estate planning documents (4)
    A. Wills
    B. Trusts
    C. Personal care documents

D. Marital agreements
E. Durable power of attorney for property
F. Business agreements

81. Overview of the federal unified tax system (4)
    A. Unified transfer tax system
    B. Generation-skipping transfer tax

82. Federal gift taxation (4)
    A. Basic concepts
    B. Techniques for managing gift tax liability
    C. Analysis and calculation of federal gift tax liability

83. Federal gross estate (4)
    A. Inclusions in a decedent's gross estate
    B. Exclusions from a decedent's gross estate

84. Valuation techniques and the federal gross estate (4)
    A. Valuation of specific property interests
    B. Valuation techniques

85. Federal estate tax deductions (4)
    A. Defining the gross estate
    B. Deductions (debts and expenses)
    C. Adjusted gross estate
    D. Deductions (marital/charitable)
    E. Taxable estate
    F. Adjusted taxable gifts
    G. Tax base

86. Calculation of federal estate tax liability (4)
    A. Steps to calculate the estate tax
    B. Various credits affecting the estate tax calculation (unified credit, state death tax, prior transfer, etc.)

87. Characteristics and tax aspects of property interests (4)
    A. Title forms
    B. Other interests
    C. Advantages and disadvantages of forms of property interests
    D. Taxation aspects
    E. Recommendation and justification of the most appropriate form of property interests

88. Probate (4)
    A. Probate process
    B. Advantages and disadvantages of probate
    C. Techniques of avoiding probate
    D. Recommendation and justification of the most appropriate probate avoidance techniques

89. Liquidity planning (4)
    A. Sale of assets
    B. Life insurance
    C. Special techniques for closely-held business owners (e.g., § 6166, 303, 2032A and buy-sell agreements)

90. Powers of appointment (4)
    A. Use and purpose in estate planning
    B. General and special (limited)
    C. "5 & 5" power (§ 2041(b)(2))
    D. Federal gift and estate tax implications

91. Features of trusts (4)
    A. Classification of trusts
    B. Characteristics of selected trust provisions
    C. Rule against perpetuities

92. Taxation of trusts and estates (4)
    A. Income tax implications of trusts
        1) Exemptions
        2) Simple and complex trusts
        3) Distributable net income
    B. Federal gift tax implications of trusts
    C. Federal estate tax implications of trusts
    D. Income tax implications of estates
    E. Recommendation and justification of the most appropriate trust
    F. Excise tax on retirement plans at death

93. Estate freeze issues
    A. Limitations on corporate and partnership freezes (§ 2701)
    B. Trust freezes (§ 2702 including qualified personal residence trusts)

94. Life insurance for estate planning (4)
    A. Advantages and disadvantages of specific life insurance techniques in estate planning
    B. Life insurance trusts
    C. Ownership, beneficiary designation and settlement options
    D. Gift and estate taxation of life insurance
    E. Recommendation and justification of the most appropriate life insurance technique

95. Gifts (4)
    A. Suitability of gifts for client and recipient
    B. Techniques for gift-giving

96. Taxation of gifts (4)
    A. Income taxation of lifetime transfers
    B. Federal gift taxation of lifetime transfers
    C. Circumstances causing inclusion of gifts in gross estate
    D. Calculation and analysis of the effect of a lifetime gift program

97. Recommendation and justification of the most appropriate property to give as a gift (4)
    A. Selection of the most appropriate property to give as a gift
    B. The most appropriate lifetime gift-giving techniques
    C. Justification of the lifetime gift-giving techniques selected for the client's situation

98. Marital deduction and bypass planning (4)
    A. Characteristics of the marital deduction
    B. Recommendation and justification of property interests that qualify for the marital deduction
    C. QTIP planning and the prior transfer credit
    D. Special planning for non-U.S. spouse

99. Federal estate tax implications of the marital deduction and bypass planning (4)
    A. Federal estate tax implications of using the marital deduction
    B. Calculation of increased wealth transfer generated from modifying a client's estate plan

100. Recommendation of the most appropriate marital or non-marital transfer (4)

A. Factors to consider in selecting the optimum mix of marital and non-marital transfers
B. Selection of the most appropriate single or combination of marital and/or non-marital transfers for a client's situation
C. Justification of the marital and non-marital transfer techniques selected for the client's situation

101. Estate planning for nontraditional relationships (4)
   A. Children of another relationship
   B. Cohabitation
   C. Adoptions
   D. Same sex relationships
   E. Communal relationships

102. Charitable contributions and transfers (4)
   A. Considerations for contributions and transfers
   B. Requirements for a gift to qualify for a charitable deduction
      1) Charitable remainder trusts
      2) Charitable lead trusts
   C. Tax and non-tax characteristics of specific forms of charitable transfers including alternative minimum tax considerations
   D. Charitable income tax deduction limitations
   E. Calculation of the maximum total and/or maximum current year income tax deduction for a client's situation
   F. Recommendation and justification of the most appropriate property and form of charitable transfer

103. Intra-family business and property transfers (4)
   A. Characteristics of intra-family transfers
   B. Federal income, gift and estate tax implications of intra-family transfers
   C. Recommendation and justification of the most appropriate intra-family business and property transfer technique

104. Postmortem planning techniques (4)
   A. Characteristics of postmortem estate planning techniques
   B. Determination of whether a client qualifies for special tax treatment
   C. Recommendation and justification of the most appropriate postmortem planning technique

105. Planning for incapacity (4)
   A. Definition of incapacity
   B. Care of client's dependents
   C. Personal care of incapacitated client
   D. Care of incapacitated client's property

106. Special topics in estate planning (4)
   A. Divorce/remarriage
   B. Selection of fiduciaries and guardians

Version: 8/98

2

Regulation of Financial Planners

Jeffrey B. Kelvin and David M. Cordell

Chapter Outline

Financial planning is an emerging profession that continues to evolve. Because of the proliferation of financial planners that began in the late 1970s, regulation of financial planners has become an increasingly important topic to investors, consumer advocates, regulatory authorities, elected officials, and financial planners themselves. This chapter reviews federal legislation and regulatory actions that govern the activities of financial planners.

A good example of the rapidly changing regulatory environment is an important piece of legislation that Congress passed and the president signed in October 1996. As explained later in the chapter, the Investment Advisers Supervision Coordination Act of 1996 changed the regulatory environment significantly. As of July 1997, the Securities and Exchange Commission (SEC) no longer requires financial planners with less than $30 million of assets under management to register with the SEC as investment advisers. Exceptions to this exemption include advisers to investment companies and financial planners in states that have no investment adviser laws. In effect, regulation of "small" investment advisers becomes the exclusive purview of the states.

When reading about the development of the regulatory environment, keep in mind the size distinction that determines whether a financial planner needs to register as an investment adviser at the federal (SEC) level after July 1997. Although many practitioners will find that registration with the SEC is no longer necessary, most will find that state requirements for investment advisers are quite similar to federal requirements.

HOW FINANCIAL PLANNERS BECAME INVESTMENT ADVISERS

In the late 1970s and early 1980s when the proliferation of financial planners, plans, and products became evident, several committees in Congress grew concerned that, due to this growth in the industry, additional regulation would be necessary. There was talk in Washington at that time of new statutes and regulations to specifically cover the activities of financial planners so that consumers could be adequately protected. Much of this talk, of course, was precipitated by relatively isolated horror stories involving fraud and abuse.

The SEC became alarmed at the prospect of new legislation in this area since the agency felt that regulation of financial planners was its turf. When taking this attitude with Congress, the SEC was urged to develop a clear and concise position on the subject of what specific activities undertaken by financial services professionals would trigger the application of the existing federal securities laws. This was felt by the Congress to be an approach that could remove the need for new legislation.

SEC Release No. IA-770

The Securities and Exchange Commission took the position that the *Investment Advisers Act of 1940* was the statutory body of law that should control the area of regulation of financial planners. It is true that this legislation had been enacted 40 years earlier in a postdepression era during which a legislative framework to police and control the activities of discretionary money managers was the primary objective. However, the SEC in the early 1980s took the position that this same statute should be applied to the activities of financial planners. In August 1981, the Securities and Exchange Commission released its famous *Release No. IA-770.* This pronouncement set forth three separate tests which were to be applied to the activities of financial planners. In the event that all three tests were answered in the affirmative, the SEC took the position that the Investment Advisers Act of 1940 would apply to the planner's activities. If, however, any one of the three tests could not be answered in the affirmative, the Investment Advisers Act of 1940 would not apply to these professional activities. Let us review these three tests separately.

Advice or Analyses about Securities

The first test under IA-770 set forth the question of whether the financial services professional provides "advice or analyses" about a security. Since the term *security* is very broadly defined for federal securities law purposes, it can include a great many financial instruments in addition to the best-known securities, like common stocks or bonds. For example, the definition includes a certificate of deposit, commercial paper, a limited partnership, or even variable life insurance or variable annuity products. The official definition of the term *security* as set forth by Sec. 80b-2(a)(18) of the Investment Advisers Act of 1940 is as follows:

> Any note, stock, Treasury stock, bond, debenture, evidence of indebtedness, certificate of interest or participation in any profit-sharing agreement, collateral trust certificate, preorganization certificate or subscription, transferable share, investment contract, voting-trust certificate, certificate of deposit for a security, fractional undivided interest in oil, gas, or other mineral rights, or in general, any instrument or interest commonly known as a *security*, or any certificate of interest or participation in, temporary or interim certificate for, receipt for, or guarantee of, or warrant or right to subscribe to or purchase any of the foregoing.

It is clear, based on the breadth and scope of the definitions under this first test, that financial services professionals will invariably become involved with providing advice about securities.

The Business Standard

The second test as set forth by SEC Release IA-770 concerns whether the financial services professional is presented to the public as being "in the business" of providing advice about securities. This issue is answered by examining how the practitioner's services are communicated to the public. What is printed on the practitioner's business card or on the front door of the office? What does the telephone book advertisement say? How is the telephone answered? What is stated on the business card and letterhead? In short, does the practitioner raise any implication that he or she provides any advice about securities? All of these factors are pertinent in deciding whether the financial services professional is "in the business" of providing advice about securities.

The Compensation Test

The last test contained in the SEC release is perhaps the simplest one to apply, and yet the least understood. The issue concerns compensation received by the practitioner, and the test is met regardless of the source of payment. Therefore, although a practitioner who charges a fee to a client for the provision of investment advice will easily meet the third test of IA-770, one who charges no fee but does receive a commission on the sale of a securities product will also meet this test. Actually in the current environment it is practically impossible for a financial services professional to fail to meet this third test.

If all three of these tests are applicable to the specific activities of a financial services professional, the terms and provisions of the Investment Advisers Act of 1940 will apply.

SEC Release No. IA-1092 Reaffirms IA-770

SEC Release No. IA-770 was a landmark ruling from the SEC. As the financial planning profession continued to emerge in the mid to late 1980s, many individuals and groups called upon the Securities and Exchange Commission to comment once again on the three tests that had been set forth by IA-770 a few years earlier. It was felt by some that the original three-test approach might no longer be held applicable by the SEC. In October 1987, in response to multiple requests from various segments of the financial services community, the Securities and Exchange Commission issued *Release No. IA-1092.* This pronouncement is significant since it totally reaffirms the three-prong approach that had earlier been set forth by IA-770.

Therefore the original application by the Securities and Exchange Commission of the three-test approach still applies. As a practical matter, any financial services professional who by reason of his or her activities must answer all three tests in the affirmative will have activities subjected to the Investment Advisers Act of 1940 at the federal level.

In addition to total reaffirmation of the three-step test of IA-770, however, IA-1092 devoted renewed attention to the antifraud provisions of the Investment Advisers Act of 1940. These provisions are designed to protect consumers who use the services of investment advisers.

The 1987 release cites *SEC v. Capital Gains Research Bureau*, a Supreme Court case discussing the antifraud provisions. That case held that "an investment adviser is a fiduciary who owes his client an affirmative duty of utmost good faith, and full and fair disclosure of all material facts." As a general matter, the release states that an adviser must disclose to clients all material facts regarding potential conflicts of interest. In this way, the client can make an informed decision about entering into or continuing an advisory relationship with the adviser.

The release includes selected interpretive and no-action letters illustrating the scope of the duty to disclose material information in certain situations involving conflicts of interest. Additional disclosure might be required, depending upon the circumstances, if the investment adviser recommends that clients execute securities transactions through the broker/dealer with which the investment adviser is associated. In addition, the investment adviser is required to inform clients that they may execute recommended transactions through other brokers or dealers.

Release IA-1092 goes on to set forth specific examples of situations that require full disclosure on the investment adviser's filing statement with the SEC. Points raised by IA-1092 in the antifraud/full disclosure area include the following:

- An adviser who intends to implement, in whole or in part, the financial plan prepared for clients through the broker/dealer or insurance company with which the adviser is associated, must inform the clients that in implementing the plan the adviser will also act as agent for that firm.
- An investment adviser who is also a registered representative of a broker/dealer and who provides investment advisory services outside the scope of employment with the broker/dealer, must disclose to advisory clients that the advisory activities are independent of employment with the broker/dealer. Additional disclosure might be required, depending upon the circumstances, if an adviser recommends that a client execute securities transactions through the broker/dealer with which the adviser is associated. For example, an adviser is required to fully disclose the nature and extent of any personal interest in such a recommendation, including any compensation that would be received from the broker/dealer in connection with the transaction. In addition, an adviser is required to inform clients that they may execute recommended transactions with other broker/ dealers.
- A financial planner who recommends and uses only the financial products offered by the broker/dealer by which the financial planner is employed should disclose this practice and inform clients that the plan may be limited by such products.
- An investment adviser must not effect transactions in which he or she has a personal interest if this could result in the adviser's preferring his or her own interest to that of the advisory clients.
- An adviser who structures personal securities transactions and then trades on the market result caused by his or her recommendation to clients must disclose this practice.
- An investment adviser must disclose his or her personal securities transactions that are inconsistent with the advice given to clients.

- An investment adviser must disclose compensation received from the issuer of a security that the adviser recommends.

Exclusions and Exemptions from the Investment Advisers Act of 1940

It should be noted that despite the foregoing, there are six excluded areas of activities specifically set forth in Section 202(a) (11) of the Investment Advisers Act of 1940. These exclusions could have the effect of eliminating the need for the financial services professional to be subjected to the mandates of the statute. The six excluded areas are

- any bank or bank holding company as defined in the Bank Holding Company Act of 1956 that is not an investment company
- any lawyer, accountant, engineer, or teacher, if the performance of advisory services by any of these is solely incidental to the practice of his or her profession
- any broker, dealer, or registered representative thereof whose performance of advisory services is solely incidental to the conduct of his or her business as a broker or dealer and who receives no "special compensation" for his or her services
- the publisher of any newspaper, news magazine, or business or financial publication of general or regular circulation
- any person whose advice, analyses, or reports relate only to securities that are direct obligations of or obligations guaranteed as to principal or interest by the United States of America
- such other persons not within the intent of the law as the Securities and Exchange Commission may designate by rules and regulations or order

There are five other groups of individuals who, although they fall within the definition of investment adviser, are nevertheless exempt from registration under section 203(b) of the Investment Advisers Act of 1940:

- any investment adviser whose clients are all residents of the state within which the investment adviser maintains the principal office and place of business and who does not furnish advice or issue analyses or reports with respect to listed securities or securities admitted to unlisted trading privileges on any national securities exchange.
- any investment advisers whose only clients are insurance companies.
- any investment adviser who, during the course of the preceding 12 months, has had fewer than 15 clients and who neither present themselves to the general public as investment advisers nor act as investment advisers to any investment company registered under the Investment Company Act of 1940.

- any investment adviser that (1) is a charitable organization or is employed by a charitable organization and (2) provides advise, analyses, or reports only to charitable organizations, or to funds operated for charitable purposes, and
- any investment adviser that provides investment advice exclusively to church employee pension plans

In summary, the five groups of individuals discussed in the preceding paragraph are exempt from registration with the Securities and Exchange Commission even though they are considered investment advisers under the act. They must still comply with the act's antifraud provisions. On the other hand, an individual who falls into the first group of exception categories mentioned above will not be covered by the antifraud provisions and the Investment Advisers Act of 1940 does not apply to any of their activities.

INVESTMENT ADVISERS SUPERVISION COORDINATION ACT OF 1996[1]

After years of dispute about the direction of regulation of investment advisers, the Congress passed and the president signed the *Investment Advisers Supervision Coordination Act (Coordination Act),* which was part of the *National Securities Market Improvement Act of 1996.* The Coordination Act, which became effective in July 1997, gives authority to the SEC to deny adviser registration to felons within 10 years of conviction, and mandates a consumer hotline for inquiry concerning disciplinary actions and proceedings against registered investment advisers and associated persons.

However, the most important aspects of the Coordination Act and SEC Release No. IA-1633 (which specifies final rules relating to the Coordination Act) concern allocating the regulation of investment advisers between the SEC and state authorities based on the level of assets under an adviser's management. The result is that investment advisers, and thus financial planners, need to register with either the SEC or state authorities, but not with both.

State versus SEC Registration

In general, the Investment Advisers Act of 1940, as revised by the Coordination Act, requires investment advisers, and thus financial planners, to register with the SEC if they are

- investment advisers defined under Section 202(a)(11);
- not excepted from the definition of investment adviser by Section 202(a)(11)
- not exempt from SEC registration under Section 203(b); and
- not prohibited from SEC registration by new Section 203A.

The first three items above were discussed earlier in this chapter. It is the fourth item that the Coordination Act added to the mix. Essentially, new Section 203A of the Advisers Act specifies four types of advisers that are *not* prohibited from SEC registration:

- advisers that have "assets under management" of $25 million or more;
- advisers to registered investment companies;
- advisers that are not "regulated or required to be regulated" as investment advisers in the state where they maintain their "principal office and place of business"; and
- advisers that are exempted from the prohibition by SEC rule or order.

Advisers with $25 Million of Assets under Management

In general, advisers with less than $25 million of assets under management are regulated by state authorities, unless they operate in 30 or more states or meet other requirements described later. Advisers with more than $30 million in assets under management must register with the SEC. If assets under management are between $25 million and $30 million and they have no other basis for eligibility for SEC registration, they can elect either state or SEC registration. The purpose of this window is to protect advisers from going back and forth between state and SEC registration merely because of volatility in the securities market or changes in the client base.

Defining Assets under Management. *Assets under management* is defined in Section 203A(a)(2) as the "securities portfolios with respect to which an investment adviser provides continuous and regular supervisory or management services." Thus, two determinations must be made before the value of an account can be counted toward meeting the $25 million threshold:

- Is the account a securities portfolio?
- Does the account receive continuous and regular supervisory or management services?

Under new SEC rules, securities portfolios include only those accounts of which at least 50 percent of the value consists of securities. Cash or cash equivalents may be treated as securities when making this calculation.

The question concerning continuous and regular supervisory or management services is more complicated. In general, accounts over which advisers have discretionary authority and for which they provide ongoing supervisory or management services are considered to receive continuous and regular supervisory or management services. An adviser will be deemed to provide continuous and regular supervisory or management services to a non-discretionary account if the adviser has an ongoing responsibility to select or make recommendations—based upon the needs of the client—as to specific securities or other investments the account may purchase or sell. If such recommendations are accepted by the client, the adviser is responsible for arranging or effecting the purchase or sale. Other factors that should be considered in deciding whether an account qualifies include

- Terms of the advisory contract. A provision in the contract that the adviser provides ongoing management services suggests that the adviser does provide continuous and regular supervisory or management services. Other provisions in the contract, or the actual management practices of the adviser, may rebut this suggestion.
- Form of compensation. A form of compensation based on the average value of assets under management over a specified period of time would suggest that the adviser provides continuous and regular supervisory or management services. On the other hand, a form of compensation based upon time the adviser spends with a client during a client visit would suggest otherwise.
- The management practice of the adviser. The extent to which the adviser actively manages assets or provides advice bears on whether the services are continuous and regular supervisory or management services. However, infrequent trades (such as those based on a "buy and hold" strategy, for example) should not be the sole basis for a determination that the services are not provided on a continuous and regular basis.

Calculation of Assets under Management. Once a determination is made that an account is a "securities portfolio" that receives "continuous and regular supervisory or management services," the value of the account may be included in "assets under management." If, however, the adviser provides continuous and regular supervisory or management services for only a portion of the account, only the portion of the account that receives such services should be included as assets under management. Current market value of the account should be determined using the same method as that used to determine the account value reported to clients or fees for investment advisory services.

Frequency of Determination. The continuing eligibility of an adviser to remain registered with the SEC must be determined once annually at the time the adviser updates its Form ADV, which is discussed later in this chapter. Thus, the registration status of an adviser whose assets under management falls below $25 million will not be affected unless the assets remained below $25 million after the end of the adviser's fiscal year. To allow an adviser facing potential cancellation of its SEC registration sufficient time to register under applicable state statutes, the SEC has adopted a "grace period" of 90 days after the date the adviser was required to file its updated Form ADV indicating that it would not be eligible for SEC registration.

Rule 203A-4 provides a *safe harbor* from the requirement to register with the SEC for state-registered advisers, if the advisers reasonably believe that they are not required to register with the SEC because they have less than $30 million of assets under management. No such similar safe harbor exists for an adviser that registered with the SEC under the mistaken belief that it had greater than $25 million in assets under management.

A state-registered adviser generally is required to register with the SEC "promptly" when the prohibitions of Section 203A no longer apply (for example, the adviser obtains $30 million of assets under management) unless the adviser is registered in a state that requires new Schedule I of Form ADV (or a substantially similar form or rule) to be filed and annually updated. Such an adviser may (but is not required to) postpone SEC registration until 90 days after the date the adviser is required to report $30 million or more of assets under management to its state securities authority.

Advisers to Registered Investment Companies

Any adviser that provides advisory services to a registered investment company pursuant to a contract (including a "sub-adviser") must register with the SEC regardless of the amount of assets under management. To qualify as an investment company adviser, the adviser must provide advisory services to an investment company that is registered under the Investment Company Act of 1940, and is operational, that is, has assets and shareholders other than organizing shareholders.

Advisers That Are Not Regulated or Required to Be Regulated by a State

Two types of advisers are not "regulated or required to be regulated" by a state and thus must register with the SEC:

- advisers with their principal office in Wyoming (the only state that has not enacted investment adviser statutes as of this writing); and
- advisers with their principal office in a foreign country.

The SEC's Rule 203A-3(c) defines *principal office and place of business* as the "executive office of the investment adviser from which the officers, partners, or managers of the investment adviser direct, control, and coordinate the activities of the investment adviser."

Advisers That Are Exempt from Prohibition on SEC Registration

Section 203A(c) authorizes the SEC to exempt advisers from the prohibition on registration if the prohibition would be "unfair, a burden on interstate commerce, or otherwise inconsistent with the purposes" of that section. The SEC used this authority to exempt, in Rule 203A-2, four categories of investment advisers from the prohibition from registering with the SEC (thereby effectively requiring them to register with the SEC):

- Nationally recognized statistical rating organizations, including ratings agencies, such as Moody's and Standard & Poors, that are registered as investment advisers.
- Pension consultants, including advisers of government plans and church plans, if the aggregate value of "assets of plans" receiving such services is at least $50 million. (Note that the exemption is available to advisers to employee benefit plans—not to plan participants.)
- Certain affiliates that directly or indirectly control, are controlled by, or are under common control with an investment adviser that is eligible to register (and is, in fact, registered) with the SEC. The exemption is available only if the principal office and place of business of the adviser is the same as that of the affiliated registered adviser. Control is defined as the power to direct or cause the direction of the management or policies of the adviser, whether through ownership of securities, by contract, or otherwise.
- Certain start-up investment advisers which have a reasonable expectation of eligibility to register with the SEC within 120 days.

Other Aspects of the Coordination Act

Section 203A(b) preempts the application of state laws requiring "registration, licensing, or qualification" to advisers registered with the SEC. In Release No. IA-1633, the SEC explained that Section 203A(b) "preempts not only a state's specific registration, licensing, or qualification requirements, but all regulatory requirements imposed by state law on SEC-registered advisers relating to their advisory activities or services, except those provisions that are specifically preserved" by the Coordination Act. The Coordination Act preserved three provisions of state investment adviser laws with respect to SEC-registered advisers:

- A state may enforce anti-fraud prohibitions, thus allowing a state to continue to investigate and bring enforcement actions with respect to fraud or deceit against an investment adviser or a person associated with an investment adviser.
- A state may require the filing of any documents filed with the SEC, solely for notice purposes, and a consent to service of process.
- A state may require the payment of filing, registration, or licensing fees. For three years after the enactment of the Coordination Act, if an adviser fails to pay the required fees, a state may require the registration of such adviser with the state.

Investment Adviser Representatives of SEC-Registered Advisers

The application of state law has been narrowed, but not eliminated, with respect to investment adviser representatives of SEC-registered advisers. Only representatives who deal directly with individual clients are subject to state registration requirements. In those cases, the representative will have to register only in the state(s) in which he or she has a place of business. If the representative is located only in states that do not register investment adviser representatives, then the representative is not subject to state registration requirements.

Supervised Persons. Section 203A(b) preempts state law with respect to *supervised persons* of SEC-registered advisers, except that a state may continue to license, register, or otherwise qualify any supervised person who is an investment adviser representative and has a place of business located within that state. New Section 202(a)(25) defines supervised person to mean a "partner, officer, director (or other person occupying a similar status or performing similar functions), or employee of an investment adviser, or other person who provides investment advice on behalf of the investment adviser and is subject to the supervision and control of the investment adviser."

Investment Adviser Representative. Rule 203A-3(a) defines *investment adviser representative* as a supervised person of an investment adviser if clients who are natural persons represent more than 10 percent of the clients of the supervised person. (Rule 203A-3(a)(1).) In 1998 Release No. IA-1733 recognized that advisers with only a few institutional clients were unduly burdened by the 10 percent rule. It specified that supervised persons can have the greater of five natural person clients or the number of natural person clients permitted under the 10 percent allowance, without being subject to state qualification requirements. High net worth individuals (those that may enter into performance fee contracts under Rule 205-3) are excluded from treatment as natural persons. Supervised persons may rely on the definition of "client" in Rule 203(b)(3)-1 to identify clients, except that supervised persons need not count clients that are not United States residents.

The rule contains exceptions for (1) supervised persons who provide advice to natural persons, but who do not, on a regular basis, solicit, meet with, or otherwise communicate with clients are excepted from the definition of "investment adviser representative," and (2) supervised persons who provide only impersonal investment advice. The SEC has defined *place of business* as an office at which the representative regularly provides investment advisory services, solicits, meets with, or otherwise communicates with clients, and any other location that is held out to the general public as a location at which the representative provides investment advisory services, solicits, meets with, or otherwise communicates with clients. (Rule 203A-3(b).)

Solicitor. A solicitor who is a partner, officer, director, or employee of an SEC-registered adviser is subject to state qualification requirements only if the solicitor falls within the definition of "investment adviser representative" under Rule 203A-3(a). A third-party solicitor for an SEC-registered adviser (that is, a solicitor who is not a partner, officer, director, or employee of the adviser) is not an investment adviser representative, and is subject to state qualification requirements to the extent state investment adviser statutes apply to solicitors. In some cases, a solicitor may solicit on behalf of both a state-registered adviser and an SEC-registered adviser. The SEC believes that the Coordination Act does not preempt states from subjecting such a solicitor to state qualification requirements.

What Federal Laws and Regulations Apply to State-Registered Advisers?

Although state-registered advisers are no longer subject to many provisions of the Investment Advisers Act or SEC rules, some provisions still apply.

- Section 206 continues to make it unlawful for any investment adviser to engage in fraudulent, deceptive, or manipulative practices.
- State-registered advisers continue to be subject to Section 204A's requirement to establish, maintain, and enforce written procedures reasonably designed to prevent the misuse of material nonpublic information (insider trading).
- State-registered advisers continue to be subject to Section 205, which contains prohibitions on advisory contracts that (1) contain certain performance fee arrangements, (2) permit an assignment of the advisory contract to be made without the consent of the client, and (3) fail to require an adviser that is a partnership to notify clients of a change in the membership of the partnership.
- State-registered advisers continue to be subject to Section 206(3), which makes it unlawful for any investment adviser acting as principal for its own account to knowingly sell any security to, or purchase any security from, a client, without disclosing to the client in writing before the completion of the transaction the capacity in which the adviser is acting and obtaining the client's consent. This limitation also applies if the adviser is acting as a broker for a person other than the client in effecting such a transaction.

Provisions of State Law Modified by the Coordination Act

State securities regulators may not enforce any law or regulation that would require an adviser to maintain books and records in addition to those required by the state in which the adviser has its principal place of business. Neither may state securities regulators enforce any law or regulation that would require an adviser to maintain a higher minimum net capital or to post any bond in addition to any that is required by the state in which the adviser has its principal place of business. These limitations apply only if the adviser is registered or licensed in the state in which it maintains its principal place of business, and is in compliance with the appropriate requirements of that state.

The Coordination Act also relieves advisers from some regulatory burden by establishing a *national de minimis standard* which states that investment advisers may not be required to register in any state unless the adviser has a place of business in the state, or, during the preceding 12-month period, has had more than five *clients* who are residents of the state. For purposes of counting clients for the national de minimis standard, the following will be deemed a single client: any natural person, and

- any minor child of the natural person;
- any relative, spouse, or relative of the spouse of the natural person who has the same principal residence;
- all accounts of which the natural person and/or the persons referred to above are the only primary beneficiaries; and
- all trusts of which the natural person and/or the persons referred to above are the only primary beneficiaries.

In general, this definition recognizes the family as an economic unit, and gives the adviser greater latitude in staying within the de minimis standard. The following will also be considered single clients:

- A corporation, general partnership, limited partnership, limited liability company, trust (other than a trust referred to above) or other legal organization that receives investment advice based on its investment objectives rather than the individual investment objectives of its shareholders, partners, limited partners, members, or beneficiaries; and
- Two or more legal organizations referred to above that have identical owners.

The Coordination Act did not affect the application of state law to investment adviser representatives of state-registered advisers. Thus, for example, a state may continue to require representatives of a state-registered adviser to register even if they do not have a place of business in the state, have less than six clients in the state, or do not meet the federal definition of investment adviser representative in Rule 203A-3(a).

Another change instituted by the Coordination Act relates to advisers to ERISA plans. ERISA permits employee benefit plan trustees to appoint certain entities as investment managers to manage plan assets, and that trustees delegating responsibilities to investment managers receive protection from liability with respect to investment decisions made by the investment managers. The Coordination Act amended Section 3(38)(B) of ERISA to include in the definition of *investment manager* investment advisers registered under the laws of any state, as well as federally-registered investment advisers and other types of entities. The definition of investment manager was amended to ensure that small investment advisers not registered with the SEC could serve as investment managers and would not be disadvantaged under ERISA. This amendment contains a sunset provision of 2 years from the date of enactment, which was October 11, 1996.

RESPONSIBILITIES OF INVESTMENT ADVISERS WHO MUST REGISTER WITH THE SEC

Each state that regulates investment advisers creates its own set of rules and responsibilities, but states will increasingly adopt standards similar to those required by the SEC. For those financial planners who are subject to SEC regulation, there are seven separate categories of responsibilities that need to be met: registration, record keeping, charging of fees, assignment of contracts, use of labels, delivery of brochures, and avoidance of fraudulent practices. These responsibilities are discussed in the following sections of this chapter.

Registration as a Registered Investment Adviser with the SEC

Financial services professionals who meet the IA-770 and IA-1092 tests and who are not exempt by The Coordination Act must comply with the mandates of the Investment Advisers Act of 1940. The chief requirement is that the practitioner become a *registered investment adviser (RIA).* This is a burdensome administrative undertaking and is accomplished by completing what is known as *Form ADV.* A one-time filing fee (currently $150) must accompany the application. The form itself is complicated and will be rejected by the Securities and Exchange Commission's Office of Applications and Reports Services unless completed correctly in each and every regard. Form ADV itself is divided into two broad parts.

The first part of the form asks generalized questions, such as the name, location, and fiscal year of the applicant's business, the form of the business (that is, corporation, partnership, or sole proprietorship), the background of the applicant and any others associated with the applicant, and whether the applicant and the people associated with him or her have ever been convicted of crimes or are subject to certain injunctions. Part I also contains questions relative to the types of clients for which the applicant will provide discretionary or any other account management services.

The second part of the form requires more detailed and extensive information. This information includes the specific types of services offered by the applicant, a detailed explanation of the fee structure, the basic method of operation of the applicant's business, and even questions dealing with the kind of direct involvement the applicant has in securities transactions for clients. Part II also asks for the names of business associates of the applicant within the securities industry, additional information on the applicant, and, if certain additional conditions are met, a balance sheet.

If the Securities and Exchange Commission finds that the applicant has satisfactorily met the general standards upon which the registration is normally accepted, it must grant the RIA registration within 45 days of the filing date or, in the alternative, must begin proceedings to determine whether registration should be denied. As a practical matter, registration will be denied if these general standards have not been met or if the Securities and Exchange Commission determines that registration, if granted, would immediately be subject to suspension or revocation. This could be the result if, for example, the SEC discovers that the applicant has failed to disclose a prior securities law conviction. Note, though, that the SEC's acceptance of a registration says nothing about the applicant's competence.

Record-Keeping Responsibilities

Once the application of the registered investment adviser has been approved, the postregistration phase of compliance begins. One of the more significant elements of this postregistration phase is the record-keeping responsibility. It must be noted that there is a 16-step record-keeping requirement with which financial services professionals who are registered investment advisers must comply. Included as part of this is compliance with the *Insider Trading and Securities Fraud Enforcement Act of 1988.*

Specifically, *Sec. 204* of the Investment Advisers Act of 1940 provides the following:

> Every investment adviser who makes use of the mails or any means or any instrumentality of interstate commerce in connection with his, her, or its business as an investment adviser shall make and keep for prescribed periods such records, furnish such copies thereof, and make and disseminate such reports as the Securities and Exchange Commission, by rule, may prescribe as necessary or appropriate in the public interest or for the protection of investors. All records of such investors and advisers are subject at any time, or from time to time, to such reasonable periodic, special, or other examinations by representatives of the Securities and Exchange Commission as the Commission deems necessary or appropriate in the public interest or for the protection of investors.

The Securities and Exchange Commission has promulgated a detailed series of record-keeping requirements with which each and every registered investment adviser must comply. As mentioned above there are 16 separate things that must be done in order for the registered investment adviser to be totally in compliance in the postregistration phase. These 16 requirements are as follows:

- *Journal requirement:* Keep a journal in accordance with generally accepted accounting principles.
- *Ledger requirement:* Maintain a ledger in accordance with generally accepted accounting principles.
- *Securities purchased record:* Keep a complete record of all securities you have purchased or recommended.
- *Retention of canceled checks:* Save all your canceled checks and bank statements for a 5-year period.
- *Retention of paid and unpaid bills:* Assemble and save all documentation of paid and unpaid bills.
- *Retention of trial balances and financial statements:* Retain all trial balances and financial statements for a 5-year period.
- *Retention of written communication:* Keep records of all written communications you send to advisory clients and those sent to you by advisory clients.
- *Records of discretionary accounts:* Maintain a list of all accounts in which you have discretionary power.
- *Evidence of discretionary authority:* Retain all documents that grant you discretionary authority.
- *Retention of written agreements:* Save all written agreements executed between you and the advisory client.
- *Retention of communications recommending specific securities:* Keep a record of all advertisements, notices, or circulars, sent to 10 or more persons, that recommend specific securities to clients.
- *Record of securities transactions where RIA has direct or indirect ownership:* Maintain a separate record of all of your recommendations that have been made to an advisory client concerning specific securities in which you have direct or indirect beneficial ownership.
- *Record of securities transactions where RIA has direct or indirect ownership but is primarily engaged in business other than advisory services (for example, life insurance, tax planning, etc.):* Comply with the requirements of the previous item even if you are not primarily involved in investment advisory activities.
- *Retention of written disclosure statements (brochures):* Keep copies of brochures given to clients. Keep signed receipts for the brochures from all advisory clients.
- *Retention of disclosure documents:* Retain copies of all disclosures signed by paid solicitors who refer business to you.
- *Insider-trading compliance:* Comply in every respect with the mandates of the Insider Trading and Securities Fraud Enforcement Act of 1988, as will be discussed below.

- *Record of rate-of-return calculations:* Retain complete documentation of any calculation of the performance or rate of return of managed accounts and securities recommendations.

SEC chairman Arthur Levitt has indicated in a letter to registered investment advisers that they should disclose to clients their preparedness to deal with the so-called Year 2000 (Y2K) problem. The Y2K problem refers to the fact that most computers are not capable of representing years subsequent to 1999 correctly, thus invalidating data and many types of calculations. The SEC's Release No. IA-1769 further requires planners to report their Y2K readiness to the SEC.

Because each and every practitioner who operates as a registered investment adviser will be subjected to an SEC examination, it is imperative that professional advisers totally comply with these record-keeping mandates. There are both civil and criminal penalties available to the regulators as a method of enforcing these rules.

Discouraging Insider Trading: Written Policies and Procedures

Many observers consider insider trading to be a direct threat to the continued integrity of securities markets and, by extension, to the entire financial system.

Another mandate of the Insider Trading and Securities Fraud Enforcement Act of 1988 is that investment advisers must have written policies and procedures that reduce the likelihood of insider trading. An historical perspective will help explain how this requirement arose.

Legislative history shows that when the Securities Exchange Act of 1934 was being debated, insider trading was one of the major issues even back then. However, it was not until 1968 that there was finally a court decision which held that the use of inside information was a violation of federal securities laws (*SEC v. Texas Gulf Sulfur Company*). Since that case was handed down, Sec. 10(b) of the Securities Exchange Act of 1934 (particularly Sec. 10(b)-5) has provided a legal underpinning for the majority of the insider-trading cases brought by the Securities and Exchange Commission.

Congress enacted the *Insider Trading Sanction Act of 1984* which, among other things, gave the SEC the authority to seek the imposition of civil penalties against insider-trading violations for as much as three times the profit gained (or loss avoided) as a result of the unlawful purchase or sale of securities. The government felt that such a provision would act as a deterrent. Of course, insider-trading problems increased, causing Congress to enact the Insider Trading and Securities Fraud Enforcement Act of 1988. Since registered investment advisers are viewed as being in a particularly vulnerable position within the insider-trading context, special provisions of the 1988 statute were enacted to deal specifically with the activities of registered investment advisers.

FOCUS ON ETHICS
Legal Compliance and Ethics

Financial services is a highly regulated industry subjected to intense scrutiny by legislators, regulators, and the media. The media coverage has been intensive, high profile, and negative. A major theme within the industry has been legal compliance. For example, financial planners often feel constrained by home-office demands for prior approval of written sales materials and presentations.

The demand for legal compliance must be maintained. While the services of financial planners are greatly needed by the public, the industry cannot expect to survive, let alone thrive, if it is losing the struggle of acting legally.

Financial planners help clients make their financial dreams become reality. The effective planner must understand a client's financial capability, obligations, and willingness to assume risk. In short, the planner must understand the client's financial aspirations in such depth that they can be converted into achievable goals. To succeed, the financial planner must *earn* the trust and respect of the client. How is this done?

Being in legal compliance is merely the minimum boundary of acceptability. The effective financial planner will strive for a higher standard. It may be to live by The American College's Professional Pledge, The Code of Ethics of the Society of Financial Service Professionals, The International Association for Financial Planning Code of Professional Ethics, or the Code of Ethics and Professional Responsibility of the CFP Board of Standards. On an introspective level, a worthy standard is a personal code of ethics that surpasses what others might impose on themselves.

Specifically, the 1988 insider-trading statute added Sec. 204A to the Investment Advisers Act of 1940, which provided the following:

> Every investment adviser subject to the Investment Advisers Act shall establish, maintain, and enforce written policies and procedures reasonably designed to prevent the misuse in violation of this act or the Securities Exchange Act of 1934, of material, nonpublic information by such investment adviser or any person associated with the investment adviser. The Securities and Exchange Commission as it deems shall adopt rules or regulations to require specific policies or procedures reasonably designed to prevent misuse in violation of this act or the Securities Exchange Act of 1934 of material, nonpublic information.

It should be noted that there are regulatory, civil, and even criminal penalties under Sec. 204A for failure to comply with this new statute section of the 1940 law. There is even a special bounty provision in Sec. 204A which grants authority to the SEC to award payments to persons who provide information concerning insider-trading violations. At the sole discretion of the SEC, the individual can receive up to 10 percent of the penalty imposed or settlement reached.

As a practical matter, insider-trading legislation imposes liabilities not only on broker/dealers and registered investment advisers but also on their employees for misuse by such employees of confidential information if the employer has failed to have effectively policed employee activities within the framework of insider trading. The insider-trading statute requires all employers to develop a compliance plan. Every registered investment adviser must have a plan in place.

It is possible to engage in insider trading in many different ways. Examples include conversations with officers of a company with whom the adviser regularly deals or just a normal conversation with clients (for example, "I'm taking my company private in a few months").

It is also possible for employees to receive inside information and act on it without the knowledge of the registered investment adviser. Therefore the RIA must have a plan. Also, when the RIA firm adopts policies, they must actually be adopted with a view that they will genuinely be enforced. If these policies are adopted pursuant to the statute but are never actually enforced, that can be worse than never having adopted a plan in the first place. An actual policy statement needs to be drafted and enforced. Management of the RIA must provide all employees with copies of the policy statement. This, in effect, is evidence of compliance.

To summarize, there are four basic types of requirements within the context of insider-trading compliance. These are

- development of written policies and procedures setting forth the legal prohibitions against insider trading, explaining key concepts underlying these prohibitions, and including any additional restrictions of the firm on insider trading and related activities
- communication of those policies and procedures to employees and supervisors throughout the firm who may learn material nonpublic information as a result of their positions at the firm
- implementation of those policies and procedures through assignment of specific responsibilities to supervisory personnel
- establishment of monitoring mechanisms to increase the likelihood that the firm will prevent, or at least detect, trading and tipping that is not in compliance with the policies and procedures

Fee Restrictions

The 1940 Advisers Act prohibited an investment adviser from basing fees on any share of the capital appreciation of all or any portion of the client's funds unless the advisory contract related to the investment of assets in excess of $1 million. In 1985, the SEC adopted Rule 205-3, which allowed registered investment advisers to charge "performance fees" (also referred to as "incentive fees"), but only if the RIA is "managing $500,000 of a client's assets" or "reasonably believes" that the client has a net worth of at least $1 million. Rule 205-3 also required that clients be advised by brochure that the performance-based fee arrangement "may create an incentive for the RIA to make investments that are riskier or more speculative than would be the case in nonperformance-based situations."

In 1998 the SEC issued Release No. IA-1731, which modified Rule 205-3 by raising the "client's assets" figure to \$750,000 and the net worth figure to \$1.5 million. Release No. IA-1731 also eliminated the disclosure requirements of Rule 205-3, noting that they were duplicative of the general obligation of advisers to deal fairly with clients and make full and fair disclosure of compensation arrangements.

Assignability of Investment Advisory Agreements

Sec. 205 of the Investment Advisers Act prohibits an investment adviser from assigning or transferring an investment advisory contract unless the client expressly consents to such transfer. Congress, in enacting such a provision, wanted to make sure that an adviser would not be able to shift his or her existing responsibilities to some other practitioner or adviser without first obtaining the original client's full consent to the new relationship. Therefore if an existing registered investment adviser wants, for example, to retire, shut down operations, or move to some other location, such practitioner cannot assign the existing professional relationship to another without first obtaining the existing client's full consent to the assignment.

Prohibition of Labels

Sec. 208(c) of the Investment Advisers Act of 1940 provides that it shall be unlawful for any person registered as an investment adviser to represent that he or she is an "investment counsel" or to use the name "investment counsel" unless (1) his or her principal business consists of acting as an investment adviser and (2) a substantial part of that business consists of rendering investment supervisory services.

Although in the form of a no-action letter and not as an actual provision of the Investment Advisers Act of 1940, the SEC has also taken the position that a practitioner must not use the initials "RIA" after his or her name. The SEC was aware of a growing trend within the financial planning community of practitioners using the "RIA" initials after their names as some form of designation—such as CLU or ChFC. Specifically, the SEC stated that, since successful acquisition of professional designations such as CLU or ChFC requires the passing of rigorous course examinations, it would be misleading to use the initials "RIA" after a practitioner's name, in light of the fact that no courses or examinations are required (at least at the federal level) in order to obtain this status. However, in a somewhat surprising conclusion, the SEC announced that it would permit use of the complete phrase "registered investment adviser" after a financial planner's name.

Brochure Rule

In SEC Release No. IA-664, the Securities and Exchange Commission set forth Rule 204-3, which has become known as the brochure rule. Essentially any practitioner who is a registered investment adviser must deliver a written brochure to each and every client.

Since January 30, 1979, when the U.S. Securities and Exchange Commission promulgated SEC Release No. IA-664, all registered investment advisers have been required to deliver a written disclosure statement to each and every client. This concept requires every investment adviser to deliver a special disclosure statement not only to existing clients to whom investment advice has been given, but also to prospective clients. This disclosure must be delivered to clients or prospective clients either (1) within 48 hours of entering into an investment advisory agreement or (2) when the contract is entered into if the client can terminate such contract within 5 days.

Compliance with the brochure rule can be accomplished either by providing the client with a copy of part II of the Form ADV or, in the alternative, by preparing a separate narrative statement containing each and every piece of data that appears as part of part II of the Form ADV. The SEC seems to prefer the former approach.

There are 13 basic categories of data that the brochure must communicate to the financial planning client:

- types of clients
- source of information, method of analysis, and investment strategy
- business background and education
- other securities industry activities
- conditions for managing accounts
- review procedures
- advisory fee structure
- types of securities about which advice may be provided
- minimum educational standards imposed on associates/employees
- other business activities with which the planner may be involved
- interest in securities transactions
- brokerage discretion
- balance sheet in the event that the registered investment adviser maintains custody or possession of the client's funds or securities or requires prepayment of advisory fees 6 months or more in advance, and such fees are in excess of $500 per client

In summary, therefore, the brochure rule requires the registered investment adviser to deliver either part II of the Form ADV or the substitute brochure to the client or prospective client. It must also be noted, however, that if a continuing relationship exists between the registered investment adviser and the client, the RIA must offer to deliver an updated version of the brochure to the client at the end of each fiscal year. This portion of the brochure rule differs from the initial requirement in that, rather than the registered investment adviser being required to actually deliver the brochure disclosure statement to the client, it is satisfactory to merely offer to deliver such brochure in subsequent years.

The Antifraud Provisions

Sec. 206 of the Investment Advisers Act of 1940 has come to be known as the antifraud portion of the act. Specifically, it provides the following:

It shall be unlawful for any investment adviser, by use of the mails or any means or instrumentality of interstate commerce, directly or indirectly:

a. to employ any advice, scheme, or artifice to defraud any client or prospective client;
b. to engage in any transaction, practice, or course of business which operates as a fraud or deceit upon any client or prospective client;
c. to act as principal for his own account, knowingly to sell any security to or purchase any security from a client, or to act as broker for a person other than such client, knowingly to effect any sale or purchase of any security for the account of such client, without disclosing to such client in writing before the completion of such transaction the capacity in which he or she is acting and obtaining the consent of the client to such transaction. The prohibitions of this paragraph shall not apply to any transaction with a customer of a broker or dealer if such broker or dealer is not acting as an investment adviser in relation to such transaction.
d. to engage in any act, practice, or course of business which is fraudulent, deceptive, or manipulative. The Securities and Exchange Commission shall, for the purposes of this paragraph (d) by rules and regulations define and prescribe means reasonably designed to prevent such acts, practices, and courses of business as are fraudulent, deceptive, or manipulative.

These antifraud provisions of the Investment Advisers Act of 1940 have been interpreted to mean that the investment adviser becomes a *fiduciary* who owes the client "an affirmative duty of utmost good faith and full and fair disclosure of all the material facts." The antifraud provisions of the act also deal quite extensively with conflict of interest issues and, in general, hold the investment adviser to an exceedingly high standard of fiduciary responsibility.

The antifraud provisions of the act may even become operative in situations in which a securities transaction per se has not taken place. In essence, the SEC has decided that since Sec. 206 of the act does not refer to "dealings in securities" as most other general antifraud provisions in the federal securities law do, Sec. 206 is much broader and can be applied to transactions in which fraudulent conduct arose out of the investment advisory relationship between an investment adviser and his, her, or its clients, even if the conduct did not involve a securities transaction.

STATE REGULATION OF FINANCIAL PLANNERS

This chapter has been focused on the regulation of financial planners within the framework of the federal securities laws. It must be noted, however, that there are a whole separate series of regulatory responsibilities stemming from the various state securities laws and state securities commissions. At this time, 49 states require the registration of investment advisers. Some of the states single out the activities of financial planners as part of this requirement, while other jurisdictions merely lump the concept of financial planner and investment adviser together. It should be noted, however, that state registration sometimes involves a series of procedures that are even more difficult than those that exist at the federal level.

For example, many states require a minimum capitalization amount as a prerequisite to granting investment adviser registration approval. Some states require a bond and an audited financial statement to accompany the application as well. Almost every state requires that the participants in the registered investment advisory operation have certain NASD registration, such as the series 63 (uniform state securities test), series 22 (limited partnership/direct participation test), or series 65 (investment adviser) examination. In addition, the state securities commissions, unlike the SEC, will want to see all contracts, disclosure statements and documents, and literature used by the RIA/financial planner with the client. It is inadequate for the financial services professional to focus only on the federal regulatory implications of providing financial planning advice since the state component of the overall scheme is just as relevant.

CONCLUSION

Any argument that the financial planning industry is unregulated must be dismissed as unfounded. This chapter has focused on the various systems used to regulate financial planning professionals. There is obviously a highly comprehensive system of regulation involving a variety of legal and regulatory mandates at both the federal and state level. The financial services professional must become familiar with these responsibilities and must grow accustomed to complying with these mandates on a continuing basis.

NOTES

1. This section was adapted from *The Great Divide: Amendments to the Investment Advisers Act and Related Commission-Rulemaking* which was written by Robert E. Plaze and Catherine M. Saadeh of the SEC's Division of Investment Management in September 1997 and posted on the Internet at http://www.sec.gov/rules/extra/grtdiv.htm.The authors did not participate in this adaptation and are not responsible for any misinterpretation of the original document.

3

Ethics and Professionalism

Robbin Derry, Ken Cooper, and Ronald F. Duska

Chapter Outline

An important consideration in the financial planning environment is ethics and professionalism. While clearly a separate topic from meeting client needs and legal and regulatory concepts, ethics and professionalism are closely related to both. First, a significant obligation of a professional is service to others, which is of paramount concern in ethics. Financial professionals, as agents who are required to consider their clients' best interests, are necessarily involved in an ethical dimension. Second, since law is primarily a codification of ethical principles, the understanding of the relationship of legal compliance to ethics is crucial. Hence an analysis of what ethics is and how it relates to the law and client needs is an important enterprise for the financial adviser.

The financial services field has been plagued by ethical lapses. Charges of improper conduct appear all too frequently. In the life insurance industry, opinion polls document that the majority of consumers trust their own agents, but there is widespread distrust of agents in general. The Insurance Information Institute recently completed a biannual consumer survey giving the life insurance industry its lowest favorability rating in a 26-year span.[1]

This decline in public confidence is related to the many charges and millions of dollars in fines and other penalties that have been assessed. These transgressions are frequently amplified by media coverage.

How can this be happening to the financial services industry? Ethical standards represent the basis for client trust, an essential ingredient in successful financial planning. The American College Code of Ethics brochure includes the following statement:

> Throughout the life span of The American College education and ethics have been inextricably combined. Dr. Solomon S. Huebner, the pioneering educator who founded the College, seldom spoke of education without also speaking of ethics. To him a professional relationship between agent and client had to be based on sound ethical principles.[2]

Whether motivated by the desire to avoid the current ethical problems or the attractiveness of the industry's cultural heritage, the financial planner will benefit by developing an understanding of ethics and professionalism. This chapter will explore

- the role of ethics
- the codification of standards of conduct
- the quality of professionalism
- the practice of ethical decision making
- ethical issues in financial services

THE ROLE OF ETHICS

There was a time when the search for a practical way to describe applied ethics seemed analogous to the familiar story of the three blind men's attempt to describe an elephant. There are still many views on what the "ethics elephant" looks like.

Most of our conscious encounters with ethics occur when we observe ethical violations: a public official is caught accepting a bribe; physicians are accused of performing unnecessary surgery; the media stages an event or betrays a trust to grab a headline; and a salesperson misleads a client to ensure the completion of a sale. This tabloid approach, while unfortunately real, only provides a negative glimpse of ethics. Ethics can and should be viewed as a positive influence.

In its most abstract form, ethics is just one of several branches of philosophy. It is that part concerned with moral behavior, that is, the product of moral standards and moral judgment. As Socrates said, "We are discussing no small matter, but how we ought to live."[3]

Deciding "how we ought to live" is the foundation of ethics. If we approach it conscientiously, the results will appear in daily conduct. Each person takes his or her morality to work each day. Regardless of how clear personal standards may be, on the job we soon discover that colleagues, competitors, and clients are governed by what appears to be a different vision of "how we ought to live." Sometimes the vision is considerably different. Regardless, ethics needs to be understood as a powerful element in the financial planning environment.

Ethics is the glue that holds our entire economic and free enterprise system together. Without ethical behavior business deals would collapse, working conditions would be intolerable, and trust would be nonexistent. In business activities people act based on the trust that their associates will behave ethically. When an employee is assigned a task, the supervisor trusts that the employee will not misuse the information, the time, or the resources that accompany the task. A life insurance agent and a client make a verbal agreement to meet again after the agent has had a chance to analyze the client's needs. The agent trusts that the client will come to the meeting and listen to the needs analysis, while the client trusts that the agent will keep personal information confidential. When a manager offers a bonus for high performance, subordinates trust that the reward will indeed be forthcoming upon achievement of such performance. All day people act in ways that demonstrate a trust in the fundamental assumptions of fair treatment, honest communication, accurate representation of intentions, and the avoidance of deception.

Certainly there are unethical people that we have learned not to trust. There are many situations in which it is wise to be cautious. But in situations where there is little trust, it is more difficult to make agreements or to conduct business. Business diminishes and disintegrates without trust. The behavior of untrustworthy individuals and organizations is too unpredictable to risk involvement. When a person lies (deceives, cheats, or steals), it is difficult to restore trust in that individual. If a business develops a reputation for fraud and deception, it is extremely challenging for that business to overcome that reputation. With the erosion of confidence, customers, suppliers, stockholders, and even potential employees will take their resources elsewhere.

Ethics is not public relations. It is not about creating a good image, nor is it a luxury that a company may indulge in after it meets the critical bottom line. Ethics is about how people conduct business, every hour of every day. It is about prompt response to client complaints and honest feedback to subordinates, peers, and superiors. Ethical behavior is being honest with ourselves and others. It involves the quality of the work to which individuals put their names. It is giving clients all the information they need to make decisions that are in their best interest.

The concept of ethics represents a set of fundamental assumptions that underlie nearly all relationships and transactions within society. These are assumptions about the way we treat people: what our rights and the rights of others are, where our individual rights end and the rights of others begin, how individual and community property ought to be treated, and what constitutes fair and equitable treatment of all people.

Discussing ethical conflicts is one important way that people can express their moral values to those with whom they live and work. If trust in ethical behavior facilitates and underlies all economic transactions, then people must be sure to build ethical behavior into their business decisions and operations. Only if they integrate an awareness of ethics into their daily work lives will they create a working environment that is founded on strong ethical principles.

What about competitive business practices? Isn't business fundamentally about trying to gain the advantage over competitors? Does ethical behavior put a manager at a competitive disadvantage?

A manager, an insurance agent, a financial planner, or an investment adviser can be ethical, competitive, and tough about goals all at the same time. Business is not just about competition. It is also about cooperation. It is about meeting the needs of customers. It is about making deals that work for the good of as many people as possible. If a business focused entirely on competing with rivals and neglected its customers, the business would quickly fail.

Honest competition is healthy, contributing to a stronger economy, higher quality service, and a better selection of consumer products. However, competition is not the fundamental purpose of business, and some aspects of competition are destructive.

Ethical behavior implies doing what is right, and that is sufficient justification. Two pragmatic reasons also justify ethical behavior in business. The first reason is that ethical expectations and trust serve to hold business, the economy, and society together. To the extent that people act unethically, these systems fail. The outcome may be that our own business systems falter as a result of distrust, deception, or a lack of consumer confidence. Adherence to ethical business practices adds a cornerstone to the foundation of any business organization.

The second reason to be ethical in business practices is that individual actions create the work environment in which people spend most of their waking hours. People are constantly creating their own living and working context by how they treat others, by statements they make, by attitudes they hold, and by the practices they condone. Ethical behavior profoundly improves their quality of life.

THE CODIFICATION OF STANDARDS OF CONDUCT

Each person is the major contributor in shaping his or her environment. A person's initiatives or reactions to ethical challenges determine the character of all his or her relationships. If people lie, cheat, and steal, they are then living in a lying, cheating, and stealing environment. An ethical environment is the only possible one in which society can progress economically, physically, morally, and spiritually. This is the ethical responsibility: to actively create a context in which everyone can survive. The fulfillment of this responsibility requires people to assess the ethical implications of all actions, the long-term costs, and the alternatives as well as to listen to others who are affected.

The practical result of this process is the development of frames of reference that citizens use to make decisions. Societal units such as nations develop laws that represent a framework based on what the governing unit considers to be minimal standards of conduct. Penalties are established, often severe, to discourage people from violating laws. Frequently industries and/or specific business organizations develop standards of conduct known as codes of ethical conduct, statements of values, rules of conduct, etc. Since people always aspire to standards more demanding than the law, these standards become the benchmark against which the organization's ethical conduct is measured. It follows that we, as individuals, often have our own codes of ethical conduct. One of the early studies on business ethics done by Raymond Baumhart found that the number one influence on a business executive's ethical decision making was a personal code of behavior.[4]

Law and ethics are both standards of conduct that govern a nation, the morality of an organization, and the moral actions of individuals. Those desiring to be a part have more or less voluntarily accepted the standards.

There are other ways to examine the relationship between law and ethics. Figure 3-1 shows that law and ethics overlap, but each has its own domain as well. The dotted lines at the intersection of law and ethics represent their mutable boundaries. Laws are largely ethical standards that society has codified in order to insist on and enforce certain behaviors. Ethical issues that are deemed sufficiently important may become laws; laws considered to be excessive or intrusive may be either ignored or struck down in court proceedings.

FIGURE 3-1
Relationship between Law and Ethics

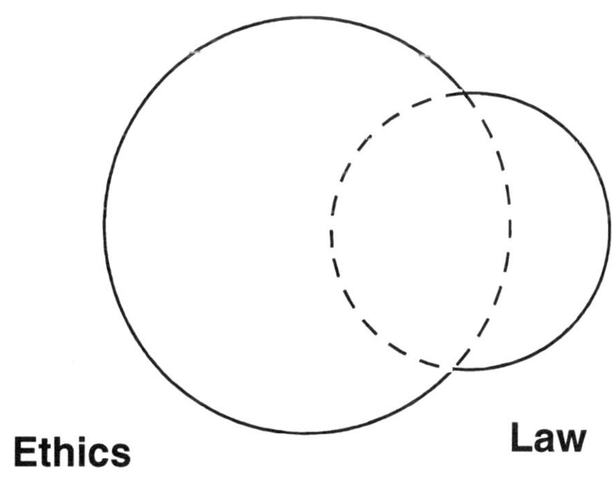

The specific areas of business law and business ethics overlap in similar ways, as shown in figure 3-2. In the area at the intersection of business law and business ethics are such issues as fulfilling contractual agreements, nondiscriminatory treatment of different racial groups in hiring and promotion decisions, and meeting minimal quality-control standards in manufacturing processes.

Within the realm of business ethics (outside the realm of business law) are such issues as the acceptable level of toxic waste to emit or dump into the environment when one knows that the legal standards are inadequate or nonexistent. Other examples are low-level but constant verbal abuse in the workplace, manipulative sales practices, and intimidation of subordinates.

In the purely legal realm are trade regulations, product specifications, and contractual relationships with suppliers, customers, the community, shareholders, and investors. Many "purely legal" rules quickly become ethical issues if they are violated, intentionally misinterpreted, or ignored. In fact, laws represent codified ethical standards. They are the minimum moral requirements that we have agreed to demand for society as a whole.

FIGURE 3-2
Relationship between Business Law and Business Ethics

Both diagrams help to focus on a common misunderstanding. The term *compliance* is often used as if it were synonymous with *ethics*. Compliance means obedience to the law. A "compliance" emphasis may even undermine ethics, because it is targeted at meeting legal requirements rather than addressing the causes of ethical misconduct.

Lynn Sharp Paine states that "legal compliance is unlikely to unleash moral imagination or commitment. The law does not generally seek to inspire human excellence or distinction. Those managers who define ethics as legal compliance are implicitly endorsing a code of moral mediocrity for their organizations."[5]

"You can't legislate morality" is a popular saying. But morality, or the definition of right and wrong behavior, is precisely the focus of the American legal system. Laws regarding stealing, killing, invading another's privacy, defrauding, and misrepresenting intentions all reflect ethical rules. If these are violated, a penalty is imposed on the violator. So society *does*, in fact, *legislate* the most important aspects of morality.

It is true, however, that society cannot legislate *all* morality. Laws cannot be made to cover every situation that arises. Laws cannot mandate decent treatment and concern for other human beings, although that is certainly an ethical issue. If an attempt were made to define and mandate all moral behavior, it would be impossible to enforce. Furthermore, citizens in democratic countries generally prefer fewer laws and greater personal freedom. With a significant increase in laws governing individual behavior, courts and prisons would be even more crowded. People want a certain amount of personal independence to resolve their ethical dilemmas, but they also need to adhere to some common moral standards, since their decisions about such dilemmas inevitably affect others. Similarly, of course, their ethical decisions affect us, and we expect them to adhere to a shared morality as well.

The law is relatively clear-cut. Lawyers, police officers, and court officials are all employed to provide guidance on how to follow the law. Although lawyers don't always agree and the body of law is always evolving, there is a concrete and accessible legal system.

Ethical rules, however, are not as clear-cut. An ethical problem is not as easily defined as a legal problem. A situation that raises ethical conflicts for Susan may not raise any such conflicts for John. This is because they each have a different sense of responsibility associated with particular moral values. For example, honesty to Susan may mean that she should give her true opinion when colleagues ask her what she thinks. Honesty to John may mean that he is always at work on time and never takes sick days unless he is completely incapable of coming into the office. If Susan doesn't share John's interpretation of honesty, she will feel no ethical dilemma at all about taking a sick day to go for a hike in the woods. And John may feel that it is perfectly acceptable, even moral, to politely lie about a colleague's poor performance. They both would agree that honesty is an important ethical standard, but they would disagree on the situations that raise conflicts over that value.

As this example shows, ethical behavior is not as readily defined as legal behavior. There is no concrete body of ethical standards that serves as recourse in ethical dilemmas. However, there are commonly accepted standards regarding the basic norms governing the moral life. These include such rules as

- Don't kill.
- Don't cause pain.
- Don't disable.
- Fulfill obligations.
- Don't cheat.
- Don't deceive.

Some of these are laws, while others are not. They are all commonly held expectations about life in our society, reflecting our values of individual rights and obligations to others. These values and the resulting moral rules extend into the realm of business, since business operates within the larger realm of society as a whole.

Financial Services Codes of Ethics

To ensure as much freedom to its citizens as possible, nations establish laws as a minimum standard, the "moral mediocrity" that Paine addressed earlier. Many aspire to much higher standards. Within the financial services industry, codes of ethics have been developed by most organizations. These are the equivalent to a binding organizational moral law.

The American College, the Society of Financial Service Professionals (formerly the American Society of CLU & ChFC), the IAFP, and the Certified Financial Planner Board of Standards have all developed strong, binding codes of ethics. Each of these codes, which appear in appendixes 3A, 3B, 3C, and 3D, emphasizes the importance of understanding the client's needs and acting to fulfill those needs.

The American College Code of Ethics

The American College Code of Ethics, which is reproduced in appendix 3A, was adopted in June 1984. Although only actions that occur after October 1, 1984, are subject to the code, the standards established by the code apply to students in the CLU and ChFC programs who matriculated on July 1, 1982, or later. All earlier CLU and ChFC matriculants were invited to subscribe to the code and to accept its mandates voluntarily. The jurisdiction of the College does not extend to pre-1982 matriculants who have not consented to be bound by the code.

The Code of The American College consists of two parts: a professional pledge and eight canons. The pledge reads:

> In all my professional relationships, I pledge myself to the following rule of ethical conduct: I shall, in light of all conditions surrounding those I serve, which I shall make every conscientious effort to ascertain

and understand, render that service which, in the same circumstances, I would apply to myself.

These are the eight canons:

I. Conduct yourself at all times with honor and dignity.
II. Avoid practices that would bring dishonor upon your profession or The American College.
III. Publicize your achievement in ways that enhance the integrity of your profession.
IV. Continue your studies throughout your working life so as to maintain a high level of professional competence.
V. Do your utmost to attain a distinguished record of professional service.
VI. Support the established institutions and organizations concerned with the integrity of your profession.
VII. Participate in building your profession by encouraging and providing appropriate assistance to qualified persons pursuing professional studies.
VIII. Comply with all laws and regulations, particularly as they relate to professional and business activities.

The sanctions that may be imposed by The American College for violation of its code of ethics include temporary or permanent suspension of the right to use the CLU designation, the ChFC designation, or both. The college may also relay its decision to other parties, such as government agencies and relevant institutions or organizations.

The Society of Financial Service Professionals Code of Ethics

The code of the Society of Financial Service Professionals (the Society) is similar in spirit but differs in style and content. The Society's code, which is reproduced in appendix 3B, is made up of two imperatives, each having four guiding statements and numerous interpretations. The first imperative is: "To competently advise and serve the client." Competent advice and service should be "in the client's best interest," which should take precedence in any conflict of the agent's and client's interests. Society members must also respect the client's confidentiality and render continuing advice and service. To best serve the client *competently,* the member must maintain and improve his or her professional abilities through continuing education.

The second imperative is: "To enhance the public regard for professional designations and allied professional degrees held by members." Enhancement of public regard entails that the member be law-abiding and maintain his or her integrity and professionalism, encourage others to continue their education, and not detract from other professionals.

The members of the American Society are expected to be professional standard-bearers. It is in this context that the second imperative is particularly relevant. This imperative is more than a concern for the image of the American Society and the field as a whole. It also reinforces the importance of acting in ways that will be seen to be entirely ethical even when exposed to the bright light of public scrutiny. Often unethical actions are taken when it is thought that no one will know. Under this imperative, actions or decisions that a financial services professional would not want to defend in public are completely unacceptable. In addition, the Guides elaborate behaviors that the American Society feels are consistent with its goals and standards.

The International Association for Financial Planning Code of Professional Ethics

The IAFP's Code of Professional Ethics, reproduced in appendix 3C, prescribes two kinds of standards—canons and rules. The seven canons serve as model standards of exemplary professional conduct. Each canon is further explained by one or more rules, which represent specific standards that are mandatory and enforceable by the IAFP.

Canons emphasize placing public interest above the planner's interest, following all laws and regulations, and taking care to avoid conduct or activity that would cause harm to those who rely on the planner's professional judgment and competence. The canons also stress professionalism, including maintaining and improving knowledge, skills, and competence. Improving public understanding of financial planning is another notable area addressed by the canons.

To provide guidance to IAFP members, a set of ethics policies and procedures gives detailed information about the handling of complaints. Included is a list of the possible actions that the IAFP can take against a member found in violation of the code.

The Certified Financial Planner Board of Standards Code of Ethics

A third code is the Code of Ethics and Professional Responsibility adopted by the Certified Financial Planner Board of Standards, which is reproduced in appendix 3D. It consists of two parts: principles and rules. The principles are statements expressing the ethical and professional ideals expected of CFP designees. The rules provide practical guidelines derived from the principles. The principles mention character traits the CFP should possess: integrity, objectivity, competence, fairness, confidentiality, professionalism, and diligence. What the seven principles require is that the CFP designee offer services with integrity and honesty, treating all interested parties fairly and not misrepresenting products. The service should be competent and diligent, that is, prompt and thorough. Adherents make decisions with objectivity, which requires putting the client's needs to the forefront, and in a professional manner, always respecting the client's confidentiality. Each of these seven principles is supplemented by detailed rules that tell how they are to be applied.

Practical Application

What do these codes mean in terms of daily professional practice? The American College pledge says, "I shall . . . render that service which . . . I would apply to myself." The Society of Financial Service Professionals' code calls for putting the client's interest before one's own. The CFP code calls for the practitioner to act "in the interest of the client." Though not identical, all mandate something like the Golden Rule, "Do unto others as you would have them do unto you."

To offer a client the same thorough attention to detail that a financial planner would apply to an investment for himself or herself is no small requirement. Think about the kind of service a planner would give to himself or herself and to close relatives or friends. The planner would make absolutely certain to understand all the apparent and hidden costs. The planner would want to know how much it would cost now and whether the cost over the life of the product would be fixed or variable. The planner would want to clearly understand the potential risks of the investment or policy. So much for the inappropriate derivative sales, churning of investment accounts, or needless life insurance policy replacements we have witnessed lately.

If a product is interest-sensitive, is the planner (or the client) able to regularly monitor its financial stability? What are the costs of withdrawal? Does the planner understand the potential benefits of the product in the short term as well as in the long term? Does he or she know exactly how to maximize those benefits or what actions to take to reduce the potential harms? The planner would not go into an investment or policy purchase without making use of as much knowledge about the product as he or she was able to responsibly acquire.

One of the benefits of being in the financial services business is having access to information and knowledge that the general public doesn't have. Some clients have a particularly strong interest in knowing all the professional details, but some clients simply aren't interested in details. But the agent relationship requires that the practitioner make that knowledge available to help the client make better-informed investment decisions.

The American College's professional pledge says that the financial services professional will render that service to clients that he or she would expect. It is the professional's responsibility to present the information in a way that clients can understand and use in their decision making.

Of course, a financial planner cannot force someone to listen. Nonetheless, it is definitely the planner's obligation to provide the client with the needed information and to present this information in a manner that the client can understand. And the professional should help the client understand why he or she needs the information about the product and what its financial effect will be in the short and long term.

Focus on the Client

The pledge also stipulates that the financial services professional will take into account the conditions surrounding the client and that the professional "shall make every conscientious effort to ascertain and understand" such conditions. This means one cannot simply "sell off" products and be a salesman. There must be what is known as "consultative" or "client-focused" planning or selling. Such an approach requires the practitioner to gather as much information as possible from the client about needs, goals, interest, and assets in order to put together an investment or insurance package that will best meet the client's needs.

The sale of products is essentially client-driven. Practitioners must approach clients with a willingness to listen carefully. Clients can best provide the information regarding their own needs and goals. Clients may also think that they know which product best fits those goals, but practitioners should keep the client focused on articulating needs and goals so they can find the best product or service to match those goals.

Consultative planning or selling is a sound approach to building good relationships with clients and selling life insurance and other financial products. It is also an ethical requirement because of the nature of the client-planner relationship. Most practitioners have the dual role of agent for a financial services company and agent for the client. As the agent of the company, they must accurately represent the company's products or services to the client. Most financial services professionals who deal primarily with the products of one company feel that their obligation to the company is to look to those products first to meet their client's needs and go outside their home company for products only if an appropriate policy or investment is not available with that company.

This traditional approach serves several purposes. First, the planner is able to gain in-depth knowledge of the products of one or two companies, which would be nearly impossible if a person tried to cover all the products on the market. This knowledge enables the planner to serve the client better. Second, it saves the financial planner extensive research time to be able to work from a body of familiar products. Of course, in some instances this could be detrimental to a client who needs more extensive research to find just the right product. It is important that the planner honestly inform the client of the planner's primary relationship with a particular company. The client should understand that these products are the ones that the planner will research and present in most cases. It is deceptive and clearly unethical to fail to disclose that primary relationship.

The financial planner is also an agent for the client. The client trusts the agent with confidential information. Courts have increasingly found that the common law understanding of the word agent is "agent of the client." Courts have held that when a financial services professional induces reliance on his or her expertise, that person incurs liability for decisions made on the basis of the expertise. When a financial planner says in effect to a client, "I am your agent," the planner does indeed take on the responsibilities and liabilities of an agent of the client.

Many educators, speakers, and managers stress the importance of selling a financial service or product solely on the basis of client need. Selling on any other basis, such as the needs and interests of the salesperson, the sales manager, or the company, makes no sense in the long term. The salesperson may be persuasive enough to make fast sales in order to meet a bonus deadline, or the company may be promoting a particular product with higher commission rates. But unless the product really meets the needs of the client over the long term, that client will not keep up the payments, which ends up being costly for the company. Clients who feel that they were sold products that did not meet their needs are not likely to be repeat customers. A client will not refer friends and relatives to a salesperson if the client doesn't believe in the salesperson's ability to listen carefully and respond. So while the short-term sales may look good, the long-term financial position of the salesperson, the selling agency, and the selling company are hurt by any sales that do not meet client needs. The same arguments, of course, support continuing attention to the changing needs of clients over time.

In summary, it is both ethically required and financially wise for the financial planner to thoroughly understand the client's needs and act to fulfill those needs as much as possible. The codes of ethics of The American College, the Society of Financial Service Professionals, the IAFP, and the Certified Financial Planner Board of Standards reinforce this standard.

To take actions that would enhance public regard for the profession (which is even more demanding than enhancing public regard for oneself) is to act in ways that are commonly regarded as highly professional. As shown in the next section, professionalism requires competence and reliability. These characteristics are integral to upholding the ethical expectations of The American College, the Society of Financial Service Professionals, the IAFP, and the CFP Board.

THE QUALITY OF PROFESSIONALISM

The adjective *professional* is loosely attached to many careers and is used in significantly different ways. An example would be the professional athlete who is highly skilled, but the determining factor is that he or she gets paid. Amateur athletes, regardless of how talented, are not professional because they are not compensated.

Today there is much discussion about the professional politician. This is a person who has chosen politics as a career. Frequently the term is used in a derisive way to describe a politician who is more interested in manipulating the system for personal gain than developing public policy.

There are a few occupations that are widely viewed as professions. Included on most lists are doctors, lawyers, and clergy. Similar status is often given to pharmacists, engineers, and architects. Still others could be added to the list.

What do people mean when they say, "She is a real professional" or "His behavior was completely unprofessional"? What is commonly understood as professional conduct?

In the first example the positive connotation includes such characteristics as job proficiency, reliability, dedication, thoroughness, dependability, a commitment to providing good service, and an awareness that one's quality of performance affects the reputations of others.

In contrast, the term *unprofessional* suggests shoddy or careless performance; a lack of concern for customers or clients; disregard for the reputation of a larger group of people; and a narrow, selfish concern for one's own well-being.

Burke A. Christensen, JD, CLU, former general counsel and vice president of the Society of Financial Service Professionals, suggests that "a professional is

Characteristics Defining a Professional

- Specialized knowledge not generally understood by the public
- Threshold entrance requirement
- Sense of altruism
- Code of ethics

a person engaged in a field that requires (1) specialized knowledge not generally understood by the public, (2) a threshold entrance requirement, (3) a sense of altruism, and (4) a code of ethics."[6]

Of these requirements, numbers one and four are immediately evident in the financial services field. Certainly financial consultants and insurance agents have a specialized knowledge not generally understood. Holders of CLU, ChFC, and CFP designations and members of the Society also adhere to professional codes of ethics.

The CLU, ChFC, and CFP designations represent a kind of threshold entrance requirement, even though there are many successful people working in the field who have not earned them. In addition to a professional designation or degree, however, thorough and continuing education in the fundamentals of the financial services profession is an important aspect of meeting clients' needs. This field is increasingly competitive and complex. Federal and state regulations are constantly evolving. Understanding these changes is essential to providing sound advice to clients. The truly professional financial adviser must in some way meet both an entrance requirement of foundational education and a requirement of continuous professional education.

Requirement number three, a sense of altruism, is the characteristic that facilitates adherence to the codes of ethics. Altruism is defined as an unselfish regard for the welfare of others.

The requirement of altruistic behavior may contradict many assumptions about business and competition. But altruism is only one characteristic of a professional, not the only characteristic. A professional is not required to entirely give away services or resources without self-regard. The professional is required to adhere to ethical standards unselfishly, to take others' needs and views into account. The welfare of others is as important as the professional's own. Altruism does not supplant the professional's own welfare, but it does balance it.

Altruism does not allow one to focus exclusively on one's own success and well-being. Altruism does facilitate the achievement of the characteristics commonly expected of a professional: competence, reliability, and high ethical standards. While altruism is an unselfish concern for others, it is clearly not without its benefits to the altruist. Demonstration of concern for others often wins great trust and reliance. However, it is the worst kind of hypocrisy to feign altruism in order to create the image of trustworthiness and reliability. The image of altruism is quite different from deeply felt altruism, and the false image will inevitably be uncovered to reveal the underlying motivations. Such deception is not worth the personal and professional cost.

The important questions facing professionals are twofold. What environment do we want to create? What environment do we want to work in? This is quite different from the question, how do we want to be perceived? The former questions are about daily choices and our expectations of others. The latter question is about image.

Insurance and financial services professionals are understandably concerned about their image in American society. But working merely to improve the image is the wrong approach. The critical issue is what these professionals are doing, not what people think they are doing. Professional respect and credibility for this field will follow professional behavior. Adherence to the highest ethical standards as elaborated here will contribute significantly toward the achievement of professional behavior and subsequently to professional respect.

THE PRACTICE OF ETHICAL DECISION MAKING

Making ethical decisions is easy when the facts are clear and the choices are evident. However, the situation is often clouded by ambiguity, incomplete information, multiple points of view, and conflicting responsibilities. In such situations—which managers experience all the time—ethical decisions depend on both the decision-making process itself and on the experience, intelligence, and integrity of the decision maker.[7]

The development of sound moral judgment requires education and practice. Moral education begins in childhood and extends throughout life. The quality of that education varies with many environmental factors. The examples from which people learn to pattern their lives range from tenderness to brutality, from consideration to greed, from fairness to bigotry. How people are affected and how those around them respond teach enduring lessons.

Accordingly the practice of ethical decision making is influenced by environmental pressures and expectations. In work organizations, these are aspects of the prevailing "organizational culture." Loyalty, for example, may be more highly valued than candor. Short-term sales performance may be more readily rewarded than superior quality service over the long term. Such rewards teach individuals what is acceptable behavior within that system. These messages may influence the moral reasoning process that is used in ethical dilemmas.

This section addresses how to make ethical decisions and how organizations can better integrate ethical decision making into daily operations. The improvement of ethical practice in the workplace must take place on both the individual and the organizational levels. Individuals are ultimately the decision makers, but they are influenced by organizational goals and pressures. Individuals often make decisions within the context of particular organizational roles that they would not make in their personal lives. Therefore it is critical to examine the organizational factors in ethical dilemmas. It is also important that individuals have a reliable method of making ethical decisions. Both the organizational and individual contributions to ethical practice will be addressed here.

Individual Decision Making

Most ethical decisions are made spontaneously by drawing on a usually reliable intuitive sense of what is right. It usually directly or indirectly reflects the values of the prevailing religion and the national culture. As decisions become more challenging due to significance or complexity, solutions are developed through thoughtful reflection. Decisions are made by examining a particular issue in light of the decision maker's personal values. Normally a frame of reference is developed and consistently employed. Examples include the following guidelines:

- Would your decision satisfy the Golden Rule?
- Would you want your decision to appear on the evening news?
- Is the decision consistent with the teaching of the (religious) faith?

Other frameworks are more elaborate but manageable. Members of Rotary International are encouraged to adopt this four-step frame of reference:

- Is it the TRUTH?
- Is it FAIR to all concerned?
- Will it build GOODWILL and BETTER FRIENDSHIPS?
- Will it be BENEFICIAL to all concerned?

Dr. Norman Vincent Peale and Ken Blanchard have developed a three-step ethics check:

1. Is it legal?
2. Is it balanced?
3. How will it make me feel about myself?[8]

Finally, Laura Nash has developed an elaborate framework for examining the ethics of a business decision, as shown in table 3-1.[9]

TABLE 3-1
Twelve Questions for Examining the Ethics of a Business Decision

1. Have you defined the problem accurately?
2. How would you define the problem if you stood on the other side of the fence?
3. How did this situation occur in the first place?
4. To whom and to what do you give your loyalty as a person and as a member of the corporation?
5. What is your intention in making this decision?
6. How does this intention compare with the probable results?
7. Whom could your decision or action injure?
8. Can you discuss the problem with the affected parties before you make your decision?
9. Are you confident that your position will be as valid over a long period of time as it seems now?
10. Could you disclose without qualm your decision or action to your boss, your CEO, the board of directors, your family, society as a whole?
11. What is the symbolic potential of your action if understood? If misunderstood?
12. Under what conditions would you allow exceptions to your stand?

When confronted with a difficult ethical dilemma, it is beneficial to have a frame of reference that leads to systematic analysis. The selected method will vary in complexity and underlying values. Each person must find the approach that, when applied, leads to acceptable and dependable decisions.

Ethical Decision Making in Organizations

Organizations, it is sometimes argued, are only paper entities; they do not make policies or shape lives and careers. It is always individuals, not organizations, who make decisions and take actions.

However, when individuals take on jobs and roles in an organization, their decisions and actions are influenced by ethical codes and organizational goals. That is appropriate to a large extent. When a person is paid to do a particular job in order to meet the company's stated goals, it is reasonable to expect him or her to perform in accordance with the objectives of the position.

Because of the influence of the organization's expectations on individual action, it is worthwhile to carefully consider the role of the organization in the ethical decision making that occurs daily. There are three critical steps to follow in analyzing and improving the level of ethical decisions within a work organization: (1) communicate clear ethical goals and standards, (2) create positive reinforcement and rewards for ethical behavior, and (3) recognize and remove barriers to good ethical decisions.

Steps Toward Ethical Decision Making in Organizations

- Communicate clear ethical goals and standards
- Create positive reinforcement and rewards for ethical behavior
- Recognize and remove barriers to good ethical decisions

Communicate Clear Ethical Goals and Standards

The first step is to communicate ethical standards. They must be practical, specific, and clear. Many corporate mission statements and ethical codes include a commitment to "the highest standards of business ethics." But what does that really mean in practice? In order to fulfill goals set forth in a mission statement, detailed operating strategies need to be established throughout all levels of the company. Broad ethical principles must be defined in more specific terms for each work environment.

There are many issues in our daily work lives that need the spotlight of ethical analysis. Here are some examples of ethical actions that might be taken in specific work situations:

- Solicit and hear constructive criticism from subordinates.
- Respond to customer complaints within 24 hours.
- Be alert to and eliminate destructive stereotypes.
- Give credit for ideas where credit is due.
- Create opportunities for growth for subordinates.
- Develop products and systems that are need-driven.

These might seem to be remarkably small issues, but it is the small daily events that affect the work environment and therefore determine how much work actually gets done daily. When a company is committed to ethical actions and standards on a daily basis, there is no question about how the company is to respond in a time of crisis. Everyone knows what the standards are because the expectations for ethical behavior have been clearly communicated by words and repeated actions.

Communicate Clear, Positive Reinforcements and Rewards for Ethical Behavior

Once specific ethical standards have been articulated, how can they be implemented? The second step is to create reinforcement and rewards for the desired behavior. A frequent concern about rewards for ethical behavior is the difficulty in measuring such behavior. However, if clear standards and expectations have been set in advance, it is not difficult to assess whether these have been achieved consistently.

A discussion of ethical issues and potential ethical conflicts in an organization's meetings will encourage individuals to raise their concerns and to share their reasoning. This step alone accomplishes small miracles in the workplace. Moral stress results in high turnover rates, while the freedom to discuss ethical issues is a major contribution to alleviating moral stress. This forum also provides the leader of the meeting with the opportunity to articulate ethical standards.

Good ethical decisions and consistent actions can be rewarded with greater access to resources and opportunities. Recognition and appreciation in either a public or private setting increase employees' awareness of the value of ethical behavior to the company.

FOCUS ON ETHICS
Professionalism Begins with Ethics

Writing with the financial services industry in mind, Dr. Ronald C. Horn, CPCU, CLU, Williams Professor of Insurance Studies at Baylor University, developed a list of seven characteristics that he considered necessary for a particular occupation to be considered a profession.[10] First on Horn's list was a commitment to high ethical standards. The complete list follows:

- a commitment to high ethical standards
- a prevailing attitude of altruism
- mandatory educational preparation and training
- mandatory continuing education
- a formal association or society
- independence
- public recognition as a profession

Compare this list with Christensen's four characteristics of a professional listed earlier. Both lists emphasize that ethical standards are a critical component of a professional.

There are numerous ways to communicate that ethical thinking is critical to the success of the organization. But if clear ethical policies are not established and adherence to them is not rewarded, no one inside or outside the company will recognize the importance of the ethical standards in daily operations.

Recognize and Remove Barriers to Good Ethical Decisions

The third step is to observe and revise all organizational practices and systems that are inhibiting good ethical decision making. Consider such practices as wide-spread inability to talk about ethics in the workplace, a culture that values toughness over the ability to recognize and reason through moral problems, reprimands within departments for raising problems that need to be addressed, closed doors instead of open doors.

In many organizations the reward system, including the compensation system, contributes to unethical behavior because it creates pressure to shortcut ethical considerations for success. In this case, it is important to evaluate the barriers to changing those aspects of the reward system that contribute to unethical actions. Why has the system been perpetuated? Who has vested interests in the system as it exists? Have there been any attempts to change it in the past? If there are obvious ethical "costs," what are the offsetting "benefits" to continuing the system as it is?

Barriers to ethical actions may take the form of peer pressure, as is often the case in, for example, the perpetuation of discrimination. Or the barriers may exist because there are financial or other benefits accruing to managers in powerful decision-making positions, who therefore protect their interests in the current system.

Another useful aspect to consider when assessing the barriers is to ask who gets rewarded. What are the characteristics of those who are promoted in this organization? What have they done to earn promotions? What are their selling techniques? Are they straightforward and honest or manipulative and deceptive? What are the reputations of the successful people?

When one looks around and asks why individuals are not acting up to their highest moral ideals in an organization, there are often many apparent explanations. If these "justifications" for unethical actions are not addressed, the strong ethical standards articulated in the corporate mission statement or code of conduct will never be implemented.

ETHICAL ISSUES IN FINANCIAL SERVICES

It is often suggested that almost any issue potentially has ethical dimensions. Every industry has practices that warrant scrutiny from an ethical perspective. Recent events have made some of the financial services transgressions abundantly clear. Legal actions and the media interpretations of them have been significant factors in the public's diminished confidence in the financial services industry. A frequently heard explanation is that industry ethical problems can be traced to a small group of individuals who have acted improperly. So the argument continues that the overwhelming majority of industry personnel have high ethical standards. If we could just get rid of those bad apples or could identify them before they were hired, the problem would go away.

No one will argue with the bad apple theory. There *are* a few individuals in the industry who are responsible for many of the high-visibility ethical problems. The solution is not as simple as it may appear, however.

Prosecutors and regulatory agencies have made it clear that simply to punish or dismiss a few people won't solve the problem. Who hired them? Who trained them? Who provided the sales scripts and brochures? Who provided the illustration framework and recommended the variables to be inserted? Indeed, everyone must assume responsibility to restore ethical respectability.

Many regulators and consumer advocates assert that restoring ethical health to the financial services industry requires actions that span the boundaries of any single organization. They point out that this is a highly competitive industry where the successful are well compensated. This structure, left unregulated, will always have more than its share of ethical problems. The issue, this argument continues, is not one of a few bad apples or a few bad companies. It is a systemic problem that must be tightly regulated at the state or perhaps even at the federal level. If it isn't, the industry is doomed, or at the least, alternative distribution systems with different compensation scales will replace the existing one.

How can we be certain who is right? Odds are that no one argument is the complete truth, but there are two crucial things to remember. The first is the importance of providing each client with the needed financial protection. The second is that this high-quality service should be provided as efficiently as possible. The client deserves both. Today's ethical issues should be viewed for what they are—signals of imperfection and the impetus for improvement.

There have been several surveys undertaken to determine what the industry's major ethical issues are. The results vary little from one survey to the next. Count on each to include the misuse of illustrations leading to deceptive sales documents and presentations, investment churning, life insurance policy replacements, and disclosure. In addition, there are issues that cut across industry lines, such as discrimination and stereotyping.

Inappropriate Illustrations

The use of nonguaranteed and noncurrent rates as illustrations in selling interest-sensitive life insurance and other products can conflict with The American College's, the Society's, the IAFP's and the CFP Board's codes of ethics as well as with standards of professionalism. Sometimes the illustrations are unrealistic. Is the nonguarantee disclosure statement adequate? Often it is not, because of the usual problems with small print. Is the client really clear about the security of the investment and its historic earnings record? Only the most honest and realistic illustrations meet the requirements of the codes of ethics and the standards of professional competence and reliability. It is often impossible to argue that the client is being given all necessary information.

If further evidence is needed to demonstrate the unethical foundation of improper illustrations, consider the long-term effects on the companies who mislead clients as to the potential return on their investments. The number and cost of problems facing companies that have consistently oversold clients is staggering.

This issue leads in nearly all the industry's ethical issues surveys. The Society of Financial Service Professionals has been a leader in helping industry personnel effectively and ethically use illustrations. An example is the life insurance illustration questionnaire (IQ), which is reproduced in appendix 3E. IQ helps agents to recognize and evaluate ethical aspects of illustrations by addressing questions from five categories: general, mortality, interest or crediting rates, expenses, and persistency. Because of the popularity of variable life insurance and the great potential for illustration abuse with that product, the Society developed the variable life insurance illustration questionnaire (VIQ), which is reproduced in appendix 3F. VIQ addresses the same factors as IQ except that investment performance replaces interest or crediting rates. While no single approach will provide an instant solution to the illustration abuses, IQ and VIQ are welcome attempts to deal directly with an ethical problem.

Churning

Churning is the process of generating brokerage commissions through unnecessary securities transactions. Churning is associated with discretionary accounts, in which the broker can make transactions without consulting the client. The act of advising a client to make unnecessary transactions is also churning.

Selling a stock and then purchasing another stock with very similar characteristics is an example of churning. The transaction transfers wealth from the client to the broker in the form of commissions without improving the client's portfolio. Further, such transactions may create undesirable tax consequences.

The first and most important question is, Is it in the client's interest? Does this activity fulfill the requirements of professionalism: demonstrating reliability and competence and responding to a client's needs? It often fits none of these. If competent, the financial adviser or sales representative would not be changing advice every few weeks or months.

The temporary success of financial advisers who churn their clients' accounts is based on deception. The adviser induces trust in his or her ability to achieve the client's objectives. Only when this trust is given is the adviser able to persuade the client that constant sales and acquisitions are in the client's interest.

In reality these actions only benefit the adviser or broker. The entire practice may be unethical for several reasons: wrongfully inducing trust, breaching that fiduciary trust, and often harming the client financially. Harming the client has long-term detrimental effects on the company and the industry as well.

Replacement and Twisting

Replacement is the process of terminating a life insurance policy and buying another. Although there are cases that are beneficial to clients, replacement in this context refers to situations in which the salesperson generates commissions by actions that work to the client's detriment. For example, the salesperson may suggest cashing in a whole life policy and replacing it with a term policy. In the short run, it may appear that the client can buy more coverage for less money while freeing up some cash. In the long run, the cost of insurance may prove to be much higher.

Since states are the primary insurance regulators, legal definitions of replacement vary considerably. Insurance agents and financial planners must abide by the laws in the appropriate jurisdiction. Still, from an ethics standpoint, the obvious question emerges: Is the new policy clearly in the client's interest? If the replacement is not absolutely in the client's best interest—and usually it isn't—the proposed action is not ethical. Use this line of reasoning. Would you be prepared to see this action become widely available and practiced by all persons? What could an organization do to create reinforcements for new sales and eliminate rewards for replacement selling?

Twisting is a form of replacement in which the agent induces the policyowner to drop an existing policy from another company through misrepresentation or incomplete information. Twisting is illegal in all states.

The Society of Financial Service Professionals has developed an extremely helpful document called *Replacement Questionnaire (RQ)—A Policy Replacement Evaluation Form,* which is reproduced in appendix 3G. Using RQ helps advisers and insurance agents recognize important issues and evaluate whether replacement is truly in the client's best interest.

Inadequate Disclosure

What information does the client need in order to make a good decision about a product or service being recommended? If the financial planner, agent, or adviser has a greater financial interest in one product than another but does not disclose that to a client, is the client misled that an unbiased presentation of each product is being given? What is the client's interest? What is truly in the professional's interest? Reliability and honesty contribute to trust. Does the client always want to know or need to know? Probably not, but the client should know by the professional's behavior that he or she can ask for and receive any information that is relevant to a decision. It is part of maintaining trust.

Discrimination and Stereotyping

In all workplaces, it is important to be alert to one's own biases and stereotypes. Are we open to hiring, training, and supporting people of different ethnic and religious backgrounds? Do we assume that some people will be more successful than others? Do we provide men and women with similar opportunities and resources? Are we aware of the effects of sexist language? Are we alert to our own assumptions about different groups of people?

The demographics of the workforce have changed dramatically. A large majority of the entering workforce consists of groups that are minorities or treated as minorities: women, blacks, Hispanics, and Asians. These groups bring different backgrounds and cultural training to many relatively homogeneous environments. These groups are still underrepresented at the higher levels of the corporate world, giving evidence of continuing discrimination.

As has been seen from the codes of ethics, the demands of professionalism, and the method of impartial legislation, ethical judgments require the financial services professional to take into account the perspective of others, whether they are the needs and interests of the client or those of all affected persons. The professional who learns to do this should increasingly outgrow discriminatory assumptions and practices. Discrimination and stereotyping are based on ignorance, fear, and inappropriately narrow views of others different from ourselves. These practices are extremely destructive to society.

Our most significant ethical responsibility is to create an environment in which we can all survive. To achieve this, we must take actions that increase trust, meet the needs of those who have put their trust in us, and build organizational systems that encourage reliable, trustworthy, and competent behavior.

Other Issues

These five issues should not be considered a comprehensive listing of the ethical issues facing the financial services industry today. Others have suggested that any such listing should include rebating, commission design, keeping oneself informed, disclosure of all conflicts of interest, competition bashing, concealing product limitations, incompetence, and misrepresentation of one's ability to provide a service.

The ethical challenge is great. The industry demands respect, trust, integrity, and honesty. Reaching for higher ethical standards is in everyone's best interests. Likewise, it is the responsibility of every financial services employee.

NOTES

1. Michael Quint, "Images of Life Insurance Takes a Hit in a Consumer Survey," *New York Times,* September 28, 1994, p. D5.
2. *The American College Code of Ethics,* a brochure published by The American College.

3. James A. Rachels, *The Elements of Moral Philosophy* (New York: McGraw-Hill, 1986), p. 1.
4. Raymond Baumhart, "How Ethical Are Businessmen?" *Harvard Business Review,* July-August 1961, p. 7.
5. Lynn Sharp Paine, "Managing for Organizational Integrity," *Harvard Business Review,* March-April 1994, p. 111.
6. Burke A. Christensen, *Journal of the American Society of CLU & ChFC,* January 1990, p. 21.
7. Kenneth Andrews, "Ethics in Practice," *Harvard Business Review,* September-October 1989, p. 100.
8. Kenneth Blanchard and Norman Vincent Peale, *The Power of Ethical Management* (New York: Morrow, 1988), p. 27.
9. Laura Nash, "Ethics Without The Sermon," *Harvard Business Review,* November-December 1981, p. 81.
10. Ronald C. Horn, *On Professions, Professionals, and Professional Ethics* (Malvern, PA: American Institute for Property and Liability Underwriters, Inc., 1978), p. 40.

Appendix 3A

The American College Code of Ethics

Throughout the life span of The American College, education and ethics have been inextricably combined. Dr. Solomon S. Huebner, the pioneering educator who founded the College, seldom spoke of education without also speaking of ethics. To him a professional relationship between agent and client had to be based on sound ethical principles.

At the College courses and designations have changed over the years, but the ethical emphasis has remained constant and all new students enter a designation program aware that it involves more than just education.

Until recently that has been enough.

Now a new climate surrounds financial services. Institutional lines and prerogatives have become blurred. The role of those who serve the financial needs of the public has changed. Competition has increased. New products and services abound.

In this climate the College feels an imperative to be more forceful in the application of long-standing ethical principles. What was once a matter of persuasion is now a matter of requirement.

RATIONALE FOR THE CODE OF ETHICS

The College's major programs are of two distinct types. Some lead to degrees that are based solely on educational achievement and have no postgraduation ethical requirements. Those that lead to designations, however, have not only educational and experience prerequisites but also ethical requirements that continue beyond graduation and require the maintenance of ongoing standards of conduct. The display of a designation is a continuing representation that the holder will act competently and ethically in all professional relationships.

Before conferring a designation, the College has historically examined the experience as well as the educational and ethical qualifications of candidates for its designations. Unless an individual acted fraudulently to obtain a designation, no postgraduation action to remove a designation was ever taken. However, since the adoption in June 1984 of the College's Code of Ethics, the board of trustees has acted to assure postconferment fidelity to the ethical standards that accompany Huebner School designations.

THE PROFESSIONAL PLEDGE AND THE CANONS

The Code consists of two parts: the Professional Pledge and eight Canons.

The Pledge to which all Huebner School designees subscribe is: "In all my professional relationships, I pledge myself to the following rule of ethical conduct: I shall, in light of all conditions surrounding those I serve, which I shall make every conscientious effort to ascertain and understand, render that service which, in the same circumstances, I would apply to myself."

The eight Canons are:

I. Conduct yourself at all times with honor and dignity.
II. Avoid practices that would bring dishonor upon your profession or The American College.
III. Publicize your achievement in ways that enhance the integrity of your profession.
IV. Continue your studies throughout your working life so as to maintain a high level of professional competence.
V. Do your utmost to attain a distinguished record of professional service.
VI. Support the established institutions and organizations concerned with the integrity of your profession.
VII. Participate in building your profession by encouraging and providing appropriate assistance to qualified persons pursuing professional studies.
VIII. Comply with all laws and regulations, particularly as they relate to professional and business activities.

ADMINISTRATION

The certification officer of the College is empowered by the board of trustees to implement the Code by investigating complaints and reports of violations, which may originate with state commissioners of insurance, other public and judicial bodies, individuals, and established institutions or organizations. In certain instances the College itself may initiate action based on an apparent violation.

Violations that may cause the certification officer to begin an investigation include conviction of a misdemeanor or felony, suspension or revocation of a license, or suspension or revocation of membership in an established institution or organization.

Although only actions that occur after October 1, 1984, are subject to the Code, the standards established by the Code apply to students in the CLU and ChFC programs who matriculated on July 1, 1982, or later. All earlier CLU and ChFC matriculants were invited to subscribe to the Code and to accept its mandates voluntarily. Jurisdiction does not extend to pre-1982 matriculants who have not consented to be bound by the Code. The Code of Ethics also applies to students in the RHU and REBC programs who matriculated on January 1, 1996, or later.

PROCEDURES

I. Initiation of Action

The College, acting through the certification officer, investigates all alleged violations of its Code that are reported by state or federal authorities, individuals, and/or established financial services institutions or organizations.

II. The Certification Officer

A. The certification officer of the College makes a preliminary appraisal to determine whether
   1. the complaint involves a violation of the Code
   2. there is sufficient evidence for presentation to the certification committee

B. The certification officer determines the facts of the complaint by
   1. reviewing the charges with the complainant(s)
   2. relaying the complaint to the person charged and permitting him or her to respond
   3. examining all the facts that appear relevant to the complaint

C. After completing the above steps the certification officer
   1. determines whether to discontinue action or to present the case to the certification committee
   2. transmits the determination in writing to all parties involved in the complaint
   3. reviews the earlier steps if new information comes to light
   4. prepares the file and presents the complaint to the certification committee if the case so warrants

III. The Certification Committee

A. Membership. The certification committee is composed of a chairperson who must be a trustee of the College and three to five members, including one senior administrative officer of the College. (Note: The College's legal counsel may serve in an advisory role.)

B. Duties
   1. The certification committee reviews the case and requests any additional information that it considers necessary.
   2. After reviewing the case, the certification committee may either dismiss the complaint or decide that the Code has been violated and impose an appropriate sanction.
   3. The decision is conveyed in writing to all parties involved in the complaint.

C. Action. The certification committee decides to impose a sanction only by unanimous vote.

IV. Sanctions

A. The certification committee may order suspension or revocation of the right to use the CLU designation, the ChFC designation, the RHU designation, the REBC designation, or a combination of designations. The suspension or revocation notice is sent by registered mail.
B. If no appeal is received, a copy of the suspension or revocation notice is sent to the complainant(s) and made a part of the College's permanent records.
C. The College reserves the right to transmit the decision to other parties.

V. Appeals
A. A suspension or revocation may be appealed by notifying the certification committee chairperson in writing within 30 days of receiving the suspension or revocation notice.
B. When an appeal is received, the chairperson of the certification committee notifies the chairman of the board of trustees, who appoints a hearing committee composed of no fewer than three members who may be trustees but not College staff members. The members may have no prior connection with the case or with any company with which the appellant has been associated.
C. The certification officer or a member of the certification committee who voted the sanction presents the case and may answer questions but may not participate in the deliberations.
D. The appellant may present his or her position, call witnesses, and point to the alleged errors in the decision.
E. If the appellant is represented by counsel, the hearing committee must also be so represented. Counsel to the committee may be present to clarify issues even if the appellant is not represented.
F. A recorder who is not a member of the hearing committee keeps minutes of the proceedings.
G. The hearing committee sets the rules for conduct of the hearing.
H. A majority vote based on information provided during the hearing is required and is final and binding on the College and the appellant.
I. The decision and statement of reasons for the decision is sent by the hearing committee chairperson to the College. The certification officer notifies the appellant and the complainant(s) of the committee's decision by registered mail within 15 days of the hearing.
J. The College reserves the right to convey the decision to other parties.

Appendix 3B

The Society of Financial Service Professionals Code of Ethics

Men and women who have chosen to enter into membership in the Society of Financial Service Professionals voluntarily bind themselves to the Code of Ethics of their professional organization.

The purpose of the Code is to give further force to the Pledge taken by all holders of the CLU and ChFC designations and to provide a series of standards by which those involved in providing insurance and financial planning and economic security may conduct themselves in a professional manner. The Code is founded upon the two ethical imperatives of competent advice and service to the client and enhancement of the public regard for the CLU and ChFC designations.

Competent advice and service to the client is at the very essence of any professional calling. Enhancement of the public regard for professional designations gives voice to the concept that in accepting Society membership, an obligation is also accepted to all other holders of similar and allied professional designations and degrees.

In its design, the Code presents the two ethical Imperatives, supported by Guides which give specificity to the Imperatives and interpretive comment which is intended to aid in a uniform understanding of the Guides.

A violation of the Code would expose a member to sanctions which range from reprimand to revocation of membership in the American Society. A member is in violation of the Code when a final judgment is made that the member has breached an ethical imperative through failure to adhere to one or more of the Guides.

For ease of drafting and reading, the masculine gender and singular number have been used. When appropriate, masculine is to be read as feminine and singular as plural. The word "client" is used under the First Imperative since standards concerning advice and service have greatest applicability to the relationship of client to professional insurance and financial services practitioner.

FIRST IMPERATIVE:

To competently advise and serve the client . . .

Guide 1.1:
A member shall provide advice and service which are in the client's best interest.
Interpretive Comment.

A. A member possessing a specific body of knowledge which is not possessed by the general public has an obligation to use that knowledge for the benefit of the client and to avoid taking advantage of that knowledge to the detriment of the client.
B. In a conflict of interest situation the interest of the client must be paramount.
C. The member must make a conscientious effort to ascertain and to understand all relevant circumstances surrounding the client.
D. A member is to accord due courtesy and consideration to those engaged in related professions who are also serving the client.
E. A member is to give due regard to any agent-principal relationship which may exist between the member and such companies as he may represent.

Guide 1.2:
A member shall respect the confidential relationship existing between client and member.
Interpretive Comment.

A. Competent advice and service may necessitate the client sharing personal and confidential information with the member. Such information is to be held in confidence by the member unless released from the obligation by the client.

Guide 1.3:
A member shall continue his education throughout his professional life.
Interpretive Comment.

A. To advise and serve competently, a member must continue to maintain and to improve his professional abilities.
B. Continuing Education includes both the member adding to his knowledge of the practice of his profession; and, the member keeping abreast of changing economic and legislative conditions which may affect the financial plans of the insuring public.
C. A member may continue his education through formal or informal programs of study or through other professional experiences.

Guide 1.4:
A member shall render continuing advice and service.
Interpretive Comment.

A. Advice and service, to be competent, must be ongoing as the client's circumstances change and as these changes are made known to the member.

B. A client with whom a member has an active professional relationship is to be informed of economic and legislative changes which relate to the client-member relationship.

SECOND IMPERATIVE:
To enhance the public regard for professional designations and allied professional degrees held by members . . .

Guide 2.1:
A member shall obey all laws governing his business or professional activities.
Interpretive Comment.

A. Business activities are non-personal activities carried on outside the life insurance community; professional activities are non-personal activities carried on within the life insurance community.

B. A member has a legal obligation to obey all laws applicable to his business and professional activities. The placement of this Guide within the Code raises this obligation to the level of an ethical obligation.

Guide 2.2:
A member shall avoid activities which detract from the integrity and professionalism of the Chartered Life Underwriter designation, the Chartered Financial Consultant designation, or any other allied professional degree or designation held by members.
Interpretive Comment.

A. Personal, business, and professional activities are encompassed within the scope of this Guide.

B. Activities which could present a violation of this Guide might include:
   (1) A member's failure to obey a law unrelated to the member's business or professional activities.
   (2) A member impairing the reputation of another practitioner.
   (3) A member unfairly competing with another practitioner.
   (4) Actions which result in the member discrediting his own reputation.
   (5) A member discrediting life underwriting as a profession, the institution of life insurance or the Society of Financial Service Professionals.
   (6) A member advertising the Chartered Life Underwriter or Chartered Financial Consultant designation or membership in the Society in an

undignified manner, or in a manner prohibited by the Bylaws of the Society.

Guide 2.3:

A member shall encourage others to attain the Chartered Life Underwriter and/or the Chartered Financial Consultant designations.

Interpretive Comment.

A. Enhancement of the public regard for the CLU and ChFC designations depends upon a continuing increase in the number of holders of the designations who are available to advise and serve the public.

B. Encouraging others who might be qualified to enter into a practice is one hallmark of a professional.

Guide 2.4:

A member shall avoid using the Chartered Life Underwriter or Chartered Financial Consultant designation in a false or misleading manner.

Interpretive Comment.

A. The CLU and ChFC designations are granted by the American College to specified individuals. Acts which directly or indirectly extend the member's personal designation to others would present a violation of this Guide.

B. Chartered Life Underwriter (CLU) or Chartered Financial Consultant (ChFC) may not be used in a name of a business in a manner which would reasonably lead others to conclude that someone other than the named member held the designation. Example:

(1) John Jones, CLU, & Associates is permissible.

(2) John Jones & Associates, Chartered Financial Consultants, is not permissible.

Appendix 3C

*IAFP Code of Professional Ethics and Ethics Policies and Procedures**

IAFP CODE OF PROFESSIONAL ETHICS

Introduction

The objective of the Code of Professional Ethics is to specify and set forth the means to enforce the minimum ethical conduct expected of all members as professionals, and to facilitate voluntary compliance with standards considerably higher than the required minimums.

Accordingly, the Code prescribes two kinds of standards: Canons and Rules of Professional Conduct.

The Canons serve as model standards of exemplary professional conduct. They express the general concepts and principles from which more specific Rules are derived.

The Rules are specific standards of a mandatory and enforceable nature. They prescribe the absolute minimum level of conduct required of every member.

In addition to the Canons and Rules, the Ethics Committee has developed a set of Ethics Policies and Procedures to guide members, the committee and staff in the application and enforcement of the Code of Professional Ethics.

Although the official Code of Professional Ethics consists of all Canons and Rules, only a violation of the Rules will constitute sufficient grounds for disciplinary action. The Canons and Ethics Policies and Procedures are used by the Ethics Committee to apply and interpret the Rules uniformly, with reference to the general principles and concepts they embody. The Ethics Committee may also refer to applicable rulings in previous cases brought before the Committee, as well as relevant published opinions of the Ethics Committee.

The Code of Professional Ethics, including the Canon and Rules of Professional Conduct, is shown below.

The Code of Professional Ethics

The reliance of the public and the business community on sound financial planning and advice imposes on financial planning professionals an obligation to maintain high standards of technical competence, morality, and integrity. To this end, the following Code of Professional Ethics serves as the guiding document.

Canon 1

Members should endeavor as professionals to place the public interest above their own.

Rules of Professional Conduct:

R1.1

A member has a duty to understand and abide by all Rules of Professional Conduct which are prescribed in the Code of Professional Ethics of the Association.

R1.2

A member shall not directly or indirectly condone any act which the member is prohibited from performing by the Rules of this Code.

Canon 2

Members should seek continually to maintain and improve their professional knowledge, skills, and competence.

Rules of Professional Conduct:

R2.1

A member shall keep informed on all matters that are essential to the maintenance of the member's professional competence in the area in which he/she specializes and/or claims expertise.

Canon 3

Members should obey all laws and regulations and avoid any conduct or activity which would cause unjust harm to those who rely upon the professional judgment and skill of the members.

Rules of Professional Conduct:

R3.1

A member shall be subject to disciplinary action for professional misconduct and has the duty to know and abide by the laws and regulations and all legal limitations pertaining to the member's professional activities.

R3.2

A member shall place the needs and best interest of the client above the needs and interests of the member, the member's employees or business associates in all cases; and

shall not allow the pursuit of financial gain or other personal benefit to interfere with the exercise of sound professional judgment and skills.

R3.3

In the conduct of business or professional activities, a member shall not engage in any act or omission of a dishonest, deceitful or fraudulent nature.

R3.4

A member shall not knowingly misrepresent or conceal any material limitation on the member's ability to provide the quantity or quality of service that will adequately meet the financial planning needs of the client.

R3.5

In marketing a product, a member shall not knowingly misrepresent or conceal any material limitations on the product's ability to meet the financial needs of the client, and shall scrupulously avoid any statements which are likely to mislead the client regarding to future results of any recommendation.

R3.6

A member has the duty to disclose fully and accurately the material facts representing the true costs, benefits, and limitations of any service or product recommended; and disclose any actual or potential conflict of interest that could impair objectivity.

R3.7

A member shall not disclose to another person any confidential information entrusted to or obtained by the member in the course of the member's business or professional activities, unless a disclosure of such information is required by law or is made to a person who necessarily must have the information in order to discharge legitimate occupational or professional duties.

R3.8

In the rendering of a professional service to a client, a member has the duty to maintain the type and degree of professional independence that (a) is required of practitioners in the member's occupation, or (b) is otherwise in the public interest, given the specific nature of the service being rendered.

Canon 4

Members should be diligent in the performance of their occupational duties.

Rules of Professional Conduct:

R4.1

A member shall competently and consistently discharge the member's occupational duties to every employer, client, purchaser, or user of the member's services, so long as those duties are consistent with what is in the client's best interests.

R4.2

In the making of oral or written recommendations to clients, a member shall (a) distinguish clearly between fact and opinion, (b) base the recommendations on sound professional evaluation of the client's needs, and (c) support the recommendations with appropriate research and adequate documentation of facts.

Canon 5

Members should assist in improving the public understanding of financial planning.

Rules of Professional Conduct:

R5.1

A member shall support efforts to provides lay persons with objective information concerning their financial planning needs, as well as the resources which are available to meet their needs.

R5.2

A member shall not misrepresent the benefits, costs, or limitations of any financial planning service or product, whether the product or service is offered by the member or by another individual or firm.

Canon 6

Members should use the fact of membership in a manner consistent with the Association's Rules of Professional Conduct.

Rules of Professional Conduct:

R6.1

A member shall not misrepresent the criteria for admission to Association membership, which criteria are (1) active participation in the financial services industry; and (2) a written commitment to abide by the Bylaws and the Code of Professional Ethics of the Association.

R6.2

A member shall not misstate his/her authority to represent the Association. Specifically, a member shall not write, speak, or act in such a way as to lead another to believe that the member is officially representing the Association, unless the member has been duly authorized to do so by the officers, directors or Bylaws of the national Association.

R6.3

A member shall not use the fact of general membership in the Association for commercial purposes. A member may use the fact of general membership for the following noncommercial purposes: in resumes, prospectus, and in introductions if the speaker clearly states that the opinions and ideas presented are his/her own and not necessarily those of the Association. Fact of Division membership may be used by an individual in the Practitioner Division,* or by a company in the Corporate or Broker-Dealer Divisions.†

R6.4

A member or prospective member applying for Association membership shall not misrepresent any credentials or affiliations with other organizations.

Canon 7

Members should assist in maintaining the integrity of the Code of Professional Ethics of the Association.

Rules of Professional Conduct:

R7.1

A member shall not sponsor as a candidate for Association membership any person who is known by the member to engage in business or professional practices which violate the Rules of this Code.

---

* Individual members in the Practitioner Division (those who have met the necessary requirements of the Division and have signed the Practitioner Division Certificate) may use fact of membership in the following manner:

Member, Practitioner Division, International
Association for Financial Planning

Members of the Practitioner Division should contact the compliance department of their broker-dealer to make sure any state or NASD regulatory concerns are addressed before using fact of membership for commercial purposes.

† Companies in the Corporate and Broker-Dealer Divisions may use fact of membership as follows:

Member, Corporate Division, International Association
for Financial Planning;

Member, Broker-Dealer Division, International
Association for Financial Planning

R7.2

A member possessing unprivileged information concerning an alleged violation of this Code shall, upon request, reveal such information to the body or other authority empowered by the Association to investigate or act upon the alleged violation.

R7.3

A member shall immediately notify the IAFP Ethics Committee of any accusation or actual violation of the code of ethics of a professional credentialing organization to which they are subject and forward complete details to IAFP.

R7.4

A member shall immediately notify the IAFP Ethics Committee of any revocation or suspension by a state or federal licensing or regulatory agency of an investment adviser, securities, or insurance license and forward complete details to IAFP.

ETHICS POLICIES AND PROCEDURES

Introduction

The purpose of the Ethics Policies and Procedures is to provide guidance to IAFP members, the Ethics Committee, and staff in the application and enforcement of the IAFP Code of Professional Ethics. All of the policies in this document are consistent with the Canons and Rules of Professional Conduct embodied in the Code. The procedures are designed to ensure fairness and due process in the enforcement of the Code.

Ethics Committee Policies

These policies do not provide guidance on specific behavior, but clarify how the Code will be applied by the Ethics Committee to typical situations faced by IAFP members. The policies will be amended as needed by the Ethics Committee.

1. A finding by a professional credentialing organization that an IAFP member has violated that organization's code of ethics will create a presumption that the member also violated the IAFP Code of Professional Ethics. Specifically, the presumption will be that Rule 3.1 of Canon 3 was violated.

2. A finding by a state or federal licensing or regulatory agency that results in the revocation or suspension of an investment adviser, securities or insurance license or registration for any reason other than a technical violation* will create a presumption that the member violated the IAFP Code of Professional Ethics. Specifically, the presumption will be that Rule 3.1 of Canon 3 was violated.

Procedures

1. An ethics file will be opened on an active IAFP member or lapsed member by the IAFP Ethics staff (not by a chapter) when one or more of the following takes place:

    a. A written complaint (either by letter or using IAFP's Ethics Complaint Form) is received from a consumer.
    b. A written complaint is received from a member.
    c. A member alerts the Ethics Committee in writing on a membership application, renewal form, or Consumer Referral Program affirmation statement that a possible ethics violation may have occurred.
    d. The Ethics Committee is alerted by a professional credentialing organization of findings and action taken against an IAFP member in the enforcement of that organization's code of ethics.
    e. Information is obtained from a state or federal licensing or regulatory agency that an IAFP member's license or registration has been revoked or suspended.
    f. Information is obtained from a published source, such as a newspaper, magazine, news release, broadcast report, or electronic communication, about a possible violation by an IAFP member of the Code of Professional Ethics.
    g. The Ethics Committee initiates an action based on other information about a possible violation by an IAFP member of the Code of Professional Ethics.

2. When a written complaint is received from a consumer or a member alleging a violation of the Code of Professional Ethics by a member who is subject to a professional credentialing organization, or who holds an investment adviser, securities or insurance license, the Ethics staff will:

    a. Advise the complainant that the Ethics Committee will review the complaint only after the appropriate professional credentialing organization and/or licensing or regulatory agency has completed its review and taken action.

* A "technical violation" generally includes violation of rules related to recordkeeping, continuing education, and other administrative requirements.

b. Therefore, the complainant will be advised that they can either forward their complaint to the appropriate professional credentialing organization and/or licensing or regulatory agency, or the Ethics staff will forward their complaint.
c. Open an ethics file on the member against whom the complaint has been received and forwarded.

3. When an ethics file is opened on an active member who is admitted to the IAFP Consumer Referral Program, the Ethics staff will flag and note that member's record in the database to indicate that the Ethics Committee is conducting an investigation into a possible violation(s) of the Code of Professional Ethics. The member will be temporarily suspended from participation in the program until the Ethics Committee completes a preliminary review of the case at its earliest convenience, based upon information available at that time. Upon that review, the Ethics committee can:

   a. Remove the temporary suspension from the Consumer Referral Program; or
   b. Leave the temporary suspension in place until the case is disposed of.

4. If information about a lapsed member is received that would result in the opening of an ethics file, the Ethics staff will flag and note that lapsed member's record in the database so the case can be reviewed in the event the lapsed member reapplies for membership.

5. The Ethics staff will review the complaint and/or information received and will seek any additional information that is needed from the complainant, member, credentialing organization, or licensing or regulatory agency so the Ethics Committee can conduct a thorough review of the facts and circumstances before deciding the case.

6. The Ethics staff may, in consultation with the Chairman of the Ethics Committee, recommend immediate dismissal of the case if it is determined that the complaint and/or information does not constitute a violation of the Code of Professional Ethics.

7. The Ethics staff will send a certified letter to the member against whom a complaint or information from a crendentialing organization, licensing or regulatory agency, or publication has been received. The letter will outline the allegations and the Rules of Professional Conduct that may have been violated and will request a written response from the member within 60 days of receipt of the letter. A copy of the letter to the member will also be sent to the complainant. If the member does not respond within the 60 days, the

Ethics Committee will consider that a violation of the Code and will take appropriate action.

8. The Ethics staff will review the written response and all other documentation submitted by the member and will request any additional information needed for the Ethics Committee to conduct a thorough review of the case.

9. The Ethics staff will schedule a conference call of a subcommittee of the Ethics Committee, appointed by the Chairman, to conduct a hearing for the purpose of an initial review of the case. The complainant, if any, will be offered an opportunity to participate in this hearing to answer questions from the subcommittee and to provide additional information the subcommittee needs before forwarding the case to the Ethics Committee. The member will also be offered an opportunity to participate in this hearing to answer questions from the subcommittee and to provide additional information the subcommittee needs before forwarding the case to the Ethics Committee.

   Important note: The purpose of this hearing is to conduct an initial review of the facts and circumstances of the case. While the member will be afforded due process to ensure a fair resolution of the case, this hearing is not a judicial proceeding. It is for the purpose of clarifying the information submitted by the complainant and/or member.

10. After all information is gathered and the initial hearing is conducted, the case will be presented to the Ethics Committee at its next scheduled meeting (usually conducted by conference call). The Ethics Committee will review the facts and circumstances of the case in light of the Canons and Rules of Professional Conduct of the IAFP Code of Professional Ethics and, in consultation with these Ethics Policies and Procedures, may take any of the following actions:

    a. Dismiss the case with no action.
    b. Delay the case until further information is received.
    c. Issue a Letter of Reprimand to the member. The Letter of Reprimand will be kept in the member's file.
    d. Suspend the member's participation in the IAFP Consumer Referral Program (if applicable) for a period of time deemed appropriate by the Ethics Committee.
    e. Suspend the member's membership in the association for a period of time deemed appropriate by the Ethics Committee.
    f. Suspend the member's participation in the IAFP Consumer Referral Program (if applicable) for a period of time deemed appropriate by the Ethics Committee, and suspend the member's membership in the association for a period of time deemed appropriate by the Ethics Committee.

g. Terminate the member's participation in the IAFP Consumer Referral Program (if applicable).
h. Terminate the member's participation in the IAFP Consumer Referral Program (if applicable), and suspend the member's membership in the association for a period of time deemed appropriate by the Ethics Committee.
i. Terminate the member's membership in the association.

11. The Ethics staff will notify the member by certified letter of the Ethics Committee's decision. A copy of the letter will also be sent to the complainant, if any.

12. Any prospective member whose membership is withheld, or existing member whose membership is suspended or to whom a letter of reprimand is issued, should be given the opportunity to request in writing a reconsideration of the decision, within 60 days after receiving the decision of the Ethics Committee.

    After 60 days, if the Committee has not received a written request for reconsideration from the member or prospective new member, the decision of the Committee is final.

    Such request must contain specific responses to the action taken by the Ethics Committee by providing either:

    a. information relevant to the specific rules violations contained in the Ethics Committee's decision; and/or

    b. specific rebuttal to the rules violation citing where the member, or prospective new member, feels that the Ethics Committee did not properly interpret the facts of the situation.

    The Committee will reconsider its decision once.

13. If the Ethics Committee's decision is to terminate the member's membership in the association, the member will have 30 days from the date of the letter to request a review of the case by a Disciplinary Appeals Board as provided for in the IAFP Bylaws.

14. If the Ethics Committee's decision is to terminate the member's membership in the association, and if the Disciplinary Appeals Board decides to uphold the termination of the member's membership in the association, the member's name and the fact of his/her termination will be published in the official membership publication of the association.

15. If the decision of the Ethics Committee is anything other than dismissal of the case, the Ethics staff will flag and note the member's record in the database appropriately.

16. Ethics case files will be maintained separate from member files, will be retained for three years and then destroyed.

Appendix 3D

Certified Financial Planner Code of Ethics and Professional Responsibility*

CONTENTS

CODE OF ETHICS AND PROFESSIONAL RESPONSIBILITY

PREAMBLE AND APPLICABILITY

The *Code of Ethics and Professional Responsibility* (Code) has been adopted by the Certified Financial Planner Board of Standards, Inc. (CFP Board) to provide principles and rules to all persons whom it has recognized and certified to use the CFP certification mark and the marks CFP and Certified Financial Planner (collectively "the marks"). The CFP Board determines who is recognized and certified to use the marks. Implicit in the acceptance of this authorization is an obligation not only to comply with the mandates and requirements of all applicable laws and regulations but also to take responsibility to act in an ethical and professionally responsible manner in all professional services and activities.

For purposes of this Code, a person recognized and certified by the CFP Board to use the marks is called a CFP designee or Certified Financial Planner designee. This Code applies to CFP designees actively involved in the practice of personal financial planning, in other areas of financial services, in industry, in related professions, in government, in education, or in any other professional activity in which the marks are used in the performance of their professional responsibilities. This Code also applies to candidates for the CFP designation who are registered as such with the CFP Board. For purposes of this Code, the term CFP designee shall be deemed to include candidates.

COMPOSITION AND SCOPE

The Code consists of two parts: **Part I—Principles** and **Part II—Rules.** The Principles are statements expressing in general terms the ethical and professional ideals expected of CFP designees and which they should strive to display in their professional activities. As such the Principles are aspirational in character but are intended to provide a source of guidance for a CFP designee. The comments following each Principle further explain the meaning of the Principle. The Rules provide practical guidelines derived from the tenets embodied in the Principles. As such, the Rules set forth the standards of ethical and professionally responsible conduct expected to be followed in particular situations. This Code does not undertake to define standards of professional conduct of CFP designees for purposes of civil liability.

Due to the nature of a CFP designee's particular field of endeavor, certain Rules may not be applicable to that CFP designee's activities. For example, a CFP designee who is engaged solely in the sale of securities as a registered representative is not subject to the written disclosure requirements of Rule 402 (applicable to CFP designees engaged in personal financial planning) although he or she may have disclosure responsibilities under Rule 401. A CFP designee is obligated to determine what responsibilities the CFP designee has in each professional relationship including, for example, duties that arise in particular circumstances from a position of trust or confidence that a CFP designee may have. The CFP designee is obligated to meet those responsibilities.

The Code is structured so that the presentation of the Rules parallels the presentation of the Principles. For example, the Rules which relate to Principle 1—Integrity, are numbered in the 100 to 199 series while those Rules relating to Principle 2—Objectivity, are numbered in the 200 to 299 series.

COMPLIANCE

The CFP Board of Governors requires adherence to this Code by all those it recognizes and certifies to use the marks. Compliance with the Code, individually and by the profession as a whole, depends on each CFP designee's knowledge of and voluntary compliance with the Principles and applicable Rules, on the influence of fellow professionals and public opinion, and on disciplinary proceedings, when necessary, involving CFP designees who fail to comply with the applicable provisions of the Code.

TERMINOLOGY IN THIS CODE

Client denotes a person, persons, or entity for whom professional services are rendered. Where the services of the practitioner are provided to an entity (corporation, trust, partnership, estate, etc.), the client is the entity, acting through its legally authorized representative.

Commission denotes the compensation received by an agent or broker when the same is calculated as a percentage on the amount of his or her sales or purchase transactions.

Conflict(s) of interest(s) denotes circumstances, relationships or other facts about the CFP designee's own financial, business, property and/or personal interests which will or reasonably may impair the CFP designee's rendering of disinterested advice, recommendations or services.

Fee-only denotes a method of compensation in which compensation is received solely from a client with neither the personal financial planning practitioner nor any related party receiving compensation which is contingent upon the purchase or sale of any financial product. A *related party* for this purpose shall mean an individual or entity from whom any direct or indirect economic benefit is derived by the personal financial planning practitioner as a result of implementing a recommendation made by the personal financial planning practitioner.

Personal financial planning or **financial planning** denotes the process of determining whether and how an individual can meet life goals through the proper management of financial resources.

Personal financial planning process or **financial planning process** denotes the process which typically includes, but is not limited to, the six elements of establishing and defining the client-planner relationship, gathering client data including goals, analyzing and evaluating the client's financial status, developing and presenting financial planning recommendations and/or alternatives, implementing the financial planning recommendations and monitoring the financial planning recommendations.

Personal financial planning subject areas or **financial planning subject areas** denotes the basic subject fields covered in the financial planning process which typically include, but are not limited to, financial statement preparation and analysis (including cash flow analysis/planning and budgeting), investment planning (including portfolio design, i.e., asset allocation, and portfolio management), income tax planning, education planning, risk management, retirement planning, and estate planning.

Personal financial planning professional or **financial planning professional** denotes a person who is capable and qualified to offer objective, integrated, and comprehensive financial advice to or for the benefit of individuals to help them achieve their financial objectives. A financial planning professional must have the ability to provide financial planning services to clients, using the financial planning process covering the basic financial planning subjects.

Personal financial planning practitioner or **financial planning practitioner** denotes a person who is capable and qualified to offer objective, integrated, and comprehensive financial advice to or for the benefit of clients to help them achieve their financial objectives and who engages in financial planning using the financial planning process in working with clients.

PART I—PRINCIPLES

Introduction

These Principles of the Code express the profession's recognition of its responsibilities to the public, to clients, to colleagues, and to employers. They apply to all CFP designees and provide guidance to them in the performance of their professional services.

Principle 1 — Integrity

A CFP designee shall offer and provide professional services with integrity.

As discussed in Composition and Scope, CFP designees may be placed by clients in positions of trust and confidence. The ultimate source of such public trust is the CFP designee's personal integrity. In deciding what is right and just, a CFP designee should rely on his or her integrity as the appropriate touchstone. Integrity demands honesty and candor which must not be subordinated to personal gain and advantage. Within the characteristic of integrity, allowance can be made for innocent error and legitimate difference of opinion; but integrity cannot co-exist with deceit or subordination of one's principles. Integrity requires a CFP designee to observe not only the letter but also the spirit of this Code.

Principle 2 — Objectivity

A CFP designee shall be objective in providing professional services to clients.

Objectivity requires intellectual honesty and impartiality. It is an essential quality for any professional. Regardless of the particular service rendered or the capacity in which a CFP designee functions, a CFP designee should protect the integrity of his or her work, maintain objectivity, and avoid subordination of his or her judgment that would be in violation of this Code.

Principle 3 — Competence

A CFP designee shall provide services to clients competently and maintain the necessary knowledge and skill to continue to do so in those areas in which the designee is engaged.

One is competent only when he or she has attained and maintained an adequate level of knowledge and skill, and applies that knowledge effectively in providing services to clients. Competence also includes the wisdom to recognize the limitations of that knowledge and when consultation or client referral is appropriate. A CFP designee, by virtue of having earned the CFP designation, is deemed to be qualified to practice financial planning. However, in addition to assimilating the common body of knowledge required and acquiring the necessary experience for designation, a CFP designee shall make a continuing commitment to learning and professional improvement.

Principle 4 — Fairness

A CFP designee shall perform professional services in a manner that is fair and reasonable to clients, principals, partners, and employers and shall disclose conflict(s) of interest(s) in providing such services.

Fairness requires impartiality, intellectual honesty, and disclosure of conflict(s) of interest(s). It involves a subordination of one's own feelings, prejudices, and desires so as to achieve a proper balance of conflicting interests. Fairness is treating others in the same fashion that you would want to be treated and is an essential trait of any professional.

Principle 5 — Confidentiality

A CFP designee shall not disclose any confidential client information without the specific consent of the client unless in response to proper legal process, to defend against charges of wrongdoing by the CFP designee or in connection with a civil dispute between the CFP designee and client.

A client, by seeking the services of a CFP designee, may be interested in creating a relationship of personal trust and confidence with the CFP designee. This type of relationship can only be built upon the understanding that information supplied to the CFP designee or other information will be confidential. In order to provide the contemplated services effectively and to protect the client's privacy, the CFP designee shall safeguard the confidentiality of such information.

Principle 6 — Professionalism

A CFP designee's conduct in all matters shall reflect credit upon the profession.

Because of the importance of the professional services rendered by CFP designees, there are attendant responsibilities to behave with dignity and courtesy to all those who use those services, fellow professionals, and those in related professions. A CFP designee also has an obligation to cooperate with fellow CFP designees to enhance and maintain the profession's public image and to work jointly with other CFP designees to improve the quality of services. It is only through the combined efforts of all CFP designees in cooperation with other professionals that this vision can be realized.

Principle 7 — Diligence

A CFP designee shall act diligently in providing professional services.

Diligence is the provision of services in a reasonably prompt and thorough manner. Diligence also includes proper planning for and supervision of the rendering of professional services.

PART II — RULES

Introduction

As stated in **Part I — Principles,** the Principles apply to all CFP designees. However, due to the nature of a CFP designee's particular field of endeavor, certain Rules may not be applicable to that CFP designee's activities. The universe of activities performed by CFP designees is indeed diverse and a particular CFP designee may be performing all, some or none of the typical services provided by financial planning professionals. As a result, in considering the Rules in Part II, a CFP designee must first recognize what specific services he or she is rendering and then determine whether or not a specific Rule is applicable to those services. To assist the CFP designee in making these determinations, this Code includes a series of definitions of terminology used throughout the Code. Based upon these definitions, a CFP designee should be able to determine which services he or she provides and, therefore, which Rules are applicable to those services.

Rules That Relate to the Principle of Integrity

Rule 101

A CFP designee shall not solicit clients through false or misleading communications or advertisements:

(a) *Misleading Advertising:* A CFP designee shall not make a false or misleading communication about the size, scope or areas of competence of the CFP designee's practice or of any organization with which the CFP designee is associated; and

(b) *Promotional Activities:* In promotional activities, a CFP designee shall not make materially false or misleading communications to the public or create unjustified expectations regarding matters relating to financial planning or the professional activities and competence of the CFP designee. The term "promotional activities" includes, but is not limited to, speeches, interviews, books and/or printed publications, seminars, radio and television shows, and video cassettes; and

(c) *Representation of Authority:* A CFP designee shall not give the impression that a CFP designee is representing the views of the CFP Board or any other group unless the CFP designee has been authorized to do so. Personal opinions shall be clearly identified as such.

Rule 102

In the course of professional activities, a CFP designee shall not engage in conduct involving dishonesty, fraud, deceit or misrepresentation, or knowingly make a false or misleading statement to a client, employer, employee, professional colleague, governmental or other regulatory body or official, or any other person or entity.

Rule 103

A CFP designee has the following responsibilities regarding funds and/or other property of clients:

(a) In exercising custody of or discretionary authority over client funds or other property, a CFP designee shall act only in accordance with the authority set forth in the governing legal instrument (e.g., special power of attorney, trust, letters testamentary, etc.); and
(b) A CFP designee shall identify and keep complete records of all funds or other property of a client in the custody of or under the discretionary authority of the CFP designee; and
(c) Upon receiving funds or other property of a client, a CFP designee shall promptly or as otherwise permitted by law or provided by agreement with the client, deliver to the client or third party any funds or other property which the client or third party is entitled to receive and, upon request by the client, render a full accounting regarding such funds or other property; and
(d) A CFP designee shall not commingle client funds or other property with a CFP designee's personal funds and/or other property or the funds and/or other property of a CFP designee's firm. Commingling one or more clients' funds or other property together is permitted, subject to compliance with applicable legal requirements and provided accurate records are maintained for each client's funds or other property; and
(e) A CFP designee who takes custody of all or any part of a client's assets for investment purposes, shall do so with the care required of a fiduciary.

Rules That Relate to the Principle of Objectivity

Rule 201

A CFP designee shall exercise reasonable and prudent professional judgment in providing professional services.

Rule 202

A financial planning practitioner shall act in the interest of the client.

Rules That Relate to the Principle of Competence

Rule 301

A CFP designee shall keep informed of developments in the field of financial planning and participate in continuing education throughout the CFP designee's professional career in order to improve professional competence in all areas in which the CFP designee is engaged. As a distinct part of this requirement, a CFP designee shall satisfy all minimum continuing education requirements established for CFP designees by the CFP Board.

Rule 302

A CFP designee shall offer advice only in those areas in which the CFP designee has competence. In areas where the CFP designee is not professionally competent, the CFP designee shall seek the counsel of qualified individuals and/or refer clients to such parties.

Rules That Relate to the Principle of Fairness

Rule 401

In rendering professional services, a CFP designee shall disclose to the client:

(a) Material information relevant to the professional relationship, including but not limited to conflict(s) of interest(s); changes in the CFP designee's business affiliation, address, telephone number, credentials, qualifications, licenses, compensation structure, and any agency relationships, and the scope of the CFP designee's authority in that capacity.

(b) The information required by all laws applicable to the relationship in a manner complying with such laws.

Rule 402

A financial planning practitioner shall make timely written disclosure of all material information relative to the professional relationship. In all circumstances such disclosure shall include conflict(s) of interest(s) and sources of compensation. Written disclosures that include the following information are considered to be in compliance with this Rule:

(a) A statement of the basic philosophy of the CFP designee (or firm) in working with clients. The disclosure shall include the philosophy, theory and/or principles of financial planning which will be utilized by the CFP designee; and
(b) Resumes of principals and employees of a firm who are expected to provide financial planning services to the client and a description of those services. Such disclosures shall include educational background, professional/employment history, professional designations and licenses held, and areas of competence and specialization; and
(c) A statement of compensation, which in reasonable detail discloses the source(s) and any contingencies or other aspects material to the fee and/or commission arrangement. Any estimates made shall be clearly identified as such and shall be based on reasonable assumptions. Referral fees, if any, shall be fully disclosed; and
(d) A statement indicating whether the CFP designee's compensation arrangements are fee-only, commission-only, or fee and commission. A CFP designee shall not hold out as a fee-only financial planning practitioner if the CFP designee receives commissions or other forms of economic benefit from related parties; and
(e) A statement describing material agency or employment relationships a CFP designee (or firm) has with third parties and the fees or commissions resulting from such relationships; and
(f) A statement identifying conflict(s) of interest(s).

Rule 403

A CFP designee providing financial planning shall disclose in writing, prior to establishing a client relationship, relationships which reasonably may compromise the CFP designee's objectivity or independence.

Rule 404

Should conflict(s) of interest(s) develop after a professional relationship has been commenced, but before the services contemplated by that relationship have been completed, a CFP designee shall promptly disclose the conflict(s) of interest(s) to the client or other necessary persons.

Rule 405

In addition to the disclosure by financial planning practitioners regarding sources of compensation required under Rule 402, such disclosure shall be made annually thereafter for ongoing clients. The annual disclosure requirement may be satisfied by offering to provide clients with the current copy of SEC form ADV, Part II or the disclosure called for by Rule 402.

Rule 406

A CFP designee's compensation shall be fair and reasonable.

Rule 407

Prior to establishing a client relationship, and consistent with the confidentiality requirements of Rule 501, a CFP designee may provide references which may include recommendations from present and/or former clients.

Rule 408

When acting as an agent for a principal, a CFP designee shall ensure that the scope of his or her authority is clearly defined and properly documented.

Rule 409

Whether a CFP designee is employed by a financial planning firm, an investment institution, or serves as an agent for such an organization, or is self-employed, all CFP designees shall adhere to the same standards of disclosure and service.

Rule 410

A CFP designee who is an employee shall perform professional services with dedication to the lawful objectives of the employer and in accordance with this Code.

Rule 411

A CFP designee shall:

(a) Advise the CFP designee's employer of outside affiliations which reasonably may compromise service to an employer, and

(b) Provide timely notice to the employer and clients, unless precluded by contractual obligation, in the event of change of employment or CFP Board licensing status.

Rule 412

A CFP designee doing business as a partner or principal of a financial services firm owes to the CFP designee's partners or co-owners a responsibility to act in good faith. This includes, but is not limited to, disclosure of relevant and material financial information while in business together.

Rule 413

A CFP designee shall join a financial planning firm as a partner or principal only on the basis of mutual disclosure of relevant and material information regarding credentials, competence, experience, licensing and/or legal status, and financial stability of the parties involved.

Rule 414

A CFP designee who is a partner or co-owner of a financial services firm who elects to withdraw from the firm shall do so in compliance with any applicable agreement, and shall deal with his or her business interest in a fair and equitable manner.

Rule 415

A CFP designee shall inform his or her employer, partners or co-owners of compensation or other benefit arrangements in connection with his or her services to clients which are in addition to compensation from the employer, partners or co-owners for such services.

Rule 416

If a CFP designee enters into a business transaction with a client, the transaction shall be on terms which are fair and reasonable to the client and the CFP designee shall disclose the risks of the transaction, conflict(s) of interest(s) of the CFP designee, and other relevant information, if any, necessary to make the transaction fair to the client.

Rules That Relate to the Principle of Confidentiality

Rule 501

A CFP designee shall not reveal—or use for his or her own benefit—without the client's consent, any personally identifiable information relating to the client relationship or the affairs of the client, except and to the extent disclosure or use is reasonably necessary:

(a) To establish an advisory or brokerage account, to effect a transaction for the client, or as otherwise impliedly authorized in order to carry out the client engagement; or
(b) To comply with legal requirements or legal process; or
(c) To defend the CFP designee against charges of wrongdoing; or
(d) In connection with a civil dispute between the CFP designee and the client.

For purposes of this rule, the proscribed use of client information is improper whether or not it actually causes harm to the client.

Rule 502

A CFP designee shall maintain the same standards of confidentiality to employers as to clients.

Rule 503

A CFP designee doing business as a partner or principal of a financial services firm owes to the CFP designee's partners or co-owners a responsibility to act in good faith. This includes, but it not limited to, adherence to reasonable expectations of confidentiality both while in business together and thereafter.

Rules That Relate to the Principle of Professionalism

Rule 601

A CFP designee shall use the marks in compliance with the rules and regulations of the CFP Board, as established and amended from time to time.

Rule 602

A CFP designee shall show respect for other financial planning professionals, and related occupational groups, by engaging in fair and honorable competitive practices. Collegiality among CFP designees shall not, however, impede enforcement of this Code.

Rule 603

A CFP designee who has knowledge, which is not required to be kept confidential under this Code, that another CFP designee has committed a violation of this Code which raises substantial questions as to the designee's honesty, trustworthiness or fitness as a CFP designee in other respects, shall promptly inform the CFP Board. This rule does not require disclosure of information or reporting based on knowledge gained as a consultant or expert witness in anticipation of or related to litigation or other dispute resolution mechanisms. For purposes of this rule, knowledge means no substantial doubt.

Rule 604

A CFP designee who has knowledge, which is not required under this Code to be kept confidential, and which raises a substantial question of unprofessional, fraudulent or illegal conduct by a CFP designee or other financial professional, shall promptly inform the appropriate regulatory and/or professional disciplinary body. This rule does not require disclosure or reporting of information gained as a consultant or expert witness in anticipation of or related to litigation or other dispute resolution mechanisms. For purposes of this Rule, knowledge means no substantial doubt.

Rule 605

A CFP designee who has reason to suspect illegal conduct within the CFP designee's organization shall make timely disclosure of the available evidence to the CFP designee's immediate supervisor and/or partners or co-owners. If the CFP designee is convinced that illegal conduct exists within the CFP designee's organization, and appropriate measures are not taken to remedy the situation, the CFP designee shall, where appropriate, alert the appropriate regulatory authorities including the CFP Board in a timely manner.

Rule 606

In all professional activities, a CFP designee shall perform services in accordance with:

(a) Applicable laws, rules, and regulations of governmental agencies and other applicable authorities; and
(b) Applicable rules, regulations, and other established policies of the CFP Board.

Rule 607

A CFP designee shall not engage in any conduct which reflects adversely on his or her integrity or fitness as a CFP designee, upon the marks, or upon the profession.

Rule 608

The Investment Advisers Act of 1940 requires registration of investment advisers with the U.S. Securities and Exchange Commission and similar state statutes may require registration with state securities agencies. CFP designees shall disclose to clients their firm's status as registered investment advisers. Under present standards of acceptable business conduct, it is proper to use registered investment adviser if the CFP designee is registered individually. If the CFP designee is registered through his or her firm, then the CFP designee is not a registered investment adviser but a person associated with an investment adviser. The firm is the registered investment adviser. Moreover, RIA or R.I.A. following a CFP designee's name in advertising, letterhead stationery, and business cards may be misleading and is not permitted either by this Code or by SEC regulations.

Rule 609

A CFP designee shall not practice any other profession or offer to provide such services unless the CFP designee is qualified to practice in those fields and is licensed as required by state law.

Rule 610

A CFP designee shall return the client's original records in a timely manner after their return has been requested by a client.

Rule 611

A CFP designee shall not bring or threaten to bring a disciplinary proceeding under this Code, or report or threaten to report information to the CFP Board pursuant to Rules 603 and/or 604, or make or threaten to make use of this Code for no substantial purpose other than to harass, maliciously injure, embarrass and/or unfairly burden another CFP designee.

Rule 612

A CFP designee shall comply with all applicable post-certification requirements established by the CFP Board including, but not limited to, payment of the annual CFP designee fee as well as signing and returning the Licensee's Statement annually in connection with the license renewal process.

Rules That Relate to the Principle of Diligence

Rule 701

A CFP designee shall provide services diligently.

Rule 702

A financial planning practitioner shall enter into an engagement only after securing sufficient information to satisfy the CFP designee that:

(a) The relationship is warranted by the individual's needs and objectives; and
(b) The CFP designee has the ability to either provide requisite competent services or to involve other professionals who can provide such services.

Rule 703

A financial planning practitioner shall make and/or implement only recommendations which are suitable for the client.

Rule 704

Consistent with the nature and scope of the engagement, a CFP designee shall make a reasonable investigation regarding the financial products recommended to clients. Such an investigation may be made by the CFP designee or by others provided the CFP designee acts reasonably in relying upon such investigation.

Rule 705

A CFP designee shall properly supervise subordinates with regard to their delivery of financial planning services, and shall not accept or condone conduct in violation of this Code.

Appendix 3E

Introduction to the Life Insurance Illustration Questionnaire (IQ)

The Life Insurance Illustration Questionnaire (IQ) is an educational tool; its use by companies or agents is entirely voluntary.

The purpose of the IQ is to help the reader understand the different non-guaranteed performance assumptions which insurance companies use to design and create sales illustrations. The IQ may be particularly useful to agents, their clients (under the agent's guidance) and the clients' other advisors.

It has been developed for non-SEC regulated products. The reader should understand that sales illustrations are useful in developing the best combination of policy specifications to achieve the buyer's objective. However, illustrations have little value in predicting actual performance or in comparing products and companies.

Most life insurance products sold today have adjustable pricing. This can be accomplished either as a traditional "participating" product or as a product with "non-guaranteed pricing elements" such as changeable interest crediting rates, mortality charges, expense charges, etc. All adjustable pricing products incorporate some guarantees. However, the sales illustrations are usually designed to present potential benefits and costs under a set of non-guaranteed assumptions more optimistic than the guarantees. The insurance company generally limits its responsibility to the guarantees. So the risks associated with the possible inability of a product to achieve the higher illustrated benefits, or lower illustrated costs, than those generated by the guarantees are borne by the policyholder. A study of the responses to the IQ should help the reader better understand those risks.

Life Insurance Illustration Questionnaire

Information about this response:

Contact Person: ______________________ Date Completed: ________________

Policy(ies) Covered: ____

Are there any more IQs that cover other policies of this Company?

❑ No ❑ Yes ______ (how many)

Do the illustration(s) covered by this IQ response comply with the NAIC Life Insurance Illustrations Model Regulation?

❑ No ❑ Yes

In the following responses, "scale" means the scale of dividends or other non-guaranteed elements used in the illustrations.

SOCIETY OF
FINANCIAL SERVICE
PROFESSIONALS ™

A National Organization of
Insurance and Financial Advisers

Revised 4/96

I. General

1. With respect to participating policies, does the company employ the contribution principle*? If not how do practices differ?
   *The contribution principle calls for the aggregate divisible surplus to be distributed in the same proportion as the policies are considered to have contributed to the divisible surplus.

2. With respect to non-participating policies:

   a) Describe the non-guaranteed elements.

   b) What is the company's policy and discretion with respect to the determination and redetermination of non-guaranteed pricing elements?

3. Do any of the experience factor(s) underlying the scales of dividends or other non-guaranteed elements used in the illustration differ from actual recent historical experience? If so, describe.

4. Is there a substantial probability that the current illustrative values will change if actual recent historical experience continues unchanged?

5. Is it company policy to treat new and existing policyholders of the same class the same or consistently with respect to the underlying factors used in pricing? Please elaborate.

6. With respect to joint and survivor policies, describe all the effects of the first death on the policy and any riders (e.g., change in cash values, mortality charges, premiums).

II. Mortality

1. Do the mortality rates underlying the scale used in the illustration differ from actual recent historical company experience? If so, describe. Define actual recent historical experience (e.g., company experience for the last 5 years).

2. Does the illustration assume mortality improvements in the future? If so, describe.

3. Do the mortality or cost of insurance charges used in the illustration include some expense charge? If so, describe.

4. Do the underlying mortality rates vary by product (e.g., whole life, universal life, survivorship life), policy size or by any other feature (e.g., term riders)? If so, specify. (Provide general description of differences - not the actual rates used).

5. Indicate the approximate duration, if any, when all underlying mortality rates vary only by attained age (i.e., when does select become ultimate?).

III. Interest or Crediting Rates

1. The interest rate used in the dividend scale or credited in the illustration is (does):

   a) ☐ a Portfolio rate (Describe) ☐ an Investment Generation ("New Money") rate (Describe) ☐ Other (Describe)

   b) ☐ a Gross rate ☐ a Net rate, which is net of
   ☐ investment expenses
   ☐ income taxes
   ☐ profit or expense charges
   ☐ other ______________

   c) Include ☐ Realized ☐ Unrealized ☐ No Capital Gains.

   If capital gains are included, describe the general method (e.g., smoothed over ____ years).

2. Do the interest rate(s) reflect the earnings on all invested assets? A portion of the assets? New investments over certain number of years? (If so, specify number of years.) An index? (If so, briefly describe.)

3. At any policy duration, do the company investment earnings rates required to support the scale used in the illustration exceed the company's actual recent historical earnings rate on the investment segment backing that block of policies?

4. Does the interest rate used in the underlying scale reflected in the illustration vary between new and existing policies? Describe.

5. Except for any impact of using an investment generation approach, do the interest rates used in the scale reflected in the illustration vary by policy duration? Describe.

6. Do the illustrated interest rates vary by product, class or otherwise? Describe.

7. How does individual policy loan activity affect the illustrated interest rates? Describe.

Revised 4/96

IV. Expenses

1. Do the expense factors used in the scale reflected in the illustration represent actual recent historical company experience? If so, what is the experience period? If not, describe the basis under which the experience factors are determined.

2. Are the expense factors based on a ❑ fully allocated ❑ marginal or ❑ generally recognized approach, as defined in the NAIC Model Regulations?

3. Are the expense charges used in the underlying scale reflected in the illustration adequate to cover the expenses incurred in sales and administration? If not, how are remaining expenses covered (e.g., charges against interest rate, increased mortality charges)?

4. How are investment expenses and all taxes assessed?

5. Are expense factors used in the scale reflected in the illustration different for new and existing policies? If so, describe.

6. Do the expense factors underlying the scale reflected in the illustration vary by product, class or otherwise? If so, describe.

7. Do the expense charges used in the dividend scale or charged in the illustration vary by duration after the initial expenses are amortized? If so, describe.

V. Persistency

1. If the actual persistency is better than that assumed, would that negatively affect illustrated values?

2. Persistency bonuses are generally amounts illustrated as being paid or credited to all policyholders who pay premiums for a specified number of years. Does the illustration involve such a bonus?

   a. If so, is it ❑ on-guaranteed or ❑ guaranteed?

   b. Is there any limitation on company discretion in deciding whether to pay or credit the bonus?

   c. What conditions must be met to pay or credit the bonus?

   d. What is its form (e.g. cash amount, additional interest credit, refund of mortality and/or loading charges)?

   e. Does the company set aside any reserve or other liability earmarked for future bonuses?

Appendix 3F

Introduction to the Variable Life Insurance Illustration Questionnaire (VIQ)

The Variable Life Insurance Illustration Questionnaire (VIQ) is an educational tool; its use by companies or agents is entirely voluntary.

The purpose of the VIQ is to help the reader understand the different non-guaranteed performance assumptions which insurance companies use to design and create variable sales illustrations. The VIQ may be particularly useful to agents, their clients (under the agent's guidance) and the clients' other advisors.

The reader should understand that variable sales illustrations and actual historical performance may be useful in selecting a policy and the investment mix most appropriate to the purchaser's investment risk tolerance. However, illustrations do not predict actual future performance nor can they be used as the primary basis of comparing products and/or companies.

In general, life insurance products sold today typically have adjustable pricing. This can be accomplished either as a traditional "participating" product or as a product with "non-guaranteed pricing elements" such as changeable interest crediting rates, mortality charges, expense charges, etc.

For variable life insurance ***products***, the investment risk is generally transferred to the policyowner; mortality and expense charges are typically subject to the carrier's actual ongoing experience.

Sales ***illustrations*** are usually designed to present potential benefits and costs under a prescribed set of investment assumptions in conjunction with projections of non-guaranteed mortality, expense and persistency factors.

The risks associated with the possible inability of a product to achieve the illustrated benefits and/or illustrated costs are borne by the policyholder. The insurance company generally limits its responsibility to the guarantees contained in the policy. Both the death benefit and cash value in a variable life insurance policy generally vary with future investment performance of the funds selected by the policyowner.

A study of the responses to the VIQ should help the reader better understand the risks assumed by the policyowner.

Variable Life Insurance Illustration Questionnaire

Information about this response:

Company: ______________________________

Date Completed: ______________________________

Contact Person: ______________________________

Policy(ies) Covered: ______________________________

Are there any more VIQs that cover other policies of this Company?

No ❑ Yes ❑ Describe:

SOCIETY OF
FINANCIAL SERVICE
PROFESSIONALS ™

A National Organization of
Insurance and Financial Advisers

(VIQ 9/96)

Notes:

1) Variable life insurance policies do not - as of 9/15/96 - fall within the scope of the NAIC Insurance Illustration Model Regulations. At such time that Illustration Regulations apply to Variable Life Illustrations, this VIQ will be modified as necessary.

2) In the following responses, "scale" means the scale of dividends or other non-guaranteed elements used in the illustrations.

I. General

1. With respect to participating policies, does the company employ the contribution principle* ? If not how do practices differ?
   *The contribution principle calls for the aggregate divisible surplus to be distributed in the same proportion as the policies are considered to have contributed to the divisible surplus.

2. With respect to policies with non-guaranteed pricing elements other than dividends:

   a) Describe the non-guaranteed elements.

   b) What is the company's policy and discretion with respect to the determination and redetermination of non-guaranteed pricing elements?

3. Do any of the experience factor(s) underlying the scales of dividends or other non-guaranteed elements used in the illustration differ from actual recent historical experience? If so, describe.

4. Except for investment performance, is there a substantial probability that the current illustrative values will change if actual recent historical experience continues unchanged?

5. Is it company policy to treat new and existing policyholders of the same class the same or consistently with respect to the underlying factors used in pricing? Please elaborate.

6. If this VIQ response includes policies issued on a joint and survivor basis, describe all the effects of the first death on the policy and any riders (e.g., change in cash values, mortality charges, premiums).

II. Mortality

1. Do the mortality rates underlying the scale used in the illustration differ from actual recent historical company experience? If so, describe. Define actual recent historical experience (e.g., company experience for the last 5 years).

2. Does the illustration assume mortality improvements in the future? If so, describe.

3. Do the mortality or cost of insurance charges used in the illustration include some expense charge? If so, describe.

4. Indicate the approximate duration, if any, when all underlying mortality rates vary only by attained age (i.e., when does select become ultimate?).

5. Do the underlying mortality assumptions for the illustration differ from those for otherwise corresponding non-variable policies and, if so, how?

III. Investment Performance

1. Does the policyowner assume all of the investment risk?

   ❑ Yes ❑ No

   Please explain.

2. Is the original or initial death benefit guaranteed regardless of investment performance?

   ❑ Yes for ____ years or to age ____ ❑ No

   If yes, under what conditions is the guarantee effective (e.g., premiums at a specified yearly and/or cumulative level, or more, must be paid prior to the end of the guarantee period)?

IV. Expenses

1. Do the expense factors used in the scale reflected in the illustration represent actual recent historical company experience? If so, what is the experience period? If not, describe the basis under which the experience factors are determined.

2. Are the expense factors based on a ❑ fully allocated ❑ marginal or ❑ generally recognized approach, as defined in the NAIC Model Regulations?

3. Are the expense charges used in the underlying scale reflected in the illustration adequate to cover the expenses incurred in sales and administration? If not, how are remaining expenses covered (e.g., charges against separate accounts, increased mortality charges)?

4. How are investment expenses and all taxes assessed? Are the fund expenses in the illustration based on an average of all funds, or on specific funds?

5. Are expense factors used in the scale reflected in the illustration different for new and existing policies? If so, describe.

6. Do the expense factors underlying the scale reflected in the illustration vary by product, class or otherwise? If so, describe.

7. Do the expense charges used in the dividend scale or charged in the illustration vary by duration after the initial expenses are amortized? If so, describe.

8. Do the underlying expense assumptions for the illustration differ from those for otherwise corresponding non-variable policies and, if so, how?

V. Persistency

1. If the actual persistency is better than that assumed, would that negatively affect illustrated values?

2. Persistency bonuses are generally amounts illustrated as being paid or credited to all policyholders who pay premiums for a specified number of years. Does the illustration involve such a bonus?

   a. If so, is it ❑ non-guaranteed or ❑ guaranteed?

   b. Is there any limitation on company discretion in deciding whether to pay or credit the bonus?

   c. What conditions must be met to pay or credit the bonus?

   d. What is its form (e.g., cash amount, additional investment credit, refund of mortality and/or loading charges)?

   e. Does the company set aside any reserve or other liability earmarked for future bonuses? Describe.

3. Do the underlying persistency assumptions for the illustration differ from those for otherwise corresponding non-variable policies and, if so, how?

(VIQ 9/96)

Replacement Questionnaire (RQ)

A Policy Replacement Evaluation Form

To CLUs/ChFCs:

Replacing an existing life insurance policy with a new one generally is not in the policyholder's best interest. New sales loads and other expenses, the new company's right to challenge a death claim during the suicide and contestibility periods, changes in age or health and the loss of important grandfathered rights are some of the obvious reasons that **most replacements cannot be justified.** On the other hand, there may be circumstances where a replacement is in your client's best interest. The ethical agent will provide his or her client with the impartial information needed to make an informed decision, including reasons the client should not replace the current policy and/or how to modify the existing policy to accomplish their goals. The need for additional coverage is not, by itself, a justification for replacement.

This Form is designed to assist you in evaluating some of the facts and circumstances that a policyholder should take into consideration when addressing the possibility of replacing a life insurance policy. It can be used for both internal and external replacements. **The definition of "replacement" is much broader than the cancellation of one policy and the issuance of another.** The legal meaning of the word "replacement" is determined by state law and varies substantially by state. You should be familiar with your own state's definition of the word. However, for purposes of simplifying the definition, we may think of "replacement" in general terms as an action which eliminates the original policy or diminishes its benefits or values. Examples of this are policy loans, taking reduced paid-up insurance or withdrawing dividends. Since no form can cover every possible situation, you may need additional material to enable your client to make a truly informed decision.

Please note that "illustrated" results in this Form are always nonguaranteed. Also, keep in mind that different companies use different assumptions in preparing illustrations and that illustrations alone should never be used to compare policies. However, current in-force illustrations for the existing policy and current illustrations for the proposed policy must be provided to the client, showing the effects of applicable surrender charges. In situations where the current policy will be changed, but not terminated, comparisons should include in-force ledgers of the policy before and after the change, if available. Reduced scale illustrations (or illustrations with lower yield assumptions) should be provided on both existing and proposed policies to demonstrate volatility in the performance of nonguaranteed policy elements under different circumstances. The reduced scale illustrations should be consistent with those required by the NAIC model illustration regulations, when effective.

This Form is intended for evaluation purposes. It is not a substitute for state replacement requirements. This Form is not designed for direct use with clients. Further, if either the existing or proposed policy is variable life insurance, use of this Form with the client must be approved by your broker-dealer.

SOCIETY OF
FINANCIAL SERVICE
PROFESSIONALS ™

A National Organization of
Insurance and Financial Advisers

Replacement Questionnaire (RQ)

A Policy Replacement Evaluation Form

A. 1. What does the policyholder want to achieve that the existing policy cannot provide?

____

____

____

2. Has the current carrier been contacted to see if the policy can be modified to meet the policyholder's objectives?

____

B. 1. Recognizing that the replacement of an existing policy generally results in the reduction of cash surrender value as a result of new acquisition costs, what is the cash surrender value of:

a. The original policy **immediately** before replacement ________________
b. The original policy **immediately** after the replacement ________________
c. The proposed policy **immediately** after the replacement ________________

These cash surrender values should be obtained directly from the insurance carrier's policyowner service department and not from an illustration, since illustrations typically reflect end of year values.

2. Illustrations should **never** be the sole criteria for evaluating a replacement. Additionally, Illustrated Cash Values and Illustrated Death Benefits are **never** reliable predictions of future results. If these non-guaranteed values and benefits are the basis for considering a replacement, the agent should attempt to know and understand the underlying assumptions in both the inforce illustration for the current policy, as well as the sales illustration for the proposed policy. In addition to reviewing illustrations, the agent should attempt to obtain an Illustration Questionnaire (IQ), which may be available directly from the companies or may be requested through the client. The agent and the client should be aware that there may be differences in the assumptions used by each company which may render a comparison based upon such illustrations invalid.

How many years from now before the proposed policy's cash surrender values and death benefits exceed those benefits in the current policy?

a. Guaranteed Cash Surrender Values ______ years and subsequent.
b. Guaranteed Death Benefits ______ years and subsequent.
c. Illustrated Cash Surrender Values ______ years and subsequent.
d. Illustrated Death Benefits ______ years and subsequent.

3. If the proposed policy is a variable life policy, what gross yield rate is being assumed? ____%

   What is your justification for that rate? ____________________

C. 1. Describe the differences in the plans of insurance. ____________________

   ____

2. Describe any term riders or term elements (above the base policy). Include the ratio of the initial term amount to the total death benefit and any term rate guarantees which may or may not be included.

   Current policy: ____________________

   Proposed policy: ____________________

3. Other than term riders, what riders do the policies include?

   Current policy: ____________________

   Proposed policy: ____________________

4. How long is the initial death benefit **guaranteed** to be in force at the **illustrated** premium?

   Current policy: ______ years. Proposed policy: ______ years.

5. What premium is necessary to **guarantee** coverage at initial/current levels for life?

   Current policy: $__________. Proposed policy: $__________.

D. 1. Is there a potential taxable gain if the current policy is replaced?

   ❑ YES ❑ NO If yes, how is it to be managed?

   ____

2. If there is a taxable gain, **and if there is a loan,** how is the loan to be managed?

   ❑ The new policy will assume the existing loan.

   ❑ The loan will be repaid.

   ❑ The policyowner will recognize taxable income.

E. Is an IRC Sec. 1035 exchange planned to preserve basis? ❑ YES ❑ NO

F. If a replacement is under consideration because a more favorable rate classification is available, has a reduction or removal of the rating on the existing policy been requested? If so, what was the result. If not, explain why such a request has not been made.

   ____

G. Does the proposed policy qualify as life insurance under IRC Section 7702?

   ❑ YES ❑ NO

H. What is the issue date of the current policy? ______________________

The following "grandfathered" features will be lost if the policy is replaced. (See Appendix for explanation of items 3-9.)

1. The current policy is incontestable by the insurance company. ❑ YES ❑ NO
2. The period has expired during which the insurance company can deny policy benefits in the event of the insured's suicide. ❑ YES ❑ NO

The current *life insurance policy* was issued on or before:	YES	NO	The current *annuity policy* was issued before:	YES	NO	The current *second to die policy* was issued before:	YES	NO
3. 8/06/63	❑	❑	6. 10/21/79	❑	❑	9. 9/14/89	❑	❑
4. 6/20/86	❑	❑	7. 8/14/82	❑	❑			
5. 6/20/88	❑	❑	8. 2/28/86	❑	❑			

I. If the current policy is term, is a conversion to permanent insurance available? ❑ YES ❑ NO
If so, other than the suicide and incontestable provisions would a conversion to permanent insurance be more advantageous?

❑ YES ❑ NO Explanation: ____

____

J. Financial Strength Ratings. Much has been made of ratings in the last few years; financial strength is important, but it is not the sole determining factor in selecting a life insurance company. A drop in ratings alone generally is not a sufficient reason to replace a policy. It is also important to know that there can be differences of opinion among rating agencies and that small differences in ratings generally are not significant. Furthermore, financial strength ratings are not necessarily indicative of policy performance. If reviewed with the client, a detailed explanation of the ratings must be provided in accordance with state regulations.

	Current Company Rating (Rank)*	Proposed Company Rating (Rank)	Date & Source of Answer
A. M. Best (15 ranks)	________	________	____________
Duff & Phelps (18 ranks)	________	________	____________
Moody's (19 ranks)	________	________	____________
S & P Claims Paying Ability** (18 ranks)	________	________	____________

* For example, an AA rating from S & P is the third highest **rank** out of 18 possible ratings.

** S & P offers two rating services. Claims Paying Ability is on a par with the other services listed here; S & P's Qualified Solvency Rating is a much differently oriented rating and is inappropriate for use in this context.

K. Policy loans:	Current Policy	Proposed Policy
1. Gross rate	________	________
2. Fixed or Variable?	________	________
3. Permanent policies: Direct Recognition?	________	________
4. Universal life, etc. a. Current spread?	________	________
b. Is spread guaranteed?	❑ YES ❑ NO	❑ YES ❑ NO

L. Additional remarks:

____

____

____

____

Appendix
Grandfathered Features Explanation
(See question H.)

3. The current policy was purchased on or before 8/6/63, so IRC Section 264(a)(3) which limits deductions for interest indebtedness does not apply. If the current policy has met the "four out of seven" test of IRC Section 264(c)(1), interest on indebtedness is deductible to the extent otherwise allowed by law. Personal interest deductions are generally denied for tax years beginning after 1990, irrespective of when the policy was purchased. IRC Sec. 163(h)(1).

4. The current policy was purchased on or before June 20, 1986. Certain policies purchased for business purposes after this date have a $50,000 ceiling on the aggregate amount of indebtedness for which an interest deduction is allowed. IRC Sec. 264(a)(4).

5. Policy was issued on or before 6/20/88 and is not subject to Modified Endowment Contract rules. IRC Sec. 7702A. Substantial increases in the death benefits of grandfathered contracts after 10/20/88 may cause the imposition of the MEC rules. H.R. Conf. Rep. No. 1104, 100th Cong., 2d Sess. (TAMRA '88) reprinted in 1988-3 CB 595 - 596.

6. Variable annuity contracts purchased before 10/21/79 are eligible for a step-up in basis if the owner dies before the annuity starting date. IRC Sec. 72; Rev. Rul. 79-335, 1979-2 CB 292.

7. An annuity issued prior to 8/14/82 is subject to more favorable (basis out first) cost recovery rules for withdrawals. IRC Sec. 72(e). Such policies are not subject to the 10% penalty on withdrawals made prior to age 59 1/2. IRC Sec. 72(q)(2).

8. To the extent contributions are made after 2/28/86 to a deferred annuity held by a non-natural person (such as a business entity), the contract will not be entitled to tax treatment as an annuity. IRC Sec. 72(u).

9. A survivorship life policy issued prior to 9/14/89 is not subject to the 7-pay MEC test if there is a reduction in benefits. IRC Sec. 7702A(c)(6).

This Appendix is provided for educational purposes only.
You should seek competent legal counsel before
applying this to any specific situation.

SOCIETY OF
FINANCIAL SERVICE
PROFESSIONALS ™

A National Organization of
Insurance and Financial Advisers

4

Effective Communication in Financial Counseling

Lewis B. Morgan

Chapter Outline

INTRODUCTION[1]

Many people take communication for granted. After all, it is an activity that most of us have engaged in since our childhood years, so why not take it for granted? The sad truth, however, is that many of us are ineffective communicators simply because we make that very assumption.

Communication is far too important a skill, especially in the field of counseling, to treat lightly. It is the single most critical skill that a counselor brings to a counseling session.

The purpose of this chapter is to examine the communication process as it typically exists in a counselor-client relationship. Our goal is to enable financial planners to become exceptionally effective communicators in their dealings with clients. Perhaps you already consider yourself to be effective in the area of communication; however, there are probably aspects of the communication process in which you can improve. This chapter will attempt to bring these aspects into sharper focus and provide you with techniques for becoming the very best communicator/counselor that you have the potential of being.

The chapter begins with a delineation of the various types of structured communication: interviewing, counseling, and advising. From there it proceeds to some of the essentials inherent in financial counseling: structuring the counseling relationship; establishing rapport; and dealing with resistance. Next it looks at some of the characteristics of effective counseling: unconditional positive regard, empathy, genuineness, and self-awareness.

The second part of the chapter focuses on basic communication principles and skills such as nonverbal communication, using the skills of attending to a client, listening and then responding to a client, and asking effective questions.

THREE TYPES OF STRUCTURED COMMUNICATION

Laypeople often use the terms interviewing, counseling, and advising interchangeably; yet each term has characteristics that are uniquely its own and that differentiate it from the other two. Let us look at each of these three terms and see how they are alike and how they are different.

Three Types of Structured Communication

- Interviewing
- Counseling
- Advising

Interviewing

One of the most common forms of structured communication is interviewing. Interviewing can be defined as a process of communication, most often between two people, with a predetermined and specific purpose, usually involving the asking and answering of questions designed to gather meaningful information. For example, a television sports announcer might interview a coach at halftime to get information about what mistakes his team made in the first half, what he plans to do differently in the second half, and how he hopes to win. Or an interview might take place in a personnel office where a job applicant is interviewed for a position with the firm. The interviewer will want to know the following: What assets will the applicant bring to the job? What is her employment history? Where does she see herself fitting into the firm? What salary does she expect? In both instances cited, there is a specific purpose to the interview in that relevant information is being sought through a question-and-answer dialogue.

Stewart and Cash, in their book, *Interviewing: Principles and Practices,* refer to two basic types of interviews: the directive and nondirective interview.[2] In the directive interview, the interviewer directs and controls both the pace and the content to be covered. It is a much more formalized and structured style of interaction. Often the interviewer even completes a questionnaire form as the interviewee answers pointed questions—for example, What is your age? Where do you live? Where was your last job? What is the highest level of education completed? The advantages of the directive interview are that it can be brief and that it provides measurable data. Its disadvantages are that it is often inflexible and does not allow the interviewee to choose topics for discussion.

The nondirective interview, on the other hand, allows both the interviewer and the interviewee a wider range of subject areas to be discussed, and the interviewee usually controls the pacing and purpose of the interview. Thus the advantages of the nondirective interview include greater flexibility, more in-depth responses, and the potential of a closer relationship between interviewer and interviewee. Its disadvantages are that it consumes more time and often generates data that are difficult to measure objectively.

All interviews, whether directive or nondirective, share common characteristics. Interviews typically take place in a formal and structured setting. Questions are the primary source of communication used by the interviewer. The subject matter discussed is specific to the overall purpose of the interview, and digressions from the subject are usually not encouraged. Finally, the interview is usually a relatively short-term relationship between interviewer and interviewee.

Counseling

The second term, counseling, is often confused with interviewing, even though they are not synonymous. Counseling implies help giving, often of a psychotherapeutic nature, and the help-giving aspect is more than implied in counseling; it is built in and an integral part of the process. Simply stated, a counselor's job is to provide assistance to clients as they explore their present situations, begin to understand where they are in relation to where they would like to be, and then act to get from where they are to where they want to be. Even though this may sound like a simple process, it is not. It usually is a long-term process, typified by struggles, setbacks, and, eventually, insights leading to an ultimate change in behavior as clients strive to live more fulfilling lives.

While financial counseling takes place over a period of time, the interview is usually a one-time interaction. As such, an interpersonal relationship develops between counselor and client, something that usually does not occur in an interview. When we discussed interviewing, we stated that the question was the primary stock-in-trade of the interviewer. While questions are also utilized in counseling, they are not the primary response modality. In certain counseling settings such as mental hospitals and mental health clinics, an intake interview constitutes the first step in the therapeutic process. In this intake interview, many personal questions are asked, either in a written or oral format, but once the intake procedure is concluded, the communication assumes a different form. While questions may still be asked periodically, they are not the predominant form of counselor response. A counselor may paraphrase what the client has said, reflect a feeling, share feedback or perceptions, clarify, summarize, interpret, provide information, and confront. In short, counseling is not as stylized as interviewing because the format is less formal and less structured. Much more of the humanness of both the counselor and the client comes into focus, all with the purpose of providing help to the client.

Advising

Still a third type of structured communication is advising, which is often confused with counseling. In fact, many people who are unfamiliar with counseling think that what they will receive is advice. Perhaps one reason for this misconception stems from the journalistic proliferation of advice such as is offered in newspaper columns by "Dear Abby" and her sister, Ann Landers. This is not to say that advice is never offered by counselors, because it is; but most counselors believe that the very best kind of advice is self-advice, rather than expert advice.

Several situations might require such advice. A college student planning a program of studies is typically assigned an academic adviser in his or her major field of study. The adviser's role is, simply, to advise the student about program sequence, course prerequisites, specific course content, graduation requirements, and possible career opportunities in the major area. In short, the adviser is the expert and, as such, provides excellent advice. A tax adviser might provide advice on tax shelters, investments, tax deferral, and so on. In both instances, advisers know much more about their field of expertise than do their clients, and their clients use this knowledge in order to reach decisions.

In financial counseling, there are bound to be occasions when counselors give advice. After all, financial counselors are the experts and thus their advice has proven value. The danger in offering advice too soon in the counseling relationship is that the client's ability to make decisions is discounted in favor of the expert's opinion. Perhaps the best way to give advice, if advice is given at all, is to hear clients out first in order to understand their situation more completely and to assess their goals, and then to explain what alternatives or options are available.

Advice giving remains a controversial issue in counseling literature. Its critics maintain that advice fosters dependency and robs clients of the right to make decisions for themselves. It is important for each counselor to question his or her haste in offering ready answers to somewhat complex situations. Is there some inner need like dominance or control being satisfied? Is the advice giver willing to assume the responsibility for another person's life? Is the advice giver projecting his or her own needs, problems, or values into the advice?

So while it is true that many people come to a financial counselor ostensibly looking for advice or the right answer, it is also true that many people choose not to take the advice when it is offered, or if they do take the counselor's advice and later discover that it was unsound, they rightfully blame the counselor.

There is a place for tentative suggestions that leave the final decision about courses of action entirely up to the client. In this manner, clients are free to make decisions that are right for them and thus assume the responsibility for their own lives. Advisers who do this are functioning in a wholly professional and ethical manner.

ESSENTIALS IN FINANCIAL COUNSELING

In the preceding section we differentiated the three types of planned, purposeful communication: interviewing, counseling, and advising. Each one of these types of communication can be found in the financial counseling relationship. For instance, interviewing in the form of data collection for a fact finder might well constitute the early stages of the communications process. After the data are collected, the second phase would probably consist largely of counseling—listening closely to the client and trying to understand the client's inner world of needs, desires, fears, attitudes, values, and goals. The third and final stage of communication in financial counseling would undoubtedly include giving expert advice, or at least carefully exploring possible alternatives for achieving the client's objectives. Let us look at the dynamics of communication and how it works in actual practice.

Structure

In any kind of planned and purposeful communication setting, the first element that needs to be attended to is structuring. Structuring serves to determine both the format and the subject matter of the interaction that is to follow. The counselor's task is to make the purpose of the session clear to the client at the outset. This would include the inevitable introductions, an explanation of the process involved, a discussion of forms that are used and the amount of time that will be required, a discussion of the confidential nature of the relationship, and some prediction of what kinds of outcomes the client might reasonably expect. This structuring need not be lengthy and cumbersome; in fact, it is far better to structure in a clear, straightforward, and succinct fashion. Consider the following example of structuring:

Counselor: "In order for me to be able to provide the best possible service for you, we'll probably need to see each other on three or four separate occasions, although I want you to know that I'm available to you as often as you need me. Today I thought we'd start by getting some information about your financial situation. To do this, I'll use the fact finder pages, which will remain confidential between the two of us. As we go about our business together, I suspect that we'll be able to come up with a financial plan that will be sensible and help you meet your goals. Do you have any questions?"

The counselor's approach in the foregoing example is friendly and promises cooperation. The client is made to feel important, that he or she is the focal point of the counseling situation. The statement offers hope that the results of client counseling will meet the needs and goals of the client.

In the early stages of counseling, the client may be apprehensive or uncertain about how to begin. A good guide to follow is to begin where the client is. If the client is, in fact, anxious at the outset, some time should be spent discussing the mere difficulty of getting started. Talking about this will invariably alleviate most of the client's anxieties. It is important to keep in mind that whenever feelings emerge, it is best to focus upon those feelings rather than ignore them. If, for example, a client, in the middle of a session, appears distressed over some aspect of his or her situation (for example, an impending divorce), some time must be given to discussing these feelings. Until the feelings are addressed and expressed, a further discussion of content is unproductive and meaningless.

Rapport

Rapport is best established through the personhood of the financial counselor. Attributes that go a long way toward a rapprochement between counselor and client would include a friendly and interested concern; an unhurried, leisurely pace; an accepting, nonjudgmental attitude; attentive, active listening; and an egalitarian relationship. In such a climate, clients are free to be themselves, since they don't have to be afraid that what they say will be evaluated in a negative way by the counselor. Furthermore, they begin to realize that the ultimate responsibility for planning, setting goals, and taking action rests with them and not the counselor.

Perhaps the most important attribute of personhood in establishing rapport is the financial counselor's acceptance of the client and the client's awareness of this acceptance. This attitude stems from a sincere desire on the part of the counselor to respect the uniqueness of each client and a genuine wish to be of help. And it might be well to add that accepting others is easier said than done, especially with people who are markedly different from us in terms of their values, attitudes, socioeconomic status, and so on. Despite this difficulty, it is absolutely imperative that counselors accept their clients, because unless a client feels accepted by his counselor, the relationship will never really become a partnership of equals.

Recognizing Resistance

Resistance often occurs in even the best of counseling relationships. It can be expressed as either overt or covert hostility toward the counselor. Open hostility is the easiest type to recognize and, in most cases, to handle. We all know what angry people look and sound like: their faces become flushed; their jaws tighten; they clench their fists; their voices rise; their language becomes more expressively angry. The only effective thing to do at this point is to reflect this anger, as in saying, "I can sense your anger. You don't like what I've just said, do you?" This allows clients to vent whatever pent-up feelings of anger they have, and the anger slowly begins to dissipate and then the behavior can become more rational.

Covert hostility is more difficult to recognize and can be more difficult to deal with, since clients themselves may not even be aware of their anger. Some indications of covert hostility are missed appointments; being late for appointments; being sarcastic or cynical; being overly genteel or polite; not getting down to business. Whatever the evidence of covert hostility is, the best approach is *not* to interpret the behavior for the client as latent hostility or passive-aggressiveness but simply to focus on the behavior itself and let the client analyze or interpret it. For instance, the counselor might say, "I've noticed that whenever we talk about your spouse's handling of the family budget, you become sarcastic. What do you think might be going on?" Again, this helps the client to focus on the feedback received and allows angry feelings to be vented. Resistance must be addressed as directly as possible if any good is to come of the counseling relationship.

Other types of resistance behaviors that counselors might encounter during counseling relationships would include withdrawal or passivity; dwelling in fantasy or nonreality; ambivalence or vacillation; and the use of inappropriate humor, to name a few. As mentioned, the counselor should not analyze or interpret a client's resistance behavior since analysis tends only to raise the client's defensiveness. Instead the counselor should be aware of what is occurring, note whether it is a recurrent pattern, and at an appropriate point share such observations in a nonjudgmental manner with the client.

Common Areas of Resistance

Client resistance is almost a given in a financial counseling relationship, probably because clients, when they enter into a counseling relationship, yield a certain amount of their privacy and personal power over the situation to the counselor. Resistance is a way of defending oneself, or restoring some of the balance of power to oneself. Certain discussion areas, because of their sensitive nature, seem to be particularly vulnerable to client resistance.

One such sensitive subject area is death and dying. Because of its uncertainty, death is extremely anxiety-producing to some people. Dr. Elisabeth Kübler-Ross, an eminent authority on death and dying, postulates that there are five stages that a person facing death passes through: denial, anger, bargaining, depression, and acceptance. The first four of these stages are all different forms of resistance that the person uses for self-protection. Financial counselors, when discussing future plans with older people, need to be particularly sensitive to the feelings of their clients. Counselors must listen and observe very closely what clients communicate when discussing death and dying. Counselors must be empathetic to feelings and communicate accurately what is heard and observed. A genuine concern for the feelings and attitudes of clients must be manifested. Counselors must also be aware of their own feelings about death, so that they do not interfere with what clients are feeling and attempting to communicate.

Counselors can help to restore some control over the future by involving clients fully in decision making and planning for contingencies. This allows clients to feel useful, worthwhile, and somewhat in control of their situation.

Another area where resistance may be encountered involves marital tensions, such as separation/divorce, parent-child disputes, sex, the empty-nest syndrome, and midlife crises. While financial counselors are not expected to be highly qualified marriage or family counselors, they should be astute enough to recognize when a married couple is resisting because of an underlying, unexpressed marital problem. And once it is recognized, counselors should be willing and able to focus with the couple on the problem area. Otherwise, if the problem is ignored, whatever decisions are reached will be less valid than those that would be reached after a full airing of the problem. Besides providing a possibly welcome catharsis for the couple, focusing on the problem can enable them to muster their forces in order to arrive at a mutually satisfactory solution. In counseling couples who are in disagreement on a crucial subject, the counselor needs to listen closely to what both partners have to say. It is far too common, unfortunately, to let the more dominant partner do most of the speaking and deciding. Since the outcome of the decision affects both partners, both should be involved in the discussion. To do any less almost guarantees an unsatisfactory conclusion.

Another sensitive area involves the executive who has failed to attain the degree of success he had dreamed of in his profession. His dreams shattered and unfulfilled, he may resort to cynicism, biting sarcasm, or empty humor in an attempt to endure it. Rather than laugh along with him, the effective counselor *reflects* the underlying feeling to let the client know that he or she understands his disappointment. A simple statement like, "I suppose it's a bitter pill to swallow when you've worked so hard to see your personal hopes go unfulfilled," allows your client to feel understood and appreciated. More often than not, the client will begin to discuss more openly how he feels. And once people are able to express their feelings, they are well on the way to addressing their problems in an effective manner.

Resistance behaviors, in any case, are a certain tip-off that the client is having difficulty subscribing to the counselor's line of reasoning. It does no good for the counselor to proceed with business as usual, ignoring the obvious resistance; nothing can be accomplished as long as the resistance continues. The resistance must be dealt with openly and objectively if there is any chance that it will be diminished, allowing the participants to get on with the business at hand.

PROFILE OF THE EFFECTIVE COUNSELOR

The main thing a counselor brings to the counseling hour is himself or herself. Financial counselors, first and foremost, must be themselves in their relation to and interaction with their clients. Each counselor is a human being, complete with strengths and frailties. But each counselor is also a professionally trained individual, a person who, ideally, enjoys listening to and trying to understand other people and to accept them as they are. The effective counselor is also sincere and genuine in attempting to help others learn how to help themselves. This attitude generates interesting, challenging, and highly gratifying work; and it is—more than anything else—hard work when done professionally.

Carl Rogers, in his classic book, *Client-Centered Therapy,* postulated that there are three conditions necessary to bring about constructive client change: (1) unconditional positive regard, (2) accurate empathy, and (3) genuineness.[3] Most counseling theorists agree that if an effective counselor-client relationship is to exist, the counselor must value the client as a unique individual (unconditional positive regard), must be able to perceive and understand what the client is experiencing (accurate empathy), and must be open and spontaneous (genuine).

A constructive counselor-client relationship serves not only to increase the opportunity for clients to attain the goals that are important to them, but also serves as a model of a good interpersonal relationship. Some questions that all counselors ought to ask themselves from time to time are the following:

- Knowing yourself, do you think it will be possible for you to value your clients, especially those who think, feel, and act differently from you?
- How easy or difficult will it be for you to view the world from another's perspective without imposing your own standards, beliefs, and attitudes on that person? Will your own values, ideas, and feelings hinder your understanding of another person?
- How open do you care, or dare, to be with a client? Will you be able to just be yourself, or will you role-play how you think a professional counselor should be?

These are important questions to consider before engaging yourself in the dynamics of a counseling relationship. Far too many financial counselors assume that they have the right kind of personality to counsel others without ever scrutinizing themselves in the same way.

Let us examine the three core conditions to which Rogers refers, and a fourth condition, self-awareness.

Four Characteristics of the Effective Counselor

1. Unconditional positive regard
2. Accurate empathy
3. Genuineness
4. Self-awareness

Unconditional Positive Regard

This quality is often misconstrued as agreement or disagreement with the client. Rather, it is an attitude of valuing the client, or being able to express appreciation of the client as a unique and worthwhile person. Liking and respecting another person have a circular effect. When you value clients, your sense of liking will be communicated to them; this by itself will enhance their feelings for themselves and add to their appreciation of themselves as worthwhile human beings.

Accurate Empathy

Accurate empathy means that your sense of the client's world fits the client's self-image. This gives clients the feeling that you are in touch with them. When clients say something like, "Yes, that's it," or "That's exactly right," it indicates that your response was right on target, and that they feel you are closely following and understanding them.

Learning to understand is not an easy process. It involves the capacity to lay aside your own set of experiences in favor of those of your clients—as seen through their eyes, not yours. It involves skillful listening so you can hear not only the obvious, but also the subtleties of which even the client may be unaware.

Developing accurate empathy also means identifying and resolving your own needs so they do not interfere with your understanding of the feelings and concerns of your client. The counselor who identifies too strongly with the client's state, however, impedes rather than facilitates the counseling objective.

Genuineness

Genuineness means, simply, that the counselor is a "real" person, that is, there is no facade, no role-playing of what a professional counselor is considered to be. Professional counselors are wholly aware of themselves and their feelings, thoughts, values, and attitudes. More importantly, counselors who are genuine are not afraid to express themselves openly and honestly at all times. Financial counselors do not have to become something different for each client with whom they have a relationship. They are role-free; they are themselves at all times.

A counselor who is genuine communicates in a spontaneous and expressive manner and does not conceal anything, is open and willing to listen to whatever the client is willing to discuss, and is consistent. He or she does not think or feel one thing but say another.

One author suggests that effective counselors can

- express directly to others whatever they are experiencing
- communicate without distorting their messages
- listen to others without distorting their messages
- be spontaneous instead of planned or programmed
- respond openly in a specific and concrete manner
- be willing to manifest their own vulnerabilities and frailties
- learn how to be psychologically close to others
- commit themselves to others

A tall order? Perhaps. And yet, for a financial counseling relationship to be effective, it is mandatory that counselors allow themselves to be genuine with their clients. Otherwise, the relationship deteriorates into a charade of two human beings playing prescribed roles with each other, and this defeats the purpose.

Self-Awareness

There is general consensus among counselor-educators that counselors need to be highly aware of themselves and particularly aware of their own attitudes and values. Counselors who are aware of their own value systems have a better chance of avoiding the imposition of their values onto their clients. This quality is of vital importance since we want to help our clients make decisions that stem from their own value systems, rather than from ours. The more we know about ourselves, the better we can understand, interpret, evaluate, and control our behavior and the less likely we are to attribute aspects of ourselves to the client, a rather common defense mechanism known as projection. Before we can be aware of others, it is essential that we be solidly grounded in self-awareness.

Barbara Okun, in her book, *Effective Helping,* suggests that counselors should continually try to determine their own needs, feelings, and values by answering the following questions:[4]

- Am I aware when I find myself feeling uncomfortable with a client or with a particular subject area?
- Am I aware of my avoidance strategies?
- Can I really be honest with the client?
- Do I always feel the need to be in control of situations?
- Do I often feel as if I must be omnipotent in that I must do something to make the client "get better" so that I can be successful?
- Am I so problem-oriented that I'm always looking for the negative, for a problem, and never responding to the positive, to the good?
- Am I able to be as open with clients as I want them to be with me?

The adage "Know thyself" should apply to financial counselors and other helping professionals even more than it does to the population at large. A very large part of our responsibility as counselors is to know ourselves as thoroughly as possible, so that we are then able to provide the very best kind of objective, informed counseling to our clients. A counselor who has "blind spots" about himself or herself will surely be less effective in a helping situation than a counselor who is comfortably self-aware. This is not to say that the counselor is a problem-free, completely self-actualized individual; rather, it means that the counselor is a human being, with a multitude of strengths and even some weaknesses, but the weaknesses are known by the counselor and do not interfere with the dynamics of counseling another person.

Orientation to Values

As human beings, we have value systems that are the result of years of living on this planet. Many of our values are inculcated in us by our parents, by schooling, by religion, by our peers, and by society. However they come to us, they are as much a part of us as our physical and psychological characteristics. This is not to say that they are a permanent, static part of our being, because our values can, and do, change. A vivid example of this type of change came during the 1960s and early 1970s when a whole society's value system was rocked to the core by momentous events such as the assassinations of the Kennedys and Martin Luther King, Jr., the civil rights movement, the war in Vietnam, the women's rights movement, and the Kent State killings. This truly was a time when an entire nation's value system was challenged, and as a result, certain of our long-cherished values were thrust into a state of flux and some ultimately changed. And what happened to the nation was repeated many times over with many individuals in our midst. People who at first accepted the Vietnam War as a rightful intervention by a powerful nation into the affairs of a far-off country slowly changed their feelings about not only that war, but armed conflict in general. And virtually the same thing happened on other controversial issues such as abortion, human rights, euthanasia, and drugs.

The point is that values, while deeply internalized, are not immutable. Counselors need to remind themselves of this fact as they work with clients who are confused and afraid in approaching important decisions. While it is true that we are in many ways a reflection of our past history, we are—or can be—much more than that. There is no need to be shackled to our past. We can, if we choose, overcome our past and live new lives, based upon who we are now and what we believe in and hold to be valuable to us both now and in the future. This is a liberating concept and, as such, frees individuals to think, feel, and behave in ways that are compatible with their present being, rather than dooming them to repeat the past and live in ways that are no longer meaningful.

The financial counselor's role in this situation is to act as a catalyst rather than as a maintainer of the status quo. The implied danger, of course, is that counselors might try to force change in their clients' values and attitudes where none is desired or sought after, or that counselors might subtly or not so subtly try to impose their values on clients. Both of these dangers must be consciously guarded against. What counselors must do is listen carefully to clients as they sift through the various value choices faced, so when clients must finally make the choice, it can be done freely, without encumbrances from the past. Clients must actually be opened up to the freedom of making choices that are relevant and meaningful to their very existence. Good counselors have a knack for being able to do this.

Differences in Values

Each of us has within us a hierarchy of values that makes order of our lives. An older executive facing retirement might, for example, rank security above risk taking when deciding how to invest money. On the other hand, a younger financial counselor might rank risk taking above security in the hierarchy of values. What happens, then, when the risk-taking counselor sits down to counsel the security-minded preretirement executive? If the counselor is sensitive and understanding, he or she will listen to the older person, and try to get a sense of what is important to the client, what the client is willing and unwilling to do. The effective financial counselor does not try to sell the client a product that the counselor believes is right but that the client believes is wrong, unsafe, or risky.

Counseling is caring, and caring means that the counselor cares enough—has enough faith in the client's worth as a unique human being—to permit that client to make value choices that fit his or her value system. The financial counselor can and should provide information that will help the client make the choice, but the choice ultimately belongs with the client, not the counselor. Only in this way are we counselors.

In addition to the differences in values, which often are reflective of the differences in age between counselor and client, we should also consider several other "isms"—sexism and racism—and how they impinge upon the counselor-client relationship. Let us look first at sex differences. Sexist counseling occurs when the counselor uses his or her own sex ideology as a framework for counseling. In the field of financial counseling this might take place when a male counselor discourages a female client from doing something that has traditionally been thought to be in the man's world, such as returning to work while there is an infant at home to be cared for. This kind of subtle advice giving, besides reflecting the obvious sex-role bias of the counselor, is not in keeping with what is happening in many households today. Further, it is intrusive in that the responsibility for making that decision is clearly the client's and not the counselor's. It is critical that counselors learn to recognize their own biases and sex-role stereotypes and not inflict them upon people whom they are trying to help.

In the case of married couples, financial counselors typically counsel both husband and wife. It is important to understand what both partners have to say. It is far too common to defer to the male of the household, the perceived "breadwinner," without taking into consideration what the female spouse has to contribute. When both husband and wife are in complete agreement, no problem exists. But when they disagree—and this is often communicated through nonverbal signals like a sigh, a frown, or an angry glance—it is important to make a point of bringing the subject up for a full discussion. It is far better to spend whatever time it takes to bring both partners to a mutually acceptable decision than to proceed with one person's plan of action, knowing that it doesn't satisfy the other person.

Racism, despite notable progress in the civil rights movement over the past two decades, is still with us in many forms. Counselors engage in racism when they limit the choices of their clients based solely on their clients' race, or when they make faulty assumptions about their clients because of racist stereotyping.

The issue of whether white counselors can be effective in a relationship with African Americans or Hispanics has been the subject of much research, though no conclusive findings exist. An effective counselor should be able to work with people of all races, since all people seem to have the same basic psychological needs and problems. Counselors need to be conscious of their own biases regarding race and to guard against allowing their biases to adversely affect the quality of the counseling relationship. The counseling strategies employed should not differ with regard to the race of the client, any more than they should not differ depending on the sex, age, or religion of the client.

BASIC COMMUNICATION PRINCIPLES

In the previous section we discussed the attributes of an effective counselor. In this section we will explore communication as a process and attempt to relate fundamental principles of communication to effective financial counseling. An effective counselor is also an effective communicator.

Communication is often thought of as one person sending a message through both verbal and nonverbal channels to another person or persons with the intention of evoking a response. A speaker asks, "How are you?" and the listener (or receiver of the communication) answers, "Just fine—except for my back."

Effective communication takes place when the receiver interprets the sender's message in precisely the same fashion in which the sender intended it. Difficulties in communication arise when the receiver misunderstands and/or misinterprets the sender's message. Since any individual's intentions are private and rarely clearly stated, the receiver of the message has the difficult job of decoding the message without knowing for a fact what the sender's intentions are.

In addition, communication failures can also be attributed to the wide variety of stimuli with which individuals are bombarded during the course of a conversation. People try to communicate while watching television or listening to the radio, or they attempt to conduct two conversations simultaneously. But all noise is not auditory; some is emotional in nature. For example, labor-management negotiations are often fraught with suspicion and mistrust. Prejudices and biases, then, are emotionally built-in stimuli that interfere with objective listening and effective communication.

Related to this communication failure is the sad but simple truth that individuals listen in order to evaluate and render judgment about the speaker, which, in turn, makes the speaker guarded and defensive about what he or she is attempting to communicate. Perhaps the best example of this type of ineffective communication is a city council meeting, where one side advocates the raising of taxes, while the other side interrupts, casts aspersions, and generally fights for all it is worth against the tax hike. Whenever there are two people, or two groups, each with a strong vested interest in an emotional issue, the likelihood of there being clear communication is virtually nil.

Communication, even in the best of circumstances, should not be taken for granted. Let us look now at some basic principles of communication theory.

- Communication is learned through experience, but experience itself does not necessarily make one an effective communicator. As children, we learn how to communicate by imitating our models—parents, brothers, sisters, neighbors, playmates, babysitters. Unfortunately, not all of our models are effective communicators; thus, we acquire poor habits of communication early, and those habits, like all habits, are difficult to break. A child reared in a home where everyone talks at the same time and no one listens carries this model upon leaving the home.
- The meaning of words is illusory; words do not mean—people do. Words are merely symbols. Consider, for example, a simple word like rock. The teenager immediately thinks of loud music; the geologist thinks of a hard object created millions of years ago; the burglar thinks of a diamond ring; the old lady thinks of her favorite chair, and so on. The point is that a word can have almost as many meanings as there are people who use it.
- Language is learned; thus, in a sense, we are programmed, and the meaning of words stays within us for future reference. This programming is extremely helpful since, once we learn a word, it

usually remains ours for a lifetime. However, this programming can also serve as an impediment to open communication with others, in that we often refer back to our original conceptions of words without thinking how others might interpret them. For example, the word girl, once used to refer to any female, is now clearly inappropriate in referring to an adult woman in this age of women's rights.

- No two people are programmed alike; therefore no symbol can always be interpreted the same way. Individuals differ in the nature and degree of their understanding. We perceive things differently, from our own frame of reference, so meanings differ.
- It is impossible for any individual to encode or process all parts of a message. Besides the fact that words are often inadequate in describing accurately what we are feeling or thinking, there is also the problem of distortion, that is, an individual's altering the event to suit his or her own purposes. But even if we have the precise word and communicate it without distortion, we still are faced with the problem of the receiver's receiving it in the same way in which it was intended.
- Some experts claim that the single greatest problem with communication is the assumption of it. Too many people assume that their messages are automatically understood. We also sometimes assume that our perceptions are more right than the perceptions of someone else. Where human communication is concerned, no assumptions can or should be made.
- We can never not communicate. Anything we say or do can be interpreted in a meaningful way as a message. Even during periods of silence, communication takes place. Nonverbal behavior (which will be discussed in some detail shortly) such as eye contact, facial expressions, gestures, body posture, voice inflections, hesitations, and the like, all speak volumes. In fact, most sociological research claims that approximately two-thirds of the total message is communicated via nonverbal channels, especially where human emotions are concerned.
- Listening is communication, too. Unfortunately, not everyone is a good listener; yet, that should not be too surprising, since listening as a communication skill is rarely, if ever, taught formally. To speak precisely and to listen carefully present a real challenge to all of us. The way in which we listen and respond to another person is crucial for building a fulfilling relationship. When we listen carefully, with understanding and without evaluation, and when we respond relevantly, we implicitly communicate to the speaker, "I care about what you are saying, and I'd like to understand it."
- The most effective communication occurs when the receiver of a message gives understanding responses, sometimes called paraphrases.

A client might say, "I don't know. . . . I doubt that we can afford to send both of our kids to college." A financial counselor using an understanding response would respond to the above statement with, "So you're just not sure you have the resources for a college education right now." While it might be tempting to try to convince the clients at this juncture that there is a way to finance their children's college education, the understanding response communicates a desire to understand the clients without evaluating these statements as right or wrong. It also helps the counselor to see the expressed ideas and feelings of clients from their point of view.

- Personalizing messages enhances the communication process and the counseling relationship. The hallmark of personal statements is the use of the personal pronouns, I, me, and my. Using generalized pronouns such as everyone, anyone, or somebody to refer to your own ideas only tends to confuse clients and, hence, results in ambiguity and faulty understanding. Personal statements like, "I can appreciate your concern over not having adequate resources," reveals your own feelings to clients and increases the personal quality of the relationship.

ELEMENTS OF NONVERBAL BEHAVIORS

As mentioned above, clients communicate many feelings and attitudes to counselors through nonverbal behaviors, including (but not limited to) fear, anxiety, sincerity, confusion, anger, aggression, happiness, hostility, interest, boredom, and concern. The two main sources of nonverbal behaviors are the *body* and the *voice*. From these two sources come seven types of nonverbal signs of meaning: *body position*, *body movement*, *gestures, facial expressions, eye contact, voice tone*, and *voice pitch*. Each of these types of nonlinguistic signs conveys a wealth of information to the observant financial counselor. It should be noted that the counselor's first impressions of the meaning or significance of any body language must be checked out against other clues given by the client.

Elements of Nonverbal Behaviors

- The body
  - –Positions
  - –Movements
  - –Gestures
  - –Facial expressions
  - –Eye contact
- The voice
  - –Tone
  - –Pitch

The Body

When learning to improve one's ability to observe the nonverbal behaviors of clients, it is important to notice the various ways by which the body actually communicates, either in agreement or in variance with what is actually said. In particular, the counselor should notice and learn to interpret the communications that are transmitted by the client's body positions and movements.

Positions

Overall body posture is the first thing the observant counselor notices. Clients who sit erect and comfortably are usually relaxed. If they lean slightly forward, it is usually a sign of interest and involvement in the counseling session. If they slouch, or seem to draw away from the counselor, they may have no interest or trust in the counselor—or they may be bored. Good client posture may indicate self-assurance and positive self-esteem. Poor posture may signal a lack of self-assurance or low self-esteem.

The counselor should also notice the position of the client's arms and legs. When the legs are uncrossed and the arms are positioned comfortably at the sides, the client is usually relaxed and open. Tightly crossed arms and legs, on the other hand, may indicate distrust or unreceptiveness. The facial position of the client should also be noticed. Most people's faces are expressive of a wide range of ever-changing feelings. The client whose face appears frozen in one position may be signaling fear, anxiety, or anger, or some other prepossessing feeling that could become a block or obstacle to open communication with the counselor.

Movements

The client who frequently changes body positions may be indicating physical or emotional discomfort, or a lack of interest. The counselor should take note of such movements and try to relate them to information gleaned later.

There is reason to believe that body language may be more honest or pure than verbal communication. In certain positive, straightforward human experiences we know that it is. The impulsive hug or kiss of greeting for people we care for is the most obvious example. But people also communicate through the body when they don't want to communicate, or when they are hiding or contradicting themselves. For example, a client may say, "No, I'm not nervous about investing in a tax shelter," while biting his nails, pulling at his hair, or fidgeting distractedly. People often say what they think they may be expected to say in a given situation or context, not realizing what they may actually be communicating through body language.

Gestures

Hand and arm gestures are usually used to illustrate or accent verbal statements. Hands clasped so tightly that the knuckles are whitened and taut certainly signify something, perhaps fear or anxiety. While jerky hand and arm gestures may indicate anxiety, smooth and flowing gestures usually mean that the client is relaxed and interested in the counseling session. Frequent crossing and uncrossing of the legs, or bouncing a leg that is crossed, may indicate nervousness, boredom, or lack of interest.

Facial Expressions

The financial counselor can learn much from a client's facial expressions. Look for frowns, smiles, or nervous habits, such as biting the lips. Look especially to see if the client's facial expressions change as topics change, and note whether the expression is appropriate or incongruent. For example, if the client talks about anger, does she appear angry? If she facially expresses disgust about her husband's spendthrift ways, do her intentions in her last will and testament reflect that feeling by providing for her children through a trust, rather than leaving everything outright to her husband?

Eye Contact

Eye contact, or the lack of it, in the counseling session can indicate the client's feeling. If the client's eyes are downcast and rarely meet the gaze of the counselor, the client could be shy, anxious, or fearful (though not necessarily toward the counselor). On the other hand, if the client stares or glares constantly at the counselor, anger or hostility could be indicated. If the client's eyes rove all around the room, looking at the walls and ceiling while the counselor is filling out the data-gathering form, there could be a serious lack of interest in the relevance of data gathering. A client who is open and interested in the counseling session will usually meet the gaze of the counselor. This eye contact of the client usually indicates interest in the session and a positive and concerned attitude toward counseling. Needless to say, reciprocity from the counselor is likely to be perceived by the client in the same way.

The Voice

Nonverbal voice clues can be observed in the tone and pitch of the client's voice. Tone and pitch are qualities of the voice that may indicate the speaker's feelings, quite apart from what is actually said. They should be observed closely.

The Tone

Tone is loudness or softness. The client who talks very loudly or shouts may be indicating anger or hostility. The client who talks very softly may be exhibiting fear or shyness.

The Pitch

Pitch is the quality of a voice that indicates how high or low the voice is on a musical scale. A high-pitched voice may indicate anxiety, fear, or anger. A low-pitched voice may indicate either comfort or control of strong emotions.

Obviously, some people's voices are naturally louder than others. The natural pitch of different voices also varies greatly. The point is not to type these differences but to observe and determine which vocal qualities are natural to a particular client so as to recognize variations. If these vocal qualities do vary during counseling sessions in relation to personal and financial details, they can be important clues to the strong emotions that often affect a client's motivations, needs, and objectives. The counseling sessions themselves are often an inducement to clients to open up and give vent to feelings about their financial condition. Thus voice tone and pitch are important factors for counselors to observe and consider in relation to all other clues that characterize the client and reveal the individual's self-image.

Interpreting the Meaning of Nonverbal Behaviors

It is important for financial counselors to note that in all the descriptions above of nonverbal behaviors, of body language, we have stated that a behavior may or usually does indicate one or more feelings. Nonverbal behaviors are clues that must be clearly observed and compared with what the client says in order to determine whether they are appropriate or compatible with their actions. For example, if a client blurts out, "I am furious with the broker who sold me that bunch of junk bonds last year!" and strikes the desk, the gesture is compatible with the verbal message—it agrees with what the client says. If the client makes the same statement and sits calmly smiling, however, there is incompatible behavior—the body language does not jibe with the verbal message. When the financial counselor observes incompatible behavior of this sort in a client, it should be mentioned to the client in order to clarify which element of the communication is correct.

Nonverbal behaviors are clues or indicators. While they signify something, their meanings can be clouded by incompatibility, distortion, or vagueness. Premature assumptions about what they really mean would be as unprofessional as failing to notice them altogether. For example, a client's palsied hands might be due to one or more of the following causes: nervousness, fear, Parkinson's disease, too much coffee, chemical poisoning, or alcoholism. The client who always talks loudly may be either angry or hard of hearing, or merely an overbearing individual. The client who shows no interest in counseling may be worn out with worrying whether his recent commodities futures trading is going to wipe him out with margin calls, or whether he should buy term or whole life for estate liquidity, or whether he will have an estate. He may be on tranquilizers over worry about a son and heir who himself abuses drugs. For any number of reasons the client may need psychological counseling or therapy before he can undertake financial counseling. In short, not all the problems that clients may bring to financial counseling sessions are financial in origin or nature. When present, these nonfinancial problems will distort client messages and add to the difficulties of clarifying them.

Observant counselors need to be astute enough to discern from among all the verbal and nonverbal clues and be aware that in most client cases there will be a mixture of compatible and incompatible evidence. Counselors thus understand who clients are, where they are, where they want to go; and can then suggest the optimal ways to help each one get there. *Do not assume that you know what a given behavior means.* Check it out and clarify your perception with each client.

And do not forget that as a counselor *you* communicate in both verbal and nonverbal ways, too, just as the client does, and that your communications behaviors very much affect the client. This is particularly true of nonverbal messages. Therefore any of the communications and psychological considerations in this chapter that you may agree are important with respect to the client are also important for you. As a financial counseling professional you will want to remove from your own behaviors those elements that present obstacles and barriers to successful communication with the client and with other professionals with whom you deal. The client is then more likely to accept your role in the counseling situation and, ultimately, the plan you develop for meeting his or her financial needs and objectives. Similarly, other professionals whose expertise you will often need to call upon in developing and implementing a plan will respect your role as a financial counselor and planner.

ATTENDING AND LISTENING SKILLS

Paying attention to clients is the first necessary component in good communication. No matter how expert your other communication skills are, if you are inattentive to your clients' verbal and nonverbal behaviors, you are apt to lose them at the very outset. How often have you been in the company of another person who shies away from looking at you, who glances nervously at his wristwatch, who interrupts you, and who, literally and figuratively, turns his back to you? Surely, if you have had this kind of experience, you can recall how uncomfortable and ill at ease you were with this inattentive behavior.

If a counselor's goal is to understand clients, the counselor must first pay close attention to or focus on their verbal and nonverbal messages. Poor attending and poor listening lead to poor understanding.

FOCUS ON ETHICS
How Ethical Behavior Improves Communication

Sometimes words are insufficient. Many clients misunderstand the specifics of the plan recommended by a financial counselor. This problem is compounded when complex financial instruments are required to implement the plan. It is much like drivers and automobiles. Most drivers really need transportation, and cars solve this problem, however, that doesn't mean that drivers understand how their cars operate.

A financial planner once stated that there are two essential rules for effectively dealing with a client. The first is to earn his/her trust because trust breaks down communication barriers. Different counselors may accomplish this in different ways, but the client must feel free to ask the challenging questions and continue to probe until a satisfactory level of understanding is achieved. When there are limits to what the client can understand, earned trust is essential.

The second rule is to maintain trust, a critical factor in the counselor-client relationship. Although clients do not fully understand, they should not fail to act. Indeed, if they understood every aspect of financial planning, they would not need a planner. Clients often make decisions based solely on their trust in their financial adviser.

There is no better way to earn and maintain trust than to develop an unassailable reputation for ethical and professional behavior. A valuable side benefit is improved communication.

Physical Attending

Gerard Egan, a renowned counselor-educator, categorizes attending behavior into (l) physical attending, or using your body to communicate and (2) psychological attending, or listening actively. He uses the acronym, SOLER, as a reminder of the five basic attributes associated with physical attending. Let us look at these five attributes.

- S: Face the other person *squarely*.

When there is face-to-face, direct contact, the communication process is enhanced. You communicate nonverbally to the other person, "I'm here with you; I'm tuned-in and ready to face the issues with you head-on." Turning your body away lessens your involvement with the other person.

- O: Adopt an *open* posture.

There is something to be said about receiving a person with open arms. Crossed arms and crossed legs can inadvertently communicate a holding-off of the other person. An open posture—open arms and uncrossed legs and an open smile—communicates receptiveness to the other person and, hence, increases good communication and decreases defensiveness.

- L: *Lean* toward the other person.

This is another physical signal of interest, involvement, caring. Two people who care about each other, when involved in conversation, almost always can be seen leaning toward each other. On the other hand, two people who are observed leaning away from one another, or sitting rigidly straight in their chairs, seem to be either bored or disinterested, or extremely cautious and defensive about getting involved with each other.

- E: Maintain good *eye* contact.

Good eye contact consists of looking at another individual when you are in conversation. Poor eye contact consists of rarely looking at the other person, or looking away when he or she looks at you or staring constantly with a blank expression on your face. The eye contact should be natural and spontaneous. Since you are interested in your client, you will want to use your eyes as a vehicle of communication.

- R: Be *relaxed* while attending.

It is possible to be both intense while focusing on the client and relaxed at the same time. A nervous, fidgety, or rigid counselor communicates these feelings to the client. A counselor who sits in a casual fashion, who speaks naturally and spontaneously, and who uses natural gestures has the advantage of being free to focus intently upon the client and his or her communication, as well as helping to facilitate naturalness and spontaneity in the client.

SOLER: The Acronym for Physical Attending

S: Face the other person *squarely.*
O: Adopt an *open* posture.
L: *Lean* toward the other person.
E: Maintain good *eye* contact.
R: Be *relaxed* while attending.

As has been mentioned previously, it is impossible not to communicate, so as a counselor you might as well use your body—gestures, posture, eyes—to communicate whatever message you wish to communicate. Otherwise, the body may communicate something you do not wish to communicate. In other words, try to make your body work for you in behalf of your counseling relationship.

Active Listening

So far, attending has been described as a physical activity; active listening brings in the psychological activity involved in attending. Many of us take listening for granted, but there is a distinct difference between simply hearing and actively listening. Hearing means the receiving of auditory signals. A person says, "I have a bad headache," and we hear that message and respond, "That's too bad," or "Here, have a couple of aspirin." An active listener, on the other hand, might respond, "You look as though it's really getting you down." In short, the active listener responds not only to the verbal message received through the auditory channel, but also to the unspoken, or nonverbal message, communicated by the sender's body, facial expression, or tone of voice.

Active listening, then, means putting the nonverbal behavior, the voice, and words together—all the cues sent out by the other person—to get the essence of the communication being sent. An active listener is an understanding listener, one who attempts to see the world from the other's frame of reference. If you can state in your own words what the other person has said, and that person accepts your statement as an accurate reflection of what he or she has said, then it is safe to say that you have listened actively and understood with accuracy.

But it must be stated that active listening is not merely parroting another's words—a computer can be (and has been) programmed to do that. Active listening means involving yourself in the inner world of another person while, at the same time, maintaining your own identity and being able to respond with meaningfulness to the messages of that other person.

Responding during Active Listening

As indicated above, active listening is hard work and requires intense focusing and concentration. Years of not listening have made most of us poor listeners. We are distracted easily; we tend to evaluate and judge what is being said while it is being said, so that we are framing our own responses to the speaker's statement before the speaker is finished talking and, thus, we miss the message.

There are several simple ways of responding to people so that they feel accepted and understood. Let us look at some of these response modalities.

Perhaps the simplest response modality is what Allen Ivey refers to as "minimal encouragers to talk," or "continuing responses." Nonverbally, if you want someone to continue talking, you might smile or nod your head to communicate agreement and/or understanding. Equally as effective in communicating your understanding is a minimal encourager like "uh-huh," "mmmm," "then?" "and . . . ?" These relatively unobtrusive responses encourage the speaker to continue talking. They communicate to the speaker, "Go on, I'm with you."

Another type of response that enhances communication is the *restatement-of-content* response. The rationale for restatement is to let speakers hear what they have said on the assumption that this may encourage them to go on speaking, examining, and looking deeper. Restatement communicates to the client, "I am listening to you very carefully, so much so that I can repeat what you have said." The most effective restatements are those that are phrased in your own words, a paraphrase of what the speaker has stated. To do this effectively, we must temporarily suspend our own frame of reference and attempt to view the world from the other person's perspective. Suppose the client says to you, "I'm really in a financial bind, what with taxes, inflation, fuel bills; I don't know how we make it from one month to the next." An accurate restatement might be expressed, "So things are tough for you financially. It seems like you can't make ends meet." The client, hearing this understanding response, is encouraged to delve more deeply into the situation, feeling that the counselor has, indeed, heard the message on the same wavelength upon which it was transmitted. The bond between client and counselor is, thus, strengthened, and greater opportunities for creative problem solving are opened up.

Just as we manifest understanding for our clients by responding to the content of the message, so may we also show our understanding of the client's experience by responding to the feelings expressed. Sometimes feelings are expressed directly, and at other times they are only implied or stated indirectly. In order to respond to a person's feelings, we must observe the behavioral cues like tone of voice, body posture, gestures, and facial expression, as well as listen to the speaker's words. Consider this client statement, "Within the next few months, we need to buy a new refrigerator and another car. [Sighs] I just don't know where the money is going to come from." A *reflection-of-feeling* response might go, "You sound pretty hopeless about your financial state. It sure is hard to break even, let alone get ahead, these days." Again, by responding in an empathic way to the client's statement, you communicate a deep understanding of the person's experience; in addition, you progress one step further by addressing the nonverbalized feelings. We illustrate to the client that we understand so well what he or she is stating that we can paraphrase both words and feelings. It is helpful to both the client and the counselor to struggle to capture in words the uniqueness of the client's experience. The most effective types of understanding responses capsulize both the feeling and the content of the client's message. The basic format for this type of response is "You feel __________ [feeling] because __________ [content]."

This response enables clients to get in closer touch with the feelings that are an outgrowth of their situations. And that, in turn, facilitates the working through of the problem, because the counselor involves clients in exploring themselves in the problem. Because you have accurately understood and responded to them, clients will go on to share other personal experiences that bear upon the presented problem.

A word might be added here about the difficulties that some people have in dealing with feelings, either their own or the feelings of others. Problems often arise in interpersonal relationships because one or more of the involved persons choose to repress, distort, or disguise their feelings rather than admit that feelings are present and then discuss them openly. This is particularly true of so-called negative feelings like anger, sadness, anxiety, frustration, discomfort, and confusion. In actuality, no feelings are negative since they all are part of being human. In any case, counselors who wish to communicate effectively need to address their own feelings as well as those of their clients. The mutual expression of feelings is an integral part of building a close, trusting, caring relationship.

Two other types of understanding responses need to be mentioned. Each is related to the restatement-of-content and the reflection-of-feeling responses; yet, there is a subtle shade of difference. First is the *clarifying response* that tends to amplify the speaker's statement. The clarifying response does not add anything new to what the speaker has said; it simply expands what has already been stated. The counselor attempts to restate or clarify for the client what the client has had some difficulty in expressing clearly. It is akin to a translation of the client's words into language that is more familiar and understandable to both client and counselor. Suppose a client says, "I'm not sure. Nothing makes sense anymore. Things get more confusing the more I think about them. It's a real puzzle to me." A counselor, by way of clarification, might say, "I can sense your bewilderment. Let me see if I can help out. From what you've said previously, I get the impression that you want to get your mortgage straightened out before you increase your monthly savings. Is that it?" If the financial counselor has, indeed, been following the flow of the client's experience, this statement will help to clarify the client's confusion over the situation. To the extent that the counselor's response is on target, the puzzle becomes suddenly clear and more readily solved.

Another side to the clarifying response concerns the counselor's need to have things clarified. When the counselor is puzzled, then it is certainly legitimate to ask for clarification as, "I'm sorry. I don't follow what you're saying. Can you make that more clear for me?"

Clarified responses are helpful because they:

- facilitate client self-understanding
- attend especially to the client's feelings
- communicate the counselor's understanding
- move the client toward a clearer definition of the problem

The other type of understanding response is *summarization.* Summaries are especially helpful toward the end of an interview, since they focus and capsulize a series of scattered ideas to present a clear perspective. The summary has the effect of reassuring clients that you have been tuned in to their many messages. For the counselor, it serves as a check on the accuracy with which the various messages have been received.

It is often better to have the client do the summarizing. In this way, the client maintains the responsibility for bringing the messages together into a meaningful conclusion. As in clarifying, themes and emotional overtones should be summarized, and the key ideas should be synthesized into broad statements reflecting basic meanings. An example of an effective summary might be: "So today you described your overall financial situation as bleak, although you think you might be able to increase your savings if you could refinance your mortgage. I know you're rightly concerned about that." If the financial counselor has accurately summarized the essence of the interview, the client then has a better handle on the intricacies of the situation, and a resolution is closer at hand.

What we have covered thus far are the basics of nonverbal behaviors, the skills of attending and active listening, and the five basic types of responses associated with active listening: "minimal encouragers to talk," restatement of content, reflection of feeling, clarification, and summarization.

Five Types of Responses Associated with Active Listening

1. "Minimal encouragers to talk"
2. Restatement of content
3. Reflection of feeling
4. Clarification
5. Summarization

The element common to all five of these response modalities is that the counselor follows, or tracks, the client's lead. This response communicates a high level of understanding and enables the client not only to experience what it feels like to be understood, but also to progress further toward an ultimate resolution of the situation. Now we will explore other types of responses in which the counselor, to a certain extent, takes the lead and deviates somewhat from the client's preceding responses.

COUNSELOR LEADING RESPONSES

When the financial counselor decides to make a leading response, it is the counselor's frame of reference that comes into focus. Up to this point, the counselor's responses have followed from the client's statements, but here the emphasis shifts. An obvious danger of this shift is that the counselor may move in a direction in which the client is not yet ready or willing to move. Despite this danger, if the counselor has followed the client closely so far, and if a good relationship has been established, then this different kind of response should not threaten the client, as long as it is interposed carefully and tentatively.

The first of the leading responses is known simply as explanation. Explanation is a relatively neutral description of the way things are. It deals in logical, practical, factual information. It is often offered at the client's request, although there are instances when the counselor will offer an explanation without its being requested. A client may be confused by some terminology that the counselor has used and ask, for example, "Exactly what is an annuity?" The counselor's explanation should be simple, concise, and comprehensible. Long-winded explanations tend to become vague and hard to follow. The counselor should also guard against explaining things in a condescending, patronizing, or pedantic tone. The best explanations are those that are exchanged between equal partners (not superior-subordinates) in a relationship.

Another type of leading response is the interpretive response. Interpretations can be particularly risky when the counselor goes too deep too soon, or when the interpretation is off base. Interpretations often come across as sounding overly clinical, diagnostic, and authoritarian. Despite these drawbacks, interpretations can be extremely effective responses because they often cut to the heart of the matter. When the interpretation makes sense to the client, it definitely accelerates the interview. We should keep in mind that the goal of all interpretive efforts is self-interpretation by the client in order to increase the client's ability to act effectively. The following is an example of a facilitative interpretation:

Client: "I'm not sure whether I want to retire early. I like to keep busy, and I don't know what I'd do with all that free time."

Counselor: "So the prospect of an early retirement is a bit frightening. Maybe you're afraid that you'd just waste your time away?"

Notice that the financial counselor's interpretation did not stray too far from what the client had said. The counselor used the words "frightening" and "afraid," but probably did so on the basis of some fear or trepidation detected in the client's voice. Further, the counselor responded tentatively, using qualifiers like "a bit" and "maybe," and converted the second statement into a question by a raised voice at the end of the sentence. This enables the client to assimilate the counselor's response without feeling as though it has been offered as a fiat from above. The client, thus, is free to accept, modify, or deny the counselor's interpretation, and this is very important. If the counselor's interpretation is inaccurate, it is far better to discover that early than to proceed indefinitely along the wrong path.

A third type of leading response frequently employed by counselors is reassurance, or encouragement. A reassuring response is designed with the intention of making the client feel better, to bolster his or her spirits, and to offer support in a time of need. It communicates clearly to the client that "I am here by your side, ready to aid you in any way that I can." As a means of helping, however, the reassuring response tends to be merely a temporary measure. It is akin to offering a tissue to someone who is crying; the crying may stop temporarily, but the underlying causes have been left untouched. For this reason the counselor must be careful not to use reassurance indiscriminately. The understanding (reflection-of-feeling) response discussed in the previous section on active listening is far more effective when emotions surface. The understanding response communicates accurate empathy; the reassuring response offers only sympathy, and very few people like to feel pitied. Contrast the effect of these two different kinds of responses on our hypothetical client:

Client: "I get so furious whenever my broker ignores me! It's almost as though I don't exist!"

Counselor: (using reassuring response): "Well, don't feel so bad. It doesn't do much good to get so worked up. Try not to worry about it, and you'll feel better."

Counselor: (using reflection of feeling): "I can feel the rage as you speak. You feel like a nonperson around your broker, that you are not getting adequate service for the money you are paying, and that infuriates you."

The first counselor response patches a Band-Aid on a deep wound and is therefore ineffectual. The second response reflects the deeply felt anger and, in so doing, helps the client work through the anger. Reassurance, while not a harmful response, promises pie in the sky and delivers nothing.

The final type of leading response is called advice, or suggestion. Many people actively seek the advice of others, possibly hoping that the advice giver will make the difficult decision for them, or solve their problems for them. And, as chance or human nature would have it, there is certainly no dearth of people in this world willing to dole out free advice. In a financial counseling relationship, however, the best kind of advice is self-advice. Counselors who have been responding in an understanding fashion are already well on their way toward helping clients discover, in their own way and in their own time, what advice is best for them. There are times within a counseling relationship when proffering advice is acceptable, but these times are few. When advice is given, it should be offered tentatively, in the form of a suggestion, or several suggestions, about which the client has the final decision. Otherwise, the counselor not only leads, but takes over the ultimate responsibility for the client's financial plan, and each person has the right to formulate his or her own plan. Advice giving robs the client of this right.

Counselor Leading Responses

- Explanation
- Interpretive
- Reassurance/encouragement
- Advice/suggestion

In the next section, we will look at still another type of counselor response—perhaps the most commonly used response—the question. Questions come in many varieties, some much more effective in communication than others.

THE QUESTION

The question is surely one of the most timeworn response modes used by financial counselors. Many counselors see their main role as an interviewer or an interrogator. The question seems appropriate only when it is an honest attempt to gather information that the counselor requires and to which the client has access. Unfortunately, the question is not always used in this fashion. Moreover, the question-answer dialogue sets up a pattern of communication that is difficult for the participants to break: the client waits for the inevitable question; the question comes, followed by the answer (and not much more), and then comes the wait for the next question. Questioning almost always casts the counselor in the role of authority figure and the client in the role of a somewhat passive subordinate, certainly not the type of interpersonal relationship conducive to effective counseling.

Despite the disadvantages of the question mentioned above, there are times when only a well-phrased question will suffice, particularly when we are seeking data from the client. Even here, though, there is a qualitative difference among the various types of questions that might be asked. Several categories of questions will be discussed in the following section.

Open-ended versus Closed-ended Questions

Ideally, questions posed by the counselor should be open-ended and should call for more than just a yes or no response on the part of the client; otherwise, they tend to stifle interaction. The open-ended question allows the client to select a response from his or her full repertory. The closed-ended question limits the client to a specific, narrow response, often either a yes or a no. The open-ended question solicits the client's opinions, thoughts, ideas, values, and feelings. The closed-ended question typically solicits singular facts or one-word replies.

Contrast the differences in the following sets of questions. The first question in each set is closed-ended; the second question in each set is open-ended.

1. a. Are you ready to start an investment program?
   b. How do you feel about starting an investment program?
2. a. Have you given any thought to retirement?
   b. What thoughts do you have about retirement?
3. a. Are you afraid to start saving something now?
   b. Why have you decided to wait to start saving?

As can be readily seen from the above examples, the open-ended questions ask for more complete, comprehensive information. In a way, they force the client to formulate thoughts, ideas, and feelings into fully rounded responses. On the other hand, the closed-ended questions solicit only a one-word or short-answer response, requiring little thought and offering virtually no feedback.

Leading Questions

Other types of closed-ended questions that are not only ineffective but also manipulative are those termed leading questions. These questions usually begin with, "Don't you think . . . ," or "Do you really feel . . . ." More often than not they lead the client toward a conclusion that the counselor (not the client) has already formulated, so that there is the element of dishonesty in even asking the question. It is far more effective, and honest, for the counselor to rephrase the leading question into a declarative statement in the form of sharing a perception or opinion with the client. Consider the following leading questions:

"Don't you think you should start an investment program now?"
"Do you really feel that $100 a month is enough?"
"Are you sure you've considered all possibilities?"

With just a bit of reflection, we can see that the counselor is actually saying:

"I think you ought to start an investment program now."
"I don't feel that $100 a month will be enough."
"I'm sure there are other possibilities you haven't considered."

The latter statements are much more honest and to the point than the questions from which they stem. Generally speaking, declarative statements communicate far more clearly than the manipulative leading questions. A good rule of thumb to follow in everyday intercourse is to make as many statements as possible and save the questions for honest information seeking.

The Either/Or or True/False Question

Another kind of relatively ineffective question is of the either/or or true/false variety. While this question is not quite as closed-ended as the leading question, it is only slightly less closed, since it limits the client to only two options. For example:

"Do you plan to stay in this house or move to an apartment?"
"Are you more apt to take a risk or play it safe?"

Clients might prefer both options, or neither, or a third or fourth option; but here they are forced to choose from what we have offered them. The world is not simply black or white; there are various shades of gray; yet, when we phrase questions so that clients are forced to choose from one of two options, we are restricting the clients' responses. We can improve on the preceding examples by asking:

"What are your plans after retirement regarding housing?"
"How do you usually make your decisions?"

Again, we see that by opening up the question we allow clients to respond freely from their own frame of reference, and not from ours. And this is what good interviewing is all about.

Why Questions

Even though why questions can be classified as open-ended questions and, thus, theoretically sound, such is not the case. On the surface, questions beginning with why appear to be legitimate enough, signifying the inquiry into causal relationships, as in, "Why are you planning to retire at age 62?" Unfortunately, why questions carry with them a connotation of implied disapproval by the questioner, thus forcing the person being asked the question to justify or defend his or her thoughts, ideas, or actions. Even when that is not the meaning the questioner intends, that is generally how the why question is received. The why question tends to question the client's motivation (or lack of motivation) and, thus, creates a certain defensiveness.

Perhaps the chief reason that why questions are received so poorly dates back to the manner in which parents put children on the spot: "Why didn't you pick up your room?" "Why don't you have your shoes on?" "Why can't you be more careful?" And, of course, this line of inquiry is later picked up by teachers with students: "Why don't you have your homework?" "Why didn't you study for this test?" In short, as children we learned that when an adult asked us a question beginning with why, it meant, "Change your behavior; think as I think; behave the way adults do." And we carry that lesson with us throughout life, usually responding to why questions in a defensive, negative manner.

So unless there is a valid reason for asking a why question and when no other type of question will suffice, it is generally better to avoid why questions.

Question Bombardment

Still another kind of faulty questioning technique occurs when we ask double, triple, or even quadruple questions without waiting for a response. This is frequently referred to as question bombardment. As absurd as this may sound, it occurs far too frequently in interviews to escape comment. For example: "What type of investment program appeals to you most—stock, municipal bonds? Or would you rather look into annuities? When do you think you'd be ready to begin?" The first question in the series is open-ended in nature and can stand by itself quite well; yet the interviewer isn't content to let well enough alone, but instead tacks on other, more restricting closed-ended questions. The result is that the client is caught in a hailstorm of questions all at one time and, more often than not, gets the opportunity to respond to only one of the several questions asked. If more than one question needs to be asked, it is better to form separate questions, waiting for a full response to each question before going on to the next one. The other issue to be addressed, though, is whether so many questions need to be asked in the first place.

Concluding Remarks

Questioning is a major component in the repertory of most interviewers. Yet that need not be so. If we wish to become better communicators, one thing that we can do is to convert some of our questions (especially closed-ended, leading, either/or, and why questions) into statements. With a statement, we assume responsibility for what we say. With a question, we shift the responsibility to the

Categories of Questions

- Open-ended questions
- Closed-ended questions
- Leading questions
- Either/or and true/false questions
- Why questions
- Question bombardment

other person, which may sometimes be necessary. Far too often, however, we simply shirk our own responsibility for, and involvement in, the interaction when we revert to questioning. As stated previously, counseling is not the same as interviewing. If we hope to do counseling, we need to do far more than simply ask one question after another.

NOTES

1. Portions of this chapter dealing with elements of nonverbal behaviors have been excerpted from a two-part article entitled "Practical Communications Skills and Techniques in Financial Counseling," by Dale S. Johnson, PhD, CFP, published in *The Financial Planner,* 11, no. 6 (June 1982): pp. 98-105, and 11, no. 7 (July 1982): pp. 62-71. They are reprinted by arrangement with the editor of that journal.
2. Charles J. Stewart and William B. Cash, *Interviewing Principles and Practices,* 7th ed. (Dubuque, IA: Brown & Benchmark, 1993).
3. Carl R. Rogers, Library of Congress #51-9139. 1951.
4. Barbara F. Okun, *Effective Helping: Interviewing & Counseling Techniques,* 4th ed. (Pacific Grove, CA: Brooks-Cole Publishing Co., Division of Wadsworth, Inc., 1992).

5

Risk Tolerance in Financial Decisions

Michael J. Roszkowski

Chapter Outline

INTRODUCTION

Investments are characterized by different levels of risk and potential return. Both ethical and regulatory principles require that the financial planner recommend only those products and investment strategies that are *suitable* given the client's investment objectives, financial capacity to absorb a loss, and psychological propensity for risk taking. The goal is to deliver the most return for the amount of tolerable risk. Proper asset allocation requires a determination of the client's risk tolerance.

At the 1995 IAFP Conference for Advanced Planners, Eleanor Blayney, a member of the IAFP Ethics Committee, reported that 90 percent of the cases under review by her committee involved suitability. Ms. Blayney stated that: "In every case, no risk-tolerance instrument was ever used. I have to wonder how much more favorably disposed I would have been if I could have seen a documented effort to make that risk assessment."

It is encouraging to see that there is growing recognition of the need to understand the psychological factors involved in investment decisions. For example, the *Journal of Financial Planning* now has a regular feature called "Money & Soul" that examines the behavioral issues in financial planning. A recent (March 1997) cover story, titled "Inside the Minds of Clients," dealt with the processes investors use to make financial decisions. James G. Powers, in his *Best's Review* article (December 1996), proposed that a source of problems with life insurance policy illustrations could be avoided if an agent considers the client's risk tolerance needs in the life insurance selling process. He argues that for risk-averse clients, illustrations should not deviate much from a guaranteed rate of return. The more risk-tolerant client, on the other hand, can be shown projections that deviate further from the guaranteed rate.

Financial services professionals of all types, therefore, need to understand risk tolerance and convey to their clients its significance in reaching proper investment decisions. Determining a client's level of risk tolerance, while extremely important, is also one of the most difficult tasks facing the financial planner. Done properly, however, it will improve relationships with clients and lessen the possibility of litigation by those who have invested beyond their comfort level.

Although it may appear to be a rather simple topic, risk tolerance is an extremely complex phenomenon. It is an area of interest for many academic disciplines—notably economics, psychology, finance, and management science. Each field has a different tradition and approaches risk tolerance from a different perspective. This chapter integrates the relevant research from all these disciplines and thereby reveals areas of professional disagreement. (More information appears in the references listed at the end of this chapter.)

Specifically, this chapter examines how people view risk and how they process information about risk factors. It explores the reasons people either minimize or maximize the objective level of risk in a situation. It also identifies demographic and personality characteristics that have been linked to risk tolerance. Finally it considers various approaches to assessing a client's risk-taking propensity and notes their relative merits and drawbacks.

Hopefully, after completing this study, financial planners will better understand why clients accept or refuse risk, and they will be able to use this information to serve their clients more effectively.

RISK AVERSION, RISK SEEKING, AND RISK INDIFFERENCE

It is generally accepted that people react differently to risk. Some are always willing to accept it; others are always ready to reject it. It is best to think of reactions to risk as a *continuum*. Individuals on the one end are known as "risk seekers" (or risk tolerant), while those on the other end are known as "risk averters" (or risk rejecters). People in the middle are referred to as "risk indifferent." Frequently the terms *aggressive* and *conservative* are used to describe investors who are, respectively, risk seeking and risk averse. According to conventional wisdom, investment decisions involve a trade-off between risk and expected return. Risk-averse investors prefer low risks and are therefore willing to sacrifice some expected return in order to reduce the variation in possible outcomes.

The *majority* of the population is thought to be closer to the risk-averter end of the continuum. For example, a study conducted by the Life Insurance Marketing and Research Association (LIMRA) asked survey participants if they would be willing to take risks for higher yields. The answers were to be given on a 10-point scale where 1 indicated "not willing" and 10 stood for "very willing." Whereas 45 percent of the people rated themselves 1, 2, or 3, only 11 percent rated themselves 8, 9, or 10. The remaining 44 percent used the middle values (4 through 7) to describe themselves. Security is a fundamental human need, as revealed in various surveys conducted over the years.

The generally negative view people hold about exposing themselves to the risk of a loss is, in fact, the basis for all sorts of consumer warranties. Is it any wonder that advertisements allowing for a "risk-free 30-day examination period" are so appealing for all products, including insurance policies?

Why are some people more willing than others to take risks? Various factors contribute to the attitude of risk acceptance. They include biological makeup, upbringing, and other life experiences.

Loss Aversion

People's unwillingness to accept losses is a fundamental part of their attitude toward risk. Although it is typically stated that most people are *risk* averse, it is really more appropriate to say that they are *loss* averse.

In finance and related disciplines risk aversion means the preference for certain outcomes over uncertain outcomes. Conversely, risk seeking refers to a preference for uncertain outcomes over certain outcomes. Studies have demonstrated conclusively that people are indeed cautious when faced with a choice between certain and uncertain gains. That is, they most often select the certain gain, even if it is smaller. However, when the two alternatives are a choice between a relatively small but certain loss and a relatively larger but only probable loss, most people are risk takers. In other words, they are willing to risk a large loss rather than accept a smaller but certain loss. For illustrative purposes, consider the following problems posed by psychologists A. Tversky and D. Kahneman. First look at problem 1, which consists of the following two choices, A and B.

Problem 1

Choice A: a sure win of $3,000

Choice B: an 80 percent chance to win $4,000 (and a corresponding 20 percent chance of winning nothing)

Most people take choice A. That is, offered a choice between a relatively smaller but certain gain, and a relatively larger but nonguaranteed gain, most people elect the smaller but certain prize. Choice A is considered the risk-averse alternative, whereas choice B is the risk-seeking alternative.

Now look at problem 2, which consists of choices C and D.

Problem 2

Choice C: a sure loss of $3,000

Choice D: an 80 percent chance of losing $4,000 (and a corresponding 20 percent chance of losing nothing)

Note that the only difference between problem 1 and problem 2 is that problem 1 deals with gains and problem 2 deals with losses. That is, the probabilities and money involved remain the same as in problem 1. In problem 2 alternative C is the certain (risk-averse) choice, while D is the uncertain (risk-seeking) choice. Under the possibility of loss, most people revise their preferences; they now elect choice D. When both alternatives are unpleasant, most people are inclined to take the 20 percent gamble that they will lose nothing even though the odds are against them. In problem 2, then, they prefer uncertainty to certainty or, in other words, they are risk-seeking.

Both the preference for A and the preference for D are a manifestation of the same psychological mechanism, namely, a reluctance to sustain a loss. It is really the prospect of loss that makes one risk averse in the first problem and risk seeking in the second problem. In both cases, people don't want to give up any money. For most people, the extent of risk seeking that occurs when faced with a choice between losses is much greater than the extent of risk avoidance that occurs when the choice is between gains.

These laboratory findings have been confirmed by observing real-life activities. At racetracks, a person will gamble more money and place more bets on longshots when he or she has been losing that day. Likewise, companies take greater risks when they are in financial trouble, as when their returns are below target.

FORMAL CONCEPT OF RISK AND PEOPLE'S INTUITIVE PERCEPTION

The term *risk* has many definitions. Psychologists and other scientists have compared these definitions to people's intuitive understanding of the concept of risk. There are some striking differences.

In the field of finance, the conventional measures of investment risk are statistical concepts of variability such as standard deviation. This approach holds that any potential deviation from the expected return, whether positive or negative, contributes to the investment's riskiness. High variability in past (and projected future) returns is equated with risk.

To the average person unsophisticated about investment matters, however, the most important factor in evaluating the riskiness of an investment is the historical trend line in the return generated by the investment. If the trend is *upward*, the investment is perceived as less risky than if the trend is *downward*. Fluctuations in the return are only a *secondary* consideration.

Intuitively, then, people do accept variability of investment returns as a measure of risk, but the evidence shows that many do not treat uncertainty about *positive* outcomes as an aspect of risk. Rather, most people focus on the probability of negative returns in defining a risk. Generally people regard the word risk to mean danger or possible loss. A survey of public opinion regarding the term risk by the Insurance Information Institute further corroborates this point. Asked to indicate what the word risk connotes, most people said "danger" (84 percent) and "possible loss" (77 percent). Risk is thought to increase as bad outcomes become more likely.

With respect to investments, the danger lies in either getting less than the expected return or sustaining a loss of the principal. Surveys have demonstrated that portfolio managers and professionals who must routinely deal with capital budgeting tend to incorporate the probability of not achieving an expected (that is, target) return on an investment into their personal definition of a risky investment. However, in most other people's minds, the loss of principal is closest to their intuitive understanding of the word risk. For example, a recent study reported in the *Financial Analysts Journal* (March/April 1997) compared the definitions of investment risk held by professional portfolio managers and individual investors. The top two definitions for both groups included references to (a) a large loss and (b) return rates below target. However, the primary definition for the portfolio managers was return below target, whereas for the individual investors it was a large loss. Table 5-1 below provides the details of the results, indicating factors that the respondents said came to mind first when they thought about a "risky" investment.

TABLE 5-1

Percentage of Portfolio Managers and Individual Investors Thinking of Each Characteristic First

Characteristic Category	Portfolio Mangers	Individual Investors
Large loss	22%	40%
Return below target	25%	20%
Business risk	22%	18%
Liquidity	15%	8%
Knowledge about firm	7%	10%
Economic uncertainty	9%	4%

Note: The median number of attributes mentioned per respondent was three.

Therefore any investment product promising no loss of principal will appear safe to most consumers. Some individuals tend to draw a distinction between investing and speculating. According to this view, investments assure the safety of principal whereas speculations do not. It is no accident that mutual funds guaranteeing the return of the principal appeared after the October 1987 stock market crash.

Another difference between people's intuitive understanding of the word risk and some formal definitions of this term involves the distinction between risk and uncertainty. About 58 percent of the people questioned in the previously noted survey indicated that they associated risk with the word *uncertainty*. However, in the decision sciences, risk and uncertainty are not considered the same. There, risk refers to situations in which (1) the various consequences of each alternative are known and (2) their exact probabilities can be specified. Uncertainty, in contrast, is said to exist when the possible alternatives and their associated probabilities of occurrence are unknown.

For illustrative purposes, consider the possible outcomes that students face when they take a pass-fail examination. There are only two possible outcomes—passing or failing. Assume for a moment that someone is asked to estimate his or her chances of passing the course. If he or she can assign a probability to this event (for example, 60 percent chance of passing/40 percent chance of failing), then the exam represents a risk. If, however, the person has no way of assigning odds (being unfamiliar with the instructor's grading policies), then the exam represents an uncertainty.

Perceived versus Objective Risk

In essence, there are four dimensions to a choice involving risk: (1) the potential amount to be gained, (2) the probability of achieving this gain, (3) the amount that could potentially be lost, and (4) the probability of this loss occurring. Whether a person accepts or rejects a risk depends on his or her analysis of these four elements. In analyzing the risk, people tend to focus more on some of these dimensions than on others. Some people look most closely at the probability of winning, while others focus on the probability of losing. Still others are mainly concerned with the amounts involved.

It has been demonstrated repeatedly that the objective riskiness of a situation and one's interpretation of it, called "perceived risk," are not necessarily the same. Different people exposed to the same information interpret it differently. The objective odds are either lowered or heightened depending on the person's experiences, inclinations toward risk taking, and the particular circumstances surrounding a given situation.

LIMITATIONS IN RATIONAL THINKING

Debates abound regarding the extent of rationality shown in people's economic behavior. While some continue to view people's financial actions as *always* totally rational, recent evidence suggests less than totally rational behavior. At best, human beings act within what the Nobel prize-winning economist and psychologist Herbert Simon calls "bounded" rationality. That is, there are bounds or limits to how rational people can be. Their choices in financial matters are shaped not only by knowledge and rational thinking but also by their values and emotions.

Challenges to rationality are often reported in the behavior of the stock market. Certain research suggests that much of the volatility in the stock market is due to fads and mass psychology (that is, people doing something because others are doing it) rather than to changes in the economy or the fundamental soundness of the companies issuing the stocks. It has been observed that attitudes about the economy change faster than the economy itself. Some have likened the spread of enthusiasm and disenchantment about a given stock to the spread of an epidemic. For instance, in October 1984, a woman in New York City claimed that she found glass slivers in Gerbers baby food. Gerbers Products' stock fell 15 percent in two days. But not long thereafter it bounced back. The market crash of October 1987 can be attributed to numerous factors, but there is no doubt that investors mimicked the behavior of others in the selling frenzy.

Psychologists have conducted studies on how people perceive and process information about uncertain events. Most studies have found that people tend to violate rationality to some degree. These flaws in judgment are due in part to people's limited abilities to process information and in part to the interference of their emotions.

With respect to risky decisions, many people do not understand the laws of probability, and their ability to combine two or more probabilities is especially flawed. For example, in one study many people preferred a lottery in which they were allowed one draw out of 10 tickets to another lottery in which they were allowed 20 draws out of 100 tickets. (The 20-draw lottery is, of course, a better deal.) When processing information about probability, most people do it intuitively, rather than mathematically. Few people know how to make optimal decisions using mathematical decision rules.

Overconfidence in Intuitive Judgments

Most people, laymen and professionals alike, tend to be overconfident in their judgment, as shown in studies that ask people to make a choice and then estimate their probability of being right. These research findings indicate that if a person believes he or she has an 80 percent chance of being right, in reality this probability is only 70 percent. In other words, people are right in their judgment 7 out of 10 times rather than 8 out of 10. Errors are frequent even when one is totally certain about something. In one study, when people said something *always* happened, it actually occurred only 80 percent of the time. Likewise, when these individuals indicated that something *never* happened, it occurred about 20 percent of the time.

Typically, people use fewer clues to make a decision than they claim. The importance of minor clues is overestimated in most instances. Presenting people with more facts seems to make people feel more *confident* about their decisions, but generally the accuracy of their decisions is not enhanced greatly.

Nonrepresentative Quality of Short-Run Trends

Most people disregard "the Law of Large Numbers." They are willing to make their risk assessments on the basis of very small samples, not realizing that what is true in the *long run* may not occur in the *short run.* Most analysts believe that investors overvalue short-run economic developments. Recent events get undue emphasis in people's decision making.

The following experiment illustrates people's failure to appreciate the significance of small versus large samples. In this experiment, people were asked to indicate which of the following is more likely to be an honest coin—coin A or coin B. Remember, in a single flip of an *honest* coin there is a 50-50 chance of the coin falling on its head or tail.

Coin A: 8 heads in 10 flips
Coin B: 70 heads in 100 flips

The honest coin is more likely to be A, but many people say B because the distribution of heads and tails is closer to 50-50 for coin B. These individuals are in error, however, because they fail to appreciate the small number of flips that took place with coin A. In the *short run*, an outcome that defies what one would expect in the long run is quite possible.

Likewise, people tend to perceive patterns in totally random events. Which of the following sequences are more likely to occur by chance on six tosses of an honest coin?

Coin 1: HHHTTT
Coin 2: HTHTTH

Most people believe erroneously, that the coin 2 sequence is more likely because it appears random, whereas the sequence of coin 1 seems less likely because it looks more systematic. In reality, the sequences are equally likely to occur by chance (i.e., ½ x ½ x ½ x ½ x ½ x ½). This tendency to see a pattern where none exists is sometimes called the "hot hand" fallacy because of the almost universal belief among both players and fans that basketball players have "hot" and "cold" shooting streaks, despite statistical evidence that fails to show any marked deviations from a player's long-term shooting percentage.

Daniel Kahneman and Mark Riepe (1998) contend that the "hot hand" fallacy can be observed in the "unfounded credibility" achieved by some fund managers who are able to beat the market for only a few short years. Their skill could simply be chance.

Failure to Correctly Evaluate Exposure

Most people have a particularly hard time evaluating the true magnitude of a risk that is not constant. In one study, the participants were asked to estimate the magnitude of risks that varied in both extent of potential harm and exposure time (that is, long-duration high risk; long-duration low risk; short-duration high risk; short-duration low risk). It was discovered that people fail to factor exposure time correctly into their estimates of risk. They tend to *overestimate* the impact of short-duration high-risk events. Being in danger for a very short time is seen as much more dangerous than it really is.

Denial of Risk

High risk taking could be due to either a failure to assess the level of danger or simply a willingness or desire to engage in the activity regardless of the level of danger. The evidence suggests that people engaging in risky behaviors on a *voluntary* basis often fail to appreciate the true level of danger in the situation.

They may know the statistical odds but refuse to believe that these odds apply to them personally.

As an example, consider the results of a study sponsored by the Insurance Information Institute. It was discovered that only 58 percent of people who smoke in bed consider it to be a very risky activity, whereas 92 percent of those who do not smoke in bed find it to be so. Similar patterns were identified for activities such as gambling (35 versus 63 percent), driving a car (27 versus 39 percent), skiing (13 versus 33 percent), and investing in the stock market (26 versus 39 percent).

Frequently, people claim that there is less risk in their own personal case because their skills reduce the risky aspects of the situation. For instance, many sky divers deny that their sport is risky. To them, it is risky only if one "does not know what he or she is doing." Similar attitudes have been documented among people who speculate in the stock market and real estate. A sharp distinction is drawn by such individuals between taking risks and being foolhardy. In many cases, people have unwarranted confidence in their skill levels.

Other people deny the risk because they feel especially lucky. They believe that the odds can be beaten. Even if the odds of success are only 10 in 100, such individuals are apt to think, "Somebody has to be in that 10 percent, so why shouldn't it be me?" When the objective probability of an event is unknown, people tend to *overestimate* the probability of a desired outcome and *underestimate* the probability of an undesired outcome. Many an individual who felt that the odds could be beaten has traveled to Las Vegas in a $15,000 car and indeed has come home in a $100,000 vehicle. Unfortunately, in a majority of such cases the $100,000 vehicle was not a new car but a bus.

People's reluctance to buy insurance stems in part from such unrealistic optimism. Some agents present actuarial data to their prospects on the probability of death, disability, and hospitalization, but most prospects feel that such statistics don't really apply to them personally. Most people believe that they are less likely than average to die prematurely, be hospitalized, or become disabled. In a recent study people were presented with the statistic that during a given year approximately 19 out of every 1,000 persons would sustain a disability lasting over 3 months. (In other words, the odds of disability were 19 in 1,000.) The group was then asked to estimate their personal odds of sustaining a disability. On average, the subjects felt their personal odds to be much lower—only 6 in 1,000.

Findings indicate that people tend to especially discount very small negative probabilities, treating them as if they were nonexistent. Due to this bias in the processing of risk information, many people are reluctant to insure against low-probability events even if a catastrophic loss potential exists and the insurance is underpriced (in relation to the actuarial risk). For example, flood insurance, despite being federally subsidized, is not easy to sell. Sales do increase after a flood occurs, but only for a few months. Psychologists have examined the style of thinking that supports this undue optimism. It has been found that people tend to overgeneralize from their previous experiences. The person's thinking reflects "It hasn't happened to me yet, so it probably never will."

Two techniques might encourage the purchase of insurance coverage for underestimated perils. One, the insurance should be sold as part of a comprehensive package rather than as a separate policy. Two, a partial refund can be offered to the policyholder during years in which no claims occur.

The refunding concept can be used with other coverages as well. For insurance, some companies offer accidental death protection that offers a refund of the full premium paid if, after a certain number of years of continuous coverage (for example, 15 years), no claim is made. The same concept is being used by others to market a fully refundable homeowners insurance, even if claims have been made. The plan, of course, requires a single lump-sum, up-front premium payment that is higher than the standard annual premiums would have been.

Complete Elimination versus Reduction in Risk

Research comparing how people react to a *reduction* in a risk relative to its complete *elimination* suggests that most people place a disproportionately high value on the latter. For example, consider the following problems (cited in Kahneman and Riepe, 1998):

> You are facing a chance for a gain of $20,000. You do not know the exact probability. Consider these three pairs of outcomes:
>
> A. The probability is either 0% or 1%
> B. The probability is either 41% or 42%
> C. The probability is either 99% or 100%
>
> How much are you willing to pay to increase your probability from 0% to 1%; from 41% to 42%, and from 99% to 100%? Research shows that people will pay more to raise the probability of a desirable event from 0% to 1% or from 99% to 100% than from 41% to 42%, even though the increase amounts to 1% in all three cases.

This mindset might also have implications for the marketing of insurance products. The high value placed on the elimination of risk may explain why many people select low deductibles on property and casualty coverages, despite the relatively high premiums. Furthermore, this bias implies that the way a particular coverage's degree of protection is described to a client is very important. For instance, an insurance policy guarding against a particular peril, like fire, may be viewed as either *full* protection against the specific risk or a reduction in the overall probability of property loss. Based on the observed preference for the elimination of a risk compared to its reduction, there is a distinct marketing advantage in focusing on the coverage's *full* protection aspect.

Telling a prospective client that buying the policy will lower his or her chances of suffering property damage will have a lower inducement value than will stressing to the client that he or she has *full* protection against fire.

Availability Bias

The most well-documented bias altering people's estimates of risk is called "availability bias." It refers to the fact that events that are easy to imagine or recall will be judged as more probable than they actually are. Events that are dramatic and vivid or that receive heavy media attention are easily available to one's mind and are therefore overestimated. In contrast, events that are dull or abstract are underestimated. A few examples should help explain this particular bias.

- When asked to estimate whether the letter "K" occurs more frequently as the first letter or the third letter in an English word, most people say first. In actuality, the letter "K" appears three times more frequently in the third position of a word. The reason why most people believe otherwise is because it is a lot easier for them to think of words that start with "K."
- Which is more frequent, homicide or suicide? Most people believe that homicide is five times more frequent. Yet suicides are 30 percent more common. People tend to believe that the opposite is true because homicides are reported in the news, whereas suicides are generally not reported (unless the suicide involves a well-known personality).
- People overestimate the probability of dying from accidents in comparison to dying from illnesses. Again, this is because the media devotes more coverage to deaths resulting from events like airplane crashes than to deaths resulting from heart attacks.
- Seeing the movie *Jaws* made the public much more wary of going into the ocean than the actual probabilities of being attacked by a shark warranted.
- People who watch TV frequently tend to overestimate the degree of violence in society because of the violence that occurs on both shows and the news.
- People tend to be more influenced by personal experiences because they are more vivid. Thus research shows that people overestimate the probability of death from diseases that killed people they knew personally. They also tend to be influenced more by anecdotal evidence provided by their friends than by more representative and trustworthy information contained in statistical reports. Consequently most people when they are in the market for a car will rely more heavily on the experiences of a friend than on a consumer survey report. Another

example is that many individuals who normally did not wear a seat belt, despite repeated warnings from various governmental agencies, started to wear one when a friend or neighbor was hurt or killed because a seat belt was not worn. It was only after this personal experience that they began to wear a seat belt.

Familiarity Bias

Most people dread the unknown. Risks that are familiar are feared less than risks that are unfamiliar. For example, investors see greater risk in foreign equities than warranted based on historical returns. This fear occurs because they know less about other countries than their own country. In other words, people tend to perceive less risk in things they know. The more a person knows about a country, company, product, or situation, the lower will be his or her perception of risk. For instance, sophisticated investors tend to be more risk tolerant than naive investors. Educating clients about unfamiliar investments may lower their inherent fears.

Typically, people overreact to unexpected news. Studies show that both securities analysts and the lay public overreact to recent information, giving the new (that is, unfamiliar) information more importance than it really deserves. The impact of familiarity can be discerned clearly in both the financial industry's and investors' reactions to the October 1987 stock market drop of 508 points as compared to the drop of 200 points in October 1989. Despite reports after the "miniplunge" of 1989 that the market was fragile, most investors and their advisers were unfazed by the drop, and few advisers received any panicky telephone calls from their clients. A random survey by the publication *Financial Services Week,* conducted after the October 1989 drop, revealed a very unconcerned attitude. One financial adviser who was interviewed in the *Financial Services Week* survey summarized the situation in the following terms:

> I was so disappointed. . . . Not only did I not get any calls from clients, but Monday morning I called up a bunch of clients—I was going to calm them down and let them know that the world had not ended and their consensus was "big deal, so what?"

Illusion of Control Bias

People tend to underestimate the risk involved in activities under their control, like driving a car, relative to activities in which the control is given over to someone else, like flying as a passenger in an airplane. Ironically, the chance of being involved in a car accident driving to the airport to catch a flight is greater than the chance of the airplane crashing.

Time Horizon

In investments, differences can exist between short-run and long-run strategies to maximize return. Therefore it is critical that a time horizon be specified. For most decisions involving an element of risk, the length of the time elapsing between making the decision and the knowledge of the eventual outcome is very crucial. If the time span between these two events is long, the person is more likely to accept the risk than if the time span is relatively short. In other words, if something is imminent, there is an increased sense of danger.

People tend to psychologically overemphasize short-term risks. Some authorities have suggested that people start smoking because the threat of cancer is so far in the future. The long-term risk, although quite threatening, does not seem real to them. (This refusal to consider future risks seriously can be seen in Mark Twain's reaction to being told that, by giving up smoking and drinking, he could add another 5 years to his life. Twain's reaction was that without smoking and drinking another 5 years of living would not be worth it.)

Fortunately, there may be some synergy between people's willingness to bear risk under a broad time horizon and the performance of the riskier investment products. Analysis of historical data has shown that, from a long-term perspective, many of these products were not risky. While they show great volatility in the short run, they are less volatile in the long run. In other words, they are safer when viewed within a broadened investment time horizon.

Unfortunately for their financial well-being, people typically have a short-range rather than long-range planning horizon. The tendency to be myopic about one's investment planning horizon is well illustrated in a study conducted by psychologist R. J. Herrnstein. Herrnstein presented a group of people with the following situation: Let's suppose that you win a lottery that gives you two alternative ways, A and B, of collecting your winnings.

Situation 1

Choice A: You can collect $100 tomorrow.
Choice B: You can collect $115 a week from tomorrow.

Most of the group selected option A, despite the fact that by waiting only one more week they would have been able to earn 15 percent. (There are few investments that would pay 15 percent *per week* interest.)

Next, the people who selected choice A were presented with another hypothetical lottery, in which the two payment schedules were C and D.

Situation 2

Choice C: You can collect $100 in 52 weeks from today.
Choice D: You can collect $115 in 53 weeks from today.

Interestingly, almost all of those who selected payment schedule A now selected payment schedule D. If they were consistent in their behavior, they would have chosen C. There was the same one-week difference between A and B as between C and D. However, the one-week difference meant much more in the present than it did in the future.

Research shows that 10 to 15 years is the longest time horizon that most people consider to be practical for planning purposes. Surveys of the general public continue to find that people do recognize that upon retirement they may not have enough income to live in their present style, yet they fail to do anything to remedy the situation. The reason typically offered as justification is that they have a more pressing *immediate* crisis or concern. Many people who purchase term insurance instead of permanent insurance, intending to invest the difference in premiums, never do so because more immediate concerns always arise.

Mood

Psychologists have been studying the impact of a person's mood on his or her willingness to undertake a risk. The relationship between mood and risk tolerance is quite complex, given the results of various studies. The research shows that a good mood leads to more positive expectations and lower perceived risk. Conversely, a bad mood leads to increased estimates of risk. However, when it comes to actual behavior, a good mood does not necessarily lead to greater risk taking. While a good mood does increase willingness to take relatively *low risks*, it decreases the person's willingness to accept *high risks*. Perhaps this is because the person does not want to jeopardize his or her good mood.

Some theoreticians attribute the generally lower stock prices on Monday as compared to Friday (known as the weekend effect) to differences in people's moods on Mondays as opposed to Fridays. Monday is said to be an unpleasant day for most people, since it is the start of a work week. On Friday, though, most people are in a pleasant mood because they are anticipating the weekend. These differences in mood are believed to be reflected in stock prices. The same explanation can be extended to the observation that stock returns are generally high in January (the January effect). Since January marks the beginning of a new year, people are generally optimistic, which again shows up in higher prices.

Effects of Alcohol on Risk Taking

Studies have shown that alcohol consumption causes people to become reckless and take greater risks than they would ordinarily. An intriguing result of such experiments is that even those people who *believed* that they were drinking alcoholic beverages—when in reality they were not—also increased their risk-taking behaviors.

Parties Bearing the Consequences of a Decision

The answer to the question "Who will be affected by the consequences of my actions?" is a strong determinant of whether a risk will be acceptable or unacceptable. Individuals tend to be more risk averse if the decision's outcome will have consequences for both the individual making the decision and those the individual cares about. Decision makers are somewhat less risk averse if only the individual decision maker is affected. The *most* risk-prone decisions are made if only others will bear the consequences of the decision. For instance, managers take more risks when they invest their company's money than when they invest their own personal funds. Studies of stock market trading reveal a similar pattern. If the money being invested is his or her own, the investor requires more information before making a transaction and makes significantly fewer trades.

Group Dynamics of Risk Taking

A phenomenon studied for about 30 years concerns the difference between individual and group reactions to risk. This phenomenon, known as the "choice shift," refers to the finding that a group decision is usually more extreme than a decision favored by most members of the group when they are polled individually (before the discussion). Generally the shift is toward more risky action, although in some instances the shift is toward a more cautious attitude. (Hence, the more neutral term *choice shift* is preferred today.)

Several studies on the choice shift phenomenon bear directly on financial planning. In one study people were asked to identify the investment products that they would be willing to buy. The investments available to them ranged from low risk (no variability in their historical return patterns) to high risk (very variable, with low returns in certain years and high returns in other years). First, each person made his or her selection individually. Next, they took part in a group discussion to reach a consensus regarding their choices. While on an individual basis most members of the group wanted the less risky products, the group decision was in favor of the riskier products. There were similar results in another study where the group's task was the selection of an automobile physical damage coverage. When polled individually, the participants were willing to pay, on average, about another $48 in premiums in order to get collision coverage. As a result of the group discussion, however, the consensus was that they would be willing to pay less—only $31—for this particular coverage. In other words, the group was willing to bear more of the risk.

Possible explanations for the shift in the risky direction include the following:

- The responsibility for a decision is shared by the group, so no one person feels totally responsible if it turns out to have been the wrong one.

- The risk-tolerant members in the group are influential.
- As a result of the discussion, the group members become more *familiar* with the situation, and this lessens their inherent fears.

Mental Accounts

Various psychological experiments have been conducted to illustrate how "mental accounts" operate in people's evaluation of monetary gains and losses. One such study shows that the opportunity to save a given amount of money will be viewed quite differently, depending on what mental account a person uses to evaluate the psychological value of this money. Psychologists Daniel Kahneman and Amos Tversky asked people what they would do if they went out to buy a $125 jacket and a $15 calculator, and upon arrival at the main store they were informed by the sales clerk that the calculator was on sale for $10 at a branch store 20 minutes away. Under these circumstances, 68 percent of people were willing to drive 20 minutes to save $5.

In a second version of this same story, the $5 in savings was on the jacket rather than the calculator. (That is, the price of the jacket was $120 at the branch store and $125 at the main store. The price of the calculator was $15 at both stores.) The percentage of people willing to drive 20 minutes to save $5 under the second set of circumstances was only 29 percent.

Five dollars would be saved either way, yet the number of people willing to save this amount of money was substantially different. Why? The simple reason is that people maintain different mental accounts for the prices of jackets and calculators. Money to be gained or lost is not evaluated in a vacuum. Rather, there is always some *subjective standard* that is employed as a yardstick to gauge the value.

The concept of mental accounts has many implications for financial services practitioners. The amount of pleasure or displeasure that the appreciation or depreciation in the value of a certain asset will bring to a client is not necessarily determined by the simple dollar amounts lost or gained. Other factors will influence the client's assessment of the event. For example, did the client's neighbor (or brother or sister) do better or worse? How did a different security that the client considered purchasing fare?

It is necessary for financial services professionals to recognize that because of mental accounts their clients may have different risk-tolerance levels for different funds, depending on how they acquired the money and what they intend to do with it. Inherited versus earned money is one factor that may account for different risk-tolerance levels. Some people who inherit hard-earned money from a loved relative refuse to risk losing the principal. With money they earned personally, however, they may have less fear of potential loss. For others, the reverse may be true.

People's mental accounting for posting gains and losses does not treat money earned and money lost as equal units. Money lost carries a much heavier psychological value. For instance, making $5,000 on an investment, provided that this return is equal to what was expected, will make a client happy. Conversely, losing $5,000 on an investment will make a client unhappy. Research shows, however, that the unhappiness experienced at losing the $5,000 is greater than the happiness felt at earning $5,000. Therefore clients are apt to be more upset about a given loss than pleased about an equivalent gain. Similarly most investors feel worse if they sell a security that shortly thereafter increases in value than if they failed to buy the security in the first place.

Mental accounting may also be the underlying cause for the finding that most investors prefer cash dividends over capital gains. Dividends and capital gains are placed into separate mental accounts according to some theorists.

RISK TAKING: SITUATION-SPECIFIC OR GENERAL PERSONALITY TRAIT

Some financial planners tend to describe people as risk takers or risk averters, without considering the type of behaviors on which they base such classifications. It is as if they expect people to act in a similar manner in all aspects of life. Yet psychologists are still debating whether most people have a consistent pattern of risk taking in all realms of their lives or whether the degree of risk they are willing to assume depends on the nature of the situation. Although some evidence suggests that there is a *slight* predisposition to act in either a risk-taking or risk-averse manner in different situations, this predisposition is weak for most persons. Only persons with the personality type that psychologists call the "thrill seeker" (also known as the "sensation" or "arousal" seeker) seem to be relatively consistent.

In general, the more similar any two situations are, the greater is the consistency in risk-taking behavior in these two situations. Research has shown that essentially four major types of life situations involve risk taking:

- *Monetary* situations involve such risks as investments, gambling, or job changes.
- *Physical* situations involve risks that could result in bodily harm, such as mountain climbing or skydiving.
- *Social* situations involve risks that could lead to loss of self-esteem or another person's respect.
- *Ethical* situations involve risks in which one is faced with the prospect of compromising one's moral or religious standards or society's legal standards. (For example, trading on insider information involves an ethical risk.)

These four risk contexts have been described, based on their consequences, as the potential loss of capital (monetary risk), the potential loss of life (physical risk), the potential loss of face (social risk), and the potential loss of freedom (ethical risk).

Cases in which the level of risk taking is quite different across different contexts are not hard to find, as many people change their behavior from situation to situation. The author was told of one, a Navy pilot who had been decorated for heroism during the Vietnam War. After his discharge from the service, this individual was encouraged to begin a career in life insurance sales. His new career proved to be both financially and emotionally unrewarding, however, because he was uncomfortable with prospecting. This came as a surprise to the person's manager since there was clear-cut evidence of fearlessness and risk taking in the person's war record. The ex-pilot and his manager had a discussion about his fear of prospecting. During the course of the conversation, it became evident to the manager that it was actually a low level of social risk tolerance that accounted for this person's high physical risk tolerance during the war. The individual related that what kept him flying was the fear of disapproval by others. As he put it, whenever he got jittery about a mission and thought of turning back, all he had to do was picture the look of disapproval from his commander and fellow pilots. In this case, low tolerance for social risk was, in part, responsible for high physical risk tolerance.

One should be careful in using risk taking in nonfinancial matters to infer a level of risk tolerance for investments. Knowing that someone is a risk taker in a certain physical activity provides clues about how the individual will react in other situations that involve potential bodily harm. However, this information provides little insight as to whether this person will be willing to invest in a financially risky venture. The latter information is best determined from a knowledge of the person's typical behavior in monetary risk-taking situations. Therefore a financial planner who promotes an "aggressive" mutual fund to a skydiving club should not be surprised if the responses to the ad are not dramatically greater than responses from the general public. The best predictor of an investor's risk tolerance in a financial matter is his or her risk preference in other financial matters, rather than how the person reacts to risk in sports, social situations, and so on.

The client's risk tolerance in financial matters should be of primary concern to the financial planner, since this is the aspect of the client's situation that is within the planner's purview. However, there may be some value in looking at the client's total risk-taking disposition. First, the client could learn that he or she may not necessarily have the same propensity for risk in money matters as in physical activities or social activities. Often clients assume that they have a general predisposition to take on the same level of risk in all spheres of life. Second, consistency across different contexts may alert the financial planner to whether the individual is someone who is a thrill seeker (discussed later in this chapter).

Physical risk taking could be a relevant issue when determining a client's insurance needs. It has been shown that risk taking in the physical realm is a major factor in various types of accidents. Therefore people who have high levels of physical risk tolerance are more apt to die from accidental causes or to suffer disabling injuries from an accident. According to the *Statistical Bulletin* published by the Metropolitan Life Companies, accidents are the *leading* cause of death among children and young adults. When the U.S. population is considered as a whole, accidental death is third in line after death due to cardiovascular diseases or cancer. Deaths from motor vehicle accidents account for approximately half of the accidental deaths reported in this country. Accidental death riders and disability income insurance may be of interest to the physical risk taker, especially if the individual has, at the same time, a low level of monetary risk tolerance.

Physical risk taking is also a contributing factor in death from nonaccidental causes. Consequently risk taking in health-related matters is of increasing concern to insurance companies. It is now standard for insurance carriers to charge lower premiums for nonsmokers, and an emergent trend may be to extend similar premium reductions to people who avoid other health risks as well. Because of the AIDS epidemic, a growing area of research—some sponsored by the insurance industry—is concerned with risk taking in sexual behaviors (a form of physical risk taking).

LIFESTYLE OF THE RISK TAKER

Most of the early studies on the personality of the typical risk taker assumed that risk taking was a general personality trait rather than being specific to a particular context. Therefore the measures of risk taking used in these studies did not differentiate between attitudes toward physical, social, ethical, and monetary risk taking. As such, one needs to exercise caution in utilizing these findings in financial planning since they may apply more to one of the other categories of risk taking than to monetary risk taking in particular.

For example, the following life experiences that some researchers identify as typical of the risk taker probably apply more to physical risk takers than monetary risk takers:

- took dares as a child
- drank and smoked at an early age
- was sexually active at a young age
- enjoys dangerous leisure activities, such as mountain climbing, surfing, hang gliding, scuba diving, racing a car, motorcycling, or skydiving
- is likely to hold a job as a pilot, soldier, fireman, or policeman

Likewise, the following characteristics of risk takers may be related mostly to social risk taking:

- has a social presence
- is self-accepting

- is self-confident
- is aggressive
- is independent
- is irresponsible
- is status-seeking
- has strong leadership abilities
- is unaccepting of other people's opinions

Similarly, the finding that risk takers feel low levels of guilt for wrongdoing probably applies more to the ethical risk taker than to the physical, monetary, or social risk taker.

Other characteristics identified in this type of research may, however, also apply to monetary risk takers. Among these are the following:

- emphasizes merit rather than seniority in job promotions
- enjoys work that involves decision making
- requires little time to make a major decision
- completes tests that have a time limit very quickly, attempting to compensate for more mistakes by answering more questions
- takes a chance and guesses on tests that impose a penalty for guessing (such as the Scholastic Aptitude Test)
- is optimistic, seeing mistakes as setbacks, not personal failures
- has a low need for an ordered environment
- is able to handle stress
- is persistent

The following characteristics may also distinguish between monetary risk averters and risk takers in their outlook on life:

Risk Averter	Risk Taker
• sees risk as danger	• sees risk as challenge or opportunity
• overestimates risk	• underestimates risk
• prefers low variability	• prefers high variability
• adopts the worst-case scenario (emphasizes the probability of loss)	• adopts the best-case scenario (emphasizes the probability of a win)
• is pessimistic	• is optimistic
• likes structure	• likes ambiguity
• dislikes change	• enjoys change
• prefers certainty to uncertainty	• prefers uncertainty to certainty

Few studies have focused on the biographical and psychological characteristics of monetary risk takers per se. Research conducted by psychologist Frank Farley is an exception. His studies indicate that monetary risk takers are good money managers who spend considerable time reading about investments and related financial matters and express confidence in their money-making abilities. In contrast to the monetary risk averters, who stated that their long-term goal was happiness, the monetary risk takers listed success as their primary goal. Farley also found that monetary risk takers tend to possess leadership skills and good sales skills. For many monetary risk takers, money is the center of their lives.

A 1993 study of mutual fund shareholders, sponsored by the mutual fund industry trade association, indicates that investors with high risk tolerance have clear financial goals. They were also more likely to be raised in homes that had an interest in investing, discussed such matters, and actually invested. In describing the outcomes of their families' investments, the high risk takers were more likely to indicate that it was successful. High-risk-tolerant mutual fund owners made their own first investment at an earlier age than their low-risk-tolerant counterparts, and their first investment was more likely to be an individual stock. The first investment for low-risk-tolerant mutual fund owners was more likely to be real estate.

Compared to low and moderate risk takers, high-risk-tolerant shareholders in this study were more apt to have confidence in their ability to make their own investment decisions, rather than relying on the advice of professionals. They used magazines and newspapers as their primary source of investment information to make these decisions. High-risk-tolerant shareholders were also more likely to read the mutual funds prospectus for investing information (that is, 38 percent of the high risk takers versus 25 percent of the moderate risk takers and 13 percent of the low risk takers). The same pattern was found in the readership of investment newsletters (26 percent, 19 percent, and 15 percent respectively for high, moderate, and low risk takers.) Low risk takers, in contrast, indicated that they were confused by the multitude of investment choices, and therefore relied on others for advice; their most frequent sources of information were friends, family, and business associates. The high-risk-tolerant investors were more likely to actually adapt a long-term view of their investments, even though the low and moderate risk takers agree just as strongly that a long-term strategy leads to the best results. Low risk takers seem overly concerned about short-term fluctuations. (See figure 5-1.)

The groups were also compared on their knowledge of investment principles, and as one might expect, the high-risk-tolerant group showed the best understanding of the subject.

Another significant survey comparing the investment attitudes of risk-tolerant and risk-intolerant investors concerns their satisfaction with the returns they previously received on their investments. Whereas risk-averse investors are generally satisfied, those who are risk tolerant tend to feel that they were not adequately compensated.

FIGURE 5-1
Sources of Financial Information by Level of Risk Tolerance

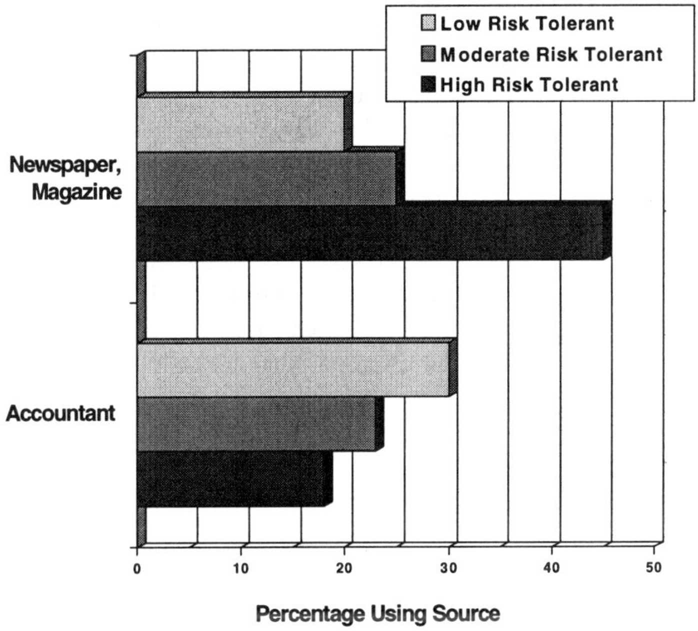

Source of data: Investment Company Institute (1993).

A study by Daniel Kahneman and Richard Thaler found differences in the type of regret experienced by risk-taking and risk-averse investors. Wealthy investors were asked to think of a bad financial decision that they now regretted, and to indicate if the regret was over one investment they made (regret of commission) or over an investment that they failed to make (regret of omission). Most of these investors reported regrets of commission, that is, about investments that they actually made. A minority, however, reported their greatest regret was about missed opportunities to make an investment. This minority constituted the risk takers in this group.

The risk takers also had another characteristic in common. Asked whether they attributed investment outcomes to luck or skill, the risk takers attributed skill to all outcomes, even the ones they regretted.

THE THRILL SEEKER

The thrill seeker is the personality type most likely to be *consistently* risk seeking across all dimensions of life, including financial matters. Sometimes a distinction is made between physical thrill seekers and mental thrill seekers. However, all thrill seekers abhor routine, be it mental or physical. These individuals are always on the lookout for experiences that offer novelty, ambiguity, complexity, and intensity. If a thrill seeker can't find excitement, he or she will create it. "In-and-out" trading in the stock market, for instance, provides many such quick thrills. For the thrill seeker, the uncertainty of an investment decision may hold as much enticement, perhaps even more, than the anticipated payoff. To the thrill seeker, money made from a safe investment does not hold as much value as the same amount of money made from a risky investment. There is some research showing that thrill seekers have a biologically based need for greater than normal levels of arousal.

Thrill seeking can have either very constructive or very destructive outlets. For example, constructive mental outlets are available in the arts or sciences, fields that reward the creative thinking characteristic of the thrill seeker. Crime, in turn, provides a common destructive outlet for both mental and physical thrill seeking. Even in prison, thrill seekers are a problem, because they continually try to escape.

It is important to realize that not everyone who takes many risks is necessarily a thrill seeker, although by definition, every thrill seeker must be considered a risk taker. How can a financial planner spot the thrill seeker? To a certain extent, the thrill seeker is a caricature of a risk taker, showing many of the same basic characteristics, but in a markedly exaggerated form. In addition to the characteristics already mentioned in defining the thrill-seeking personality, the financial planner should be alert to those that follow.

Thrill seeking is more common among men than women. Thrill seekers enjoy loud parties. They tend to be outgoing, spontaneous, and fast decision makers. In looking for a history of sensation seeking, the planner needs to check to see if the person participates in risky sports and likes to gamble, especially at blackjack. A history of traffic violations is common. Thrill seekers may associate with unconventional persons and have an intense dislike for people they perceive as boring. The thrill seeker seeks variety in his or her sex life. If the thrill seeker uses recreational drugs, a variety of drugs rather than just one drug are taken.

Thrill seekers may appear to be perfect candidates for risky investments, given their obviously high tolerance for risk. But this very desire for novel, intense, and varied experiences, may lead the thrill seeker to pursue legal action against the planner for suggesting an overly risky product if the investment does not produce the expected returns. With this type of client, the planner must take particular care in documenting due diligence.

DEMOGRAPHIC CHARACTERISTICS

Numerous studies have been conducted over the years in which risk tolerance was related to such things as wealth, education, age, gender, birth order, marital status, and occupation. The results of this research are discussed below.

Wealth

Do wealthy individuals take more risks with their money? First, a distinction must be drawn between *absolute* and *relative* risk tolerance. Absolute risk tolerance is gauged by the *amount* of wealth one allocates to risky assets. Relative risk tolerance, in contrast, is measured by the *proportion* of one's wealth allocated to risky assets. It is generally accepted that absolute risk tolerance increases with wealth, since the wealthy have more money to spend on *everything*. There is some disagreement, though, about whether relative risk tolerance increases with wealth. Several studies have addressed this question by examining people's investment portfolios. One such study, conducted by R. A. Cohn and his colleagues, found that relative risk tolerance does increase with wealth—the wealthier a person was, the greater the proportion of total wealth that person put in risky assets. For instance, if the individual's assets were above $175,000, on average, 62 percent of his or her investments were risky. If the total value of assets was below $175,000, only 42 percent of the investments were of the risky type. This pattern held even after sex, age, and marital status were taken into account. However, this relationship between wealth and risk tolerance was strongest among male investors and married investors.

Some researchers have been unable to find such relationships. One reason for the discrepancy is attributable to differences in the type of assets considered and how these assets were classified (safe versus risky). The way the primary residence is treated seems to be especially critical. Relative risk tolerance goes up with increasing wealth if housing is either excluded from the definition of wealth or classified as a riskless asset.

There is further support for a positive relationship between relative risk tolerance and wealth in studies using questionnaires as the basis for determining the degree of risk tolerance. In the survey sponsored by the Insurance Information Institute cited at the beginning of this chapter, it was reported that the wealthy were more likely to associate the word *risk* with the word *opportunity* than the other respondents. Similarly, a study of the upper affluent sponsored by the CIGNA Corporation found that the risk takers in this group were more likely to have higher incomes and were much more likely to be millionaires. The "chicken and egg" question still remains—did the wealthy become so because of their greater willingness to assume risk, or is it that they are more risk taking now that they are wealthy? That is, does having money make one more risk seeking?

How money was acquired may also be a factor in the risk-taking propensity characteristic of the wealthy. Differences in risk tolerance have been reported between those who inherited their wealth and those who made their fortune themselves. Namely, people who earned their own wealth are more risk tolerant than those who inherited their wealth.

Some evidence suggests that a majority of the millionaires alive today did not inherit their wealth. In an interview with *Financial Services Week* (March 5, 1990), consultant Steve Moeller reports that 60 percent of millionaires made their fortunes by starting their own businesses. According to Moeller, the profile of the average millionaire is as follows: married, male, 57 years old, some college education, blue-collar family background, annual income of $130,000. Millionaires who acquired their own wealth prefer to make their own decisions, so Moeller recommends that financial planners present such individuals with a variety of investment options. Other evidence indicates that those who inherit their money are more receptive to financial planning advice than those who made their money themselves.

Education

Numerous studies have found that financial risk tolerance increases with degree of formal education. Riley and Chow, for instance, looked at the percentage of total wealth held in risky assets by individuals with differing levels of education and made the following observations (table 5-2).

TABLE 5-2
Risk Tolerance and Degree of Formal Education

Education	Percentage of Wealth in Risky Assets
Less than high school	2.0%
High school diploma	3.4%
Some college	5.2%
College degree	7.9%
Post graduate	8.0%

Among the mutual fund shareholders studied by the Investment Company Institute, the percentage of investors with at least a 4-year college degree increases with risk tolerance (39 percent among the low risk tolerant, 57 percent among the moderate risk tolerant, and 66 percent among the high risk tolerant). The reason for this relationship is not entirely clear, however. Because education is correlated with income and wealth, it could be that it is the latter two variables that account for the greater risk tolerance among the better educated, rather than education *per se*. It is also possible that people with higher levels of education become familiar with the range of investment options available to them.

Age

One study of mutual fund investors asked whether they agreed or disagreed with the statement, "The older people get, the less willing they are to take investment risk." Ratings were on a scale from 0 to 10, with 0 indicating no agreement and 10 indicating strong agreement. In general respondents agreed with this statement, since the average rating was 7.6. Low-risk-tolerant, moderate-risk-tolerant, and high-risk-tolerant shareholders were compared on their opinions about this issue, and surprising differences were noted. The low-risk-tolerant investors were most likely to agree with this statement (average rating = 8.6), while the high-risk-tolerant investors were least likely to agree with it (average rating = 6.7). The moderate risk takers fell in the middle (average rating = 7.5).

Who is correct? A substantial body of research exists on the relationship between age and risk taking in all sorts of activities, financial as well as nonfinancial. The bulk of this research points to an inverse relationship between age and willingness to take risks. That is, as one gets older, one becomes more cautious. For instance, the 1993 Investment Company Institute Study of Risk Tolerance (cited previously) found that the average ages of their low-, moderate-, and high-risk-tolerant investors were 60, 51, and 42 years, respectively.

The observed relationship between financial risk taking and age has been linked to biological factors. An article published in the *Financial Analysts Journal* (November/December 1990), titled "Understanding and Assessing Financial Risk Tolerance: A Biological Perspective," reported that an enzyme, monoamine oxidase (MAO) is found in higher concentrations among the risk averse, and that MAO levels increase with age. (It was noted in jest in a review of this article in the *CFA Journal* that a practical application of this research could be a blood test to determine the client's level of risk tolerance.)

Some qualifiers are in order, however. This relationship between more advanced age and increased caution may not be as strong for monetary risks as it is for physical risks. Moreover, the relationship between monetary risk tolerance and age may be weaker among the wealthy, according to some studies. It has been suggested that when looking at the impact of age on risk taking one also needs to consider the client's particular circumstances. For instance, some financial planners report that they have encountered middle-aged couples who were previously very conservative investors but who now take an interest in aggressive investing because their obligations to raise and educate their children are at an end.

Gender

The study of psychological differences between men and women has a long history. Almost all research prior to the women's movement indicates that men are more risk tolerant than women in most aspects of life. Both biologically based and psychologically based explanations have been offered. One psychological explanation is that women have been socialized to be more dependent and risk averse.

The results of more recent studies are mixed. Some newer studies encourage consideration of age and income when looking at sex differences in monetary risk taking. While older married women are less likely to accept financial risks than their husbands, the differences in financial risk taking between younger men and women with comparable incomes are either small or nonexistent.

Polls also reveal the changing attitudes toward financial risks among women. For instance, a *Ms. Magazine* poll conducted in 1977 found that only 26 percent of their readers would invest a cash windfall rather than keep it in a savings account. When the same poll was repeated in 1988, 40 percent of the respondents indicated that they would be willing to take risks in order to obtain a higher potential return. Also stock ownership in this group increased. About 33 percent of the 1988 respondents owned stocks, compared to 24 percent of the 1977 respondents.

Other gender-related differences between men and women have also been declining. For example, a recent review of the literature found that the difference favoring males in mathematics skills was larger in studies published before 1974 than in studies published after that date.

Birth Order

Although there is only limited research on the topic, it appears that birth order is related to risk taking. Namely, the firstborn child tends to be less willing to take risks than the later-born children in the same family. The favorite explanation is that parents exert greater control over the early life of the firstborn child and instill in him or her the need to be dependable and act responsibly. To the child, this means not taking unnecessary chances.

Marital Status

Single individuals appear more risk tolerant than married individuals in some studies, and more risk averse in other studies. The reason for the conflicting results is a failure to consider whether both spouses are employed. The key is the presence of dependents, rather than marital status per se. If the individual feels that his or her actions might have negative consequences for dependents, then he or she is likely to be more cautious. In dual-income families, the spouse's level of risk tolerance may be no less than that of a single person, because neither party is the dependent under these circumstances. In fact, a dual income may increase the level of risk tolerance. For example, a study of mutual fund shareholders found that among married low-risk-tolerant investors, 61 percent of the spouses worked, compared to 73 percent of the high-risk-tolerant married households.

Other research indicates that widowed and separated people are more risk averse than either never-married persons or persons who are currently married.

Occupation

Most people spend much of their adult life working. Certainly the types of jobs they hold in some way relate to risk tolerance. Several aspects related to occupation and risk tolerance have been studied and are discussed below.

Public-Sector versus Private-Sector Employment

One important manifestation of financial risk-taking propensity is the need for job security—the greater the probability of becoming unemployed, the greater the financial riskiness in that occupation. Thus one would expect monetarily risk-averse individuals to gravitate toward jobs that offer security, even if the pay is lower. It is generally accepted that the public sector offers greater job security. A number of studies have compared the monetary risk-taking propensities of private-sector and public-sector employees. This research points to greater risk aversion among public-sector employees.

Professionals versus Nonprofessionals

According to the results of some studies, professionals (physicians, lawyers, managers, and so on) tend to be more risk taking in investment decisions than nonprofessionals (farmers, unskilled and skilled laborers, clerical workers, and so on). This disparity is perhaps due to differences in the level of sophistication about investment matters. As mentioned earlier, risk tolerance tends to increase with increased knowledge and familiarity.

Risk tolerance differences within a given profession cannot be explained in these terms, however. Certain reports indicate that professionals in private practice or professionals working for small firms are more risk tolerant than individuals in the same profession who are employed by large firms. Among physicians, differences have also been observed between surgeons and physicians in other specialties (internists, for example). Specifically, surgeons reportedly are more likely to be risk tolerant than other physicians.

Length of Job Tenure

Chances of advancement decrease the longer a person remains in one position. Remaining with the same company at the same job especially lowers one's future advancement opportunities. Again, many financially risk-averse people remain in positions that offer few possibilities for upward mobility because of financial security needs. Financial risk takers, in contrast, change jobs quite frequently (that is, they are *job hoppers*).

Management Level

Studies comparing the risk-tolerance levels of managers at different levels within an organization usually find that the risk takers hold more senior level positions, earn higher incomes, and have greater authority. Risk takers are also more likely to work as managers in small rather than large firms.

Salary versus Commission

A recent study examined the personality characteristics of job seekers and how these characteristics related to the compensation system preferred by the job seeker. It was determined that risk-averse individuals were more attracted to positions and organizations that offered a fixed rather than a contingent (upon performance) pay system. Moreover, risk-averse individuals did not consider pay level to be as important a criterion in the job they were seeking.

Monetary risk takers are well represented in occupations in which all or a substantial portion of the earnings depend on commissions. Moreover, the more successful performers in such jobs generally take higher risks. It has been found, for example, that the risk-taking individual is more likely to pursue one or two large accounts instead of a large number of small accounts.

Entrepreneurship

According to the Small Business Administration, about 75 percent of new business ventures fail within 5 years. Given the financial risks involved, one would naturally expect people who are successful entrepreneurs to be high risk takers. Surprisingly, however, research points to only a moderate propensity for taking risks among entrepreneurs. In other words, risk taking is not the characteristic that differentiates entrepreneurs from nonentrepreneurs. Rather, it seems to be the need for independence—to be one's own boss—and a need to achieve. This pattern of motivation may explain the preference for moderate levels of risk over low and high levels of risk. People with a strong need to achieve prefer moderate levels of risk where skill can have a marked influence on the outcome. In low-risk situations, everyone can achieve the desired outcome, whereas in high-risk situations, it becomes more a matter of luck than skill.

COMMUNICATING PROBABILITY STATEMENTS VERBALLY

Poor communication between client and financial adviser is responsible for many of the allegations of investment unsuitability filed against financial services professionals. Typically, the client claims that the risks of the investment were not conveyed adequately. This brings us to the issue of communicating probabilities of success and failure to one's clients.

Research indicates that people prefer to obtain information about the probability of an event in numerical form, yet are generally more comfortable describing the probability of an event to others in words rather than in numbers. Perhaps it is because in everyday situations it is not always possible to assign an exact probability to outcomes. But what does it mean to clients if their financial planner tells them that a certain investment will *probably* double their money in 6 years, while another investment offers only a *low chance* of producing this rate of appreciation?

It has been suggested that at least 282 words and phrases can be used to report the likelihood of something happening. A number of researchers have attempted to quantify these expressions by asking people questions like: "If you were told that an outcome was ______ [the blank being filled in by a word or phrase], what percentage would best represent the probability of that outcome occurring?" Table 5-3 shows the percentages that were assigned to the 18 most commonly used expressions. The intent is to provide the financial planner with a basis for determining how these terms would be understood by clients if he or she were to use them in communicating estimates of the probabilities of various investment opportunities. For example, on average, "almost impossible" is understood as having a 2 percent (2 in 100) chance of occurring. The phrases "medium chance" and "even chance," in turn, are understood to represent about a 50 percent chance of occurring.

TABLE 5-3
Relationships between Numerical Probability and Verbal Probability Statements among Mutual Fund Shareholders

Numerical	Verbal
2%	Almost impossible
5	Very improbable
10	Very unlikely; very low chance
15	Improbable; unlikely
20	Low chance
40	Possible
50	Medium chance; even chance
70	Probable; likely
80	Very possible; very probable; high chance
85	Very likely
90	Very high chance; almost certain

Source of data: Reagan, Mosteller, and Youtz (1989).

Research conducted in 1993 by the Investment Company Institute dealt with how much risk certain investment terms connoted for mutual fund shareholders.

FIGURE 5-2
Degree of Risk Connoted by Selected Investment Terms

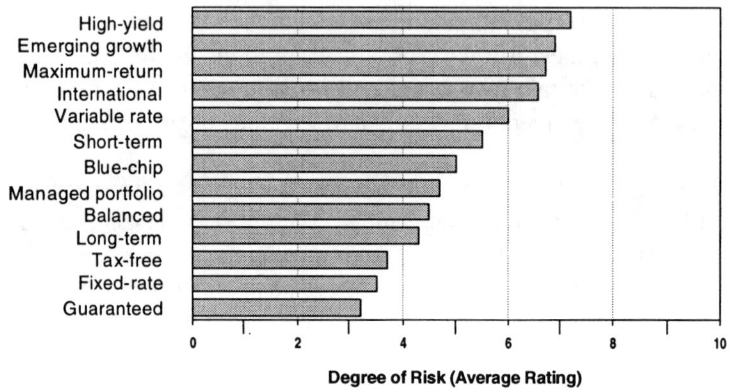

Source of data: Investment Company Institute (1993).

Participants in this study were asked to indicate, on a scale of 0 (no risk) to 10 (great risk), how much risk they associated with an investment described by the particular term. The mean ratings for the terms can be found in figure 5-2. These ratings ranged from 7.2 to 3.2, with "high yield" conveying the greatest risk and "guaranteed investment" connoting the lowest risk. Other terms suggesting high risk were "emerging growth" (6.9), "maximum return" (6.7), and "international" (6.6). Other terms suggesting low risk were "fixed rate" (3.5) and "tax free" (3.7).

It was reported that low-, moderate-, and high-risk-taking shareholders did not vary much in their assessment, other than for the term "maximum return" and "international." "Maximum return" implied *less* risk for low-risk-tolerant investors than for moderate or high-risk-tolerant investors, whereas "international" connoted more risk for the low-risk-tolerant investors relative to the other two groups.

When communicating with clients, planners need to be aware of differences in linguistic style between men and women. In the *Harvard Business Review* (September-October 1995), Deborah Tannen reports the finding that women tend to downplay their certainty about things whereas men tend to minimize their doubts.

ASSESSMENT OF THE CLIENT'S RISK TOLERANCE

Purpose of Assessment

So far, some of the factors that exert an influence of one sort or another on a person's willingness to undertake a risky course of action have been examined. Now comes the issue of assessment. How does one measure a client's *typical* level of risk tolerance? By typical, we mean the level at which the aforementioned distortions do not cause the client to make decisions that are either riskier or safer than would generally be characteristic of that individual.

One way would be to observe the client repeatedly over an extended time period in situations that are likely to reveal his or her characteristic risk-tolerance level. Of course, this approach is not really feasible since it would be unreasonably time-consuming for the financial planner and would constitute an unwarranted intrusion for the client. Some observations may even be misleading since the individual may not even be aware of the risks he or she is incurring. Consequently there is a need to estimate the client's risk tolerance within a relatively short time period.

The sections that follow review some of the available options for estimating the client's risk tolerance within a relatively short time period. All of these options call for sensitivity to appropriate cues and an ability to integrate them into a total impression of the client.

Whatever method is used, one should realize the assessment process; it is meant to help clients *understand* their own level of risk tolerance. Quite frequently, clients are not aware of how risk-tolerant or risk-averse they are. To them risk tolerance is a vague concept that requires both explanation and exploration. The purpose of assessment is not to enable the planner to *impose* his or her perceptions on the client. For example, it is inappropriate to advise the client that the choice is between "eating" (risky investments) and "sleeping" (nonrisky investments). In the end, it is the client who must decide what constitutes an acceptable level of risk. The planner's role is to help the client learn enough about himself or herself to be able to make an informed decision.

Assessment Methods

Many practitioners fail to appreciate the complexity of the task facing them in trying to determine a client's risk tolerance accurately. Considerable time and effort are required to do it correctly. The primary problem is that, frequently, the various techniques do not give the same picture of a particular person's level of risk tolerance. All too often the individual may appear to be a risk taker when assessed with one technique and a risk averter when assessed with another. For example, in one study employing 16 different assessment procedures, the percentage of people who could be classified as risk takers ranged from 0 percent to 94 percent, depending on the technique used. Practically, this means that more than one approach should be employed for an accurate assessment of a client's risk-taking propensity.

Contrasts between Qualitative and Quantitative Assessment

The assessment process can be either *qualitative* or *quantitative* in its orientation. When one relies on a qualitative approach, one typically collects the necessary information primarily through conversations with the client, without assigning numbers to the information gathered. The information is collected in an unstructured format and is evaluated on an intuitive or impressionistic basis, based on the planner's training and experience. A quantitative approach, in contrast, relies on the use of a structured format—questionnaires, for example—that allows one to translate observations into some type of numerical score. These scores are then used to interpret the client's risk-taking propensities.

Most planners do not rely on one approach to the exclusion of the other. For example, few quantitatively oriented planners are willing to surrender their professional judgment to the results of a questionnaire. It is really a matter of degree of how qualitative or quantitative one planner is compared to another. One can use a primarily qualitative approach and still not forfeit some of the advantages of quantifiable information. Questionnaires and other quantitative devices can be valuable tools in the hands of any skilled financial planner.

Often a questionnaire, or similar device, used to assess a client's risk tolerance can facilitate the beginning of a dialogue between the planner and the client. The content of the questionnaire highlights issues that the client may not have thought about. Another advantage is that a quantitative approach allows one to standardize the assessment process.

A number of limitations are inherent in a strictly qualitative approach—one in which the financial planner relies solely on the verbal comments made by a client and interprets their significance on an intuitive basis. One study found that financial planners (like all people) are overconfident about their ability to make intuitive judgments. The planners, presented with various statements that clients could make, were asked to evaluate the level of risk tolerance these statements implied on a 10-point scale, where 1 indicated low risk tolerance and 10 indicated high risk tolerance.

It is understandable that an ambiguous statement such as "Taking calculated risks is different from being rash" would receive ratings as low as 4 and as high as 8. (The average was 6.7.) However, even on more straightforward statements there was also a lack of consensus. The statement "I like to speculate on my investments," if made by a client, was interpreted, on average, as an 8.5. However, again there was diversity of opinion about its meaning. Some financial planners saw the statement as meriting only a rating of 5 whereas others assigned it a rating of 10. "Rubber yardsticks" of this type can be minimized in a quantitative-assessment approach.

When using a qualitative orientation to the assessment of risk tolerance, the planner should be familiar with good interviewing skills. There are standards for quantitative assessment procedures as well, most of which are beyond the scope of this chapter. Suffice it to say that a quantitative measurement device, such as a test or even a questionnaire, needs to be constructed very carefully. The questions should be written in such a way that they do not lead or bias the individual to answer them in a certain way. Moreover, evidence must be provided to demonstrate that the test or questionnaire does, in fact, assess the attributes it is meant to measure and that it measures them accurately on a consistent basis.

Provided that they are accurate, the best quantitative measurement devices are ones that allow the planner to compare the standing of a particular individual to a representative group. A measurement device of this sort is said to have "norms." Using such norms, one can compare the individual to the public at large, or to some subgroup. For instance, using a normed measure of risk tolerance, it is possible to see whether the client is more or less risk tolerant than people in general or to compare the client to other people of the same age and sex.

Unfortunately, most of the tests, inventories, scales, checklists, and questionnaires employed today by financial planners to measure their clients' risk tolerance have not been developed under such strict standards. A majority were created for in-house use by individual planners, brokerage houses, or mutual funds. Many of the developers of these assessment devices are probably unaware of such requirements. There is a critical need for well-constructed questionnaires that provide some evidence to support their use as measures of risk tolerance.

Most of the available assessment devices suffer from the same problems. In some, the wrong questions are asked, or they are presented in an incorrect format. Many devices are too short, thereby failing to contain an adequate representation of questions. It has been demonstrated repeatedly that answers to similar questions about risk tolerance may not concur. In order to avoid being misled by the answer to any one question, the financial planner needs to ask a *series* of questions. Some answers may underestimate the client's true level of risk tolerance, whereas others may overestimate the true level of this attribute. Other things being equal, the more questions that are used to measure a psychological characteristic, the more precise are the results.

Some questionnaires do not separate the different contexts of risk taking, so that a high score on such a questionnaire is probably better at identifying tendencies toward thrill seeking rather than high risk tolerance for investment matters. For all these reasons, one must exercise caution in using questionnaires. It is strongly recommended that the financial planner examine the content of the questionnaire. A "questionnaire" or "checklist" or "inventory" purporting to assess risk tolerance may, in fact, be measuring some other attribute.

Many techniques can be used to assess a client's risk tolerance. Some lend themselves more to a qualitative approach, whereas others call for a more quantitative approach. In the section that follows, a brief overview of the most common approaches is provided. In essence, such techniques consist of looking at the client's

- investment objectives
- preferences for various investment vehicles
- real-life choices involving risk
- attitudes toward risk
- preferences for different probabilities and payoff levels

Examination of Client Investment Objectives

Frequently clients are asked to identify their financial objectives. For example, the client may be asked to indicate how important the following are to him or her: liquidity, safety of principal, appreciation, protection from inflation, current income, and tax reduction. The client's level of risk tolerance is inferred from the answers. If the client's primary concerns are safety of principal and/or liquidity, then risk aversion is assumed. If, however, the main objectives are protection from inflation or tax relief, then the inference is that the client is risk tolerant.

Objectives, however, must not be confused with risk tolerance. There are many individuals who desire tax relief yet are quite risk-averse. One's stated objectives may, in fact, be quite incompatible with one's level of risk tolerance. In many cases the client may be unaware of this incongruity. In a sense, the client's level of risk tolerance should be the basis for evaluating how reasonable the client's objectives are. However, using objectives for the purpose of gauging risk tolerance, without any further attempts to assess actual risk tolerance, is a mistake. To do so is to have "the tail wag the dog."

Preferences for Various Investment Products

This is the most direct approach to measuring a client's risk tolerance. With this method, the client indicates the products that he or she prefers as investments. Several variations of this procedure exist. In its simplest form, the client is presented with the available alternatives and is then asked how he or she wishes to distribute available assets among these options. The products are usually presented in some rank order, ranging from very safe investments to very risky investments. Either actual (real) or imaginary funds can be used. For the latter variation of this task, the client is asked something like, "What would you do if you got a windfall?" Naturally people tend to be more daring with imaginary money than with actual money. A third variation of this approach is to ask the client to rank the products from most preferred to least preferred or to assign to each product some rating that represents the client's level of preference (for example, low, medium, or high).

The accuracy of this procedure (in all its variants) rests on the client's knowledge of the actual risk-return potential of the various investments. Preferably these differences are explained and specified to the client, since many clients may lack even basic knowledge. One should never assume that clients are highly knowledgeable about financial matters. Surveys of the general public, including the wealthy, reveal a startling level of financial ignorance.

FOCUS ON ETHICS
When Risk Attitude and Risk Capacity Collide

Consider the case of client John Doe who views himself to be highly risk tolerant in monetary matters. His existing portfolio consists of common stock investments in small, highly risky companies. A third-party evaluation of the client's risk tolerance confirms that he is among the top 5 percent in terms of his attitude toward risk. The client asks about specific, aggressive stocks. Should the planner feel free to recommend or sell high-risk investments to this client?

Now consider some additional information. The client is a 30-year-old widower with three small children. He is an aeronautical engineer employed by a defense contractor that relies entirely on the government for revenues. His total savings including his investment portfolio are less than one month's earnings, and he is not vested in his pension plan. He has no life or disability insurance. Both his father and grandfather died of heart attacks in their mid-forties.

Ask the question again: Should the planner feel free to recommend or sell high-risk investments to this client?

Clearly this client has an attitude toward risk tolerance that is at odds with his economic and family situation. Selling the client what he wants will generate a commission, but is it ethical?

Real-Life Choices Involving Risks

As with investment products, a person's past performance is no guarantee of future performance. But it has been observed that the best predictor of future behavior is typically past behavior. This notion underlies the real-life choices approach to risk-tolerance assessment. That is, factual information about the client's life is gathered and evaluated. The following lifestyle characteristics can be used to gauge a client's disposition toward monetary risk.

- *composition of present investment portfolio.* How risky is it? What percentage of total assets are in passbook savings accounts, Treasury notes, mutual funds, stocks, options and commodities, and so on? If stocks are owned, does the person use short selling and margin buying? If an annuity is owned, is it of the fixed or variable type? How satisfied or dissatisfied is the client with this type of portfolio? If changes were made to a previous portfolio, were these changes in a more conservative or more aggressive direction?

- *debt ratio.* The ratio of the client's liabilities to his or her gross assets has been used as a measure of risk tolerance. It has been suggested by some that a debt ratio over 23 percent reflects risk taking, under 8 percent is characteristic of risk aversion, and 8 percent to 23 percent suggests a risk-neutral attitude.
- *ratio of life insurance to annual salary.* The assumption is that the larger the resulting ratio, the higher the client's level of risk aversion.
- *the size of deductibles on property-liability coverage.* It has been observed that as the amount of wealth allocated to risky securities rises, so does the size of the deductible on the client's insurance coverages. Risk-tolerant individuals elect larger deductibles.
- *percentage of net wealth used for recreational gambling.* The larger the ratio is, the more risk seeking the individual is considered.
- *job tenure.* The willingness to make a voluntary job change is considered an indicator of a willingness to take financial risks. Therefore clients can be asked how many job changes they have made during the last 15 years. Over three changes is considered by some as a sign of a risk-taking attitude. Quitting a job before one has found a replacement is particularly significant. Job changes at middle age may also be especially noteworthy.
- *variations in income.* Risk-taking individuals may show greater variations in their annual income from year to year, and not always in an upward direction. The financial adviser should also look at the duration of unemployment if the client was ever unemployed. Did the individual take the first job offer he or she received during this period of unemployment or did he or she wait until a job to his or her liking was found? What was the salary of the new job the client took after the period of unemployment? If it was lower than that of the previous job, it could indicate risk aversion.
- *type of mortgage.* A willingness to undertake a variable rather than a fixed mortgage could be a sign of monetary risk taking. If the client has chosen a fixed mortgage, did he or she lock in on a guaranteed rate before settlement? Locking in is a sign of risk aversion.

Attitudes toward Risk

A method frequently used to obtain information about a client's degree of risk tolerance involves eliciting his or her attitude toward risk. Attitudes toward risk can be elicited by using either a quantitative or a qualitative approach. Questions can take on many different forms. First, clients can be asked *global* questions such as whether they view themselves as risk averters or risk takers. For example, "On a 10-point scale, where 1 is an ultimate risk averter and 10 is an ultimate risk taker, where would you place yourself?"

Second, clients can be asked about their *specific* reactions to risk. For example, does the client experience the following:

- can't sleep after making a risky investment
- has persisting second thoughts about the investment
- views risk as an opportunity rather than a danger
- gets more pleasure from making $3,000 on a risky investment than $3,000 on a safe investment
- is afraid of losing what he or she has
- is willing to borrow money to make a good investment
- believes that it is impossible to get ahead without taking chances
- agrees with the saying "Better safe than sorry"

Earlier it was noted that many questions must be asked in order to assess risk tolerance accurately. This is especially true in the case of the attitude approach to measurement. It has been found that the reason why many attitudes, as measured through questionnaires or other scales of that type, fail to predict actual behavior is because not enough questions were asked. When the number of questions was increased, there was a much better correspondence between attitude and behavior.

A major problem with the attitude approach to risk-tolerance assessment is that people want to present themselves in the best possible light to others. Any characteristic that is valued is likely to be overstated. In America it is considered more desirable to be risk-taking than risk-averse. Clients are therefore likely to exaggerate their willingness to take risks. Consequently discrepancies between verbally expressed attitudes and behavior are frequent, even if numerous questions are asked. When using this approach, one needs to ascertain how well the expressed attitudes agree with other evidence, such as factual information about the person's risk-taking proclivities.

Probability and Payoff Preferences

A variety of assessment techniques fall under this classification. Three types will be considered:

- preferences for certain versus probable gambles
- minimum required probability of success
- minimum required return

All of these methods rely on a manipulation of at least one of the four elements found in any gamble: probability of loss, probability of gain, amount to be lost, and amount to be gained. Consequently the techniques falling under this classification are best used in a quantitative approach to assessment.

Anyone using the probability and payoff-preferences approach to measuring a client's risk tolerance needs to be aware of how framing a question affects the answer, lest he or she be misled by the results. Framing refers to the finding that the same objective facts can be described either in terms of the probability of gaining or the probability of losing. Although it may not seem that—to use an analogy—describing a bottle as half empty or half full should have any marked consequences on one's choices in a risky situation, the evidence shows otherwise. To illustrate, consider research in which one group of people is informed that there is a 50 percent chance of success in a particular venture. Another group is told that this same venture has a 50 percent chance of failure. Logically, the same proportion of people in each group should be willing to take this risk. Yet this was not the case. When the risk was described (framed) in terms of the probability of success, more people were willing to take it than when this same risk was described in terms of the chances of failure. Other related research has shown that describing ground meat in terms of how lean versus how fat the product was made a big difference. To shoppers, ground meat described as 90 percent lean was seen as a better buy than the same ground meat described as 10 percent fat.

Another consideration is the "unpacking effect." This principle refers to the finding that the perceived likelihood of an event is influenced by how specifically it is described. The more specific the description becomes, the more likely it is judged to be. For example, Stanford University undergraduate students were asked to estimate the frequency of different causes of death. When asked to estimate the probability of death from a natural cause, on average, the answer was 58 percent. However, when they were requested to estimate the probability of death from a list of three possible natural causes of death—cancer, heart disease, and other natural causes—the probabilities assigned to these respective events were 22 percent, 18 percent, and 33 percent. Together, they sum up to 73 percent (22% + 18% + 33%), which is higher than the first estimate, 58 percent. In other words, the sum of the components was greater than the whole. This type of effect has been observed among both novices and experts, and in different professions, including professional options traders estimating the closing price of Microsoft stock.

Preferences for Certain versus Probable Gambles. Gambles are abstract representations of real-life situations. One very common technique is to present the client with two alternatives. One choice is a certain win, whereas the other choice offers only some probability of winning. A series of such pairs of gambles is presented. For example, the person is asked to indicate whether he or she would choose

A: a sure gain of $1,000
B: a 50 percent chance of gaining $2,000

Persons who are risk-averse chose options similar to A, whereas risk-taking individuals chose options similar to B.

On some questionnaires, these choices are woven around a story line. For example, an item of this type may be "Imagine that you are a winning contestant on a game show. Which of the following actions would you take?"

> A: Stop playing with a certain prize of $8,000 in cash.
> B: Go another round with a 50 percent chance of winning $16,000 and a 50 percent chance of winning nothing.

Minimum Probability of Success Required before Undertaking a Risky Action. A good example of a procedure relying on this approach is the "choice dilemma" questionnaire (Kogan and Wallach, 1964), often used to study the risky shift phenomenon discussed earlier. This questionnaire presents 12 situations. For each situation, two alternatives are described. One choice is risky and the other is safe. In every case, the risky course of action offers a larger potential payoff. Five odds are given for the chance of success for the risky course of action, namely 1 in 10, 3 in 10, 5 in 10, 7 in 10, and 9 in 10. The person answering the questionnaire is asked to select the odds that would make it worthwhile to take the risky alternative instead of the safe one. The situations involve a broad range of dilemmas, such as job change, heart operation, football game, marriage decision, and so on. One such question involves a business investment decision:

> Mr. E is president of a light metals corporation in the United States. The corporation is quite prosperous and has strongly considered the possibilities of business expansion by building an additional plant in a new location. The choice is between building another plant in the U.S., where there would be a moderate return on the initial investment, or building a plant in a foreign country. Lower labor costs and easy access to raw materials in that country would mean a much higher return on the initial investment. On the other hand, there is a history of political instability and revolution in the foreign country under consideration. In fact, the leader of a small minority party is committed to nationalizing, that is, taking over all foreign investments.

Imagine that you are advising Mr. E. Listed below are several probabilities or odds of continued political stability in the foreign country under consideration.

Please check the lowest probability that you would consider acceptable for Mr. E's corporation to build a plant in that country.

- The chances are 1 in 10 that the country will remain politically stable.
- The chances are 3 in 10 that the country will remain politically stable.

- The chances are 5 in 10 that the country will remain politically stable.
- The chances are 7 in 10 that the country will remain politically stable.
- The chances are 9 in 10 that the country will remain politically stable.
- Place a check here if you think Mr. E's corporation should not build a plant in the foreign country, no matter what the probabilities.

The higher the odds of success the person requires, the greater the level of risk aversion. The choice dilemma is a research instrument with well-known measurement properties. However, its appropriateness for assessing monetary risk taking is questionable because this questionnaire looks at risk taking in all contexts (for example, it looks at risk taking as if it was a unitary—which it is not, as noted in the earlier discussion of the subject). Only a few of the 12 situations are concerned with financial risk taking. Furthermore, some of the items are quite dated. Nonetheless, some researchers have found it to be useful in differentiating between investors who are risk-taking from those who are risk-averse.

Minimum Return Required before Undertaking a Risky Action. An example of a question that requires an answer in terms of amount to be gained rather than in terms of probability (as was the case in the choice dilemma task) is: "You are faced with an investment opportunity in which you stand a 50 percent chance of losing half of your personal net wealth and a 50 percent chance of making a certain amount of money. How much of a return would you require in order to take this risk?" (The answers are evaluated in relation to the person's net wealth.)

Figure 5-3 provides a sample question for each of the risk tolerance estimation approaches discussed above. Appendix 5A presents The American College's Survey of Financial Risk Tolerance.

Guidelines on Assessment

The following guidelines are based on the preceding discussion of assessment, taking into consideration the information presented about risk and situational influences on risk-taking propensity:

- Focus on monetary risk taking.
- Assume the client is risk-averse, unless evidence to the contrary can be obtained.
- Remember that people are more likely to overstate than understate their risk-taking propensity.
- Keep in mind that even risk-averse individuals may be risk-seeking in situations where the choices are between losses. People are reluctant to cut their losses.

FIGURE 5-3
Sample Questions for Estimating Risk Tolerance

1. Examination of Client Investment Objectives
   Rank the following investment objectives from 1 to 6, with 1 being the most important.

   ___liquidity
   ___safety of principal
   ___protection from inflation
   ___growth
   ___current income
   ___reduced taxation

2. Preferences for Various Investment Products
   If you received a large windfall, how would you allocate it among the following (percentages must sum to 100)?

   ___% Certificates of deposit
   ___% U.S. government securities
   ___% Corporate bonds and bond mutual funds
   ___% Stock and stock mutual funds
   ___% Options
   ___% Futures contracts
   100%

3. Real-Life Choices Involving Risks
   How often have you used "short selling" or "margin buying" in stock market investments?

   ___Never ___Seldom ___Frequently ___Very Frequently

4. Attitudes toward Risk
   Do you experience anxiety or thrill when awaiting the outcome of an important investment decision?

   ___Always anxiety ___Most frequently anxiety ___Neither anxiety nor thrill
   ___Most frequently thrill ___Always thrill

5. Probability/Payoff Preferences: Certain versus Probable Gambles
   In some instances you are faced with a choice between (a) earning a certain amount of money for sure and (b) taking a risk and earning either a larger amount of money or nothing at all.
   For example, consider an investment choice between a certain gain of $50 and an 80 percent chance of earning $100. If you take the certain choice, you will get $50 for sure (no more, no less). On the other hand, if you take the 80 percent probability of earning $100, you also stand a 20 percent chance of earning nothing at all.
   For the choices shown below please indicate whether you would take the sure gain or some probability of earning twice as much (or nothing at all). Be sure to select one option for *each* pair, A through F.

Pair A: 1 A certain gain of $10,000
2 80 percent probability of gaining $20,000 (with a corresponding 20 percent chance of earning nothing)

Pair B: 1 A certain gain of $10,000
2 50 percent probability of gaining $20,000 (with a corresponding 50 percent chance of earning nothing)

Pair C: 1 A certain gain of $30,000
2 80 percent probability of gaining $60,000 (with a corresponding 20 percent chance of earning nothing)

Pair D: 1 A certain gain of $30,000
2. 50 percent probability of gaining $60,000 (with a corresponding 50 percent chance of earning nothing)

Pair E: 1 A certain gain of $50,000
2. 80 percent probability of gaining $100,000 (with a corresponding 50 percent chance of earning nothing)

Pair F: 1 A certain gain of $50,000
2 50 percent probability of gaining $100,000 (with a corresponding 50 percent chance of earning nothing)

FIGURE 5-3 (continued)
Sample Questions for Estimating Risk Tolerance

6. Probability/Payoff Preferences: Required Probability of Success

Assume you a contestant on a TV game show. After winning a prize that's equivalent to one year's salary, you are offered the option of walking away with this prize money or taking a chance on either doubling it or losing it all. What are the odds of success that you would require before agreeing to accept this gamble?

1 Would not take the bet no matter what the odds
2 9 in 10
3 8 in 10
4 7 in 10
5 6 in 10
6 5 in 10
7 4 in 10
8 3 in 10
9 2 in 10
10 1 in 10

7. Probability/Payoff Preferences: Minimum Required Return

You are faced with an investment opportunity in which you have a 50 percent chance of losing half of your personal net worth and a 50 percent chance of making a certain amount of money. What percentage expected return would you require in order to take this risk? ____%

- Start your assessment by looking at the client's demographic characteristics and personality makeup. However, remember you are dealing with an individual rather than a group. Just because a person belongs to a group that is more risk-tolerant or risk-averse than average, it does not mean that the client facing you today will necessarily follow the group pattern. The differences in risk tolerance between demographic groups are usually small, so there will be many people who do not fit the stereotype. Do not judge the individual merely by the group to which he or she belongs. Group differences simply provide you with some hunches that can be explored through the assessment process; you still need to assess the individual client.
- Look for quantitative-assessment devices that are accurate and allow you to compare the client's performance to a norm group.
- Consider the results from a questionnaire or other measurement device as only an approximation of the client's actual risk tolerance. No assessment procedure is perfect; they are all susceptible to some error.
- Diversify your methods of assessment. This will allow you to draw on the strengths of the various techniques.

- Use the information you collect to start a dialogue with the client about risk tolerance. Be sure to remember that assessing the client's risk tolerance is a cooperative venture. When an agreement is reached, ask the client to provide a written confirmation of the results of this assessment.
- Realize that biases may be operating on the client's risk perceptions (for example, familiarity, availability, and so on), which may be inflating or deflating the client's true level of risk tolerance.
- Remember that a client's propensity for risk taking does not necessarily remain constant throughout his or her lifetime. As noted throughout this chapter, changes in personal circumstances such as age, wealth, and number of dependents can produce shifts. Likewise, world events can either increase or decrease a person's level of risk tolerance. Therefore it is prudent to periodically reassess the client's risk tolerance.

EPILOGUE

One needs to recognize that knowledge about risk tolerance is still evolving. The amount of information that is available is substantial, even though many unanswered questions remain.

Even the existing body of knowledge is useless if it is not actually applied by financial planners in their dealings with clients. Loren Dunton, one of the early leaders in the development of the financial planning profession, wrote that he was frequently asked by the media to describe the difference between the approach used by financial planners and that used by other financial services practitioners. In his reply, Dunton made the following comment about financial planners: "Most of them, and all the good ones, will first find out the risk tolerance of the individual or couple they might be going to counsel" (Dunton, p. 71).

REFERENCES

Arrow, K.J. "Risk Perception in Psychology and Economics." *Economic Inquiry*, 1982, vol. 20, pp. 1–9.

Baker, M.W., and E. Kramer. *Success in America: The CIGNA Study of the Upper-Affluent.* Louis Harris and Assoc., Inc., 1987.

Barnewall, M.M. "Examining the Psychological Traits of Passive and Active Affluent Investors." *Journal of Financial Planning,* October 1988, vol. 1, no. 2, pp. 70–74.

Bellante, D., and A.N. Link. "Are Public Sector Workers More Risk Averse Than Private Sector Workers?" *Industrial and Labor Relations Review,* 1981, vol. 34, pp. 408–412.

Bjorkman, M. "Decision Making, Risk Taking and Psychological Time: Review of Empirical Findings and Psychological Theory." *Scandinavian Journal of Psychology,* 1984, vol. 25, pp. 31–49.

Blayney, E. "IAFP Conference for Advanced Planners Roundup." *Investment Advisor,* June 1995, pp. 30–37.

Blum, S.H. "Investment Preferences and the Desire for Security: A Comparison of Men and Women." *American Journal of Psychology,* 1976, vol. 94, pp. 87–91.

Bonieki, G. "What Are the Limits to Man's Time and Space Perspectives: Toward a Definition of a Realistic Planning Horizon." *Technological Forecasting and Social Change,* 1980, vol. 17, pp. 161–175.

Brockhaus, R.H., Sr. "Risk-Taking Propensity of Entrepreneurs." *Academy of Management Journal,* 1980, vol. 23, pp. 509–520.

Brown, M.S. "Communicating Information about Workplace Hazards: Effects on Worker Attitudes toward Risks." *Social and Cultural Construction of Risk,* edited by B.B. Johnson and V.T. Covello. Norwell, Mass.: Kluver Academic Publishers, 1987.

Cable, D.M., and T.A. Judge. "Pay Preferences and Job Search Decisions: A Person-Organization Fit Perspective." *Personnel Psychology,* 1994, vol. 47, pp. 317–348.

Cohn, R.A., W.G. Lewellen, R.C. Lease, and G.G. Schlarbaum. "Individual Investor Risk Aversion and Investment Portfolio Composition." *Journal of Finance,* 1975, vol. 30, pp. 605–620.

Crum, R.L., D.J. Laughhunn, and J.W. Payne. "Risk-Seeking Behavior and Its Implications for Financial Models." *Financial Management,* winter 1981, pp. 20–27.

DeBondt, W.M.F., and R. Thaler. "Does the Stock Market Overreact?" *The Journal of Finance,* 1985, vol. 40, pp. 793–808.

Deets, M.K., and G.C. Hoyt. "Variance Preferences and Variance Shifts in Group Investment Decisions." *Organizational Behavior and Human Performance,* 1970, vol. 5, pp. 378–386.

Dickson, G.C.A. "A Comparison of Attitudes towards Risk among Business Managers." *Journal of Occupational Psychology,* 1981, vol. 54, pp. 157–164.

Dowling, G.R. "Perceived Risk: The Concept and Its Measurement." *Psychology and Marketing,* 1986, vol. 3, pp. 193–210.

Dunton, L. *About Your Future.* San Diego: The National Center for Financial Education, 1988.

Erev, I., and B.L. Cohen, "Verbal versus Numerical Probabilities: Efficiency, Biases, and the Preference Paradox." *Organizational Behavior and Human Decision Processing,* 1990, vol. 45, pp. 1–18.

Farrelly, G. "A Behavioral Science Approach to Financial Research." *Financial Management,* 1980, vol. 9, no. 3, pp. 15–22.

Feinberg, R.M. "Risk Aversion, Risk, and the Duration of Unemployment." Review of Economics & Statistics, 1977, vol. 59, pp. 264–271.

Fischoff, B., and R. Beyth. "I Knew It Would Happen—Remembered Probabilities of Once-Future Things." *Organizational Behavior and Human Performance,* 1975, vol. 13, pp. 1–16.

Gooding, A.E. "Quantification of Investors' Perceptions of Common Stocks: Risk and Return Dimensions." *The Journal of Finance,* 1975, vol. 30, pp. 1301–1316.

Grey, R.J., and C.E. Gordon. "Risk-Taking Managers: Who Gets the Top Jobs?" *Management Review,* 1978, vol. 67, pp. 8–13.

Grossberg, S., and W.E. Gutowski. "Neural Dynamics of Decision Making under Risk: Affective Balance and Cognitive-Emotional Interactions." *Psychological Review,* 1987, vol. 94, pp. 300–318.

Harlow, W.V., and K.C. Brown. "Understanding and Assessing Financial Risk Tolerance: A Biological Perspective." *Financial Analysts Journal,* Nov./Dec. 1992, pp. 51–62.

Harris, L., and Associates. *Public Attitudes toward Risk.* Study No. 837008, conducted for the Insurance Information Institute, 1983.

Heflin, T.L., M.L. Power, and W.L. Dellva. "Choice Shift: Implications for Insurance Application." *The Journal of Insurance: Issues and Practices,* 1988, vol. 2, pp. 68–82.

Hensley, W.E. "Probability, Personality, Age and Risk Taking." *Journal of Psychology,* 1977, vol. 95, pp. 139–145.

Herrnstein, R.J. "Rational Choice Theory: Necessary but Not Sufficient." *American Psychologist,* 1990, vol. 45, pp. 356–367.

Hisrich, R.D. "Entrepreneurship/Intrapreneurship." *American Psychologist,* 1990, vol. 45, no. 2, pp. 209–222.

Hogarth, R. *Judgment and Choice: The Psychology of Decisions.* New York: John Wiley & Sons, 1987.

Hunter, J.E., and T.D. Coggin. "Analyst Judgment: The Efficient Market Hypothesis versus a Psychological Theory of Human Judgment." *Organizational Behavior and Human Decision Processes,* 1988, vol. 42, pp. 284–302.

Investment Company Institute. "Piecing Together Shareholder Perceptions of Investment Risk," Spring 1993.

Isen, A.M., and R. Patrick. "The Effect of Positive Feelings on Risk Taking: When the Chips Are Down." *Organizational Behavior and Human Performance,* 1983, vol. 31, pp. 194–202.

Isen, A.M., T.E. Nygren, and F. G. Ashby. "Influence of Positive Affect on the Subjective Utility of Gains and Losses: It Is Just Not Worth the Risk." *Journal of Personality and Social Psychology,* 1988, vol. 55, pp. 710–717.

Jackson, D.N., L. Hourany, and N.J. Vidmar. "A Four-Dimensional Interpretation of Risk Taking." *Journal of Personality,* 1972, vol. 40, no. 3, pp. 483–501.

Jamison, K.S. "Upscale Consumers in a Changing Marketplace." *Managers Magazine,* August 1988, pp. 20–24.

Johnson, E.J., and A. Tversky. "Affect, Generalization, and the Perception of Risk." *Journal of Personality and Social Psychology,* 1983, vol. 45, pp. 20–31.

Jones, C.P., and J.W. Wilson. "An Analysis of the January Effect in Stocks and Interest Rates under Varying Monetary Regimes." *The Journal of Finance,* 1989, vol. 12, pp. 341–354.

Kahle, L.R., and P. Kennedy. "Using the List of Values (LOV) to Understand Consumers." *The Journal of Consumer Marketing,* 1989, vol. 6, no. 3, pp. 5–12.

Kahneman, D., and A. Tversky. "Choices, Values and Frames." *American Psychologist,* 1984, vol. 39, pp. 341–350.

Kahneman, Daniel, and Mark W. Riepe. "Aspects of Investor Psychology." *The Journal of Portfolio Management,* Summer 1998, pp. 52–65.

Kogan, N., and M. Wallach. *Risk Taking: A Study in Cognition and Personality.* New York: Holt, Rinehart and Winston, 1964.

Levin, I.P., R.D. Johnson, C.P. Russo, and P. J. Deldin. "Framing Effects in Judgment Tasks with Varying Amounts of Information." *Organizational Behavior and Human Decision Processes,* 1985, vol. 36, pp. 362–377.

Levin, I.P., M.A. Snyder, and D.P. Chapman. "The Interaction of Experimental and Situational Factors and Gender in a Simulated Risky Decision-Making Task." *The Journal of Psychology,* 1988, vol. 122, pp. 173–181.

Ludwig, L.D. "Elation-Depression and Skill as Determinants of Desire and Excitement." *Journal of Personality,* 1975, vol. 43, pp. 1–22.

Lupfer, M. "The Effects of Risk-Taking Tendencies and Incentive Conditions on the Performance of Investment Groups." *Journal of Social Psychology,* 1970, vol. 82, pp. 135–136.

MacCrimmon, K.R., D.A. Wehrung, and W.T. Stanbury. *Taking Risks: The Management of Uncertainty*. New York: Free Press, 1986.

MacDonald, J.G., and R.E. Stehle. "How Do Institutional Investors Perceive Risk?" *Journal of Portfolio Management,* 1975, vol. 2, no. 1, pp. 11–16.

Mann, L., and C. Ball. "The Relationship between Search Strategy and Risking Choice." *Australian Journal of Psychology,* 1994, vol. 46, pp. 131–136.

March, J.G., and Z. Shapira. "Managerial Perspectives on Risk and Risk Taking." *Management Science,* 1987, vol. 33, pp. 1404–1418.

Markese, J.D., and G.W. Perritt. "Investment Attitudes and Portfolio Decisions of Individual Investors." *The Mid-Atlantic Journal of Business,* 1985, vol. 23, no. 2, pp. 21–31.

Masters, R. "Study Examines Investors' Risk-Taking Propensities." *Journal of Financial Planning,* July 1989, pp. 151–155.

Masters, R., and R. Meier. "Sex Differences and Risk-Taking Propensity of Entrepreneurs." *Journal of Small Business Management,* 1988, vol. 26, no. 1, pp. 31–35.

Milburn, T.W., and R.S. Billings. "Decision-Making Perspectives from Psychology." *American Behavioral Scientist,* 1976, vol. 20, no. 1, pp. 111–126.

Mongrain, S., and L. Standing. "Impairment of Cognition, Risk-Taking, and Self-Perception by Alcohol." *Perceptual and Motor Skills,* 1989, vol. 69, pp. 199–210.

Morgan, R.L., "Risk Preference as a Function of the Number of Wins and the Amount Won." *American Journal of Psychology,* 1983, vol. 96, pp. 469–475.

Morin, R.A., and A.F. Suarez. "Risk Aversion Revisited." *The Journal of Finance,* 1983, vol. 38, pp. 1201–1216.

Okun, M.A. "Adult Age and Cautiousness in Decision: A Review of the Literature." *Human Development,* 1976, vol. 19, pp. 220–233.

Olsen, R.A. "Investment Risk: The Experts' Perspective." *Association for Investment and Research,* 1997, pp. 62–66.

Plax, T.G., and L.B. Rosenfeld. "Correlates of Risky Decision Making." *Journal of Personality Assessment,* 1976, vol. 40, pp. 413–418.

Powers, J.G. "Risky Business: One Size Does Not Fit All." *Best's Review,* December 1997, pp. 84–86.

Rachlin, H., A.W. Logue, J. Gibbon, and M. Frankel. "Cognition and Behavior in Studies of Choice." *Psychological Review,* 1986, vol. 93, pp. 33–45.

Rapoport, A. "Effects of Wealth on Portfolios under Various Investment Conditions." *Acta Psychologica,* 1984, vol. 55, pp. 31–51.

Reagan, R.T., F. Mosteller, and C. Youtz. "Quantitative Meanings of Verbal Probability Expressions." *Journal of Applied Psychology,* 1989, vol. 74, pp. 433–442.

Riley, W.B., and K.V. Chow. "Asset Allocation and Individual Risk Aversion." *Financial Analysts Journal,* Nov./Dec. 1992, pp. 32–37.

Rim, Y. "Personality and Risky Shift in a Passive Audience." *Personality and Individual Differences,* 1982, vol. 3, pp. 465–467.

Roszkowski, M.J., and G.E. Snelbecker. "Effects of 'Framing' on Measures of Risk Tolerance: Financial Planners Are Not Immune." *Journal of Behavioral Economics,* 1990, vol. 19, no. 2, pp. 237–246.

—. "How Much Risk Can a Client Stand?" *Best's Review,* August 1989, pp. 44–46, 118–119.

Schaninger, C.M. "Perceived Risk and Personality." *Journal of Consumer Research,* 1976, vol. 3, pp. 95–100.

Schoemaker, P.J.H. "The Role of Statistical Knowledge in Gambling Decisions: Moment vs. Risk Dimension Approaches." *Organizational Behavior and Human Performance,* 1979, vol. 24, pp. 1–17.

Schooley, D. "Risk Aversion Measures: Company Attitude and Asset Allocation." *Financial Service Review,* vol. 5, no.2, 1996, pp. 87–99.

Schwager, J.D. *Market Wizards—Interviews with Top Traders.* New York: Simon & Schuster, 1989.

Sciortino, J.J., J.H. Huston, and R. W. Spencer. "Risk and Income Distribution." *Journal of Economic Psychology,* 1988, vol. 9, pp. 399–408.

Shefrin, H., and M. Statman. "The Disposition to Sell Winners Too Early and Ride Losers Too Long: Theory and Evidence." *The Journal of Finance,* 1985, vol. 40, pp. 777–792.

Sinn, H. "Psychophysical Laws in Risk Theory." *Journal of Economic Psychology,* 1985, vol. 6, pp. 185–206.

Slovic, P. "Information Processing, Situation Specificity and the Generality of Risk-Taking Behavior." *Journal of Personality and Social Psychology,* 1972, vol. 21, no. 1, pp. 128–134.

Slovic, P., B. Fischoff, S. Lichtenstein, B. Corrigan, and B. Combs. "Preference for Insuring against Probable Small Losses: Insurance Implications." *Journal of Risk and Insurance,* 1977, vol. 44, pp. 237–258.

Snelbecker, G.E., M.J. Roszkowski, and N. E. Cutler. "Investors' Risk Tolerance and Return Aspirations, and Financial Advisors' Interpretations: A Conceptual Model and Exploratory Data." *Journal of Behavioral Economics,* 1990, vol. 19, no. 2, pp. 377–393.

Sutton, N.A. "An Illusion of Control." *Best's Review: Life/Health Insurance Edition,* July 1987, pp. 54–58.

Svenson, O. "Cognitive Strategies in a Complex Judgment Task: Analyses of Concurrent Verbal Reports and Judgments of Cumulated Risk over Different Exposure Times." *Organizational Behavior and Human Decision Processes,* 1985, vol. 36, pp. 1–15.

—. "Time Perception and Long Term Risk." *Canadian Journal of Operations Research and Information Processing,* 1984, vol. 22, pp. 196–214.

Tannen, D. "The Power of Talk: Who Gets Heard and Why." *Harvard Business Review,* September-October 1995, pp. 138–148.

Taylor, R.N. "Psychological Determinants of Bounded Rationality: Implications for Decision-Making Strategies." *Decision Sciences,* 1973, vol. 6, pp. 409–429.

Tharp, V.K. "Winners and Losers: Attitude Makes the Difference." *Futures,* 1984, vol. 12, no. 12, pp. 54–56.

Tversky, A., and C. Heath. "Preferences and Beliefs: Ambiguity and Competence in Choice under Uncertainty." *Journal of Risk and Uncertainty,* 1991, vol. 4, pp. 5–28.

Tversky, A., and D.J. Koehler. "Support Theory: A Nonextensional Representation of Subjective Probability." *Psychological Review,* 1994, vol. 101, pp. 547–567.

Tversky, A., S. Sattath, and P. Slovic. "Contingent Weighting in Judgment and Choice." *Psychological Review,* 1988, vol. 95, pp. 371–384.

Watson, J.S. "Volunteer and Risk-Taking Groups Are More Homogeneous on Measures of Sensation Seeking Than Control Groups." *Perceptual and Motor Skills,* 1985, vol. 62, pp. 471–475.

Weinstein, N.D. "Why It Won't Happen to Me: Perceptions of Risk Factors and Susceptibility." *Health Psychology,* 1984, vol. 3, pp. 431–457.

Wicker, F.W., D. Hamman, A.S. Hagen, J. Lynn. "Studies of Loss Aversion and Perceived Necessity." *Journal of Psychology,* 1995, vol. 129, pp. 75–89.

Wiegman, O., and J.M. Gutteling. "Risk Appraisal and Risk Communication: Some Empirical Data from the Netherlands Reviewed." *Basic and Applied Social Psychology,* 1995, vol. 16, pp. 227–249.

Wiener, J.L., J.W. Gentry, and R.K. Miller. "The Framing of the Insurance Purchase Decision." *Advances in Consumer Research,* 1986, pp. 251–256.

Winger, B.J., and N.K. Mohan. "Investment Risk and Time Diversification." *Journal of Financial Planning,* 1988, vol. 1, no. 1, pp. 45–48.

Zuckerman, M. "Sensation Seeking: A Comparative Approach to a Human Trait." *Behavioral and Brain Sciences,* 1984, vol. 7, pp. 413–471.

Zuckerman, M., M.S. Buchsbaum, and D.L. Murphy. "Sensation Seeking and Its Biological Correlates." *Psychological Bulletin,* 1980, vol. 88, pp. 187–214.

Appendix 5A

Client Name/ID ____________________

FINANCIAL PLANNING

Survey of Financial Risk Tolerance

Survey of Financial Risk Tolerance

Following this introduction you will find a questionnaire titled Survey of Financial Risk Tolerance and an accompanying answer sheet. This form consists of questions based on a number of the approaches to assessing risk tolerance discussed in this chapter.

The Survey of Financial Risk Tolerance relies on direct measures of risk tolerance as well as proxy measures of this characteristic. Please understand, however, that this questionnaire, like all others, is meant to complement rather than serve as a substitute for a more comprehensive assessment (as described in this chapter). Always be sure to compare the impressions you gain using this questionnaire with other more objective evidence. For instance, one section of the questionnaire asks the client to indicate his or her preference for various investment vehicles. You should determine whether the expressed preferences match the client's actual portfolio of past and current investments. Also recognize that the score derived from this questionnaire is a composite number that can be obtained through various combinations of answers. It constitutes an attempt to represent the client's risk tolerance in the form of a single number, which may not be possible under some circumstances.

Remember too that other factors besides the person's characteristic level of risk tolerance can influence the amount of risk he or she may be willing to take. As noted previously, research suggests that people treat money differently depending on how it was acquired. Generally money that was easily earned, especially if acquired through a windfall, is more apt to be exposed to risk than money that was earned through hard labor. Likewise, since investments are likely to vary in their value and returns more sharply in the short run than in the long run, the client's investment horizon is a critical consideration. If a client is able to adopt a long-term horizon, there may be a corresponding greater willingness to take a risk.

The financial adviser therefore needs to determine the suitability of the procedure for the particular client and the client's unique situation. The Survey of Financial Risk Tolerance is intended only as a tool to assist the professional financial adviser in assessing a client's attitudes toward risk taking as part of a comprehensive review of appropriate investment choices. The survey is not intended to substitute for the professional financial adviser's judgment of his or her client's financial ability to sustain a loss and of his or her professional investment goals.

How the Survey of Financial Risk Tolerance Can Be Used

There are three ways to use the Survey of Financial Risk Tolerance, each method varying in the degree of subjectivity involved in analyzing the client's answers. The three methods, from the most subjective to the least subjective, are as follows:

- open-ended questions
- standardized response options without formal scoring
- formal scoring of the answers by The American College

Each of these methods is described below.

Open-ended Questions

It is possible to use the Survey of Financial Risk Tolerance as a list of questions to ask the client during the course of a face-to-face interview, allowing the client to respond in his or her own words. For example, "How do you react to unexpected bad financial news?" can be answered by the client in a variety of ways. The answer, of course, needs to be analyzed by the financial adviser for the degree of risk aversion it conveys. This procedure imposes minimal restraints on the client's answers and allows one to explore in depth through further questioning the reasons underlying them. But the costs are the amount of time it takes to ask the number of questions necessary to get a feel for the pattern of the client's answers and the potential for ambiguity in the answers.

Standardized Response Options without Formal Scoring

With the exception of Question 32, the standardized answers for each question are arranged on a continuum, reflecting a progression from risk-averse to risk-tolerant behaviors. The use of standardized options provides a more uniform basis for interpreting the client's responses. Again, consider our earlier example concerning the reaction to unfavorable financial news (Question 2). Note that underneath the questions there are five possible answers that the client can select, namely: "always overreact," "frequently overreact," "rarely overreact," "almost never overreact," and "never overreact." The client who is risk averse is more likely to overreact. By examining the pattern to the answers for the different questions a client provides, the financial adviser can get some sense of the client's risk tolerance. The more risk-taking options the client selects, the more risk taking he or she is likely to be.

Formal Scoring through The American College

If a financial adviser uses either of the two approaches discussed so far, it is necessary to somehow combine the answers mentally to arrive at an impression of the client's financial risk tolerance. Different people combine them differently, giving more or less weight to certain questions, which allows for subjectivity. One adviser's estimate of a particular client's risk tolerance can differ from another's, even when they ask the same questions and the client provides identical answers in each case, because each adviser may be using different formulas for the mental calculation. Often the advisers are even unable to clearly articulate the rules they use.

In order to minimize these ambiguities, The American College makes available a standardized approach to scoring. With this approach, the answers are combined using a mathematical formula. The same formula is used each time so that different clients can be compared using exactly the same standard each time.

Due to the complexity of the scoring procedure and the possibility of making errors in calculations, formal scoring of the questionnaire is available only through The American College at a charge of $12 per questionnaire. To use this scoring service, please return the completed answer sheet along with a check or money order payable to

The American College
P. O. Box 1400
Bryn Mawr, PA 19010

After the answer sheet is scored, the adviser will receive a report that will indicate the client's scores and discuss their implications. The report, which is appropriate for sharing and discussing with the client, will be returned to you within 5 working days of its receipt, in order to assist you in scheduling client meetings.

Advisers also have the option of purchasing a software package that allows them to score and print the report at their site. The cost per administration of the questionnaire is $7.80 with the $39 Introductory Package (good for 5 administrations). Also available is a 20-administration program for $100, with the cost thus being $5 per questionnaire.

To run the PC-based software the following hardware is needed:

- at least a 386 PC
- Microsoft Windows
- 4MB of RAM
- 2MB of available hard drive space
- one 3.5-inch disk drive

After the client's answers are entered, the program produces the report on command. The quality of the graphics depends on the printer.

Three scores will be reported. The first is on a scale of 0 to 100 percent and indicates the percentage of the maximum that a particular score reflects. The lowest possible score—if one were to select the most risk-averse option on all the questions—would be 0 percent. Conversely if one selected the most risk-seeking option on all the questions, the score would be 100 percent. Of course, it will be rare, if ever, that you come across a client who obtains either of those two extreme scores.

The second score provides a comparison between a given client's risk tolerance and the risk tolerance of other clients who completed this questionnaire during the initial field test of the instrument. In other words, scores are also presented in terms of percentiles. (A percentile score indicates the percentage of the comparison group that obtained scores lower than the client under consideration.)

Earlier it was noted that people show different degrees of variability in their answers to different questions attempting to assess risk tolerance. Therefore the third score produced through the formal scoring system gauges the client's consistency across different questions. Generally the more consistent the answers, the more probable it is that one can describe a client's level of risk tolerance in the form of a single number.

Technical Information about the Survey of Financial Risk Tolerance

In order to be useful, an assessment procedure must demonstrate two characteristics, *reliability* and *validity*. An assessment device that is reliable yields scores that are stable. An assessment device that is valid should actually measure what it intends to measure. Statistical procedures have been developed to gauge whether a given assessment device is reliable and valid. These techniques have been used to determine the reliability and validity of the Survey of Financial Risk Tolerance and the summarized outcomes of these studies follow. The results reported below are based on the responses of the clients of the graduates of The American College's Master of Science in Financial Services (MSFS) program.

Reliability

One method for estimating reliability involves analyzing the extent to which scale items correlate both to each other and to the total score on the specific scale. *Cronbach's Coefficient Alpha,* an index of reliability based on this procedure, can range from 0 to 1.00. Generally, in order to be considered reliable, scales used to draw conclusions about individuals should have alpha coefficients that are about .85 or higher. The computed alpha on the Survey of Financial Risk Tolerance is .91.

Another method for gauging reliability is the test-retest method, which involves administering the questionnaire to the same individuals on two different occasions. The correlation between the test and retest was .87 for the risk tolerance score and .69 for the consistency score when the survey was given to 101 persons from 7 days to 131 days apart (mean 46 days).

Validity

A number of different aspects of validity have been identified, but given the purpose of this scale, it is most important to demonstrate that the scale has criterion-related validity. Evidence for criterion-related validity can be generated by showing that the scale has the expected relationships with some other characteristics associated with risk tolerance. Therefore scores from the Survey of Financial Risk Tolerance were related to demographic information. As expected, the scores from the Survey of Financial Risk Tolerance showed

- a negative relationship with age (that is, older persons were less risk-tolerant)
- a positive relationship with income (the higher the income, the greater the risk tolerance)
- differences between occupational groups (such as retired clients being more risk-averse)
- current ownership of conservative and aggressive investments consistent with the scores

Further study of the psychometric properties of the Survey of Financial Risk Tolerance is in progress.

Client Name/ID ____________________

Survey of Financial Risk Tolerance

Directions: *Please answer all questions by circling the number in front of the answer that indicates your response.*

1. Do you experience "anxiety" or "thrill" when awaiting the outcome of an important investment decision?

1 Always anxiety
2 Most frequently anxiety
3 Neither anxiety nor thrill
4 Most frequently thrill
5 Always thrill

2. How do you react to unexpected bad financial news?

1 Always overreact
2 Frequently overreact
3 Rarely overreact
4 Almost never overreact
5 Never overreact

3. Assume you're an executive. Your company offers you two ways of collecting your bonus: either cash equivalent to 6 months' salary or a stock option with a 50-50 chance of either doubling in value or becoming worthless in the next year. Which would you take?

1 Definitely the cash
2 Probably the cash
3 Not sure
4 Probably the stock option
5 Definitely the stock option

4. Once you have made an investment decision, how sure do you usually feel that your choice was the correct one?

1 Very unsure
2 Somewhat unsure
3 Somewhat sure
4 Very sure

5. Which of the following investment portfolios do you find most appealing?

1 60 percent in low-risk,
30 percent in medium-risk, and
10 percent in high-risk investments

2 30 percent in low-risk,
40 percent in medium-risk, and
30 percent in high-risk investments

3 10 percent in low-risk,
50 percent in medium-risk, and
40 percent in high-risk investments

6. When you think of the word risk in an investment context, which of the following words comes to mind first?

1 Danger
2 Uncertainty
3 Opportunity
4 Thrill

7. How often have you invested a large sum in a risky investment primarily for the "thrill" of seeing whether it went up or down in value?

1 Never
2 Very rarely
3 Somewhat rarely
4 Somewhat frequently
5 Very frequently

8. How easily do you adapt to unfavorable financial changes in your life?

1 Very uneasily
2 Somewhat uneasily
3 Somewhat easily
4 Very easily

Client Name/ID ______________________

Survey of Financial Risk Tolerance

9. You are considering an investment that amounts to 25 percent of the funds you have allocated for investment purposes. The expected return on this investment is about twice the return you would get by placing the money into a savings account at your local bank. However, this investment, unlike a bank account, is not protected against loss of the principal. What would the chance of loss have to be in order for you to make this investment?

1 Zero
2 Very improbable
3 Low chance
4 Even chance

10. Compared to other investors, how sophisticated are you about investing money?

1 Very unsophisticated
2 Somewhat unsophisticated
3 Somewhat sophisticated
4 Very sophisticated

11. If your friends were interviewed, how would *they* describe *your* evaluation of financial risks?

1 Severely overestimates the risks
2 Somewhat overestimates the risks
3 Estimates the risks correctly
4 Somewhat underestimates the risks
5 Severely underestimates the risks

12. You are faced with a choice between (a) greater job security with a small pay raise and (b) a high pay raise but less job security. Which would you select?

1 Definitely greater job security
2 Probably greater job security
3 Not sure
4 Probably higher pay raise
5 Definitely higher pay raise

13. An investment decision involves the possibility of making an amount of money as well as the possibility of losing all or some portion of the funds invested. Some people focus more on the possibility of making money, whereas others focus more on the possibility of losing money as a result of the decision. When making an important investment decision, what dominates your thinking?

1 The potential loss, by far
2 The potential loss, somewhat more
3 The potential gain, somewhat more
4 The potential gain, by far

14. In the past what have been the outcomes of your high-risk investment decisions?

1 Almost always unfavorable
2 Usually unfavorable
3 Equal mix of favorable and unfavorable outcomes
4 Usually favorable
5 Almost always favorable

15. How long does it take you to make an important financial decision?

1 Very long time
2 Long time
3 Average amount of time
4 Short time
5 Very short time

16. Compared to other people you know, how would you rate your ability to tolerate the stress associated with important financial matters?

1 Very low
2 Low
3 Average
4 High
5 Very high

Client Name/ID ____________________

Survey of Financial Risk Tolerance

17. Some people view financial losses as personal failures. Others consider these same consequences as merely setbacks. How do you tend to view these issues?

1 Almost always as personal failures
2 Mainly as personal failures
3 Sometimes as personal failures and sometimes as merely setbacks
4 Mainly as just setbacks
5 Almost always as just setbacks

18. If you were to become unemployed, which of the following would you be most likely to do?

1 Definitely take the first job offered, even if it was not exactly what I was looking for
2 Probably take the first job offered, even if it was not exactly what I was looking for
3 Not sure
4 Probably hold out for the kind of job I really wanted
5 Definitely hold out for the kind of job I really wanted

19. What is your general outlook on the eventual outcome of your financial decisions after you make them?

1 Very pessimistic
2 Somewhat pessimistic
3 Somewhere in the middle
4 Somewhat optimistic
5 Very optimistic

20. Which of the following comes closest to your ideal employment compensation structure involving some mix of *salary* and *commissions*?

1 Entirely salary
2 Primarily salary
3 Equal mix of salary and commissions
4 Primarily commissions
5 Entirely commissions

21. What degree of risk have you assumed on your investments in the past?

1 Very small
2 Small
3 Medium
4 Large
5 Very large

22. Do you consider yourself reflective or impulsive when making investment decisions?

1 Very reflective
2 Somewhat reflective
3 Neither reflective nor impulsive
4 Somewhat impulsive
5 Very impulsive

23. You are applying for a mortgage. The interest rates have been coming down over the last several months, and there's a possibility that they may drop another percentage point in the next month. However, the possibility also exists that the rates will start climbing again. It's unclear which of the two possibilities is more likely since economists disagree in their forecasts. You have the option of locking in on the current interest rate or letting it float. If you lock in, you will get the current rate, even if interest rates go up. If the rates go down, though, you'll have to settle at the higher rate. What would you do?

1 Definitely lock in
2 Probably lock in
3 Probably let it float
4 Definitely let it float

Client Name/ID ____________________

Survey of Financial Risk Tolerance

24. Assume you are a contestant on a TV game show. After winning a prize that's equivalent to one year's salary, you are offered the option of walking away with this prize money or taking a chance on either doubling it or losing it all. What are the odds of success that you would require before agreeing to accept this gamble?

1 Would not take the bet no matter what the odds
2 9 in 10
3 8 in 10
4 7 in 10
5 6 in 10
6 5 in 10
7 4 in 10
8 3 in 10
9 2 in 10
10 1 in 10

25. Have you ever borrowed money in order to make an investment (other than a home-mortgage loan)?

1 No
2 Yes

26. How much confidence do you have in your ability to make money?

1 Very low confidence
2 Low confidence
3 Average level of confidence
4 High confidence
5 Very high confidence

27. Compared to other people you know, how much time do you spend reading about financial and investment matters?

1 Much less than most
2 Somewhat less than most
3 About the same
4 Somewhat more than most
5 Much more than most

28. Suppose that 5 years ago you bought stock issued by a company highly recommended by your financial adviser. That same year the company experienced a severe decline in sales due to poor management. The price of the stock dropped drastically, and you sold your shares at a substantial loss. The company is now restructured under new management, and most analysts expect its stock to produce better-than-average returns. Given your bad experience with this stock in the past, how likely are you now to purchase shares of this stock?

1 Definitely would not buy
2 Probably would not buy
3 Not sure
4 Probably would buy
5 Definitely would buy

29. Is it more important to be protected from inflation or to be assured of the safety of your principal?

1 Much more important to be assured of the safety of my principal
2 Somewhat more important to be assured of the safety of my principal
3 Somewhat more important to be protected from inflation
4 Much more important to be protected from inflation

Client Name/ID ____________________

Survey of Financial Risk Tolerance

30. What percent of your funds are you willing to place in investments that are of above-average risk?

1 0 percent
2 1–9 percent
3 10–19 percent
4 20–29 percent
5 30–39 percent
6 40–49 percent
7 50–59 percent
8 60–69 percent
9 70–79 percent
10 80–89 percent
11 90–99 percent
12 100 percent

31. In some instances you are faced with a choice between (a) earning a certain amount of money for sure and (b) taking a risk and earning either a larger amount of money or nothing at all.

For example, consider an investment choice between a certain gain of $50 and an 80 percent chance of earning $100. If you take the certain choice, you will get $50 for sure (no more, no less). On the other hand, if you take the 80 percent probability of earning $100, you also stand a 20 percent chance of earning nothing at all.

For the choices shown below please indicate whether you would take the sure gain or some probability of earning twice as much (or nothing at all). Be sure to select one option for each pair, A through F.

Pair A: 1 A certain gain of $10,000
2 80 percent probability of gaining $20,000 (with a corresponding 20 percent chance of earning nothing)

Pair B: 1 A certain gain of $10,000
2 50 percent probability of gaining $20,000 (with a corresponding 50 percent chance of earning nothing)

Pair C: 1 A certain gain of $30,000
2 80 percent probability of gaining $60,000 (with a corresponding 20 percent chance of earning nothing)

Pair D: 1 A certain gain of $30,000
2 50 percent probability of gaining $60,000 (with a corresponding 50 percent chance of earning nothing)

Pair E: 1 A certain gain of $50,000
2 80 percent probability of gaining $100,000 (with a corresponding 20 percent chance of earning nothing)

Pair F: 1 A certain gain of $50,000
2 50 percent probability of gaining $100,000 (with a corresponding 50 percent chance of earning nothing)

Client Name/ID ____________________

Survey of Financial Risk Tolerance

32. How likely is it that you would be willing to place one-fourth of your net wealth into each of the following classes of investments?

LOW RISK

	Very Unlikely	Somewhat Unlikely	Not Sure	Somewhat Likely	Very Likely
(a) 90-day U.S. Treasury bill	1	2	3	4	5
(b) Deposit account (savings, CD)	1	2	3	4	5
(c) Money market fund	1	2	3	4	5
(d) U.S. government bond	1	2	3	4	5
(e) Municipal bond	1	2	3	4	5
(f) Corporate bond	1	2	3	4	5
(g) Blue-chip common stock	1	2	3	4	5
(h) Convertible security	1	2	3	4	5
(i) Aggressive-growth common stock	1	2	3	4	5
(j) Venture capital	1	2	3	4	5
(k) Limited-partnership unit	1	2	3	4	5
(l) Junk bond	1	2	3	4	5
(m) Options/commodities	1	2	3	4	5

HIGH RISK

33. Diversification is typically the soundest investment strategy. However, suppose an eccentric uncle left you an inheritance of $75,000, stipulating in his will that you invest *all* the money in only *one* of the following investments. Which one would you select?

1 Savings account
2 Mutual fund (moderate growth)
3 Blue-chip common stock
4 Limited partnership
5 Naked option/commodities futures contract

34. Investments can go up and down in value. What is the maximum drop in the value of your total investment portfolio that you could tolerate before feeling uncomfortable?

1 0 percent
2 1–9 percent
3 10–19 percent
4 20–29 percent
5 30–39 percent
6 40–49 percent
7 50–59 percent
8 60–69 percent
9 70–79 percent
10 80–89 percent
11 90–99 percent
12 100 percent

35. A long-lost relative dies and leaves you her house. The house is in disrepair but is located in a neighborhood that's being rehabilitated. As is, the house would probably sell for about $75,000, but if you were to spend about $25,000 on renovations, the selling price would be approximately $150,000. However, there's some talk about constructing a major highway next to the house, which would lower its value considerably. What would you do?

1 Sell it as is
2 Keep it as is, but rent it out
3 Take out a $25,000 mortgage for the necessary renovations

Client Name/ID ____________________

Survey of Financial Risk Tolerance

36. You are offered an investment in which you stand an even chance of either losing half of your personal net worth or making a certain amount of money. What's the lowest return you would need in order to make such an investment?

1 I would not make the investment no matter what the rate of return.
2 Quadruple my net worth
3 Triple my net worth
4 Double my net worth
5 Less than double my net worth

37. What types of changes have you made in your investment portfolio in the past?

1 Always toward less risky investments
2 Mostly toward less risky investments
3 No changes or changes with no clear direction
4 Mostly toward more risky investments
5 Always toward more risky investments

38. How often have you used "short selling" or "margin buying" in stock market investments?

1 Never
2 Seldom
3 Frequently
4 Very frequently

39. Suppose you are the beneficiary of a $100,000 life insurance policy from a beloved relative. You are considering various investment possibilities, including some of very high risk. How much of this money could you lose *forever* without feeling that you were betraying your relative's motive for leaving you this sum?

1 $0
2 $1,000–$9,000
3 $10,000–$19,000
4 $20,000–$29,000
5 $30,000–$39,000
6 $40,000–$49,000
7 $50,000–$59,000
8 $60,000–$69,000
9 $70,000–$79,000
10 $80,000–$89,000
11 $90,000–$100,000

40. How do you rate your willingness to take investment risks in comparison to the general population?

1 Extremely low risk taker
2 Very low risk taker
3 Low risk taker
4 Average risk taker
5 High risk taker
6 Very high risk taker
7 Extremely high risk taker

Client Name/ID ____________________

Survey of Financial Risk Tolerance ***Demographic Data Form***

The following information will allow your risk-tolerance score to be classified by relevant demographic categories. Please be assured that this information, like your responses to the risk-tolerance questions, will remain confidential. Circle the number representing your answer or fill in the blank.

1. Sex 1 Male
   2 Female

2. Age: ______

3. Marital status

   1 Single
   2 Married
   3 Divorced
   4 Widowed

4. Numbers of dependents, including yourself:

   ______

5. Highest education level

   1 Less than high school
   2 High school
   3 Some college
   4 Bachelor's degree
   5 Master's degree
   6 Law degree
   7 Doctorate

6. Occupation

   1 An employee of a private company or business, or an individual working for wages, salary, or commissions
   2 A government employee (federal, state, county, or local)
   3 Self-employed in your own business, professional practice, or farm
   4 Retired

7. If you are an employee, how many years have you been with the same employer? ______

8. Approximate income, before taxes, from all sources. Please indicate your own income *and* total household income.

	a. Your income	b. Household income
Under $50,000	1	1
$50,000 to $99,000	2	2
$100,000 to $149,000	3	3
$150,000 to $199,000	4	4
$200,000 to $249,000	5	5
$250,000 to $500,000	6	6
Over $500,000	7	7

9. Which category describes your approximate net wealth?

   1 Under $250,000
   2 $250,000 to $499,000
   3 $500,000 to $999,000
   4 $1,000,000 to $2,499,000
   5 $2,500,000 to $5,000,000
   6 Over $5,000,000

10. Which of the following investments do you presently own? (Circle all that apply.)

   1 Life insurance
   2 Savings account or CDs
   3 Money market funds
   4 Bonds
   5 Stocks
   6 Real estate (other than primary residence)
   7 Options or futures
   8 Other (list)

   ____
   ____
   ____

Client Name/ID ____________________

Survey of Financial Risk Tolerance ***Answer Sheet***

Directions: The client has answered the questions in the survey by circling a number corresponding to his or her answer. Transfer these numbers to the appropriate spaces in the Answer columns. For scoring please return this form along with a check or money order in the amount of $12.00 to **Survey of Financial Risk Tolerance**
P.O. Box 1400
The American College
270 S. Bryn Mawr Ave.
Bryn Mawr, PA 19010

Question Number	Answer	Question Number	Answer	Question Number	Answer	Question Number	Answer
1.	_____	16.	_____	31. Pair A	_____	32. j	_____
2.	_____	17.	_____	31. Pair B	_____	32. k	_____
3.	_____	18.	_____	31. Pair C	_____	32. l	_____
4.	_____	19.	_____	31. Pair D	_____	32. m	_____
5.	_____	20.	_____	31. Pair E	_____	33.	_____
6.	_____	21.	_____	31. Pair F	_____	34.	_____
7.	_____	22.	_____	32. a	_____	35.	_____
8.	_____	23.	_____	32. b	_____	36.	_____
9.	_____	24.	_____	32. c	_____	37.	_____
10.	_____	25.	_____	32. d	_____	38.	_____
11.	_____	26.	_____	32. e	_____	39.	_____
12.	_____	27.	_____	32. f	_____	40.	_____
13.	_____	28.	_____	32. g	_____		
14.	_____	29.	_____	32. h	_____		
15.	_____	30.	_____	32. i	_____		

***Demographic Data*---**

Question Number	Answer	Question Number	Answer	
1.	_____	10. List all numbers circled in numerical order.		List other investments below.
2.	_____			__________
3.	_____			__________
4.	_____		_____	__________
5.	_____		_____	__________
6.	_____		_____	__________
7.	_____		_____	__________
8a	_____		_____	__________
8b.	_____		_____	__________
9.	_____		_____	
			_____	
			_____	

Please fill in the following to indicate where results should be sent:

Client's name ____________________ Adviser's name ____________________

Address ____________________ City __________ State __________ Zip __________

Date of administration __________ (month) __________ (day) __________ (year) __________

Identification number [ ]

Sample Report to Client

THE SURVEY OF FINANCIAL RISK TOLERANCEE REPORT FOR:

CLIENT: **I. L. Sea** ADVISER: **Mike U. Money, CLU, ChFC, MSFS**

DATE: **May 20, 1998**

YOUR ASSESSED FINANCIAL RISK TOLERANCE INDEX

Your financial risk tolerance was assessed by considering how you react in a variety of specific situations that involve financial risk, your attitudes, and your own general impression of your overall inclination to take financial risks.

If you had selected the most risky option on every question, your risk tolerance index would be 100. Conversely, selection of the least risky option on every question would result in a risk tolerance index of 0.

Although one can have a risk tolerance as low as 0 and as high as 100, most investors who have taken the survey fall between 20 and 70. The median is 43; i.e., there were as many results above as there were below 43.

Your financial risk tolerance index is 46.

YOUR SELF-IMPRESSION

The last question in the survey asked you to describe your own general impression of your risk-taking inclinations. You had the option of placing yourself in one of seven categories. You described yourself as an average risk taker.

YOUR SELF-IMPRESSION COMPARED TO YOUR ASSESSED FINANCIAL RISK TOLERANCE INDEX

The average financial risk tolerance index of survey participants in each of the seven categories is shown on the graph below. You can understand the meaning of your assessed risk tolerance by determining its place on the graph.

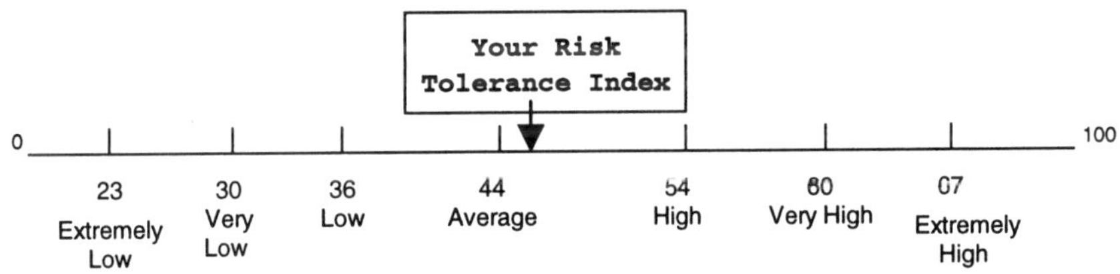

You described yourself as an average risk taker. If your perception of yourself is accurate, your results should be close to the average of 44 for that category. Based on your answers to all the financial risk tolerance questions, you are most likely to be an average to high risk taker.

YOUR RISK TOLERANCE COMPARED TO OTHER PEOPLE

Approximately 59 percent of people who have taken this questionnaire have a lower risk tolerance than yours. Conversely, about 41 percent have a risk tolerance equal to or higher than yours.

p. 2 Survey of Financial Risk Tolerance Report for: I. L. Sea

YOUR CONSISTENCY

People differ in the consistency of their financial risk-taking behaviors. The most consistent individuals show less variation in their risk-taking inclination across all the questions than the less consistent, who show greater variation in their inclinations and may even tend to seem contradictory in their responses to the questions.

You should consider the consistency of your responses across the questions in the survey. A lack of consistency could indicate that the survey results may not be a completely valid indicator of your risk-taking in all circumstances. You may take the risks in some situations, while avoiding the risks in others.

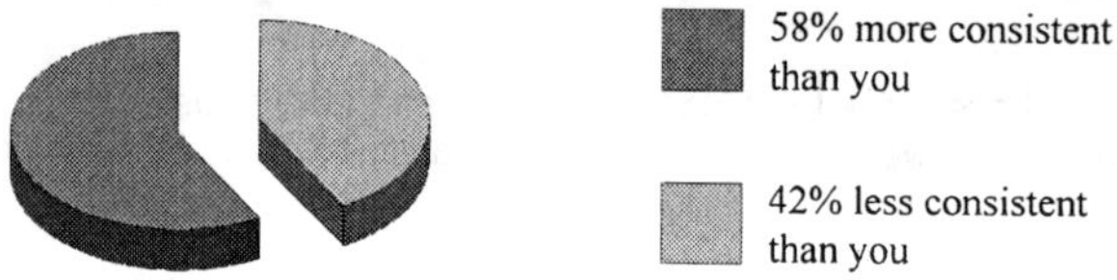

How consistent are you compared to the reference group? 58 percent were equally consistent or more consistent than you and 42 percent were less consistent than you.

COMBINATION OF RISK TOLERANCE AND CONSISTENCY

A combined graphic representation of both your risk tolerance and your consistency across questions, as previously described, is shown below.

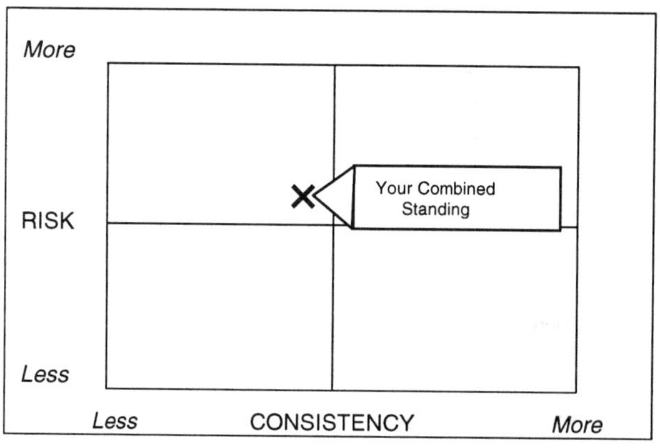

PERCENT OF QUESTIONS SKIPPED

The norms for this survey are based on those individuals who answered all of the questions. Questions that were not answered caused the results to be prorated. The more questions that were not answered, the greater the probability that the indicated norms might not be applicable to you. You skipped 0 percent of the questions.

```
p.   3  Survey of Financial Risk Tolerance Report for:  I. L. Sea
```

DESCRIPTION OF THE REFERENCE GROUP

The reference group to which you are being compared is not a randomly selected cross-section of the population. Therefore, it is critical for you to determine how applicable the percentiles are to you. Provided below is a description of the demographic characteristics of those individuals who completed the Survey of Financial Risk Tolerance.

Sex: Male: 83% Female: 17% ***Age:*** Ranged from 23 to 76, with a median of 48

Marital Status: Single: 9% Married: 84% Divorced: 3% Widowed: 4%

Number of Dependents: Median equals 3

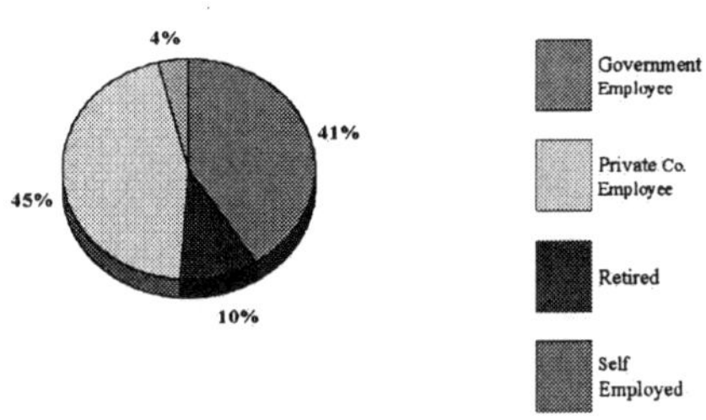

Occupation

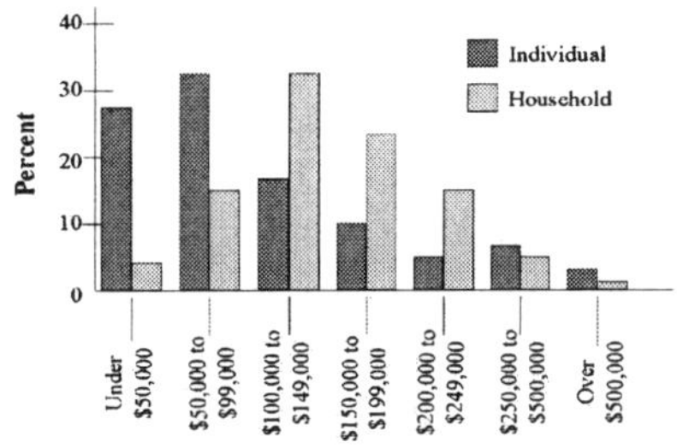

Income

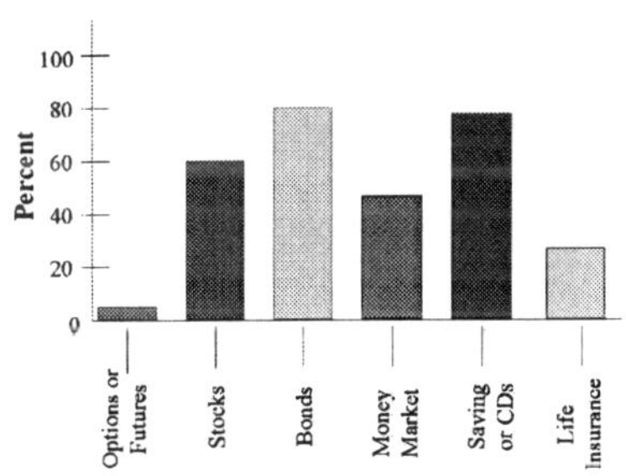

Investments

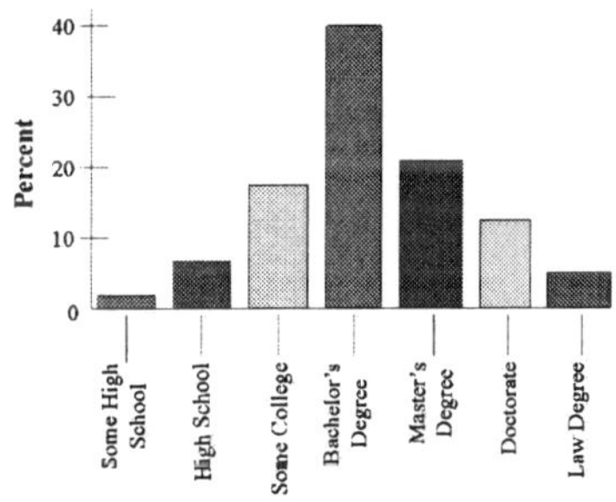

Education

PROPER USE OF THIS SURVEY

You and your financial adviser need to determine the suitability of this questionnaire for you and your unique situation. The Survey of Financial Risk Tolerance is intended only as a tool to assist you and your professional adviser in assessing your attitudes toward risk taking as a part of a comprehensive review of appropriate investment choices. The survey is not intended to substitute for either your judgment or the professional adviser's judgment of your financial ability to sustain a loss and of your personal investment goals.

6

Time Value of Money: Basic Concepts and Applications

Robert M. Crowe

Chapter Outline

THE BASICS OF TIME VALUE

Why is it that when individuals take out a loan they must repay more money than they borrowed? Why is it that a supplier of materials you use in your business offers you a discount from the full amount of the invoice if you pay within 30 days? Why does the savings and loan association credit depositors' savings accounts with interest? Why is it when you deposit a perfectly good check in your checking account the bank may deny you access to the money for a few days? Why is it inadequate for an investor to evaluate a proposed investment project on the basis of its payback period, that is, the number of years it will take for the total cash inflows from the project to equal the initial cash outlay? Why does the winner of a lottery prize of $1 million after taxes, payable in $100,000 annual installments over 10 years, actually receive less than $1 million of value?

The answer to all of these and dozens of similar questions centers on the time value of money (TVM). These questions arise in all fields of business and personal financial planning, real estate, marketing, investments, accounting, insurance, banking, and many other fields.

Some erroneously believe that a dollar is a dollar is a dollar. The fact is that dollars to be paid or received in different time periods have different values. Ask yourself these questions: When would you rather receive your federal income tax refund check—as soon as you file your return or 3 months later? When would you rather collect the rent from the tenants in your apartment building—at the beginning of each month or at the end?

Opportunity Cost

Solely on the basis of intuition, most people probably would conclude, quite properly, that they would prefer to receive money sooner rather than later. Why? Because the sooner they receive money the sooner they can use it, either by spending or investing it, for their own benefit. If they wait for the money, they incur what economists call an *opportunity cost.* The opportunity cost of an activity (in this case waiting to receive the money) is the value of the lost opportunity to engage in the best alternative activity (spending or investing the money now) with the same resource (the specified sum of money).

Conversely, most people would intuitively conclude that if they must pay out a specified sum of money, they would prefer to pay it later rather than sooner. Why? Because the longer they can delay the payment, the longer they can use the money, either spend it or invest it, for their own benefit. If they pay the money early, they incur an opportunity cost.

The Role of Interest

Since a given sum of money due in different time periods does not have the same value, a tool is needed in order to make the different values comparable. That tool is *interest.* Interest can be viewed as a way of quantifying the opportunity cost incurred by one who waits to receive money or one who gives up the opportunity to delay paying it.

For example, if you deposit $1,000 in a savings account and leave it there for one year, you expect to have more than $1,000 in the account at the end of that time. You expect your account to earn interest. By postponing the use of your money and allowing the bank to use it, you incur an opportunity cost. The bank gives you interest as compensation for your cost.

To reverse the situation, assume a loan you took out at your bank matures in one year, at which time you are obligated to pay $10,000. If you repay the loan today, one year early, you should be required to pay less than the full $10,000. If you forgo the opportunity to delay the repayment, you should be compensated in return by having the amount payable reduced.

The specific interest rate used to quantify opportunity cost is made up of two components: a risk-free rate and a risk premium. At a minimum, the opportunity cost of letting someone use your money is the rate of return you could have earned by investing it in a perfectly safe instrument. A reasonable measure of this minimum opportunity cost is the rate of interest available on 3-month U.S. Treasury bills. These bills are always available and, for all practical purposes, risk-free. At the time of this writing, 3-month T-bills were yielding between 5 and 5.25 percent on an annual basis.

In addition, most situations in which you allow someone else to use your money entail some risk of loss for you. For example, the market value of your investment instrument may decline. The purchasing power of your principal sum may be eroded by inflation. The person or organization using your funds may default on scheduled interest and principal payments. Tax laws may be changed to lower the after-tax return on your investment. These and other types of risk associated with letting someone else use your funds should be reflected in a risk premium, or in an add-on to the risk-free opportunity cost of money. Theoretically, the higher the degree of risk, the greater the risk premium and, therefore, the higher the interest rate you should require.

Simple Interest versus Compound Interest

There are two ways of computing interest. *Simple interest* is computed by applying an interest rate to only an original principal sum. *Compound interest* is computed by applying an interest rate to the total of an original principal sum and interest credited to it in earlier time periods.

To illustrate the difference, assume $100 is deposited in an account that earns 6 percent simple interest per year. At the end of each year the account will be credited with $6.00 of interest. At the end of 5 years there will be $130 in the account (if no withdrawals have been made), as shown in table 6-1.

TABLE 6-1
Accumulation of $100 in 5 years at 6% Simple and Compound Interest per Year

	Simple Interest			Compound Interest		
Year	Principal Sum	Interest	Ending Balance	Principal Sum	Interest	Ending Balance
1	$100.00	$6.00	$106.00	$100.00	$6.00	$106.00
2	$100.00	$6.00	$112.00	$106.00	$6.36	$112.36
3	$100.00	$6.00	$118.00	$112.36	$6.74	$119.10
4	$100.00	$6.00	$124.00	$119.10	$7.15	$126.25
5	$100.00	$6.00	$130.00	$126.25	$7.58	$133.83

If instead the account earns 6 percent compound interest per year it will grow to a larger amount, again as shown in table 6-1. The extra $3.83 in the account when it is credited with compound interest is interest earned on previous interest earnings.

Notice the difference in the annual amount by which the account grows when compound rather than simple interest is credited. The balance grows by a constant amount, $6.00 per year, when simple interest is credited. In the case of compound interest, however, the account balance grows by an increasing amount each year. The rate of growth, however, remains the same, 6 percent in this illustration.

Most of the day-to-day situations calling for a recognition or calculation of the time value of money involve compound interest, rather than simple interest. Hence this and the following chapter will deal only with compound interest.

Compounding versus Discounting

The process by which money today, a *present value,* grows over time to a larger amount, a *future value,* is called *compounding.* The process by which money due in the future, a *future value,* is reduced over time to a smaller amount today, a *present value,* is called *discounting.*

Figure 6-1 shows the difference between present and future value, with compound interest as the link between the two. Compounding may be viewed as a movement up the curve, while discounting may be viewed as a movement down the curve. Note also that the link between present and future value in figure 6-1 is shown as a curve, rather than as a straight line, to reflect the application of compound interest rather than simple interest. When compound interest is used, the future value rises each year by an increasing amount of money (or the present value declines by a decreasing amount of money).

FIGURE 6-1
Compound Interest as the Link between Present Value and Future Value

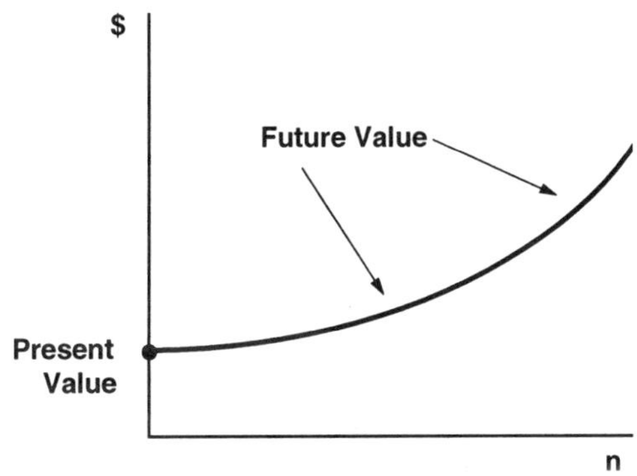

This figure depicts compound interest as the link between the two values. Dollar amounts are reflected by the vertical axis, and the number of periods during which compounding or discounting occurs is reflected on the horizontal axis. As one moves up the curve (compounding), the future value grows by increasing amounts. As one moves down the curve (discounting), the present value declines by decreasing amounts.

Two major factors influence the shape of the curve in figure 6-1. These are (1) the number of periods over which compounding or discounting occurs, and (2) the interest rate used in the compounding or discounting process. All other things being equal, the greater the number of periods, the greater the length of the curve. Consequently, as the number of periods is increased, the difference between the present value and the future value also increases. Similarly, all other things being equal, the greater the interest rate, the steeper the slope of the curve. Thus as the interest rate is increased, the difference between the present value and the future value also increases.

These relationships among the number of periods (n), the interest rate (i), the future value of money (FV), and the present value of money (PV) may be summarized as follows: in compounding, FV moves in the same direction as n and i (it increases as they increase); in discounting, PV moves in the opposite direction from n and i (it decreases as they increase).

Note that there are four key variables in the most basic problems involving the time value of money. They are the number of periods, the interest rate, the present value, and the future value. In the most basic problems, you will be given three of the variables and be called upon to solve for the fourth. In more complex time-value problems the four variables are the number of periods, the interest rate, the amount of each payment in a series of payments, and either the present value or the future value. Again, you will be given three of the variables and asked to compute the fourth. And some apparently complex time-value problems are simply combinations of two or more of these basic four-variable problems that are linked together.[1]

The Power of Compound Interest

Of course your concern with compound interest is not so much with the shape of a curve as with the effect that compound interest has on time value. That effect is extremely powerful, especially when a high interest rate or a long period of time is involved. For example, in the year 1980 the consumer price index, a fairly good measure of the rate of inflation, rose by 13.5 percent over the preceding year. If that rate of inflation had continued throughout the decade of the 1980s and into the latter half of the 1990s, the same bag of groceries that cost $100 at the beginning of 1980 would have cost about $355 in 1990! By 1999 it would have cost $1,109!

One more example will help to emphasize the point. Peter Minuit is said to have purchased the island of Manhattan in the year 1626 for about $24 worth of beads. If instead of buying Manhattan at the beginning of 1626 he had put the $24 into a bank account paying 6 percent compound interest per year and left the money there continuously, at the end of 1998, 373 years later, he would have had a bank account of almost $66 billion, if income taxes are ignored. You are invited to judge for yourself whether Peter made a wise purchase.

But to carry the illustration a step further, notice in table 6-2 how slowly Peter Minuit's account would have grown in the first 300 years. His money was on the flat part of the curve in figure 6-1. By 1925 he wouldn't even have become a billionaire. He really would have become fabulously wealthy only in the past 70 years, during which time his wealth would have grown by over $60 billion. In 1998 alone it would have increased by about $3.7 billion! (Again, an important point to remember is that the *rate* of growth of his wealth was constant throughout the period, 6 percent per year. It is the *amount* of growth that accelerates under compound interest.)

TABLE 6-2
Accumulation of $24 in 373 Years at 6% Compound Interest per Year

Year	Ending Balance
1626	$25
1675	$442
1725	$8,143
1775	$150,000
1825	$2,763,000
1875	$50,895,000
1925	$937,500,000
1975	$17,268,877,000
1998	$65,962,785,000

Effect of Income Taxes

One factor that must be considered in the analysis of several types of time-value-of-money problems is the impact of income taxes—federal, state, and local. For example, the rate of return nominally realized on most investments should be adjusted downward to an after-tax basis. Similarly, the nominal size of a payment or interest rate on a loan should be adjusted downward by the borrower if the payments are deductible for income tax purposes. We have not explicitly factored tax considerations into the problems discussed in this chapter and the next but have, instead, implicitly assumed that all values in the problems discussed are after-tax values.

Frequency of Compounding or Discounting

As you will see in the next chapter of this book, there is another factor, in addition to the interest rate and the number of years, that affects the size of the present and future values of money. That factor is the frequency with which the interest rate is applied in the compounding or discounting process.

Throughout this and most of the next chapter, it will be assumed that the interest rate is applied once per year, which is called annual compounding or discounting. You should recognize, however, that in many cases interest rates are applied several times within a year—for example, semiannually (twice a year), monthly (12 times a year), or daily (usually computed in commercial transactions by applying the interest rate 360 times per year).

All other things being equal, the greater the frequency with which compounding or discounting occurs, the greater is the effect on the growth of a future value or the decline of a present value. For example, a $1,000 principal sum that is credited with 8 percent compound interest will grow to a future value of $1,166.40 in 2 years if compounding occurs annually. If compounding occurs semiannually, on the other hand, it will grow to $1,169.86; and if compounding occurs monthly, it will grow to \$1,172.89. Conversely, the present value of \$1,000 due 2 years from now is \$857.34 if an 8 percent annual interest rate is applied once per year. If the discounting is applied semiannually, however, the present value is only \$854.80.

The explanation of why the frequency of compounding or discounting produces these results and of how to compute present and future values based on various frequencies will be deferred to the next chapter. Meanwhile, you should assume in the text and problems for each chapter that compounding and discounting occur only once per year.

Measuring the Number of Periods

Before moving on you should keep in mind one other factor regarding the compounding or discounting process—the importance of being accurate in measuring the number of periods during which the compounding or discounting occurs. That, in turn, depends on whether the process begins and ends at the beginning or the end of the periods in question.

If that sounds a bit confusing, refer back to the example of Peter Minuit in table 6-2. In that illustration, year number one was 1626, and the account balance for that year was \$25. That result occurred because it was assumed that \$24 was deposited on January 1, 1626, the *beginning* of year one, and the account balance was computed on December 31, 1626, the *end* of year one. As a consequence, year one produced approximately \$1.00 of interest.

On the other hand, what if Peter had deposited the initial \$24 at the *end* of year one? Obviously, the ending account balance for that year would have been \$24, and no interest would have been earned in that year.

The effect of this change in the assumption about when the initial deposit was made, whether at the start or the end of the first year, carries over into all remaining years. In table 6-2 the ending balance for 1998, over \$65.9 billion, was the result of compounding for 373 years, that is, from January 1, 1626, to December 31, 1998. If Peter had begun his investment just 12 months later, at the end of 1626, compounding would have occurred for only 372 years by December 31, 1998, and his account balance would have grown to only about \$62.9 billion. In other words, the 12-month delay would have cost him over \$3.7 billion of interest earnings. What a difference a year makes!

In order to be sure you are counting n, the number of periods, accurately in solving time value of money problems, it is helpful to draw time lines, such as those in figure 6-2, and to mark the timing of known dollar values in the problem with vertical arrows along the time line and the timing of unknown dollar values with question marks. The reason for drawing certain arrows below the line and others above it will be explained shortly. For the present you need only to recognize how the *timing* of each sum of money in a problem, both the known and unknown sums, is depicted on a time line. The upper time line, for example, depicts a case where you are to calculate the future value as of the beginning of the sixth period (which is the same as the end of the fifth period) of a deposit made at the beginning of the first period. The lower time line depicts a situation in which you are to compute the present value as of today (the start of period one) of a series of payments that will occur at the end of each of the next four periods. Time lines can be constructed for all types of time-value-of-money problems, as will be shown frequently throughout this chapter and the next one.

FIGURE 6-2
Time Lines as a Help in Counting Number of Periods of Compounding or Discounting

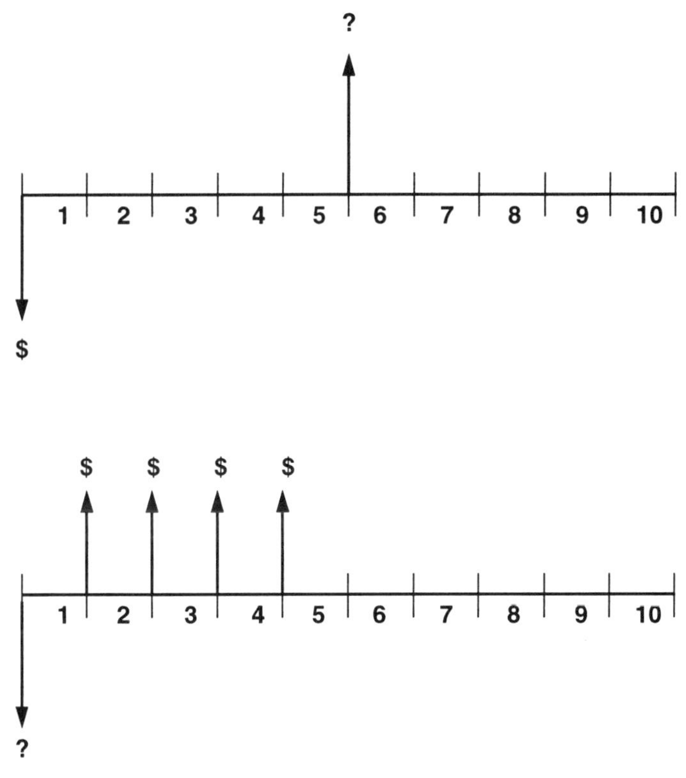

The top time line reflects a problem in which a present value is deposited at the start of period one and you are asked to solve for the future value at the start of period six, or the end of period five. The lower time line depicts a problem in which a sum of money is to be paid at the end of each of the next four periods and you are asked to solve for their present value as of the start of period one.

Plan of the Time-Value Discussion

The balance of this chapter utilizes and builds upon the elementary concepts presented thus far. Emphasis is placed upon explaining *how to solve* various types of basic problems involving the time value of money. The same emphasis is present in the following chapter, where somewhat more advanced and complex time-value-of-money problems are explained. Practical illustrations are used constantly to demonstrate principles and solution techniques. Review problems are presented at the end of each chapter so that you can test your mastery of each type of problem explained.

Although this and the following chapter deal with the interactions among numbers—dollars, interest rates, and time periods—you do not need a sophisticated knowledge of mathematics in order to perform any of the calculations. An ability to add, subtract, multiply, and divide, as well as an ability to raise a number to a power, will be helpful. Even these are not totally essential, however, if you have access to a calculator. (The procedure for raising a number to a power by means of a calculator is described in appendixes C, D, and E at the end of this book.)

These two chapters contain an explanation of several tools and can be used to solve time-value-of-money problems. At the low-tech end of the spectrum, explanations are provided for solving them by directly applying mathematical formulas to the data. A rung higher up the technological ladder is the use of tables of time-value factors of various types. Still higher on the ladder, two of the most popular electronic calculators with time-value capabilities are also explained.

The explanation of the various types of time-value problems treated in these chapters proceeds in a logical progression from the least complicated to more advanced types. The rest of this chapter deals with the future value and present value of single sums of money, as well as the future value and present value of level streams of money payments, called annuities. Chapter 7 then takes up the future value and present value of nonlevel streams of money payments. These topics are then applied to investment decisions through an explanation of discounted cash flow analysis. Then the assumption that compounding, discounting, and payments occur only once per year is dropped, and an explanation is provided on how to deal with any of the preceding types of problems where compounding, discounting, or payment frequency is greater than annual.

Now, to begin.

FUTURE VALUE OF A SINGLE SUM

The most frequently encountered and easiest to understand application of the time-value-of-money concept involves the future value of a single sum. As explained earlier, determination of a future value of a sum of money entails a process of compounding, or increasing, the present value at some interest rate for some period of time. The most common example is the growth of a sum placed in an interest-bearing savings account. Recall, for example, that in table 6-1 a $100 deposit made today (present value) will grow to $133.83 (future value) at the end of 5 years at 6 percent compound interest.

Basic Time-Value Formula

The basic formula for computing the future value of a single sum of money, from which all other time-value formulas are derived, is the following:

$$FVSS = PVSS \times (1 + i)^n$$

where

FVSS = the future value of a single sum
PVSS = the present value of a single sum
i = the compound annual interest rate, expressed as a decimal
n = the number of years during which compounding occurs

In other words, add the interest rate (expressed as a decimal) to one, and raise this sum to a power equal to the number of years during which the compounding occurs. Then multiply this by the present value of the single sum or deposit in question to compute the future value of that single sum.

For example, assume that $5,000 is placed on deposit today in an account that will earn 9 percent compound annual interest. To what amount will this sum of money grow by the end of year 7? The problem is depicted on a time line in figure 6-3.

It is important, both conceptually and mathematically, to recognize that in every time-value-of-money problem there is an implicit tradeoff over time of a sacrifice for a gain, a cost for a benefit. For example, you may be willing to loan money to a friend today (a cost or cash outflow in the present) in order to be repaid a larger amount later (a benefit or larger cash inflow in the future). Throughout the time-value-of-money discussions in this book, the nature of this tradeoff will be pointed out over and over. For purposes of consistency among the time lines used to depict various types of problems to be discussed, present values will be depicted below the line, as will periodic cash outflows. Future values and periodic cash inflows will be shown as above-the-line factors.

To return to the problem at hand, then, the $5,000 that is placed on deposit today represents a present value. The amount to which it will grow at 9 percent compound annual interest by the end of the seventh year is the future value. The basic time-value formula can be used to compute the solution as follows:

$$\begin{aligned} FVSS &= PVSS \times (1 + i)^n \\ &= \$5{,}000 \times 1.09^7 \\ &= \$5{,}000 \times 1.828039 \\ &= \$9{,}140.20 \end{aligned}$$

FIGURE 6-3
Time Line Depiction of FVSS Problem

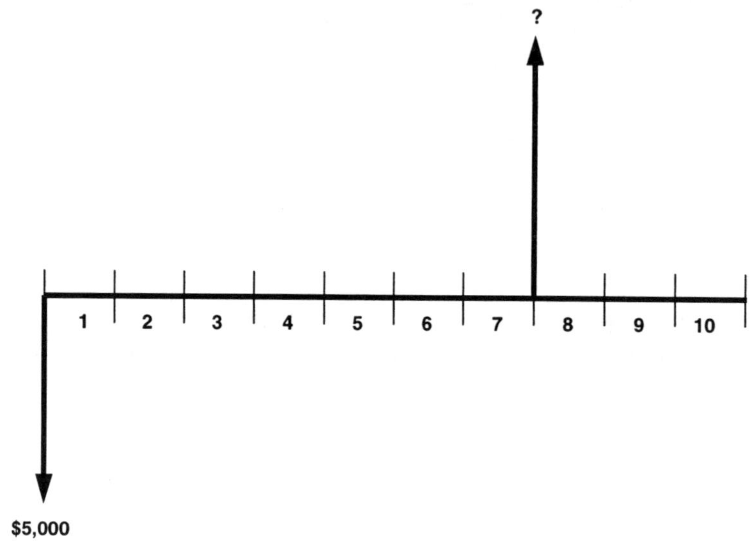

This time line depicts a problem in which a known single sum, $5,000, is deposited today, at the start of year one, and you are to calculate its future value as of the end of year seven. The time line also illustrates the basic tradeoff present in all time-value-of-money problems. Here the tradeoff is a cash outflow today (the deposit, shown below the time line) for a larger cash inflow later (the account balance at the end of the seventh year, shown above the time line).

To reiterate a point made earlier in this chapter, note what would happen to FVSS if i were more than 9 percent or if n were more than 7 years. In either case the quantity $(1 + i)^n$ would be larger than 1.828039, so that when multiplied by $5,000 the FVSS would be larger than $9,140.20. That is, future value increases as the interest rate or the number of years increases, and it falls as either of them is lowered.

FVSS TABLE

The process of raising (1 + i) to the nth power can be time consuming and tedious, as well as filled with possibilities for making arithmetic errors. To simplify the task, a table has been constructed showing the value of $(1 + i)^n$ for various rates of interest and numbers of periods. (See table B.1 in appendix B.) Excerpts from the table are presented below. All that needs to be done is to select the correct factor from the table and multiply it by the present value of the sum in question to compute its future value.

For example, look down the 9 percent column to the row for seven periods and find the factor 1.8280, virtually the same amount that was computed in the preceding example when the quantity 1.09 was raised to the seventh power.[2] What that computation and the table have disclosed is that if the present value of a single sum is one, its future value at 9 percent or seven periods is 1.8280. Since the present value of the single sum in the illustration is not one but $5,000, the factor for one must be multiplied by $5,000 to produce the future value of that sum of money, namely, $9,140.20.

Take another look at table 6-3. Note as you move from left to right across a particular row in the table, to higher and higher interest rates, the FVSS factor increases. Also, as you move from top to bottom down a particular column in the table, to higher and higher numbers of periods, the FVSS factor increases. Once again, FVSS rises as either i or n rises, and vice versa.

TABLE 6-3
Future Value of a Single Sum Factors

n/i	7%	8%	9%	10%	11%
1	1.0700	1.0800	1.0900	1.1000	1.1100
2	1.1449	1.1664	1.1881	1.2100	1.2321
3	1.2250	1.2597	1.2950	1.3310	1.3676
4	1.3108	1.3605	1.4116	1.4641	1.5181
5	1.4026	1.4693	1.5386	1.6105	1.6851
6	1.5007	1.5869	1.6771	1.7716	1.8704
7	1.6058	1.7138	1.8280	1.9487	2.0762
8	1.7182	1.8509	1.9926	2.1436	2.3045
9	1.8385	1.9990	2.1719	2.3579	2.5580
10	1.9672	2.1589	2.3674	2.5937	2.8394
11	2.1049	2.3316	2.5804	2.8531	3.1518
12	2.2522	2.5182	2.8127	3.1384	3.4985
13	2.4098	2.7196	3.0658	3.4523	3.8833
14	2.5785	2.9372	3.3417	3.7975	4.3104
15	2.7590	3.1722	3.6425	4.1772	4.7846

Computing FVSS with a Financial Calculator

A powerful tool for solving time-value-of-money problems is the financial calculator. This type of calculator greatly speeds the task of solving these problems, especially the more complex ones described later. Three of the most popular electronic calculators with finance functions currently on the market are the HP-12C Programmable Financial Calculator, the HP-17B II Financial (Business) Calculator, both produced by Hewlett-Packard Company, and the BA-II Plus calculator produced by Texas Instruments Incorporated. In this book an explanation will be furnished showing how to solve on these three calculators each type of time-value-of-money problem as it is encountered.[3] The individual keystrokes in each sequence of calculator keystrokes shown are separated by commas. If at some point in a sequence you key in an incorrect number, you can correct the mistake by immediately pressing the CLX key on the HP-12C, the left arrow or CLR key on the HP-17B II calculator, or the right arrow or CE/C key on the BA-II Plus.

Using the HP-12C

To use the HP-12C calculator to solve problems involving future value of a single sum, turn the machine on by pressing the ON key in the lower left corner of the keyboard. Next, depress the yellow f key[4] and the CLX key, which has REG printed above it. This serves to clear any data that may have been stored earlier in the financial and several other "registers" (memory units) of the machine. If you wish to clear only the financial registers, press the yellow f key and the x $\lessgtr$ y key, which has FIN printed above it, instead. (It is a good idea to get into the habit of clearing the memory of the calculator each time you use it.) Next, depress the yellow f key and the number 2. This will cause the machine to display dollar values carried to two decimal places, which is the level of precision to be used for dollar values throughout most of this chapter and the following one. (As will be explained later, other values, such as those for n and i, will sometimes be entered or displayed with other numbers of decimal places.)

By the way, what you have just done affects only the number of decimal places *displayed.* In most calculations it does not have any impact on the precision with which the machine performs the actual calculations.

The next steps are to enter the three known values in the FVSS problem, namely, PVSS, n, and i. These may be entered in any order. The language of the HP-12C, however, includes an important convention that reflects the cost-benefit tradeoff in all time-value problems referred to earlier. This convention, called the cash flow sign convention, requires that at least one (and usually only one) value entered into the calculator in a time-value problem be entered as a negative number. This is accomplished through use of the CHS (change sign) key in the top row of the keyboard. If this is not done, the cash flow sign convention usually causes solutions to problems to be displayed as negative numbers. For purposes of consistency, present values will be entered or displayed as negative numbers. Also, as will be explained later, the amount of a payment that constitutes a cash outflow in a series of payments in some types of problems will be entered or displayed as a negative number on the HP-12C.

Now take a moment to review the keys in the left-hand portion of the top row of the keyboard. These keys (n, i, PV, PMT, FV), as well as the yellow and blue functions they activate and the CHS key, will be used in solving various types of time-value-of-money problems.

To return to the example given earlier, assume you wish to know the amount to which a single sum of $5,000 will grow in 7 years at 9 percent compound interest. Since i is 9, press the 9 key, then the i key. Since n is 7, depress 7, then n. And since the sum of money today is $5,000, press 5000, CHS (since it is the present value), and PV. Finally, press FV and the answer, $9,140.20, should appear on the display.[5]

If you wish to change one of the data items in the problem, you may do so without reentering all the information. For example, if you wish to recalculate the same problem with a 12 percent interest rate, simply press 12, i, and FV. The new amount, $11,053.41, should appear on the display.

Using the HP-17B II

If you are using the HP-17B II to solve TVM problems, you should first take care of a number of housekeeping chores. Turn the machine on by pressing the CLR key in the lower left corner of the keyboard. Turn it off by pressing the colored shift key[6] just above it and then the CLR key again. (Note that OFF is printed in color above the CLR key.) Now adjust the contrast level on the display screen to one that is comfortable for you. Do this by holding down the CLR key and pressing the + key or the – key several times. Next, select the Algebraic system of entry logic by pressing shift and MODES on the DSP key. Now press the menu key, the key labeled ^, that is directly below ALG on the screen. Then press the EXIT key in the upper right portion of the keyboard. Do not change this setting—ever!

Next, set the number of decimal places to be displayed on the screen. We will use two decimal places for most dollar values in this book, so press DSP, the menu (^) key under FIX, then 2, and the INPUT key in the upper left portion of the keyboard. (In some cases, such as when dealing with large dollar amounts, we will display figures with no decimal places. In other cases, such as when calculating an interest rate, we may use four decimal places.

By the way, the setting for the number of decimal places applies only to what appears on the display. It does not normally affect the precision with which the machine performs actual calculations.

Of *extreme* importance as a housekeeping chore, you should set the HP-17B II for one payment period per year and one compounding period per year. In chapter 6 we will take up problems in which more than one payment or compounding period occurs in a year, but for now we will keep life simple. Press shift, MAIN on the EXIT key, the FIN menu key, the TVM menu key, the OTHER menu key, 1, the P/YR menu key, shift, MAIN, and CLR. Do not change this setting—ever!

One more important housekeeping chore that should be performed before every time-value problem is taken up is to clear the calculator of any data left in it from a previous problem. To do this, press shift, MAIN, the FIN menu key, shift, CLEAR DATA on the INPUT key, shift, and MAIN. Get into this habit every time you turn the calculator on and every time you wish to solve a new problem. Otherwise, you may produce incorrect results for the problem.

Now that all of the housekeeping has been taken care of, you will not need to do it again (except to clear the machine). The various settings will remain in the machine continuously, unless and until you specifically change them. So let's proceed to compute the future value of a single sum. Turn the machine on and press shift and MAIN. On the display screen you will see the calculator's main memory system. We will use only the finance menu system, so press the FIN menu key. The next level of the menu shows TVM, ICNV, CFLO, BOND, and DEPRC. In this chapter we will use only the TVM functions, so press the TVM menu key.

The next steps are to enter the three known values in the FVSS problem into the calculator. In doing so, it is important to remember the cost-benefit tradeoff present in all TVM problems as was explained earlier. Entering a number as a negative is accomplished through the use of the +/– key, which is located next to the INPUT key. For purposes of consistency, *present values* will be entered or displayed as negative numbers. Also, as will be explained later, the amount of a payment that constitutes a cash *outflow* in a series of payments in some types of problems will be entered or displayed as a negative number.

Now take a moment to review the TVM menu. The display shows one payment per year, which we entered earlier, and either END MODE or BEGIN MODE. We can ignore these modes for now, as they will not affect the calculations to be performed in this chapter. The display also shows the labels N, I%YR, PV, PMT, FV, and OTHER. The menu keys for these labels will be used to solve many types of TVM problems.

To return to the example given earlier, assume that you wish to know the amount to which a single sum of $5,000 will grow in seven years at 9 percent compound interest. Since the number of periods is 7, depress 7, then the N menu key. Since the interest rate is 9, press the 9 key, then the I%YR menu key. And since the sum of money today is $5,000, press 5000, the +/– key (since it is a present value), and the PV menu key. Finally, press the FV menu key and the answer, $9,140.20, will appear on the display.[7]

If you wish to change one or two of the data items in the problem, you may do so without reentering all the information. For example, if you wish to recalculate the same problem with a 12 percent interest, simply press, 12, the I%YR menu key, and the FV menu key. The new answer, $11,053.41, will appear on the display.

Using the BA-II Plus

In order to solve time-value-of-money problems using the BA-II Plus calculator, turn the machine on and clear the display screen by pressing the ON/OFF key in the upper right-hand corner of the keyboard. Next, clear the calculator of any previous information contained in the calculator's memory units. This is accomplished by pressing the gray key labeled 2nd in the upper left-hand corner[8] and the number 0 key, which has MEM printed above it. Then press 2nd and the FV key, which has CLR TVM printed above it. Then to complete the task, press 2nd again, followed by CE/C key with CLR Work printed above it. (It is a good idea to get into the habit of clearing the memory of the calculator each time you use it.) Next press 2nd, the decimal point key with Format printed above it, the number 2 key (for the number of decimal places desired), and finally the ENTER key. This will cause the machine to round numbers to two decimal places, which is the level of precision we will use for dollar values. (As will be explained later, other values, such as those for n and i, will sometimes be entered or displayed with other numbers of decimal places.)

By the way, what you have just done affects only the number of decimal places *displayed.* In most calculations it does not have any impact on the precision with which the machine performs the actual calculations.

The BA-II Plus uses two modes for solving the problems we will be discussing: the standard-calculator mode (which is used for routine arithmetic and for most basic time-value-of-money problems) and the prompted-work sheet mode (which is used to solve some advanced problems we will discuss later). For now, put the machine in the standard-calculator mode by pressing 2nd followed by the CPT key that has QUIT printed above it.

Take a moment to review the keys in the third row from the top of the keyboard. These keys (N, I/Y, PV, PMT, and FV), along with the 2nd key and the CPT (compute) and ENTER keys in the top row, will be used in solving various types of time-value-of-money problems.

The language of the BA-II Plus includes an important convention that reflects the cost-benefit tradeoff inherent in all time-value problems as described earlier. This convention requires that at least one (and usually only one) value entered into the calculator in a time-value problem be entered as a negative number. This is accomplished through the use of the +/– key in the bottom row of the keyboard. For consistency, present values will be entered or displayed as negative numbers. As will be explained later, the amount of a payment that constitutes a cash outflow in a series of payments in some types of problems will also be entered as a negative number on the BA-II Plus.

To return to the example given earlier, assume you wish to know the amount to which a single sum of $5,000 will grow in 7 years at 9 percent compound interest. These three known values should be entered into the calculator. They may be entered in order. Since the interest rate per year is 9 percent, press 9 and I/Y. Then enter the number of years involved by pressing 7 and N. Next is the sum of money today. Press 5,000, +/– (to change it to a negative value because it is a present value), and PV. The BA-II Plus is shipped with internal settings that assume 12 payment periods per year and 12 compounding periods per year. The following entries will convert the settings to one payment period and one compounding period per year: 2nd, P/Y, 1, 2nd, SET, ENTER, ↓, 1, 2nd, SET, ENTER, CE/C, ENTER. Finally, press CPT and FV and the answer, $9,140.20, should appear on the display.[9]

If you wish to change one of the data items in the problem, you may do so without reentering all the information. For example, if you wish to recalculate the same problem with a 5-year compounding period, simply press 5, N, CPT, and FV. The new amount, $7,693.12, should appear on the display.

Rule of 72

Occasionally you may find it necessary to obtain a precise measurement of the effect of interest in the compounding process and that a rough estimate of the future value of a single sum will suffice. In such cases a simple device called the "rule of 72" may be useful.

The rule of 72 is a quick method of estimating how long it will take for a sum to double in value at various compound interest rates. In this method the number 72 is divided by the applicable interest rate expressed as a whole number. The quotient is the number of periods in question.[10]

For example, at a compound annual interest rate of 9 percent, a $100 principal sum will double in value and reach $200 in approximately 8 years (72 ÷ 9). It will double again and reach $400 in approximately another 8 years and double still again, reaching $800, at the end of approximately 8 more years. At a compound annual interest rate of 6 percent, on the other hand, the growth of the principal sum will be slower, since it will take about 12 years (72 ÷ 6) for each doubling to occur.

Remember that the rule of 72 produces only approximations, and that for most purposes you will want to be more precise. Moreover, the amount of imprecision produced by using the rule of 72 increases as the interest rate and the principal sum are increased. (As a partial corrective measure, some prefer to divide the interest rate into the number 78 for interest rates of 20 percent or more.) More precise methods for computing the effects of compounding than the rules of 72 or 78 will be used in the balance of this chapter and the following one.

Computing n or i

In some types of problems involving future value of a single sum, FVSS and PVSS are known, as well as either i or n. The task in such cases is to use the three known values to compute the fourth.

For example, assume that you plan to deposit $1,200 in a savings account and withdraw the money when the account balance reaches $1,500. How long will you have to wait if the annual compound interest rate on the account is 7.5 percent?

The reader who is mathematically talented can solve this problem through the basic time-value formula by substituting the known values in it as shown below, and then solving for n.[11]

$$1500 = 1200 \times 1.075^n$$

Alternatively, if you happen to have an FVSS table with a column of factors for an interest rate of 7.5 percent, read down the column to find the factor closest to 1.25, which is 1500 ÷ 1200. Then read across to the years column to determine the approximate n. (From table B.1 in appendix B, you can find that the approximate n is 3 years.)

It should be obvious that neither the formula nor the table provides a quick and precise method for dealing with the problem of computing n. An electronic calculator with finance functions, however, can compute n as readily as it computes FVSS.

On the HP-12C, for example, after clearing the machine as described, enter the three known values in any order and solve for the fourth. Press 7.5, i, 1500, FV, 1200, CHS (in accordance with the machine's cash flow sign convention), PV, and n. The answer, 4.00 years, should appear on the display.

Actually this is an incomplete answer because of a design limitation of the HP-12C in dealing with this type of problem. If the answer is not an integer, or whole number, the HP-12C usually rounds the answer up to the next higher integer. This in effect means that the final year contained in the displayed value for n is actually only a partial year. (The HP-12C rounds down to the next lower integer if the portion of n to the right of the decimal point is less than .005, resulting in a slight understatement of the actual n.) If you wish a more precise value for n on the HP-12C, the best approach is to use the formula in note 11 at the end of this chapter, together with the log function of the calculator.

The HP-17B II and the BA-II Plus provide a more precise answer to the problem of computing n than does the HP-12C. If you are using the HP-17B II, set the calculator to display, say, four decimal places. Then go to the TVM menu system and clear its memory. Then use the menu keys to enter 7.5 as I%YR, 1200 as a negative PV, and 1500 as FV. Press the N menu key and the answer, 3.0855 years, will be displayed.

If, instead, you are using the BA-II Plus, after clearing the machine's display and memory and setting it to, for example, four decimal places as described earlier, press 7.5, I/Y, 1500, FV, 1200, +/–, PV, CPT, and N. The answer, 3.0855 years, appears on the display.

Instead of solving for n in a time-value problem, in many cases the task will be to solve for i. For example, what compound annual interest rate must you earn on your money if you have $6,000 to invest today and wish to have $10,000 in 5 years? Solving this type of problem is complex mathematically. Hence an explanation involving the use of a formula is not attempted here.

Use of the FVSS table to compute an interest rate is more feasible, at least for simple problems. The approach in the present example is to look across the row for the number of periods in the problem, five, until you find the FVSS factor closest to 1.6667, which is the FVSS, $10,000, divided by the PVSS, $6,000. In table B.1 in appendix B the factors 1.6474 and 1.6851 appear in the 5-year row. Look at the interest rates at the top of these columns and you can properly conclude that the interest rate in this problem is somewhere between 10.5 percent and 11.0 percent. Perhaps that is a sufficiently close approximation for some purposes. Alternatively, you could use a process of interpolation to get closer to the exact answer. Much greater convenience and precision in solving for i, however, is possible with a financial calculator.

On the HP-12C, for example, set the number of decimal places to four and enter the three known values in any order: 10000, FV, 5, n, 6000, CHS, PV, i. After a few seconds the answer should appear as 10.7566 percent. On the HP-17B II, with the calculator displaying four decimal places, clear the TVM memory and use the menu keys to enter 5, N, 6000, +/–, PV, 10000, FV, and I%YR. The answer will appear as 10.7566%. Or on the BA-II Plus, after you make sure the memory is clear, set the number of decimal places to four and press 5, N, 6000, +/–, PV, 10000, FV, CPT, I/Y to produce the answer, 10.7566 percent. (As with the HP-12C, any order in which you choose to enter the three known variables on the other two calculators is acceptable.)

PRESENT VALUE OF A SINGLE SUM

The preceding pages dealt with the question of compounding, of computing how a known single sum of money accumulates over time to an unknown future value. Now the question will be reversed. Given the future value of a single sum of money, what is it worth today? What is its present, or discounted, value?

For example, assume that in 4 years it will be necessary to spend $125,000 to replace an asset that is wearing out. How much money should be on hand today in an account earning 10 percent compound interest in order to reach that goal? Or assume that you are scheduled to receive a $75,000 lump-sum distribution from a trust 5 years from now. For how much would you sell that right today (if you are permitted to do so) if interest rates are 7 percent? (See figure 6-4.)

Using the Time-Value Formula

You learned earlier that FVSS can be found through the formula

$$\text{FVSS} = \text{PVSS} \times (1 + i)^n$$

Students of elementary algebra will recognize that this formula can be rearranged to

$$PVSS = FVSS \times \left[\frac{1}{(1 + i)^n}\right] = \frac{FVSS}{(1 + i)^n}$$

That is, FVSS multiplied by the mathematical reciprocal of $(1 + i)^n$, which is the same as dividing FVSS by $(1 + i)^n$, produces the PVSS. Discounting is thus the reverse of compounding. When compounding you should multiply the known sum by $(1 + i)^n$, whereas in discounting you should multiply it by the reciprocal of that quantity (or divide it by that quantity).

FIGURE 6-4
Time Line Representation of PVSS Problems

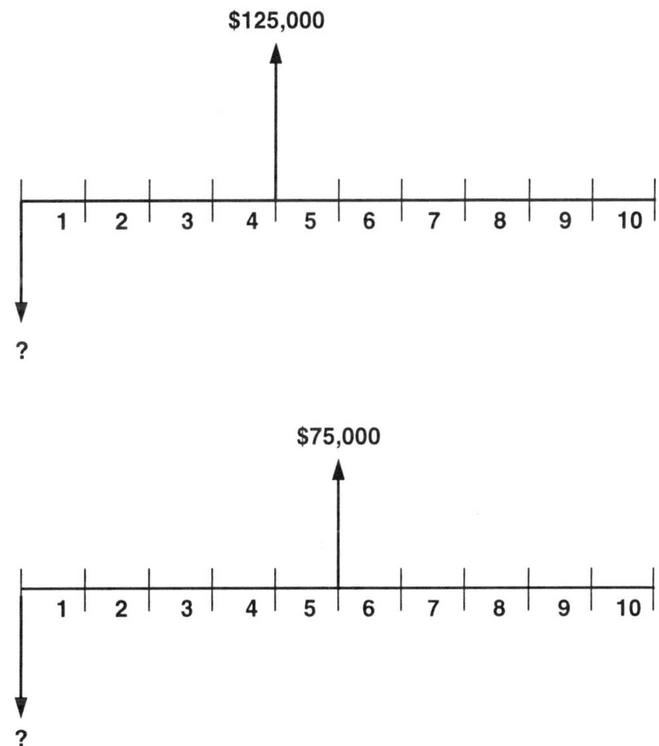

The time line on the top represents a problem in which you are asked to determine the present value of a $125,000 single sum due 4 years hence. In the time line on the bottom the problem is to compute the PVSS when FVSS is $75,000 due in 5 years.

In the top of figure 6-4, then, you need to have $125,000 in 4 years for replacement of the wearing-out asset. If you can earn 10 percent compound interest, you should set aside today a total of a little over $85,000. That is,

$$\text{PVSS} = \$125{,}000 \text{ x} \left[\frac{1}{1.10^4}\right] = \frac{\$125{,}000}{1.10^4} = \frac{\$125{,}000}{1.4641} = \$85{,}376.68$$

This amount, accumulating at 10 percent compound annual interest, will grow to the necessary $125,000 when it is needed in 4 years.

And the present value of that $75,000 trust fund distribution due to be received in 5 years, if the interest rate is 7 percent, is a little more than $53,000.

$$\text{PVSS} = \$75{,}000 \text{ x} \left[\frac{1}{1.07^5}\right] = \frac{\$75{,}000}{1.07^5} = \frac{\$75{,}000}{1.4026} = \$53{,}472.12$$

Note the effect of a change in i or n on PVSS. If either of these is increased, the denominator of the formula increases and, when it is divided into FVSS, the resulting PVSS declines. For example, the present value of the $75,000 trust fund distribution due in 5 years is only $46,569.39 if the interest rate used in discounting is 10 percent; it is still smaller, $34,987.87, if it is due in 8 years and the interest rate is 10 percent. A decrease in either i or n, on the other hand, causes PVSS to rise.

Using the PVSS Table

The calculation of present values by means of the formula is as tedious, time consuming, and susceptible to errors as is the calculation of future values. To simplify the process of computing PVSS, a table has been constructed showing the value of $1 \div (1 + i)^n$ for various rates of interest and numbers of years. (See table B.2 in appendix B.) Excerpts from that table are presented below.

This table, it should be remembered, is a direct by-product of table 6-3, which showed FVSS factors. All that was done to produce table 6-4 was to divide each factor in table 6-3 into one; that is, each PVSS factor is the reciprocal of the FVSS factor for the same n and i.

To compute the present value of a single sum, select the appropriate factor from the PVSS table and multiply it by the future value of the sum in question. For example, to the present value of $125,000 needed in 4 years and discounted at a 10 percent interest rate, look down the 10% column to the row for four periods. The factor, .6830, is multiplied by $125,000 to produce the answer, $85,375. And the present value of $75,000 to be received in 5 years and discounted at 7 percent is $53,475 ($75,000 x .7130).

Once again, review table 6-4 to see the effect of changes in n and i on PVSS. As you move down any interest-rate column to higher levels of n, the PVSS factor, and hence PVSS, declines. And as you move across the row for any number periods to higher levels of i, the PVSS factor, and hence PVSS, declines.

TABLE 6-4
Present Value of a Single Sum Factors

n/i	7%	8%	9%	10%	11%
1	0.9346	0.9259	0.9174	0.9091	0.9009
2	0.8734	0.8573	0.8417	0.8264	0.8116
3	0.8163	0.7938	0.7722	0.7513	0.7312
4	0.7629	0.7350	0.7084	0.6830	0.6587
5	0.7130	0.6806	0.6499	0.6209	0.5935
6	0.6663	0.6302	0.5963	0.5645	0.5346
7	0.6227	0.5835	0.5470	0.5132	0.4817
8	0.5820	0.5403	0.5019	0.4665	0.4339
9	0.5439	0.5002	0.4604	0.4241	0.3909
10	0.5083	0.4632	0.4224	0.3855	0.3522
11	0.4751	0.4289	0.3875	0.3505	0.3173
12	0.4440	0.3971	0.3555	0.3186	0.2858
13	0.4150	0.3677	0.3262	0.2897	0.2575
14	0.3878	0.3405	0.2992	0.2633	0.2320
15	0.3624	0.3152	0.2745	0.2394	0.2090

Computing PVSS with a Financial Calculator

Using the HP-12C to Compute PVSS

The task of computing the present value of a future sum of money is greatly simplified by the HP-12C financial calculator. As explained earlier, clear the machine and set it to display two decimal places. The next step is to enter the three known values into the machine in any order. Then press the PV button to solve for the present value of the single sum in question.

For example, assume that you own a zero coupon bond that will mature in 13 years, at which time it will pay you $1,000. Meanwhile, it will pay you nothing. What would you sell the bond for today if you believe you could invest the proceeds elsewhere and earn 9 percent compound interest?

Enter 9, i, 13, n, 1000, FV. The calculator is now programmed to compute the present value of the $1,000 due to be received in the future. Depress the PV key and the answer, $326.18, should be displayed. (Remember that the HP-12C's cash flow sign convention referred to earlier shows the answer as a negative number if all the data are entered as positive numbers.) That is, if you were to invest $326.18 at 9 percent compound interest, you would have $1,000 at the end of 13 years. (You may wish to verify this by computing the FVSS of $326.18 as explained earlier in this chapter.)

Using the HP-17B II to Compute PVSS

If you wish to use the HP-17B II to compute the present value of a single sum, set the calculator to display two decimal places. Clear the TVM menu system's memory. Then enter the three known variables in the problem by pressing the appropriate menu keys. Lastly, press the PV menu key to produce the answer.

For example, assume that you own a zero-coupon bond that will mature in 15 years for $1,000. Meanwhile, it will pay you nothing. What would you sell the bond for today if you believe you could invest the proceeds elsewhere and earn 8 1/2 percent compound interest?

Enter 15 as the N, 8.5 as the I%YR, and 1000 as the FV. Press the PV menu key to find the answer, and $294.14 will be displayed. (Remember that present values are displayed as negative numbers because the three known variables were all entered as positive numbers.) That is, if you were to invest $294.14 at 8.5 percent compound interest, you would have $1,000 at the end of 15 years. (You may wish to verify this by computing the FVSS of $294.14 as explained earlier in this chapter.)

Using the BA-II Plus Calculator to Compute PVSS

If you wish to use the BA-II Plus calculator to compute the present value of a single sum, clear the memory and set the machine to display two decimal places, as was explained earlier. Then enter the three known values into the calculator in any order. Finally, press the CPT and PV keys to compute the present value of the single sum in question.

For example, assume that you own a zero coupon bond that will mature in 6 years, at which time it will pay you $1,000. Meanwhile, it will pay you nothing. What would you sell the bond for today if you believe you could invest the proceeds elsewhere and earn 11 percent compound interest?

Enter 1000, FV, 11, I/Y, 6, N. The calculator is now programmed to compute the present value of the $1,000 due to be received in the future. Depress the CPT and PV keys and the answer, $534.64, should be displayed. (Remember that the BA-II Plus shows the answer as a negative number if all the data are entered as positive numbers.) That is, if you were to invest $534.64 at 11 percent compound interest for the next 6 years, you would have $1,000 at the end of that time. (You may wish to verify this by computing the FVSS of $534.64 as explained earlier in this chapter.)

Rule of 72

Earlier in this chapter, the rule of 72 was presented as a quick method for estimating how long it takes a sum of money to double in value. It can also be used to estimate how long it takes a sum of money to halve in value. For example, if an average annual inflation rate of 8 percent should be experienced over an extended period, a person's $50,000 salary would fall in purchasing power to $25,000 in approximately (72 ÷ 8 =) 9 years (if the salary remains at $50,000).

Computing n or i

As is true of future-value problems, it is sometimes useful to be able to compute either n or i, given the other and given FVSS and PVSS. For example, assume that you owe $5,000 to be paid in a lump sum in 2 years. The lender offers to accept $4,750 today in satisfaction of the loan. Should you accept the offer? The answer depends at least partly on the rate of return (interest) the lender is effectively offering you.

This can be determined by using table B.2 in appendix B. First divide the present value, $4,750, by the future value, $5,000. The answer is .9500. Then look across the row for two periods and find the PVSS factor closest to .9500. That factor is .9518, which is in the 2.5% column. Hence the lender is offering you about 2.5 percent per year to pay the loan early. That hardly sounds like a bargain!

Alternatively, you can use a financial calculator. Set your HP-12C to display four decimal places. Then enter 5000, FV, 4750, CHS (again, present values should be entered as negative numbers), PV, 2, n. Then press the i key to produce the answer, 2.5978 percent. Or set your HP-17B II to display four decimal places. Then press 2, the N menu key, 4750, +/– (because it is a present value), the PV menu key, 5000, the FV menu key, and the I%YR menu key. The answer is 2.5978 percent, the rate of return you would realize by paying off the loan today. Or set your BA-II Plus to display four decimal places. Then press 2, N, 4750, +/– (again, present values should be entered as negative numbers), PV, 5000, FV. Then depress the CPT and I/Y keys. The lender has offered you a compound annual rate of return on your money of 2.5978 percent.

To reverse this illustration, if you insist on obtaining an 8 percent compound annual rate of return on your money, when would you be willing to pay the lender $4,750 to discharge your $5,000 debt? If you wish to use table B.2 to find the number of periods, look down the 8% column to find the factor nearest to .9500. The closest the table comes is to .9259 in the row for one period. This means you would not be willing to pay off the loan more than one year early.

As was explained earlier, the HP-12C provides only an approximate answer to this type of problem. Press 4750, CHS, PV, 5000, FV, 8, i, n to produce the answer, one year. The HP-17B II and the BA-II Plus are more precise. Set the HP-17B II to display four decimal places. As always, clear the TVM menu. Then enter 8 as the I%YR, 4750 as the negative PV, and 5000 as the FV. Press the N menu key to produce the answer, 0.6665 years. Or set the BA-II Plus to display four decimal places, press 8, I/Y, 4750, +/–, PV, 5000, and FV. Now press CPT and N to compute the answer, 0.6665. That is, if you repay the $5,000 loan about

8 months early (two thirds of one year) for $4,750, your compound annual rate of return will be 8 percent.

FUTURE VALUE OF AN ANNUITY OR ANNUITY DUE

Earlier in this chapter we explained how to compute the future value of a *single* sum placed on deposit or paid into an account credited with compound interest. Now we will build upon and expand that case to deal with the calculation of the future value of a *series* of deposits or payments. For example, if $300 is deposited, or paid, into an account each year and is credited with 11 percent compound annual interest, how much will be in the account at the end of 6 years?

This type of problem will be referred to as a future value of an annuity (FVA) or a future value of an annuity due (FVAD) problem. An *annuity* is a series of payments of equal amounts made at the end of each of a number of periods. An *annuity due* is a series of payments of equal amounts made at the beginning of each of a number of periods.[12]

There are many personal and business situations where sums of money are invested periodically. Some corporations, for example, make available payroll deduction plans whereby employees may save for a desired objective by having a stipulated amount withheld from each paycheck and invested in U.S. government savings bonds. Many individuals deposit a pre-established amount each week or month in Christmas Club or Vacation Club accounts at banks or credit unions. Many wage earners and self-employed individuals deposit funds each year in Individual Retirement Accounts (IRAs) or Keogh plans at banks, thrift institutions, brokerage firms, insurance companies, or mutual funds. Tax-advantaged employee benefit programs such as 401(k) and tax-deferred annuity plans are vehicles for employees to make periodic deposits, often matched by employer contributions, to save for retirement. Corporate sinking fund contributions to accumulate money for the purchase of fixed assets are another example of the annuity principle.

Assumptions

To simplify the solution of FVA and FVAD problems, it will be assumed for now that the deposits or payments are made annually. This assumption will be modified in the next chapter. Also it will be assumed that the deposits all earn the same rate of compound interest, though obviously each earns it for a different length of time.

In that connection, it is particularly important in annuity problems to be accurate in measuring the length of time during which each deposit earns compound interest. One possible assumption is that the deposits are made at the beginning of each year (an annuity due); the other is that they are made at the end of each year (an annuity). The difference between the two future values, all other things being equal, can be quite large.

For example, assume five annual payments of $1,000 each earn 7 percent compound interest. At the end of the fifth year the future value of these periodic payments will be $6,153.29 if they are made at the beginning of each year versus only $5,750.74 if they are made at the end. The $402.55 difference between the two future values, FVAD and FVA, is due to the fact that each deposit earns one more year of interest under the first assumption than under the second. That is, when deposits are made at the start of each year the first deposit earns interest for 5 years rather than 4, the second for 4 years rather than 3, etc., and the last deposit earns interest for one year rather than none. (See figure 6-5.)

FIGURE 6-5
Time Line Representation of FVAD and FVA Problems

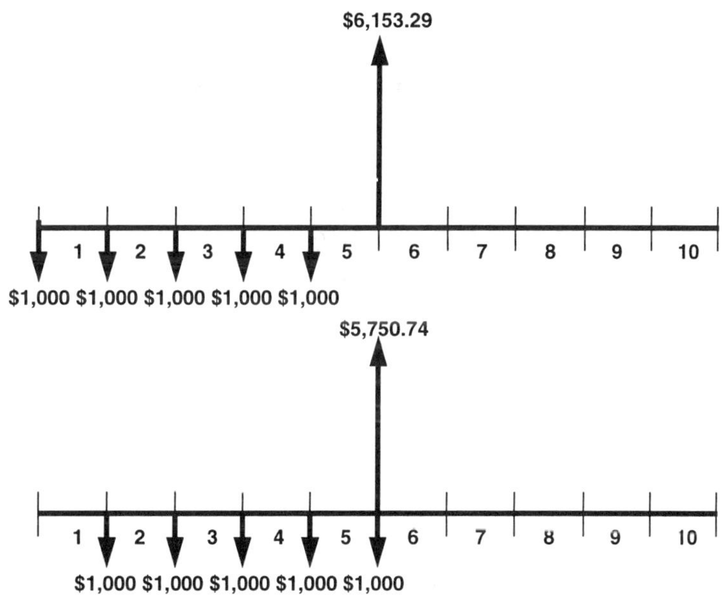

The top line depicts a problem in which $1,000 deposits are made at the beginning of each of 5 years (an annuity due), and the problem is to determine the future value as of the end of the fifth year. In the lower time line the problem is the same in all respects except that all deposits are made at the end of each of the 5 years (an annuity).

Using a Time-Value Formula

Problems calling for calculation of the future value of an annuity or annuity due can be viewed as collections of FVSS problems. Each annuity payment or deposit is a single sum that earns compound interest for a different number of years. Hence the FVA or FVAD is really the sum of a series of FVSS calculations.

To illustrate, assume that $100 is deposited at the end of each of 4 years and earns 5 percent compound annual interest. What is the total future value of these deposits at the end of the fourth year? The first deposit earns interest for 3 years (that is, from the end of year one till the end of year four). Hence its future value is

$$\begin{aligned} \text{FVSS} &= \text{PVSS x } (1 + i)^n \\ &= \$100 \text{ x } 1.05^3 \\ &= \$100 \text{ x } 1.1576 \\ &= \$115.76 \end{aligned}$$

The future value of the second deposit, which earns interest for 2 years, is

$$\begin{aligned} \text{FVSS} &= \text{PVSS x } (1 + i)^n \\ &= \$100 \text{ x } 1.05^2 \\ &= \$100 \text{ x } 1.1025 \\ &= \$110.25 \end{aligned}$$

The future value of the third deposit, which earns interest for one year, is

$$\begin{aligned} \text{FVSS} &= \text{PVSS x } (1 + i)^n \\ &= \$100 \text{ x } 1.05^1 \\ &= \$105.00 \end{aligned}$$

And the future value of the fourth deposit is $100, the same as its present value, because it earns no interest. Thus the FVA in this illustration is $431.01 ($115.76 + $110.25 + $105.00 + $100).

If, on the other hand, the deposits had been made at the beginning of each year, their future values would have been as follows:

1st	$\$100 \text{ x } 1.05^4$	=	$121.55
2d	$\$100 \text{ x } 1.05^3$	=	115.76
3d	$\$100 \text{ x } 1.05^2$	=	110.25
4th	$\$100 \text{ x } 1.05^1$	=	105.00
	FVAD	=	$452.56

As an alternative to the foregoing approach of summing the future value of each of the separate deposits, the same result can be achieved in one step by using a somewhat more complex formula for cases where the deposits are made at the end of each year.

$$\text{FVA} = \text{annual deposit x} \left[\frac{(1 + i)^n - 1}{i} \right]$$

In the previous illustration,

$$\text{FVA} = \$100 \text{ x} \left[\frac{1.05^4 - 1}{.05} \right]$$

$$= \$100 \text{ x} \left[\frac{.2155}{.05} \right]$$

$$= \$431.01$$

For cases in which the deposits are made at the beginning of each year, the same formula may be used, but with one important modification. To reflect the fact that each deposit will be credited with one extra year of interest, it is necessary to multiply the result of the preceding formula by (1 + i). That is, if deposits are made at the beginning of each year, the formula becomes

$$\text{FVAD} = \text{annual deposit x} \left[\frac{(1 + i)^n - 1}{i} \right] \text{x } (1 + i)$$

$$= \$100 \text{ x} \left[\frac{1.05^4 - 1}{.05} \right] \text{x } (1 + i)$$

$$= \$100 \text{ x} \left[\frac{.2155}{.05} \right] \text{x } 1.05$$

$$= \$431.01 \text{ x } 1.05$$

$$= \$452.56$$

A simple way to keep the FVAD calculation in mind is to calculate FVA through the end-of-year formula above. If the problem is a beginning-of-year case, multiply the result by (1 + i) to produce the FVAD.

Using a Table to Compute FVA and FVAD

Those who are somewhat less mathematically inclined may prefer to avoid memorizing and applying the formulas contained in the preceding section. They will, undoubtedly, be heartened to learn that most of the work has already been done for them, and that the results of computing the quantity

$$\frac{(1 + i)^n - 1}{i}$$

for various rates of interest and numbers of periods appear in a table. (See table B.3 in appendix B.) Excerpts from that table appear below. To compute the FVA (the future value of a series of periodic payments made at the end of each year) simply multiply the appropriate factor in this table by the amount of one of the payments. To compute FVAD, multiply the result of the foregoing calculation by (1 + i).

TABLE 6-5
Future Value of an Annuity Factors

n/i	7%	8%	9%	10%	11%
1	1.0000	1.0000	1.0000	1.0000	1.0000
2	2.0700	2.0800	2.0900	2.1000	2.1100
3	3.2149	3.2464	3.2781	3.3100	3.3421
4	4.4399	4.5061	4.5731	4.6410	4.7097
5	5.7507	5.8666	5.9847	6.1051	6.2278
6	7.1533	7.3359	7.5233	7.7156	7.9129
7	8.6540	8.9228	9.2004	9.4872	9.7833
8	10.2598	10.6366	11.0285	11.4359	11.8594
9	11.9730	12.4876	13.0210	13.5795	14.1640
10	13.8164	14.4866	15.1929	15.9374	16.7220
11	15.7836	16.6455	17.5603	18.5312	19.5614
12	17.8885	18.9771	20.1407	21.3843	22.7132
13	20.1406	21.4953	22.9534	24.5227	26.2116
14	22.5505	24.2149	26.0192	27.9750	30.0949
15	25.1290	27.1521	29.3609	31.7725	34.4054

For example, assume that an individual deposits $2,000 at the end of each year for 13 years in an IRA account earning 11 percent compound interest per year. How much will be in the account at the end of the thirteenth year? In table 6-5 or B.3, locate the FVA factor in the 11% column, row 13. The future value of these periodic deposits will be $52,423.20 ($2,000 x 26.2116). If, on the other hand, the 13 deposits are made at the beginning of each year, the FVAD will be 11 percent higher, because each deposit will earn one extra year's interest. Hence the FVAD is $58,189.75 ($2,000 x 26.2116 x 1.11).

Using a Financial Calculator to Compute FVA and FVAD

As with the types of time-value problems discussed earlier in this chapter, an electronic calculator with finance functions is a very useful tool for solving FVA and FVAD problems. Among the advantages of the calculator over formulas or tables are its great speed, its reduced likelihood of error, and the great range of values for n and i that it can handle.

Solving FVA or FVAD on the HP-12C

To use the HP-12C, clear the memory units and set the calculator to display two decimal places. In annuity and annuity due problems you will be using a new key on the top row of the keyboard, PMT (payment), to reflect the fact that a series of deposits is involved, rather than a single sum. Also when solving a problem involving a series of payments or deposits you must always remember to instruct the calculator as to whether the payments or deposits will be made at the end of each period (FVA) or at the beginning (FVAD). This will be accomplished through use of the blue g key and the blue END or blue BEG function in the top row of the keyboard.

To illustrate, assume that a young couple deposits $5,000 today and at the start of each of the next 4 years in a savings account to accumulate a down payment for a house. If the account is credited with 8 percent compound interest per year, how much of a down payment will the couple have 5 years from now? (See the time line depiction of this type of problem in figure 6-6.)

Depress the following keys to reflect the known information: 5000, CHS (because, as was noted earlier, deposits that represent cash outflows are treated as negative numbers according to the cash flow sign convention), PMT, 8, i, 5, n, blue g, BEG (because the deposits are made at the start of each of the 5 years), FV. The answer, the FVAD, $31,679.65, should appear on the display. If the deposits had been made at the end of each of the 5 years, the keystrokes would be identical except for the substitution of END for BEG after blue g. The answer under this new assumption, the FVA, would be $29,333.00. You can produce this new solution simply by pressing blue g, END, and FV, rather than reentering all the information in the problem.

Solving FVA or FVAD on the HP-17B II

If your calculator is the HP-17B II, set it to display two decimal places and clear the TVM menu system's memory. In annuity and annuity due problems, you will be using a new menu key, the one for PMT, which is located between the PV and FV menu keys, to reflect the fact that a series of deposits or payments is involved, rather than a single sum. Also, when solving an annuity-type problem, you must *always* remember to instruct the calculator as to whether the payments or deposits will be made at the end of each period (FVA) or at the beginning (FVAD). This is accomplished by going to the TVM menu, pressing the OTHER menu key, and pressing the menu key for BEG or END, as appropriate. For now set the calculator for BEG.

FIGURE 6-6
Time Line Representation of FVAD Problem

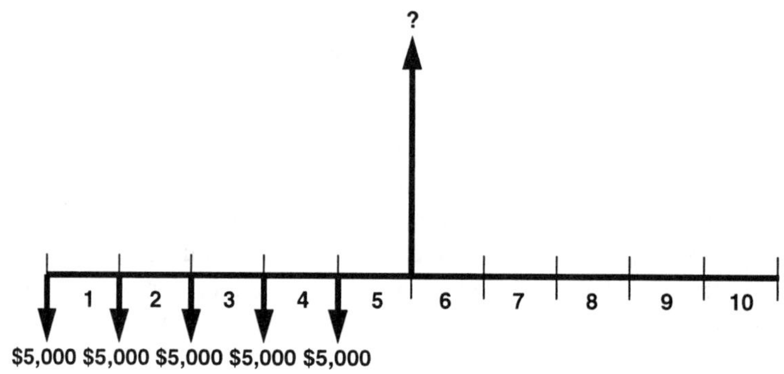

This time line depicts a 5-year annuity due. The problem is to determine the FVAD as of the end of the fifth year.

To illustrate, assume that Jack and Jill deposit $5,000 today and again at the start of each of the next four years in their credit union savings account to accumulate funds for the purchase of a piece of land. If the account is credited with 8 percent compound interest per year, how much will be in the account five years from now? (See the time line depiction of this problem in figure 6-6).

Press the following keys to reflect the known information: 5000, +/– (because, as noted earlier, deposits that represent cash outflows are treated as negative numbers), the PMT menu key, 8, the I%YR menu key, 5, and the N menu key. Now press the FV menu key and the answer, the FVAD, $31,679.65, appears on the screen. If the deposits had been made at the end of each year, rather than at the beginning, the answer, the FVA, would be 8 percent lower. You can produce the new solution without reentering all the data. Simply press the OTHER menu key, the END menu key, the EXIT key, and the FV menu key. The FVA is $29,333.00.

Solving FVA or FVAD on the BA-II Plus

If you wish to use the BA-II Plus, clear the memory units and set the calculator to display two decimal places. In annuity and annuity due problems you will be using a new key in the third row of the calculator keyboard, PMT (payment), to reflect the fact that a series of deposits is involved, rather than a single sum. Also when solving a problem involving a series of payments or deposits you must always remember to instruct the calculator as to whether the payments or deposits will be made at the end of each period (FVA) or at the beginning (FVAD). This will be accomplished through the use of the 2nd key and the BGN function printed above the PMT key.

To set the calculator to reflect when the payments occur in each period, press 2nd and BGN. The display should show either BGN or END. If the current setting is the one you want, press 2nd and QUIT. If the current setting is not the one you want, press 2nd, SET (which is printed above the ENTER key in the top row of the keyboard), 2nd, and QUIT.

To illustrate, assume that a married couple deposits $5,000 today and at the start of each of the next 4 years in a savings account to accumulate funds for their young daughter's college education. If the account is credited with 8 percent compound interest per year, how much of a college fund will the couple have 5 years from now? (See the time line depiction of this problem in figure 6-6.)

Set the calculator for beginning-of-period deposits. Then depress the following keys to reflect the known information: 5000, +/– (because, as we noted earlier, deposits that represent cash outflows are treated as negative numbers), PMT, 5, N, 8, I/Y, CPT, FV. The answer, the FVAD, $31,679.65, should appear on the display. If the deposits had been made at the end of each of the 5 years, the keystrokes would be identical except that you would set the calculator for end-of-period payments. The answer under this new assumption, the FVA, would be $29,333.00. You can produce this solution by pressing 2nd, BGN, 2nd, SET, 2nd, QUIT, CPT, FV, rather than reentering all the information in the problem.

If Number of Compounding Periods Exceeds Number of Deposits

Sometimes a problem will be encountered in which the number of periods during which compounding occurs exceeds the number of periods during which deposits are made. For example, assume that $500 is to be deposited at the end of each of the next 6 years in an account earning 8 percent compound annual interest. How much will be in the account at the end of 10 years? (See figure 6-7).

The simplest way to solve a problem of this type is to treat it as two separate problems and combine the results. The first step is to compute the FVA; the second is to treat that value as a single sum and compute the FVSS.

FIGURE 6-7
Time Line Representation of Problem Where Number of Compounding Periods Exceeds Number of Deposits

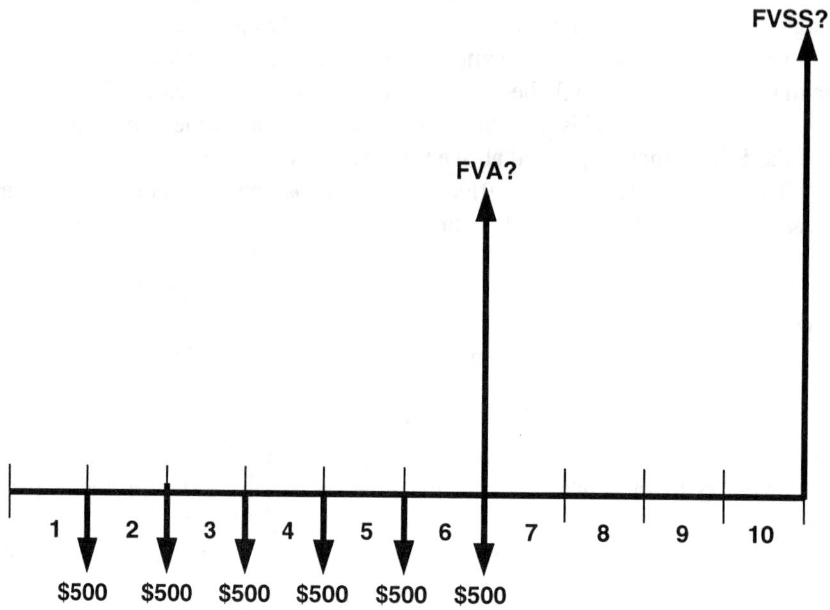

In this time line level payments are made at the end of each of 6 years. The future value of that annuity as of the end of the sixth year is then left as a single sum to accumulate until the end of the tenth year.

In this illustration, the FVA for 6 years and 8 percent interest, based on the factor from table B.3 in appendix B, is

$$\begin{aligned} FVA &= \$500 \times 7.3359 \\ &= \$3{,}667.95 \end{aligned}$$

The FVSS at 8 percent interest at the end of the remaining 4 years, using the factor from table B.1, is

$$\begin{aligned} FVSS &= \$3{,}667.95 \times 1.3605 \\ &= \$4{,}990.25 \end{aligned}$$

Solving Sinking Fund Problems

So far in this section you have learned how to compute the future value of a series of payments or deposits when the number of payments, the rate of interest, and the size of each payment are known. Sometimes, however, the facts are different, and it is the size of the periodic payment that is the unknown of the four key elements. This is often called a sinking fund payment problem.

For example, assume that a business wishes to accumulate $10,000,000 by the end of 3 years in order, at that time, to retire some of its outstanding mortgage bonds. The company plans to make three annual deposits, beginning today, into a sinking fund that will earn 9 percent compound interest. The question: How large must each of the deposits be in order to reach the target amount in 3 years?

Although the answer can, of course, be found by rearranging the FVA or FVAD formula and solving for the amount of the deposit, the use of a table or financial calculator is much more efficient. Hence only those methods will be explained here.

If you wish to use the FVA table, simply divide the target amount, the future value of the deposits, by the factor for the proper i and n. When calculating the FVA or FVAD, you *multiply* the proper factor by one of the deposits. When calculating the amount of one of the deposits, you *divide* the FVA or FVAD by the proper factor.

Since in the present illustration the sinking fund payments are to be made at the beginning of each year, you must first convert the FVA factor in table B.3 in appendix B for 3 years, 9%, which is 3.2781, into an FVAD factor. This is done by multiplying it by 1.09. The resulting FVAD factor, 3.5731, is then divided into the desired FVAD, $10,000,000, to produce the size of each deposit that will be needed to reach that goal, namely, $2,798,690.21. Three deposits of this amount, one made today and the others at the beginning of each of the next 2 years, all earning 9 percent compound annual interest, will grow to approximately $10,000,000 by the end of the third year.

Using a financial calculator is even more efficient than using table B.3, and is more precise because of a lesser problem of rounding. On the HP-12C, for example, press the following keys: 10000000, FV, 9, i, 3, n, blue g, BEG, PMT. The answer, $2,798,667.50, should be displayed on the screen (with a minus sign, in accordance with the cash flow sign convention). On the HP-17B II, set the machine for beginning-of-period payments and press 10000000, the FV menu key, 9, the I%YR menu key, 3, the N menu key, and the PMT menu key. The answer, $2,798,667.50, is displayed (with a minus sign, since these are outgoing payments). On the BA-II Plus, the same answer, again preceded by a minus sign, is found by setting the calculator for beginning-of-period payments and pressing 10000000, FV, 9, I/Y, 3, N, CPT, PMT.[13]

Variations from the foregoing sinking fund problem are problems in which the task is to compute n, the number of deposits that will be required, or i, the interest rate that must be earned on the deposits, in order to reach the target amount. For such purposes a financial calculator is the most effective tool.

Assume, for example, that you wish to accumulate $10,000 for a dream vacation in Tahiti and that you can afford to save $1,200 per year, beginning a year from now, toward that objective. If your savings earn 10 percent compound annual interest, how long will you have to wait before you can buy your airline tickets? On the HP-12C, press 10000, FV, 10, i, 1200, CHS, PMT, blue g, END, and n to produce the answer, 7 years. Or set the HP-17B II for end-of-period payments and press 10000, the FV menu key, 10, the I%YR menu key, 1200, +/–, the PMT menu key, and the N menu key. The answer, to four decimal places, is 6.3596 years. On the BA-II Plus, set the calculator for end-of-period payments and press the following keys: 10000, FV, 10, I/Y, 1200, +/–, PMT, CPT, N. The answer is 6.3596 years.[14]

On the other hand, if you insist on waiting only 5 years before going to Tahiti with your $10,000, what compound annual interest rate must you earn on your periodic deposits? On the HP-12C, press 10000, FV, 1200, CHS, PMT, 5, n, blue g, END, i. The answer, hardly encouraging, should appear after a few seconds of running time as 25.7839 percent. The HP-17B II and the BA-II Plus provide no happier an answer. With the HP-17B II set for end-of-period payments, press 10000, the FV menu key, 1200, +/–, the PMT menu key, 5, the N menu key, and the I%YR menu key. You'll have to find an investment that will earn 25.7839 percent. Or set the BA-II Plus for end-of-period payments, press 10000, FV, 1200, +/–, PMT, 5, N, CPT, I/Y to produce the answer after a few seconds, 25.7839 percent.

PRESENT VALUE OF AN ANNUITY OR ANNUITY DUE

An earlier section of this chapter contained an explanation of how to calculate the present value of a *single* sum due or needed at some time in the future. This section expands on that case and deals with the question of how to compute the present value of a *series* of level future payments. This type of problem will be referred to as a present value of an annuity (PVA) problem if the payments are to be made at the end of each period or as a present value of an annuity due (PVAD) problem if they are to be made at the beginning of each period.

To illustrate the type of problem that is the concern here, assume that an installment loan is to be repaid to you through six annual payments of $1,000 each beginning a year from now. For how much would you be willing to sell the promissory note today if you believe you can earn 8 percent compound annual interest on your money in some other investment outlet? What is the present value of this 6-year annuity discounted at 8 percent?

Assumptions

As was true in the preceding pages concerning the future value of a series of payments, it will be assumed here in the discussion of present value that each payment is made annually. This assumption will be dropped in the following chapter. In addition, it will be important to specify in each example whether the annuity payments are made at the end or at the beginning of each year. The difference in the answer can be substantial. For example, an 8-year, $1,000 annuity discounted at 6 percent has a PVA of $6,209.79, versus a PVAD of $6,582.38. (See figure 6-8.)

FIGURE 6-8
Time Line Representation of PVA and PVAD Problems

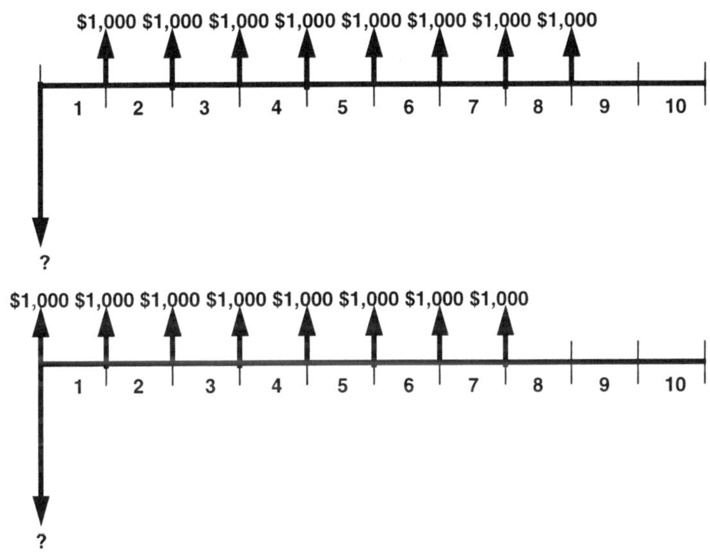

The upper time line depicts a case in which 8 annual payments of $1,000 are to be made beginning in one year, and the problem is to compute the PVA. The lower time line depicts an 8-year annuity due, in which $1,000 payments are to be made at the start of each year, and the problem is to compute the PVAD.

Using a Time-Value Formula

The basic formula for computing the present value of a single sum can also be used to compute the present value of an annuity or an annuity due. All that is needed is to calculate the PVSS for each annuity payment separately and total the results.

For example, assume that as part of a divorce settlement a father has been ordered to deposit a lump sum in trust sufficient to provide child support payments for his son. The child support payments are to be $5,000 per year for 4 years, beginning one year from today. If the amount placed in trust can be assumed to earn 7 percent compound annual interest, how much should the father place in the trust today?

Through the formula described in the discussion of the present value of a single sum, the present value of each separate payment can be found. The amount to be deposited today would be equal to the combined present value of the four payments.

Specifically, the present value of the first payment, to be made in one year, would be

$$\text{PVSS} = \text{FVSS x} \left[\frac{1}{(1 + i)^n}\right]$$

$$= \$5{,}000 \text{ x} \left[\frac{1}{1.07^1}\right]$$

$$= \$5{,}000 \text{ x } .9346$$

$$= \$4{,}673.00$$

The present value of the second, third, and fourth payments would be as shown below:

$$\text{2nd} = \$5{,}000 \text{ x} \left[\frac{1}{1.07^2}\right] = \$5{,}000 \text{ x} \left[\frac{1}{1.1449}\right] = \$5{,}000 \text{ x } .8734 = \$4{,}367.00$$

$$\text{3rd} = \$5{,}000 \text{ x} \left[\frac{1}{1.07^3}\right] = \$5{,}000 \text{ x} \left[\frac{1}{1.2250}\right] = \$5{,}000 \text{ x } .8163 = \$4{,}081.50$$

$$\text{4th} = \$5{,}000 \text{ x} \left[\frac{1}{1.07^4}\right] = \$5{,}000 \text{ x} \left[\frac{1}{1.3108}\right] = \$5{,}000 \text{ x } .7629 = \$3{,}814.50$$

The sum of these present values, the PVA, would be $16,936.00 ($4,673.00 + $4,367.00 + $4,081.50 + $3,814.50). That amount, placed on deposit today at 7 percent compound annual interest, will be just enough (well, within $.07 of just enough) to provide four annual payments of $5,000 each beginning in one year. To verify this, examine what would happen to the account each year.

Year	Beginning Balance	Interest Earnings	Amount Withdrawn	Ending Balance
1	$16,936.00	$1,185.52	$5,000.00	$13,121.52
2	$13,121.52	$ 918.51	$5,000.00	$ 9,040.03
3	$ 9,040.03	$ 632.80	$5,000.00	$ 4,672.83
4	$ 4,672.83	$ 327.10	$5,000.00	($ 0.07)

If, on the other hand, the four annual payments were to be made beginning immediately, the PVAD would be as follows:

$$\text{1st PVSS} = \$5{,}000 \text{ x} \left[\frac{1}{1.07^0}\right] = \$5{,}000 \text{ x } 1.0000 = \$5{,}000.00$$

$$\text{2nd PVSS} = \$5{,}000 \text{ x} \left[\frac{1}{1.07^1}\right] = \$5{,}000 \text{ x } .9346 = \$4{,}673.00$$

$$\text{3rd PVSS} = \$5{,}000 \text{ x} \left[\frac{1}{1.07^2}\right] = \$5{,}000 \text{ x } .8734 = \$4{,}367.00$$

$$\text{4th PVSS} = \$5{,}000 \text{ x} \left[\frac{1}{1.07^3}\right] = \$5{,}000 \text{ x } .8163 = \underline{\$4{,}081.50}$$

$$\text{PVAD} = \$18{,}121.50$$

Why would a larger amount need to be deposited in trust if the payments are to begin immediately? The total interest earnings would be lower because each withdrawal to make the child support payments would occur a year earlier than under the end-of-year assumption.

As an alternative to the foregoing approach of finding PVA or PVAD by summing the present value of each of the separate annuity payments, the same result can be achieved in one step by using the following, somewhat more complex, formula:

$$\text{PVA} = \text{annual payment x} \left[\frac{1 - \dfrac{1}{(1 + i)^n}}{i}\right]$$

Note that this formula should be used only for the case where the annuity payments are made at the end of each year.

In the child support illustration, then,

$$\text{PVA} = \$5{,}000 \text{ x} \left[\frac{1 - \dfrac{1}{1.07^4}}{.07} \right]$$

$$= \$5{,}000 \text{ x} \left[\frac{1 - \dfrac{1}{1.3108}}{.07} \right]$$

$$= \$5{,}000 \text{ x} \left[\frac{.2371}{.07} \right]$$

$$= \$5{,}000 \text{ x } 3.3871$$

$$= \$16{,}935.50$$

For cases in which the payments are to be made at the beginning of each year, the same formula may be used, but with one important modification. To reflect the fact that each payment will earn one fewer year of interest before it is distributed, it is necessary to multiply the result of the preceding formula by (1 + i). That is, if the payments are made at the beginning of each year, the formula becomes

$$\text{PVAD} = \text{annual payment x} \left[\frac{1 - \dfrac{1}{(1 + i)^n}}{i} \right] \text{x } (1 + i)$$

$$= \$5{,}000 \text{ x} \left[\frac{1 - \dfrac{1}{1.07^4}}{.07} \right] \text{x } 1.07$$

$$= \$5{,}000 \text{ x} \left[\frac{.2371}{.07} \right] \text{x } 1.07$$

$$= \$16{,}935.50 \text{ x } 1.07$$

$$= \$18{,}120.99$$

As was done in converting from FVA to FVAD, then, the way to compute PVAD is to compute PVA, and then multiply the result by (1 + i).

Using a Table to Compute PVA and PVAD

By this time it should come as no surprise to the reader that the factors generated through the foregoing PVA formula for various rates of interest and numbers of years have already been calculated. They appear in table B.4 in appendix B. Excerpts from that table are presented below. To compute the PVA, simply multiply the appropriate factor in this table by the amount of one of the annuity payments. To compute the PVAD, multiply the PVA by (1 + i).

For example, assume that you have won the lottery and will be receiving $15,000 per year, beginning in one year, for the next 10 years. What is the present value of your prize if interest rates are at 9 percent? From table 6-6 or B.4, the PVA factor for 10 years, 9%, is 6.4177. This factor is multiplied by the amount of one of the payments, $15,000, to produce the PVA, $96,265.50.

One of the few things in life that would be nicer than the lottery prize you won would be if the 10 annual payments were to begin immediately, rather than 12 months from now. In this case, the PVAD would be 9 percent higher; that is, $15,000 x 6.4177 x 1.09 = $104,929.40.

TABLE 6-6
Present Value of an Annuity Factors

n/i	7%	8%	9%	10%	11%
1	0.9346	0.9259	0.9174	0.9091	0.9009
2	1.8080	1.7833	1.7591	1.7355	1.7125
3	2.6243	2.5771	2.5313	2.4869	2.4437
4	3.3872	3.3121	3.2397	3.1699	3.1024
5	4.1002	3.9927	3.8897	3.7908	3.6959
6	4.7665	4.6229	4.4859	4.3553	4.2305
7	5.3893	5.2064	5.0330	4.8684	4.7122
8	5.9713	5.7466	5.5348	5.3349	5.1461
9	6.5152	6.2469	5.9952	5.7590	5.5370
10	7.0236	6.7101	6.4177	6.1446	5.8892
11	7.4987	7.1390	6.8052	6.4951	6.2065
12	7.9427	7.5361	7.1607	6.8137	6.4924
13	8.3577	7.9038	7.4869	7.1034	6.7499
14	8.7455	8.2442	7.7862	7.3667	6.9819
15	9.1079	8.5595	8.0607	7.6061	7.1909

Using a Financial Calculator to Compute PVA and PVAD

Use of an electronic calculator with finance functions greatly eases the task of calculating the present value of an annuity or of an annuity due. The calculator is faster, less likely to produce mistakes, and allows for the selection of more values for n and i than are likely to be found in most present value tables.

Solving PVA or PVAD on the HP-12C

Assume that a woman receives $6,000 each year from a trust. She is interested in obtaining a cash sum with which to buy a fancy new sports car. Her cousin has offered to buy from her now the present value of the next four annuity payments (the first of which will be made one year from now) discounted at 8 percent compound annual interest. How much will the woman receive if she accepts the offer?

If you are using the HP-12C, clear the memory units and set the calculator to display two decimal places. Then depress the following keys to enter the known information: 6000, CHS (because we are showing payments as negative values according to the cash flow sign convention), PMT (because the problem involves a series of payments rather than a single sum), 8, i, 4, n, blue g, END (because the payments will be made at the end of each year). The calculator is now programmed to compute the PVA. Depress the PV key and the answer, $19,872.76, should be displayed on the screen.

If the facts of the problem were revised so that the four annual payments from the trust were to begin immediately, the procedure for solving it would be identical except that the BEG key would be pressed instead of the END key. You can solve it now by pressing blue g, BEG, PV. The answer, the PVAD, is $21,462.58.

Solving PVA or PVAD on the HP-17B II

Assume that you have just won the lottery and are scheduled to receive $15,000 at the end of each of the next ten years. If the going rate of interest is 7 percent, how much have you won in present-value terms?

Clear the TVM menu system and set the calculator for end-of-period payments. Then enter the known information as follows: 10, the N menu key, 15000, the PMT menu key (because the problem involves a series of payments, rather than a single sum), 7, and the I%YR menu key. Now press the PV menu key and the answer, $150,353.72, will be displayed (as a negative, because it is a present value).

Solving PVA or PVAD on the BA-II Plus

Assume that several years ago the owner of a small business borrowed $10,000 from a relative and agreed to repay the loan in 10 equal annual installments of $1,500. Six payments now remain to be made, the first of which is due in one year. The business owner now would like to pay off the remainder of the debt. What sum should the business owner propose to the lender as a payoff figure if money is presently worth 7 percent?

If you are using the BA-II Plus, clear the memory units, set the calculator to display two decimal places, and set it for end-of-period payments (because the payments will be made at the end of each year). Then depress the following keys to enter the known information: 1500, +/– (because we are showing payments as negative values), PMT (because the problem involves a series of payments, rather than a single sum), 6, N, 7, I/Y, CPT. The calculator is now programmed to compute the PVA. Depress the PV key and the answer, $7,149.81, should be displayed on the screen.

If the facts of the problem were revised so that the remaining six annual payments were to be made beginning immediately, the procedure for solving it would be identical except that the calculator should be set for beginning-of-period payments. You can solve it now by pressing 2nd, BGN, 2nd, SET, 2nd, QUIT, CPT, PV. The answer, the PVAD, is $7,650.30.

If Number of Discounting Periods Exceeds Number of Payments

Sometimes a problem will be encountered in which the number of periods during which discounting is to occur exceeds the number of periods during which annuity payments are to be made. For example, what is the present value at a 7 percent compound annual interest rate of an income stream consisting of five annual payments of $2,000 each, the first of which will be made 3 years from now? (See the time line depiction of this type of problem in figure 6-9.)

The simplest way to solve a problem of this type, called a deferred annuity problem, is to treat it as two separate problems and combine the results. The first step is to compute the PVA; the second is to treat that value as a single sum and compute its PVSS.

In the present illustration the PVA for 5 years and 7 percent, based on the factor from table B.4 in appendix B, is

$$\begin{aligned} \text{PVA} &= \$2{,}000 \times 4.1002 \\ &= \$8{,}200.40 \end{aligned}$$

The PVSS at 7 percent for the value of an annuity that commences in 2 years (even though the first payment will not be made until the end of 3 years), based on the factor from table B.2, is

$$\begin{aligned} \text{PVSS} &= \$8{,}200.40 \times .8734 \\ &= \$7{,}162.23 \end{aligned}$$

If you are using the HP-12C, HP-17B II, or BA-II Plus calculator for this type of problem, compute the PVA in the usual manner. However, be sure to then fully clear the calculator's memory units before you proceed to the second step of the problem. Then enter the PVA you just calculated as a future value, and compute its present value in the normal way.

Note that in this solution a PVA is calculated and then discounted as a single sum for 2 additional years. The same result can be achieved if the problem is viewed as entailing the calculation of a PVAD and then discounting that single sum for 3 additional years. (Re-examine figure 6-9 to verify that a 5-year PVA discounted for an additional 2 years is identical to a 5-year PVAD discounted for an additional 3 years.)

FIGURE 6-9
Time Line Depiction of PVA or PVAD Problems Where Discounting Period Exceeds Payment Period

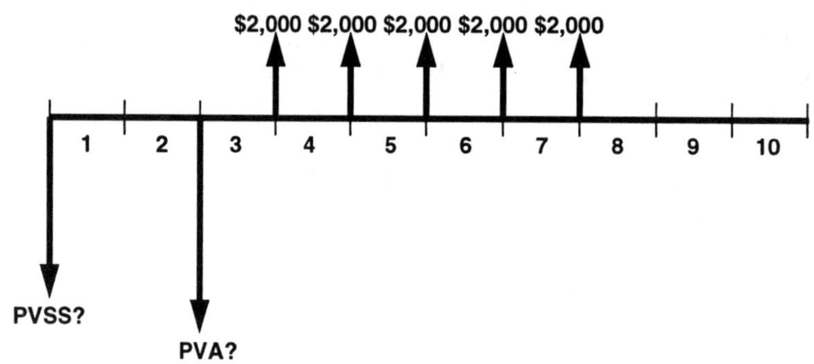

This time line depicts a case in which five annual payments of $2,000 each are to be made beginning in 3 years. The problem, which is to determine the present value of the income stream, can be divided into two parts. First determine the present value of the annuity as of the start of the annuity period, which is the beginning of year *three.* (Note: It is not the beginning of year four, even though that is when the first payment will be made.) Then compute the present value of that single sum as of today, 2 (not 3) years earlier.

Solving Debt Service/Capital Sum Liquidation Problems

Thus far you have seen how to compute the present value of a stream of equal payments when the number of payments, the rate of interest, and the size of each payment are known. Sometimes, however, it is the size of the periodic payment that is the unknown of the four key elements. A frequently encountered problem of this type is that of determining the amount of money necessary to liquidate a debt through periodic loan repayments. A similar problem is to determine how large a periodic withdrawal from a sum of capital can be in order to liquidate that sum over a given number of years.

In installment loans such as those used to finance the purchase of a house or automobile, each level periodic payment, called the debt service, consists of some repayment of the principal and some payment of interest on the remaining unpaid principal. Given the initial size of the loan, the interest rate, and the number of payments to be made, the problem is to compute the size of each required payment.[15] Such a debt service problem can be solved using PVA and PVAD factors in a manner analogous to that for solving sinking fund problems using FVA and FVAD factors as explained earlier.

For example, assume that a real estate mortgage for $50,000 bearing an 11 percent interest rate is to be repaid in 15 equal annual installments, the first to be made in one year. The question: how large must each annual installment payment be?

Although the answer can, of course, be found by rearranging the PVA formula and solving for the amount of the payment, that procedure is complex and unwieldy in comparison with using a table or financial calculator. Hence only the latter two methods are explained here.

Using the Table

In order to use the table, simply divide the original loan balance by the PVA factor for the proper i and n. When calculating the PVA, you *multiply* the proper factor by one of the payments. When calculating the amount of one of the payments, you *divide* the PVA by the proper factor.

Since in the present illustration the loan payments are to be made at the end of each year, you can use the PVA factor for 15 years and 11% shown in table B.4 in appendix B. Dividing this factor, 7.1909, into the $50,000 loan amount produces the size of the annual payment, $6,953.23. (Note, by the way, the amount of interest that will be paid on this loan. The total to be repaid will be $104,298.45, that is, 15 x $6,953.23. Since the loan principal is $50,000, the interest is $54,298.45.)

If the terms of the loan, on the other hand, had called for the first annual installment payment to be made immediately, it would be necessary first to convert the PVA factor for 15 years and 11% into a PVAD factor. This would be accomplished by multiplying 7.1909 x 1.11. The resulting PVAD factor, 7.9819, would then be divided into the $50,000 loan amount to produce the annual payment of $6,264.17. The total amount of interest to be paid in this situation would be $43,962.55, that is, ($6,264.17 x 15) – $50,000.

Using a Financial Calculator

Using a financial calculator is even more efficient, as well as being more precise, than the table because of a lesser problem of rounding. To illustrate, assume that in a negligence case a jury has awarded $125,000 to be used to support an injured child until the child reaches age 21, 11 years from now. How much will this capital sum and interest earnings thereon provide for the child per year if the fund earns 8 percent compound interest?

On the HP-12C, depress the following keys: 125000, CHS, PV, 8, i, 11, n, blue g, BEG (or END, depending on when the first withdrawal will be made), PMT. The payment under the beginning-of-year assumption is $16,212.54. Under the end-of-year assumption it is $17,509.54. Or on the HP-17B II, set the machine for beginning-of-period payments. Press 125000, +/–, the PV menu key, 8, the I%YR menu key, 11, the N menu key, and the PMT menu key. The answer is $16,212.54. Now see what the payment would be if an end-of-period assumption is used. Press the OTHER menu key, the END menu key, the EXIT key, and the PMT menu key. The answer is $17,509.54. On the BA-II Plus the same answers are found by setting the calculator for beginning- or end-of-period payments and pressing 125000, +/–, PV, 8, I/Y, 11, N, CPT, PMT.

FOCUS ON ETHICS
Ethics and the Time Value of Money

At first glance a discussion of ethics seems ill-suited to the topic of time value of money. After all, doesn't time value of money rely strictly on mathematical formulas without regard to ethical values? While it is true that mathematical formulas are amoral in and of themselves, it is also true that these formulas, improperly used, can lead to some extremely misleading results. These errant results may lead to decisions that aren't in the client's best interests.

TVM formulas are dependent on interest-rate assumptions. Higher rates of return provide more optimistic results. In a competitive marketplace, it is not uncommon for projected yields to be a determining factor as the client weighs alternative courses of action. Time-value-of-money formulas don't know one yield from another. If a salesperson offers an exaggerated yield, the formula will provide an exaggerated result. It may be the decisive factor in leading the client into an inappropriate purchase.

A $10,000 tax-deferred investment that earns 10 percent per year will grow to $67,275 in 20 years. What if a financial planner exaggerates the rate of return to 12 percent per year? The mathematical result is $96,463—a 43 percent increase in future value. Would this projection "close the sale"?

There is an old saying: "Figures don't lie, but liars figure." The ethical financial professional uses projected rates of return that are fully justified in terms of historical experience and analysis of future economic conditions.

Variations from the foregoing debt service and capital liquidation problems are problems in which the task is to compute n, the number of installment payments that will be required or possible, or i, the interest rate being charged or needed. For such purposes a financial calculator is the most effective tool.

Assume, for example, that a company plans to borrow $200,000 to expand its fleet of delivery vehicles. If the financial officer believes the company can afford to make loan repayments of $55,000 per year beginning a year from now, and if the lending institution is quoting an interest rate of 10.5 percent, how long will it take to repay the loan? On the HP-12C, press 200000, CHS, PV, 55000, PMT, blue g, END, 10.5, i, and n. The answer is five years. Or set the HP-17B II for end-of-period payments and four decimal places. Press 200000, +/–, the PV menu key, 55000, the PMT menu key, 10.5, and the I%YR menu key. Then press the N menu key to obtain the answer, 4.8172 years. On the BA-II Plus press the following keys after setting the calculator for end-of-period payments: 200000, +/–, PV, 55000, PMT, 10.5, I/Y, CPT, N. The answer is 4.8172 years.[16]

On the other hand, if the financial officer believes the company must have the loan repaid in 4 years, what interest rate must he or she obtain from the lending institution to accomplish this objective? On the HP-12C, press 200000, CHS, PV, 55000, PMT, 4, n, blue g, END, i. The answer, an unlikely 3.9245 percent, should eventually appear on the screen. Even if the borrower and lender use the HP-17B II or the BA-II Plus, they are unlikely to reach agreement on an acceptable interest rate. Set either calculator for end-of-period payments. Then on the HP-17B II press 200000, +/–, the PV menu key, 55000, the PMT menu key, 4, the N menu key, and the I%YR menu key. Or on the BA-II Plus press 200000, +/–, PV, 55000, PMT, 4, N, CPT, I/Y. After a brief delay, the 3.9245 percent rate is again displayed.

Creating an Amortization Schedule

Another useful calculation in connection with debt service problems is to generate an amortization schedule. In any installment loan, a portion of each payment is used to pay interest and the rest is applied to reduce the principal of the loan. Over the term of the loan the interest portion of the payment falls and the principal portion rises. The amortization schedule enables you to see, year by year, how much is being applied toward each.

To illustrate, assume a $1,000 loan with a compound annual interest rate of 11 percent is to be repaid in four equal annual installments beginning in one year. The amount of each payment is $322.33. How much of each year's payment will be applied to interest and how much to principal?[17]

Manual Calculation. If you are preparing the amortization schedule manually, you should set up a work sheet with column headings as shown in table 6-7.

After inserting the initial loan amount and the first year's payment, calculate the first year's interest by multiplying the 11 percent interest rate by the loan amount. This produces the figure for column (3). The balance of the payment, shown in column (4), is principal and is subtracted from the initial loan amount to produce the unpaid balance at the end of the first year, as shown in column (5). This amount is also the unpaid balance at the beginning of the second year, as shown in column (1). Again, 11 percent of this amount is the second year's interest in column (3), the remainder of the payment goes on principal in column (4), and so on through the end of the fourth and final year of the loan.

TABLE 6-7
Sample Loan Amortization Schedule

Year	(1) Unpaid Balance, Beg. of Year	(2) Payment, End of Year	(3) Interest Payment i x (1)	(4) Principal Payment (2) – (3)	(5) Unpaid Balance, End of Year (1) – (4)
1	$1,000.00	$322.33	$110.00	$212.33	$787.67
2	787.67	322.33	86.64	235.69	551.98
3	551.98	322.33	60.72	261.61	290.37
4	290.37	322.33	31.94	290.39	(.02)

Creating an Amortization Schedule with the HP-12C. If you are using the HP-12C to create an amortization schedule, note that the n key also contains a yellow AMORT (amortization) function. Note also the $x \lessgtr y$ key in the second row of the keyboard. Both of these will be used to solve the problem.

First enter the basic data about the problem in this illustration. Press 11, i, blue g, END, 1000, PV, 322.33, CHS, PMT. Now press 1 (because one payment will be made per year), yellow f, AMORT. The amount displayed, $110.00, is the first year's interest. Next press the $x \lessgtr y$ key to see the principal payment, $212.33. Then press RCL (the Recall key in the bottom row of the keyboard) and PV to show the unpaid balance at the end of year one, $787.67. Repeat the sequences as shown below to see the amounts in the following years.

Year	Keystrokes	Interest	Keystrokes	Principal	Keystroke	Unpaid Balance
2	1, yellow f, AMORT	$86.64	$x \lessgtr y$	$235.69	RCL, PV	$551.98
3	1, yellow f, AMORT	$60.72	$x \lessgtr y$	$261.61	RCL, PV	$290.37
4	1, yellow f, AMORT	$31.94	$x \lessgtr y$	$290.39	RCL, PV	($ .02)

The total interest paid during the 4 years is, thus, $289.30 ($110.00 + $86.64 + $60.72 + $31.94). The principal repaid, of course, totals (except for $.02 due to rounding) $1,000.

Creating an Amortization Schedule with the HP-17B II. In order to create an amortization schedule for this problem on the HP-17B II, set the machine to display 2 decimal places. Also set it for end-of-period payments. Then enter the basic data about this problem in this illustration: 4, the N menu key, 11, the I%YR menu key, 1000, the PV menu key, 322.33, +/–, and the PMT menu key. Now press the OTHER menu key and the AMRT menu key. Next, press 1 and the #P menu key. Now you are ready to see the year-by-year results. Press the INT menu key to see that $110 of interest is paid in the first year; the PRIN menu key to see that $212.33 of principal is paid in the first year; and the BAL menu key to see that the unpaid balance at the end of the first year is $787.67. Now press the NEXT menu key; the INT menu key to see that $86.64 of interest is paid in the second year; the PRIN menu key to see that $235.69 of principal is paid in the second year; and the BAL menu key to see the unpaid balance, $551.98, at the end of the second year. Press the NEXT and INT menu keys for the third year's interest, $60.72; the PRIN menu key for the for the third year's principal payment, $261.61; and the BAL menu key to show that $290.37 is owed at the end of the third year. Complete the schedule by pressing the NEXT menu key, the INT menu key ($31.94), the PRIN menu key ($290.39), and the BAL menu key (–$.02).

If you wish to see a summary of the results for the four years, press 4, #P, the INT menu key to see that $289.30 is paid in interest. Press the PRIN and BAL menu keys to show that the loan is repaid in full. Press EXIT twice to return to the TVM menu.

Creating an Amortization Schedule with the BA-II Plus. The procedure for creating an amortization schedule on the BA-II Plus calculator requires that you leave the machine's standard calculator mode that has been used throughout this chapter and use its prompted work sheet mode. First, however, clear the memory units and set the calculator for end-of-period payments and two decimal places. Then enter the basic data about the problem in this illustration by pressing the following keys: 1000, PV, 11, I/Y, 4, N, 322.33, +/–, PMT.

Then to create the schedule you will be using the Amort (amortization) function on the PV key, the ENTER key on the top row of the keyboard, and the down-arrow key next to the ON/OFF key. Press the following keys:

2nd, Amort	(to access the amortization prompted work sheet mode),
1, ENTER, ↓, 1, ENTER,↓	(to show the unpaid loan balance after the first payment),
↓	(to show how much of the first payment was applied to principal),
↓	(to show how much of the first payment was applied to interest),

↓, ↓, 2, ENTER, ↓	(to show the unpaid loan balance after the second payment),
↓	(to show the cumulative total applied to principal to this point),
↓	(to show the cumulative total applied to interest to this point),
↓, ↓, 3, ENTER, ↓	(to show the unpaid loan balance after the third payment),
↓	(to show the cumulative total applied to principal to this point),
↓	(to show the cumulative total applied to interest to this point),
↓, ↓, 4, ENTER, ↓	(to show an unpaid loan balance of approximately zero after the fourth and final payment),
↓	(to show the approximate cumulative total applied to principal by the end of the loan period),
↓	(to show the approximate cumulative total applied as interest by the end of the loan period).

When you have completed your review of the amortization schedule, clear this prompted work sheet and all the memory registers and return to the standard calculator mode by pressing 2nd, Amort, 2nd, CLR Work, 2nd, Quit, 2nd, and CLR TVM.

CASH FLOW STRUCTURES INVOLVING SINGLE SUMS AND ANNUITIES

Earlier in this chapter we noted that, though most time-value-of-money problems involve only four variables, sometimes they involve five variables, of which four are known and the task is to solve for the fifth. For example, a problem might involve an initial deposit of $1,000 into a savings account, annual deposits of $300 at the end of years one, 2, and 3, and compound annual interest earnings of 7 percent on all the deposits. The task might be to compute the account balance at the end of the third year.

Problems such as these are simply combinations of the types of problems you have already learned to solve. Simply divide the problem into its component parts, solve each component separately, and add the solutions together.

To illustrate, the preceding problem is made up of an FVSS problem ($1,000 for 3 years at 7 percent) and an FVA problem ($300 at the end of each year for 3 years at 7 percent). If you use tables B.1 and B.3 in appendix B to solve this problem, you will find that the future value is $2,189.47, namely,

$1,000 x 1.2250	=	$1,225.00
+ $300 x 3.2149	=	964.47
Total		$2,189.47

To revise part of this problem a bit, what if the objective is to have $2,500 in the account at the end of the third year? What initial deposit is needed, together with the three annual deposits, to reach this goal? This problem involves calculating the FVA of the three $300 deposits, subtracting it from the $2,500 future goal, and computing the PVSS of the balance. Using tables B.2 and B.3 in appendix B, you will find that the answer is $1,253.45, namely,

Future amount desired		$2,500.00
– $300 x 3.2149	=	964.47
Balance		$1,535.53
$1,535.53 x .8163	=	$1,253.45

If you are using a financial calculator, the task is somewhat simpler. In the first problem, enter –$1,000 as the PV, –$300 as the end-of-period payment, 3 as the n, and 7 as the i. Then solve for FV, which should be $2,189.51. In the second problem, enter $2,500 as the FV, –$300 as the end-of-period payment, 3 as the n, and 7 as the i. Then solve for PV, which should be –$1,253.45.

A frequent situation calling for the calculation of a fifth variable on the basis of four known variables is the computation of a bond's yield to maturity. For example, what is the yield to maturity of a $1,000 face amount bond, currently selling for $920, that will mature in six years and, in the meantime, will pay $80 of interest at the end of each year?[18] Enter $1,000 as the FV, –$920 as the PV, 6 as the n, and $80 as the end-of-period payment. Then solve for i, which is 9.83%.

PROBLEMS

1. A real estate appraiser has advised you that the value of the homes in your neighborhood has been rising at a compound annual rate of about 6 percent in recent years. On the basis of this information, what is the value today of the home you bought 7 years ago for $119,500?
2. According to the rule of 72, approximately how long will it take for a sum of money to double in value if it earns a compound annual interest rate of 4 percent?
3. Although you have made no deposits or withdrawals from your emergency fund savings account at the bank, the account balance has risen during the past 3 years from $15,000 to $17,613.62.

(a) What has been the compound annual interest rate that the bank has been crediting to your account?
(b) At that rate, how many more years will be needed until your account balance reaches $20,000?

4. There is an attractive piece of undeveloped land that you are considering purchasing. You think that in 5 years it will sell for $30,000. What would you pay for it today if you want to earn a compound annual rate of return of 12 percent on your investment?
5. Your personal net worth has risen in the past 4 years from $110,000 to $260,000 due to your shrewd investing. What has been the compound annual rate of growth of your net worth during this period?
6. You hope to accumulate $45,000 as a down payment on a vacation home in the near future.
   (a) If you can set aside $38,000 now in an account that will be credited with 8 percent compound annual interest, how long will it take until you have the needed down payment?
   (b) What if you can get 9 percent per year on your money?
7. You have decided that, beginning one year from now, you are going to deposit your $1,200 annual dividend check in a savings account at the credit union to build up a retirement fund. The account will be credited with 6 percent compound annual interest.
   (a) If you plan to retire 18 years from now, how much will be in the account at that time?
   (b) If you should decide to retire 3 years earlier than that, how much will be in the account?
8. The round-the-world trip you and your spouse intend to take on your 25th wedding anniversary, 6 years from now, will cost $22,000.
   (a) How much should you set aside each year, beginning today, to reach that objective if you can earn 9 percent compound annual interest on your money?
   (b) How will the size of the annual deposit be affected if you can earn only 8 percent compound annual interest?
9. You have just started a program of depositing $2,000 at the beginning of each year in an education fund account for your newborn son. How much will be in the account
   (a) after 11 years if it earns 8.5 percent compound annual interest?
   (b) after 13 years if it earns 8.5 percent compound annual interest?
   (c) after 18 years if it earns 7.5 percent compound annual interest and you discontinue making deposits after the fifth deposit?
10. A company leases an office building you own for $25,000 each year. The next rental payment is due in one year.
    (a) For what lump sum amount would you sell the next three payments today if you could invest the proceeds at a 12.5 percent compound annual rate of return?

(b) For what amount would you sell them if the next rental payment is due later today?

11. Which would you prefer to have: $10,000 today in a lump sum or $1,000 per year for 13 years, beginning one year from now, if interest rates are
    (a) 4 percent?
    (b) 6 percent?
12. A bank is willing to lend you $15,000 to make some home improvements. The loan is to be repaid in five equal annual installments, beginning one year from now. If the interest rate on the loan is 10 percent,
    (a) what will be the size of the annual payment?
    (b) how much of the second payment will be interest?
    (c) how much of the final payment will be principal?
13. The account in which you deposited your inheritance has a present balance of $48,000. If the account is credited with 13 percent compound annual interest and if you plan to withdraw from it $7,500 per year beginning one year from now, how long will it be before the balance is zero?
14. Suppose that a bank will lend you $10,000 if you agree to repay $4,199.31 at the end of each of the next 3 years. What compound annual interest rate is the bank charging you?
15. If you deposit $1,100 in your bank account today, and add deposits of $600 to it at the end of each of the next 9 years, and if all your deposits earn 6 percent compound annual interest, how much will be in your account immediately after you make the last deposit?

SOLUTIONS

(*Note:* Solutions to most of the problems at the end of this and the next chapter have been calculated with the answers rounded to two decimal places for dollar values and four decimal places for interest rate values and values of n. Your solutions may vary slightly from those presented due to rounding differences.)

1. The house should be worth about $179,700 today. In table B.1 of appendix B, the factor to be used is 1.5036. $119,500 x 1.5036 = $179,680.20. Or using a financial calculator, $119,500 compounded at 6 percent for 7 years produces FV = $179,683.82.
2. At a 4 percent compound annual interest rate, according to the rule of 72 it will take about 18 years for a sum of money to double in value, because 72 ÷ 4 = 18. A more precise answer, found by means of a financial calculator, is n = 17.6730.
3. (a) Your account has been credited with 5.5 percent compound annual interest. $17,613.62 ÷ $15,000 = 1.1742. In table B.1 in the 3-year row the factor 1.1742 is in the 5.5% column. Or using a financial calculator with $15,000 as the PV, $17,613.62 as the FV, and 3 as the n, i = 5.5000 percent.

(b) Your account balance will reach \$20,000 in a little more than 2 years. \$20,000 ÷ \$17,613.62 = 1.1355. In table B.1 in the 5.5% column, this FVSS factor is between those for 2 and 3 years, and is closer to that for 2 years. Through the use of a process of interpolation or use of the HP-17B II or the BA-II Plus financial calculator, you can find the precise n = 2.3731 (rounded to 3 on the HP-12C calculator).

4. You should be willing to pay about \$17,000 for the property today. In table B.2, the factor to be used is 0.5674. \$30,000 x 0.5674 = \$17,022. Or with a financial calculator, \$30,000 discounted at 12 percent for 5 years produces PV = \$17,022.81.

5. Your net worth has grown at a compound annual rate of almost 24 percent. \$110,000 ÷ \$260,000 = .4231. In table B.2 in the 4-year row, the closest factor is .4230, which is in the 24.0% column. Through a process of interpolation or the use of a financial calculator, you could calculate the precise amount, i = 23.9924 percent.

6. (a) It will take a little over 2 years to accumulate the down payment. \$38,000 ÷ \$45,000 = .8444. In table B.2 in the 8% column, this value lies between the factors for 2 and 3 years, and is closer to the 2-year factor. By interpolation or use of a financial calculator, you could find that the precise n = 2.1969. (Note, however, that the HP-12C produces an imprecise n = 3.)

   (b) With a higher rate, the waiting period is shortened to just under 2 years. In the 9% column of table B.2, .8444 lies between the factors for 1 and 2 years and is closer to that for 2 years. If you interpolate or use a financial calculator you will see that n = 1.9619.

7. (a) There will be about \$37,087 in the account at the end of 18 years. In table B.3 the correct FVA factor is 30.9057. \$1,200 x 30.9057 = \$37,086.84. Or if you use a financial calculator, FVA = \$37,086.78.

   (b) At the end of 15 years the account balance will be almost \$27,931. From table B.3 the FVA factor of 23.2760 is multiplied by \$1,200 to produce FVA = \$27,931.20. If you use a financial calculator, the more precise answer is FVA = \$27,931.16.

8. (a) You should set aside approximately \$2,683 now and at the beginning of each of the next 5 years in order to reach the target amount. In table B.3 the factor for 9%, 6 periods, is 7.5233. To convert this to an FVAD factor, 7.5233 is multiplied by 1.09 to produce 8.2004. The target amount, \$22,000, is divided by 8.2004 to produce an annuity due payment of \$2,682.80. On a financial calculator, the beginning-of-year PMT = \$2,682.78.

   (b) If only 8 percent compound annual interest is earned, the size of the needed annual deposit rises to about \$2,777. The factor is 7.3359 x 1.08 = 7.9228. Dividing \$22,000 by 7.9228 = \$2,776.80. Or on the calculator, the beginning-of-year PMT = \$2,776.79.

9. (a) After 11 years at 8.5 percent there will be approximately $37,099 in the account. In table B.3 the correct FVA factor is 17.0961. The correct FVAD factor is 17.0961 x 1.085 = 18.5493. $2,000 x 18.5493 = $37,098.54 FVAD. On the calculator, FVAD = $37,098.50.
   (b) After 13 years at 8.5 percent there will be about $48,198 in the account. From table B.3 the factor is 22.2109 x 1.085 = 24.0988. $2,000 x 24.0988 = $48,197.60 FVAD. On the financial calculator, replacing 11 with 13 as n produces FVAD = $48,197.73.
   (c) At the end of 5 years there will be about $12,488 in the account. The table B.3 factor is 5.8084 x 1.075 = 6.2440. Multiplying $2,000 by this factor produces $12,488.06 as the FVAD. This amount, carried forward as a single sum for 13 more years at 7.5 percent (see table B.1) will grow to $12,488.06 x 2.5604 = $31,974.43. If you use a financial calculator, $12,488.04 will be in the account at the end of 5 years. Clear the machine and reenter this as the PV, with 7.5 as the i and 13 as the n. FV = $31,974.54.
10. (a) You would be willing to sell the next three payments for about $59,533 today. In table B.4, the PVA factor for 3 years, 12.5% is 2.3813. $25,000 x 2.3813 = $59,532.50. On a financial calculator with $25,000 as the end-of-year PMT, 3 as the n, and 12.5 as the i, PVA = $59,533.61.
   (b) In this case the selling price would be higher, about $66,975. The PVAD factor is 2.3813 x 1.125, or 2.6790. $25,000 x 2.6790 = $66,975.00. If you use a financial calculator, the present value of the three beginning-of-year PMTs is $66,975.31.
11. (a) $10,000 now is preferable. In table B.4 the PVA factor for 4%, 13 years, is 9.9856. $1,000 x 9.9856 = $9,985.60 PVA. On the financial calculator, PVA = $9,985.65.
   (b) $10,000 in a lump sum now is even more preferable at the 6 percent discount rate. The PVA factor of 8.8527 multiplied by $1,000 = $8,852.70. On the financial calculator, PVA = $8,852.68.
12. (a) The PVA factor in table B.4 is 3.7908. The payment would be $15,000 ÷ 3.7908, or $3,956.95. On the financial calculator, with $15,000 as the PV, 5 as the n, and 10 as the i, the end-of-year PMT = $3,956.96.
   (b) and (c)
   It is possible, though cumbersome, to create an amortization schedule such as the following without using a financial calculator.

Year	(1) Balance, Beg. of Year	(2) Payment, End of Year	(3) Interest Payment 10% x (1)	(4) Principal Payment (2) – (3)	(5) Unpaid Balance, End of Year (1) – (4)
1	$15,000.00	$3,956.95	$1,500.00	$2,456.95	$12,543.05
2	12,543.05	3,956.95	1,254.31	2,702.64	9,840.41
3	9,840.41	3,956.95	984.04	2,972.91	6,867.50
4	6,867.50	3,956.95	686.75	3,270.20	3,597.30
5	3,597.30	3,956.95	359.73	3,597.22	.08

Thus the interest portion of the second payment will be $1,254.31 and the principal portion of the final payment will be $3,597.22. If you use the much faster financial calculator technique as described in the text with $3,956.96 as the end-of-year PMT, the second interest payment is $1,254.30 and the final principal payment is $3,597.23.

13. You could divide $48,000 by the $7,500 payment to produce a PVA factor of 6.4000. Then use the 13% column of table B.4 to find the n closest to this factor. The PVA factor for 14 years is 6.3025. The PVA factor for 15 years is 6.4624. Thus n is between 14 and 15 years, and is closer to 15. By a process of interpolation or by using a financial calculator with $7,500 as the end-of-year PMT, you can find the precise n = 14.5952.
14. First divide $10,000 by the $4,199.31 payment to produce a PVA (because the payments are to be made at the end of each year) factor of 2.3813. In the 3-year row of table B.4, this factor appears in the 12.5% column. Alternatively, enter the PV, n, and end-of-year PMT in a financial calculator to find that i = 12.50000 percent.
15. The FVSS of the $1,100 initial deposit after 9 years will be $1,858.45 ($1,100 x 1.6895). The FVA of the nine $600 deposits after the last deposit is made will be $6,894.78 ($600 x 11.4913). Thus the total account balance will be $8,753.23 ($1,858.45 + $6,894.78). Alternatively, on your financial calculator enter $1,100 as the PV, $600 as the end-of-period PMT, 9 as the n, and 6 as the i to find the FV, $8,753.22.

NOTES

1. Problems of this type are discussed briefly at the end of this chapter.
2. You should not be concerned with small differences among answers produced by the use of the table versus the formula or a calculator. Differences of a few cents often arise because of the lesser precision of the tables in the rounding process.
3. The descriptions provided for the solution of problems using the HP-12C, HP-17B II, and the BA-II Plus are for educational purposes only and should not be construed as an endorsement of them by either the author or The American College.

4. Several keys on the HP-12C calculator perform more than one function. This is accomplished by means of the yellow f key and blue g key on the bottom row of the keyboard. Pressing yellow f and a key causes the key to perform the function printed in yellow above that key. Pressing blue g and a key causes the key to perform the function printed in blue on the lower edge of that key. For example, press the 9, ENTER, 2, and y^x keys. The number 81, which is 9 squared, appears on the display. Now press CLX, 9, ENTER, blue g, and the same y^x key. The number 3, which is the square root of 9, appears on the display. Pressing the blue g key switched the function to be performed by the y^x key from raising the number to a power (y^x), in this case squaring it, to finding its square root $\sqrt{x}$.
5. For your convenience, appendix C lists the keystrokes to be used in solving the most common types of time-value-of-money problems on the HP-12C.
6. Several keys on the HP-17B II calculator perform more than one function. This is accomplished by the colored shift key. Pressing this key and another key causes the latter key to perform the function printed in color above it. For example, press the shift key and the CLR key, which has OFF printed above it, to turn the calculator off. Turn it on again, then press 9, shift, X (which has y^x printed above it), 4, and =. The number 6,561 appears on the display screen. You have just raised the number 9 to the fourth power (9 x 9 x 9 x 9) by means of the y^x function that is activated by the shifted X key.
7. For your convenience, Appendix D lists the keystrokes to be used in performing various housekeeping functions and in solving the most common types of time-value-of-money problems on the HP-17B II.
8. Several keys on the BA-II Plus keyboard perform two separate functions. The first function is that printed on the key. The second is that printed directly above it. This latter function performed by pressing the gray key marked 2nd in the upper left-hand corner of the keyboard, followed by the key in question.
9. For your convenience, appendix E lists the keystrokes to be used in solving the most common types of time-value-of-money problems on the BA-II Plus.
10. The rule of 72 can be used for purposes of discounting as well as for compounding, as will be explained later. In this case the result of dividing the number 72 by the interest rate is the approximate number of periods it will take to produce a present value equal to one-half the original sum.
11. Specifically, the formula is as follows:

$$n = \frac{\log\left[\dfrac{FVSS}{PVSS}\right]}{\log(1 + i)}$$

12. In some fields, such as insurance, the terms *annuity* and *annuity due* are used to refer to a series of payments the value of which includes both compound interest *and mortality* factors. Such annuities are more accurately referred to as *life annuities* or *life annuities due.*
13. If the sinking fund payments were to be made at the end of each of the 3 years, the methods of solving the problem would be slightly different. If the table is used, divide $10,000,000 by the factor in table B.3 without first multiplying the factor by 1.09. On the HP-12C, press END after blue g, rather than BEG. On the HP-17B II or the BA-II Plus, set the machine for end-of-period payments and recompute the payment. The precise answer is $3,050,547.57. The larger deposits are necessitated, of course, by the fact that each deposit will earn interest for one year less under the end-of-year assumption.
14. Technically, this answer assumes that in the seventh year a fraction of a year's interest is earned and a fraction of one annual deposit is also added to the account. Also, as was

explained earlier, the HP-12C is less precise than the BA-II Plus in solving for n. In this case, the HP-12C would give an answer of 7 years.

15. In reality, most installment loans call for monthly payments. In this chapter, however, it will be assumed that the periodic loan payments are made annually. The method for computing monthly payments will be explained in the next chapter.
16. As was explained earlier, the HP-12C is less precise than the HP-17B II or the BA-II Plus in solving for n. In this case, the HP-12C would give an answer of 5 years. Also, technically the precise answer of 4.8172 years assumes that in the final year a fraction of a year's interest is paid, as well as a fraction of a full year's loan payment.
17. The procedure for creating an amortization schedule where the loan is repaid through monthly installment payments is the same as described in this section except that (a) the figure used as the periodic payment should be the monthly payment; (b) the figure used as the interest rate should be the annual rate divided by 12; and (c) the number used as the n should be the total number of monthly payments to be made. See the discussion of simple annuities in the following chapter.
18. The solution when a bond pays interest semiannually, as is the usual case, will be explained in the next chapter.

7

Time Value of Money: Advanced Concepts and Applications

Robert M. Crowe

Chapter Outline

DEALING WITH UNEVEN CASH FLOWS

The preceding chapter included explanations of how to compute the future value and present value of an annuity (or an annuity due). By definition of the term *annuity,* the discussion dealt only with cases in which each of the payments or deposits in the series was of the same amount. This chapter begins with an explanation of how to compute the present value and future value of a stream of *uneven* payments or deposits. The ability to do so is useful in and of itself to solve several types of problems. It also is essential for evaluating various types of investments through discounted cash-flow analysis, as explained later in this chapter.

Present Value of Uneven Cash Flows

Assume that a young man will be entering college in one year. The estimated tuition is $6,000 to be paid at the start of the freshman year, $6,600 at the start of the sophomore year, $7,250 at the start of the junior year, and $8,100 at the start of the senior year. How much should be on hand today in an account earning 8.5 percent interest in order to just meet these four tuition payments as they come due? What is the present value of this series of uneven cash flows discounted at 8.5 percent?

The solution of a simple problem of this sort actually involves no techniques that have not already been covered. All that is needed is to compute the present value of each of the four tuition payments and add them together. In other words, the present value of this stream of uneven payments is simply the sum of the present values of the four single sums.

Using Time-Value Tables

Since this sequence of cash flows is fairly brief, simple tools such as a time-value formula or table can be used to compute the present value fairly quickly. Table B.2 in appendix B is used here to provide the appropriate 8.5 percent factors needed to solve the problem.

End of Year	Tuition Amount	PVSS Factor	PVSS
1	$6,000	0.9217	$ 5,530.20
2	6,600	0.8495	5,606.70
3	7,250	0.7829	5,676.03
4	8,100	0.7216	5,844.96
Total			$22,657.89

If $22,657.89 is placed on deposit today, and if 8.5 percent compound interest is earned on the account balance over the next 4 years, there will be just enough to meet each of the estimated tuition payments as they fall due. After the final payment is made, the account balance will essentially be zero. Table 7-1 shows the pattern of the account balance over the 4 years.

TABLE 7-1
Liquidation of a Capital Sum Compounding at 8.5% Interest through Uneven Cash Withdrawals

Year	Beginning Balance	Interest Earnings	Cash Withdrawal	Ending Balance
1	$22,657.89	$1,925.92	$6,000	$18,583.81
2	18,583.81	1,579.62	6,600	13,563.43
3	13,563.43	1,152.89	7,250	7,466.32
4	7,466.32	634.64	8,100	0.96

This case is an illustration of so-called *ungrouped* cash flows, which means that the cash-flow sequence includes no consecutive payments of the same amount and arithmetic sign, positive or negative. Each payment, therefore, has to be discounted separately. In some situations, however, there are *grouped* cash flows, that is, some of the consecutive payments are of the same amount and flow in the same direction, either in or out. With grouped cash flows a short cut is possible in finding the present value.

A common example of an uneven cash flow where some of the payments can be grouped is a corporate bond. For example, assume that you are considering purchasing a bond that will pay you interest of $90 per year at the end of each of the next 6 years, as well as the $1,000 face amount at the end of the sixth year.[1] If you wish to earn a rate of return of 13 percent on your money, how much would you pay for the bond? That is, what is the present value, discounted at a 13 percent annual interest rate, of this income stream, which is depicted in figure 7-1?

This series of cash flows actually consists of two components: an annuity of $90 per year for 5 years and a single sum of $1,090 at the end of the sixth year (or an annuity of $90 per year for 6 years and a single sum of $1,000 at the end of the sixth year). Hence to compute the present value of the entire sequence it is necessary to (1) compute the present value of the annuity, (2) compute the present value of the single sum, and (3) add the results together.

Again, the sequence of cash flows is rather short and simple in this illustration, so the solution can be calculated fairly quickly using time-value formulas or tables. For example, table B.4 in appendix B shows a PVA factor of 3.5172 for 5 years and 13%. Multiplied by the $90 annuity payment, this produces a PVA of $316.55. Table B.2 shows a PVSS factor of .4803 for 6 years and 13%. Multiplied by $1,090 it produces a present value of the sixth year cash flow of $523.53. Thus, the present value of the total sequence of cash flows, the price you would be willing to pay for the bond, is $840.08 ($316.55 + $523.53).

To take a different situation involving some grouped cash flows, assume you loan a sum of money to a borrower today. The repayment schedule calls for the borrower to make payments to you as follows:

End of Year	Payment Amount
1	$ 0
2	2,000
3–9	3,000
10	5,000

What is the present value of this sequence of payments, which is depicted in figure 7-2, if an 11 percent interest rate is assumed?

FIGURE 7-1
Time Line Depiction of a Bond Value

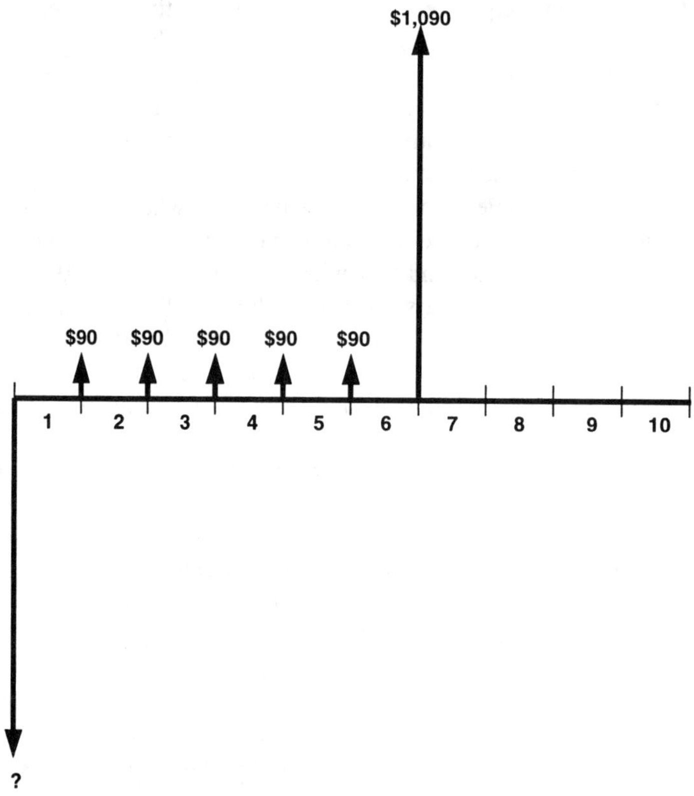

The time line depicts the uneven stream of cash flows provided by a bond—5 annual payments of $90 each and a sixth of $1,090. The problem is to compute the present value of the steam of cash flows.

FIGURE 7-2
Time Line Depiction of the Present Value of Uneven Cash Flows

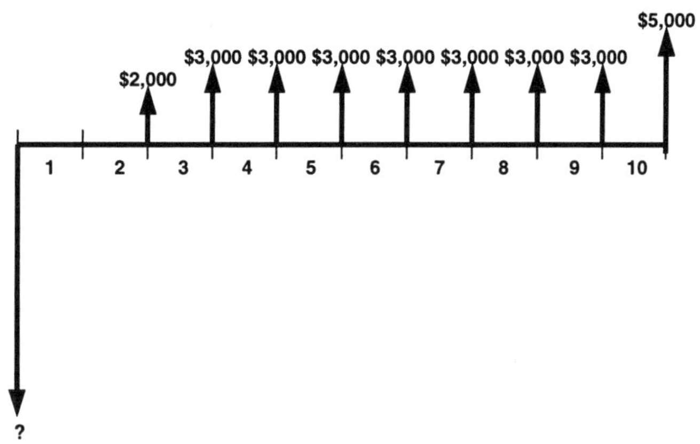

This time line shows a problem in which the task is to compute the present value of a stream of cash flows consisting of zero at the end of year 1, $2,000 at the end of year 2, $3,000 at the end of years 3 through 9, and $5,000 at the end of year 10.

The solution to this problem involves several steps. First, the $2,000 payment at the end of year 2 must be discounted. Second, the present value of a 7-year, $3,000 annuity must be computed. Third, the present value of that annuity must be further discounted as a single sum to compute its present value *today,* rather than its present value 2 years from now when the annuity begins. (Note that this annuity begins at the *start* of the third year, even though the first payment under it is not made until the *end* of the third year.) Fourth, the $5,000 payment at the end of year 10 must be discounted. Finally, the PVSS of the first payment, the twice-discounted value of the PVA of the next seven payments, and the PVSS of the ninth payment must be added together to obtain the present value of the entire series of cash flows.

Again you can use tables B.2 and B.4 to solve the problem. From the 11% column, find the appropriate factors and apply them as follows:

1. PVSS of payment at end of year 2
   $2,000 x 0.8116 = $ 1,623.20
2. PVA of payments at end of years 3–9
   $3,000 x 4.7122 = $14,136.60

3.	PVSS of PVA of payments at end of years 3–9 $14,136.60 x 0.8116 =	$11,473.26
4.	PVSS of payment at end of year 10 $5,000 x 0.3522 =	1,761.00
5.	Present value of the cash flows	$14,857.46

One last point should be made before some slightly more complex cash-flow patterns are discussed. In some problems one or more of the cash-flow amounts are negative. For example, assume you own rental property that is expected to generate net income for you of $15,000 per year at the end of each of the next 15 years, except for year 10. In that year you estimate that replacement of the heating and air conditioning units will be necessary, causing a *net cash outflow* for the year of $6,000. What is the present value of this stream of cash flow discounted at 9 percent?

In this case the only difference in procedure for finding the solution is that the present value of the net cash outflow must be *subtracted* from the aggregate present value of the net cash inflows. Specifically, in this illustration,

1.	PVA of inflows at end of years 1–9 $15,000 x 5.9952 =	$ 89,928.00
2.	PVA of inflows at end of years 11–15 $15,000 x 3.8897 = $58,345.50	
3.	PVSS of PVA of inflows at end of years 11–15 $58,345.50 x .4224 =	24,645.14
4.	Present value of cash inflows	$114,573.14
5.	PVSS of outflow at end of year 10 $6,000 x .4224 =	– 2,534.40
6.	Present value of the net cash flows	$112,038.74

As you can see, the illustrations are becoming a bit complex, and the use of tables to solve them is starting to be a little unwieldy. To reduce the difficulty, you may be able to express the cash flows of a problem in slightly different terms. For example, the preceding pattern of cash flows could be expressed as

1. an annuity of $15,000 for 15 years, and
2. an outflow of $21,000 at the end of year 10 (that is, $15,000 that needs to be subtracted out of the annuity and $6,000 that was the actual net outflow).

Calculation of the present value of this pattern of cash flows could have been completed in fewer steps than presented above.

Using a Financial Calculator to Solve Problems with Uneven Cash Flows

In the illustrative problems up to this point, the solutions were easy to find because of the short and simple patterns of payment. Tools such as time-value formulas or tables B.2 and B.4 and a simple calculator suffice in such situations for computing and totaling the present value of the individual cash flows or, in the case of groups of level cash flows, the annuities.

Often, however, a lengthy series of cash flows is involved in a problem. Frequently the series will involve many different payment amounts, some years of zero flows, and perhaps even some changes of arithmetic signs. For those cases, a financial calculator like the HP-12C, the HP-17B II, or the BA-II Plus calculator is very well suited. For problems that exceed the usually ample capacity of these calculators, a computer program may be necessary.

Ungrouped Cash Flows at End of Year. First to be explained is the use of these calculators to solve problems in which there are no consecutive cash flows of the same amount. In this circumstance, the HP-12C has the capacity to solve problems involving up to 20 cash flows that occur at the end of each year (or 21 that occur at the beginning of each year). The HP-17B II has the capacity to solve problems with up to 700 separate uneven cash flows. The BA-II Plus has the capacity, in this case, to handle up to 24 cash flows that occur at the end of each year (or 25 that occur at the beginning of each year).

To illustrate, assume an investment will produce the following pattern of net cash inflows during the next 20 years.

End of Year	Cash Flow	End of Year	Cash Flow
1	$ 500	11	$ 0
2	1,100	12	2,150
3	1,150	13	2,250
4	1,175	14	2,350
5	1,000	15	2,450
6	2,600	16	2,600
7	2,700	17	650
8	2,800	18	2,700
9	2,900	19	2,800
10	1,000	20	2,900

This set of data, together with the discount rate to be used, represents the maximum capacity that the HP-12C can handle and almost all that the BA-II Plus can handle. It barely scratches the surface of the HP-17B II's capacity. As explained below, either calculator's capacity can be expanded if some of the data consists of grouped data. Note in this problem, by the way, that some of the cash flows are of equal amounts (years 6 and 16, 7 and 18, 8 and 19, and 9 and 20).

Nevertheless, these are not grouped data because the equal amounts do not occur in consecutive years.

Using the HP-12C to Solve Problems with Uneven Cash Flows. To solve a present-value problem on the HP-12C where the cash flows are ungrouped and begin one or more periods in the future, first look at the PMT key in the top row of the keyboard. Note that it also contains a blue CFj function. (The CFj symbol stands for juxtaposed, or side-by-side, cash flows.) This function is used to enter the amount of each cash flow, including zero amounts. After all the payments in the series are entered, the discount rate is entered with the i key as usual. Finally, note that the PV key in the top row of the keyboard also contains a yellow function, NPV (net present value). The yellow f key and NPV are used to produce the solution.

To illustrate the process, assume that you have a deferred compensation agreement with your employer. Under the agreement the employer is obligated to pay you the following amounts:

End of year 1	$ 0
End of year 2	$ 75,000
End of year 3	$ 80,000
End of year 4	$ 85,000
End of year 5	$ 90,000

If you use a discount rate of 12.5 percent, what is the present value of this future income stream? Press 0, blue g, CFj. The initial year's zero value is now entered. Press 75000, blue g, CFj to reflect the amount to be received at the end of year 2. Press 80000, blue g, CFj to enter the cash inflow at the end of year 3. Enter the remaining two payments by pressing 85000, blue g, CFj, and 90000, blue g, CFj. Now enter the discount rate by pressing 12.5 and the i key. Finally, compute the present value of the income stream by pressing the yellow f key and NPV. The answer, $218,454.50, should appear on the display.

Using the HP-17B II to Solve Problems with Uneven Cash Flows. To solve a present value problem on the HP-17B II where the cash flows are uneven and occur at the end of each period, we will use the calculator's CFLO (cash flow) menu, which you will find at the same level in the menu system as the TVM menu. Press the CFLO menu key, shift, CLEAR DATA, and the YES menu key. Then press the #T? menu key. If the Time Prompting function is shown to be OFF, release the key. If not, press the #T? menu again to shut it off. Now you are ready to enter a series of ungrouped cash flows and compute their present value.

To illustrate the process, look at the brief series of cash flows in the deferred compensation agreement described in the illustration above. The HP-17B II is asking you for FLOW(0), which is the cash flow at the *start* of year one of the problem. Since there is nothing at that time in the problem you are considering, press 0 and INPUT. The calculator now is asking you for FLOW(1), which is the cash flow at the *end* of year one. Since this too is zero, press 0 and INPUT. The calculator then asks for the next cash flow, so press 75000 and INPUT. For the remaining cash flows press 80000, INPUT, 85000, INPUT, 90000, and INPUT. Now that the full series of cash flows is in the machine, press EXIT and the CALC menu key. Before you can compute the (net) present value of the series, you must tell the machine what discount rate to use. Press 12.5 and the I% menu key. Then press the NPV menu key to find the answer, $218,454.50.[2]

A sometimes useful feature of the HP-17B II is that it enables the user to check or even to alter the list of cash flows that have been entered. To review the amount of each of the flows, starting at the end of the series and proceeding back to the beginning, press the EXIT key and then press the up arrow key in the left-hand column of the keyboard several times. To change the amount of one of the cash flows, use the down or up arrow keys to display the item to be changed. Then key in the new value, press INPUT, and recompute the NPV. To delete a cash flow from the list, display the item to be eliminated and press the DELET menu key and recompute the NPV. To insert an additional cash flow, display the cash flow that follows the new one. Press the INSR menu key; then key in the new value, press INPUT, and recompute the NPV.

Using the BA-II Plus to Solve Problems with Uneven Cash Flows. If you wish to solve a present-value problem on the BA-II Plus where the cash flows are ungrouped and begin one or more periods in the future, you need to again use the prompted work sheet mode. This time, however, you do not use the amortization work sheet explained in chapter 5. Instead, you use the cash flows work sheet, which can be accessed through the CF key in the second row of the keyboard. You also use the NPV key in the same row of the keyboard to calculate the net present value of the cash flow.

To illustrate, look at the brief series of cash flows in the deferred-compensation agreement described on the previous page. If you use a 12.5 present discount rate, what is the present value of this future income stream? Press the following keys:

CF, 2nd, CLR Work	(to enter the cash flows prompted work sheet and clear it of extraneous data)
ENTER, ↓	(because there is no cash flow at the start of year one)
0, ENTER, ↓,↓	(because there is no cash flow at the end of year one and to prepare to enter the next cash flow)

75000, ENTER, ↓,↓	(to enter the first cash flow, to show that it occurred only once, and to prepare to enter the next cash flow)
80000, ENTER, ↓,↓	(to enter the second cash flow, to show that it occurred only once, and to prepare to enter the next cash flow)
85000, ENTER, ↓,↓	(to enter the third cash flow, to show that it occurred only once, and to prepare to enter the next cash flow)
90000, ENTER, ↓,↓	(to enter the final cash flow, to show that it occurred only once, and to prepare to solve the problem)
NPV, 12.5, ENTER,↓	(to tell the machine that you want to find the net present value of these cash flows discounted at 12.5 percent)
CPT	(to produce the answer)

The answer, $218,454.50, should appear on the display.

Sometimes it is useful to be able to review the cash flows that have been entered or even to revise one or more of them. To see the list again, press the CF key and move through the list by pressing the down arrow key several times. To remove a number from the list, display that number and press 2nd, DEL. Then recompute the NPV. To insert a number into the list, display the space where it is to be inserted. Press 2nd, INS, the number to be inserted, and ENTER. Then recompute the NPV.

Now you should test your skills a bit further by solving the preceding lengthy problem containing 20 cash flows. Hopefully you conclude that, if you use an 8 percent interest rate, the present value of this income stream is $16,638.51. (Did you remember to enter the zero amount in year 11?)

Solving Problems That Include Grouped Cash Flows. These three calculators can solve present value problems involving far more than 20 or 25 cash flows if the series includes some grouped data, because grouped data counts as only one cash-flow amount. For example, a cash flow of $50,000 followed by 40 annual cash flows of $2,000 involves 41 cash flows but only two cash-flow amounts. For problems that include grouped data you should enter, along with the amount of each such cash flow, the total number of times it occurs in succession, including the first time. On the HP-12C, this number is entered by means of the blue Nj function on the FV key in the center of the top row of the keyboard. On the HP-17B II, this number is entered after you have turned the #T? function to ON. On the BA-II Plus, this number is entered when you respond to the FO= prompt that appears on the display after each cash flow (other than the first one) is entered.

To illustrate the process, assume that you are considering investing in a great opportunity that yields a cash inflow to you starting next year of $6,000 per year for 5 years, followed by $4,000 per year for 10 years, followed by $2,000 per year for 15 years, followed by a lump-sum payment of $25,000. Compute the present value of this income stream utilizing an 8 percent discount rate.

On the HP-12C, begin by entering the amount of the initial inflow: 6000, blue g, CFj. Since it occurs a total of five times (including the first), press 5, blue g, Nj. Now enter the next group of inflows: 4000, blue g, CFj; and the number of times this amount occurs: 10, blue g, Nj. Enter the third group of inflows by pressing 2000, blue g, CFj, and 15, blue g, Nj. Then enter the 31st and final inflow: 25000, blue g, CFj. Finally, enter the interest rate by pressing 8 and the i key. Compute the answer by pressing yellow f, NPV and the answer, $49,920.35, should appear on the screen. You can revise the interest rate if you wish simply by entering the new rate and pressing i, yellow f, NPV.

If you are using the HP-17B II, enter the cash flow mode by pressing the CFLO menu key and clear its memory. Press the #T? menu key once or twice to turn the function that prompts you to tell how many times a particular cash flow occurs to ON. Next, press 0 and INPUT to tell the machine that there is no cash flow at the start of the first year. Now press 6000, INPUT, 5, and INPUT to tell the machine that the first cash flow is $6,000 and that it occurs for five consecutive periods. Then press 4000, INPUT, 10, and INPUT to enter the next set of cash flows. Complete the series by pressing 2000, INPUT, 15, INPUT, 25000, INPUT, 1, and INPUT. Now press EXIT, the CALC menu key, 8, the I% menu key, and the NPV menu key to produce the answer, $49,920.35. You can revise the interest rate if you wish by simply entering the new rate and pressing the I% and the NPV menu keys.

The present value of this same great opportunity can be solved with the BA-II Plus by pressing the following keys:

CF, 2nd, CLR Work, ENTER,↓	(to clear the work sheet, to show that there is no cash flow at the start of the first year, and to prepare to enter the first set of cash flows)
6000, ENTER,↓ , 5, ENTER,↓	(to enter the first set of 5 cash flows)
4000, ENTER, ↓, 10, ENTER,↓	(to enter this set of 10 cash flows)
2000, ENTER, ↓, 15, ENTER, ↓	(to enter this set of 15 cash flows)
25000, ENTER, ↓,↓	(to enter the final lump-sum payment and to prepare to solve the problem)
NPV, 8, ENTER, ↓, CPT,	(to calculate the answer at the specified discount rate)

The answer is $49,920.35. You can revise the interest rate if you wish by pressing NPV, the new interest rate, ENTER, ↓, CPT.

Cash Flows at Beginning of Year. Each of the preceding illustrations of how to use the HP-12C, the HP-17B II, and BA-II Plus involve cash flows that occur at the end of the year. If the cash flows occur at the beginning of the year, only a slight change in procedure is needed to find the present value of the payment stream. If you are using the HP-12C, take another look at the PV key, and note that it has a blue CFo function. If the problem to be solved entails cash flows at the beginning of each year, the first such flow (or group of consecutive cash inflows or outflows of equal amount) is entered by means of this blue CFo function. (The symbol CFo stands for original cash flow.) Subsequent cash flows are then entered via the CFj function in the manner described above.[3]

If you are using the HP-17B II, notice that when you enter the cash flow made by pressing the CFLO menu key, the calculator asks for the FLOW(0), the original cash flow, the cash flow at the start of the first year. If this cash flow is ungrouped data, enter the first cash flow here and proceed in the manner described above to enter the size and number of each of the subsequent cash flows. However, if the first cash flow constitutes grouped data, for example, $1,000 at the beginning of years one, two, three, and four, this data must be treated as two separate cash flows, $1,000 occurring at the start of the first year followed by a group of three additional cash flows of $1,000 each.

If you are using BA-II Plus, the procedure is a bit more complex. Notice that when you enter the cash flow prompted work sheet, the calculator asks for the CFo, the original cash flow. If this cash flow is ungrouped data, insert the first cash flow and proceed in the manner described above to enter the size and number of each of the subsequent cash flows. However, if the first cash flow constitutes grouped data, for example, $1,000 at the beginning of years 1, 2, 3, and 4, this data must be treated as two separate cash flows—$1,000 occurring at the start of year one followed by a group of three additional cash flows of $1,000 each.

To illustrate, if a 12 percent discount rate is used, what is the present value of the following series of cash flows?

Beginning of Year	Amount
1–5	$3,500
6–10	2,500
11	1,500
12	500

On the HP-12C, enter the first five cash flows by pressing 3500, blue g, CFo, 5, blue g, Nj. The next five cash flows are entered by pressing 2500, blue g, CFj, 5, blue g, Nj. The last two cash flows are entered by pressing 1500, blue g, CFj, 500, blue g, CFj. The solution is found by entering the discount rate (12 and

i) and pressing yellow f, NPV. The answer, $20,484.67, should appear on the display.

On the HP-17B II, after entering the cash flow menu system and clearing CFLO of any old data, turn on the #T? function. Enter the cash flows by pressing 3500, INPUT, 3500, INPUT, 4, INPUT, 2500, INPUT, 5, INPUT, 1500, INPUT, 1, INPUT, 500, INPUT, 1, and INPUT. Next, press EXIT the CALC menu key, 12, the I% menu key, and NPV. The answer, $20,484.67, will be displayed.

On the BA-II Plus, after entering the cash flow prompted work sheet and clearing it of any old data, enter the first five cash flows by pressing 3500, ENTER, ↓, 3500, ENTER, ↓, 4, ENTER,↓. The next five cash flows are then entered by pressing 2500, ENTER, ↓, 5, ENTER,↓. The last two cash flows are entered by pressing 1500, ENTER, ↓,↓ , 500, ENTER, ↓,↓. The solution is then found by pressing NPV, 12, ENTER,↓ , CPT. The answer, $20,484.67, should appear on the display.

Payments Growing by a Constant Percentage

In many cases time-value-of-money problems involve the need to discount to their present value a stream of payments that grows by a constant annual percentage. Adjusting for an assumed inflation rate is often the underlying motivation.

For example, assume that you wish to have an income stream of $25,000 per year in *constant purchasing power* for the next 10 years, with the first payment occurring immediately. (That is, a total of ten payments with the first one occurring right now.) How large a capital sum would you need to set aside today to meet this objective if the annual inflation rate is assumed to be 5 percent and if the principal sum to be liquidated can be assumed to produce a rate of return of 8 percent per year? What is the present value, discounted at 8 percent, of this 10-year stream of payments that rises by 5 percent per year?

You could, of course, calculate the amount of each of the 10 payments, discount each of them for the appropriate number of years, and add up the results. There is, however, a better way to produce the answer to this problem. If done manually, it involves using the following formula:

$$\text{PV} = \text{amount of 1st payment x } \frac{1 - \left[\dfrac{(1 + \text{growth rate})}{(1 + \text{i})}\right]^{\text{n}}}{(\text{i} - \text{growth rate})} \text{ x } (1 + \text{i})$$

In the present illustration, the answer is

$$= \$25{,}000 \text{ x } \frac{1 - \left[\frac{1.05}{1.08}\right]^{10}}{(.08 - .05)} \text{ x } 1.08$$

$$= \$25{,}000 \text{ x } \frac{1 - .7545}{.03} \text{ x } 1.08$$

$$= \$25{,}000 \text{ x } 8.1836 \text{ x } 1.08$$

$$= \$220{,}957.20$$

If the first $25,000 payment is to be made after one year, rather than immediately, the answer found through this formula is divided by (1 + i). In this case the present value is $204,590.00 ($220,957.20 ÷ 1.08).

Rather than laboring through the formula, you may prefer to use the HP-12C or BA-II Plus calculator to solve this problem. On the HP-12C, the keystrokes are as follows for the beginning-of-year approach:

blue g, BEG, 25000, PMT	(to enter the first payment, which is to occur immediately)
1.08, ENTER, 1.05, ÷, 1, –, 100, x, i	(to enter the adjusted discount rate)
10, n, PV	(to enter the n and produce the solution)

The answer, $220,955.95, should appear on the display. Dividing this result by 1.08 produces the end-of-year solution, $204,588.85.

If you are using the HP-17B II, return to the TVM menu system by pressing shift, MAIN, the FIN menu key, and the TVM menu key. Set the calculator for beginning-of-period payments. Then press the following keys: 25000, the PMT menu key, 1.08, ÷, 1.05, –, 1, x, 100, =. and the I%YR menu key. You have now entered the initial payment and the inflation-adjusted discount rate. Now press 10, the N menu key, and the PV menu key to produce the solution, $220,955.95. If you want to see the answer under the assumption of end-of-period payments, divide this answer by 1.08. Press ÷, 1.08, =, and the revised answer, $204,588.85, will appear on the display.

On the BA-II Plus, return to the standard calculator mode by pressing 2nd and QUIT. Set the calculator for beginning-of-year payments. Clear the calculator of extraneous data by pressing 2nd and CLR TVM. Then the keystrokes for the beginning-of-year solution are as follows:

25000, PMT	(to enter the first payment)
1.08, ÷, 1.05, –, 1, x, 100, =, I/Y	(to enter the adjusted discount rate)
10, N, CPT, PV	(to enter the n and produce the solution)

The answer, $220,995.95, should appear on the display. Dividing this result by 1.08 produces the end-of-year solution, $204,588.85.

Future Value of Uneven Cash Flows

The following pages deal with the reverse of the previous set of problems and explain how to calculate the future value of a series of uneven cash flows. The explanation is brief because the approach to solving such problems parallels that for solving present-value problems.

Assume that a business plans to make the following series of contributions to fund certain obligations under its pension plan:

End of Year	Amount
1	$30,000
2	40,000
3–5	50,000
6–10	60,000

If these contributions are credited with 10 percent interest per year, how much will be in the fund at the end of the 10th year? What is the future value of this series of uneven cash flows?

The solution of this problem entails compounding each payment from the time it is made until the end of the 10th year and totaling the results. Thus the first $30,000 should be compounded for 9 years at 10 percent to produce its FVSS. The second should be compounded for 8 years, the third for 7 years, and so on. The final $60,000 payment, of course, earns no interest because it is made at the end of the 10th year.

Using Time-Value Tables to Calculate Future Value of Uneven Cash Flows

If, as in the present illustration, the sequence of cash flows is brief and straightforward, the basic future-value formulas or tables can be used to produce a solution. For example, table B.1 in appendix B can provide the nine FVSS factors to be applied to the various payments. Alternatively, since this illustrative problem includes two sets of grouped data ($50,000 per year for 3 years and $60,000 per year for 5 years), table B.3 can be used to provide FVA factors. It must be remembered, however, that the FVA of the three payments at the end of years 3, 4, and 5 must be further compounded by means of an FVSS factor to produce the future value of these three contributions as of the end of the 10th year.

Specifically, then, the future value of this series of uneven cash flows at 10 percent can be found as shown:[4]

1. FVSS of payment at end of year 1
   $30,000 x 2.3579 — $ 70,737.00
2. FVSS of payment at end of year 2
   $40,000 x 2.1436 — 85,744.00

3. FVA of payments at end of years 3–5
   $50,000 x 3.3100 = $165,500
4. FVSS of FVA of payments at end of years 3–5
   $165,500 x 1.6105 266,537.75
5. FVA of payments at end of years 6–10
   $60,000 x 6.1051 366,306.00
6. Future value of the cash flows $789,324.75

Using a Financial Calculator to Calculate the Future Value of Uneven Cash Flows

The HP-12C and BA-II Plus calculators are not constructed to directly compute the future value of a series of uneven cash flows. However, since they do have the capability to compute the present value of a series of uneven cash flows, you can compute the single sum that is the present value of the cash flows and then compute the future value of that single sum. This provides the same result as if you calculated the future value of the cash flows directly. The HP-17B II, unlike the other machines, can produce the answer directly.

For example, assume the following sequence of cash flows:

End of Year	Amount
1	$500
2–5	600
6–8	700

Calculate the future value as of the end of year 8 using a 7 percent interest rate.

Using the HP-12C. On the HP-12C, begin by computing the present value of these cash flows as explained earlier. Press the keys as shown below.

500, blue g, CFj
600, blue g, CFj, 4, blue g, Nj
700, blue g, CFj, 3, blue g, Nj
7, i, yellow f, NPV

The present value, $3,676.43, should appear on the display. Now carry this present value forward as a single sum to the end of year 8 using the same 7 percent interest rate by pressing the following keys:

ENTER, CHS, PV, 8, n, 7, i, FV

The future value of this series of uneven cash flows, $6,316.79, should appear on the display.

Using the BA-II Plus. If you are using the BA-II Plus, compute the present value of the cash flows by pressing the following keys:

CF, 2nd, CLR Work, ENTER, ↓,
500, ENTER, ↓,↓ ,
600, ENTER, ↓, 4, ENTER, ↓,
700, ENTER, ↓, 3, ENTER, ↓,
NPV, 7, ENTER, ↓, CPT

The present value, $3,676.43, should appear on the display. Now carry this present value forward as a single sum to the end of year 8 using the same 7 percent interest rate by pressing the following keys:

STO, 1	(to store this present value in a memory register)
2nd, QUIT, 2nd, CLR TVM	(to leave the prompted work sheet mode, return to the standard calculator mode, and clear the calculator of extraneous data)
RCL, 1, +/–, PV	(to recall the stored value and enter it as the present value)
8, N, 7, I/Y	(to insert the rest of the information needed to find the future value)
CPT, FV	(to produce the answer)

The future value, $6,316.79, should appear on the display. If the cash flows in this problem had occurred at the beginning of each year, rather than the end, use the same procedure, but multiply the answer by (1 plus the interest rate).

Using the HP-17B II. On the HP-17B II, solving a future-value-of-uneven-cash-flows problem is less cumbersome. Enter the CFLO mode and clear the CFLO memory of any extraneous data. Turn the #T? function to ON. Then press the following keys:

0, INPUT
500, INPUT, 1, INPUT,
600, INPUT, 4, INPUT,
700, INPUT, 3, INPUT,
EXIT, the CALC menu key,
7, the I% menu key, and the NFV menu key

The answer, $6,316,79, will appear on the display. If the cash flows in this problem had occurred at the beginning of each year, rather than the end, use the same procedure, but multiply the answer by (1 plus the interest rate).

Deposits Growing by a Constant Percentage

Now instead of dealing with the future value of cash flows that change in an irregular manner we take up the case of the future value of cash flows with amounts that increase each year by a constant percentage. This type of problem frequently arises when someone sets up a savings plan for the attainment of a financial goal and the amount to be saved each year rises at the same rate as the person's income is expected to grow.

For example, assume that you plan to begin a program of annual saving, beginning with a $500 deposit now. Assume also that you expect your income and, hence, the amount you can save to rise by about 10 percent per year. If your savings generate a 7 percent annual rate of return, how much will be in your account at the end of 5 years? What is the future value, compounded at 7 percent interest, of this 5-year stream of deposits that rises by 10 percent per year?

You could, of course, calculate the amount of each of the five deposits, compound each of them for the appropriate number of years, and add up the results. There is, however, a faster way. This type of problem can be solved through the use of the following formula where the first deposit is made immediately:

$$\text{FV} = \text{amount of first deposit x} \left[\frac{(1 + \text{i})^{\text{n}} - (1 + \text{growth rate})^{\text{n}}}{(\text{i} - \text{growth rate})}\right] \text{x } (1 + \text{i})$$

In the present example, the answer is

$$= \$500 \text{ x} \left[\frac{1.07^5 - 1.10^5}{.07 - .10}\right] \text{x } 1.07$$

$$= \$500 \text{ x} \left[\frac{1.4026 - 1.6105}{-.03}\right] \text{x } 1.07$$

$$= \$500 \text{ x } 6.9300 \text{ x } 1.07$$

$$= \$3{,}707.55$$

If the first $500 deposit is made after one year, rather than immediately, the answer found through this formula is divided by (1 + i). In this case the future value is $3,465.000 ($3,707.55 ÷ 1.07).

If instead of using the formula you prefer a financial calculator for solving this type of problem, the HP-12C, HP-17B II, or BA-II Plus can be used. However, they can compute the solution only in the indirect manner described earlier in this chapter for calculating the future value of uneven cash flows. First compute the present compounding period.

Using the HP-12C. The HP-12C keystrokes needed to solve the present problem, based on the beginning-of-year approach, are as follows:

blue g, BEG, 500, PMT	(to enter the first deposit)
1.07, ENTER, 1.10, ÷, 1, –, 100, x, i	(to enter the adjusted discount rate)
5, n, PV	(to enter the n and produce the present value)
STO, 1, yellow f, FIN	(to preserve the present value while clearing out the financial registers)
RCL, 1, PV, 7, i, 5, n, FV	(to produce the solution)

The answer, $3,708.59, should appear on the display. Dividing the result by 1.07 produces the end-of-year solution, $3,465.97.

Using the HP-17B II. Enter the TVM menu system, clear any extraneous data, and set the machine for the beginning-of-period mode. Then press the following keys:

500, the PMT menu key	(to enter the first deposit)
1.07, ÷, 1.10, –, 1, x, 100, =, the I%YR menu key	(to enter the inflation-adjusted discount rate)
5, the N menu key, the PV menu key	(to enter the number of payments and produce the present value)
STO, 1, shift, CLEAR DATA	(to preserve the present value while clearing out the extraneous data)
RCL, 1, the PV menu key, 7, the I%YR menu key, 5, the N menu key, the FV menu key	(to produce the solution)

The answer, $3,708.59, will appear on the display. Dividing this result by 1.07 will produce the end-of-period solution, $3,465.97.

Using the BA-II Plus. On the BA-II Plus, begin by clearing the TVM registers and setting the calculator for beginning-of-period deposits or payments. Then press these keys:

500, PMT	(to enter the first deposit)
1.07, ÷, 1.10, –, 1, x, 100, =, I/Y	(to enter the adjusted discount rate)
5, N, CPT, PV	(to enter the n and produce the present value)
STO, 1, 2nd, CLR TVM	(to preserve the present value while clearing out any extraneous data)
RCL, 1, PV, 7, I/Y, 5, N, CPT, FV	(to produce the solution)

The answer, \$3,708.59, should appear on the display. Dividing this result by 1.07 produces the end-of-year solution, \$3,465.97.

EVALUATING AN INVESTMENT THROUGH DISCOUNTED CASH-FLOW ANALYSIS

One of the most common personal and business applications of time-value-of-money principles and techniques is the evaluation of a proposed investment. For example, assume that you are considering the purchase of a bond that involves a cash outlay now (the purchase price) and a series of cash inflows over several time periods in the future (the interest payments and the face amount). Or perhaps you are considering construction of an apartment building that involves a cash outlay now and perhaps again next year (the construction costs), after which you anticipate a series of cash inflows for a period of years (the rental payments). Or perhaps the investment under consideration is the purchase (cash outflow) of a piece of equipment that reduces expenses (cash inflow) over some future period.

In all of these situations there is a tradeoff: one or more cash outflows in return for one or more cash inflows. The questions: Are the inflows to be received worth the outflows expended—is it a good investment? By this point you surely understand that these questions cannot be adequately answered without taking into account the time value of money. Discounted cash-flow analysis assists you to evaluate an investment by making comparable the time value of the cash outflows and the time value of the cash inflows. It can be used to assist in deciding (1) whether a proposed investment project is an acceptable one and (2) how to rank several competing investment opportunities in terms of their relative acceptability.

Of course there is more to evaluating an investment than simply crunching some numbers through various time-value-of-money formulas, tables, or calculator functions. The degree of certainty in amount, timing, and duration associated with various cash outflows and inflows, as well as the tax aspects, must also be considered. Evaluation of tax elements is beyond the scope of this chapter. Risk considerations, however, are incorporated in the interest rate that is used in discounted cash-flow analysis.

As you will see, the mechanics of discounted cash-flow analysis are quite straightforward when the pattern of the cash outflows and inflows is simple. Calculations become more complex when the amounts vary from year to year, and still more complex when cash flows are positive in some years and negative in others. This chapter deals with simple discounted cash-flow analysis situations first, followed by gradually more complicated cases.

Discounted Cash-Flow Techniques Defined

There are two commonly used techniques for discounted cash-flow analysis: calculation of an investment's net present value (NPV) and its internal rate of return (IRR).

Net Present Value

The *net present value* of an investment is defined as the present value of the stream of cash inflows minus the present value of the stream of cash outflows, with both present values calculated on the basis of an appropriate rate of interest. The discount rate used might be the minimum rate of return that is acceptable to an investor in light of his or her assessment of the riskiness of the investment; the cost of capital the investor has to raise in order to make the investment; or the rate available on an alternative acceptable investment involving a similar degree of risk.

If the result of the NPV calculation is positive, that is, if the present value of the inflow stream exceeds the present value of the outflow stream, the investment is a good one. It provides a net addition to the wealth (in a time-value sense) of the investor in the amount of the positive remainder. A positive NPV means that the rate of return provided by the investment (whatever that rate is) exceeds the discount rate being used as the benchmark. If the NPV is negative, the reverse is true and the investment will result in a net reduction in the wealth (in a time-value sense). And if the NPV is zero, the investment neither adds to nor subtracts from the investor's wealth (in a time-value sense), so that it is a matter of indifference as to whether the investment should be made.

Internal Rate of Return

The *internal rate of return* on an investment is the interest rate that equates the present value of the stream of cash inflows to the present value of the stream of cash outflows. If that rate is larger than the minimum rate deemed acceptable by the investor, the investment is a good one and should be pursued. If not, it should be rejected. Criteria for determining an acceptable minimum rate of return are the same as those described in connection with the net present value technique.

Similarity of the NPV and IRR Techniques

Note that the NPV and IRR methods of evaluating an investment are very similar. In computing NPV the investor specifies the minimum acceptable interest rate and determines whether at that rate the present value of the inflows exceeds the present value of the outflows. In computing IRR the investor computes the interest rate that makes the present value of the inflows equal to the present value of the outflows; that is, the investor computes the interest rate that produces an NPV of zero.

As a general rule, when used to evaluate a particular investment the two techniques will lead the investor to the same conclusion if the same data is used. If the NPV is positive, the IRR normally is acceptable and the investment is an attractive one. Conversely, if the NPV is negative, the IRR normally is unacceptable and the investment should be rejected. When used to rank several investments as to their relative acceptability, however, there are situations in which the NPV and IRR techniques produce different results using the same data. In most cases the NPV method is more reliable for ranking several competing investment possibilities. The project with the largest NPV should be ranked first, the one with the next largest NPV should be second, and so on.

Computing Net Present Value: Simple Problems

Consider this very simple investment: You are evaluating the purchase of a piece of equipment that costs $10,000. It provides a net cash flow of $4,000 per year at the end of each of the next 4 years, after which it will have no value. Is this a worthwhile investment if your cost of capital is 10 percent per year?[5]

Depicted on a time line, the cash flows associated with this project appear as shown in the upper half of figure 7-3 on the following page. The single component of cash outflow, $10,000 occurs immediately, so its present value is $10,000. The four inflows of $4,000, totaling $16,000, constitute a 4-year annuity to be discounted at 10 percent. You have already learned how to calculate a PVA by several methods. For example, using table B.4 in appendix B you can find the 10%, 4-year PVA factor of 3.1699. Multiplying this factor by the $4,000 annuity payment produces a PVA of $12,679.60. Subtracting the present value of the outflow, $10,000, you find that the project has a positive NPV of $2,679.60. Your wealth will increase (in a time-value sense) by this amount if you invest in the project. So far, then, calculation of NPV involves nothing that you have not already learned.

If the problem is made a bit more complex by involving uneven cash flows, the calculation is still similar to the procedures explained earlier. The lower half of figure 7-3 shows a modification to the preceding case by including a pattern of increasing cash inflows totaling $16,000. The present value of the income stream, discounted at 10 percent, can be found by one of the methods described earlier. For example, using the basic formula to compute a PVSS, you can find the present value of each inflow and total them to produce the solution.

$$\text{Amount x } \frac{1}{(1 + i)^n} = \text{PVSS}$$

$$\$2{,}500 \text{ x } \frac{1}{1.10} = \$\,2{,}272.73$$

$$\$3{,}500 \text{ x } \frac{1}{1.10^2} = 2{,}892.56$$

$$\$4{,}500 \text{ x } \frac{1}{1.10^3} = 3{,}380.92$$

$$\$5{,}500 \text{ x } \frac{1}{1.10^4} = \underline{3{,}756.57}$$

$$\text{Total} \qquad \$12{,}302.78$$

Subtracting the present value of the outflow stream, \$10,000, you find that this investment has a positive net present value of \$2,302.78. (It should not be surprising that the NPV with the increasing pattern of cash inflows, \$2,302.78, is less than the NPV for the previous case of level cash inflows, \$2,679.60, that totaled the same amount, \$16,000.)

FIGURE 7-3
Time Line Representation of NPV Problem: Level and Uneven Inflows

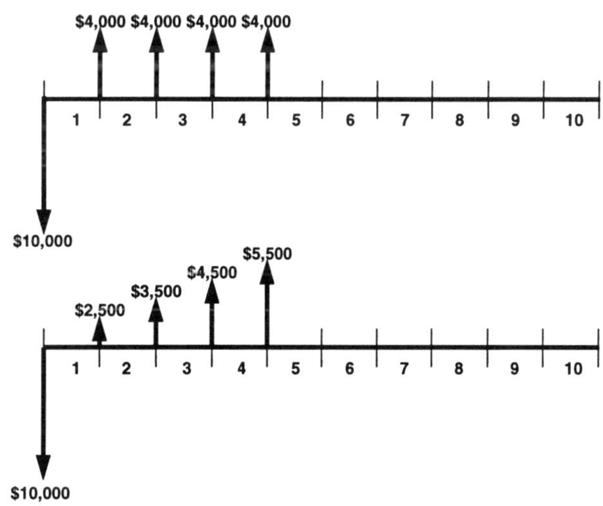

The upper time line depicts an investment that entails an initial cash outflow of \$10,000 and a level stream of four \$4,000 cash inflows. In the lower time line the initial cash outflow is the same but the four cash inflows follow an increasing pattern over time.

An additional level of complexity is introduced into the problem if it is assumed that a series of cash outflows is required before the series of cash inflows begins. See, for example, figure 7-4 below, in which the top time line depicts a project calling for 3 years of uneven cash outflows ($2,000, $1,000, and $500), followed by 5 years of cash inflows ($500, $1,000, $2,000, $2,000 and $3,000). Here the only new procedure is that you must subtract the present value of the series of outflows from the present value of the series of inflows. Note also from the time line when the outflows are assumed to occur (at the *beginning* of years one, 2, and 3) and when the inflows are assumed to occur (at the *end* of years 3, 4, 5, 6, and 7).

FIGURE 7-4
Time Line Representation of NPV Problem: Series of Outflows and Inflows and Years of Zero Outflows or Inflows

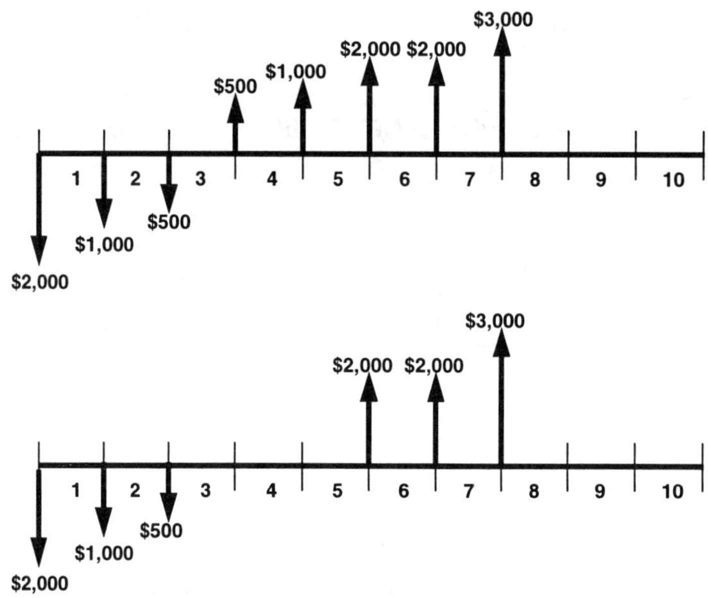

The top line depicts an investment that entails a decreasing series of cash outflows followed by an increasing series of cash inflows. The lower line depicts a similar situation except that there is a gap of 3 years between the last outflow and the first inflow.

Based on the use of table B.2 in appendix B, the procedure for finding the solution to this problem, with a discount rate of 8 percent, for example, is as follows:

1. Calculate and sum the present value, discounted at 8 percent, of each of the inflows:

$ 500 (in 3 years)	x .7938	=	$ 396.90
$1,000 (in 4 years)	x .7350	=	735.00
$2,000 (in 5 years)	x .6806	=	1,361.20
$2,000 (in 6 years)	x .6302	=	1,260.40
$3,000 (in 7 years)	x .5835	=	1,750.50
Total			$5,504.00

2. Calculate and sum the present value, discounted at 8 percent, of each of the outflows.

$2,000 (in 0 years)	x 1.0000	=	$2,000.00
$1,000 (in 1 year)	x .9259	=	925.90
$ 500 (in 2 years)	x .8573	=	428.65
Total			$3,354.55

3. Subtract the result of step two from that of step one to produce the positive NPV of $2,149.45.

One more complicating factor may be the presence of one or more years in which there is no cash outflow or inflow. This does not change the procedure for solving the problem, but it does require a little extra care to make sure the inflows and outflows are being discounted for the correct number of years. For example, if the last illustration is changed so that there is no cash inflow at the end of years 3 and 4 (see the bottom time line in figure 7-4), the NPV, on the basis of an 8 percent discount rate, is as follows:

1. Present value of inflows

$2,000 (in 5 years) x .6806	=	$1,361.20
$2,000 (in 6 years) x .6302	=	1,260.40
$3,000 (in 7 years) x .5835	=	1,750.50
Total		$4,372.10

2. Present value of outflows

$2,000 (in 0 years) x 1.0000	=	$2,000.00
$1,000 (in 1 year) x .9259	=	925.90
$ 500 (in 2 years) x .8573	=	428.65
Total		$3,354.55

3. Net present value $1,017.55

The final bit of complexity to be introduced at this point is the presence of one or more cash outflows after the stream of cash inflows has begun. Any inflows and outflows that occur in the same year should be netted against each other. This may result in: a net cash inflow that is smaller than it otherwise would have been; a net cash inflow that is zero; or a net cash outflow. The first two results involve no new procedures in finding the NPV. The third result requires a little extra work. (As you will see later, this result may greatly complicate the task of computing an internal rate of return.)

Consider, for example, an investment that calls for the following pattern of cash flows (see figure 7-5):

Beginning of Year	Cash Flow
1	$3,000 outflow
2	$2,000 outflow
3	$ 0
4	$1,000 inflow
5	$2,000 outflow
6	$3,000 inflow
7	$3,000 inflow
8	$3,000 inflow

In this case the only new procedure for solving the problem is that you must remember to add the present value of the initial outflows in years one and 2 to the present value of the outflow that occurs at the beginning of year 5. If, for instance, a 7 percent discount rate is assumed, the present values based on table B.2 in appendix B are as shown below:

1. Present value of inflows

$1,000 (in 3 years) x .8163	=	$ 816.30
$3,000 (in 5 years) x .7130	=	2,139.00
$3,000 (in 6 years) x .6663	=	1,998.90
$3,000 (in 7 years) x .6227	=	1,868.10
Total		$6,822.30

2. Present value of outflows

$3,000 (in 0 years) x 1.0000	=	$3,000.00
$2,000 (in 1 year) x .9346	=	1,869.20
$2,000 (in 4 years) x .7629	=	1,525.80
Total		$6,395.00

3. Net present value $ 427.30

In the net present value illustrative problems up to this point, the solutions were fairly easy to find because of the short pattern of cash flows. As explained earlier, tools such as the time-value formulas or tables B.2 and B.4 in appendix B and a simple calculator suffice for computing and totaling the present values of the individual cash flows or, in the case of a series of level cash flows, the annuity.

As net present value problems start to become more involved, however, the use of formulas or tables starts to be cumbersome. At that point a calculator like the HP-12C, the HP-17B II, or the BA-II Plus, or perhaps even a computer, becomes necessary.

FIGURE 7-5
Time Line Representation of NPV Problem: Series of Outflows followed by Year of Zero Flow followed by Series of Inflows Interrupted by Outflow

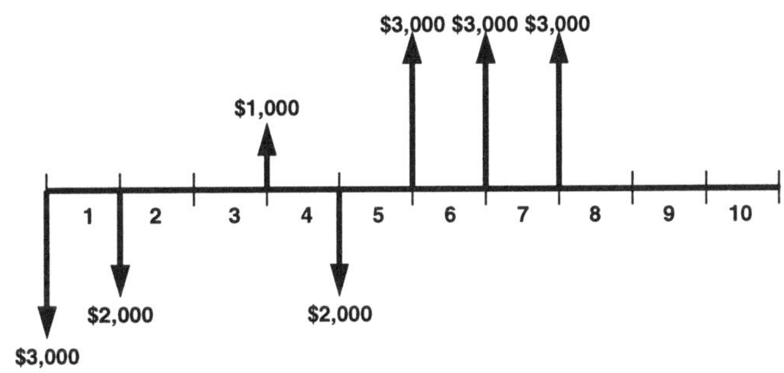

This line shows a series of decreasing cash outflows followed by one year in which there is no net inflow or outflow. Thereafter comes one year of a net cash inflow and one of a net cash outflow. Finally, 3 years of level net cash inflows occur.

Computing Net Present Value: Complex Problems

Ungrouped Cash Flows

Now we will take up somewhat more complicated problems. First explained is the use of calculators to solve NPV problems in which there are no consecutive cash flows of the same amount and sign. To solve an NPV problem on the HP-12C where the cash flows are ungrouped, the procedure is the same as that explained earlier in this chapter. You use the blue CFo and CFj keys in the top row of the keyboard. In addition, you need to use the CHS key to enter outflows as negative numbers. You enter the discount rate using the i key as usual. Finally, you use the yellow f key and the NPV function to produce the solution. To solve the same type of problem on the HP-17B II or the BA-II Plus, you use the cash flow prompted work sheet explained earlier in this chapter. In addition, however, you use the +/– key to enter outflows as negative numbers. You enter the discount rate into the work sheet just as before and use the CPT and NPV keys to produce the answer.

To illustrate the process, assume you have been asked to make a $75,000 loan. The borrower agrees to the following repayment schedule:

End of year 1	$ 0
End of year 2	$ 15,000
End of year 3	$ 20,000
End of year 4	$ 25,000
End of year 5	$ 30,000

Should you enter into this loan if you insist on a rate of return of at least 11 percent on your investment? On the HP-12C, press 75000, CHS, blue g, CFo. The initial outlay (at the beginning of the first year) has now been entered as a negative amount. Press 0, blue g, CFj to reflect the fact that in the first year following the initial outlay there is no net cash inflow or outflow. Press 15000, blue g, and CFj to enter the positive cash inflow at the end of year 2. Enter the remaining three inflows by pressing 20000, blue g, CFj; 25000, blue g, CFj; and 30000, blue g, CFj. Now enter the minimum acceptable rate of return by pressing 11 and the i key. Finally, compute the NPV by pressing the yellow f key and NPV. The answer, –$13,930.02, should appear on the display.

On the HP-17B II, enter the CFLO menu system and turn off the #T? function. Then press 75000, +/–, and INPUT. The initial outlay (at the beginning of the first year) has now been entered as a negative amount. Press 0 and INPUT to reflect the fact that in the first year following the initial outlay, there is no net cash inflow or outflow. Press 15000, and INPUT to enter the positive cash inflow at the end of year two. Enter the remaining three inflows by pressing 20000, INPUT, 25000, INPUT, 30000, and INPUT. Now press EXIT and the CALC menu key. Enter the minimum acceptable rate of return by pressing 11 and the I% menu key. Finally, press the NPV menu key to produce the answer, –$13,930.02.

If you use the BA-II Plus, press CF, 2nd, CLR Work. Then press 75000, +/–, ENTER,↓. The initial outlay (at the start of the first year) has now been entered as a negative amount. Press 0, ENTER, ↓, ↓ to reflect the fact that at the end of the first year there is no net cash inflow or outflow. Then enter each of the remaining cash inflows by pressing 15000, ENTER, ↓, ↓, 20000, ENTER, ↓, ↓, 25000, ENTER, ↓, ↓, and 30000, ENTER, ↓,↓. Now press NPV, 11, ENTER, ↓, CPT. The answer, –$13,930.02, should appear on the display.

Obviously this project should be rejected since, in light of the time value of money, it would cost you almost $14,000. This project would be unacceptable even if you were willing to settle for as little as a 5 percent rate of return. On the HP-12C press 5, i, yellow f, NPV; on the HP-17B II, press 5, the I% menu key, and the NPV menu key; or on the BA-II Plus press NPV, 5, ENTER, ↓, CPT. Note that the net present value even at this rate is negative $44.46.

Grouped Cash Flows

These financial calculators can solve NPV problems involving more cash flows if there is grouped data. As explained earlier in this chapter, for such problems you should enter, along with the amount of each cash flow, the total number of times it occurs in succession, including the first time.

To illustrate the process, assume that you are considering investing in an oil exploration limited partnership that you believe will entail the following cash flows:

Initial outlay	$ 50,000
Inflows at end of years 1–5	$ 0
Inflows at end of years 6–9	$ 6,000
Inflow at end of year 10	$ 60,000

Is this investment acceptable if you insist on a rate of return of at least 12 percent per year?

After clearing the HP-12C, begin by entering the amount of the initial outflow: 50000, CHS, blue g, CFo. Now enter the first group of inflows by pressing 0, blue g, CFj. Since this amount will occur a total of five times (including the first), press 5, blue g, Nj. Now enter the next group of inflows: 6000, blue g, CFj, and the number of times it occurs: 4, blue g, Nj. Then enter the last inflow, 60000, blue g, CFj. Finally, enter the required interest rate by pressing 12 and i. Compute the answer by pressing yellow f and NPV and the answer, –$20,340.76, should appear on the screen. Another investment to be avoided!

If you are using the HP-17B II, enter the CFLO menu system and turn on the #T? function. Now enter the initial outflow by pressing 50000, +/–, and INPUT. Then enter the first group of inflows by pressing 0 and INPUT. Since this will occur a total of five times (including the first), press 5 and INPUT. Now enter the next group of inflows: 6000, INPUT, 4, and INPUT. Then enter the last inflow: 60000, INPUT, 1, and INPUT. Then press EXIT, the CALC menu key, 12, and the I% menu key. Press the NPV menu key to produce the answer, –$20,340.76. This is a "great" investment that you definitely don't need!

Or if you are using the BA-II Plus, enter the cash flow prompted work sheet and clear it of extraneous data. (You didn't have to be reminded, did you?) Then press the following keys:

50000, +/–, ENTER, ↓, 0, ENTER, ↓, 5, ENTER, ↓, 6000, ENTER, ↓, 4, ENTER, ↓, 60000, ENTER, ↓, 1, ENTER, ↓, NPV, 12, ENTER, ↓, CPT

The answer, –$20,340.76, should appear on the screen. An investment you can get along without!

Computing Internal Rate of Return

Recall the definition of the second technique for discounted cash-flow analysis. The internal rate of return generated by an investment is the interest rate that equates the present value of the cash inflows and outflows, producing a net present value of zero. If the IRR exceeds the investor's minimum desired rate of return, the investment is an attractive one. If it equals the minimum desired rate, the investor should be neutral toward the project. If the IRR is below the minimum desired rate, the investment is unattractive.

The mathematics of computing the IRR of an investment are extremely complex. The process is essentially one of trial and error. To solve the problem manually, you must begin with an estimate of what the IRR might be.[6] (Some authors suggest that a 10 or 15 percent rate is usually a reasonable starting point.) Discount the cash inflows and outflows to their present values using that rate and compare. If the present value of the inflows exceeds the present value of the outflows (that is, if there is a positive NPV at that rate), the rate being used is below the actual IRR, so you must select a higher rate and repeat the calculations. (Remember the present values move in a direction opposite than that of interest rates. Here you are looking for a smaller net present value, namely, zero, so you must increase the interest rate being used.) On the other hand, if with a given interest rate the discounted cash outflows exceed the discounted cash inflows (that is, if there is a negative NPV), you must select a lower interest rate and repeat the calculations. Continue this trial and error process, using higher and lower interest rates to discount the cash flows, until the resulting NPV is equal to or very close to zero. The rate producing this result is the IRR, which is an average rate of return over the period under consideration, weighted to reflect the amount and timing of the various cash flows.

Using a Time-Value Table

Time-value tables can be used to solve only very simple IRR problems. To illustrate, assume that an investment today of $10,000 will produce cash inflows of $2,739.80 at the end of each of the next 5 years. What is the internal rate of return on this investment?

Begin with a guess that it is 10 percent. At that rate, using table B.4 in appendix B you can find that the present value of the annuity in this problem is $10,386.03 ($2,739.80 x 3.7908). The net present value is positive (namely, $386.03), so you need to raise the discount rate and redo the calculation. At a rate of 12.5 percent the PVA is $9,755.33 ($2,739.80 x 3.5606), so the NPV is now negative. Try 11 percent, and you find that the NPV is $126.03 ($2,739.80 x 3.6959 – $10,000). You are getting closer, so try a rate of 11.5 percent. Here the present value of the inflows is $10,000.00 ($2,739.80 x 3.6499). Bingo! The internal rate of return is 11.5 percent.

Obviously the process of computing the internal rate of return is extremely tedious if done in this manner. Imagine, for example, if the project involves a series of uneven cash outflows, a lengthy series of uneven cash inflows, and an occasional year of zero inflows or outflows. By the time you finish doing and redoing all the computations, the investment opportunity will have passed you by.

Also, of course, it is impossible to calculate very precise IRR answers using tables B.2 and B.4. They show an array of interest rates only in intervals of half percentage points. A process of interpolation is necessary to come closer to the precise IRR if an interest rate doesn't happen to fall neatly on one of the tabular rates.

Using Financial Calculators to Solve IRR Problems

The procedure for solving IRR problems with financial calculators is very similar to that for NPV problems. The only differences in the procedure are as follows:

1. When solving for IRR you do not need to enter a discount rate, since this is what you are trying to find. Therefore skip the next-to-last portion of the NPV sequence.
2. On the HP-12C, instead of pressing yellow f and the NPV function after all the data have been entered, press yellow f and the IRR function, which is located on the FV key.
3. On the HP-17B II, instead of pressing the NPV menu key after all the data have been entered, press the IRR% menu key, which is immediately to the left of the I% menu key.
4. On the BA-II Plus, instead of pressing NPV, the discount rate, ENTER, ↓, CPT after all the cash flows have been entered, simply press IRR in the second row of the keyboard and CPT.

For example, to solve an earlier illustrative problem (a single outflow of $10,000 followed by five inflows of $2,739.80 each), set the calculator to display four decimal places. Then on the HP-12C press the following keys: 10000, CHS, blue g, CFo, 2739.80, blue g, CFj, 5, blue g, Nj, yellow f, IRR. Or on the HP-17B II, turn the #T? function on and press 10000, +/–, INPUT, 2739.80, INPUT, 5, INPUT, EXIT, the CALC menu key, and the IRR% menu key. On the BA-II Plus press 10000, +/–, ENTER, ↓, 2739.80, ENTER, ↓, 5, ENTER, ↓, IRR, CPT. (Normally it is necessary for you to wait for several seconds for the answer to appear because the complex mathematical characteristics of the IRR calculation.) Eventually the answer, 11.4997 percent, should be displayed on the screen. (Note the added precision of the financial calculators versus table B.4. In fact, if you set any of the calculators to display eight decimal places, the maximum capacity in this case, you will see that the IRR is 11.49974092 percent.)

To take a more involved example, assume that an investment you are considering involves a $60,000 initial outlay and the following series of cash flows:

End of Year	Cash Flow	End of Year	Cash Flow
1	$2,000 inflow	6	$10,000 outflow
2	$9,000 inflow	7	$11,000 inflow
3	$9,000 inflow	8	$ 0
4	$9,000 inflow	9	$12,000 inflow
5	$9,000 inflow	10	$30,000 inflow

The keystrokes on the HP-12C are as follows:

Initial outlay	60000, CHS, blue g, CFo,
Year 1	2000, blue g, CFj,
Years 2–5	9000, blue g, CFj, 4, blue g, Nj,
Year 6	10000, CHS, blue g, CFj,
Year 7	11000, blue g, CFj,
Year 8	0, blue g, CFj,
Year 9	12000, blue g, CFj,
Year 10	30000, blue g, CFj

Then press the yellow f key and IRR. After the machine runs for several seconds, the answer, 4.6664 percent, should be displayed.

The keystrokes on the HP-17B II, with the #T? function turned on, would be as follows:

Initial outlay	60000, +/–, INPUT,
Year 1	2000, INPUT, 1, INPUT,
Years 2–5	9000, INPUT, 4, INPUT,
Year 6	10000, +/–, INPUT, 1, INPUT,
Year 7	11000, INPUT, 1, INPUT,
Year 8	0, INPUT, 1, INPUT,
Year 9	12000, INPUT, 1, INPUT,
Year 10	30000, INPUT, 1, INPUT

Then press EXIT, the CALC menu key, and the IRR% menu key. The answer will be displayed very quickly as 4.6664%.

The keystrokes on the BA-II Plus, after entering CF, 2nd, and CLR Work, are as follows:

Initial outlay	60000, +/–, ENTER, ↓,
Year 1	2000, ENTER, ↓, ↓,
Years 2–5	9000, ENTER, ↓, 4, ENTER, ↓,
Year 6	10000, +/–, ENTER, ↓, ↓,
Year 7	11000, ENTER, ↓, ↓,
Year 8	0, ENTER, ↓, ↓,
Year 9	12000, ENTER, ↓, ↓,
Year 10	30000, ENTER,↓

Then press IRR and CPT. After a few seconds the answer, 4.6664 percent, should be displayed.

Problems in Decision Making Based on IRR

The internal rate of return provided by potential investments must be used with caution as a basis for decision making. This is especially true when the IRR is used as a means of ranking competing investment opportunities.

One situation in which an evaluation based solely on comparative IRRs may lead to an incorrect decision is the case of mutually exclusive investment projects that are of substantially different magnitudes. Assume, for example, that you can invest in either of two pieces of equipment for your business, but the investment in one eliminates the possibility of investing in the other for some technical reason. Assume also that you have or can borrow enough money so that you are free to invest in either piece of equipment. The total cash flows from the two projects, A and B, are shown below. Neither piece of equipment has any salvage value.

Beginning of Year	Cash Flow (A)	Cash Flow (B)
1	$5,000 outflow	$50,000 outflow
2	$3,000 inflow	$25,000 inflow
3	$4,000 inflow	$35,000 inflow
4	$5,000 inflow	$45,000 inflow

The IRR from project A is 54.0603 percent, while that from project B is only 42.9811 percent. Does this mean that project A is preferable? Not necessarily. For example, if the money to meet the initial outflow is borrowed at a 10 percent rate of interest, it may be preferable to invest in project B. On the basis of a 10 percent discount rate, the NPV of project B is $35,462.06, whereas that of project A is only $4,789.63. In other words, project B increases your wealth (in a time-value sense) by more than seven times the amount project A provides. A more modest rate of return on a large project may be preferable to a higher rate of return on a small project. (Note, however, that this illustration deals with *mutually exclusive* projects. In other cases, the wise decision might be to invest in both projects.)

A second situation in which a decision based solely on IRR may be incorrect is when mutually exclusive potential investment projects entail substantially different cash-flow patterns. Assume that two competing investment opportunities, C and D, are expected to produce the total cash flows shown below. Assume also that the two projects are mutually exclusive because you are able to borrow only $30,000, the amount of the initial cash outlay for each. The interest rate the lender charges and therefore the discount rate you decide to use in evaluating the two projects is 12 percent per year.

Beginning of Year	Cash Flow (C)	Cash Flow (D)
1	$30,000 outflow	$30,000 outflow
2–5	$11,000 inflow	$ 5,000 inflow
6–20	$ 0	$ 5,000 inflow

The IRR from project C is 17.2968 percent, while that from project D is only 15.6071 percent. The NPV of project D, however, is $6,828.88 at a discount rate of 12 percent, whereas it is only $3,410.84 for project C. Once again, the project with the lower IRR provides a greater addition to your wealth (in a time-value sense).

If all of this isn't sufficiently confusing, assume a different discount rate, such as 19 percent, for the calculation of the NPV of the two projects. Under that assumption, project C has both the better IRR and the better (actually, the less bad) NPV.[7]

There is also a difficulty in relying solely on IRRs when deciding between investment opportunities that have substantially different durations. The IRR method includes no explicit assumption about how the rate of return funds released from a short duration project can be reinvested. In the preceding example, project D generates an annual IRR of over 15 percent for 19 years. Project C provides an annual IRR of a bit over 17 percent, but for only 4 years. Assume that the rates of return available on investments of comparable risk fall substantially during the next few years. This means that the heavy early cash inflows from project C have to be reinvested at rates so unattractive that the combined IRR from project C and its successor(s) over the full 19 years will be less than its 4-year IRR, and perhaps even less than the 19-year IRR of project D.

Another limitation of the IRR method for comparing investment projects involves the question of financing costs of cash outflows that may be associated with one or both of the projects. Consider the following set of cash flows from investment projects E and F.

Beginning of Year	Cash Flow (E)	Cash Flow (F)
1	$10,000 outflow	$10,000 outflow
2	$ 1,000 inflow	$ 0
3	$ 5,000 outflow	$ 0
4	$ 5,000 inflow	$ 0
5	$ 5,000 inflow	$ 0
6	$ 5,000 inflow	$ 3,000 inflow
7	$ 5,000 inflow	$13,000 inflow

On the surface, project E appears to be clearly preferable. Its IRR is 9.7283 percent versus 8.4315 percent for project F. And if a reasonable discount rate is used, such as 8 percent, for calculating NPV, project E wins again, $837.31 versus $233.95.

But notice that project E requires a $5,000 cash outflow at the beginning of year 3. Presumably that amount will have to be borrowed at some rate of interest or taken out of another investment where it is earning a rate of return. In either case there is a cost to the investor, either a direct cost or an opportunity cost, arising from the need to cover the cash outflow. If interest rates should rise substantially during the first 2 years of the project, that cost alone might be sufficient to drive the actual IRR of project E below that of project F.

A final problem to be discussed here concerning the IRR method is that it is possible for a project to have more than one IRR, each of which is mathematically correct. It is also possible that an investment may have no IRR within the realm of real numbers. A mathematical explanation of how these results can be produced is beyond the scope of this book. They can arise, however, whenever the stream of outflows and inflows involves more than one change of sign between negative and positive (for example, one or more outflows followed by one or more inflows followed by one or more outflows, as is the case in connection with project E).

How can you tell whether an investment may have more than one internal rate of return? Look over the pattern of net cash outflows and inflows. Often there is only one change of sign in these net flows over the lifetime of the investment. The sequence might begin with one or a few periods of net cash outflows (minus signs) that are followed by a series of net cash inflows (plus signs), perhaps with an occasional net inflow of zero (still a plus sign), until the project is concluded. Where there is only one sign change, there is only one internal rate of return. If there is more than one sign change, however, there *may* be more than one IRR, or there may be no IRR at all. A number of answers may be mathematically correct—but none of them will be of much help as a basis of making an intelligent decision.[8]

If you are using the HP-12C, HP-17B II, or BA-II Plus to compute the IRR of an investment, the calculator will usually let you know if it is having trouble computing the one-and-only correct internal rate of return and will display an error message.

What should you do about these problems of using IRR as a basis for deciding about an investment? One simple solution is to punt. Perhaps you should forget about trying to use IRR as a method of evaluating the particular investment. Rather, use the NPV method. Another approach is to use one of several *modified* IRR methods. Many textbooks on investments and managerial finance contain explanations of these modified IRR methods.

Modified Internal Rate of Return (MIRR)

A modified internal rate of return calculation entails (a) reducing a series of cash flows having multiple sign changes to one that has only one sign change; and (b) specifying the reinvestment rate that will apply, rather than assuming that the project's IRR will be the applicable reinvestment rate. In these ways, MIRR may be superior to IRR, while still expressing the solution as the familiar yield or rate of return that decision makers sometimes prefer to the fuzzy notion of NPV.

The first step in computing a project's MIRR is to select a rate, usually a conservative (low) one, at which it is safe to assume that the project's cash inflows can be reinvested until the end of the project. The second step is to compute the future value (sometimes called the *terminal value*) of all those inflows as of the end of the project's life. The third step is to discount (find the present value of) all the project's outflows back to the origination point of the project. The final step is to compute the annual rate of return represented by the difference between the present value of the outflows and the future or terminal value of the inflows over the life of the project.

To illustrate, assume that a proposed investment is likely to entail the following series of cash flows:

Initial outlay	$ 1,500,000
Inflow at end of year 1	$ 125,000
Outflow at end of year 2	$ 150,000
Inflow at end of year 3	$ 0
Inflow at end of year 4	$ 200,000
Inflow at end of year 5	$ 1,900,000

If a safe reinvestment rate of 5 percent is assumed, what is this investment's MIRR?

(a) The future or terminal value of the inflows at 5 percent is $125,000 for four years plus $200,000 for one year plus $1,900,000, or a total of $2,261,938.28.

(b) The present value of the outflows at 5 percent is $1,500,000 plus $150,000 for two years, or a total of $1,636,054.42.

(c) The life of the project is five years.

(d) In the calculator, insert $2,261,938.28 as the FV, $1,636,054.42 as the negative PV, and 5 as the n. Solve for i, which is 6.6932%. This is the modified IRR based on an assumed 5 percent reinvestment rate.

The use of MIRR doesn't solve all the problems that arise when comparing mutually exclusive projects. For example, an investment with a high MIRR and a low NPV might be less desirable than one with a lower MIRR and a higher NPV. Therefore, NPV is still the most reliable tool for ranking competing investments. MIRR is often, however, an improvement over IRR in such circumstances.

INCREASING THE COMPOUNDING, DISCOUNTING, OR PAYMENT FREQUENCY

All the explanations and illustrations so far in this and the preceding chapter are based on the assumption that compounding and discounting occur once per year. In reality, however, compounding and discounting often occur more frequently than annually. For example, a certificate of deposit may be credited with compound interest on a monthly basis. A NOW (negotiable order of withdrawal) account may earn daily compound interest. The present value of the income from a corporate bond typically is computed on a semiannual discounting basis.

In addition, all of the explanations of problems involving periodic payments thus far have been based on the assumption that payments are made annually. Often, however, such payments occur more than once per year. Installment loan payments, for example, are frequently made monthly. Bond interest payments are usually made every 6 months. Deposits into the savings accounts of many people are made weekly.

The remainder of this chapter examines the effect on the interest rate and therefore on the time value of money resulting from compounding or discounting more often than annually. It also contains an explanation of how to solve problems involving a series of level payments that occur more often than once per year, regardless of how often compounding or discounting takes place.

Nominal versus Effective Interest Rates

As you know, compounding results in the conversion of interest earnings into principal. For example, if $100 is deposited today and subsequently credited with $7.00 of compound interest, the principal on which future interest is credited rises to $107. The $7.00 of interest converts into principal.

If compounding occurs annually, when does interest convert into principal and begin to earn interest on itself? Obviously the conversion and thus the capacity for increased interest earnings occur after one year, again after 2 years, and so on. If, on the other hand, compounding occurs on a monthly basis, when does interest convert to principal and thus begin to earn interest on itself? The conversions occur after one month has elapsed, again after 2 months, 3 months, and so on.

Of course the greater the frequency in which compounding occurs, the smaller the dollar amount of interest earned and converted into principal on the occasion of each compounding. Naturally the amount of interest a given amount of principal can earn in a week is less than it can earn in a month at any given stated or nominal annual interest rate. Nevertheless, all other things being equal, the more frequently compounding occurs per year, the greater the *total* amount of interest credited to an account during the year. To illustrate, table 7-2 shows the amount of interest credited during one year to a $5,000 deposit with a stated or nominal 9 percent annual interest rate applied with various frequencies during the year.

TABLE 7-2
Total Interest Credited to a $5,000 Deposit during One Year at 9% Stated Annual Interest Rate and Various Compounding Frequencies

Compounding Frequency	Interest Earnings
Annually	$450.00
Semiannually	460.13
Quarterly	465.42
Monthly	469.03
Weekly	470.45
Daily*	470.81

*Based on 360 days per year[9]

Technically, of course, compounding can occur even more frequently than daily—every hour, every minute, every second, or even more frequently than that. And as the frequency continues to increase, so does the total interest credited. The upper limit of the total interest credited to a sum of money for a particular stated or nominal annual interest rate occurs in the case of continuous compounding, wherein interest is compounded an infinite number of times per year, rather than at discrete time intervals. Continuous compounding is a theoretical concept useful principally in the study of advanced financial topics, but it also has some practical applications since financial institutions occasionally credit interest to customer accounts on a continuous basis.

From the figures in table 7-2 it should be obvious that a stated or nominal annual interest rate does not necessarily reflect the true or effective interest rate. You have seen that a 9 percent nominal annual rate produces any of six separate interest earnings in a year, depending on the frequency in which compounding occurs. Hence it is important to distinguish between the nominal or stated annual rate (9 percent in this illustration) and the true or effective annual rate (also known in some instances as the yield, or the annual percentage rate or APR).

When compounding occurs once per year, the nominal and effective annual rates are identical. In table 7-2, when annual compounding is applied, the $5,000 deposit earns $450, exactly 9 percent. In all other cases it earns more than $450 (more than 9 percent) because compounding occurs more than once per year.

The *effective annual interest rate* is defined as the annual rate that produces in one compounding the same amount of interest as does the nominal annual rate with its compounding frequency. For instance, the 9 percent nominal annual rate in table 7-2 when compounded quarterly produces $465.42 of interest. Thus the effective annual interest rate is 9.3084 percent ($465.42 ÷ $5,000). Similarly, the 9 percent nominal annual rate compounded daily generates $470.81 of interest. Thus the effective annual rate is 9.4162 percent ($470.81 ÷ $5,000).

Calculating the Effective Annual Rate

The effective annual interest rate can be computed for any nominal rate and compounding frequency by the following formula:[10]

$$i_{eff} = \left[1 + \frac{i_{nom}}{f}\right]^f - 1$$

where i_{eff} is the effective annual rate,
i_{nom} is the nominal annual rate, and
f is the compounding frequency per year

Thus, for example, a 9 percent nominal annual rate compounded monthly represents an effective annual rate of

$$i_{eff} = \left[1 + \frac{.09}{12}\right]^{12} - 1$$
$$= 9.3807\%$$

As an alternative to using this formula, you can calculate the effective interest rate for any nominal annual rate and compounding frequency by using the HP-12C, HP-17B II, or BA-II Plus calculators. To illustrate, assume that a 7 percent nominal rate is to be compounded weekly. Set the HP-12C calculator to display four decimal places. Then press the following keys:

blue g, END, 7, ENTER	(to enter the nominal rate)
52, n, ÷, i	(to enter the weekly frequency of compounding)
100, CHS, ENTER, PV, FV, +	(to produce the effective rate)

The answer, 7.2458 percent, should appear on the display.

If you are using the HP-17B II, set it to display four decimal places. Then enter the interest rate conversion menu system by pressing the ICNV menu key, which is next to the TVM menu key. Then press the PER menu key, since in this, and almost all problems, compounding is periodic, rather than continuous. Then press 7 and the NOM% menu key to enter the nominal rate; 52 and the P menu key to enter the weekly frequency of compounding; and the EFF% menu key to produce the effective annual rate, 7.2458 percent.

If you use the BA-II Plus, set the calculator to display four decimal places. Then press 2nd and I Conv, which is located on the number 2 key. Press 2nd, CLR Work to remove any extraneous data. Then press 7, ENTER, ↓, ↓ (to put the nominal rate into the machine), 52, ↑ (to put the number of compounding periods per year into the machine) and CPT. The answer, 7.2458 percent, should appear on the display.

For those who do not wish to use either a formula or a financial calculator to determine the effective interest rate, appendix F will be of some help. It contains a table showing the effective annual interest rates that correspond to a number of nominal annual rates and commonly used compounding frequencies. The table also includes the effective rate for the unusual case of continuous compounding.

To illustrate further the difference between the nominal and effective annual rates of interest, the following list shows the effective rate for a nominal rate of 7 percent with various compounding frequencies:

7% annually	=	7.0000% effective rate
7% semiannually	=	7.1225% effective rate
7% quarterly	=	7.1859% effective rate
7% monthly	=	7.2290% effective rate
7% weekly	=	7.2458% effective rate
7% daily (360)	=	7.2501% effective rate

Again it is clear that, for a particular nominal annual interest rate, the true or effective rate rises as the frequency of compounding per year increases. Note, however, that the increase in the effective rate becomes smaller and smaller with each increase in compounding frequency. In the above list, for example, the change from annual to semiannual compounding increased the effective rate by .1225 percentage points (7.1225–7.0000). The change from semiannual to quarterly compounding changed the effective rate by only .0634 percentage points (7.1859–7.1225); and the change from quarterly to monthly compounding increased it by only .0432 percentage points (7.2290–7.1859).

Another point worth noting concerning nominal versus effective annual interest rates is that sometimes a low nominal rate with a high compounding frequency produces a higher effective rate than a high nominal rate with a low compounding frequency. For example, assume that you plan to deposit $10,000 in an interest-bearing account for one year. Bank A pays interest of 8 percent compounded semiannually. Bank B pays 7.9 percent compounded daily (360 days per year). Where should you put your money? If you use the formula described earlier or a financial calculator, you will find that the effective rate in Bank A is 8.1600 percent. Bank B, on the other hand, pays an effective rate of 8.2195 percent. That is an extra $5.95 credited to your $10,000 deposit if you go to Bank B.

Impact of Compounding Frequency on Future Values

Because the effective interest rate rises as the frequency of compounding increases, so does the future value of a single sum. The same is true of other future values described in this and the previous chapter. For example, the future value of an annual annuity or of a series of annual uneven cash flows rises as compounding frequency increases. Conversely in sinking fund problems the size of the annual payment needed to reach a targeted future amount diminishes as the frequency of compounding and the effective interest rate increase. Finally, the number of years or annual payments needed to reach a particular future value decreases as the frequency of compounding and the effective interest rate increase.

Impact of Discounting Frequency on Present Values

You probably have already guessed that increasing the frequency of discounting has the opposite effect on present values than increasing the frequency of compounding has on future values. This again follows from the preceding discussion of nominal versus effective interest rates.

To illustrate, calculate the present value of $100 due in one year at 7 percent. Discounted annually, you know that the effective rate is 7 percent. The present value of $100 for one year at 7 percent is $93.46. Discounted quarterly, however, the effective rate is 7.1859 percent. The present value of $100 for one year at 7.1859 percent is $93.30. And discounted monthly the effective rate is 7.2290 percent, which produces a present value of $93.26. Generalizing from these results, then, you can conclude that, all other things being equal, an increase in the frequency of discounting increases the effective interest rate and, therefore, reduces the present value of a single sum. The same is true of the present value of an annual annuity or of a series of annual uneven cash flows. Conversely, in debt services problems, an increase in the frequency of charging interest per year, all other things being equal, increases the amount of the loan payments per year. Finally, the number of years it takes to pay off a loan or to liquidate a principal sum increases as the frequency of charging or crediting interest per year increases, all other things being equal.

Calculating Future and Present Values

When you encounter a time-value-of-money problem in which the interest rate is compounded or discounted more than once per year, there are two basic ways of solving it: (1) use the effective rate or (2) adjust the nominal rate and number of periods.

Using the Effective Rate

The first basic approach is to solve the problem by computing the effective interest rate as explained earlier. Then use the effective rate in the same way you have learned to use the nominal annual interest rate throughout this and the preceding chapter.

To illustrate, \$500 will grow to what amount in 3 years at 6 percent interest compounded quarterly? The effective rate is 6.13636 percent. Therefore you can use this rate in place of 6 percent in the FVSS formula:

$$\begin{aligned} \text{FVSS} &= \$500 \text{ x } 1.0613636^3 \\ &= \$500 \text{ x } 1.19562 \\ &= \$597.81 \end{aligned}$$

Or what is the present value of a 5-year annuity of \$2,000 if it is discounted at 8 percent weekly? The effective rate is 8.32205 percent. Therefore you can use this rate in place of 8 percent in the PVA formula:

$$\begin{aligned} \text{PVA} &= \$2{,}000 \text{ x } \frac{1 - \dfrac{1}{1.0832205^5}}{.0832205} \\ &= \$2{,}000 \text{ x } \frac{1 - \dfrac{1}{1.49137}}{.0832205} \\ &= \$2{,}000 \text{ x } \frac{1 - .67053}{.0832205} \\ &= \$2{,}000 \text{ x } 3.9590 \\ &= \$7{,}918 \end{aligned}$$

Instead of using a formula, you can solve these problems by means of your financial calculator. Again, however, first calculate the effective rate. Then follow the normal series of keystrokes for the particular type of problem inserting the effective rate, rather than the nominal rate, as the interest rate.

Using a present-value or future-value table usually is infeasible if you follow this first method. Most tables, including those in appendix B of this book, fail to provide the needed factors for the fine gradations of effective interest rates. For example, there is no set of FVSS factors in table B.1 for an interest rate of 6.13636 percent. Similarly, there is no set of PVA factors in table B.4 for an interest rate of 8.32205 percent.

Adjusting the Nominal Rate and Number of Periods

The second basic way of solving these kinds of problems involves using the nominal annual rate, rather than the effective rate. In this case, two adjustments must be made. First, the problem's nominal annual interest rate must be *divided* by the number of compounding or discounting periods per year. This reflects the fact that only a fraction of the annual rate will be applied each time compounding or discounting occurs during the year. Second, the number of years in the problem must be *multiplied* by the number of compounding or discounting periods per year. This reflects the total number of times that compounding or discounting of the fractional annual rate occurs. Note, then, that if this approach is used, the number that is divided into i and the number that is multiplied by n are always the same (four for quarterly compounding or discounting, 12 for monthly, 360 for daily, etc.).

To illustrate this approach of solving time-value problems, compute the FVSS of $100 at 8 percent compounded quarterly for 20 years. Instead of the usual formula

$$\text{FVSS} = \$100 \text{ x } 1.08^{20} = \$466.10$$

the formula is

$$\text{FVSS} = \$100 \text{ x } 1.02^{80} = \$487.54$$

That is, the 8 percent annual rate is divided by 4 and the 20-year period is multiplied by 4.

If you wish to calculate by means of the formula the present value of $3,000 due 6 years hence with a discount rate of 12 percent applied monthly, the usual formula

$$\text{PVSS} = \$3{,}000 \text{ x} \left[\frac{1}{1.12^{6}}\right] = \$1{,}519.89$$

is replaced by

$$\text{PVSS} = \$3{,}000 \text{ x} \left[\frac{1}{1.01^{72}}\right] = \$1{,}465.49$$

The 12 percent annual rate is divided by 12 and the 6-year period is multiplied by 12.

If you prefer to use tables rather than formulas to calculate present and future values, the same two adjustments must be made. For example, if the nominal annual interest rate in a problem is 6 percent compounded quarterly for one year, use the tabular factor not for 6 percent and one period but for 1.5 percent (6% ÷ 4) and four periods (1 x 4). Or if a problem involves a nominal rate of 9 percent discounted semiannually for 8 years, use the tabular factor not for 9 percent and 8 periods but for 4.5 percent (9% ÷ 2) and 16 periods (8 x 2).

One difficulty you may encounter in attempting to use tables in this way is that the adjusted nominal rate may not be listed. For example, an 11 percent rate that is compounded monthly would require a set of factors for an adjusted nominal rate of 9.1667 percent. A 12 percent nominal rate that is compounded weekly would require a set of factors for an adjusted nominal rate of .2308 percent. There is no easy way to overcome this difficulty.

A second difficulty you may encounter in using the tables is that when n is multiplied by the number of compounding or discounting periods in a year, the resulting number of periods may be greater than those shown in the table. For example, assume you wish to calculate the future value of $2,000 at the end of 5 years at 18 percent interest compounded monthly. The factor needed from table B.1 is for 1.5 percent (18% ÷ 12) and 60 periods (5 x 12). The table, however, shows factors for only 50 periods. This difficulty is overcome simply by multiplying factors for any 2 years in the 1.5 percent column in which the combined number of periods equals the desired number of periods. For example, multiply the factor for 50 years by that for 10 years to produce a 60-year FVSS factor at 1.5 percent of 2.4431 (2.1052 x 1.1605). This, multiplied by $2,000, produces the FVSS, $4,886.17. The same technique may be used in conjunction with table B.2 to compute the factor for any number of periods needed to solve a PVSS problem. *It cannot be used in this way, however, to solve annuity problems through tables B.3 or B.4.*

Assume that instead of formulas or tables you wish to use a financial calculator. The only new procedure when using financial calculators for problems involving compounding more often than annually is to make the two adjustments referred to above: (1) divide the nominal annual i by the compounding frequency and (2) multiply the number of years by the compounding frequency. These adjustments may be made mentally before data is entered or they may be made on the calculator itself as part of the data entry process. The latter approach is illustrated here because the numbers are a bit too complex to compute mentally.

How can you calculate the amount to which $15,000 will grow in 4 years at an 8 percent nominal annual interest rate if compounding occurs on a weekly basis? The solution process entails entering the initial sum as a present value, entering 4 years of weekly compounding as the number of periods, and entering 1/52 of 8 percent as the weekly interest rate.

The sequence of keystrokes for solving this problem on the HP-12C is as follows:

15000, CHS, PV	(to enter the initial deposit)
4, ENTER, 52, x, n	(to enter the number of compounding periods)
8, ENTER, 52, ÷, i	(to enter the weekly interest rate)
FV	(to produce the solution)

The answer, $20,651.84, should be displayed.

The HP-12C has one additional feature that provides a useful shortcut when solving problems involving monthly compounding (or discounting). Note that the n key also has a blue 12x function and the i key has a blue 12÷ function. These serve to automatically adjust n and i to a monthly basis.

To illustrate, assume you wish to calculate the payment amount at the end of each month on a $9,000, 4-year automobile loan carrying a nominal annual interest rate of 8.8 percent compounded monthly. Press the following keys:

blue g, END	(to set the payment mode to the end of the month)
9000, CHS, PV	(to enter the loan amount)
8.8, blue g, i	(to enter the monthly interest rate)
4, blue g, n	(to enter the number of payments)
PMT	(to produce the solution)

The answer, $223.11, should appear on the display.

Users of the HP-17B II will recall from chapter 5 that they were instructed to set the calculator for one payment per year and one compounding period per year and not to change this setting—ever! But now we are dealing with payments that occur and compounding that takes place more than once per year. Should the calculator setting be changed? Though doing so will produce a correct answer, we recommend strongly against it. Our experience has been that users of the calculator often forget to change the settings back to once per year/once per year after solving a problem, and they forget to check these settings for accuracy the next time they try solving a problem, with the result that solutions to subsequent problems are wildly incorrect. Therefore, we prefer to set the calculator for one payment per year and one compounding period per year and not to change that setting—ever!

How, then, does one deal with payments and compounding that occur more frequently than annually? The answer is to enter the number of periods, not the number of years, as the value of N, and the periodic interest rate, not the nominal annual rate, as the value of I%YR. For example, to find the future value of $15,000 in four years at 8 percent compounded weekly, the keystrokes on the HP-17B II in the TVM menu system are as follows:

15000, +/–, the PV menu key	(to enter the initial deposit)
4, x, 52, =, the N menu key	(to enter the number of compounding periods)

8, ÷, 52, =, the I%YR menu key	(to enter the weekly interest rate)
the FV menu key	(to produce the solution)

The answer, $20,651.84, is displayed.

Those who are using the BA-II Plus calculator will recall from chapter 5 that they were instructed to set the calculator for one payment per year and one compounding period per year and not to change this setting—ever! But now we are dealing with payments that occur and compounding that takes place more than once per year. Should the calculator setting be changed? Though doing so will produce a correct answer, we recommend strongly against it. Our experience has been that users of the calculator often forget to change the settings back to once per year/once per year after solving a problem, and they forget to check these settings for accuracy the next time they try solving a problem, with the result that solutions to subsequent problems are wildly incorrect. Therefore, we prefer to set the calculator for one payment per year and one compounding period per year and not to change that setting—ever!

How, then, does one deal with payments and compounding that occur more frequently than annually? The answer is to enter the number of periods, not the number of years, as the value of N, and the periodic interest rate, not the nominal annual rate, as the value of I/Y. For example, to find the future value of $15,000 in four years at 8 percent compounded weekly, press the following keys:

15000, +/–, PV	(to enter the initial deposit)
4, x, 52, =, N	(to enter the number of compounding periods)
8, ÷, 52, =, I/Y	(to enter the weekly interest rate)
CPT, FV	(to produce the solution)

The answer, $20,651.84, should appear on the display screen.

Interpreting the Results of the Calculations

When the solution to a time-value-of-money problem is a value for i, I/Y, n, N, or PMT, remember that these are *periodic* values. Therefore, if the compounding or discounting frequency is other than annual, these solutions are also other-than-annual values. To convert the solution to an annual basis, therefore, it must be adjusted by, in the case of monthly results, a factor of 12. For example, if a monthly payment is $800, the amount paid per year is $800 x 12 = $9,600. Similarly, if the number of monthly payments is 24, the number of years during which payments will be made is 24 ÷ 12 = 2.

Also, if the solution to a time-value-of-money problem is a value for i, I%YR, or I/Y, it too is a *periodic* value. If its frequency is other-than-annual, such as monthly, it too should be converted to an annual basis. However, it is insufficient to merely multiply the periodic interest rate value by, in this case, 12, since the result of such a multiplication would be a *nominal* annual rate (often called the APR, or annual percentage rate, by financial institutions). A more accurate result is found by then converting that nominal annual rate to an effective annual rate as described earlier.

Assume you wish to compute the annual interest rate on a $1,000 loan that calls for 12 monthly payments of $99, beginning one month from the date of the loan. When you enter the data into your calculator, you initially find as the solution a rate of 2.7553 percent. This, however, is a monthly rate. Multiply it by 12 to find the annual rate, 33.0631 percent. Then convert this to an effective annual rate as explained earlier. The effective annual rate on this loan is 38.5634 percent.

FOCUS ON ETHICS
The Impact of Inflation

The financial planner must never lose track of the impact of inflation. If a couple planning to retire in 20 years projects its annual needs at $50,000, that projection is in the current year's dollars. If inflation is estimated at 3 percent per year, at the retirement date the inflation-adjusted needs will be $90,000! Twenty years into retirement (40 years from today), the adjusted income requirement at 3 percent annual inflation would be $163,000! Viewed another way, a $50,000 income in 40 years will have purchasing power equal to only $15,000 in today's dollars.

Often planners supply future projections of mutual fund or insurance cash values with specific rate-of-return assumptions. Often the projected accumulation is extremely large, and the client is lulled into a dangerous complacency because inflation is ignored.

Unfortunately, fully informing the client of the perils of inflation often (unintentionally and ironically) results in scaring the client into inaction. This may mean a loss of income for the planner. Regardless of this possibility, the planner's ethical responsibility is clear. Inflation is a critical factor that must be addressed in any financial projections. Withholding this information is the same as misinforming the client.

Annuity Payments Occurring Other Than Annually

Thus far we have examined problems in which compounding or discounting occurs more frequently than once per year. A related but separate topic is the question of annuity payments that occur more frequently than once per year. (Uneven cash flows that occur other than annually are not dealt with in this book.)

Simple Annuities and Simple Annuities Due

A *simple annuity* or *annuity due* is one in which the frequency of payments and the frequency of compounding or discounting are identical. An example of a simple annuity is a series of six quarterly deposits credited with interest quarterly, beginning 3 months from now. Likewise, a simple annuity due is a series of 15 monthly payments discounted on a monthly basis, beginning immediately. All of the annuity topics discussed so far involved simple annuities or simple annuities due because both the payment frequency and the compounding or discounting frequency were identical, once per year.

The calculation of the present or future value of a simply annuity or a simple annuity due when payments are more frequent than annual involves the same tools and procedures as you have already learned. The same formulas you use for computing FVA, FVAD, PVA, and PVAD can be used; the same FVA and PVA tables can be used; the same keystrokes can be used on the HP-12C, HP-17B II, or the BA-II Plus—*except for two adjustments.* First, the figure you use as the n should always be the total number of *payments* in the problem, not the number of years. Second, the figure you use as the i should always be the *periodic* interest rate, not the annual rate. For example, in a problem that involves 3 years of quarterly payments and a 16 percent interest rate compounded quarterly, n is 12 and i is 4 percent. Or in one that involves 5 years of monthly payments and a 6 percent interest rate compounded monthly, n is 60 and i is .5 percent.

A corporate bond is a frequently encountered security that includes a simple annuity with payments occurring other than annually. For example, assume that a bond provides semiannual interest payments of $40 for ten years, beginning six months from now, as well as payment of the $1,000 principal sum at the end of the tenth year. If bonds with a similar degree of riskiness are yielding 11 percent, what should you pay for this bond? The present value of 20 payments of $40 each should be found based on a 5.5 percent discount rate. To this should be added the present value of the $1,000 final payment, also discounted at 5.5 percent for 20 periods. On a financial calculator, enter 40 as the end-of-period PMT, 1000 as the FV, 5.5 as the i, 20 as the n, and find the PV, or intrinsic value of this bond, $820.74.[11]

Now assume that you buy this bond for $821 and hold it for three years, at which time it is called by the issuing corporation for $1,040. What has been your annual yield to the call date? On a financial calculator, enter 821 as the PV, 1040 as the FV, 40 as the end-of-period PMT, and 6 as the n. Find i, the period interest rate, 8.47%. Now convert this periodic rate to an effective annual rate. Find the nominal annual rate by doubling 8.47 to 16.94 percent. The effective annual yield to call of a nominal annual 16.94 percent received semiannually is 17.66 percent.

You can also calculate the n, i, or PMT in a simple annuity or annuity due involving other-than-annual payments. Use the same tools you would use if the payments were annual. Again, however, the item you input or compute as n is always the total number of payments, not the total number of years. The item you input or compute as i is always the periodic interest rate, not the annual rate. And the item you input or compute as PMT is always the single periodic payment, not the sum of the payments per year.

Complex Annuities and Complex Annuities Due

A *complex annuity* or *annuity due* is one in which the frequency of payments and the frequency of compounding or discounting are different. For example, a complex annuity due is a series of 14 monthly deposits that are credited with interest daily, beginning immediately. Likewise, a complex annuity is a series of 10 semiannual lease payments that are discounted on an annual basis, beginning 6 months from now.

The mathematics of solving problems involving complex annuities are fairly complicated and generally beyond the scope of this book. Here we deal with only two types of complex annuity problems, computing the FVA or FVAD and the PVA or PVAD. The tool described for finding the solution to each is a formula, although a calculator is also needed, especially to facilitate raising certain numbers to a power.

In order to solve problems involving complex annuities, it is necessary to introduce one new variable that has not been used in any of the problems heretofore. That new variable, which we shall label as "c," is the number of times that compounding or discounting occurs in *each payment interval.* The value of c is found by dividing the frequency of compounding or discounting per year by the frequency of the payments per year. For example, if compounding occurs monthly and annuity payments are made quarterly, c = 3. Or if discounting occurs semiannually and annuity payments are made weekly, c = 1/26.

The formula for computing the future value of a complex annuity is presented below. In it, as in simple annuities, i is the periodic interest rate and n is the total number of annuity payments.

$$\text{FVA} = \left[\frac{(1 + i)^{n \times c} - 1}{(1 + i)^{c} - 1}\right] \text{x amount of one deposit}$$

To illustrate, assume that $70 is deposited into a savings account every 6 months for 5 years. The first deposit is made 6 months from now. Interest is credited to the account at a 12 percent nominal annual rate, compounded monthly. How much will be in the account at the end of 5 years? Substituting in the formula, we have

$$\begin{aligned}\text{FVA} &= \left[\frac{1.01^{10 \times 6} - 1}{1.01^{6} - 1}\right] \text{x } \$70 \\ &= \left[\frac{.8167}{.0615}\right] \text{x } \$70 \\ &= 13.2797 \text{ x } \$70 \\ &= \$929.58\end{aligned}$$

If in this illustration the first deposit is made immediately rather than 6 months from now (if the problem called for finding FVAD), one further step is necessary. The value of the FVA has to be increased in a manner analogous to that used for annual annuities due. Specifically, the adjustment to be made is

$$FVAD = FVA \times (1 + i)^c$$

Again, remember to use the periodic interest rate for i in making this adjustment. In this illustration, then,

$$\begin{aligned} FVAD &= \$929.58 \times 1.01^6 \\ &= \$929.58 \times 1.0615 \\ &= \$986.75 \end{aligned}$$

That is, the account balance is 6.15 percent higher because an extra 6 months of interest is earned at a 12 percent nominal annual rate compounded monthly.

Next we turn to calculating the present value of a complex annuity. The formula is presented below. As before, n is the total number of payments, i is the periodic interest rate, and c is the discounting frequency per payment interval.

$$PVA = \text{amount of one payment} \times \left[\frac{1 - \dfrac{1}{(1 + i)^{n \times c}}}{(1 + i)^c - 1} \right]$$

To illustrate, assume that during the first 3½ years after you retire you want to have interest income of \$250 per month, beginning one month after your retirement date. Also assume that the principal sum to be liquidated in order to provide this income can be invested at a nominal annual rate of 6 percent, compounded quarterly. How large a principal sum will you need on the date you retire? What is the present value of this complex annuity? Substituting in the formula, we have

$$\begin{aligned} PVA &= \$250 \times \left[\frac{1 - \dfrac{1}{1.015^{42 \times 1/3}}}{1.015^{1/3} - 1} \right] \\ &= \$250 \times \left[\frac{1 - .8118}{1.0050 - 1} \right] \\ &= \$250 \times 37.64 \\ &= \$9,410.00 \end{aligned}$$

If the \$250 of monthly income is to begin on your retirement date, rather than one month later (if the problem called for calculating the PVAD rather than the PVA), one further step is necessary. The value of the PVA has to be increased in a manner analogous to that used for annual annuities due. Specifically, the adjustment is

$$PVAD = PVA \times (1 + i)^{c}$$

Again, remember to use the periodic interest rate in making this adjustment. In this illustration, then,

$$\begin{aligned} PVAD &= \$9{,}410 \times 1.015^{1/3} \\ &= \$9{,}410 \times 1.0050 \\ &= \$9{,}457.05 \end{aligned}$$

The principal sum has to be about .5 percent higher because one month of interest earnings is lost on a 6 percent annual rate compounded quarterly.

PROBLEMS

1. The divorce is final and you have been awarded the following alimony: \$5,000 at the end of each of the next 3 years, plus \$6,000 at the end of each of the following 5 years, plus \$7,000 at the end of each of the following 10 years. If you remarry, however, you receive no further alimony. Measured in terms of present value and a discount rate of 6.5 percent, what will your wedding cost if you remarry today?
2. To convince yourself of the wisdom of your recent decision to quit smoking (and this time you really mean it), you plan at the end of each of the next 5 years to put into a savings account earning 6 percent compound annual interest the money you would have spent on cigarettes. You anticipate that the amounts of the five deposits will be \$400, \$450, \$500, \$550, and \$600. If all goes according to plan, how much will be in your account after 5 years?
3. Which of the following income streams would you rather have if interest rates currently are 7 percent?

Beginning of Year	Cash Flow		End of Year	Cash Flow
1	\$2,000		1	0
2	\$2,500		2	0
3	\$3,000	OR	3	\$5,500
4	\$3,000		4	\$5,500
5	\$3,000		5	\$5,500

4. Your race horse is a sure thing to win $60,000 for you at the end of each of the next 3 years, after which you believe that the horse will be able to earn about $10,000 per year in stud fees at the end of each of 5 years. If you insist on a compound annual rate of return of at least 20 percent, what would you accept for the horse today?
5. Tuition at the university your daughter will be attending next year is expected to be $11,000 at that time and to rise by about 8 percent per year thereafter. You plan to set aside today a capital sum that, invested at 6 percent interest, will be just sufficient to pay her tuition in full at the start of each of the 4 years. How large a capital sum is needed to accomplish this objective?
6. Your goal is to have accumulated a capital sum of $75,000 when you retire 12 years from now. You plan to make an initial deposit of $2,000 today, and on each of the following 11 annual anniversary dates you will deposit an amount that is 10 percent higher than the previous year's deposit. If your deposits earn 7 percent interest per year, will you reach your goal?
7. You have just made a loan of $85,000 to a friend, who has agreed to the following repayment schedule:

End of year 1	$ 5,000
End of year 2	$ 10,000
End of year 3	0
End of year 4	0
End of year 5	$100,000

   (a) What is your internal rate of return?
   (b) What is the net present value of this investment if 10 percent is your minimum acceptable compound annual rate of return?
8. Tax reform legislation notwithstanding, you have located an exotic tax-sheltered investment opportunity. For an initial outlay of $50,000 and an additional $10,000 5 years from now, you will receive the following income stream:

End of years 1–4	$ 7,500
End of years 6–10	$ 8,000

   What is the internal rate of return on this investment?
9. You are debating whether to invest $100,000 in a piece of equipment that will produce the following cost savings for your business:

End of years 1–3	$ 30,000
End of year 4	($ 10,000)
End of years 5–7	$ 20,000

(a) What is the internal rate of return?
(b) What is the net present value if you discount the cash flows at the 8 percent compound annual interest rate you would have to pay in order to finance the purchase of the equipment?

10. Use the formula or your financial calculator to compute the effective annual interest rate when a nominal annual rate of 18 percent is compounded
    (a) semiannually
    (b) quarterly
    (c) monthly
    Check your answers by comparing them with table F in appendix F.
11. Where should you put your money: in a certificate of deposit that will earn 9.75 percent compounded daily (360 days) or in one that will earn 10 percent compounded semiannually?
12. (a) Show which is the larger amount: the future value of a 10-year, $2,000 annual annuity growing at a nominal annual interest rate of 5 percent compounded weekly or one growing at a nominal annual interest rate of 5 percent compounded monthly.
    (b) Show which is the larger amount: the present value of a 6-year, $3,000 annual annuity discounted at 11 percent applied monthly or one discounted at 11 percent applied quarterly.
13. Assume that you plan to save for Junior's college education by depositing $200 per month for the next 12 years in a savings account, beginning immediately. The account is expected to earn a nominal annual rate of 6 percent, compounded monthly. How much will be in the account at the end of the 12th year?
14. What is the present value of a stream of 10 quarterly payments of $500 each, beginning 3 months from now, if an annual discount rate of 16 percent is applied semiannually?

SOLUTIONS

1. Not counting the cost of the gown, the organist, the flowers, the photographer, and so on, the wedding will cost you $64,287.34 in lost alimony, computed as shown below, using factors in tables B.2 and B.4.

The present value of the first series of payments is $13,242.50.	($5,000 x 2.6485 = $13,242.50)
The present value of the second series of payments as of the beginning of year 4 is $24,934.20.	($6,000 x 4.1557 = $24,934.20)
The present value of this amount as of the beginning of year one is $20,640.53.	($24,934.20 x .8278 = $20,640.53)

The present value of the third series of payments as of the beginning of year 9 is \$50,321.60.	(\$7,000 x 7.1888 = \$50,321.60)
The present value of this amount as of the beginning of year one is \$30,404.31.	(\$50,321.60 x .6042 = \$30,404.31)
The total present value of the three series of payments is \$64,287.34.	(\$13,242.50 + \$20,640.53 + \$30,404.31 = \$64,287.34)

If you used a financial calculator, the present value of these uneven cash flows is \$64,290.04.

2. The future values of these five items of ungrouped data, based on FVSS factors in table B.1, are as follows:

\$400 x 1.2625	=	\$ 505.00
\$450 x 1.1910	=	535.95
\$500 x 1.1236	=	561.80
\$550 x 1.0600	=	583.00
\$600 x 1.0000	=	600.00
Total future value		\$2,785.75

Use of a financial calculator in the way described in this chapter would produce a future value of the same amount.

3. Using PVSS and PVA factors from tables B.2 and B.4, you can compute the present value of the income stream on the left as \$11,694.02.

\$2,000 x 1.0000	=	\$ 2,000.00
\$2,500 x .9346	=	2,336.50
\$3,000 x 2.6243 x 1.07 x .8734	=	7,357.52
Total present value		\$11,694.02

The present value of the income stream on the right is higher, \$12,606.35.

\$5,500 x 2.6243 x .8734 = \$12,606.35

If you use a financial calculator, the income stream on the left is worth \$11,694.34 and that on the right is worth \$12,606.99.

4. Based on the appropriate PVA and PVSS factors from tables B.2 and B.4, the horse's present value is

\$60,000 x 2.1065	=	\$126,390.00
\$10,000 x 2.9906 x .5787	=	17,306.60
Total present value		\$143,696.60

This would be your minimum selling price. (On the HP-12C, HP-17B II, or BA-II Plus, the answer is $143,695.67).

5. The answer may be found through the formula for calculating the present value of a series of payments that grow by a constant percentage. Specifically,

$$PV = \$11{,}000 \text{ x} \left[\frac{1 - \left[\frac{1.08}{1.06}\right]^4}{(.06 - .08)} \right] \text{x } 1.06$$

$$= \$11{,}000 \text{ x} \left[\frac{1 - 1.0776}{-.02} \right] \text{x } 1.06$$

$$= \$11{,}000 \text{ x } 3.8817 \text{ x } 1.06$$

$$= \$45{,}260.62$$

But since the first payment is not due for one year, this result should be divided by 1.06 to produce the answer, $42,698.70. Alternatively, if you use the appropriate keystrokes on the HP-12C, HP-17B II, or the BA-II Plus, the answer that appears on the display is $45,261.02. Dividing this by 1.06 produces the answer, $42,699.08.

6. You will not reach the $75,000 goal with the planned funding pattern. The answer may be found through the formula for calculating the future value of a series of deposits that grow by a constant percentage and that begin immediately. Specifically,

$$FV = \$2{,}000 \text{ x} \left[\frac{1.07^{12} - 1.10^{12}}{.07 - .10} \right] \text{x } 1.07$$

$$= \$2{,}000 \text{ x} \left[\frac{2.2522 - 3.1384}{-.03} \right] \text{x } 1.07$$

$$= \$2{,}000 \text{ x } 29.5400 \text{ x } 1.07$$

$$= \$63{,}215.60$$

Or if you use the appropriate keystrokes on the HP-12C, HP-17B II, or BA-II Plus, the answer that appears on the display is $63,218.22.

7. (a) Even for a fairly simple set of cash flows such as this one, a financial calculator is the most practical means of calculating the IRR. The keystrokes for the HP-12C are as follows: 85000, CHS, blue g, CFo, 5000, blue g, CFj, 10000, blue g, CFj, 0, blue g, CFj, 2, blue g, Nj, 100000, blue g, CFj, yellow f, IRR. On the HP-17B II, with the #T?

function turned off, the keystrokes in the CFLO menu system are as follows: 85000, +/–, INPUT, 5000, INPUT, 1, INPUT, 10000, INPUT, 1, INPUT, 0, INPUT, 2, INPUT, 100000, INPUT, 1, INPUT, EXIT, the CALC menu key, and the IRR% menu key. The keystrokes for the BA-II Plus are as follows: 85000, +/–, ENTER, ↓, 5000, ENTER, ↓, ↓, 10000, ENTER, ↓, ↓, 0, ENTER, ↓, 2, ENTER, ↓, 100000, ENTER, ↓, IRR, CPT. The answer is 6.9171%.

(b) With the above data still in the machine, on the HP-12C press 10, i, yellow f, NPV. On the HP-17B II, press 10, the I% menu key, and the NPV menu key. Or on the BA-II Plus press NPV, 10, ENTER, ↓, CPT. The answer is –$10,097.95.
Alternatively, the NPV can be found by using present value factors from table B.2.

$5,000 x .9091	=	$ 4,545.50
$10,000 x .8264	=	8,264.00
$100,000 x .6209	=	62,090.00
Present value of inflows		$74,899.50
Present value of outflows		–85,000.00
Net present value		–$10,100.50

8. On the HP-12C press 50000, CHS, blue g, CFo, 7500, blue g, CFj, 4, blue g, Nj, 10000, CHS, blue g, CFj, 8000, blue g, CFj, 5, blue g, Nj, yellow f, IRR. On the HP-17B II, the keystrokes in the CFLO menu system with the #T? function turned on are as follows: 50000, +/–, INPUT, 7500, INPUT, 4, INPUT, 10000, +/–, INPUT, 1, INPUT, 8000, INPUT, 5, INPUT, EXIT, the CALC menu key, and the IRR% menu key. On the BA-II Plus press 50000, +/–, ENTER, ↓, 7500, ENTER, ↓, 4, ENTER, ↓, 10000, +/–, ENTER, ↓, ↓, 8000, ENTER, ↓, 5, ENTER, ↓, IRR, CPT. The answer probably is 3.3231%. Because the income stream involves more than one sign change, however, there may also be a negative IRR, though this is unlikely.
9. (a) The internal rate of return may be found on the HP-12C by pressing 100000, CHS, blue g, CFo, 30000, blue g, CFj, 3, blue g, Nj, 10000, CHS, blue g, CFj, 20000, blue g, CFj, 3, blue g, Nj, yellow f, IRR. If you are using the HP-17B II, you can find the IRR by entering the CFLO menu system, turning on the #T? function, and pressing the following keys: 100000, +/–, INPUT, 30000, INPUT, 3, INPUT, 10000, +/–, INPUT, 1, INPUT, 20000, INPUT, 3, INPUT, EXIT, the CALC menu key and the IRR% menu key. Or you can find the IRR on the BA-II Plus by pressing 100000, +/–, ENTER, ↓, 30000, ENTER, ↓, 3, ENTER, ↓, 10000, +/–, ENTER, ↓, ↓, 20000, ENTER, ↓, 3, ENTER, ↓, IRR, CPT. The answer is 10.6118% (but see solution 8 above).

(b) With the above data still in the HP-12C, press 8, i, yellow f, NPV. On the HP-17B II, with the above data still in the machine, press 8, the I% menu key, and the NPV menu key. Or if you use the BA-II Plus, with the above data still in the machine press NPV, 8, ENTER, ↓, CPT. The answer is $7,847.48. Alternatively, the NPV can be found by using PVSS and PVA factors from tables B.2 and B.4.

$30,000 x 2.5771	=	$ 77,313.00
$20,000 x 2.5771 x .7350	=	37,883.37
Present value of inflows		$115,196.37
$100,000 x 1.0000	=	$100,000.00
$10,000 x .7350	=	7,350.00
Present value of outflows		$107,350.00
Net present value		$ 7,846.37

10.

(a) $\left[1 + \frac{.18}{2}\right]^{2} - 1 = 18.81000\%$

(b) $\left[1 + \frac{.18}{4}\right]^{4} - 1 = 19.25186\%$

(c) $\left[1 + \frac{.18}{12}\right]^{12} - 1 = 19.56182\%$

11. Take the 10 percent rate. The 9.75 percent CD pays an effective rate of

$$\left[1 + \frac{.0975}{360}\right]^{360} - 1 = 10.2397\%$$

whereas the 10 percent CD pays an effective rate of

$$\left[1 + \frac{.10}{2}\right]^{2} - 1 = 10.2500\%$$

12. (a) Weekly compounding will produce the larger FVA because the effective annual interest rate is 5.12458 percent, versus 5.11619 percent for monthly compounding. Substituting these effective rates in the FVA formula, we have

$$\$2{,}000 \text{ x } \left[\frac{1.0512458^{10} - 1}{.0512458}\right] = \$25{,}302.55$$

versus

$$\$2{,}000 \text{ x } \left[\frac{1.0511619^{10} - 1}{.0511619}\right] = \$25{,}292.63$$

(b) Discounting on a quarterly basis will produce the larger PVA. The effective rate for quarterly discounting is 11.46213 percent, versus 11.57188 percent for monthly discounting. Substituting these effective rates in the PVA formula, we have

$$\$3{,}000 \text{ x } \left[\frac{1 - \left[\frac{1}{1.1146213^{6}}\right]}{.1146213}\right] = \$12{,}524.44$$

versus

$$\$3{,}000 \text{ x } \left[\frac{1 - \left[\frac{1}{1.1157188^{6}}\right]}{.1157188}\right] = \$12{,}485.23$$

13. If you use the FVAD formula, the answer for this simple annuity is

$$= \$200 \text{ x } \left[\frac{1.005^{144} - 1}{.005}\right] \text{ x } 1.005$$

$$= \$200 \text{ x } \left[\frac{1.0508}{.005}\right] \text{ x } 1.005$$

$$= \$200 \text{ x } 210.16 \text{ x } 1.005$$

$$= \$42{,}242.16$$

Table B.2 cannot be used to solve the problem because it does not contain a factor in the .5% column for an n of 144.

The HP-12C, HP-17B II, or the BA-II Plus can also be used. Remember that n or N is 144 and i or I/Y is .5. The answer displayed will be $42,240.18.

14. In this problem the annuity is a complex annuity. The value of c is 2 ÷ 4, or ½. Substituting in the formula for the PVA of a complex annuity, we have

$$= \$500 \text{ x } \left[\frac{1 - \left[\frac{1}{1.08^{10 \text{ x } 1/2}} \right]}{1.08^{1/2} - 1} \right]$$

$$= \$500 \text{ x } \left[\frac{1 - .6806}{.0392} \right]$$

$$= \$500 \text{ x } 8.1480$$

$$= \$4,074.00$$

NOTES

1. Most corporate bonds pay interest semiannually. For purposes of simplicity, however, annual payments are assumed here. A later section of this chapter deals with compounding and discounting where cash flows occur more frequently than once per year.
2. In some cases you might at this point want to calculate an annuity, that is, a series of level payments, that would have the same net present value as the uneven cash flows in the machine. If so, simply press the NUS (net uniform series) menu key to produce the answer, \$61,353.83. A five-year annuity of this amount, discounted as 12.5 percent, has a present value of \$218,454.50.
3. Alternatively, you could compute the present value under the end-of-year approach referred to in note 1, and multiply the result by (1 + i).
4. You may have noticed that this cash flow can be restated in terms that are easier to handle if you are using tables.

   \$30,000 for 10 years
   +\$10,000 for 9 years
   +\$10,000 for 8 years
   +\$10,000 for 5 years
   Compute the future value of each annuity and add them together.
5. In this and in all investment opportunities being evaluated, care must be exercised to be sure that all relevant elements of the cash inflow and outflow streams are considered and discounted property. Don't forget to include, when appropriate, such items as shipping and installation costs of a proposed new piece of equipment, maintenance costs, income taxes, salvage value, and so on. In the illustrations in this portion of the chapter it is assumed that all such considerations have already been accounted for in the numbers being used.
6. As seen later in this chapter, this is not usually necessary when using the HP-12C, HP-17B II, or BA-II Plus calculator's IRR function.
7. For more on this phenomenon, review the subject of NPV profiles in college-level financial management textbooks.
8. For an interesting example of multiple IRRs, see Roger H. Allen, *Real Estate Investment and Taxation,* 2d ed. (Cincinnati: South-Western Publishing Co., 1984), p. 205. An illustration developed by Robert J. Doyle, formerly of the faculty of The American College, is presented showing an investment that has several internal rates of return. The cash flows used in the illustration are (\$1,000), \$3,600, (\$4,310), and \$1,716. An investment with this set of cash flows has IRRs of 10 percent, 20 percent, and 30 percent. Each of those rates, when used to discount the cash flows, produces an NPV of zero.

9. Financial institutions typically use a 360-day year as the basis for daily compounding calculations. This produces a slightly smaller annual interest, all other things being equal, than if they were to use a 365-day year.
10. The mathematics of calculating the effective rate manually when compounding is continuous are too complex to be dealt with in this book. The procedure for calculating it by using the HP-12C or BA-II Plus calculators, however, is included in appendixes C and E.
11. The three financial calculators dealt with in this text also have separate systems for computing various bond values. Consult the owner's manual for details.

8

Information Technology

Edmund W. Fitzpatrick

Chapter Outline

INTRODUCTION

Most financial services professionals have an idea of what *information technology* is. The term brings to mind computers, telephone, fax, and e-mail communication, laser printers, and even electronic bulletin boards. Information technology encompasses all these and much more. Indeed, it is becoming so pervasive that, whether people realize it or not, information technology is changing the way they live, work, and spend their leisure time. For example, information technology even affects many of the cars people drive on their daily commute—nearly all new cars have computer-controlled engines.

Information technology is causing profound changes in financial services. The way in which financial services are being provided to consumers is changing, and the way financial services professionals perform their functions is also changing. For example, today a financial services professional may use a computer graphics package to create a dramatic graphic presentation of complex concepts and relationships that apply to a client's personal finances. Or perhaps a computerized imaging system is used that captures all of a client's documents (wills, trust documents, etc.) on a computer's hard disk. This puts all documents electronically at a financial planner's fingertips and does away with manually handling thousands of pages of printed material.

Definition of Information Technology

Isolated examples cannot convey the full picture of the pervasiveness and growing impact of information technology. A careful reading of a definition of information technology can give a clearer notion of the broad scope it encompasses and a deeper understanding of its implications for financial services. Here is a definition of the term information technology:

> *Information technology* is the application of science to solving the problems of collecting, classifying, storing, retrieving, and disseminating knowledge.

Notice that the definition refers to the *application* of science. As science advances, technology seeks to apply the new scientific results. Today most financial services firms make use of technology that was unavailable or too costly only a few years ago. And a few years from now, firms will be using technology that is unavailable or too costly today.

Impact of Personal Computers

One of the most dramatic changes in the financial services industry has been the extent to which personal computers (PCs) have been adopted and put to use for client financial planning and other purposes. Financial planners, recognizing the potential contribution PCs and spreadsheets could make in client data analysis and in planning, were among the first financial services practitioners to adopt this new technology. Soon there was an array of specially designed stand-alone financial planning software packages available for use on personal computers. Acquiring this software made it possible for financial planning offices to generate their own financial plans in-house. Virtually overnight, financial planners were able to improve the services they provided to their clients.

This chapter attempts to provide basic information that financial planners should know in order to make the most effective use of technology in their practices. The benefits of technology are discussed, particularly the impact of technology on sales, office efficiency, and client relations. Broad trends occurring in the field of information technology are also discussed (including pricing trends). And a major portion of this chapter describes various types of computer hardware and software and contains suggestions to be borne in mind when purchases of these items are being considered. Finally the chapter concludes with a discussion of the risks and challenges associated with technology that the financial services professional will need to confront.

TECHNOLOGY AS AN INVESTMENT

It is difficult to find a modern-day financial planning office that is not computerized. The problem today is not whether a financial planning office should be computerized but what new technology the office should use. There is so much new technology becoming available that it is difficult to evaluate and determine what will be most cost-effective.

Good managers and financial services specialists do not blindly accept new technology, despite the hoopla that may surround its announcement. The question that must always be asked concerns opportunity cost: Will this investment yield the larger return for the firm or individual planner?

At the outset it seemed very clear that PCs, along with their word-processing and spreadsheet capabilities, were easily justifiable investments because their benefits far outweighed their cost. However, it was less clear, in those early years, how personal computer technology might contribute more directly to financial services. In particular, there was much interest in how personal computers could support the primary function of attracting new business to a financial services office. Studies by sales personnel helped to answer that question.

Technology and Sales

One of the most important attempts to answer questions regarding the use of PCs by salespersons was a study done in 1980 by Booz, Allen & Hamilton, Inc. Almost 20 years ago, it was already clear that PCs would soon be within the financial reach of even small professional service offices. In the study, Booz, Allen & Hamilton, Inc., investigated whether greater use of technology could improve the performance of "knowledge workers," such as financial planners and insurance sales representatives. The study, funded by some 40 major corporations, looked at a variety of industries, including insurance.[1]

The study generated time profiles of sales representatives before and after a program to improve their performance through greater use of information technology. Table 8-1 provides a comparison of the before and after profiles.[2]

TABLE 8-1
Use of Sales Representative's Time

Activity	Before	After
Effective prospecting/sales	18%	40%
Ineffective prospecting/sales	18%	10%
Servicing	39%	25%
Administration	19%	15%
Training	6%	10%

Use of sales representative's time before and after the introduction of computer hardware-software technology (desktop PCs for sales support and service in the office and portable PCs for sales representatives in the field).

Source: Booz, Allen & Hamilton, Inc.

As table 8-1 suggests, the use of new technology (specifically desktop and portable PCs) by agents and office support personnel significantly increases the amount of time a financial services professional is able to devote to effective marketing activities. If financial services professionals double the time they spend on these key activities, it follows that they should be able to substantially increase, if not double, their revenue.

Based on this major study, it appears to be in the financial planning office's best interest to keep abreast of new technology and seek to encourage its effective use by managers, planners, and support staff. Subsequent studies have confirmed that expanded use of information technology can substantially increase the amount of time a planner or sales representative spends on activities directly related to generating incremental revenue. The implications are clear. Higher productivity leads to higher revenues.

GE Information Services, a component of General Electric Company, has published data showing that sales force automation has benefited the salesperson as well as the company (see table 8-2.).[3] GE Information Services found that, with automation, salespersons generally spend less time prospecting and doing administrative tasks and more time on sales visits, creating proposals, and closing orders. Salespersons actually increased the amount of time spent on sales visits by 50 percent.

Table 8-2 compares salespersons' use of time before and after the implementation of new technology.

TABLE 8-2
Use of Salespersons' Time

Activity	Before	After
Sales visits	30%	45%
Customer prospecting	20%	10%
Servicing	20%	15%
Administration	20%	15%
Proposal generation and order closing	10%	15%

Use of sales representatives' time before and after the introduction of computer hardware-software technology.

Source: GE Information Services

These and other studies demonstrate that it is possible for new technology to dramatically improve the effectiveness of a financial services office. Whether the benefits of the technology are actually realized depends on many factors. For example, if technology is inappropriately used, the investment may be wasted. Potential benefits are so substantial that financial services firms and individual practitioners should be motivated to do what it takes to select and properly implement the appropriate technology.

Technology and Office Systems

Due to technological advancements, much of the communication between financial services firms and home offices (assuming there is one) is now electronic. It takes the form of fax communications, e-mail, and computer networks. A growing portion of communication is automated electronic communication—that is, direct communication between a local financial planning office computer and a company computer. Much of this local-headquarters communication is done to exchange client information and to avoid the costs and errors associated with duplicate keyboard-entry of data.

For example, insurance policy application data typed into a computer in a financial planning office may be sent electronically to a home-office computer. There is no need for rekeying the data at the home office. Similarly, a home-office computer may update client databases nightly in local financial planning offices by sending them a variety of data, ranging from policy tracking data to the latest performance results on investments made for their clients.

A great majority of local financial planning offices have more than one PC, and most of them also have a local area network—or LAN—that links all of the computers in the office together. Data exchanges between a home-office computer and a LAN can update the home-office computer as well as each computer networked into the local financial planning office's LAN.

Home-office computers are generally part of a home-office computer communications network. In other words, the home-office communications computer may be linked to many PCs and terminals throughout the home office. This means, for example, that an expert in small company pension plans could send a recommended plan directly to a person in a local office. The pension plan would be sent from the pension expert's PC via the home-office computer communications network to the local office's LAN and through the LAN to the specific PC of the local office planner requesting the pension plan.

Technology and the Client

It is very probable that the consumer will gradually enter into the financial services computer communications network. Starting in the 1980s, many consumers began to automate their lives. This automation has taken many forms, such as evermore sophisticated telephone systems, satellite and cable television systems, home personal computers, video games, and PC-based information services. American Online is the market leader in PC-based on-line services, and industry giant Microsoft has developed a network that will coordinate closely with Microsoft software. These and many other vendors allow a customer to use a PC at the office or in the home for banking, investing in mutual funds, buying and selling securities, and performing many other activities. They also provide ready access to the Internet, an interactive network of databases that includes considerable investment information.

As the first video games and personal computers became available to households in the early 1980s, a major study was conducted to determine how widely certain technology-based services might be accepted by consumers. More specifically, 700 demographically balanced households in four states were studied in an attempt to forecast the acceptance of certain technologies that would become available to homes by the 1990s, such as banking, investing, and purchasing insurance using a color-screen PC. Here, in table 8-3, are some results of the study.[4]

TABLE 8-3
Results of Household Survey of Expected Use of Selected Technology-Based Services

	Definitely in Use	Very Likely to Use	Somewhat Likely to Use
Banking/bill paying	40%	32%	17%
Insurance	8%	27%	27%
Investments	7%	27%	31%

Source: Booz, Allen & Hamilton, Inc.

With about two-thirds of households at least *somewhat likely to use* home computers for insurance and investment purposes, the local financial services planners need to plan with the view that eventually there will be direct electronic links with consumers. Computer information services for consumers are rapidly evolving. As financial services offices consider further automation, they should be aware that individual clients, as well as business clients, may increasingly find it convenient to use electronic means for such things as requesting financial information and initiating or effecting financial transactions of all types. A computer on one's desk is closer than the nearest automatic teller machine or the nearest financial services office!

There were some differences among age groups (not shown in table 8-3) concerning electronic financial services. As expected, the interest in electronic services was strongest among those under age 45. However, researchers were surprised that the over-age 55 group showed a higher level of interest than the 45–55 age group. The researchers speculated that perhaps electronic delivery appeals more to the older group because they are less mobile. Of course, it could also be that this group has more discretionary funds and is more interested in the services because of a concern about financing their retirement.

The point is that the financial services professionals should think about the possibility of inviting a new party to participate in their computer communications network—clients and prospective clients.

Indeed, the consumer is already able to engage in computer-to-computer exchanges with financial services firms. Many financial services firms now accept and respond to buy-sell orders sent to them via personal computers. As these links with financial services firms grow, it is reasonable to expect that a growing number of clients will seek computer links with financial planners, investment advisers, fund managers, insurance agents, tax advisers, and others.

DYNAMICS OF INFORMATION TECHNOLOGY

The manifestations of information technology are ever-changing. There are always new and improved versions on the drawing boards. This makes it difficult and cost-prohibitive for a firm to always have the latest technology. And, of course, information technology means more than PCs for the financial services firm. Recall the definition given earlier. Notice that the definition is broad, encompassing telephone systems, facsimile (fax) systems, computers, computer software programs, printers, telecommunications networks, video systems, and other forms of information storage, retrieval, manipulation, and communication.

Converging Technologies

It is difficult enough for the financial services firm to stay abreast of individual types of technology, such as computer technology and telephone technology. Adding to that difficulty is a trend for different technologies to be combined. One piece of equipment, for example, may be the product of several different technologies, each of which has its own path of development. Computer, video, facsimile, telephone, and other technologies may be incorporated in a single computer system that may be purchased by the financial planner.

There are many examples of how personal computers benefit from converging technologies. The benefits are perhaps most clear in the convergence of computer and telephone technology.

For example, a personal computer's database capability is constantly expanding. It can hold massive amounts of information about each client, including client telephone numbers. When the planner wishes to call a client, the computer can automatically retrieve the number from its database, dial the number, and display helpful information for the planner such as notes regarding the last telephone discussion the planner had with the client.

Another example of the benefits of the convergence of computer and telephone technologies is networking. Computer networking via phone lines is one of the most important developments in the past few years. Networks enable computers located in different offices, buildings, cities, or states to "talk" to each other, thus allowing financial planners to work together on the same spreadsheet or other project, update each other's files, send and receive e-mail, and send and receive fax communications by computer.

A third example of the benefits of the convergence of computer and telephone technologies is seen in the ability to send sophisticated computer-generated graphics and sounds over fiber optic telephone cables. At a time when computers are gaining powerful graphics capabilities, old wire telephone lines are being replaced by fiber optics cables, which have the enormous capacity necessary for carrying computer-generated graphics and sounds. Now we are beginning to see electronically-stored multimedia client files that contain data, documents, pictures, and voice/video segments sent from one location to another via internal or external cable. Although other technological convergences are taking place (for example, video and computer technology), the combining of computer and telephone technology will probably have the biggest impact on the planner in the near future.

Multimedia Computers

By combining with other technologies, the PC has become a multimedia work and education station. It is possible, for example, to watch a television or video show in a small window on your computer screen while using the remainder of the screen for other work. High fidelity stereophonic sound capabilities are being incorporated into PCs, which make it possible for a PC to "speak" text from its own database and produce other sound effects that relate to a graph or other image being displayed on the screen. Voice-recognition technology, which allows voice control of the PC, has become a reality. And massive data storage media, which can store such applications as an entire encyclopedia on a CD-ROM disk a few inches in diameter, are now being offered as PC components.

The multimedia PC is becoming an important product communication tool. It can be used to teach, for example, financial professionals about new products, how to identify clients that will benefit from these products, and how to present the products so that clients recognize the values. The multimedia approach immerses the financial professional in the subject matter and produces both a clearer understanding and a better feel for the product.

Increasing competition in financial services markets makes it more important for financial services professionals to keep their skills up-to-date through participation in continuing education programs. Multimedia PCs, which include sound and color video as well as student-testing capabilities, play an important role in the continuing education of professionals.

The multimedia PC is also likely to become a medium for *client* education and communication. For example, it could present client education programs on retirement planning, education funding, estate planning, and other topics. Such programs could require active responses from clients to make the education programs more interesting and to help ensure the client's understanding.

As various technologies develop, the multimedia PC continuously adds other capabilities. Converging or combining technologies often has this synergistic effect—that is, more is accomplished when individual technologies work together than when they work alone. It is in the interest of the financial services firm to keep abreast of PC developments and to be ready and able to take advantage of cutting-edge technology. Individual financial planners need to keep abreast of the direction of new technology because it will be a factor in their long-term success.

Network Infrastructure

As mentioned earlier, many of the personal computers used by financial services firms are part of one or more computer networks. A planner's computer may be part of a LAN (local area network) that makes certain resources available to the planner or a WAN (wide area network) that makes even more resources available to the planner. The planner's PC, LAN, or WAN may be further connected to other information resource networks in other cities, such as a portfolio updating service or home-office communications system. Because networks are connecting to other networks, the PC in one network becomes more powerful as it is able to tap into a wider range of other networks.

In view of the growth of networking and the decreasing cost of information technology, personal computer systems can be expected to gain access to larger amounts of information. Computer databases at the planner's fingertips will become more comprehensive and contain text, graphics, voice messages, video cuts, and other forms of expression. And rather than having so much information that it becomes overwhelming to the computer user, the database search, retrieval, and analysis capabilities have become much more user-friendly and selective due to advances in computer software.

COMPUTER HARDWARE

Computer systems can be divided into two primary categories of components, hardware and software.

- *Hardware* is any part of the computer a person can see or touch. For example, a monitor, a floppy disk, and a printer are all hardware.
- *Software* is any part of a computer that a person cannot see or touch. The most important software takes the form of computer programs. A computer program may be stored, for example, on a floppy disk, in the computer memory, or on a magnetic tape. The medium that holds the program (software) is hardware.

An old rule of thumb used in designing and purchasing computer systems is first to choose the software and that will indicate what type of hardware is needed. In an environment as dynamic as financial services, the purchase decision is more complicated than that. Most of the important software is regularly upgraded and, in the process, demands more computer resources. Therefore, regardless of the software one may decide to use today, the upgraded software likely to be in use 2 or more years from now will be much more demanding of the hardware. A computer that can handle today's software may be obsolete in terms of the upgraded software in only one or 2 years. It is better to initially buy more computer capacity than necessary in the hope of having adequate computer hardware for at least 4 or 5 years.

Therefore, a better method of determining what computer hardware to purchase is to choose the software as well as to look at trends in both technology and financial services. It is important to research both the capacity of the hardware and the technology it incorporates. The planner should purchase enough capacity to handle expected growth over the next 3 to 5 years. More importantly, the planner needs to make sure that he or she buys the latest practical and affordable hardware technology available because most competitive new software is designed to run on the latest hardware technology. Obviously, it is better to delay technological hardware obsolescence (and the need to purchase new hardware) as long as possible.

Computer Chips

An important computer hardware characteristic is the semiconductor or chip.

> The *chip* is the microprocessor—the heart of the computer. It is the component that allows software to manipulate the data.

Much research and development is directed at producing faster and more powerful chips. Older technology, such as 8086, 8088, 80286, and 80386 chips are totally obsolete and cannot run most of the software currently being produced. Even computers based on the 80486 chip struggle when running commonly used business software packages. By the end of 1998 most new desktop computers utilized Intel Corporation's Pentium or Pentium II chips or comparable chips manufactured by AMD or Cyrix.

Just as no one blows a bugle to announce when the stock market is about to rise or fall, there is no clear signal when a planner should move up to the next chip in purchasing a PC. Often the reason for replacing a computer is based on components other than the chip, and often the reason is more imagined than real. There are, however, two indications that the planner should watch for prior to upgrading: (1) increased advertising of computers based on a newer chip and (2) a narrowing of prices between computers based on the current dominant chip and the newer chip.

Microprocessor Speed (MHz)

Why does one computer take 20 minutes to calculate a large spreadsheet while another computer does it in seconds? The answer is likely that one uses an old, slow chip and the other uses a new, fast chip.

The measure of how fast a chip can process data is in megahertz, abbreviated as MHz. One MHz equals one million cycles per second. The MHz rating is often referred to as a computer's *clock speed.* A PC's megahertz rating is generally stated in the literature that accompanies the PC. In general, the newer generations of chips have higher MHz ratings because they process data faster than the older generations of chips. In general, it is advantageous for the planner to purchase the PC with the higher (or highest) MHz rating available.

Entry-Level PC Characteristics

The state of the art in computer hardware seems to change almost daily. Fortunately, the entry-level computer for financial planners is a bit more stable, if more subjective.

By the end of 1998, a bare-bones, entry-level desktop computer for financial planners might have contained the following characteristics, although the list may seem woefully out of date by the time you read it:

- Pentium chip operating at 266 MHz
- 32MB of RAM
- 6 gigabyte hard disk drive
- Multimedia capability
- Fax/modem meeting the V.90 standard
- 4 expansion slots
- 1 parallel port and 2 serial ports
- 15" noninterlaced, .28 dot pitch, SVGA color monitor

RAM (Main Memory)

RAM stands for random access memory. It refers to the main memory of the computer, where the computer temporarily stores computer programs and data while it is working with them. DRAM or dynamic RAM, is the most common type of computer memory. (When the computer is turned off, all data and programs that were placed in RAM are lost unless they were saved on a permanent storage medium, such as a hard disk or floppy disk.) The greater the computer's main memory capacity, the better, because a computer with a large memory can[5]

- receive and use larger programs
- hold copies of more than one program in main memory, thereby allowing more than one program to be run at a time
- operate faster and more efficiently
- use new, sophisticated software, such as Windows, which requires a lot of main memory
- hold images for creating graphs and animation
- work with and manipulate more data

A minimum of 32MB (32 megabytes) of RAM is recommended, especially if Windows 95, Windows 98, or another graphical user interface program will be used. If extensive *multitasking* (running more than one application at a time) is desired, 64MB is recommended, which will permit relatively large applications to run simultaneously.

Whether the initial RAM selected is 32MB, or more, it is important that main memory be expandable by simply plugging additional chips into the computer's central board. Future memory-hungry applications could require this much memory, if not more.

Hard Disk: 6.0 Gigabyte

A hard disk is a *permanent* storage medium for computer programs and data. Most planners keep a copy of all of their important software on the hard disk. They also may keep a great deal of data on the hard disk, including their full client database.

An average printed page requires about 2 kilobytes (2,000 bytes) of storage space. Therefore, one megabyte (1,000,000 bytes) of space on a hard disk can hold about 500 pages. A hard disk with a minimum capacity of 6.0 gigabytes (6,000 megabytes) is recommended. Windows-based applications demand a lot of hard disk space, and even CD-ROM software (discussed later) places large files on the hard disk. In addition, planners have a tendency to acquire additional software over time and to continuously add to their client data. It is much less costly on a per-megabyte basis to buy a larger hard disk at the start than to have to buy a second hard disk later because the planner ran out of space on the first hard disk.

Most manufacturers package desktop computers with hard disks of at least 4 gigabytes. Since new software tends to take up large amounts of storage and since the incremental cost of a larger hard disk on a new computer is very small, selecting a larger hard disk is prudent.

Multimedia Capability

Software manufacturers are increasingly using *CD-ROM* (compact disc, read-only memory) technology to market their programs. Software CDs are identical to audio compact discs and can hold over 600 MB of programs and data. This capability makes CD-ROM particularly attractive for delivering multimedia programs—those using sound and graphical and photographic images. So-called writeable CD-ROM drives allow planners to store and archive large amounts of data on CD-ROM disks, which is especially valuable for duplicate, off-site storage.

FOCUS ON ETHICS
Ethics and Technology

Ethics is important when considering technology for several reasons. First, a client may have blind faith in what the computer produces. The challenge is that, even if the software is extremely sophisticated, the planner must be able to explain to the client what the computer results mean. Beforehand, the planner must understand the logic the software uses in analyzing and producing results. This means, for example, that for large, comprehensive financial planning software systems, the planner will need to spend some time learning to understand the logic used in each planning area and how the planning areas interrelate.

Second, it is easy to use assumptions that make the forecasted results look better. For example, a higher assumed interest rate can change an insurance policy illustration from one that will not sell to one that will. The temptation to enhance results is great, especially when competitors may be doing it.

Third, financial planning software often includes numerous rules of thumb and other general assumptions that the planner can adjust to fine-tune the software to the client's situation and the planner's own philosophy. Adjustments the planner makes can easily bias the analysis, resulting in increased fee and/or commission income. Again, the temptation is great, but the planner benefits more in the long run by abiding by codes of ethics and always putting the client's interests first.

Fourth, output almost always requires interpretation. The planner is responsible for interpreting the output and applying it to the specific needs of the client. Sometimes the output is misleading.

Finally, the ease with which modern day technology can produce reports magnifies another critical issue, confidentiality. The client is entitled to it and ethical responsibility demands it. Information, whether stored in hard copy, floppy disks, or hard drives, needs the proper controls to protect the client's right to confidentiality.

Since financial software often employs the human voice or sound effects, the computer must contain a *sound card* to reproduce the software's audio. The de facto standard for sound cards is Soundblaster compatibility, a reference to a predominant brand of sound card popularized by computer game users. Although more expensive sound cards are capable of producing audiophile-quality output, financial software typically does not require high fidelity sound. Likewise, the *speakers* required for multimedia need not be capable of premium quality reproduction.

Fax/Modem

A fax/modem attached to a telephone line allows a computer to send, receive, and electronically store faxes. If two computers have modems, files can be transferred between them. Accessing on-line information services, such as America Online or the Microsoft Network, requires a modem, as does connecting to the Internet. These services provide immense sources of information for financial practitioners.

Since most users of on-line information services are charged according to the length of time they are connected to the service, the fax/modem's speed should be at least 56,000 baud (56K) and meet the V.90 standard. Large offices and heavy users of on-line services may justify the extra cost.

Four Expansion Slots

An *expansion slot* is merely a place inside the computer box into which a board can be plugged to give the PC added capabilities. The cover must be taken off the computer box in order to plug a board into a slot. There are many different kinds of boards, such as a LAN (local area network) board, AM/FM tuner board, TV/video board, and others. Sometimes a combination of functions is included on a single board so it requires only one slot.

The number of expansion slots a planner needs depends on what he or she plans to do with the computer and how well equipped the computer is. In most cases, four expansion slots are adequate.

One Parallel Port, Two Serial Ports

A *port* refers to an electronic plug-in place on the computer. A *parallel* port refers to a connection for a multiwire cable (its wires are actually in parallel), which typically is attached to a printer. Data are sent to the printer through all the wires simultaneously—that is, in parallel. A *serial* port refers to a connection for sending data over a single line—that is, in serial fashion. A serial port is often used to connect a modem, mouse, or printer that has a serial connector.

A PC should have at least one parallel port and two serial ports, since there are usually one parallel and two serial devices to be connected to the PC. Adding a greater number of devices will require adding more parallel and/or serial ports. Often a board purchased for a different purpose will include a serial port as a no-cost extra. However, a board can be purchased specifically to add one or more ports to a PC.

Color Monitor: 15", High-Resolution, Super VGA (1024 x 768), Noninterlaced, .28 Dot Pitch

The term *monitor* refers to the visual display screen associated with the personal computer. A planner or planner support person may spend many hours each day looking at a PC monitor. Therefore it is usually worth investing in a monitor that will provide a clear, pleasant, flicker-free display. A Super VGA (SVGA) monitor with 1,024 x 768-pixel resolution is, at this writing, a high resolution monitor available at a practical price. It can handle a great majority of the graphics needs of planners.

Noninterlaced refers to the way the monitor scans the image and noninterlaced monitors are more likely to seem flicker-free, a desirable attribute. *Pitch* refers to how close together the tiny dots are that are used to paint images on the screen. To avoid grainy images, the dot pitch should be .28 millimeters or smaller. If multitasking is common, a 17" or larger monitor will allow the user to take better advantage of the graphical user interface. The additional cost is minimal. An obvious negative point is that a larger screen takes up more room on the desk.

Desktop PC versus Portable PC

Portable computers also continue to be improved. The term *portable,* as used here, includes notebook as well as the much smaller subnotebook and PDA (personal digital assistant) computers. Caution must be exercised when purchasing any portable. Manufacturers seek to put as many of the capabilities of the desktop PC into the portable as possible. However, in order to make the capabilities fit, many manufacturers have incorporated a variety of compromises that affect the way portables operate. Planners should inquire about possible compromises before purchasing any portables.

Some portables, for example, have smaller keyboards, which require that certain keys serve dual purposes. Software is generally designed with the desktop PC keyboard in mind, not the special keyboard arrangements found on many portables. Consequently, some software does not run properly on some portables because the keys have different purposes.

Another important difference is that portable PCs by and large do not have the expandability of desktop PCs. Portables may have only one or two expansion slots available. Also the slots may be smaller than the standard size used in desktops, so only an expansion board purchased from the manufacturer of the portable will fit. Expect to pay a high price for such a board. Also, expect to have relatively few types of these nonstandard-size boards available for purchase, compared to an almost unlimited number of standard-size boards for desktop PCs.

A number of manufacturers are producing high-quality color portables. Many use an active-matrix LCD technology that produces bright, saturated, and flicker-free color screens that compete visually with the standard VGA color monitors. The visual impact of these portables makes it possible to deliver compelling presentations on the road. Indeed, some portables provide multimedia capability—that is, they can present stunning color displays with accompanying sound.

Local Area Networks (LANs)

The discussion at the beginning of this chapter cites the growth of computer networks, including local area networks (LANs). The LAN is the form of network system that will most affect the planner's day-to-day activities. Because of the benefits, it is likely that a great majority of planners will eventually make use of a LAN.

A LAN is made up of both hardware and software. The hardware generally includes a board that is inserted into each PC and cables that physically connect each PC to the other PCs or to a server computer. A *server* functions as the LAN manager and the repository of the resources available to all connected PCs. The most common LAN configuration is for the PCs in an office or building to be connected by cable to a powerful server. Each linked PC is still able to function as a stand-alone, but the LAN gives the PCs the added capability of communicating with other linked computers and of using the LAN's resources.

A LAN makes it possible for every PC user in the firm to share the same central database system—the one on the LAN's server computer. A planner (or production assistant) can use his or her own computer to store, search, and retrieve data from the server's database just as if that database was on the user's own PC. In addition to sharing the LAN's central database, the planner can have different, private databases on his or her own linked personal computer.

As stated above, an important advantage of the LAN is that all PCs linked to it can share the resources attached to the LAN. For example, any PC in the LAN could have access to a color printer or fax machine attached to the LAN or to powerful analytic, illustration, and desktop publishing software on the LAN server's hard disk.

A LAN can make a contribution to balancing the firm's workload. For example any person can be authorized to enter data into a particular client's record using any PC in the LAN. Similarly, any person can be authorized to retrieve and display (or print out) data regarding a specific client, using any PC in the LAN. This translates into better support for the planner, quicker and more responsive client service, and a means to balance workloads in the firm.

A LAN also can provide a measure of control over the software used by individual planners and their assistants. Any firm-approved software can be housed in the LAN's server computer and made available to all planners and their assistants via linked PCs. This lessens the likelihood that a planner or assistant will use other software that could expose the planner and the firm to legal risks.

Financial planning firms of all sizes have installed or are considering installing a LAN. Even small offices with as few as two or three PCs may benefit from a LAN.

Computer Printers

Financial planners know the importance of computer printers. A computer printer is usually attached by cable to one or more PCs or to a LAN and is used for producing a wide variety of printouts, including letters, proposals, reports, and other communications meant for clients and prospects. Since the printed document represents the planner and the firm, most planners seek to have at least one computer printer that can produce letter-quality copy.

Dot Matrix Printers

Before the nonimpact printers (such as laser printers) improved and became available at an acceptable price, financial planners were generally limited to dot matrix printers (or the super slow daisy wheel printers). A dot matrix printer is an impact printer. Small, separate pin-like hammers strike the printer ribbon against the paper, causing letters and other images to be formed. Many of these dot matrix printers come very close to producing letter-quality copy—so close that some are advertised as letter quality. However, few financial services professionals believe the copy produced by the printers is of sufficient quality for use in preparing client documents.

Dot matrix printers have three advantages: speed, flexibility, and price. They can print up to 400 characters per second in draft mode, although often only about 100 characters per second in letter-quality mode (which is still faster than some nonimpact printers). Dot matrix printers are versatile in what they can print, from almost any size character to specially designed symbols and creative graphics. They can also print multipart (carbon and noncarbon) forms. While the 24-pin printer can produce relatively high-quality copy, the nonimpact printers, such as the laser printer, can produce higher quality copy that many planners prefer to use with clients.

Nonimpact Printers

Nonimpact printers include ink-jet, color thermal, and laser printers. The primary advantage of these printers is that they generally produce higher quality copy than the 24-pin dot matrix printers. They are called nonimpact printers because they do not have pins or other parts that physically strike a ribbon or paper.

Laser Printers. The laser printing process resembles the operation of a photocopy machine. A laser beam is directed across the surface of a light-sensitive drum and fired as necessary to record a page image onto the drum. The image is then transferred to paper. Lasers are popular printers because of their high-quality output, relative speed, and reasonable cost.

Ink-Jet Printers. Ink-jet printers use little jets that selectively spray ink on the paper to form characters and other images. They offer near-laser quality at a significantly lower price. One advantage is that many ink jets can print in color.

Portable Bubble Jet Printers. Portable bubble jet printers are small and can be carried in a briefcase or taken along on client calls. They operate on a battery or AC power and produce relatively high-quality output suitable for clients.

Color-Thermal Printers. Color-thermal printers create vivid color images by melting wax or plastic, one color at a time, onto specially coated paper. They are especially good for preparing transparencies because the colors remain bright when projected onto a screen.

COMPUTER SOFTWARE

It is the software that makes the computer hardware work. Since financial services practitioners rely so much on computers, the importance of using proper software cannot be overemphasized. Software can make a difference between the success or failure of an office.

A financial planner does not have to become an expert on computer software. Rather, what is required is that the planner

- have a clear understanding of his or her own business, including the functions, goals, and objectives
- have a basic conceptual knowledge of how technology can support those functions and objectives
- select qualified computer professionals to assist in designing and periodically reviewing the selected computer hardware and software
- learn to ask computer professionals a lot of questions concerning how software and hardware can make the planner's practice more efficient and more effective

In the following discussion of software, the emphasis is on conveying conceptual information to the reader. The objective is to help the reader, as a financial planning professional, know what is currently possible with technology and what may be possible in the future. Hopefully, this information will encourage and assist the planner to ask the right questions when talking with computer professionals about the possible use of new technology.

Three Classes of Software

In general, software can be grouped into three classes:

- *systems software.* Each personal computer, minicomputer, and main frame computer has an *operating system,* which is the most basic layer of software used by the computer. For PCs the dominant system software is Microsoft's DOS (Disk Operating System). Microsoft's Windows—the current version is Windows 98—is the de facto standard *graphical user interface* (GUI). Windows works in concert with DOS to create a more *user-friendly* environment. GUIs, like Windows, allow the user to operate the computer by selecting pictures (icons) from menus and pushing (clicking) the buttons on a mechanical device called a *mouse.* Windows is a *multitasking* environment, meaning that the operator can run more than one application at a time. For example, the user can run a word-processing package and a spreadsheet package at the same time, and import a table from the spreadsheet into the word-processing document.
- *applications programs.* Applications programs are programs designed to meet the immediate needs of the computer user to solve specific classes of problems. For example, a financial planning program will help solve client financial planning needs, a client management database system will help the planner manage data better, a spreadsheet program will support financial analyses and accounting needs, and a word-processing program will help meet client communication needs. Many of these programs are commercially available off-the-shelf. Sometimes applications programs are developed in-house for personal or business needs.
- *utility programs.* Utility programs can be thought of as individual service programs. They include programs that will undelete a file that was accidently deleted, unformat a disk that was accidently formatted, diagnose and fix a hard disk problem, and so on. Many utility programs are sold commercially, others are offered as shareware or public domain programs.

Importance of Applications Programs

The computer programs of greatest importance to financial planners are applications programs. Certain general-purpose applications are found in so many financial service practitioner's offices that they are almost considered standard. Probably the most common types of general-purpose software programs used by planners are

- word-processing software
- spreadsheet software
- database software
- graphics software
- communication software

In addition to these general-purpose programs, planners tend to have a number of applications programs that relate specifically to the planning areas they specialize in, such as software for financial planning, retirement planning, estate planning, portfolio management, and income tax management.

Selecting Applications Programs

Needless to say, there are thousands of applications programs available to planners. Whether or not a planner should use a particular program depends on the quality and characteristics of the program in relation to the planner's needs.

Unfortunately, even when a planner has a clear picture of his or her needs, it is difficult to gain a clear picture of a computer program's pluses and minuses without trying it out for a while. Descriptions from vendors and software demo disks are oriented toward selling the software; they are not designed to provide a balanced presentation of the advantages and the disadvantages of the program.

Trial Periods

For expensive and specialized financial software, vendors often provide restricted demonstration versions for a small fee. Some vendors even permit a 30-day trial period although there may be a charge of $25 or so to screen out those who are not really serious about buying the software. Unfortunately, it may not be possible to test the software properly within 30 days. The problem is the amount of time it may take to learn how to use the software before it can be properly tested under normal conditions at the planner's office.

Also, there is the practical question of how much data can be input into a trial program for a 30-day test. Considering a new client database management program, it might be impractical if not impossible to move an entire client database into a new database system to see how the system operates under typical workload conditions. Nevertheless, enough of a database needs to be moved to the new system so that some idea can be gained of how well the new software handles a planner's demands.

A trial period can be costly to the planner because of the number of hours that one or more persons must devote to learning the software, entering test data into it, and then trying it out under regular and stress conditions. Therefore it is important that the planner makes a thorough pretrial evaluation to be sure that the new software is worth the time and effort necessary to try it out.

Database Software

Database management software is one of the most important types of software systems for financial services professionals. The purpose of database management software is to facilitate the storage and selective retrieval of management data and client information. Typically a database holds the names, addresses, telephone numbers, and other data on each client and prospect. It also holds information on each product and service offered by the planner.

Once the data is entered, database management programs allow the planner to search the database to identify clients or prospects who meet certain criteria, such as those who will be reaching age 62 within the next 5 years or those who have parents as dependents. After a specific group of clients or prospects is identified and selected, the names and addresses of the individuals who meet the criteria may be automatically inserted in form letters or printed on labels or envelopes. The entire process, from identifying qualified persons to preparing personalized letters and envelopes, is often accomplished entirely by using database software.

Another feature of client database management programs is that they usually permit the planner to keep extensive notes on telephone conversations or other correspondences with clients and prospects. Many have features for making notes and leaving reminders to follow up on a prospect or client contact. Typically, notes and reminders are placed in an electronic calendar or scheduler, entered into the client's file, and printed on a daily or weekly basis as a guide for the planner.

The most advanced client database management software will permit images to be stored in the database. For example, a client's will, complete with signatures, can be scanned into the database with a hand scanner or page scanner. When the planner needs to see the will, the computer will retrieve it from the database and display it on the screen. Pictures of the client and his or her family can be included in the database, if the planner wishes.

Categories of Database Software

Database management systems fall into three general categories:

- general purpose
- special purpose
- component of comprehensive system

General-Purpose Database Management Software. A general-purpose database management system is software that can be purchased from a local computer store or computer mail-order center. The advantage of such software is that you can customize it to your way of doing business. You do not have to accept someone else's notion of what data you should keep, what reports you can generate, and so on. The disadvantage of general-purpose database management software is that someone must take the time to customize the software to the firm's liking. Unfortunately, customization of this software can be a technically demanding and time-consuming task.

Special-Purpose Database Management Software. There are many commercially available special-purpose database management software packages. Usually they are the result of a computer software firm taking a general-purpose software package and tailoring it for a particular purpose. Many packages focus on keeping track of interactions with clients and prospects. They are referred to as client database management software or, simply, client management software. Literally thousands of other special-purpose database management software programs exist that focus on asset management, portfolio management, and financial planning.

Comprehensive Planning System Component. Comprehensive financial planning software is designed to produce comprehensive personal and business financial plans. The top-of-the-line comprehensive financial planning software systems generally have database management capabilities or interface with database management software packages. The database for clients includes all of the personal, financial, and business data pertaining to each client. The planner can search the database using a single criterion or a combination of criteria. For example, the planner could do a single-criterion search to identify clients who own a particular stock and then do a multi-criteria search among those stockholders to identify clients in regard to, say, income, age, net assets, or zip code.

A comprehensive planning system may have a database that is so slow that it is not possible to use it while discussing matters on the telephone with a client. The database may be designed strictly for use during planning. On the other hand, vendors of such software have been concerned about a planner's need for data retrieval speed and flexibility while using the telephone. Some vendors have taken steps to add speed, either via an interface with another database program or by making changes in the comprehensive planning system. This aspect—database retrieval speed and flexibility—should be discussed with a vendor before purchasing the vendor's software.

Spreadsheet Software

Spreadsheet software provides the computer user with the equivalent of an accountant's or bookkeeper's work sheet. The spreadsheet stores formulas and data and automatically does speedy calculations. This electronic work sheet is divided into columns and rows, each of which has its own identification. The place where a column and row intersects is called a *cell.* Cells contain math formulas, data, or label names.

An illustration of a very simplified spreadsheet is provided in table 8-4. In this case, there are four columns, A through D, and nine rows, 1 through 9. Notice that cell A2 (where column A and row 2 meet) contains a label, "STOCK." Many other cells also contain labels. Cells B4 through B7 and C4 through C7 contain numbers. Cells D4 through D7 and D9 contain formulas, which you cannot see. Only the results of those formulas are shown in the cells. The formula in D4, for example, is: +B4*C4. This means that the data in cell B4 is multiplied by the number in cell C4 and the results are shown in cell D4.

TABLE 8-4
Illustration of a Simple Spreadsheet

	A	B	C	D
1		NUMBER	COST PER	TOTAL
2	STOCK	SHARES	SHARE	COST
3				
4	IBM	500	103	51,500
5	DIG EQUIP	100	79	7,900
6	ATT	300	23	6,900
7	H-P	1,000	32	32,000
8				
9	TOTAL:			$98,300

If you type a new number in B4 (that is, increase or decrease the number of IBM shares), the results in D4 and D9 will automatically change. Similarly, if you type a different number in C4 (to change the IBM share price), the results in D4 and D9 will automatically change. Spreadsheets can be very complex, involving hundreds or even thousands of interrelated formulas. The advantage of the computer spreadsheet is that, regardless of its size, the entire spreadsheet can be automatically recalculated whenever data is changed. This is a very powerful tool for financial analyses, updating portfolios, and conducting what-if analyses.

Planning versus Data Management Software

Financial planning software can be essential in developing the initial personal or business financial plan and in keeping it up to date through periodic revision. A major advantage of comprehensive and integrated financial planning systems is that a change in one planning area will automatically make needed adjustments in other planning areas. For example, if an asset is earmarked for one purpose, the software will not permit it to be advertently earmarked for a second purpose. This is helpful when the planner and client are determining how to allocate new savings and investments. By being able to coordinate and relate thousands of items of information in all major planning areas, the comprehensive financial planning system is a key software system for financial planners.

While comprehensive planning software is strong in financial analysis and planning, it is often weak in speed and flexibility of database access, asset allocation planning, and portfolio updating. Many planners, therefore, acquire additional computer programs to help meet these other needs.

As stated earlier, financial planning software systems are often not suited to supporting day-to-day dealings with clients and prospects. The database component is often too slow to use while actually meeting with a client or talking to the client on the telephone. For speedy database support, many planners turn to client database management software because it is specifically designed to assist the planner (or support person) as he or she interacts with clients and prospects.

A second drawback of many comprehensive financial planning systems is that they are weak in helping the planner determine asset allocation based on each client's risk tolerances and expectations of return on investment assets. At best, the systems allow the user to impose arbitrary rules of thumb for investment allocations, and typically cannot access or process necessary historical performance data to develop, optimize, and periodically measure the performance of a market-efficient portfolio. This had led some planners to acquire software aimed specifically at asset allocation.

Finally, some comprehensive financial planning software cannot automatically update market prices on the client's financial assets. This creates a problem in keeping the portfolio values up to date, and it means the planner is usually unable to tell the client the current value of his or her portfolio. Again, planners often look to other software to meet their portfolio updating needs.

The most common software obtained by planners to augment their financial planning software is a client management database software package. Selecting a client management database package that meets the firm's requirements and that the planners and staff feel comfortable with is important because client management software is used extensively, virtually every day.

In general, a client management software system should

- support a wide range of client services and fee billings
- target and support effective communication with potential clients
- track all of the firm's communications and marketing developments
- provide cash and investment allocation, management, tracking, and performance reporting
- provide interface and data exchange with financial planning software (currently or as a planned enhancement)
- account for the entire staff's time and billable hours

Of central importance, the client management software should either share or be able to communicate directly with the database used for comprehensive financial planning. If they cannot use the same database, the client management database must be kept current and it must be able to update the financial planning database when it is time to create or revise a financial plan.

Selecting Client Management Software

After the planner or firm has established objectives and has at least a preliminary determination of hardware/software requirements, it is possible to start to review and evaluate client management software packages. The following material is divided into two sections. The first section identifies currently available capabilities of client management software. A planner or firm may review these capabilities to aid in developing a preliminary shopping list of desired features. The second section deals with general considerations for selecting the software after the desired capabilities have been determined.

Evaluating Capabilities and Features

The following summary outlines capabilities to look for and evaluate in client management software. Capabilities are discussed under category names commonly used in client management software packages:

- *automatic "to do" calendar.* The "to do" calendar represents a group of related capabilities generally associated with time and task management.
- *client billing/staff time management.* Basically, the client billing/staff time management capabilities are specialized accounting tools and track fees, commissions, and client accounts.
- *client information management.* Capabilities that are grouped in this category emphasize ease and speed of accessing and updating database information. They also include telephone communication tools and mailmerge word processing and printing.
- *asset and risk management.* Capabilities grouped in this category are generally aimed at portfolio management. The software functions may include asset allocation, asset management, portfolio optimizing, and portfolio performance measurement features. Note that no single software program generally includes all of these capabilities. Note also that some programs do not track insurance and annuity products.
- *reporting.* Flexibility of generating reports is desirable. It is impossible to forecast all the types of reports one may be called upon to generate.
- *interfaces with financial planning software.* An important capability is the ability of client management software to smoothly interface with primary financial planning software, such as the comprehensive financial planning system. Ideally, the two software systems should share the same database or be able to update each other's database. In addition, the client management software should be capable of exporting and importing data to and from spreadsheets and other important software programs (word processing and graphics files, for example). This avoids multiple entries of the same data, reduces entry errors, and helps to maintain a central client information base, rather than a number of databases with overlapping data.

- *export and import of data files.* Most of the client management software systems use industry standard file formats for their databases and for importing and exporting data. When industry standard formats are used, there is less dependence on one vendor. Therefore, if the vendor who developed a planner's database software goes out of business, the planner will need to switch to another vendor's software. If both software packages use industry standard formats, it greatly simplifies the task of transferring data from the old to the new program.

Selection Criteria

Once the planner and/or firm has examined and evaluated the capabilities of several client management programs, the final selection of one or more of these software packages should take into account the computer hardware expected to be used, other software that the planner or firm owns or plans to acquire, and general business practices.

The paragraphs below contain ideas that various financial planning practitioners and software consultants have generated. Every firm is different, so any suggestion or idea from an external source needs to be evaluated in terms of its suitability or appropriateness to a particular situation.

- For asset allocation software, the firm's choice should be based on two major components: (1) a cost-benefit analysis relative to the number and quality of investment advisory clients it has and (2) the breadth and depth of historical data on asset classes and issues the firm requires for fully optimizing client investment portfolios.
- Unless only one person will ever use a client and asset management program (an unrealistic assumption), it should be a network version to provide staff access through multiple keyboards, thus avoiding having to install multiple printers and other components for individual users. This capability is especially important in a transactions-oriented practice.
- Even if the firm uses another brand of network software, it is usually advisable for the client and asset management program to be compatible with the latest Novell Netware software because it is a benchmark of the network operating system's compatibility with the computer and other hardware.
- Plan to use a client and asset management program as a major application in a multitasking operating environment, most likely Windows, so that more than one application program can be run simultaneously and immediately accessed. This is especially valuable for quickly and easily accessing data from different sources while on the telephone with a client.
- Stand-alone asset allocation and portfolio performance measurement programs are not likely to be used on a daily basis. Therefore they may

not need to be network versions and they may not need to be run in a multitasking mode. Although their reports can, and in many cases should, be presented to clients, their best use is usually as analytical tools used by the planner to (1) make investment recommendations within a diversified portfolio modeled on the client's risk and return parameters and (2) measure the performance, over time, of portfolios and individual issues within portfolios.

- Data that can be entered in client and asset management programs should include essential information for updating financial plans with the current status of investment assets. Therefore, make sure client and asset management programs interface (or soon will) with the comprehensive financial planning system that is now being used or being considered.
- Keep in mind that not all available client and asset management programs combine the same levels of capabilities and that not all provide the same degree of performance tracking and reporting.

FINANCIAL AND TAX PLANNING SYSTEMS

Financial and tax planning capabilities are available as a part of comprehensive integrated financial planning systems, "quick" planning programs, and stand-alone programs for focused planning.

Comprehensive Integrated Systems

Comprehensive and fully integrated systems are relatively few in number. Many of them include most of the applications required in a practice.

The term *integrated,* as used in financial and tax planning software, came into being when software vendors began to combine several applications into a single packaged system. An advantage is that data is entered once and then shared throughout the software system's various computations, calculations, projections, and reports. Because comprehensive integrated systems cover all the major planning areas, they appeal to planners with large client bases who produce and periodically update a large number of financial plans. The top-of-the-line comprehensive integrated systems may also appeal to planners who serve a few substantial clients rather than a larger number of clients.

Integrated data entry and processing is defined in various ways by vendors. Some vendors claim (or imply) that entry or financial asset data automatically generates the tax consequences. Unfortunately, that is not always the case. Entering additional information may be necessary to produce accurate consolidated financial and tax results.

Integration is meaningful and reliable only when initially entered data includes (or can include) all related items required for processing and tracking the data and producing accurate reports. In a truly integrated system, reports should keep continuous accounts of all cash flows, investment assets, and associated tax consequences. Beware of claims of "complete integration" when the entered data items on actual data gathering sheets and screen input fields reveal that the program is too simplistic to support its claims.

Comprehensive and fully integrated financial planning systems permit the user to choose configuration of related and linked software applications that will perform most of the tasks normally associated with analyzing, developing, and reporting on clients' current and projected financial and tax liability positions. Comprehensiveness of software is measured by the quality and depth of the program of all focus areas of planning.

Typically, a comprehensive integrated system includes programs that

- collect and organize client information
- prepare financial and tax profiles
- project these profiles into a finite future (at least 5 years)
- create alternative profiles (what-if modeling) for analyzing potential consequences of various planning assumptions (such as death, disability, retirement, estate planning, inflation, and asset growth rates)
- produce a series of textual and numeric reports that recompute and reprocess all information already entered in the system
- merge financial profile computations with formatted text from a word processor

These systems generally include or can be interfaced with

- sophisticated word-processing applications with dictionary, thesaurus, and desktop printing features
- high-level financial and tax analysis programs
- graphics programs which produce graphs, charts, and visual presentation materials
- client and asset tracking and management programs or facilities (usually an integrated database)—or, alternatively, interface capabilities with stand-alone client and asset management programs

In addition to numerical report content with textual headnotes, most of the systems also provide more extensive analytical text or client education boilerplates that can be customized, replaced, or added by the user.

The most widely used integrated systems are packaged with most of the essential elements of a comprehensive system in place. Several can be interfaced with some commonly used database and spreadsheet software systems and with alternative word-processing and graphics programs. Interfaces with these systems have been developed by the vendors of client and asset management programs.

Any one of the top-of-the-line comprehensive systems could possibly fulfill the basic processing and reporting needs of a financial planning practice. Nevertheless, each system should be examined for as close a correlation as possible between the practice's requirements and the system's capabilities.

> *NOTE:* Integrated data entry in financial planning software should be evaluated in relation to the quality and meaningfulness of system processing, tracking, and reporting of entered items. This means that the two most important criteria in evaluating them are (1) the breadth, depth, and interrelatedness of entry items for assets, cash flows, and taxes and (2) the breadth, depth, interrelatedness, and accuracy of reporting on these entered items. Data entries for all information for which the practice requires processing and reports for financial planning purposes should be accepted by the system. Generally, the best way to evaluate a system's processing and reporting capabilities is through careful, detailed examination of the data-entry sheets provided for collecting client information, the data-entry screens in the system itself, and the reports the system produces. The user should be able to track each data item from its initial entry to its appearance or processed result in all relevant printed reports. If these details in the system seem inadequate, extensive hands-on testing will not be worthwhile.

Beyond basics, systems from different vendors can be quite different from one another. They vary in their planning approach, comprehensiveness, implementation of reliable federal and state tax computations, flexibility, ease of use, and user support. They also vary widely in the breadth, depth (different than mere volume), and understandability of the reports they produce. Some include *expert system programming,* which is a set of decision rules activated by certain entered information to provide automated analyses and planning recommendations. These recommendations are based on what an expert might recommend as a general rule of thumb.

Modular and "Quick" Financial Planning Systems

Downsized versions of most integrated systems have been developed by unbundling (modularizing) the comprehensive systems or by creating comprehensive "quick" planning systems that use summary data rather than detailed data. By selecting modules as needed, the planner can employ a graduated approach by starting with the basic computation, projection, and reporting capabilities and, later, adding other application modules, such as word processing, graphics, long-range planning, estate planning, and client and asset management. The "quick" planning versions of integrated systems appeal to financial services professionals who do not wish to provide in-depth plans or whose focus is primarily product marketing. These versions require fewer data entries and produce less extensive computations and projections.

Stand-Alone Programs for Focused Planning

One of the limitations of comprehensive, integrated financial planning systems is that they do not go into great depth in each financial planning area. There are several reasons why the planning depth in each area is limited. One reason is that most clients do not need in-depth planning in all areas. A second reason is that any single software system that went into great depth in every planning area would be so large that it could not be accommodated by, or effectively run on, most personal computers.

Since some clients do need in-depth planning in some areas, stand-alone focused planning software is available. Stand-alone programs for focused planning software are designed exclusively for single financial planning areas, such as retirement planning, education funding, estate planning, and tax planning.

Many of these packages are the most powerful and sophisticated financial planning and analyses software programs available for individual areas of financial planning. Therefore, a specialist in estate planning will often acquire a leading stand-alone package that focuses on estate planning, while a tax specialist will obtain one that focuses on tax planning.

There are many lightweight focused planning software systems available. Professional planners need to understand the limitations of such programs. Light-weight systems can be used for generating rough approximations or obtaining ballpark results. Since they generally require only a small amount of data to be entered, they lack precision and cannot be used in complex situations. As always, the planner needs to understand the limitations, as well as the capabilities, of the software that is used with clients.

Even the most sophisticated stand-alone focused planning software system requires that only data relevant to the particular planning area of interest be entered. For example, retirement planning software may require little if any data related to education funding. A disadvantage is that using more than one focused planning program for the same client generally requires separate data entries. While much of the data entered will be different because different planning areas are involved, there will nevertheless be some redundant data entry.

On the other hand, some of the stand-alone software systems use data and file formats that are compatible with commonly used database and spreadsheet programs. This means that data can be transferred from the focused software program to a spreadsheet program for additional analysis or inclusion in a special report.

TECHNOLOGY COST TRENDS

The common pattern for computer hardware prices is to trend downward year after year. PCs became popular in the early 1980s when the prices of computer processors dropped to the point where they became affordable to large numbers of people. Facsimile machines represent an old technology and their sales were modest for decades. Then, when their price dropped within reach of almost any office a few years ago, their sales skyrocketed. Now all desktop computers and a vast majority of laptop computers include fax-telephonic capability. Similarly, computer printers, including laser printers that produce outstanding print output, sell at a fraction of their 1980s prices and offer better quality.

Like computer hardware, computer software tends to trend downward in price. New spreadsheet and database software packages, for example, are continuously becoming available with greater capabilities than prior software and with lower prices. One reason why many companies are moving processing tasks off mainframe and minicomputers and onto PCs and local area networks is because the price of PC software is more affordable.

Given that better and cheaper software and hardware are always in the pipeline, when should a financial services firm purchase new technology? Should it be early, when it is most expensive—or later, when its price has dropped? This is a trade-off decision that only the individual firm and planner can answer. Current technology often provides an important competitive advantage and enhances the firm's productivity. If the technology is effectively used, it might more than pay for itself in a relatively short period of time.

BENEFITS OF TECHNOLOGY

The use of information technology—and more specifically the use of computer technology—offers a number of important benefits to the financial planning firm. By far the most important overall benefit is that it can be the means for a firm to remain competitive or gain a competitive advantage in financial services markets. On a more elemental level, the benefits of computer technology are the following:

- improved quantity and quality of work
- increased sales
- reduced costs
- conserved time
- reduced exposure to legal liability

The fundamental characteristic of information technology is speed—speed of information retrieval, speed of analysis, speed of electronic communication between databases, and so on. In fractions of seconds a computer can perform tasks that would otherwise be impossible or impractical for a person to do manually or with a hand calculator. This capability means more clients are served and more sales are closed per month—all at a lower cost.

Another benefit is that properly programmed computers almost never make mistakes. Humans are prone to error, partly because mechanical and repetitive tasks tend to bore us. A computer cannot get bored; it can perform the same task thousands of times, in exactly the same way, without making a mistake. In addition, the computer can serve as a quality control monitor of human tasks. It reminds us of what we must do (for example, to make certain telephone calls), how to do it (by suggesting what we should say or do), and when to do it (with an automated "to do" calendar).

Computers also help protect planners from lawsuits. Once the financial planning software system has been tested and approved for use within a financial services firm, it generally can be relied upon to repeatedly perform highly complex analyses and produce consistent and reliable results. Having an approved means for doing complex, demanding financial analysis helps reduce the firm's exposure to lawsuits for errors and omissions. This is a valuable benefit, considering the litigious nature of our society and the high cost of errors and omissions lawsuits.

The technology—primarily computers and software—makes it possible for financial planning practitioners to perform tasks and functions they otherwise could not perform. Many practitioners would find it impractical and too costly to offer comprehensive financial planning services without computer systems. Similarly, powerful client management software can make it practical for the financial services professional to communicate frequently and effectively with clients and to otherwise be of service to them. A variety of management software makes it possible for the firm's managers to more effectively monitor and control business activities.

RISK ASSOCIATED WITH TECHNOLOGY

Nothing is ever entirely risk free. Many problems that have occurred with new technology can be traced to poor planning and faulty decision making. Unfortunately, however, some problems may be encountered when adopting new technology despite the best planning and decision-making methods. It is a good idea to anticipate them. Here are some typical problems associated with the adoption of new technology.

Misuse Due to Inadequate Training

Information technology provides powerful tools for financial analyses in such areas as insurance needs, tax strategies, investments, education funding, pension planning, and estate planning. It is not uncommon for a firm or agency to underestimate the amount of training needed to properly use these tools. If a planner is not properly trained in the use of a particular software system, the result may be that the client is poorly served and the risk of incurring a lawsuit is increased.

Pervasive Data Input Errors

A major benefit of integrated computer systems is that the data only has to be input once and then it can be used for many purposes. There is no wasted effort in rekeying data for new uses. By the same token, this means that if a data input error is made, it will be reflected system-wide. There are usually safeguards against the entry of incorrect data, but not all types of errors are identifiable. For example, one software system requires that certain data be entered in order for it to proceed, or it may not accept data unless the data is entered in a specified format (for example, all the data entered must be numeric). The software has no way of determining, though, that the $8,000 figure keyed in should have been $80,000.

Poor Vendor Support

Poor vendor service or an unexpected end to vendor support (due to business failure of the vendor, for example) can have serious negative effects on a planning firm that is relying upon the vendor to keep its software or hardware operating. Malfunctioning software or hardware often means an inability to serve clients properly. Therefore care must be exercised in selecting the vendors as well as the products. It is not always possible to forecast that a particular vendor will decide to abandon one line of business to pursue another. If you own a product that can be serviced by someone else, the problem might be solved easily. If you own a product that no one else can service, the problem might be expensive and time-consuming to solve.

Do-It-Yourself Software Problems

Some individuals like to develop their own software. Also, some software vendors offer to customize their software to the individual firm. In either case, the software needs to be formally tested; software needs to be accurate, reliable, and ethically sound before it is used with client data. Many financial services firms do not have the time or knowledge to test the software. Often the safer alternative for such a firm is to purchase software that has already been properly tested.

CHALLENGES TO THE PLANNER AND FIRM

Information technology presents certain challenges to financial services planners and firms. Planners and firms that rise to these challenges and are eager to embrace new technology will gain the competitive advantage. Note that there are four challenges, as described below.

Understanding the Technology

The financial services practitioner, particularly if he or she is in a management position, must take the steps to learn what new technology can and cannot contribute. This knowledge is essential if the planner and firm are to remain competitive by making wise and cost-effective technology decisions. This does not require that the planner be an engineer or otherwise acquire a lot of technical knowledge. It does require that the planner is informed about relevant, recent technology. A planner can stay informed by attending seminars and courses, joining user groups, and subscribing to appropriate computer publications.

Selecting Appropriate New Technology

At some point, the planner and firm will need to select and install new technology. The planner should have sufficient general knowledge to know how the new technology will contribute to his or her business. However, when mission-critical hardware or software is involved, a planner should not—unless he or she possesses exceptional technical knowledge or the technology is simple—make final purchase or installation decisions without the informed counsel of a consultant. It is worthwhile insurance to engage a consultant who has expertise in the technology being acquired. The consultant can help make the final purchase decision and help plan and perhaps do the installation of the hardware and/or software.

Properly Training Yourself and Your Staff

Does your assistant *really* know how to use the word-processing software? Do you? Does anyone *really* understand and know how to use that new financial planning software or the old graphics software package your office acquired? Why does it seem to take forever to update data in your new client database management system? Just as it is a mistake for the planner to be poorly trained in financial planning, it is a mistake to overlook the critical roles of support persons and training they need to perform their tasks.

Too often, a planner and the support staff will tough it out and try to each themselves how to use new hardware and software technology. Letting people train themselves, though, can be risky. They may train themselves incorrectly or overlook critical fine points that contribute most to improving productivity.

Many vendors provide excellent training programs designed specifically for people who purchase their software. Training is especially important when complex financial planning software is involved. Also, many technical education firms as well as most community colleges, 4-year colleges, and universities offer one-, two-, and three-day training programs on widely used software, including specific word processing, spreadsheet, database, and graphics programs. The payback for training can be almost immediate—perhaps within the week!

Avoiding Creeping Technological Obsolescence

Since technology has such an important role in the competitiveness of the financial planner, the planner needs to monitor whether he or she is keeping up with the latest practical technology. Failure to keep up means creeping technological obsolescence and gradual loss of competitiveness. The important task of monitoring can be done by periodically reexamining the effectiveness of the technology being used, keeping up with what technology other successful planners are using, and watching what is currently being offered by vendors. From time to time, the planner will find it advantageous to acquire new software and/or hardware and perhaps revise the way financial planning services are being offered and rendered. Indeed, identifying significant improvements that can be achieved by using new technology is important because technology is one of the least costly ways to improve individual and group productivity.

CONCLUSION

Information technology is a force for change in financial services. It impacts marketing and sales, office operations, and client services.

Financial planners and firms need to embrace new technology and learn to use it effectively—not simply as a tool for eliminating manual tasks and reducing costs, but as a vital means for gaining a competitive advantage in increasingly competitive markets. The overriding challenge for planners and financial services firms is to determine how to invest in new technology wisely.

Moreover, planners and firms need to learn how to use their computers to interact with other organizations that are likely to be highly automated. Major financial services firms, especially insurance companies, have already invested substantially in developing sophisticated systems to accomplish mission-critical functions, such as the developing of new and better products and the managing of client data. Being able to electronically communicate with those sources of products and services will be increasingly important to planners and their clients.

NOTES

1. Harvey L. Poppel and Bernard Goldstein, *Information Technology* (New York: McGraw-Hill, 1987), pp. 18–23.
2. Ibid., p. 26. Data provided by Booz, Allen & Hamilton, Inc., 1983.
3. Source is GE Information Services (Rockville, Maryland), as reported in "Tools for Better Sales Management," *Inbound/Outbound Magazine,* October 1991, pp. 40–43.
4. Ibid., pp. 53–55. Report of Booz, Allen & Hamilton, Inc.'s HIS Study in 1982.
5. Based on Sarah E. Hutchinson and Stacey C. Sawyer, *Computers: The User Perspective* (Homewood, Ill.: Irwin, 1990), p. 165.

9

Income Tax Planning

James F. Ivers III

Chapter Outline

INTRODUCTION

> *I am proud to be paying taxes in the United States. The only thing is—I could be just as proud for half the money.*
>
> *Arthur Godfrey*

It is said that the only things that are certain in life are death and taxes. Although death would seem to be more certain than anything, it's likely that even Houdini would have had trouble defying Uncle Sam. At the least, it would take a highly accomplished escape artist to evade both the federal income tax *and* a jail cell.

In any event, such extremes are not advisable, for a variety of legal, ethical, and moral reasons. Yet, it is perfectly acceptable (and perhaps even commendable) to use every legal means to minimize payment of the federal income tax.

This chapter will outline the most important basic concepts of our federal income tax law. It will not deal with advanced tax planning. It will provide, however, a firm grasp of fundamental concepts—always an excellent foundation to build upon. More advanced texts present planning techniques that are available to avoid paying taxes. Some tax-avoidance techniques (many call them loopholes) must be left to the experienced tax professional to recommend and implement.

However, a working knowledge of the tax law will enable the financial services professional to help clients, as well as to help the professional know what he or she knows or doesn't know. This will help make situations that call for a tax expert more recognizable. Therefore the purpose of this chapter is to explain basic income tax concepts, and to introduce the reader to the ways in which taxpayers can plan for tax avoidance.

THE PRINCIPLE OF GROSS INCOME

To learn about the federal income tax law, the student should begin with an understanding of the term *gross income*. Basically, gross income includes every item of value, whether consisting of money or other property, that is either made available to or comes into the possession of the taxpayer. In other words, anything of value is considered to be gross income for income tax purposes unless—and this *qualification* is very important—the Internal Revenue Code contains a specific provision that *excludes* a particular item from the taxpayer's gross income.

This is why the provision in the Internal Revenue Code that provides the gross income rule is referred to as a "shotgun" clause. Although the provision lists 15 different items that are includible in a taxpayer's gross income, the provision states that gross income includes, *but is not limited to*, these items. Gross income means "all income from whatever source derived."

However, certain items of money or other property are not includible in a taxpayer's gross income. These items include gifts, income from tax-exempt bonds, workers' compensation benefits, and many other items. Such items are called *exclusions* from gross income. It is important to remember that the reason such items are excluded from a taxpayer's gross income is that there is a specific section in the Internal Revenue Code that says so. In other words, no item of money or other property can be excluded from gross income unless there is a code provision stating that it is to be excluded. Therefore it is fairly simple in most cases to determine whether an item is includible in the taxpayer's gross income.

It is important to distinguish the concept of an *exclusion* from that of a *deduction* for tax purposes. An exclusion is an item of value that the taxpayer *receives* that is not includible in the taxpayer's gross income. A deduction, on the other hand, is an item of *expense* (not an item of receipt) that reduces the amount of income that is subject to tax.

> *Example:* Cheryl has the following items of income and expense for the current year: $35,000 in salary from her job as a paralegal, a $5,000 gift from her aunt, and an alimony payment of $3,000 to her former husband. The $35,000 of salary is includible in Cheryl's gross income. The $5,000 gift is not includible in her gross income because there is a provision in the Internal Revenue Code that says that gifts are not includible in the recipient's gross income. The $3,000 alimony payment is deductible from Cheryl's gross income in determining how much of Cheryl's income will actually be taxed, because the Internal Revenue Code contains a provision that states that alimony payments are generally deductible.

EXCLUSIONS FROM GROSS INCOME

There are many items that the Internal Revenue Code states are *excludible* from a taxpayer's gross income. Among these items are the following:

- gifts and inheritances
- income from certain bonds issued by states and municipalities
- workers' compensation benefits
- life insurance proceeds
- benefits paid from medical expense insurance policies
- social security benefits (for taxpayers below certain income levels)
- amounts received under certain dependent-care-assistance programs and educational assistance programs
- certain qualified scholarships

The specific rules determining how and to what extent these items are excludible from gross income are covered elsewhere, such as in The American College's course Income Taxation. At this point, it is important for the student to understand only the concept of an exclusion, and how exclusions are used in the overall process of computing an individual's tax liability. An item that is excludible generally does not have to be reported in any way on the taxpayer's return.

DEDUCTIONS

As previously stated, a deduction is an item of expense that reduces the amount of the taxpayer's income that is subject to tax. There are many different items that are *deductible* for federal income tax purposes. However, before some of these items are listed and explained, the concepts of *adjusted gross income* and *taxable income* should be understood.

Adjusted Gross Income

Adjusted gross income is an intermediate calculation that is made in the process of determining an individual's income tax liability for a given year. Why is such an intermediate calculation necessary or useful? For purposes of the tax law, adjusted gross income (AGI) is used as a base amount to determine how the taxpayer must treat certain *other* items for tax purposes. For example, adjusted gross income is used to calculate the maximum amount of charitable contributions that may be deducted by an individual in a given year (generally 50 percent of the individual's AGI).

Taxable Income

Taxable income is the amount of income that will actually be subject to tax in a given year. How does taxable income differ from adjusted gross income? Taxable income is the taxpayer's adjusted gross income, reduced by certain deductions that are taken only after the individual's adjusted gross income has been computed. In other words, in the computation of an individual's tax liability, there are two basic types of deductions. The first type consists of those deductions that are subtracted from gross income to determine AGI. The second type consists of those deductions that are subtracted from AGI to determine taxable income. The first type is known as *above-the-line deductions,* while the second type is known as *below-the-line deductions.*

What is the significance of this distinction? There are two basic reasons why the distinction is important. The first is that above-the-line deductions will change how certain *other* items on the individual's return are treated. This is so because, as previously stated, AGI is used as a base for defining or limiting how and to what extent certain other items may be excluded or deducted on the individual's return. The second reason relates to the concept of the standard deduction.

FOCUS ON ETHICS
The Ethics of "Playing the Odds"

Every year at tax time the media highlights the probability that certain categories of taxpayers will be audited. Usually the likelihood is quite low, and this can cause some clients to suggest "liberally interpreting" the tax law for their own financial gain. Among the myriad of possible approaches are deducting personal travel expenses by suggesting that they were business related, showing phony charitable donations and failing to report cash income.

Financial planners have a responsibility to assist clients in legally minimizing their taxes, and tax counseling can be one of the most significant contributions a financial planner can make. However, it is obvious that planners must never participate or condone fraudulent behavior. Regardless of the odds, an improper action could be disastrous to the client financially and legally, not to mention the impact on reputation. The same is true for the advising financial planner.

The Standard Deduction

The standard deduction is a fixed amount that the individual may claim in lieu of claiming itemized deductions on Schedule A of Form 1040. *Itemized deductions,* or deductions taken on Schedule A, include charitable contributions, deductions for interest payments, taxes, casualty losses, certain business expenses of employees, and other items. The amount of the standard deduction depends on whether the individual is filing the return as a single taxpayer, an unmarried head of household, a married taxpayer filing jointly, or a married taxpayer filing separately.

If the individual is entitled to claim itemized deductions that, when added together, are more than the amount of his or her standard deduction, then the individual will deduct his or her itemized deductions and not claim the standard deduction. The standard deduction amounts are indexed annually for inflation.

All itemized deductions are below-the-line deductions (deductions taken in calculating taxable income). However, if these items were above-the-line deductions (deductions taken in determining adjusted gross income rather than taxable income), the taxpayer would deduct these items *regardless* of whether he or she claims the standard deduction. The standard deduction can be taken *in addition to* other deductions. This is the second important difference between above-the-line and below-the-line deductions. The first type are deductible regardless of whether the individual claims the standard deduction. The second type may be claimed only in lieu of the standard deduction.

Categories of Deductions

Before we discuss the various types of deductions that are allowable under federal tax law, it is important to remember that a deduction may be claimed only if there is a specific provision in the Internal Revenue Code that allows it. If there is no provision in the Code regarding a given item, no deduction may be claimed for that item.

Stated broadly, there are three basic categories of deductions allowable to individual taxpayers. The first category includes deductions for expenses that are incurred in the course of carrying on a trade or business. For example, the cost of employees' salaries or advertising would fall into this category. These are referred to as business deductions. The second basic category includes deductions for expenses that are incurred in the course of an activity that is not a trade or business, but is engaged in for the purpose of producing income and making a profit. An example of a deduction falling into this category is an expense incurred in connection with the maintenance of a taxpayer's investments, such as a fee for investment advice. The third basic category includes deductions for expenses that are simply personal, family, or living expenses. Although the Code provides a general rule that these expenses are nondeductible, there are several important exceptions to the general rule. Personal expenses that *are* deductible within limitations include charitable contributions, medical expense deductions, and interest payments for home mortgages and education loans. However, many of these personal deductions are subject to limitations as to what and how much can be deducted.

Whenever the client or adviser is determining whether a given item of expense is deductible, certain questions should always be asked. Obviously, the first and most basic question is whether the Code allows a deduction for the item. A second important question is what basic category the expense falls under; in other words, whether it is a business expense, an expense for the production of income, or a personal expense. A third question is whether the deduction is an above-the-line or below-the-line deduction. It is always important for tax planning purposes to know where an item will appear on the individual's tax return.

A fourth question that should be asked is whether there is a particular restriction or limitation on the deductibility of the item. For example, certain deductions such as the medical expense deduction and the casualty loss deduction are subject to a *floor.* This floor is based on a percentage of the taxpayer's adjusted gross income. If the taxpayer's expenses in a given category are less than the applicable floor, no deduction will actually be allowed for the expenses.

> *Example:* Trish has medical expenses of $5,000 this year. Medical expenses are deductible, but only to the extent they exceed 7.5 percent of the taxpayer's adjusted gross income. Trish's adjusted gross income this year is $70,000. Although Trish has $5,000 of medical expenses, her deduction for these expenses is zero because the amount of the expenses ($5,000) is less than 7.5 percent of her adjusted gross income ($5,250).

Other types of restrictions may apply to particular deduction items. For example, cash contributions to a public charity are generally deductible, but only up to a maximum of 50 percent of an individual's adjusted gross income for any given year. Contributions in excess of that amount must be carried over to future taxable years. In the case of charitable contributions, the individual's adjusted gross income provides a *ceiling* for the deduction, rather than a floor.

Under present law, there is also an *overall* limitation on an individual's total itemized deductions. The overall limitation applies to all itemized deductions except medical expenses, casualty and theft losses, and investment interest expenses. The overall limitation is also based on adjusted gross income. It applies to individuals with adjusted gross income above a specified amount that is adjusted annually for inflation. Itemized deductions are disallowed or "phased out" to the extent of the individual's AGI in excess of the specified amount multiplied by 3 percent. Up to 80 percent of a taxpayer's itemized deductions can be disallowed under this rule. It applies after all other limitations and restrictions on the deductions have been taken into account.

Another type of restriction that may apply to a deduction is a dollar-amount restriction. An example of this restriction is the rule for deducting interest payments on a taxpayer's first mortgage on his or her principal residence. Generally such payments are deductible, but only with respect to a maximum of $1 million of loan principal. If the first mortgage exceeds $1 million, a corresponding portion of the interest deduction is disallowed. Note that in the case of the deduction for home mortgage interest, the dollar amount limitation is based on the amount of the loan principal, not the amount of the interest expense itself. Another example of a dollar-amount limitation is the limitation on deductible individual retirement account (IRA) contributions that may be claimed by individuals who are not covered by employer-provided retirement plans and by certain other individuals whose income falls within specified ranges.

Yet another type of restriction on the deductibility of certain expenses is a percentage limitation. For example, business entertainment expenses are generally deductible, but the deduction is limited to 80 percent of the actual expenses. There are many other ways in which the Internal Revenue Code limits the claiming of deductions.

Depreciation: A Special Type of Deduction

Not all tax deductions represent actual out-of-pocket expenses. Some deductions are allowable even though they represent no corresponding cash outlay. These are often referred to as *paper deductions,* because they represent or are related to some entry on the books of a taxpayer's business or investment activity, but they are not a cash-flow item.

What is the nature of these items? And why are they allowable as deductions against a taxpayer's income? What these items represent is a measure of a gradual decrease in the value or usefulness of property owned by the taxpayer. But they are only an arbitrary measure of such a decrease in value or usefulness. They are not a real-life measure of such a decrease.

The most important noncash deduction is the deduction for depreciation. The depreciation deduction allows a taxpayer to recover the cost of certain property for tax purposes by allowing the taxpayer to deduct a specified portion of the cost of the property each year against the taxpayer's income. The reason why such a deduction is allowed is that the cost of property that is used in business or for income-producing purposes should be deductible, but the deduction should be spread out over the useful life of the property.

Generally capital expenditures, such as those made for the purchase of a building or piece of equipment, are not deductible for income tax purposes. This is so because a capital expenditure is not considered to be an operating expense of a business, but a more long-term investment in an asset. As such, the capital expenditure would normally be recovered for tax purposes only when the asset is sold. In other words, the amount of the capital expenditure becomes the taxpayer's *tax basis* in the asset. This basis will be subtracted from the amount realized when the asset is sold to determine how much of the sale proceeds should be taxed.

But the depreciation deduction allows the taxpayer to deduct portions of the capital expenditure *before* the asset is sold, that is, on an annual basis. The theory is that the asset experiences wear and tear while it is being used by the taxpayer, and therefore there should be a deduction allowed for such wear and tear. However, in reality, the asset might actually be *appreciating* in real economic terms in spite of the wear and tear it is experiencing. This can happen with many types of assets, but is particularly common with real estate. In such a situation, the taxpayer is receiving a tax deduction, which is supposed to represent a *decrease* in the property's value, while the property is actually *increasing* in value.

Any depreciation deductions claimed with respect to an asset are subtracted from the taxpayer's *income tax basis* in the asset. This means that when the asset is sold later, the amount of depreciation deducted is, in effect, recouped by the government because the portion of the sales proceeds that is taxable will be increased. But, in the meantime, the taxpayer has enjoyed the economic benefit of the tax deductions for depreciation. The concept of basis will be discussed in more detail later in this chapter.

Because depreciation is a deduction that often does not represent economic reality, there is an element of social policy behind its presence in the tax law. That policy is to stimulate investment in business assets and assets held for the production of income.

What types of assets are eligible for this *cost recovery* that results from the depreciation deduction? There are two basic requirements. The first is that the asset must be used either in the taxpayer's business or in some other activity intended to produce income for the taxpayer. Assets held for personal use are not eligible for the deduction. The second requirement is that the asset must have a limited useful life in order to qualify. This requirement explains why land, for example, does not qualify for a depreciation deduction. Land is considered to be an asset that does not wear out.

There are some fairly complicated rules that determine how much of a qualifying asset's cost can be claimed each year as a depreciation deduction. These rules are based on two factors: the number of years over which the cost of the asset will be deducted, and the percentage of the cost of the asset that will be deducted each year. The details are beyond the scope of this chapter. In summary, however, it is fair to say that the depreciation deduction is especially beneficial to taxpayers because it allows them to save tax dollars without a corresponding cash outlay in the year of the tax saving.

PERSONAL AND DEPENDENCY EXEMPTIONS

Each individual taxpayer is allowed to claim a personal exemption for himself or herself. A married couple filing jointly may claim an exemption for each spouse. The amount of the exemption or exemptions is subtracted from adjusted gross income in the process of computing taxable income. Personal exemptions are *not* itemized deductions claimed on Schedule A of Form 1040, however. Therefore either the standard deduction or itemized deductions may be claimed in addition to the taxpayer's exemptions. Individual taxpayers are also permitted to claim an additional exemption for each *dependent* individual who is supported by the taxpayer. There are strict rules regarding whom a taxpayer may claim as a dependent and under what circumstances. The exemption amount changes annually by way of an inflation adjustment.

In addition, under current law taxpayers at certain income levels lose a portion of their personal exemption amounts. The amount lost is equal to 2 percent of the applicable personal exemption amount for every $2,500 (or *any fraction* thereof) by which the taxpayer's adjusted gross income exceeds a specified threshold amount. The threshold amounts are based on filing status and are also adjusted annually for inflation. This phaseout of exemption amounts applies separately to each and every exemption the taxpayer is entitled to claim. Simply stated, upper income taxpayers can lose all or part of the personal and dependency exemptions that they would otherwise be permitted to claim without this provision.

TAX RATES

Once the taxpayer's gross income has been determined, all deductions allowable in determining adjusted gross income are subtracted from gross income. Next, all deductions and exemptions allowable in determining taxable income are subtracted from adjusted gross income. The resulting figure is the taxpayer's taxable income. This is the figure to which the income tax rates are applied to determine the amount of income tax payable for the year. For individual taxpayers, a 15 percent rate is first applied to a specified amount or bracket of taxable income. Then the 28 percent rate is applied to the next bracket of income, followed by 31 percent, 36 percent, and 39.6 percent for subsequent brackets. The rate applicable to each successively higher income bracket is called the *marginal tax rate.* The amount of income taxed at each marginal rate is called the *marginal tax bracket.*

The brackets of taxable income to which the various rates are applied depend on the individual's *filing status.* As previously described, an individual taxpayer is categorized within one of four filing status categories: a single taxpayer, a married taxpayer filing jointly, a married taxpayer filing separately, or an unmarried head of household. The amount of taxable income that will fall into each tax bracket depends upon the individual's filing status. The brackets are also indexed annually for inflation.

It should be noted that an upper income taxpayer's actual *effective* tax rate may be higher than the maximum *statutory* marginal rate of 39.6 percent. This can happen as a result of the tax rules that *reduce* a taxpayer's itemized deductions and personal exemption amounts as the taxpayer's adjusted gross income *increases*. The actual *effective* rate for upper income taxpayers depends on the level of income, the amount of deductions, and the number of exemptions the taxpayer is entitled to claim. The calculation of the actual effective rates for upper income taxpayers is beyond the scope of an introductory chapter on taxation such as this one.

TAX CREDITS

Once the tax rates have been applied to an individual's taxable income, the resulting figure is the individual's tentative tax. However, this tentative tax can be reduced if the individual is eligible to claim any income tax credits.

It is important to understand the difference between a tax *deduction* and a tax *credit*. As explained earlier, a deduction is an item of expense that reduces the amount of income that is subject to tax. A credit, on the other hand, is a dollar-for-dollar reduction of the actual tax payable. Therefore a tax credit, if available, is of more value to the taxpayer than a deduction of an equal amount.

> *Example:* JoAnne has $90,000 of adjusted gross income this year. She has a deduction of $5,000 for her home mortgage interest payments. JoAnne is also entitled to claim a tax credit of $5,000 for rehabilitation work she performed on a certified historic structure that she owns. Assume JoAnne's marginal tax rate is 31 percent. Her deduction reduces her income subject to tax by $5,000, thereby resulting in a tax savings of $1,550 ($5,000 x .31). However, her tax credit is applied *directly* to her tentative tax, thereby resulting in a tax savings equal to the amount of the credit, $5,000. Credits currently available to individual taxpayers include the tax credit for children, the adoption credit, and the "Hope" and "Lifetime" education credits.

THE ALTERNATIVE MINIMUM TAX (AMT)

The AMT is a *separate* and *parallel* system of income taxation to the regular system. It applies to any taxpayer whose tax liability under the parallel system is greater than the liability for that year under the regular income tax system. In other words, the taxpayer pays the AMT amount if the AMT is greater than the regular tax. Therefore it follows that the computational process for determining the AMT is a different process from that used in determining the regular tax. The deduction rules are different. The credit rules are different. The tax rates are different.

The purpose of the AMT is to make certain that taxpayers who enjoy certain tax benefits will not be permitted to reduce their tax liability below a minimum amount by claiming certain tax deductions. For example, one thing that the AMT rules do is to add back certain deductions for AMT purposes that are allowable to the taxpayer for regular tax purposes. These items that are deductible for the regular tax, but face different rules under the AMT, are referred to as *tax preference items.* These items generally produce no benefit to the taxpayer under the AMT system as they would under the regular system.

The tax rate under the AMT system is applied to income subject to the AMT. For individuals, there are two brackets with rates of 26 percent and 28 percent respectively. For corporations, it is a flat rate of 20 percent except for small corporations, which are not subject to AMT. Note that although the AMT tax *rates* are lower than in the regular system, the tax *payable* may be greater. If so, the AMT must be paid instead of the regular tax.

For purposes of this chapter, the reader should simply be aware that the AMT tax system exists, and that certain taxpayers with certain types of deductions will be subject to it. The details for calculating the AMT and the various rules for determining what goes in and out of the AMT tax base are found in the more advanced texts. A basic understanding of these rules is important for the financial services professional.

CONCEPT OF THE TAXABLE YEAR

Individuals file tax returns on an annual basis. For the vast majority of individuals, income tax is calculated based upon a calendar-year period. However, many partnerships and corporations (as well as a small number of individuals) report their tax liability based upon a 12-month period that does not coincide with the calendar year. Such a period is referred to as a fiscal year. In the past, the use of a fiscal year for tax purposes by a business entity provided an opportunity for deferring taxable income. This was accomplished by paying or crediting income to a partner or shareholder in the beginning of a calendar year that was actually earned by the business during its fiscal year, which began several months before the onset of the calendar year. However, such techniques have been virtually eliminated by strict new rules governing the election of a fiscal year for tax purposes.

THREE IMPORTANT ISSUES

The preceding material has been an overview of the process by which an individual's tax liability is computed. To more fully understand the income tax system, it is helpful to think about three basic issues in addition to understanding the computation process. These three issues are (1) what is taxed? (2) to whom is it taxed? and (3) when is it taxed? There are important tax law doctrines that clarify each of these issues.

The What Question: The Economic Benefit Doctrine

The question of *what* is taxed has already been discussed in the section of this chapter that describes the concept of gross income. In general, anything of value received by the taxpayer is taxed. Any event or transaction that confers an economic benefit on the taxpayer will result in gross income to the taxpayer, as long as the economic benefit is certain and can be measured. For example, suppose the Carroll Corporation sets up a trust for one of its key employees, Toby. The terms of the trust provide that in 2 years Toby will receive $20,000 a year for a 10-year period. Toby's right to the money is nonforfeitable and the trust assets are not otherwise available to the Carroll Corporation in any way. Even though Toby is not receiving any money currently, the Carroll Corporation has conferred an economic benefit upon Toby that is certain and can be measured using time-value-of-money calculations. Therefore Toby will be taxed currently on the present value of the payments to be made in the future. Note that the result would be different if the payments were contingent on the rendering of future services by Toby, or if the assets of the trust were available to the Carroll Corporation or its creditors for use other than to pay Toby. This is an example of the *economic benefit* doctrine, which holds that a taxpayer must pay tax whenever an economic benefit has been conferred on the taxpayer, regardless of whether the taxpayer has actually received any cash or property. Another example of the application of this doctrine is the case in which an employer pays life insurance premiums on a policy covering the life of an employee who has the right to name the beneficiary under the policy. The employer in such a case has conferred an economic benefit upon the employee (life insurance coverage) that is subject to income tax.

The To Whom Question: The Doctrine of the Fruit and the Tree

There are many types of assets that produce income that is taxed. The asset producing the income may be a corporate bond that pays interest. Or it may be a piece of real estate that generates rental income. Or it may be an individual, whose knowledge or expertise generates income from sales or services. In any event, the tax principle that applies is this: Income is to be taxed to the person who *earns* it, or to the person who *owns* the *asset* that produces it. In other words, for income tax purposes, the "fruit" comes from the "tree" that produced it, and must be taxed accordingly.

> *Example:* Sandra owns a $1,000 bond issued by the Merlin Corporation. Sandra clips the interest coupons from the bond and gives them to her son, Brett. Brett receives the interest income. Sandra retains ownership of the bond itself. In spite of the fact that Brett has received

the income, Sandra is still taxed on it because she owns the asset that produced the income.

Similarly income from personal services is taxed to the person who earns it. The fruits of an individual's labor cannot be assigned to another individual for tax purposes. For example, assume an insurance agent irrevocably assigns in writing her right to future commissions from one of her client's policies to her daughter. Will her daughter be taxed on the income? The answer is no. The individual who earned the income must be taxed on it. This principle is often referred to as the doctrine of *assignment of income*.

The When Question: The Doctrine of Constructive Receipt

The current use of money is valuable. Therefore if taxation can be deferred, the taxpayer gains a monetary benefit through the use of tax money until it is paid to the government later. As a result, taxpayers may try to use techniques that defer the receipt of income until a later tax year in order to defer the payment of tax on the income. An important doctrine that limits the use of such techniques is referred to as the doctrine of *constructive receipt*.

Under the doctrine of constructive receipt, the taxpayer is deemed to have received income for tax purposes when it is either credited to the taxpayer's account, set apart for the taxpayer, or otherwise made available to be taken into the taxpayer's possession.

> *Example:* John, a life insurance agent, filed a policy application with his company in November of last year. In December, the policy was issued, and a commission check was made out to John. John did not pick up the check until January of this year, even though he could have easily picked it up in December. John must report this income on last year's tax return under the doctrine of constructive receipt, even though John did not *actually* receive the income until this year.

It is important to know, however, that if there is any condition or restriction that limits the taxpayer's right to receive the income, the doctrine of constructive receipt will not apply.

> *Example:* Natalie is a real estate agent. In November of last year, her client signed an agreement to purchase a home that Natalie listed. The sale is closed on January 2 of this year. Although Natalie was fairly certain in November that she would receive her commission, the client still had to go through with the closing in order for Natalie's rights to her money to become unconditional. Therefore the doctrine of constructive receipt does not apply to Natalie and she will be taxed on the commission in the year she actually receives it.

BASIC INCOME-TAX-PLANNING CONCEPTS

Although the Tax Reform Act of 1986 was highly touted as a breakthrough in simplifying the federal income tax system, much complexity remains in the understanding and application of the Internal Revenue Code. Because of this complexity, many highly intelligent people devote their professional lives to the process of trying to figure out how the Code can be analyzed (and, in some cases, manipulated) to save some tax money for their clients. This is fine and good, as long as the tax is saved through tax *avoidance* (reasonable interpretation of the tax laws), and not through tax *evasion* (ignoring or flouting of the tax laws).

As previously stated, sophisticated tax planning is not the subject of this chapter. However, it should be helpful to outline some of the basic concepts that are used in tax planning to illustrate how tax lawyers and other tax professionals think in their efforts to help clients.

Income and Deduction Shifting

The purpose behind income-shifting techniques is this: Get taxable income into the hands of a taxpayer who is in a lower tax bracket than the taxpayer who would otherwise have to report the income. The result is that less tax is paid on the income. For example, a taxpayer in a 31 percent marginal tax bracket will pay $3,100 in tax on $10,000 of additional income. However, a taxpayer in the 15 percent bracket will pay only $1,500 of tax on the same $10,000 of income. Expressed as a percentage, the lower bracket taxpayer pays 52 percent less tax on the same income than would the higher-bracket taxpayer. Although the tax rates are much more compressed now than they were under previous tax law, income shifting can still provide substantial savings.

What, then, are some of the income-shifting techniques that are available? Perhaps the simplest one is an outright gift of property. As previously discussed, income is taxed to the person who owns the asset that produces the income. If the asset is transferred by gift, the donee will be taxed on income generated by the asset. However, the *gift* tax consequences of giving away property to shift the *income* tax burden must always be considered. Gift taxes are discussed in chapter 13 of this text.

For planning purposes, the converse of income shifting is deduction shifting. Deduction shifting is a simple, yet frequently overlooked, planning technique. Here, the idea is to shift deductions to a taxpayer who is in a higher tax bracket than the taxpayer who would otherwise claim the deduction. As a result, the deduction is taken against income that would be taxed in a higher bracket, thereby resulting in a greater tax savings.

> *Example:* Marjorie is ill and must enter the hospital for an extended stay. The cost of her care is only partially covered by insurance. Although Marjorie has some assets, she is not working and does not have much income. Her mother, Ruth, is in the 31 percent tax bracket

and also has enough medical expenses of her own this year to claim a medical expense deduction. Marjorie is Ruth's dependent for tax purposes, and therefore, Ruth can deduct medical expense payments she makes for Marjorie's care. If Ruth pays for Marjorie's care, there will be a tax savings of 31 cents for every dollar of expense. If on the other hand Marjorie paid for her own expenses, there would be little or no tax savings.

Avoiding Limitations on Deductions

As was explained earlier in this chapter, although many types of expenses are deductible for income tax purposes, there may be limitations on how much of a given expense may actually be deducted. One common way that the law limits deductions is through the use of a *deduction floor.* You will recall that the taxpayer is allowed to deduct items that are subject to the floor, but only to the extent those items *exceed* a specified percentage of income (specifically, adjusted gross income in most cases).

For example, there is an entire group of deductions that are claimed by individual taxpayers on Schedule A of Form 1040 that are referred to as *miscellaneous itemized deductions.* This group of deductions includes employee business expenses, fees for safe deposit boxes, fees for investment and individual tax advice, and several other items. First, all of the taxpayer's deductions that fall within this group are added together. Then, the taxpayer's adjusted gross income is multiplied by 2 percent. The resulting figure is subtracted from the total of the items in the group to determine how much the taxpayer can actually deduct. The result is that the taxpayer is permitted to deduct miscellaneous itemized deductions only to the extent they exceed this 2 percent floor.

How can taxpayers avoid this floor? With respect to some deductions that fall within this category, it is impossible to avoid the floor itself. However, if adjusted gross income can be *reduced* in a year in which the taxpayer has these items, a greater portion of the items will be deductible, since the floor will be less. How, then, can AGI be reduced? By maximizing above-the-line deductions, as previously discussed. If a taxpayer has miscellaneous itemized deductions and wishes to minimize the effect of the 2 percent floor, it may be appropriate to *bunch* the taxpayer's above-the-line deductions into a given year to reduce AGI. Conversely, it may also be helpful to bunch a greater number of the miscellaneous itemized deductions subject to the floor into one year. The result of this technique would be that some deductions that would be lost under the floor if claimed in next year's return can actually be deducted if taken this year, because the floor has already been exceeded.

Other deductions that are subject to a floor include the medical expense deduction (7.5 percent of AGI) and the deduction for personal casualty losses (10 percent of AGI).

Example: Lynn, who is the sole proprietor of a small business, accidentally rinses her diamond ring down the drain this year. Lynn's husband paid $10,000 for the ring as an anniversary present. Lynn and her husband file a joint return and are in the 28 percent tax bracket. The ring is not insured. Lynn and her husband have $60,000 of AGI for the year. Therefore $6,000 of their casualty loss deduction will be lost under the 10 percent floor ($60,000 x .10). However, if Lynn made a deductible contribution of $5,000 to her Keogh account this year, the couple's adjusted gross income would be reduced to $55,000. Then, only $5,500 of the casualty loss deduction would be lost under the floor ($55,000 x .10). As a result, the Keogh contribution produces a tax savings of $140 ($500 x .28) in addition to the tax benefit produced by the Keogh contribution itself.

The same technique (reducing AGI) is also helpful in avoiding the overall limitation or "phaseout" of itemized deductions, mentioned earlier.

Deferral and Acceleration Techniques

Deferral of income and acceleration of deductions are basic and common tax planning techniques. These techniques are based on the time value of money. If income can be deferred to a later year, the tax payable on the income is also deferred and the taxpayer has the use of that money for a longer time. Similarly, if deductible expenses are accelerated into an earlier tax year, the tax saving from those deductions is realized sooner, thereby giving the taxpayer the use of that money sooner. However, it is important to note that most tax deductions are attributable to actual out-of-pocket expenses. Therefore the expense itself involves the loss of use of money, which over the same time period will be greater than the benefit realized by the tax savings. The point is to not let the tax "tail" wag the overall financial "dog."

What, then, is the potential benefit of accelerating deductions? The benefit lies in a differential with respect to the comparative time periods. For example, if a taxpayer makes a deductible expense in December of this year rather than in January of next year, the taxpayer has lost the use of the money spent only for one additional month. However, the tax savings generated by the expense gives the taxpayer the use of the tax savings for an entire additional year, as compared to making the expense in January. In such a situation, the taxpayer does in fact gain a net benefit from accelerating the expense.

Example: Harry makes a $10,000 deductible business expense in December of this year. Harry's marginal tax bracket is 31 percent. By making the expenditure in December of this year rather than January of next year, Harry postpones the payment of $3,100 in taxes ($10,000 x .31) for one year. Assume Harry can invest money for one year at 8 percent annual interest. Harry will have $248 ($3,100 x .08) that he would not have if he had deferred the expense until next year. However, by paying the $10,000 in December instead of January, Harry loses one month's interest on the $10,000. This amount is $67 [($10,000 x .08) ÷ 12]. But note that Harry is still ahead $181 ($248 – $67) by accelerating the deductible expense and, in effect, deferring the payment of taxes on $10,000 of income for one year.

The Passive-Loss Rules

There are special limitations on the deductibility of so-called *passive losses.* These tax losses are typically generated by activities in which the taxpayer has an ownership interest, but does not participate in the activity of the business. For example, suppose a taxpayer owns an interest in a limited partnership that invests in rental real estate. Assume that the depreciation deductions and other deductions generated by the partnership properties exceed the income generated by the properties. Therefore for tax purposes, the partnership generates losses.

Under tax laws in effect before the Tax Reform Act of 1986, there were few limitations on the deductibility of such items by taxpayers owning interests in limited partnerships and other activities in which the taxpayer did not participate. Because these investments allowed taxpayers to *write off* the tax losses against salary and other types of income, they were referred to as *tax shelters.* Tax shelters were a very important weapon in the tax-avoidance arsenal.

Under current law, however, there are strict limitations on the deductibility of losses generated by tax-shelter investments. These rules are intended to prevent taxpayers from investing in activities merely for tax purposes, as distinguished from the actual economics of the investment. There are complicated rules and definitions as to what constitutes a passive activity that will be subject to the strict deduction rules. The basic rule, however, is that tax losses generated by passive activities can be deducted only against income generated by the taxpayer's passive activities, and not against salary or other income of the taxpayer.

There are qualifications, exceptions, and certain significant loopholes to these rules. This is one of those areas of the tax law that is a specialty in itself. In fact, some specialists in this area have trouble understanding the rules, which are complicated by hundreds of pages of Treasury regulations. For purposes of this chapter, the reader should simply be aware that if a taxpayer invests in an activity in which the taxpayer does not participate, and the activity generates tax losses, the deductibility of those losses is limited by some very strict rules. Activities deemed to be passive include most rental activities in which the taxpayer owns an interest. However, investments in publicly traded stocks and bonds are not covered by these rules, because these are not the type of investments that usually produce tax losses on an annual basis.

Tax-Exempt Transactions

Perhaps one of the best types of tax planning techniques is that of creating a transaction that produces a monetary benefit without the taxpayer being taxed on that transaction. Within this general category there are two basic types of transactions. The first is where taxation is altogether *eliminated*, and the second is where taxation of the transaction is merely *deferred*. The first type can be described as a tax-exempt transaction. Such transactions are generally based on some specific exclusion from gross income.

An example of a tax-exempt transaction is the receipt of income from a public-purpose municipal bond. The income from such bonds is excludible from the taxpayer's gross income for federal income tax purposes. You will remember that *all* income is includible in gross income unless there is a provision in the Code that specifically excludes it. There is such an exclusion for certain municipal bond income (IRC Sec. 103).

Financial market forces generally dictate that unless the taxpayer is subject to the highest marginal income tax rate (currently 39.6 percent), the interest rate on such bonds will not be higher than the after-tax rate on taxable obligations. Therefore such investments are generally of interest only to higher-bracket taxpayers.

Another example of a tax-exempt monetary gain is the exclusion of the first $250,000 ($500,000 if married, filing jointly) of gain on the sale of a personal residence if certain requirements are met.

Nonrecognition Transactions

There are many types of transactions in which taxation is merely deferred rather than eliminated. These transactions may generally be referred to as *nonrecognition transactions.* Typically such a transaction involves the sale or exchange of property at a gain realized by the taxpayer. However, because of a provision in the Internal Revenue Code, the *realized* gain is not currently *recognized* (reportable on Form 1040).

How do such transactions merely *defer*, rather than *eliminate*, taxable gain? In order to understand the mechanics of the nonrecognition transaction, the basic tax treatment of a sale or exchange of property must be understood.

Computation of Gain or Loss

When property is sold, it is necessary to determine what portion of the sale proceeds will be subject to taxation. In general, the gain realized from a sale of property is equal to the total amount realized from the sale, minus the taxpayer's *basis* in the property.

What does the term *basis* mean? Broadly stated, basis is the amount that the taxpayer has invested in the property. Therefore basis is generally the amount that the taxpayer paid for the property, plus the cost of improvements to the property, if any. Stated another way, the basis of property is generally equal to its cost. As a result, the gain realized from a sale of property is the sales price minus the taxpayer's cost.

> *Example:* Nancy bought 1,000 shares of stock in Cleanseco, Inc., a household cleanser manufacturer, 2 years ago. She paid $5,000 for the

stock. This year, she sells the Cleanseco stock for $10,000. The amount realized from the sale is $10,000. Nancy's basis is $5,000. Therefore the realized gain from the sale is $5,000 ($10,000 – $5,000).

The fact that the portion of the sales price that represents a recovery of the taxpayer's *basis* is not taxable illustrates a basic principle of tax law, namely, that money received that represents a *return of capital* is not treated as gross income. The Internal Revenue Code contains many provisions which reflect this basic principle. It is really a matter of common sense: Getting back money that the taxpayer has invested in property should not result in taxation, because there has been no profit returned to the taxpayer, only the original investment.

How Nonrecognition Transactions Differ from Taxable Transactions

Some sales and exchanges are governed by specific provisions in the Internal Revenue Code, which provide that the gain *realized* shall not be *recognized* (that is, reported on Form 1040 and taxed). It has been stated above that the purpose of these transactions is not to *eliminate* taxation, but merely to *defer* it. How is this accomplished?

The answer to this question relates to the taxpayer's basis in property. Generally a taxpayer's basis in property is equal to the cost of the property. In the case of an exchange of property, the taxpayer's cost for the property received in the exchange is really the fair market value of the property surrendered in the exchange. However, if the exchange is one in which gain is not recognized, the taxpayer's basis in the new property will generally be the *same* as the taxpayer's basis in the old property. This preserves the unrecognized gain and allows that gain to be taxed when the *new* property is later sold in a taxable transaction.

Example: Robert owns a condominium that he holds as a rental property. He paid $100,000 for the property and added $20,000 worth of improvements. The value of the property is now $180,000. Robert exchanges the property for another condominium in a transaction that qualifies for nonrecognition treatment under the Internal Revenue Code. The property received in the exchange is also worth $180,000. Robert's realized gain is $60,000 ($180,000 value of property received minus $120,000 basis in property given up). Robert's recognized gain is zero because the exchange qualifies for nonrecognition treatment. However, Robert's basis in the new property will be the same as his basis in the old property ($120,000). As a result, if the new property is sold later, the gain that would have been recognized if the exchange was taxable earlier will be recognized *later*, when the new property is sold. On the other hand, if the exchange was taxable, Robert would pay tax currently on the $60,000 of gain, but he would have a basis of $180,000 in the new property.

Clearly, the *deferral* of taxation in such a transaction has significant value. Moreover, the deferred gain may never be taxed if the taxpayer does not sell the property received in the exchange later. The intent of the nonrecognition provisions is merely to defer taxation. But there is no assurance that Uncle Sam will ever get his tax money, particularly if the taxpayer keeps the new property until death.

The example above is just one type of transaction that qualifies for nonrecognition. Other examples include exchanges of insurance policies and involuntary conclusions. These transactions, and the specific rules that govern their tax treatment, are beyond the scope of this chapter.

Transactions That Result in a Taxable Loss

Some sales of property will result in a loss rather than a gain to the selling taxpayer. This will happen when the amount received for the property is less than the taxpayer's basis in the property. In such cases, the amount of the loss will generally be deductible for income tax purposes if the property sold is either business property or property held for the production of income. If the property is held for personal use, the loss resulting from a sale of the property is generally nondeductible.

> *Example:* Alexandra owns stock in the Hi-Five Corporation, a publicly traded corporation that sells sneakers. Alexandra paid $5,000 for the stock 2 years ago. This year, she sells the stock for $3,500. Alexandra has a realized loss of $1,500 ($5,000 basis minus $3,500 amount realized). Alexandra may deduct the $1,500 loss on her tax return this year.

Ordinary versus Capital Gain and Loss

Some different rules apply to sales of a taxpayer's assets, depending on whether the gain or loss is treated as an *ordinary* gain or loss or a *capital* gain or loss.

Capital Gain versus Ordinary Income

As most financial services professionals know, one of the most important pieces of the federal tax law puzzle is the broad scope of social policy considerations. In other words, what politicians perceive to be a policy that will get them elected often finds its way into the tax laws. One of the policy issues that is a continuous source of controversy and change is the question of whether *capital gain* should be taxed at the same rates as *ordinary income.*

What is the difference between capital gain and ordinary income? Basically capital gain is income that is realized through the sale or exchange of a capital asset. The definition of a capital asset does appear in the Internal Revenue Code, although the Code defines a capital asset by stating what it is *not* rather than what it *is*. In any event, a capital asset can generally be described as any property held by the taxpayer other than property held for sale by the taxpayer, or intellectual or artistic property created by the taxpayer. Special tax rules apply to the sale of property used by a taxpayer in a trade or business. These rules will be discussed below.

The social policy issue surrounding the sale of capital assets is this: Should the sale of such assets receive a tax break relative to other kinds of income? Those who answer yes argue that capital-gain tax relief encourages savings and investment. They also argue that full taxation of capital gain subjects taxpayers to what is really a tax on inflation, rather than one on real economic gains.

How does a capital-gain tax break favor savings and investment? Stocks, bonds, real estate, and other investment-type assets generally are treated as capital assets. When an investor sells such an asset, a greater portion of the amount realized from the sale will remain in the investor's pocket if favorable tax treatment applies to the realized gain. Therefore the investor has a higher rate of return on the investment, which presumably provides an incentive to save rather than spend.

In addition, it is argued that a portion of the increase in value of an investment-type asset is attributable to inflation, rather than to real economic appreciation. Therefore, the argument goes, taxing the full amount of gain when the asset is sold is confiscatory, because the portion of the gain attributable to inflation has conferred no real economic benefit upon the taxpayer who is paying tax on it.

These theories have helped to introduce varying legislative measures over the years that provide relief for the taxation of capital gain. For example, through the use of an exclusion from gross income for a specified percentage of an individual's capital gain or a lower tax rate on capital gain, a lower tax bill on the overall gain results.

For individual taxpayers, the maximum rate applicable to capital gains on assets held more than 12 months is generally 20 percent, as opposed to the maximum marginal rate of 39.6 percent that is applicable to ordinary income. Collectibles and real estate gains resulting from "unrecaptured" depreciation are taxed at higher rates. Additional rules are scheduled to take effect in the future that will provide even lower maximum rates for gains on assets held for more than 5 years. As with other provisions in the tax law, legislative change is the norm.

What are the arguments *against* favorable tax treatment for capital gain? The principal argument is that a preferential treatment for capital gain favors wealthy taxpayers at the expense of the average citizen. The theory goes that most stocks and bonds and other investment assets are owned by the rich, and that by taxing gains from the sale of these investments at a lower effective rate, the government is playing Robin Hood in reverse: stealing from the poor to feed the rich.

Draw your own conclusions.

Tax Treatment of Capital Losses

When a capital asset is sold at a loss rather than at a gain, special rules do apply under current law. Basically capital losses can be deducted only against the taxpayer's capital gains. In other words, a taxpayer cannot deduct a large capital loss from the sale of a stock investment against his or her wages for the year. However, in the case of individual taxpayers only, $3,000 of capital losses in excess of capital gains can be deducted against the taxpayer's other income. Any remaining capital losses can be carried over to future tax years.

Sec. 1231 Assets: Depreciable Property and Real Property Used in a Trade or Business

This class of assets receives different tax treatment, depending on whether the asset is sold at a gain or at a loss. If the asset is sold at a gain, the gain is treated as a capital gain. If the asset is sold at a loss, the loss is treated as an ordinary loss, not as a capital loss.

What is the significance of this hybrid form of tax treatment? The most important thing is that the sale of an asset falling into this category is *not* subject to the limitations that apply to the deductibility of capital losses. Therefore if such an asset is sold at a loss, the loss can be deducted against the taxpayer's salary or other income.

If the asset is sold at a gain, the gain will be treated as capital gain. Even though there is currently no partial exclusion or other preferential treatment available for capital gains, capital-gains treatment can provide a benefit for taxpayers who have capital *losses* for the year. Why? Because the capital losses can be deducted against capital gains, but not against ordinary income.

> *Example:* Pat sells a piece of machinery this year that is used in his business. The machinery is sold at a gain of $40,000. Pat also has a capital loss of $40,000 this year from a sale of stock from his investment portfolio. Because the gain from the sale of the machinery is treated as capital gain and not ordinary income, Pat can deduct his stock losses in full against the gain from the sale of the machinery.

The assets that receive this hybrid form of tax treatment include all depreciable property plus land that is used in the taxpayer's business (land is not depreciable for tax purposes). These so-called Sec. 1231 assets provide the best of both worlds for taxpayers, and the rules that govern them are designed to stimulate investment in assets that are used in the conduct of a business.

TAXABLE ENTITIES

Most of the discussion in this chapter has focused on the individual taxpayer who receives income from salary, investment, or a sole proprietorship. However, the individual is not the only taxpayer under the federal income tax system.

Trusts, estates, and corporations also are subject to the federal income tax. However, certain corporations can make an election to have their shareholders taxed on the corporation's taxable income. This is called a *subchapter S election.* The effect of such an election is to have the corporation treated for tax purposes very much like a partnership. Like a partnership, a corporation that makes an S election is not subject to income tax at the entity level. Rather, the owners of the business pay the taxes. Partnerships and S corporations are often referred to as *pass-through entities,* because the responsibility for paying their taxes is passed through the entity to the owners of the entity.

However, trusts, estates, and corporations other than S corporations do pay taxes. There are special rules that apply to each of these entities that do not apply to individual taxpayers. In addition, each of these entities has a tax rate structure that is different from the rate structure applicable to individual taxpayers.

CONCLUSION

This chapter has outlined basic income tax concepts and planning techniques that should be familiar to financial services professionals. Much more can be learned about each of these topics by the financial services professional. Although many loopholes under prior law have been closed by recent legislation, income tax planning is still a crucial element of financial planning.

10

Insurance Planning: The Risk Management Process

Charles E. Hughes

Chapter Outline

Personal financial planning represents an integrated approach to the development and implementation of plans for the achievement of individual or family financial objectives. Although financial objectives may differ in terms of individual circumstances, goals, attitudes, and needs, all integrated plans should include an analysis and recommendations that satisfy the individual protection objectives.

While plans for the accumulation of wealth may be more exciting, the protection of that accumulated wealth cannot be overlooked. Most people work to acquire assets (wealth) such as homes, automobiles, savings, and investments, but the pleasure associated with this wealth is sometimes interrupted by the chilling thought that some event over which there is little or no control could cause assets to be damaged or destroyed. To find some method of protecting assets, or preserving the wealth represented by those assets, is the challenge people face, that is, the risk they face.

As will be seen in more detail in chapter 12, the meaning of the term *risk* as applied to investments relates to the uncertainty of growth or decline in income or principal. Another type of risk, identified as *pure risk,* differs in meaning in that the uncertainty associated with it involves *only the chance of loss.* In this definition the possibility of gain is essentially absent, and all that remains is the alternative of loss or no loss (no change).

To illustrate the concept of pure risk, suppose a client owns a home and is concerned about the possibility of damage or destruction due to fire. What are the possible outcomes? Either a fire occurs and causes damage that results in a loss, or no fire occurs and there is no change or loss. The uncertainty as to the outcome is the pure risk that the client faces. While there is risk in that the home could appreciate or depreciate in market value, this is the investment type of risk and not pure risk. Reference made to risk for purposes of discussion in this chapter and the next will be to pure risk, and this risk is defined as uncertainty as to financial loss.

Technically, a function of insurance is to reduce or replace uncertainty. However, insurance, especially property and liability insurance, is more understandable if its function is stated as a reimbursement for the loss sustained. Loss is the undesirable end result of risk and is defined as the decrease or disappearance of value, usually in an unexpected or relatively unpredictable manner. For example, when fire damages or destroys a home, the owner suffers a financial loss at least equivalent to the cost necessary to repair or replace the damaged property. This type of loss is in the pure-risk category.

How is the financial services professional to approach his or her clients' pure-risk situations? The process of risk analysis and control, normally referred to as risk management, has been developed for application in business situations. Much of the same process applies to the management of risk at the individual or family level. This chapter will provide an introduction to the use of the risk management process as an integral part of financial planning for individuals and families. Since the use of insurance is a major tool in managing pure risks, this chapter includes some introductory comments about insurance. Chapter 11 will focus primarily on the insurance coverages available to deal with pure risks that may confront clients.

RISK MANAGEMENT PROCESS

The risk management process is a systematic approach to the discovery and treatment of risks facing individuals and families. It is a modification of the risk management functions performed for business organizations by risk managers, consultants, and practitioners in the field. This process includes three steps: (1) risk analysis, (2) risk-treatment planning, and (3) risk-treatment plan implementation.

Steps in Risk Management

- Risk analysis
- Risk-treatment plan
- Risk-treatment plan implementation

Risk Analysis

The first step in the risk management process is to analyze the risks the client faces. *The identification* of risks is the first function in this analysis. Identification might also be considered the most important function, since there is really no need for additional action (until or unless the event does occur) if the risk has not first been identified. A systematic approach is helpful in discovering all of the significant risks the client faces.

The second function in risk analysis is the *measurement* of the losses associated with the identified risks. Once the risks have been identified and an appropriate value determined as a measurement of the possible loss, the final function in risk analysis is to evaluate the potential financial impact such losses would have upon the client.

Risk-Treatment Planning

The second step in the risk management process is risk-treatment planning, which is the evaluation of the alternative techniques for handling risks. Although various methods of loss control and loss financing will be described briefly in this chapter, the major emphasis will be placed on the use of insurance as a risk-treatment technique.

Risk-Treatment Plan Implementation

The final step in the risk management process involves the collection of data from the first two steps and the formulation of recommendations for the risk-treatment plan. In addition, this step includes both assistance in the implementation of the plan and the task of continuously monitoring the selected plan to determine its effectiveness and to review the risks upon which the plan is based.

With this brief overview of the risk management process in mind, each of these three steps will now be discussed in greater detail.

RISK ANALYSIS

As mentioned above, the first step in the risk management process is to analyze the risks that the individual faces. This step includes the identification of risks, measurement of loss, and evaluation of the financial impact of the risk.

Risk Identification

To identify potential risks, a checklist of all the losses that could possibly be incurred by an individual or family is useful to the planner. This provides him or her with a systematic approach to discovering the potential losses faced by the particular client.

The initial step in developing this checklist is to establish some basis for classifying the risks to be identified. For example, one method would be to group the risks into categories according to the general nature of the loss. These categories could include: (1) physical damage to assets, (2) loss of possession by fraud or criminal violence, (3) loss of ownership through an adverse judgment at law, (4) loss of income resulting from damage to the property of others, (5) loss of income because of a personal disablement, and so on. Unfortunately, this technique could become unmanageable and even confusing.

Categories of Potential Risks: Nature of Loss

- Physical damage to assets
- Loss of possession by fraud or criminal violence
- Loss of ownership through adverse legal judgment
- Loss of income resulting from damage to property of others
- Loss of income through personal disablement

Another method of categorizing risks is to establish general headings under which would be listed events that would (1) decrease assets, (2) decrease income, (3) increase expenses, or (4) increase liability. An advantage of this method is its emphasis on outcomes. For example, under the category of decreased assets, the planner would be concerned with identifying the assets owned, used, or in the possession of the individual or family that would cause this client to experience a loss should a particular event occur. For example, suppose the client owns an automobile. Could that automobile (asset) be damaged or destroyed? If the answer is yes, the client is exposed to the risk of a decrease in the value of that asset. Therefore, the automobile would be listed under the decreased assets category of risk. (At a later stage in the risk management process the planner will also need to examine what could cause this automobile to be damaged or destroyed and to give some thought to the dollar amount of the loss that would be suffered by the client should the event occur.)

Categories of Potential Risks: Financial Outcomes

- Decreased assets
- Decreased income
- Increased expenses
- Increased liability

The planner should also list ownership of the automobile under the Increase Liability category since an adverse judgment could be rendered against the client because of the ownership of that automobile.

This same process could be completed for each of the four risk categories. As another example, the possibility that a client will be injured or become ill would be listed under both the Decrease Income and Increase Expenses categories of risk. The occurrence of the event would result in an increase in expenses for the client's medical care and the possibility of a decrease in income because of the inability to continue to work during a period of disability.

This whole process can be continued until the planner eventually ends with a rather lengthy list of possible losses or risks that the individual or family faces.

Another method of classifying loss exposure is on the basis of the following outline:

1. property losses
   a. direct losses associated with the need to replace or repair damaged or missing property
   b. indirect (consequential) losses, such as additional living expenses that are caused by the direct loss
2. liability losses arising out of damage to or destruction of others' property or personal injuries to others
3. personal losses
   a. loss of earning power because of premature death, disability, periods of unemployment, or superannuation
   b. extra expenses associated with injuries or periods of sickness

Categories of Potential Risks: Types of Loss

- Property losses
- Liability losses
- Personal losses

Clients are exposed to direct loss through the ownership of real and personal property. Real property typically consists of the client's dwelling, and personal property includes such items as household goods, clothing, and automobiles. Indirect losses are associated with the loss of use of property (normally indirect losses are associated with real property rather than personal property because of the ease in quickly replacing most types of personal property). In addition to the indirect loss referred to as additional living expenses, other types of consequential losses include debris removal costs, rental income losses, and demolition losses. Of these, additional living expenses and debris removal are the more important losses for most individuals and families.

The ownership, maintenance or use of an automobile is the best known source of liability loss. However, individuals should be aware of the fact that potential losses also arise out of the ownership, maintenance, or use of real property and out of personal activities. It should also be noted that workers' compensation statutes can give rise to an exposure in certain states when a client has household employees.

Examples of personal losses include the loss of continuing income to family members upon the breadwinner's retirement or premature death. In addition, increased expenses associated with medical care for hospitalization and physician expenses are types of personal losses.

FOCUS ON ETHICS
When Responsibility Exceeds Knowledge

When financial planners address a client's financial security, they often emphasize future income production and protection. The goal is to produce a level of wealth that will generate a sufficient stream of income that will prepare the client for retirement or will ensure a chosen lifestyle should there be an interruption in income production.

Commission-based financial planners are rarely licensed to sell property and casualty insurance and frequently overlook the threat posed by property destruction or major liability claims. An underinsured home destroyed by fire or natural disaster can destroy the best financial plan. The same can happen if the client is underinsured and loses a major liability suit resulting from an accident, professional negligence, or other reason.

The financial counselor must sensitize the client to these needs as well. Insurance can minimize the client's liability, property, and casualty losses. Protecting the client's assets is an essential part of financial planning. Just because the planner is less knowledgeable in these areas does not reduce the need or the responsibility.

When this type of classification system is used, the exposures to risk can be listed in an abbreviated fashion. For example, when the risk involves possible damage or destruction to the dwelling, the use of the word *dwelling* can be appropriate. The underlying questions associated with the single word to identify a risk could include such things as the number of dwellings involved, where the dwellings are located, and, if the dwellings are exposed to loss, what could conceivably cause the loss.

For this last question, some individuals conducting risk surveys prefer to actually list the causes of loss. The advantage in listing the various causes of loss is the ability to better analyze the potential loss associated with a particular risk. However, a primary disadvantage of this approach is the tendency of some financial planners to rely heavily on only those causes of loss that are insurable, and to forget to list causes of loss that are not considered insurable.

The decision of whether to list causes of loss in the identification of risks will be at the discretion of the individual making the risk analysis survey. Those who are skilled in identifying all the possible causes of loss to a particular asset will probably prefer to simply list that asset. An insurance salesperson conducting the survey might prefer to identify causes of loss to help select the proper insurance coverage to meet the particular risk. The financial services professional should select the risk identification procedure with which he or she is most comfortable.

Completing the Risk Analysis Checklist

How does the planner go about completing the checklist of potential risks? If a comprehensive checklist is available, and if it has been completed and the information required has been obtained from the client, the completion of the checklist should be rather easy. Since the planner is attempting to identify the client's property and activities that give rise to risk, it might be possible for the planner to simply sit back and think about the risk exposures. However, to ensure that risk exposures will not be overlooked, it is necessary to become more involved. This involvement should include a visual inspection of the client's property or a lengthy discussion with the client in order to obtain answers to the questions in the survey form.

Some risk analysis surveyors like to use an insurance survey form. However, it should be reemphasized that this type of form is normally designed to discover needs for insurance coverages and not to identify all the potential loss situations. Some surveyors prefer their own checklist form, such as the one contained in appendix 10A, and financial services professionals would probably incorporate a few additional questions necessary to prepare a complete list of all risks in the client's situation. If there are any doubts about the identification of risks, the financial planner should seek additional assistance from someone experienced in this task.

The first phase of risk analysis can now be completed. To illustrate how this might be done, assume that the circumstances of a client are as follows: Burt Beamer, aged 45, has a wife, aged 43, a son, aged 18, and a daughter, aged 16. Burt is a manager for a local firm and currently earns $78,000 annually. The Beamers purchased a home 5 years ago for $225,000. Last year they purchased a small cabin in the mountains for $45,000. They plan to use this cabin as much as possible during the summer months and occasionally on weekends during the balance of the year. They are also thinking about renting the cabin out periodically during the summer season. The Beamers own two automobiles, a 3-year-old station wagon and a one-year-old foreign compact.

Although this is a simplified example, a partial listing of the risks that the Beamer family faces is shown in table 10-1. In actual practice the planner should seek additional information from the Beamer family to complete the list of exposures. The planner would want to include other assets or property that might be owned or used by the Beamers. He or she would also be concerned with expanding the liability exposure to include any possible business pursuits and to investigate any other liability exposures, such as the use of nonowned autos. In this illustration, personal risks are limited to the premature death of Burt. In practice this area would be expanded to include premature death of Burt's spouse, risks associated with the loss of earning power because of periods of disability, the incurring of additional expenses for medical costs associated with accidents or illnesses, and the need for income at retirement. Even the needs under the premature death category might be expanded beyond those shown in this illustration.

TABLE 10-1
Risk Identification (Type of Risk)

Property risks
- Direct losses
  - Dwelling
  - Cabin
  - Furniture, clothing, etc. (dwelling)
  - Furniture, clothing, etc. (cabin)
  - Automobiles
- Indirect losses
  - Additional living expenses
  - Debris removal

Liability risks
- Owned premises (dwelling, cabin)
- Owned automobiles
- Personal activities

Personal risks
- Premature death (of Burt)
  - Cash for clean-up fund
  - Education fund
  - Mortgage redemption fund
  - Lifetime income for spouse

The risk-identification process may appear to be a relatively simple task. Some financial services professionals and clients may feel that it is a waste of time to formalize the risk-identification process. They need only be reminded that forgetting or neglecting the wrong risk could have disastrous financial consequences.

Risk Measurement

The second function of risk analysis is the measurement of the losses associated with the identified risks. As will be shown in table 10-2, the measurement of loss exposures should be the maximum possible loss associated with the event.

Theoretically, risk measurement should include information on loss severity and probability of occurrence. Measuring loss probabilities requires the compilation and interpretation of statistics, and in the single-risk situation associated with individuals and families, probabilities have little application. Also, in most single-risk situations the frequency of losses is so low that it does not permit the accumulation of sufficient data to have any degree of reliability. Therefore the major emphasis should be on the severity of the loss. When dealing with individual risks, it is safest to assume total loss and identify this as the maximum possible loss.

Property Risks

The easiest asset to measure for loss purposes is cash; each one dollar bill is worth one dollar (except, of course, when it is numismatic property or when problems of foreign exchange enter the picture). For property other than cash, however, risk measurement problems begin to emerge. Three key terms of the measurement process that need to be understood are (1) actual cash value, (2) replacement cost, and (3) depreciation.

Actual cash value is an insurance term used in many property insurance contracts. These contracts often limit the insurer's liability for damaged property to its actual cash value at the time of loss. Actual cash value has generally been defined as replacement cost less a reduction resulting from depreciation and obsolescence. This is normally expressed simply as

$$\text{Actual cash value} = \text{Replacement cost} - \text{Depreciation}$$

Actual cash value is sometimes a difficult measurement to understand, primarily because of the confusion that arises from the interpretations of *replacement cost* and *depreciation.* Although useful life is frequently used as a guideline in measuring depreciation, depreciation as a factor in measuring actual cash value differs from depreciation in an accounting sense. Depreciation is a function of the age of the asset, its use, its condition at the time of loss, and any other factor causing deterioration. In addition, anything that causes the property to become obsolete in any fashion is also included in the depreciation determination for purposes of calculating actual cash value.

Replacement cost is that cost necessary to replace or repair the damaged asset. For personal property this is replacement with a comparable asset at the current price. In the calculation of actual cash value, replacement cost would be reduced for the comparable age of the damaged property. For example, assume that an auto that had been purchased new 3 years ago for $11,995 was completely destroyed in an accident. The same auto purchased today would cost $15,000, which would be its replacement cost. The actual cash value is an amount sufficient to replace the destroyed auto with one of like age and condition. Note, however, that depreciation is deducted from the current price, not the original price. It is immaterial that the damaged auto cost $11,995 new 3 years ago. The actual cash value is $15,000 (replacement cost) less an allowance for depreciation.

When replacement cost is used for real property, such as a dwelling, it is normally interpreted to mean the *cost to rebuild the same type dwelling on the same site for the same type of occupancy and with materials of like kind and quality*. If the replacement cost for the dwelling is determined to be $160,000 and depreciation is $17,200, the measurement of the actual cash value will be

$$\begin{aligned}\text{Actual cash value} &= \text{Replacement cost} - \text{Depreciation}\\ &= \$160{,}000 - \$17{,}200\\ &= \$142{,}800\end{aligned}$$

There are several ways of estimating replacement cost. One method used for dwellings is to take the original construction cost and adjust it by one of the published construction cost indexes. A second method is the unit-measurement technique, a tabular process of calculating a base cost value by using a square-foot calculation for a given type of construction and type of dwelling (one-story, two-story, and so on), and then applying a geographic location adjustment factor to that value. A variation of this begins with a counting of rooms in the dwelling. Perhaps the most accurate valuation method is to have a complete survey made by a professional appraiser qualified to prepare replacement cost values. This would probably include a detailed physical inspection and study of any plans available in order that a complete list of labor and material costs could be determined.

Replacement cost has become the more practical measure of the maximum possible loss associated with a client's real property in pure-risk situations, especially when insurance is determined to be the technique most appropriate to treat the particular risk. Sometimes there is a temptation to use market value as the measurement of loss for real property. While this is the value that is most familiar to consumers and owners of real estate, market value is closely linked to supply and demand conditions, and caution should be exercised in using this value as the measurement of maximum possible loss for pure-risk situations.

Remember that pure risk is the possibility of loss or no loss; the concern is for the damage or destruction of property, not its transfer of ownership.

Methods of Estimating Replacement Cost

- Adjustment of original cost by published construction cost indexes
- Unit measurement: base cost per square foot for dwelling and construction type, adjusted by geographic location factor
- Survey by professional appraiser

Actually, destruction of real property from a pure-risk standpoint might even increase the market value of the property and therefore result in a profit to the owner. For example, suppose a dwelling is situated on a lot at a well-traveled intersection. This property would have market value based on its potential sale as a commercial establishment. If a fire totally destroyed this dwelling, the owner might actually realize an increase in market value for the property since the purchaser would not have to bear most of the cost of demolition in order to prepare the site for a new commercial building. However, if the owner is not interested in selling the property and wants to make the dwelling habitable again, the loss is the cost to repair the damage—the pure risk. This is measured on a replacement cost basis, which may differ substantially from market value.

For insurance purposes, the measurement of loss for personal property such as furniture and clothing has traditionally been the item's actual cash value. Actually, however, the maximum possible loss is the replacement cost of the particular item. For an extra premium, most insurance companies will provide replacement cost coverage on personal property. For this reason, and for the purpose of showing the value differences, the maximum possible loss for personal property (and for real property as well) is measured on both a replacement cost and actual-cash-value basis. An example of this is shown in table 10-2.

The loss measurement for personal property is further complicated by the fact that most clients do not keep an accurate list of all the personal property they own. For this reason, it is suggested that the data-gathering questionnaire used in the risk-identification function include a listing of specific items of property or clusters of types of property as an aid in formulating a closer approximation of the personal property owned by the client. Then the task becomes one of attaching a value, either replacement cost or actual cash value, to the items of personal property.

The measurement of loss to automobiles tends to be less complex than the measurement of value for a dwelling or personal property. Replacement cost, the

TABLE 10-2
Risk Identification and Measurement

Type of Risk	Maximum Possible Loss	
	Actual Cash Value	Replacement Cost
Property risks		
Direct losses		
Dwelling	$160,000	$200,000
Cabin	30,000	42,000
Furniture, clothing, etc. (dwelling)	60,000	90,000
Furniture, clothing, etc. (cabin)	4,000	7,500
Automobiles	19,000	28,000
Indirect losses		
Additional living expenses		9,600
Debris removal		3,500
Liability risks		
Owned premises (dwelling, cabin)		unlimited
Owned automobiles		unlimited
Personal activities		unlimited
Personal risks		
Premature death (of Burt)		
Cash for cleanup fund		50,000
Education fund		78,000
Mortgage redemption fund		137,000
Lifetime income for spouse		$1,100,000

cost of purchasing a brand new automobile of the same type, would be the maximum possible loss. However, since physical damage insurance for automobiles is written on an actual-cash-value basis, the loss measurement should be listed on this basis as well as on the replacement cost value. This will indicate for the owner the difference between the actual loss and the amount that the owner can reasonably expect to recover from an insurer. Values for automobiles are published in various "books" that provide a close estimate of the current actual cash value. However, it should be understood that the figures published in these books are for vehicles in average condition and may not apply to specific automobiles.

Finally, for measurement purposes some loss exposures listed under the property risk category are not costs of replacing property but are indirect expenses incurred because of damage to property. The best example of this for most individuals is the category of additional living expenses. These are the costs over and above normal living expenses that would be necessary to provide living accommodations, food, and transportation if a dwelling could not be occupied due to damage or destruction. An estimate of these expenses should be made as the measurement of this loss exposure.

Liability Risks

The measurement of liability risk is somewhat similar to that of indirect additional living expenses since they are both estimates of future dollar amounts. No perfect method has been developed for measuring the maximum possible dollar loss that individuals can suffer from the liability exposure. A client can enter into certain contractual arrangements that will limit the extent of liability, but in most cases the liability loss will depend upon the severity of the future accident and the amount the court awards to the injured parties (or the amount of the out-of-court settlement agreement).

It could be argued that the maximum possible liability loss is limited to the current accumulated wealth of the individual. To a certain extent this is correct since the balance of a judgment could be discharged by a declaration of bankruptcy. Unfortunately, the stigma of bankruptcy that would remain could hamper future business and personal activities. In addition, bankruptcy might not be permitted as a way of discharging some liability judgments. Since a liability loss could range anywhere from a few dollars to $1 million or more, it is appropriate to recognize some uncertainty about the measurement of the liability loss and to identify this amount as "unlimited."

Personal Risks

There are several ways of measuring the loss associated with personal risks. For example, the loss associated with premature death might simply be the aggregate dollar amount that would have been provided to the survivors by the deceased (presumably the breadwinner) on an annual basis over the future productive lifetime of that individual. The *human-life-value method* of measuring loss due to premature death is based on a calculation of the present value of a given dollar amount annually over a given number of years at some assumed interest rate.

Another common method of measuring the loss associated with premature death is to determine, at some assumed interest rate, the principal sum necessary to provide interest earnings comparable to the dollar contributions that would have been made to the survivors by the deceased. When this method is utilized, other sources of income and other income-producing assets can be considered in arriving at the final capital sum required.

Another method of determining the loss associated with premature death (and the method used in this chapter) is to identify and attach a dollar amount to the specific financial needs of the survivors. For the Beamer family, the lump-sum cash needs are identified in table 10-2 as a cleanup fund, education fund, and mortgage redemption fund. The income need was identified as a lifetime income for the surviving spouse.

In table 10-2, the dollar amount shown for the cleanup fund is an estimate of the amount needed for last illness expenses, funeral costs, outstanding debts, probate expenses, federal and state estate and inheritance taxes, and so forth. The dollar amount for the education fund is the present value of the projected future costs of educating the two Beamer children. Planning for future education expenses has become a common part of the financial planning process, and the dollar amount needed for this item would most likely be provided in some other part of the total financial planning process. If not, some time should be spent in developing an estimate of these costs. The amount for the mortgage is typically the current unpaid balance shown in the amortization schedule.

The measurement of the amount needed to fund the lifetime income for the surviving spouse requires calculations beyond the scope of this chapter. In the planner's discussions with the client it was determined that, in the event of his premature death, Burt wanted his widow to have the equivalent purchasing power of $4,000 per month throughout her lifetime. To calculate the present value of a principal sum needed to satisfy this objective, it is necessary to make assumptions regarding future rates of inflation and future rates of interest earnings. For this case, these assumptions were 4.5 percent and 6.5 percent, respectively. It was also assumed that upon reaching age 65 Mrs. Beamer would qualify for an inflation adjusted benefit equal to $1,000 per month from Burt's social security. Based on these assumptions and a projection of Mrs. Beamer's longevity of life, the current principal sum needed is calculated to be $1,100,000. This is the amount entered in table 10-2 as the maximum possible loss for the personal risk exposure.

At this point, the risk identification and measurement functions can be completed. Table 10-2 illustrates the maximum possible loss values that were determined for the partial list of risks facing the Beamer family.

Risk Evaluation

Once all the risks have been identified and an appropriate value has been determined as the measure of the maximum possible loss, the final function in risk analysis is to evaluate these risks from the standpoint of their potential financial impact upon the client. The financial services professional can assist in this process by having the client assess the seriousness of each potential loss on his or her financial status and by ranking the various risks according to their severity. One method of showing this is to categorize losses as *serious, moderate,* or *minimal* depending on each client's circumstances. The risks listed for the Beamer family in table 10-2 are evaluated using this method in the Risk Impact Chart (table 10-3).

TABLE 10-3
Risk Impact Chart

Serious
- Liability losses
  - Owned premises (dwelling, cabin)
  - Owned automobiles
  - Personal activities
- Property losses
  - Dwelling
  - Cabin
  - Furniture, clothing, etc. (dwelling)
- Personal losses
  - Cash for cleanup fund
  - Mortgage redemption fund
  - Lifetime income for spouse

Moderate
- Property losses
  - Furniture, clothing, etc. (cabin)
  - Automobile (foreign compact)
  - Additional living expenses
- Personal losses
  - Education fund

Minimal
- Property losses
  - Debris removal
  - Automobile (station wagon)

One additional comment should be made about the evaluation of risks. It is a mistake to view these risks as isolated individual events; for example, the fire that causes damage to the dwelling should not be considered as a loss isolated from the concurrent loss due to fire damage of the furniture contained in that dwelling. All the losses that may result from a single event should be combined into one unit to obtain a true measure of the maximum possible loss. Therefore the fire damage to the dwelling and furniture should be considered as one loss and the combined total should be utilized to determine the total financial impact on the individual or family.

RISK-TREATMENT PLANNING

The second step in the risk management process is determining what to do about the risks enumerated in the risk-analysis step, that is, evaluating the alternative techniques for handling risks. The techniques typically available to individuals and families are grouped in two categories: loss control and loss financing.

Loss Control

Loss control (sometimes referred to as risk control) is concerned with the precontact, contact, and postcontact stages of losses that could have an adverse financial impact upon the individual or family. Loss control is concerned with reducing the probability that events resulting in financial loss will occur and minimizing the magnitude of those losses that do occur.

Many items of real or personal property can be repaired or replaced if they are damaged or destroyed, but even when property is covered by an insurance policy financial loss may result since many insurance policies leave a portion of the loss unreimbursed. In some cases, damaged property cannot be repaired or replaced, nor can a proper substitute for that property be found. Losses associated with injury or death can be compensated with money, but regardless of the sum, money is frequently not the true measure of the loss in these situations. Therefore as these brief examples indicate, loss-control activities are an important part of risk management. Three loss-control techniques are examined: risk avoidance, loss prevention, and loss reduction.

Risk Avoidance

The objective of risk avoidance is the elimination of the given activity or condition that gave rise to the risk so that the possibility of a loss becomes nonexistent. While this method is potentially the most powerful risk-treatment action, in many ways it is a very difficult treatment technique for an individual or family to practice. For example, if an individual is concerned about the liability loss exposure that arises from the ownership or use of an automobile, the application of risk avoidance would call for the complete elimination of the ownership and use of automobiles. In today's society this could be an extremely difficult objective to accomplish. Furthermore, if an individual currently owns an automobile, a strict interpretation of the avoidance technique would require the individual to demolish the automobile rather than to sell it and thereby transfer the risk to someone else, a practice that is difficult to accept in reality.

To take a more practical case, the existence of a swimming pool in one's backyard increases the liability exposure on the premises. An individual concerned about this liability exposure would practice avoidance by never purchasing a home that had a swimming pool in the backyard, never installing a swimming pool in the backyard, or filling in or destroying a swimming pool that currently exists in the backyard.

Similarly, certain types of animals are known to be vicious or to become vicious at times. Risk avoidance would be practiced by never owning such an animal or by destroying such an animal if currently owned. Concern about the possibility of a valuable fur coat being damaged or stolen would cause an individual practicing risk avoidance to resist purchasing a fur coat or to destroy any such coat that is currently owned. The same would be true for many other types of personal property.

Sometimes individuals can practice risk avoidance when the risk concerns the ownership of real property, for example, by living in rented property rather than owning a home. Although the individuals in this example avoid the loss exposures associated with the ownership of real property, they should be made aware that some of the same types of loss exposure may be acquired through the rental of property. In other words, the avoidance of one risk may create another.

Obviously then, risk avoidance can be a difficult risk-treatment technique to apply. It is most effective if considered in the planning stages, that is, when a client is contemplating the purchase of a home or an auto, rather than after the fact when demolition of the asset might be the only avoidance alternative. In any case, it is virtually impossible to avoid all risks and it is therefore necessary to consider techniques that will forestall or minimize the losses.

Loss Prevention

Loss prevention, the attempt to control inescapable risks and forestall losses, must precede the occurrence of a loss and is directed at reducing the frequency of loss. Loss-prevention actions tend to be directed at hazards or conditions that increase the likelihood of a loss occurring. For example, since smoking in bed tends to increase the likelihood of fire, and smoking itself tends to increase the likelihood of future medical complications, a loss-prevention action for both of these risks would be to stop smoking. Similarly, since consumption of alcohol combined with driving can increase the likelihood of an automobile accident, loss prevention would be practiced by not consuming alcoholic beverages or by not driving after having done so.

While these examples are "don't do" activities, loss-prevention actions can also be positive in nature. For example, the construction of a fence around the swimming pool in one's backyard is an action designed to make it more difficult for individuals to gain access to the pool and therefore reduces the likelihood of a liability loss due to someone's use of the swimming pool without the property owner's knowledge. Some other examples of loss prevention activities include the following: proper servicing of one's automobile in order to reduce the possibility of an accident due to mechanical failure, taking a driver education program in order to reduce the frequency of accidental losses, keeping matches out of a child's reach in order to prevent fire, and picking up a child's toys from the floor and the steps to prevent someone from stepping on one of the toys and causing a fall and a potential injury.

It is sometimes difficult to measure the effectiveness of loss prevention activities since most types of losses occur infrequently. It is also difficult to know how many times loss did not occur because prevention measures were introduced. The goal of loss prevention activities is to eliminate the occurrence of the event, but since not all loss exposures can be totally prevented, some effort should also be made to minimize the magnitude of the loss.

Loss Reduction

Loss reduction is a technique directed at reducing loss severity. It can be used before, during, or after a loss has occurred and is designed to minimize the magnitude of the loss and its financial impact on a family or individual.

Two examples of loss reduction actions directed at the possibility of fire are maintaining fire extinguishers in the home to extinguish flames before they spread and cause extensive damage to the property and installing smoke detectors to alert inhabitants that there is a fire so that they may extinguish the fire or call the fire department. Note, however, that these methods have no value as loss reduction unless they are properly serviced and all household members are instructed in their use. Also, although it is discussed here as a risk reduction action, installing smoke detectors also serves as a loss-prevention action since individuals should be instructed to vacate the property when the alarm sounds, thereby reducing the likelihood of death or injury due to fire. Most insurance companies now give a small discount in the premium for the proper installation of smoke detectors.

Loss-Control Techniques

- Risk avoidance
- Loss prevention
- Loss reduction

Loss-Control Planning

The techniques of risk avoidance, loss prevention, and loss reduction should not be considered separately; the best alternative is often a combination of these actions. In the evaluation of a particular risk, three questions should be asked. Can this risk be avoided? If not, how can the loss be prevented? If the event and a loss do occur, how can the loss be minimized?

There are costs associated with initiating and maintaining loss-control activities. These costs should be compared with the benefits of the loss-control action. This may be difficult to evaluate, and some judgment may be necessary to make a positive decision to engage in loss control when costs appear high relative to benefits.

Loss Financing

Since some losses will occur, it is necessary to plan how to fund these losses. Although several techniques are used by individuals, the primary methods are retention, insurance, and, in some situations, noninsurance transfer. This last technique is examined first.

Noninsurance Transfer

Although insurance is the form of risk transfer most commonly practiced, there are noninsurance means of transferring risk. Noninsurance transfers are useful but are more often initiated by businesses than by individuals; individuals are more frequently the recipients of the transfer. For example, when someone orders merchandise through a catalog, the supplier may ship the goods F.O.B. point of origin. This means that the supplier has transferred to the purchaser responsibility for damage to the goods while in transit. As a second example, transportation companies may use a bill of lading to limit their liability. The limit is usually expressed in dollars per unit of weight, and if the limitation is low, some of the risk of damage to the goods being transported may have been shifted to the owner of those goods. A third case may occur when property is left in the custody of others for such purposes as storage, cleaning, or repair. Normally, it is possible to have the bailee, the temporary custodian of the property, assume full responsibility for such property.

When one party assumes the liability of another for bodily injury or property damage as an incidental obligation in contracts dealing with services, premises, or products, the transfer is typically referred to as a *hold-harmless agreement.* Such agreements are common in business-to-business dealings, and perhaps more common than generally realized in business-to-individual dealings. One example of the latter is the leasing of dwellings or apartments. Under the lease the landlord may be able to transfer to the tenant financial responsibility for damage to the property and for bodily injuries to third parties that, in the absence of the lease, would be borne by the landlord. Although the landlord is still legally liable to these third parties, the tenant can agree by means of the lease to finance any losses that may otherwise have to be paid by the landlord.

Retention

Many individuals purchase insurance for pure risks and fail to consider other loss-financing techniques. Yet it is obvious that everyone retains some risks, either consciously or unconsciously. Voluntary risk retention can be a useful tool of risk management. However, involuntary or unintentional risk retention due to failure to identify exposures can be a serious problem.

Risk retention is the process of financing or paying one's own losses, and as such is frequently referred to as self-assumption of risk or self-insurance (although this is technically incorrect). In cases where retention is consciously practiced, an individual may set aside funds earmarked for a particular risk. When the loss occurs, these funds are available to pay for the amount lost. However, this formal method of employing retention is rarely practiced—most retention is practiced informally by covering losses with funds in a savings account, by borrowing, or by paying for the loss on an out-of-pocket basis.

People may choose risk retention when the maximum possible loss is too small to cause financial hardship—few people would insure against the risk of accidental loss of a 98-cent ballpoint pen. Conversely, risks for which the maximum possible loss is quite large may be retained because the probability of the loss is extremely small. There is some danger in this practice for individuals since the application of probability is not appropriate for the single exposure unit of the individual. For example, a young person might decide not to purchase life insurance because of the small probability of death at a young age. Retention of the risk for this reason could have very serious consequences.

Retention is frequently practiced even when insurance is purchased for a particular risk. For example, a deductible may apply to losses covered by the insurance policy purchased, in which case the insured is retaining the first dollar amount of the loss. Similarly, the exposure to loss by causes excluded under an insurance contract is retained by the policyowner. These loss exposures may have to be retained by the policyowner simply because there is no alternative. Retention is also practiced when insurance policies exclude the loss to certain types of property or property at certain locations. Other provisions or exclusions in insurance policies may also preclude coverage for particular types of loss. Explaining the need for this sort of retention to purchasers of insurance is an important service provided by the financial services professional.

Insurance

The discussion of insurance in this chapter is designed to provide an understanding of insurance as a risk-treatment technique. As a risk-financing method, insurance involves a transfer of the financial burden of risk through a contract for a price (premium). In addition, insurance is a loss-sharing device and a system for reducing risk. This and the following section briefly examine some of the fundamental principles underlying the insurance technique. Applications of the insurance technique will be the topic of chapter 11.

Definition of Insurance. There are many definitions of insurance. Insurance is sometimes defined as the business of transferring pure risks by means of a two-party contract. Transfer, then, is the primary function according to this definition, and this is accomplished through use of a contract. A characteristic that distinguishes the insurance technique from other transfer devices is that insurance is practiced as a business.

In the two-party contract, the person who transfers the risk is known as the *insured,* and the party who assumes the risk is the *insurer.* The function of the insurer is to accept the pure risks of many individuals. Since the act of transferring risk does not affect the possibility of the loss, insurance does not replace the need for loss control. However, an interesting phenomenon takes place as the insurer accepts a greater number of similar risks: risk is actually reduced.

To understand this last statement, it is necessary to review the insurance process. As insurers accept insureds, they pool those with similar characteristics, and the combination of many similar exposure units permits the operation of the law of large numbers. From a statistical standpoint, as the number of exposure units increases, the deviation of actual from expected experience diminishes. As the potential margin of error decreases, so also does uncertainty about losses. This increased knowledge allows the insurer a greater predictability of probable losses and results in a reduction of risk for the insurer.

This increased knowledge of probable loss frequency and severity also means that the insurer can determine a more suitable charge (premium) for accepting the transfer of risk from the insured. The premium becomes a known cost (in most cases), which replaces the unknown cost of a potential loss. The insurer, in effect, collects a small premium from many and redistributes most of it to the few who suffer loss.

The definition of insurance can be summarized in either a process or functional fashion. As a process, insurance is a transfer of pure risk to a professional risk bearer. From a functional standpoint, insurance is the substitution of a small, certain loss for the possibility of a large, uncertain loss.

Subjects for Insurance. During the risk-identification function, dwellings, personal property, automobiles, and similar items were listed as risks subject to damage or destruction. However, the underlying question is, what would cause these losses to occur? The causes of loss must be considered in order to determine whether the insurance technique is actually available as a method for treating these particular risks. Insurance does not cover every loss that can occur: insurers look for characteristics that allow a given cause of loss to qualify as an insurable one. Although there are insurable causes of loss that fail to meet every requirement, the following are examples of characteristics that insurers find desirable.

The first desirable characteristic for an insurable cause of loss is the existence of a large number of homogeneous exposures (exposures that have approximately the same expectations of loss). This is necessary to permit the operation of the law of large numbers, discussed earlier, and to allow the insurer to achieve a meaningful estimate of probable losses and to maintain equity among insureds.

A second desirable characteristic is that the cause of loss insured against should be accidental and unintentional; that is, the insured should not have control over when the loss occurs. It should be fortuitous or subject to chance. If a deliberately caused loss were to be paid, moral hazard would be substantially increased.

Third, an insurable cause of loss should produce a loss that is definite as to when it occurred and how much was lost. While difficult to satisfy, these requirements are nevertheless important since their absence may introduce an element of moral hazard and make coverage questions difficult to resolve.

A fourth important characteristic of an insurable cause of loss is that the exposed units should be independent. For example, the destruction of one insured dwelling should not affect the probability that another will burn. The group of insureds should not be exposed to an incalculable catastrophic hazard. If catastrophic occurrences are predictable, however, the cause of loss may be insurable.

Loss-Financing Techniques

- Noninsurance transfer
- Voluntary risk retention
- Insurance

Loss-Financing Planning

The evaluation of loss-financing techniques is an important step in risk-treatment planning. It begins with an evaluation of the client's capacity to safely assume certain risks so that retention can be practiced at its most effective level. Where retention cannot be practiced, the transfer technique can sometimes be applied.

Although noninsurance transfer of risk is not widely used by individuals, it can be an effective means of financing losses. However, noninsurance transfers should be approached cautiously. The parties to whom risk financing is transferred may be unable to fund losses, thereby rendering the transfer ineffective. Finally, the price of transfer should be compared with other techniques for treating the risk.

There is also a price associated with the use of insurance as a loss-financing technique. The premiums for insurance should be reasonable in relation to the potential financial loss, and the cost should be compared with the cost of alternative techniques. Most individuals have only a limited number of premium dollars with which to purchase protection against insurable losses. The usc of premium dollars to protect against relatively small potential losses generally results in failure to cover more significant loss causes. This problem can be overcome by employing the *large-loss principle*.

The use of insurance is best suited to the handling of low-frequency, high-severity risks. The large-loss principle suggests that, in the purchase of insurance, first priority should be given to exposures that might cause significant financial loss. As noted earlier, the definition of a large loss differs among individuals. However, risks listed as serious during the risk evaluation process should, by implication, be large losses and should receive first priority in the use of insurance.

Risk-treatment planning is an extremely important stage in the risk management process. The evaluation of risk treatment alternatives leads to decisions on implementation of specific programs that may affect the continued solvency and well-being of families and individuals.

SELECTING THE INSURANCE TECHNIQUE

Insurance will play a major role in risk treatment for most families and individuals. Because of this, it is imperative that all financial services professionals have some understanding of how insurance functions and of the principles underlying insurance contracts.

Many questions arise about the use of insurance as a method of treating risk. For example: Under what circumstances would the insurer be responsible for the loss? What events, causes of loss, property, or sources of liability are covered? Whose life or health is covered? What persons, losses, locations, and time period are covered? Are there any special conditions that do not fall into any of these categories that may suspend or terminate the coverage? If the insurer is responsible for the loss, how much will it pay? And finally, what steps must the insured take following a loss? These are just a sampling of questions that may arise in any discussion of insurance. They cannot all be answered here, but the next section of this chapter will review some of the basic components of an insurance contract, the important principle of indemnity, and some material vital to the adjustment of losses under insurance contracts.

Insurance Contract Components

The provisions in an insurance contract are typically classified into four categories: declarations, insuring agreements, exclusions, and conditions. Some contracts clearly label these categories. In others, the divisions are not clearly discernible, but the content of these categories can be found in the contract.

Declarations

The declarations page is extremely important and should be reviewed thoroughly whenever an insurance contract is issued. This page clearly identifies the insured, describes the property, activity, or life being insured, and states the types of coverages purchased, the applicable policy limits, and the term of the coverage. The information that completes the declarations page is typically obtained from the application for the insurance coverage. It is typically the only material that is typed in the printed policy. It is important that this material be verified for its completeness and accuracy.

Insuring Agreement

The insuring agreement states what the insurer promises to do. In a life insurance policy, for example, the insurer simply promises to pay the face amount on due proof of the death of the insured. An automobile insurance policy may have several insuring agreements—for example, for liability coverage the agreement might state that the company will pay damages for which the insured becomes legally responsible because of an auto accident. The homeowners policy states that the insurance company insures against risks of direct loss. Typically, the insuring agreement describes the characteristics of the events covered under the contract. Certain terms used in the contract may also be defined in this section.

Exclusions

The coverage provided by an insurance contract is limited by exclusions. They may exclude certain causes of loss, property, sources of liability, persons, losses, locations, or time periods.

There are many reasons for exclusions in insurance policies. An exclusion may be contained in one policy because it is more appropriate for coverage to be provided in a different policy. For example, damage to automobiles is excluded from homeowners policies because such damage would more appropriately be covered in an automobile insurance policy. Some losses are excluded because the cause of loss does not meet the characteristics for being insurable (as discussed earlier), and some losses, such as ordinary wear and tear of property, should not be expected to be covered by insurance. Another example, the freezing of an automobile radiator is not covered because an insured could easily prevent this loss with proper servicing of the automobile. Other types of losses are excluded because they are the concern of only a handful of people who can obtain separate coverage on those specific exposures. An example of this would be the exclusion in automobile policies for travel in Mexico.

An understanding of exclusions by financial services professionals and their clients is even more important when a particular policy is an "all risks" contract. Policies that purport to cover all risks typically do not really do so; they usually state that they cover all risks "except," and then go on to list exclusions. The homeowners policy is a good example of this. For years some forms of homeowners policies were referred to as providing all risks coverage. Although the exclusions were clearly indicated, the implications associated with providing all risks coverage created loss adjustment problems and litigation. The broad coverage now provided by these homeowners policies is against the "risks of direct loss." The policy then goes on to list causes of loss that are not covered.

Sometimes the wording of an exclusion is difficult for the purchaser of the insurance to understand. For example, the purchaser of a health insurance policy may not understand that preexisting conditions are not covered. Exclusions provide an excellent opportunity for the financial services professional to educate consumers by going through the exclusions listed in the client's policy.

Conditions

The conditions define terms used in other parts of the contract and may describe the rights and obligations of the insured and the insurer following a loss. They may also prescribe certain events or actions that must be satisfied before the insurer is liable for a loss. Examples of some conditions are discussed later in this chapter.

Other Components

There are many other provisions in the insurance contract that are important to an understanding of the coverage provided (one of these, policy limits, will be discussed later in this chapter). In addition, it is common to have one or more endorsements or riders attached to the insurance policy. Endorsements and riders modify the contract in some fashion such as by adding or deleting coverage, changing the description of the locations or property covered, or placing restrictions on what the insurer may or may not do.

Insurance Contract Components

- Declarations
- Insuring agreement
- Exclusions
- Conditions
- Other components

Principle of Indemnity

Many property, liability, and health insurance policies are contracts of indemnity. The principle of indemnity, often said to be the cardinal principle of insurance, states that a person may not collect more than his or her actual loss in the event of the occurrence of an insured peril (cause of loss). Indemnity contracts require the insurance company to reimburse the insured for the "actual cash value" of the loss sustained. As noted earlier, some insurance policies, such as homeowners policies, settle losses on the basis of replacement cost rather than actual cash value. Although this is a violation of the principle of indemnity, it has become an accepted practice. Other policies, such as life insurance contracts, simply pay the dollar amount stipulated on the face of the contract since life insurance contracts are not intended to be interpreted as contracts of indemnity.

The enforcement of the indemnity principle in insurance contracts includes three additional concepts: insurable interest, subrogation, and duplicate insurance. The purpose of these concepts is to minimize the possibility that the insured will profit from the occurrence of the event covered in the insurance contract.

Insurable Interest

A legal requirement under the *principle of insurable interest* is that the insured be able to demonstrate a loss to himself or herself in order to collect under the contract. Insurable interest is that relationship to the person or thing insured that the law requires so that the contract is not a mere wager. The basis for insurable interest in property and liability contracts includes (1) a property right, (2) a contract right, and (3) legal liability. If insurance is to be purchased, an insurable interest is essential (although in property and liability insurance the insurable interest need exist only at the time of loss and not at the inception of the contract).

Although life insurance is not considered a contract of indemnity, the requirement of an insurable interest does apply. It is generally accepted in law that an individual has an unrestricted insurable interest in his or her own life. Beyond this, the basis for the existence of an insurable interest can be found in a close family relationship or a financial relationship. A major difference between a life insurance contract and a property or liability insurance contract is that for life insurance the insurable interest must exist only at the inception of the contract.

Subrogation

Subrogation is a process in insurance whereby the insurer is substituted for the insured for the purpose of claiming indemnity from a third person for a covered loss. Once the insurance company pays a loss to an insured, the insurer takes over the rights of that insured to recover from a third party for the loss. For example, if a client's automobile is damaged in an accident where the other party is clearly at fault, the client may wish to avoid possible delays in repairing the auto by having his or her own insurance company pay for the damage under the collision coverage. Once this settlement has taken place, the client's insurance company can begin proceedings against the party at fault in an attempt to recover the amount paid to the client. The client is not able to recover twice—once from his or her own insurance company and again from the wrongdoer. Subrogation reinforces the principle of indemnity by preventing double recovery.

Duplicate Insurance

Finally, the inclusion of clauses in insurance contracts regarding the existence of other insurance minimizes the possibility that the insured will profit from the occurrence of an event. Typically such clauses provide that policies covering the same risk must share in the loss on some predetermined basis. The purpose is to discourage the insured from taking out duplicate policies with different insurers in the expectation of recovering more than his or her actual loss.

Loss Adjustments

The natural presumption among those who purchase insurance is that the insurance company will pay or reimburse the insured if a loss is suffered. Earlier in this chapter it was stated that insurers collect small premiums from many clients and redistribute them to the few who suffer loss. This functional interpretation of insurance is widely accepted. However, it should also be understood that the insurer is under no obligation to do anything until it has been notified of a loss. When and how this notification takes place and what the amount of the loss payment will be are questions important for the client's understanding of the way insurance contracts fulfill their promises, and for the purpose of counseling clients in their effective purchase of insurance.

Initiating the Loss Adjustment

Insurance contracts contain conditions setting forth the procedures that the insured must follow in submitting a claim. They may be very simple, as in a life insurance policy where the requirement is the submission of due proof of death. While some major medical policies may include a provision stating that a notice of claim must be submitted in writing within 20 days after the commencement of any loss covered by the policy, most current major medical policies simply include a provision stating that notice of a claim may be submitted as soon as is reasonably possible. Once a notice of claim has been received, the major medical policy states that the company will then furnish to the claimant such forms as are necessary to complete the proof of loss. This written proof of loss must then be completed and furnished to the insurance company within 90 days.

Homeowners and personal auto policies contain conditions setting forth the insured's duties after a loss (or accident) occurs. The first requirement is normally prompt notice to the company (or agent). This requirement is followed by a list of additional duties, such as notification of the police if the cause of loss is theft or cooperation with the insurance company in the investigation, settlement, or defense of any claim or suit where third parties might be involved. Eventually, the insurance company requires some form of written proof of loss. If personal property is included in the loss, the insurer will most likely ask for an inventory of the damaged property. Preparing such an inventory can be a difficult task since people tend not to remember all details about all their personal property, as was indicated earlier in this chapter in the identification of risks function in the risk management process.

The period following an event that causes loss can be very stressful. During this period the financial services professional should provide as much assistance as possible to aid the client in processing a claim with an insurance company. If the financial services professional represents an insurance company, he or she should be thoroughly familiar with the requirements of that company in the total claim process in order to readily give a client proper assistance.

Policy Limitations on Amounts Payable

After the required notice of claim and proof of loss have been filed, the insured and insurer move into the settlement phase of the loss adjustment. Unfortunately, insureds are sometimes not happy with the loss adjustment, often because of a general lack of understanding of the provisions and clauses contained in the insurance contract. One of the most common causes of disagreement over the amount of a loss settlement results from the actual-cash-value basis for settling many property damage claims, since insureds prefer that the item be replaced or simply that replacement cost be the basis of settlement.

Policy Limitations on Amounts Payable

- Deductibles
- Time limitations
- Dollar limitations
- Coinsurance

There are several other clauses contained in insurance contracts that also act to limit the amount payable under the policy. These include deductibles, time limitations, dollar limitations, and coinsurance clauses. Of these, the deductible is perhaps the most visible limiting clause and the most easily understood by insureds. The deductible is simply the amount of money that must be paid by the insured before the insurance company will become liable on the loss. Time limitations also affect the total amount of dollar coverage and are quite common in health insurance contracts, for example, where benefits are payable only for a stated number of days, weeks, or months. Time limitations may also be used to restrict benefits to the amount of time it would take under normal conditions to repair or replace damaged property. Most insurance contracts provide for maximum dollar limits for recovery of losses.

A coinsurance feature means different things in different insurance policies. For example, in major medical health insurance policies, coinsurance refers to a sharing of the costs—for example, 80 percent to be paid by the insurer and 20 percent by the insured—typically between the deductible and the maximum dollar limit in the policy. With this feature the insured is thus required to participate in the costs of medical care.

The coinsurance provision in property insurance policies is quite different. Here, coinsurance penalizes an insured who does not carry a sufficient amount of insurance in relation to the value of the insured property. Under these conditions, the insured shares in the loss only if the requirements of the coinsurance provision are not satisfied.

Although homeowners policies do not contain a coinsurance clause, the loss settlement provisions are very similar. Homeowners policies require that, at the time of loss, the amount of insurance carried on the damaged dwelling be 80 percent or more of the full replacement cost of the dwelling at the time the loss occurs. If the amount of insurance carried is less than 80 percent of the replacement cost, the insurer agrees to pay the greater of the actual cash value of the loss or a proportion of the cost to repair or replace the dwelling determined by the ratio of the amount of insurance carried to the amount of insurance required. This can be expressed as a formula:

$$\frac{\text{Amount of insurance carried}}{\text{Amount of insurance required}} \text{ x Loss} = \text{Recovery}$$

The following example will illustrate the operation of this loss settlement provision. As indicated in table 10-2, Burt Beamer's dwelling has a replacement cost value of $200,000. If Burt carried at least 80 percent of this value ($160,000) on the dwelling, a loss to the dwelling would be settled on the replacement-cost basis, subject, of course, to the policy limit. However, if Burt carried less than $160,000, there would be a calculation of both the replacement cost value of the damage and the actual cash value of the damage sustained. Suppose Burt carried $120,000 on the dwelling and suffered a loss with a replacement cost value of $20,000. The application of the above formula would be as follows:

$$\frac{\$120{,}000}{\$160{,}000} \text{ x } \$20{,}000 = \$15{,}000$$

If the actual cash value of the loss is greater than $15,000, the loss is settled on that actual-cash-value basis. If actual cash value is less than $15,000, the loss recovery is $15,000. Note that in this situation Burt Beamer would be sharing in the loss because an inadequate amount of insurance to value was carried. As illustrated in this example, it is important to understand replacement cost on dwellings and to make sure that clients purchase a sufficient amount of insurance for their homeowners coverage on the dwelling.

RISK-TREATMENT PLAN IMPLEMENTATION

The final step in the risk management process is implementing the program of loss control and loss financing that has been formulated to meet the identified risks. Here the discussion will be limited to selecting the proper insurance coverage and the role financial services professionals play in this plan implementation.

Preparing the Plan

The financial services professional is now ready to formulate a plan for the utilization of insurance as a technique for treating the risks faced by the client. In performing this step, he or she should be concerned with matching particular insurance policies to the various risks identified and measured in the risk-analysis step.

An important step in proposing insurance coverages to meet specified risks is to rank in order of importance the various insurance policies available. One practical approach to identifying a rank or priority for the various insurance coverages is to list the risks according to the seriousness of their financial impact upon the client. This was done for the Beamer family in table 10-3, where risks were listed according to the categories *serious, moderate,* and *minimal.* The first priority in the use or purchase of insurance should be the risks identified as "serious."

One technique for exhibiting a plan of insurance utilization to the client is to list the insurance contracts according to their desirability as methods of meeting identified risks. This can be done by breaking down into the categories of *essential, desirable*, and *available* the insurance contracts that would take priority in the utilization of the client's premium dollars.

A sample of a listing of insurance policies for the Beamer family is shown in table 10-4. This list does not mention insurance coverage for two of the loss exposures that were identified as being in the serious category: liability at premises owned and liability arising out of personal activities. A financial services professional who understands the homeowners policy would realize that these liability loss exposures are covered by section II of the homeowners policy, but the client might assume that important risks have been forgotten. For this reason it would be appropriate that the listing of insurance policies, at least in the essential and desirable categories, include a brief description of the recommended insurance contracts. For example, where a homeowners policy has been recommended, the description should include the identification of property covered, limits on property, liability coverage, and the various extensions of coverage provided in this comprehensive package policy.

Since the description of insurance policies is the subject of chapter 11, the descriptions for the Beamer family have been omitted from table 10-4. However, since the current replacement cost of the dwelling does appear, a dollar amount can be shown that will satisfy the loss settlement provision in the contract (a minimum of 80 percent of the replacement cost), with the replacement cost as the maximum. Dollar values can be inserted for the liability limits in the homeowners policy and the personal auto policy, but these will have to be coordinated with the requirement of the personal umbrella liability policy.

The whole life insurance policy on Burt Beamer's life is for the purpose of satisfying the cash need for the cleanup fund. The face amount for this policy was taken from table 10-2, but a different face amount could appear because of other cash needs for the Beamer family that could be integrated into this policy. The amount of the mortgage redemption policy would depend on the current outstanding indebtedness. The income need for Burt's survivors is based on the objectives and assumptions developed earlier in this chapter.

TABLE 10-4
Insurance Planning

Essential
1. Personal auto policy—$300,000 liability
2. Homeowners form 3—$180,000 dwelling
   $100,000 liability
3. Personal umbrella liability—$2 million
4. Dwelling form on cabin—$40,000
5. Whole life insurance policy on Burt—$50,000
6. Life insurance on Burt—$1,100,000 to provide lifetime income to surviving spouse

Desirable
1. Dwelling form for personal property (cabin)—$4,000
2. Personal auto policy—ACV for physical damage to compact auto
3. Mortgage redemption policy—$137,000

Available
1. Personal auto policy—ACV for physical damage to station wagon
2. Life insurance on Burt—$78,000 for education fund

A plan to use insurance as a technique for treating risks cannot be formulated in isolation from other parts of the financial plan or from insurance the client may already have. For example, it is highly probable that the client already has purchased a homeowners policy, an auto policy and life insurance. The client's employer probably provides employee benefits for health care financing, life insurance, income replacement for periods of disability, and retirement, and social security will provide income during retirement. The financial plan may indicate techniques other than insurance for the attainment of desired retirement income levels.

The end result of insurance planning should be an integrative approach to solving the protection needs of the client. It should indicate what gaps or overlaps exist in present insurance coverage, reinforce the value of insurance protection, and enhance the overall validity of the financial services professional's interest in serving the needs of the client.

Role of the Financial Services Professional

The role of the financial services professional in risk-treatment plan implementation can take several different directions. First, he or she may feel that the task is complete at the presentation of the risk-treatment plan and request that the client implement the plan in conjunction with a professional insurance specialist. A second alternative is to provide complete assistance to the client in the implementation of the plan. If the financial services professional is a licensed insurance agent, the type of assistance provided should be obvious.

The role of the financial services professional who is not a licensed insurance agent will, of necessity, be much more general than the role of a licensed agent. There are three areas in which such a financial services professional can provide clients with information about insurance companies: financial stability, services provided, and premium costs for the coverage proposed.

Although there are various types of insurance companies, as the companies grow in size, the distinction between stock and mutual, for example, tends to become less distinct. Rather than attempting to differentiate between the types of companies, the financial services professional should identify financially stable firms and be able to state with some confidence that the selection of a given company is satisfactory from a financial stability standpoint. As a minimum reference on a particular company, the financial services professional may consult a publication such as *Best's Insurance Reports* for a description of an insurer's management, general underwriting policy, and present financial data.

Service is a second area to consider in the selection of insurance. Service takes many forms, including the ability to provide the type of insurance coverage desired, fairness in settling claims, and provision of efficient policyowner assistance. If the company cannot provide the specific insurance contract that is desired, there is little need to go beyond this point. However, if the desired policy is available, the professional should know how the policyowner is going to be serviced in the future. An important area of service is claims payment and administration. The financial services professional should seek information about the company's ability to handle all claims and its inclination to provide the proper claim service. The client will also be interested in miscellaneous administrative services, such as changes in the policy, the address, or the named insureds. The company should be able to provide prompt and courteous service. For claims and policyowner services the client will deal with an agent or a company representative.

The third area to consider is cost. In insurance planning for individuals, the only element of cost is typically the premium outlay (perhaps net of dividends) necessary to purchase the desired insurance protection. This may involve some balancing between the insurance transfer and the level of retention (deductibles and policy limits). In reality, decisions of this nature would be considered in the risk-treatment planning step of the risk management process. To assist the client, the financial services professional should provide representative insurance premium figures, or at least establish a contact with someone who could provide the appropriate premium quotations.

The financial services professional has identified and measured risks and recommended a risk-treatment plan. Proper assistance in the purchase of insurance protection and other risk-treatment techniques must follow.

Role of Financial Services Professionals Who Are Not Licensed Property/Casualty Insurance Agents

- Identify financially stable insurers
- Screen insurers for service quality
- Compare costs

ROLE OF RISK MANAGEMENT IN FINANCIAL PLANNING

Risk management has become integral to maintaining the financial stability of business enterprises. An adaptation of the risk management process is also an appropriate vehicle to combat the undesirable consequences of pure-risk situations facing individuals and families. However, the management of property, liability, and personal risks is an area that is sometimes overlooked in financial planning, especially by those professionals who are not specialists in insurance. It is, nevertheless, a vital function in the overall planning process.

Premium expenditures are small in comparison to the disastrous financial effects that accompany the occurrence of insurable risks that are inadequately protected against. It is as important that accumulated wealth be protected as it is for that wealth to grow and provide income. Risk management is the vehicle with which to properly structure that protection.

Appendix 10A

RISK IDENTIFICATION QUESTIONNAIRE

(Individual Form)

Developed by Charles E. Hughes

____
(Name)

____
(Mailing Address)

____

____
(Phone Number)

REAL PROPERTY

Address of principal residence ______________________________

____

This is a single family dwelling __________duplex______apartment unit____condominium_____

other (describe) ______________________________

Address of all additional locations:

Seasonal residence ______________________________

Farm ______________________________

Income property ______________________________

Vacant land ______________________________

Other property interests ______________________________

Property Owned	**Principal Residence**	**Other (identify)**	
Residence—square ft.			
Number of stories			
Type of construction			
Year built			
Original building cost			
Date purchased			
Purchase price			
Actual cash value			
Replacement cost (excl. land value)			
Current mortgage			

Describe detached garage or other buildings on the same premises.

____

If any of these properties were rented rather than owned, what amount of rent would probably be charged?

____

If any occupied property would become untenantable because of damage or destruction, what monthly expenses over and above current living expenses would be incurred? ______________

____

Provide a copy of the latest appraised value excluding land or property. ______________

Property Rented

Single family dwelling ______________duplex __________apartment ______________

Monthly rent ____

Lease termination date ____

If premise becomes untenantable because of damage or destruction, does lease require continuation of rent?

____

Income Property	**Location 1**	**Other**
Number of units		
Type of commercial use		
Rental income—annual		
Monthly rates		

If all leases could be cancelled and rewritten today, what change would there be in annual rental income and rate per unit? ____

Land	**Farm**	**Vacant Land**
Number of acres		

General

Occupation and other business pursuits (describe duties) ______________________________

____

Amount of largest personal check likely to be drawn ______________________________

Number of credit cards ____________Number of fund transfer cards ______________

Number of full-time servants ______________part-time ______________

Number of caretakers or other household employees ______________________________

PERSONAL PROPERTY

	Principal Residence		Secondary Residence	
Estimated Value of	Actual Cash Value	Replacement Cost	Actual Cash Value	Replacement Cost
a. Silverware, pewter				
b. Linens (including dining and bedroom)				
c. Clothing (men's, women's, children's)				
d. Rugs (including floor coverings and draperies)				
e. Books				
f. Musical instruments (including pianos)				
g. Television sets, radios, record players, and records				
h. Paintings, etchings, pictures and other objects of art				
i. China, glassware (including bric-a-brac)				
j. Cameras, photographic equipment				
k. Golf, hunting, fishing, and other sports equipment				
l. Refrigerators, washing machines, stoves, electrical appliances, and other kitchen equipment				
m. Bedding (including blankets, comforters, covers, pillows, mattresses, and springs)				
n. Furniture (including tables, chairs, sofas, desks, beds, chests, lamps, mirrors, and clocks)				
o. Business property				
p. All other personal property (including wines, liquors, foodstuffs, garden and lawn tools and equipment; trunks, traveling bags; children's playthings; and miscellaneous articles in basement and attic)				
Total Estimated Value				

Special Items

Jewelry and watches:

a. Describe each item ______________________

b. Original cost of each ______________________

c. Appraised value (obtain appraisal) ______________________

d. Where kept (safe-deposit box) ______________________

Furs:

a. Describe each article of fur ______________________

b. Original cost of each ______________________

c. Appraised value (obtain appraisal) ______________________

d. Where stored (limit of liability per receipt) ______________________

Describe and value other items of unusual value:

a. Stamp collections ______________________

b. Fine arts ______________________

c. Paintings ______________________

d. Antiques ______________________

e. Securities ______________________

Boats or marine equipment:

a. Length and type of boat ______________________

b. Size of motor ______________________

Miscellaneous Items

Dogs, saddle horses, and other pets (pedigreed) ______________________

____

Contents of barns, sheds, and other outbuildings ______________________

____

Value of children's property away at school ______________________

____

Airplanes, motorcycles, and motorized scooters ______________________

____

Location, nature, and value of property in storage warehouses: furs in storage, sports equipment at clubs, silver in safe-deposit vaults, etc. ______________________

____

Cash on hand ______________________

Automobiles

	#1	#2	#3
Year and make			
Body style/model			
Identification number			
Name of registered owner			
Purchase date (new/used)			
Purchase price			
Actual cash value (current)			
Use of automobile			
Distance to work			
Where garaged (if other than principal residence)			
Trailers—Type			
Weight			
Axles			

Describe all recreational vehicles ______________________________

____

____

Do you ever rent an automobile? __________ Length of typical rental period ______

Describe your use of company-owned vehicles ______________________

____

PREMATURE DEATH

	You	Spouse
Lump-Sum Cash Needs		
Cleanup fund. Includes unpaid last illness expenses, burial costs, federal and state taxes, probate costs, and other unpaid bills or debts	$	$
Mortgage. The remaining balance, (Assumes that preference is to pay off mortgage. If not, mortgage payments should be included in income needs.)	$	$
Education fund: Estimated present value of future costs to educate children	$	$
Emergency fund. Used for unexpected expenses not readily payable from current income	$	$
Other	$	$
Totals	$	$

Income Needs

Level of income desired for each category (based on current purchasing power)

Survivors

Lifetime monthly income to surviving spouse	$
Additional monthly income to family during child-raising years (dependency period)	$
Monthly income during first 2 years after death (readjustment period)	$

DISABILITY

Estimated monthly income needed if disability occurs today $ ______

MEDICAL EXPENSE

Estimated cost of major illness requiring extended hospitalization and physician care $ ______

RETIREMENT

Desired monthly income at retirement $ ______

11

Insurance Planning: Survey of Insurance Coverages

Charles E. Hughes

Chapter Outline

As pointed out in the preceding chapter, insurance is an appropriate technique for treating many of the pure risks facing most individuals and families. For this reason the financial services professional needs an understanding of what insurance contracts provide and cover and how insurance premium dollars can most effectively be utilized in treating a client's identified risks. The previous chapter contained a brief introduction to insurance. This chapter takes the next step by providing an overview of several types of insurance policies and describing some of the possible problem areas and special situations that may require further examination before recommending an insurance solution. The purpose is to provide the financial services professional with knowledge that will be of assistance in the counseling of clients and in dealing with insurance specialists brought in to assist in this process.

Unraveling the complexity of insurance coverages would require more than a few pages in one chapter. Since this chapter covers several major lines of insurance, the detail in the analysis of specific contracts is minimized so that a greater variety of contracts can be included within a limited space. The chapter begins with homeowners insurance, followed by auto insurance and excess liability coverage, and then treats life insurance, disability, and medical expense insurance coverage.

HOMEOWNERS INSURANCE

A few years ago, purchasing property insurance on a dwelling simply meant buying a fire insurance policy. Today, the convenience and cost savings of packaging together various types of insurance coverage has won wide acceptance among the buying public. Most individuals now purchase homeowners policies.

The homeowners policy is a package of insurance coverage on the dwelling and personal property combined with liability coverage. There is more to the purchase of a homeowners policy, however, than simply an individual's wish to buy one. These policies come in a variety of forms, and it is necessary to understand the differences among them to be able to recommend the form that provides the coverage the client desires. All homeowners forms include liability coverage, so much of the decision of which form to recommend is based on differences in the property coverage section of the policy. However, as will be illustrated later, proper liability coverage is vital to the final composition of the policy.

The basis for the discussion of homeowners insurance policies in this chapter is the program introduced and made available by the Insurance Services Office (ISO). The ISO format has been adopted by many insurance companies throughout the country. There are, however, insurance companies that use their own policy forms, and regional or state variations that modify the basic forms.

Homeowners policies are available for owner-occupied dwellings (defined as containing one or two living units) used principally as private residences. Although endorsements are available to provide coverage for three- or four-family dwellings, the owner-occupant of a larger building cannot purchase a homeowners policy on the building. In this situation a tenants form is available. Likewise, unit owners of condominiums or cooperative apartments have a special homeowners form available.

The first decision to make is which homeowners policy to recommend. For the nonowner client this is no problem since the only form available is the broad Form HO–4 (sometimes referred to as the *renters policy*). Condo and cooperative unit owners should use Form HO–6. The broad Form HO–2, special Form HO–3, and modified basic Form HO–8 (basic Form HO–1 has been withdrawn in most states) are available for owner-occupants of dwellings. One basis for determining which form to recommend is to compare the breadth of coverage for losses to the dwelling.

[*Note:* The correct number for HO–3 is HO 00 03 04 91. However, HO–3 will be used here, as will HO–2, and so forth.]

Homeowners Policy Forms

HO–1—broad form (withdrawn in most states)
HO–2—broad form
HO–3—special form
HO–4—broad form for renters
HO–6—broad form for condominium and cooperative unit owners
HO–8—modified basic form

Causes of Loss

The descriptive titles given to homeowners forms—basic, broad, and special—help to identify a basic difference among homeowners policies, at least as far as breadth of coverage on the dwelling is concerned. The major concern here is the determination of the causes of loss provided by the policy. Since, if the policy has not been endorsed, the causes of loss for damage to personal property are virtually the same in all forms, the selection process centers on dwelling coverage.

At one time, property insurance policies were written on the basis of a single cause of loss, such as fire or windstorm. If protection against damage caused by some other peril (defined as *cause of loss*) was desired, it could be added by endorsing the policy. As more and more perils were added they began to be grouped together. For example, several perils, including wind, hail, explosion, riot, and smoke, were grouped together in what was referred to as the *extended coverage endorsement.* The basic form of the homeowners (HO–1) provided coverage for a combination of fire, the extended coverage perils, and a few other perils. The present Form HO–8 is a modification of the basic form.

The *broad form* used in homeowners policies is simply the basic form with an addition of several perils and an expansion of the scope of others. For example, in the basic form loss caused to the dwelling by a vehicle is excluded if the vehicle is owned or operated by a resident of the premises. The broad form removes that exclusion and extends coverage to damage caused by vehicles.

Examples of perils added by the broad form include the weight of ice, snow, or sleet and the accidental discharge or overflow of water or steam.

The financial services professional should read policy provisions concerning these and other perils very carefully to determine exactly which losses are covered and under what conditions such coverage is afforded. While this chapter does not go into that detail, the financial services professional should realize that these policies will respond only to losses caused by the specific perils identified in the policy. This is referred to as the *named-peril approach* to providing insurance protection.

The *special form* of the homeowners policies is written on what is called an "all-risks" basis. However, this is a misnomer since not all losses are covered. *All risks* really means that a loss is covered unless it is specifically excluded, which is how the insuring agreement of the special form now reads. Insurance is provided against risks of direct loss to property, and the policy then goes on to indicate that losses caused by listed occurrences or circumstances are not insured. Although the first list that appears is not lengthy, a later part of the homeowners policy lists exclusions applicable to all forms. Therefore, although the special form provides the broadest coverage available on dwellings, it does not cover all risks. While the term *all risks* is still widely used by insurance people, the use of *special form* is more appropriate with the general public.

The comparison of homeowners forms normally results in a choice between the broad Form HO–2 and the special Form HO–3. While the difference in premiums between these two forms is generally moderate, and either would suffice for most clients, recommending the broader coverage provided by HO–3 is usually preferable. The important point is that the client understand that there is a possibility that a given loss to the dwelling might not be covered even by this policy.

Property Coverages

Homeowners policies contain two sections: section I for property coverage and section II for liability coverage. Unless indicated otherwise, the following discussion of property coverages is limited to Forms HO–2 and HO–3. The five major categories of coverage contained in section I of these policies are dwelling, other structures, personal property, loss of use, and additional coverages.

Homeowners Property Coverages

- Coverage A—dwelling
- Coverage B—other structures
- Coverage C—personal property
- Coverage D—loss of use
- Additional coverages

Dwelling—Coverage A

Dwelling coverage requires the selection of a limit or dollar amount of insurance coverage. This is the only part of section I for which the insured *must* choose a limit of coverage. The limits for all other property covered by the homeowners policy are either a fixed-dollar amount or a fixed percentage of the limit on the dwelling. However, some of these limits can be changed by the insured.

A recommendation of the proper limit of coverage that the client should purchase on the dwelling should be made with care. If a loss should occur to the dwelling it will be settled on a full replacement-cost basis if, at the time of loss, the amount of insurance carried is equal to 80 percent or more of the full replacement cost of the dwelling (see chapter 10 for a discussion of this loss-settlement provision). If the current replacement cost of the dwelling is $200,000, a minimum limit of coverage on the dwelling of $160,000 and a maximum limit of $200,000 should be recommended. In most cases it would be appropriate to recommend the selection of a limit closer to the top of the range.

One reason for recommending a limit of coverage on the dwelling close to the dwelling's replacement cost is the fact that the insured must practice retention for any amount not insured. Second, the cost of replacing the damaged property will be measured at the time of loss, and costs could rise between the inception of the policy and the time of loss. This could result in a loss penalty if the amount of insurance carried is not sufficient to satisfy the loss-settlement provision. One way to protect an insured against such a penalty is to place an inflation guard endorsement on the policy. This endorsement periodically and automatically increases the limit of coverage on the dwelling, typically on a specified percentage or construction-cost-index basis. The purpose is to maintain adequate coverage when inflation increases replacement costs. Some insurance companies are now offering coverage that guarantees the full cost of replacing the damaged dwelling even if that cost exceeds the coverage A limit. When this coverage is available, the company typically requires an original coverage A limit equal to 100 percent of the value of the dwelling.

Other Structures—Coverage B

Coverage B provides insurance on other structures located on the premises that are not attached to the dwelling. These include detached garages or tool-sheds and such things as fences, driveways, and retaining walls. Unless increased by the insured, the amount of coverage is 10 percent of the limit on the dwelling. Losses to these other structures are settled on a replacement-cost basis.

Other structures on the premises used for business purposes are excluded and must be insured separately. Structures rented to others are also excluded; however, coverage is provided if the structure is rented to a tenant of the dwelling or if the structure is used solely as a private garage.

Personal Property—Coverage C

Personal property includes the items normally contained in a dwelling, such as furniture, appliances, and clothing, and property stored in a garage, other structure, or outdoors. Unless increased, the limit of coverage on personal property is 50 percent of the dwelling limit, and coverage is provided worldwide. However, when an insured has personal property normally situated at a secondary residence, coverage on such property is limited to either 10 percent of the coverage C limit or $1,000, whichever is greater.

Internal Limits. Personal property is subject to internal limits of coverage on various items. Some examples of these internal limits include

- $200 on money, bank notes, bullion, gold other than goldware, silver other than silverware, platinum, coins, and medals
- $1,000 on watercraft, including their trailers, furnishings, equipment, and outboard motors
- $1,000 for loss by theft of jewelry, watches, and furs
- $2,500 for loss by theft of silverware, silver-plated ware, goldware, gold-plated ware, and pewterware
- $2,500 on property on the *residence premises,* used at any time or in any manner for any *business* purpose
- $250 on property away from the *residence premises,* used at any time or in any manner for any *business* purpose

For the average homeowner, these internal limits create little concern either because such property is not owned or because, if it is owned, values tend to be within the set limits. When the financial services professional identifies situations where client asset values exceed these limits, it is appropriate to suggest alternative ways of treating the exposure. For some property, such as money, it may be impossible to insure the potential loss above some moderate limit. Other types of property on which these internal limits apply can more appropriately be covered in an insurance policy separate from the homeowners policy. This is true, for example, of a watercraft that exceeds the value of coverage provided in the homeowners policy. (The liability exposure discussed later in this chapter is another reason for the use of a separate policy for watercraft.) Another example includes all the property items where the internal limit applies only to theft. Items of jewelry, furs, and silverware, for example, are common targets of theft. When the values of these items exceed the internal limits, a recommendation of separate and increased coverage would be appropriate.

The limits for some of these types of property can be increased by endorsement to the homeowners policy. Whether the property is covered by an endorsement or by a separate insurance policy, it is important to remember that such property may no longer be covered by the provisions of coverage C. The limit selected for this property should therefore be the full desired limit of that property.

The internal limit on business property is somewhat broader than some homeowners may believe. It applies not only to the conduct of a business on the premises, but also to work brought home from the office, which sometimes includes expensive equipment. While some business property, such as books of account, drawings, and computer tapes or other software media that contain business data, is specifically excluded, the cost of blank recording or storage media and prerecorded computer programs available on the retail market is covered.

Modifying Coverage C. Personal property is covered on an actual-cash-value basis. Sometimes it is desirable to place this coverage on a replacement-cost basis, which can be done by endorsement for an additional premium. To qualify for this broader loss-settlement protection, many companies require either that the limit of coverage on the dwelling equal 100 percent of the dwelling's replacement value or that personal property coverage equal 70 percent of the amount carried on the dwelling (coverage C is normally 50 percent of coverage A). Since the replacement cost of personal property will be greater than its actual cash value, it makes sense to increase coverage C when loss settlement will be based on replacement cost.

Another modification that can be made in coverage C is to extend coverage to a "risks of loss not otherwise excluded" basis. This modification, available only for HO–3, makes coverage on personal property comparable to the coverage on the dwelling.

Loss of Use—Coverage D

The primary loss-of-use coverage is for additional living expenses—those increased costs necessary to maintain normal living standards when the insured's dwelling is uninhabitable because of damage caused by a covered cause of loss. The automatic limit for this coverage is 20 percent of the coverage applicable to the dwelling, subject to a time limit of the period required to repair or replace the damage or to permanently relocate, whichever is shortest.

If a part of the residence premises is rented or held for rental to others, loss-of-use coverage is extended to the fair rental value of the rented portion. In effect, this coverage provides a continuation of the rent payment, less a deduction for expenses that do not continue. Coverage for additional living expenses or fair rental value is also provided if action by a civil authority prohibits the insured from using the residence premises because of direct damage to a neighboring premises that was caused by a covered peril in the insured's policy.

Additional Coverages

There are several additional coverages included in the property section of homeowners policies, some of which provide an additional amount or limit of insurance. Each of these additional coverages should be reviewed carefully to determine what is and is not provided. For example, additional coverage is extended for trees, shrubs, and plants, but only when damage is caused by a list of specified perils. Unfortunately, wind, a common cause of damage to trees, is not among the listed perils.

The cost of removing debris following a loss is another additional coverage. The reasonable expense of removal is paid as part of the loss. However, if the direct loss to the property equals or exceeds the policy limit applicable to that property, an additional amount of coverage is granted for the cost of removing the debris. The additional amount in these situations is limited to 5 percent of the amount of coverage applying to the direct loss.

Another example of the additional coverages contained in homeowners policies is a provision that pays up to $500 for losses resulting from theft or unauthorized use of credit cards or fund-transfer cards, for losses from forgery or alteration of any check or negotiable instrument, and for losses related to the acceptance of counterfeit currency (U.S. or Canadian). While some people may believe there is no need for this coverage because of the apparent limitation of $50 that a card issuer may recover from the cardholder in cases involving lost or stolen cards, this $50 applies per card, and a loss could be substantially greater than anticipated. Moreover, with the extension of this coverage to fund-transfer cards, forgery, and counterfeit paper, this can be a valuable extension of coverage.

A final example of the additional coverages included in the property section of homeowners policies is for landlord's furnishings. This coverage provides up to $2,500 for losses to appliances, carpeting, and other household furnishings in an apartment that is regularly rented or held for rental to others. However, it is important to note that this coverage applies only to an apartment on the residence premises. Damage to the property must be caused by one of the perils listed for this additional coverage. Theft is not one of the listed perils.

Property Coverages—Other Forms

In addition to homeowners Forms HO–2 and HO–3, there are several other homeowners forms and other ways of writing property coverages.

Form HO–4

This form is designed primarily for tenants who occupy residential rental property. It parallels HO–2 except that there is no coverage on the dwelling or other structures. The purchaser of HO–4 selects an amount of coverage on personal property (coverage C), and loss of use (coverage D) is then 20 percent of this amount.

There is typically no need for tenants to purchase insurance on the building. However, tenants sometimes install, at their own expense and for their exclusive use, improvements and alterations to the apartment or dwelling. The tenant's interest in these additions is covered up to 10 percent of the personal property limit. This amount may be increased by endorsement.

Sometimes an owner-occupant of residential property that is not eligible for homeowners coverage, such as a multiple-unit apartment building, will purchase a Form HO–4. Property coverage on the building would be purchased separately on a non-homeowner policy basis.

Form HO–6

HO–6 is for condominium unit owners and cooperative apartment occupants. Although the building itself is not covered (this is the association's responsibility), there is coverage for additions and alterations similar to those mentioned above for HO–4. The limit for this coverage is $1,000. Whether this amount is sufficient depends largely on how the association insurance on the building is written.

If the association insurance covers the entire unit, including all interior fixtures, wiring, decorating, etc., the unit owner may not need more than the $1,000 limit. However, if the association insures only the original construction and not improvements or additions made by the unit owner, the unit owner may need additional coverage. Sometimes the association insurance is what is referred to as "bare walls" coverage. If so, the unit owner must insure the entire interior, including all fixtures, interior partitions, paint or paper on the walls, etc. Since much more than $1,000 of coverage may be necessary to cover the unit owner's interest adequately in this case, the limit can be increased to meet this need.

The purchaser of Form HO–6 must select the amount of the limit on personal property coverage C. Then, 40 percent of that amount is automatically provided for loss-of-use coverage D.

Form HO–8

As discussed earlier, the loss-settlement provision applicable to dwellings covered by homeowners policies requires insurance equal to at least 80 percent of the replacement cost of the dwelling. In some cases, especially for older homes, replacement cost might be considerably higher than the market value of the home. Since it would not be logical for many homeowners to purchase insurance on a home in an amount two or three times its market value, Form HO–8 provides a partial solution to the problem.

HO–8 provides insurance on the dwelling and other structures on the basis of the cost of repairing or replacing the property using common construction materials and methods. Since this eliminates the replacement-cost condition, the owner can purchase a lesser amount of coverage on the dwelling without being exposed to the penalty for underinsuring.

The HO–8 form is not as broad as other homeowners forms—for example, only the basic perils apply to this form, coverage on personal property is not worldwide, and theft coverage is more limited—yet HO–8 can serve a useful purpose in the right situation.

Dwelling Program

Many dwellings do not meet the eligibility requirements to qualify for homeowners insurance coverage. As one way of making property coverage available for such dwellings, the Insurance Services Office developed a series of forms in what is called the *dwelling program.* Under this program, property coverage on dwellings, other structures, and personal property, as well as additional living expenses and rental value can be provided. In general, the coverage provided under the dwelling program is narrower than that provided by the homeowners program. A fundamental difference is the fact that the dwelling program does not include the theft, liability, or medical payments coverage that homeowners policies do. Another difference is that in the dwelling program, an insured who desires to include personal property in a policy covering the dwelling must separately select a stated limit, whereas in the homeowners policy the selection of a limit on the dwelling automatically establishes a limit on the personal property.

As an example of how this dwelling program might be used, recall the cabin owned by the Beamer family as a secondary residence (see chapter 10). Although the cabin might qualify for homeowners coverage, the Beamers had already purchased a homeowners policy on their principal residence, so a homeowners policy on the cabin would duplicate some coverage. (Some companies will write a homeowners policy on the secondary residence and give a premium credit for the section II coverage discussed below.) An alternative solution for the Beamers is to purchase a dwelling program policy on the cabin. Also, since the homeowners policy contains only a small amount of coverage on personal property located at a secondary location, the Beamers could add a separate amount of additional personal property coverage for the cabin on the dwelling program policy.

Liability Coverages

Personal liability insurance provides protection for activities and conditions at the premises where the insured maintains a covered residence and for personal activities of the named insured and members of the insured's family anywhere in the world. All homeowners policies contain the same liability coverage. Section II of the homeowners policy contains two principal parts, coverage E—personal liability, and coverage F—medical payments to others. As with the property section, this section also includes some additional coverages.

Homeowners Liability Coverages

- Coverage E—personal liability
- Coverage F—medical benefits to nonresidents
- Additional coverages

Coverage E is similar to other liability insurance policies. Protection is provided for legal liability involving bodily injury or property damage, but not for personal injury. The latter includes such injuries as libel, slander, violation of privacy, malicious prosecution, and wrongful entry. These may be added by endorsement or covered under the umbrella liability policies discussed later in this chapter. The standard liability limit is $100,000 per occurrence, but may be increased for a relatively small additional charge.

Coverage F provides medical benefits to persons, other than residents of the insured household, who suffer bodily injury at an insured location or who are injured because of an insured's activities away from the insured location. The basic limit for coverage F is $1,000 per person. This amount is available for all necessary medical expenses incurred with 3 years of the date of the accident. Benefits under this coverage will be paid whether or not the insured is legally liable.

Exclusions

The liability section of the homeowners policy has always been considered as providing very broad coverage. In fact, when this coverage is purchased as a separate insurance policy it is referred to as comprehensive personal liability. Nevertheless, as with all policies that are considered to provide broad coverage, what is not covered is of extreme importance. Some of the exclusions found in homeowners policies should be expected, such as war and nuclear exposure. Others should be anticipated because the exposure can be covered with a different policy, such as the motor vehicle, aircraft, and workers' compensation exposures. It should also be anticipated that losses that are intentionally caused should not be covered, nor should bodily injury to an insured.

Certain exclusions are particularly important for the financial services professional to understand in order to assist a client in reorganizing or modifying coverage or in obtaining the proper coverage in some other fashion. Three of these exclusions relate to business pursuits, watercraft, and property damage.

Business Pursuits. Bodily injury or property damage arising out of or in connection with a business engaged in by an insured is excluded under the liability and medical coverages of homeowners policies. Most people are unaware that such part-time activities as baby-sitting, lawn mowing, and snow shoveling, or even ongoing hobbies or child care might result in liability losses that are not covered by the homeowners policy. The business exclusion centers on the definition of *business activity.* Basically, if there is an expectation of profit or gain, and evidence of continuity of the activity, the exclusion can be expected to apply and either a separate liability coverage or an endorsement to the homeowners policy will be needed.

Many home-business liability exposures can be covered by using endorsements to the homeowners policy, such as the permitted incidental occupancies residence premises endorsement or the business pursuits endorsement. However, care should be exercised in the use of endorsements since, for example, the business pursuits endorsement does not provide coverage if the business is owned by the insured. It is applicable to those situations where an insured is conducting business in the home for an outside employer. If the business is owned by the insured, a separate business-liability insurance policy should normally be obtained, but liability coverage for something like child care in the home can be covered by an endorsement to the homeowners policy.

A second part of the business exclusion applies to the rental or holding for rental of any part of any premises by an insured. This exclusion does not apply, however, if the rental is (1) on an occasional basis if used only as a residence, (2) in part for use only as a residence as long as the renting family unit has no more than two roomers or boarders, and (3) in part as an office, school, studio, or private garage. For an example of this last case, if the garage is rented out to a person for the purpose of conducting a radio repair shop, no coverage is provided. If the garage is rented for the purpose of parking an automobile, coverage is extended to the property owner. In some cases an endorsement for structures rented to others will be necessary.

Finally, it should be understood that the homeowners policy does not provide coverage for loss arising from the rendering of or failure to render professional services. Separate professional liability insurance is required for clients who have this exposure.

Watercraft. The homeowners policy provides only limited liability coverage for ownership or use of watercraft. No liability coverage applies to any watercraft owned by an insured if it is an inboard or inboard-outdrive type of any size, a rented inboard or inboard-outdrive boat with more than 50 horsepower, or an owned or rented sailboat 26 feet or more in length. Also, if the boat that is owned by the insured is powered by outboard motors with more than 25 total horsepower, there is coverage only if the boat is acquired during the policy period or, if acquired prior to the policy period, if the boat was declared at the inception of the policy or if the insured notified the insurer in writing within 45 days of acquiring the outboard motors. Use of borrowed, nonowned watercraft is covered, and use of rented watercraft is covered if size specifications are met.

The liability coverage provided by homeowners policies for watercraft is suitable for many owners of small boats. However, as the size increases, so does the need to change the insurance coverage. Although liability coverage can be added by endorsement to the homeowners policy, individuals who also want coverage for damage to the boat in excess of that provided under the property section of the policy should be advised to purchase a separate boat or yacht policy.

Property Damage. There are some exclusions contained in section II that are directed specifically at damage to property. One of these states that property damage to property owned by the insured is not covered, which seems logical since such property should be covered in section I. This exclusion does not, however, prevent recovery by one insured for damage to that insured's property by another person who also is an insured under the policy.

Another liability exclusion applies to damage to property rented to, occupied by, used by, or in the care of the insured. This exclusion does not apply if the damage is caused by fire, smoke, or explosion (some insurers include water damage in this list). This exclusion is most significant for tenants who may be liable for damage to the apartment they rent and less significant when personal property is involved because coverage C insures personal property owned or used by an insured.

Additional Coverages

As with section I there are several additional coverages contained in section II. Two of these are examined here.

Damage to Property of Others. This provision makes it possible to pay small property damage claims without needing to prove the loss was caused by the negligence of the insured. Payment of up to $500 per occurrence is made on a replacement-cost basis.

Since property subject to this provision may already be covered under section I of the homeowners policy, payment under this additional coverage is in addition to any section I coverage. As might be expected, this provision does not apply to property owned by an insured or for any loss arising out of a business engaged in by an insured.

Loss Assessment. One exclusion that was not discussed earlier is for the insured's share of any loss assessment that would be charged against any member of an association, corporation, or community of property owners. For example, if a liability claim has been successfully made against a condominium association, the association assesses its members for any sum needed to satisfy the claim. This type of assessment is excluded from coverage by the homeowners policy.

An additional coverage contained in the homeowners policy gives back to the insured the benefit of payment for assessments of the nature just excluded above. This coverage will pay up to $1,000 as the insured's share of a loss assessment resulting from bodily injury or property damage not excluded by the policy. This benefit also covers assessments based on the association's liability arising out of an act of an unpaid elected director, officer, or trustee of the association.

This completes the discussion of homeowners insurance coverage. The homeowners policy has become a major risk-financing tool for property and liability risks facing individuals and families. It is important that financial services professionals, even those who have no direct relationship to the sale of insurance, have some knowledge of the breadth and complexity of this major insurance policy.

AUTOMOBILE INSURANCE

There are various forms of automobile insurance available today. However, like the homeowners policies just discussed, the Insurance Services Office (ISO) form will be the basis for description in this chapter. This is called the Personal Auto Policy (PAP). In most cases, the policy forms used by insurance companies that do not use the ISO form are very similar to this form. The PAP contains four coverages: liability, medical payments, uninsured motorists, and damage to your auto.

Personal Auto Policy Coverages

- Part A—liability coverage
- Part B—medical payments coverage
- Part C—uninsured motorists coverage
- Part D—coverage for damage to your auto

In addition to the basic coverages, several states have enacted statutes requiring that so-called no-fault benefits be added to the policies. Also, because of the many variances among state requirements, most PAP policies contain endorsements that modify the standard policy to satisfy local requirements regarding terminology or provisions in the policy. Finally, the PAP differs from the homeowners policy in that the insured, for the most part, may choose the coverages he or she desires and must choose an amount of insurance for each coverage.

Liability Coverage

The insuring agreement for the liability coverage provided by the PAP states that the insurance company will pay damages for bodily injury or property damage any insured becomes legally responsible for because of an auto accident. Part A of the PAP contains a single limit, such as $100,000 or $300,000, as the maximum amount that will be paid for all damages resulting from any one accident.

Who Is an Insured?

The PAP identifies the named insured (the person named on the declarations page) and any other family member as insureds for the liability exposure arising from the ownership, maintenance, or use of *any* auto. This means that autos both owned and not owned by the named insured are covered. A family member in this case is anyone who is related to the named insured by blood, marriage, or adoption and who resides in the named insured's household. Other persons are also covered by the named insured's PAP for liability arising out of the use of the insured's *covered auto.*

A covered auto is any vehicle shown in the declarations of the policy. It also includes any trailer the named insured owns. If the insured purchases an additional vehicle during the policy period, it will be covered automatically as long as the insurance company is notified of this addition within 30 days. If the new vehicle is a replacement auto, the insurance company must be notified within 30 days only if the insured desires to add or continue coverage for damage to the auto.

Clearly, the insuring agreement for the liability coverage portion of the PAP is broadly stated to provide coverage for a wide mix of individuals and autos. As might be expected, there are several exclusions applicable to this broad coverage.

Exclusions

Examples of exclusions contained in the liability section of the PAP include intentionally caused bodily injury or property damage, damage to property owned or transported by an insured, and vehicles with fewer than four wheels. There are other exclusions, but only two of these are discussed here.

The PAP excludes coverage for property damage to property rented to, used by, or in the care of an insured. However, this exclusion does not apply to a residence or private garage. In other words, there is coverage if the insured rams a covered auto into the door of a garage he or she rents. At one time another exception to this exclusion applied to autos that were borrowed or rented; although this has since been removed, a few insurance companies have retained the old exception. Therefore the financial services professional should look closely at this exclusion. The current PAP does not provide liability coverage for damage to borrowed or rented vehicles. (See the discussion under Damage to Your Auto later in this chapter.)

The second exclusion has two parts. The first part excludes liability coverage for the ownership, maintenance, or use of any vehicle owned by the named insured or spouse that does not qualify as a covered auto. The intent here is to avoid situations where an insured might own two vehicles but insure only one of them with the expectation that he or she would be covered regardless of which vehicle was being driven. Both vehicles must be insured for coverage to be applicable.

The second part of this exclusion applies to an auto that is furnished or available for the regular use of the named insured or spouse, such as an auto provided by an employer. The insured's PAP excludes liability coverage in such situations. Although the employer's policy would probably provide adequate coverage, this exposure should be examined very carefully. If needed, there are endorsements to the PAP that will provide additional liability coverage for this type of situation.

Medical Payments Coverage

Under the medical payments coverage of the PAP, the insurer will pay reasonable expenses incurred for necessary medical and funeral services because of bodily injury *sustained by an insured.* Subject to certain exclusions, benefits are payable to the named insured and family members if injured while occupying any motor vehicle designed for public roads or if struck by a motor vehicle. This coverage differs from medical payments coverage under the homeowners policy where the named insured and members of the household are not covered, and coverage applies to other persons injured on the premises or because of an insured's activities. In the PAP, medical expenses of other persons are also covered, but only while they are occupying the covered auto. Where no-fault benefits are required, medical payments coverage is normally replaced by the no-fault coverage.

Uninsured Motorists Coverage

Uninsured motorists coverage is a rather unique addition to the PAP policy. It basically provides that if an insured sustains bodily injury (some states also include property damage) in an auto accident where the other driver was at fault (negligent), but where that driver does not have insurance, the insured may recover from his or her own insurance company those sums he or she is legally entitled to recover. In effect, the insured looks to his or her own insurance company to receive what a negligent, uninsured motorist cannot provide.

An uninsured motorist is the owner or operator of an uninsured motor vehicle, which includes vehicles for which there is no applicable liability insurance, as well as hit-and-run vehicles and vehicles for which the liability coverage is not available because the insurer is insolvent or denies coverage. An uninsured motor vehicle also includes vehicles that are insured but have liability limits less than the bodily injury liability specified in the financial responsibility law of the state in which the insured's covered auto is principally garaged.

Some states require that uninsured motorists coverage be included in all auto insurance policies containing liability insurance. Some states stipulate that this coverage is mandatory unless the insured rejects it in writing, while still other states simply consider this an optional coverage.

The limit of liability for uninsured motorists coverage is typically the required limit of the financial responsibility law in the insured's state. However, an option to increase this limit up to the limit the insured has purchased for part A—Liability is available. When this limit is increased, the policy is normally changed by endorsement to provide a combination benefit called *uninsured/underinsured motorists coverage.* The uninsured benefit remains as above. The underinsured benefit provides payment when the at-fault driver or owner has liability insurance at least equal to the financial responsibility limit but less than the limit carried by the insured.

The underinsured motorist benefit becomes an excess amount over the at-fault party's liability insurance up to the amount of the loss or maximum limit carried by the insured. For example, suppose the required liability limit is $25,000 and the named insured carries $100,000. If the named insured suffers bodily injuries in an auto accident and the at-fault driver has no insurance, the named insured would receive $25,000 from his or her own insurance company under the uninsured motorists coverage and the balance of the loss, up to $75,000 (for a total maximum of $100,000), from the underinsured motorists benefit. If the at-fault driver carries liability insurance of at least $25,000, that person's insurance would respond to that limit and the injured party's underinsured motorists coverage would pay the balance of the loss up to the policy limit.

Damage to Your Auto

The physical damage coverage of the PAP is referred to as part D—Damage to Your Auto. The two primary coverages in this part of the policy are *collision* and *other than collision.* The latter has historically been called "comprehensive" and is still referred to in this way by many in the insurance business. *Collision* is defined as the upset of the covered auto or its impact with an object or another vehicle. *Other than collision* is every other cause of loss except collision. In effect, the combination of the two parts provides coverage on an all-risks basis. This, however, means that exclusions listed in the policy should be carefully examined.

Exclusions and Limitations

Several exclusions in this part of the PAP are directed at special types of equipment that may be included within or as part of the auto. For example, damage to custom furnishings or equipment, such as facilities for cooking or sleeping frequently found in pickups or vans, and loss to electronic equipment that receives or transmits audio, visual, or data signals are not covered. This exclusion applies to the increasingly popular telephone in the auto. Coverage for this type of property can be provided by an endorsement to the PAP or by separate insurance coverage. (The 1991 edition of the homeowners policy extends coverage to portable electronic devices, such as car phones, while used in an auto. The base limit for this coverage is $1,000.) Other types of exclusions in the physical damage part of the PAP include damage caused by wear and tear, freezing, breakdown, and war.

The limit of liability for physical damage claims is the lesser of the actual cash value of the stolen or damaged property and the amount necessary to repair or replace the property. In addition, the damage amount is subject to a deductible that, within limits, can be selected by the named insured. A single deductible may apply to all losses or different deductibles may apply to collision losses and other than collision losses. An increase in the amount of the deductible can often result in a substantial premium savings.

Nonowned Autos

Although this part of the PAP is called Damage to *Your* Auto, coverage is also extended to nonowned autos. A nonowned auto is defined as any private passenger auto, pickup, van, or trailer not owned by or furnished or available for the regular use of an insured. By definition, nonowned auto also includes a temporary substitute auto, used when a covered auto is out of normal use because of breakdown, repair, servicing, loss, or destruction. In one of the strange anomalies of the PAP, a temporary substitute auto is defined as a covered auto in the liability part of the policy, but becomes a nonowned auto in the physical damage part. This underscores the need to study the PAP in its entirety.

Under the physical damage part of the PAP, coverage for nonowned autos is equal to the broadest of any auto having physical damage coverage. This means that when an insured has only other than collision on one auto and both other than collision and collision on another auto, both the collision and the other than collision coverages would apply to a nonowned auto. The coverage provided by this policy is excess over other applicable physical damage insurance. For example, if an insured borrows a neighbor's auto to run an errand and carelessly collides with a tree, the neighbor's physical damage coverage applies first, and the insured's coverage is excess. However, if the neighbor did not carry physical damage coverage, the insured's policy would pay for the collision damage.

Automobiles that are leased on a long-term basis (6 months or more) should be described on the declarations page just as an owned auto would be. Physical damage to an auto that is rented on an occasional basis is covered by the PAP if the insured carries the physical damage coverage. Sometimes a client will ask if it is necessary to purchase the *collision damage waiver* (CDW) when renting an auto on a short-term basis. This is a difficult question to answer. It would appear that it should not be necessary to purchase the CDW because of the duplication of coverage with the client's PAP. However, the physical damage coverage of the PAP does not provide for the loss-of-use claims that car rental agencies consider a part of the loss to be reimbursed by the renter. Also, the rental agency typically wants payment on the spot to repair or replace the auto immediately, while the client's insurer might want to assess the damages and circumstances before approving payment. For these reasons, the purchase of the CDW may be justified. The cost of this coverage over the duration of the rental must also be considered.

The wording of the CDW varies among auto rental agencies. In most cases there are conditions under which the waiver does not apply, such as while driving in a reckless manner, driving under the influence of drugs or alcohol, or even using the vehicle off paved roads. In these cases the CDW would not respond, but the client's PAP has no similar restrictions. Therefore, the CDW should be recommended to the client, since overlapping coverage is preferable to a gap in coverage. A "yes" to the client's question contains much protection for both the client and the financial services professional.

No-Fault Benefits

Approximately half the states have adopted some form of no-fault automobile insurance plan. Under a pure no-fault plan, legal liability arising out of automobile accidents would be abolished, and anyone suffering a bodily injury loss in an automobile accident would collect from his or her own insurance company. None of the plans now in existence have gone to this extreme. Rather, the right to sue another party either has not been altered or has been modified to eliminate suits for which losses are below a certain dollar limit (called a *threshold*) or below some verbalized statement regarding the severity of the injury. No-fault benefits typically include some combination of medical expenses, lost wages, replacement of services, survivors' benefits, and funeral expenses.

In those states with no-fault laws, individuals either must be offered the coverage or are required to carry insurance to compensate themselves, their families, and possibly passengers in their autos for their own bodily injuries. This is accomplished by adding the required endorsement to the PAP.

UMBRELLA LIABILITY INSURANCE

The homeowners and automobile insurance policies are the basic coverages for most individuals and families. There are situations or possible loss exposures where these two policies are not adequate, and additional types of policies, such as for aircraft, watercraft, business pursuits, or other exposures are needed. Sometimes it is the need for liability limits greater than these two basic policies provide that creates a demand for additional coverage. One policy that is becoming increasingly popular for this purpose is the *personal umbrella liability policy,* also called *excess liability* or *personal catastrophe liability insurance.*

While there is no standardized personal umbrella liability insurance policy, a few generalizations can be made.

These policies provide excess liability limits over underlying liability coverage limits and, in most cases, broader coverage than the underlying policies. Umbrella liability policies typically provide a liability limit of $1 million or more, often up to a maximum of $5 or $10 million. The insured is required to carry certain underlying liability policies and limits—for example, a homeowners policy with a liability limit of $100,000 and an automobile liability policy with a single limit of $300,000. Other coverages may also be required if the exposures exist.

With respect to the underlying coverages, the umbrella liability policy provides excess coverage. For example, if an individual has an automobile liability policy with a single limit of $300,000 and an umbrella liability policy with a limit of $1,000,000, the first $300,000 of any claim arising out of an automobile accident would be payable under the automobile policy, and the balance (up to the policy limit) would be payable under the umbrella policy. Therefore, the insured would have total coverage amounting to $1,300,000.

An important point to remember about underlying coverage is the fact that the agreed-upon limit of the underlying coverage *must* be maintained by the insured. If the insured in the above instance had reduced the auto liability limit to $100,000 rather than the required $300,000, the umbrella coverage would still pay toward the claim as if the $300,000 limit had been maintained—in other words, the insured would have to pay $200,000 of the claim.

The umbrella policy also covers situations not covered by underlying insurance policies, such as personal injury in the form of libel, slander, and invasion of privacy; auto liability outside the United States and Canada; or liability for damage to property in the insured's care, custody, or control. When the umbrella policy does provide coverage in these cases, it drops down to provide primary coverage over the insured's retained limit. A retained limit is like a deductible that must be paid by the insured. This can be as low as $250, but is typically in the $500 to $1,000 range.

Umbrella liability policies do contain some exclusions. Some typical ones are intentional acts, amounts payable under workers' compensation laws, business pursuits, and damage to the insured's own property. Professional liability may also be excluded, but insurance companies are now offering this coverage if the insured carries an underlying professional-liability policy.

The umbrella liability policy enables an individual to have virtually all-risk liability insurance at a very reasonable cost. The financial services professional should consider recommending this coverage to all clients.

LIFE INSURANCE

The purchase of life insurance should focus on satisfying the financial needs identified for individuals and families. Some of these needs, such as cash for the cleanup fund or for lifetime income for a surviving spouse, continue to exist for many years and can be considered permanent needs. Others, such as the income need during the dependency period or the financial need associated with fixed periods of indebtedness, tend to disappear eventually and are considered temporary needs. These two types of needs influence the choice of an appropriate type of life insurance to recommend.

The insuring agreement in life insurance policies states that the company will pay the face amount (or some designated amount) upon the death of the insured. This death benefit can be viewed simply as the claim payment that is to be made if the contingency insured against occurs, much like a claim payment on a homeowners policy for damage to a dwelling. Just as property insurance is thought of as providing protection, this same approach can be applied to life insurance where the amount to be paid at death can be viewed as protection. Some forms of life insurance place primary emphasis on this protection element.

There is another side to life insurance, however. A client purchasing life insurance frequently gives consideration to the desire for the accumulation of wealth or the need for a cash fund at some known future date, such as retirement. In this instance life insurance is similar to a savings fund, and some forms of life insurance combine this savings element with the protection element.

The process of selecting the appropriate life insurance policy to meet the identified needs and objectives of the client is complicated by the vast array of life insurance policies available in the marketplace. It is important to understand the differences between the various types of life insurance policies in order to make the proper recommendation.

Types of Life Insurance

This section reviews the basics of traditional term and whole life policies and discusses universal life policies. There are numerous variations between these three types of life insurance, and there are many other policies that do not fit precisely into one of these categories. It is impossible to cover all of them in the short amount of space available in this chapter.

Term Life

Term life insurance provides protection for a limited period of time. If the insured dies during that period, the specified amount (normally the face amount of the policy) will be paid to the designated recipient (beneficiary). If the insured survives for the stated period of time, the policy expires and all obligations of the insurance company terminate. The stated period of time in term life insurance policies is expressed as a number of years (such as 1, 5, or 20), or until a certain age of the insured (such as to age 60 or age 65). Because of these features, term insurance is well suited to situations where there is a temporary need for protection.

The death benefit, or face amount of the policy, normally remains constant throughout the life of the term policy. However, term life is also written on a decreasing death-benefit basis or, with some companies, on an increasing basis. Sometimes, term insurance is written as a rider or supplement to another life insurance policy, normally to a policy of the whole life variety.

A decreasing term policy may be appropriate for needs that decline over time—such as the principal sum necessary to provide income over a shorter and shorter dependency period or a debt that is being liquidated, such as a mortgage. However, since the principal sum of a mortgage does not reduce on a straight-line basis, a mortgage life insurance policy should have a similar death-benefit structure.

An increasing term life insurance policy might be used (typically in conjunction with a whole life policy) when the insured wants the death benefit to equal the original face amount of the policy plus all premiums that have been paid. Another use is when the insured would like to have the death benefit keep abreast of some index, such as the cost of living.

Because it provides protection only for a limited period of time, initial premium rates per $1,000 of coverage are lower for term life insurance than for other life products issued at the same age. If the term coverage is to be continued for another term, the premium rate will increase to reflect the current age of the insured. Although these increases may be nominal at the younger ages, they increase rapidly at older ages.

If an individual has purchased a short time span for the term policy, such as 1, 5, or 10 years, the inclusion of a renewability provision should be considered. This provision allows the insured to renew the policy without showing evidence of insurability. This could be a valuable provision if the insured's health should begin to deteriorate when there is still a need for the protection.

Another provision that should be considered for inclusion with the issuance of a term policy is the conversion privilege. This feature permits an insured to exchange the term policy for a whole life policy or another cash-value insurance contract without evidence of insurability.

In addition to the uses of term life insurance already mentioned, it should be recognized that term insurance can be the basis for one's future permanent insurance program. This is true, for example, when a client needs a large amount of life insurance but can afford only relatively small premiums at the present time. For this reason financial services professionals should conduct periodic reviews with their clients.

Whole Life

There are two features that distinguish whole life from term life insurance. One is, as the name implies, that it is insurance for the whole of life. The policy provides for the payment of the face amount upon the death of the insured regardless of when death occurs. A second feature is the fixed-premium nature of the policy. The premium remains constant throughout the premium payment period of the contract, rather than increasing periodically as is the case with term insurance. (Some whole life policies, such as modified whole life insurance, change premiums as specified in the contract.)

The existence of a fixed premium over a long period of time results in the establishment of the predominant feature of whole life insurance—a savings element. Since premiums during the early years of a whole life policy exceed what is necessary to pay death claims, this excess is set aside and accumulates for the benefit of the insured. This savings element is normally referred to as the policy *cash value* (policy reserves are not discussed in this chapter).

The existence of the cash value buildup alters the structure of the death benefit under whole life policies and provides special benefits to the policyowner. The death benefit for whole life policies remains constant through time. However, since the cash value, or savings element, of the policy increases through time, the protection element decreases. In effect, whole life insurance is a combination of decreasing protection and increasing savings, with the sum of the two elements equaling the face amount of the policy.

The other important aspect of the existence of cash values is the fact that policyowners may have access to those funds. One way to do this is to utilize the policy loan values, which may be borrowed at the request of the policyowner. Although interest is charged on the amount borrowed, there is no requirement that the principal or interest on a scheduled basis be repaid. Any unpaid policy loan or interest will, however, reduce the future death benefit.

FOCUS ON ETHICS
Focusing on the Client's Need

One of the charges frequently made against life insurance agents is that whole life policies are often proposed when term coupled with some form of investment would have provided better results for the client. The logic of this criticism is based on the logic that the agent earns a higher commission on whole life and therefore emphasizes it in sales. Often this ethical criticism fails to consider important factors such as tax deferral, risk, purpose of the insurance purchase, and length of time the insurance is needed.

The real issue is the importance of clearly focusing on the client's need. Consider a single-earner family with young children and a limited budget. Their primary life insurance need is to replace the breadwinner's income in case of premature death. The amount of the insurance need is calculable and the funds available are limited. If a life insurance agent encourages purchase of an insufficient amount of cash value life insurance instead of a sufficient amount of lower-cost term insurance, that agent has ignored the client's need. The agent would then have traded compassion, integrity, and professionalism for commissions.

If a client died and was underinsured because the agent had failed to focus on the client's need, the result would be more than an ethical lapse. It would be a financial catastrophe for an entire family.

The second way to access the savings or cash values is through exercising the policy nonforfeiture options. One of these options is for the policyowner to surrender the contract and receive its surrender value, which is the cash value. Since surrender of the policy cancels the protection element of the insurance when there may still be a need for the coverage, two additional nonforfeiture options are designed to continue a death benefit for the policy. The first of these permits the policyowner to elect to exchange the cash surrender value for paid-up insurance of the same type as the original policy. Paid-up insurance means that no more premiums will be required. As should be expected, since no further premiums will be paid, the face amount of the paid-up policy will be less than the original policy face amount. However, this nonforfeiture option may be appropriate where a smaller amount of whole life insurance would be satisfactory and the client desires to discontinue premiums, for example, when he or she reaches retirement age.

The second option permits the policyowner to exchange the cash value for term insurance for the full face amount of the original policy. As with all term policies, the length of the term coverage will be determined by the age of the insured and the premium dollars available from the cash value. The important point here is that the full face amount continues for some specified period of time. Therefore this option may be appropriate when the need for maximum protection continues to exist, but the premium-paying capacity does not.

Whole life insurance policies can be distinguished by the length of the premium-paying period. When the premium is to be paid as long as the insured is alive, the whole life policy is referred to as a *straight life policy* (sometimes called *ordinary life* or *continuous premium whole life*).

When an applicant, prior to the issuance of a life insurance policy, decides that he or she would prefer to pay premiums only for a specified number of years, a policy can be issued to satisfy that desire. A policy of this nature is referred to as a *limited-payment policy.* Premiums can be scheduled to be paid for a specified number of years or until the attainment of a specified age, typically age 65. These policies involve a higher premium and a more rapid buildup of cash values than a straight life policy. Also, when the premium-paying period is completed, the policyowner has a paid-up policy for the original face amount. This contrasts with the reduced paid-up policy that results from exercising the nonforfeiture option.

The most extreme form of limited-payment life insurance is single premium whole life. This policy involves one premium payment at the inception of the contract. As might be expected, the emphasis in this type of life insurance policy is the savings element rather than the protection element. In fact, because of interest-rate levels that were available during the 1980s, the savings element was viewed more as an *investment* than as long-term savings. Changes in certain aspects of the federal income tax treatment of life insurance in 1988 have taken most of the luster from single premium whole life insurance policies.

The shorter the premium-paying period for whole life insurance, the smaller the face amount that can be purchased for a given amount of premium.

Therefore, in planning for the use of whole life insurance it is necessary to clearly identify the client's objectives. Since whole life is most appropriate for permanent needs, the trade-off between a high amount of protection and a rapidly accumulating savings element should be considered carefully.

Universal Life

Although universal life policies can properly be classified as whole life policies, they are singled out in this chapter as an example of the flexible premium variety of life insurance policies. Universal life policies require a stipulated premium payment during the first year of coverage. After the first year, the premium on this type of policy is truly flexible. Policyowners may pay whatever amounts at whatever times they wish, or even skip premium payments, as long as the cash value is large enough to cover required policy charges.

Each year the policyowner of a universal life policy receives a report illustrating the flow of funds during the year. This report shows the amount in the cash value account at the beginning of the period, the reduction in this account due to mortality charges and expenses (if any), and the interest earnings credited to the account. This type of detailed information is not generated for traditional whole life policyowners.

Universal life policies offer two death-benefit designs, usually labeled as options A and B. Option A provides a constant or level death benefit, like that of traditional whole life policies. However, at older ages the death benefit begins to increase because of the technical need to satisfy the Internal Revenue Code definition of life insurance. Option B provides a death benefit that at any time is equal to the sum of the original face amount of the policy and the accumulating cash value. The death benefit continues to increase as long as the cash value increases.

In addition to flexibility with regard to premium payments, universal life policyowners may also change the face amount of the policy. Decreases in the policy death benefit can be made by policyowner request at any time. However, evidence of insurability may be required if an increase in the death benefit, other than that indicated above, is requested.

Some argue that the universal life policy is the only policy a person will need over an entire lifetime. They base the argument on the flexibility in premium payments and death benefits, which allows adjustments to be made to fit the client's needs at any time in the life cycle. Therefore, the universal life policy is one that should be understood by all financial services professionals.

Annuities

Life insurance can be considered a technique used to accumulate or create wealth. The growth of cash values can be considered the accumulation of wealth while the cash payment upon the death of the insured is the creation of wealth. Sometimes the wealth already exists for a client, and there is a desire to systematically liquidate that wealth. That is a function that can be performed by annuities.

An annuity provides for the systematic liquidation of a principal sum over a period of time, usually for the lifetime of the annuitant (the recipient of the payments). Annuities are similar to life insurance in that they can be purchased either by a single premium or on an installment premium basis. When annuities are purchased by a single premium, periodic benefit payments to the annuitant can either begin immediately or be deferred to commence at some future specified time. Annuities can be purchased to provide periodic payments of a guaranteed fixed amount or a variable amount. When the variable annuity is elected, the periodic payment depends on the performance of an underlying investment portfolio, typically common stocks.

Under a pure or *life annuity,* payments cease upon the death of the annuitant, with no further obligations placed on the insurance company. Most annuity purchasers dislike this contingency basis and prefer arrangements that will guarantee payments to the annuitant's survivors on some basis. This can be accomplished through the election of guaranteed payments for a certain period of time or through the selection of a cash or installment refund arrangement. Another alternative is the *joint-and-survivor annuity* based on the lives of two or more annuitants, such as a husband and wife.

A knowledge of annuities is important in understanding some forms of pension plans. Their general use in retirement planning is discussed in chapter 13. However, since cash values in life insurance were discussed in this chapter, the financial services professional should recognize that retirement purposes can be served through the purchase of individual life insurance policies. At some time in the future, the accumulated savings element in whole life policies can be exchanged, typically at net cost, for an annuity to provide income to a client for the purpose of supplementing social security and other sources of retirement income.

DISABILITY INCOME INSURANCE

One of the more frequently overlooked personal risk exposures is the loss of wages or earnings during periods of disability. Most people seem to be aware of the medical care costs associated with accident or illness and of the total discontinuation of earnings because of premature death, but tend to overlook the seriousness of the possible loss of income because of disability. At most ages the likelihood of a serious, long-term disability is considerably greater than the probability of death.

The financial services professional should begin the process of satisfying the need for income replacement due to serious disability by examining the client's employee benefit package. This was not suggested for life insurance because group life benefits tend to be small in relationship to the total need. However, in disability income-replacement situations, the combination of social security disability benefits and employer-provided salary continuation or disability income benefits may provide most or all of the replacement income needed. Individual disability income insurance is one tool that can be used as an additional source for the replacement of earnings lost during periods of disability.

Definition of Disability

When it is determined that there is a need for additional income-replacement protection, the financial services professional should review the key features of disability income insurance policies before making a recommendation to the client. One of these features is the definition of *disability*.

Total Disability

Definitions of disability in disability income policies are based on the ability of the insured to perform certain occupational tasks. One definition, typically called the *any occupation* definition, states that insureds are considered to be totally disabled when they cannot perform the major duties of any gainful occupation that their education, training, or experience makes them reasonably suited for.

A somewhat less restrictive definition is usually referred to as the *your occupation* definition. According to this definition insureds are deemed to be totally disabled when they cannot perform the major duties of their regular occupations. For purposes of this definition, the regular occupation is the one engaged in when the disability begins. Since this definition would allow an insured to work in some other capacity and still be entitled to benefits, insurers modify the definition slightly by adding that the insured may not work in any other occupation. In virtually all definitions of disability, insurers add a provision stipulating that the disabled person must be under the care and attendance of a physician.

Partial Disability

After the totally disabled person has begun the recovery process, there may be a period of time during which he or she may be able to return to work on a limited basis. Since the person no longer satisfies the definition of total disability, *partial disability coverage* was designed to provide a reduced benefit during this period of recovery. Partial disability is usually defined in terms of time as well as duties: a typical definition may state that, although the insured has returned to work, he or she is unable to perform all of the major duties of his or her occupation or is unable to work on more than a half-time basis.

Partial disability benefits are typically a percentage of the total disability benefit. They are also paid for a limited time period, typically 6 months.

Residual Disability

The concept of *residual disability* is used as a replacement for the partial disability provision as a method of paying benefits to a disabled insured who has returned to work with a reduced capacity. Although the definition of residual disability may include terms regarding occupational performance like those in total or partial disability, an added dimension refers to a reduction in income. For example, a definition might state that residual disability means that the insured can engage in his or her regular or another occupation, but because of the accident or sickness, income has been reduced by at least 20 percent of the insured's prior income.

Residual disability benefits are payable in proportion to the reduction in earnings and are usually limited to the benefit period of the basic plan. Residual and partial disability coverages are separate add-ons to the total disability income insurance plan.

Key Coverage Provisions

There are several key coverage provisions that should be considered in evaluating the suitability of an individual disability income insurance plan for a client. These include the elimination period, the benefit period, the benefit amount, and the terms of renewability.

Key Disability Income Insurance Coverage Provisions

- Elimination period
- Benefit period
- Benefit amount
- Terms of renewability

Elimination Period

The elimination period is the number of days that must elapse between the start of disability and the start of benefit payments. It is sometimes called the waiting period or simply the deductible stated in time rather than dollars. The intent of this provision is to avoid coverage of the short-term illness or injury that temporarily disables an insured and for which retention is more economical than insurance.

Elimination periods are generally available for periods ranging from 30 days to one year. The length of time recommended to a client should depend on the availability of other funds to support a risk retention program. For example, if a client's employer provides a salary continuation plan that will compensate the employee in full for 6 months, there is little need to add an individual disability income insurance policy that will pay benefits at the end of 30 days. However, if a short-term disability would cause financial hardship, a 30-day elimination period might be very appropriate. As with any deductible, the longer the elimination period selected, the lower the premium.

Benefit Period

The benefit period is the length of time during which income benefits will be paid. This ranges anywhere from 2 years in duration to until the insured reaches age 65, or even for the insured's entire lifetime. Historical data indicate that most disabilities are of short duration, but the likelihood of full productive recovery diminishes as the length of the disability increases. This means that long-term disabilities will be more devastating and that insurance is usually the best tool for dealing with this contingency. Therefore the recommended benefit period should be of long duration. Of course, the longer the benefit period, the higher the premium, but a long elimination period might offset part of this higher cost.

Benefit Amount

Individual disability income policies are written to provide a fixed amount of monthly benefit. When disability income insurance is provided on a group basis, it is common to include reference to the total of all such benefits not exceeding some percentage of the insured's earnings. Some policies purchased on an individual basis may still contain a similar reference to a relationship of earnings to insurance. For most individually purchased policies, however, the benefit amount is not adjusted for changes in the insured's earnings or for other disability income insurance that may be payable, except as discussed earlier for residual disability benefits.

Insurance companies limit the amount of disability income coverage they will write so that the total benefit from all sources does not exceed a given percentage of the insured's earned income—about 65 percent for individuals in higher income brackets. One reason for this limitation is the fact that individually purchased disability income benefits are not taxable income to the recipient. Another reason is the potential disincentive for a disabled person to return to work if benefit payments are too high relative to predisability income.

Another limiting factor in purchasing disability income insurance is the maximum dollar benefit that companies are willing to write. This creates problems for higher income clients since they are unable to purchase an adequate level of benefit amount. The maximum benefit available tends to be in the \$10,000 to \$12,000 per month range for the more favorable risk classifications. The higher the benefit amount, the higher the premium.

Terms of Renewability

State laws specify that individually purchased disability income policies (and medical expense policies) must indicate the basis upon which the insured can continue the contract, a very important consideration to the insured.

Many disability income policies can be canceled or renewal refused at the option of the insurer. If the client wishes to have some assurance of continuation, either a guaranteed renewable or a noncancelable contract should be purchased.

Under a guaranteed renewable contract the insurer reserves the right to change premium rates for all insureds of the same class but cannot cancel or refuse to renew the policy. Under a noncancelable policy the insurer can neither change premium rates nor cancel the policy. A noncancelable policy costs more than a comparable guaranteed renewable one.

MEDICAL EXPENSE INSURANCE

The second major type of health insurance coverage is medical expense insurance. This is the insurance to pay hospital bills, physicians' costs, and various other expenses related to periods of sickness or injury. For many individuals and families this coverage is provided through an employer-sponsored employee benefit program, though in some cases it will be necessary to supplement the benefits provided by such a plan. Usually the only way for a financial services professional to analyze the benefits provided is through reading the employee handbook. If there are gaps or insufficient coverage, proposals should be made to overcome deficiencies.

One factor that may create problems in analyzing and making coverage recommendations of medical expense insurance is the lack of uniformity among individual medical expense insurance policies. Although certain state-mandated benefits or required provisions must be included, many variations still exist.

A strategy that should be considered in reviewing and recommending medical expense insurance is to give first priority to protecting against catastrophic loss. For this reason, the discussion that follows emphasizes major medical coverage.

Major Medical Coverage

Basic medical expense insurance policies typically cover only one or two kinds of medical expense. An example of this is the separate policy issued to provide benefits for expenses associated with hospital confinement. This policy, referred to as a *basic hospital expense policy,* reimburses the insured for room-and-board charges up to a specified number of dollars per day for a specified number of days. As an additional benefit this policy might pay for general nursing, medicines, and other miscellaneous hospital charges. A separate basic surgical expense policy might also be purchased to cover fees charged by a surgeon, normally on some specific schedule basis. Other single-purpose medical expense policies might also be purchased.

In this kind of setting, the concept of major medical expense insurance was developed. Although separate basic medical expense policies could have been, and often were, combined into one policy, gaps or overlaps often existed. Because of the need to overcome this problem and to provide coverage broader in scope than that provided by these basic expense policies, major medical expense insurance policies were designed and introduced. They provide a broad range of coverage for virtually all kinds of expenses associated with illness or injury. Another, and perhaps more compelling reason for the emergence of major medical policies, was the limited dollar amount provided for benefits under the basic policies. Major medical expense policies offer much higher limits on benefit amounts.

Major medical policies are issued in two formats: as a supplemental policy superimposed over existing basic policies or as a combination of the basic and major medical into one policy. The latter is normally called *comprehensive major medical expense coverage.* Although major medical policies differ among companies, they tend to have several characteristics in common.

Maximum Limit

The first characteristic of major medical expense policies is the high aggregate limit available for benefits. These limits range from $10,000 to $1 million or more and some policies provide an unlimited benefit amount. The limit stated in the policy can be applied on a per disability basis, a calendar-year basis, a lifetime basis, or on some other basis.

Major medical policies may contain certain internal limits, such as a maximum rate for daily hospital room-and-board charges or for charges for surgical procedures. Internal limits are designed to minimize possible abuses of the broad coverage and benefits in major medical policies and to keep premiums within acceptable limits.

Deductibles

The second characteristic common to major medical policies is the deductible. Several types of deductible provisions are found in individual major medical policies. A deductible may apply to each separate illness or may have to be satisfied once in any given calendar year. The policy may include a family deductible that requires a flat dollar amount per year for a family regardless of the number of claims or that eliminates the deductible after two or three members of the family have paid it. Individual major medical policies may also contain a common accident provision stipulating that only one deductible has to be satisfied if two or more family members are injured in the same accident.

The deductible for comprehensive types of individual major medical policies might range from $500 to $10,000 or more. A very high deductible might be appropriate for a client who has ample financial resources to absorb large medical expenses or for a client who has group medical expense coverage that provides only limited benefits. When a major medical plan is superimposed over a basic plan, the deductible is normally quite small ($100 or $250) and applies after basic benefits are exhausted and before major medical benefits begin. This type of deductible is referred to as a *corridor deductible.*

Coinsurance

The third key characteristic of major medical expense insurance is the coinsurance provision (sometimes called a *percentage participation clause*) that requires the insured to pay part of eligible medical expenses in excess of the deductible. A typical provision requires the insured to pay 20 percent (or 25 percent) of the expenses eligible for payment by the insurer. For example, if a client who has a $250,000 major medical policy with a $1,000 deductible and a 20 percent coinsurance provision incurs $21,000 of eligible medical expenses, the client will pay the $1,000 deductible plus 20 percent of the remaining $20,000 of expenses or a total of $5,000.

Some major medical policies contain a stop-loss limit, which modifies the coinsurance provision when an insured's out-of-pocket eligible expenses reach a designated level. At that point the percentage participation by the insured ceases, and the insurer begins paying 100 percent of the eligible expenses. In the above example, if the client had a stop-loss limit of $2,000, the client's total payment for the claim would have been $3,000 rather than $5,000. The deductible is not affected by the stop-loss limit. Therefore, in this example, the client would pay the $1,000 deductible and the $2,000 stop-loss limit for a total of $3,000.

An understanding of these three common characteristics of major medical expense insurance—maximum benefit amounts, deductible, and coinsurance—is fundamental to an appreciation of this important coverage. Any individual medical expense coverage, like disability income insurance, must be closely integrated with employee benefit packages provided through the workplace.

Planning for Older Ages

As individuals approach age 65 they may have a tendency to downplay the need for medical expense planning because of the mistaken belief that medicare takes care of everything. It does not, as can be seen in the discussion in chapter 13. This means that financial services professionals and their clients must understand medicare benefits and plan how medical expenses that are not covered can be dealt with in the most effective way. This also means that the financial services professional must keep abreast of frequent changes in the medicare benefit structure, such as the legislation of 1988 and its repeal in 1989.

Insurers provide medicare supplements or medigap policies to cover expenses not paid by medicare. These policies vary from those that cover just the hospital deductible and copayment requirements of medicare to those that provide broad benefit structures covering expenses that exceed medicare allowances, and in some cases, health care expenses that are not covered at all by medicare.

Another segment of medical care that is now receiving greater emphasis is the expense of long-term stays in nursing homes. Medicare provides limited benefits for these expenses at best, and in some situations no benefits are provided at all. Insurance policies have been developed to provide the funding for long-term care not covered under medicare or other medical expense policies. For the most part these policies are new and evolving, and coverage is gradually becoming broader and less expensive. Any policy that alleges that it meets the need for long-term care costs, however, should be examined carefully to make sure it actually does meet the client's needs.

A CAUTIONARY NOTE

A survey of insurance coverages such as the one presented in this chapter can only begin to touch on the basics of individual insurance coverages available to meet the pure risk situations facing clients. Furthermore, each client situation presents different problems to solve. For the financial services professional, this chapter should be considered only as a brief introduction to insurance that provides a basic foundation for the discussion of insurance with clients and a sense of how insurance can be used to meet client needs. It is not, however, a solution to all the questions that arise about insurance.

12

Investments and Investment Planning

William J. Ruckstuhl

Chapter Outline

THE MEANING OF INVESTMENT

Often we hear comments such as, "My investments in municipal bonds have performed spectacularly," or "I think that investments are just too risky for me." Rarely, if ever, do we hear, "I invested money in my savings account today." That is because most people do not view a savings account as an investment. They are inclined to think that investments must be stocks, bonds, or some other exotic item, such as futures, options, or master limited partnerships. What actually is considered an investment depends on the definition employed by the individual investor.

When economists define the term *investment,* they focus on additions to the nation's stock of capital assets. Thus new buildings, equipment, and additions to inventory constitute the major elements of the economic definition. This view, however, is not appropriate for an understanding of personal investments.

For our purpose, investment is defined as the purchase of an asset by an individual or an institution with the expectation that the asset acquired will increase (or hold) its value and/or generate a current income flow commensurate with its risk. The asset may be tangible or intangible. Examples of tangible investment assets include land, buildings, art objects, antique furnishings, set and unset jewels, precious metals, and collectibles such as stamps and coins. Intangible assets are shares of stock, bonds, money in a savings account, or other financial assets. Money in a non-interest-bearing checking account, however, does not qualify as an investment within this definition because its value will not increase and indeed can decrease because of the ravages of inflation. Further, the account does not provide any return (income) to the depositor.[1]

Investment versus Speculation

When an investment is made, there is the anticipation that a return commensurate with the investment's risk will be earned. This is also true for speculation. Moreover, both investment and speculation can have a short-term time horizon. What, then, is the basic difference between investing and speculating? Short-term investments entail relatively low risk and therefore earn a relatively low return. Speculation, on the other hand, is an effort to obtain a high return in a short period of time by purposely buying (selling) tangible or intangible assets whose value is very uncertain over the next few days, weeks, or months. An example of speculation is buying stock in a corporation considered to be the object of a bidding war between two or more potential acquirers.

Since the distinction between investment and speculation rests on the expected return in the short run, a particular asset could be acquired by both an investor and a speculator at the same time for different reasons. The speculator anticipates a short-term upward movement of the asset's market price and expects to dispose of the asset when the price change occurs. The investor, on the other hand, seeks a long-term return and expects to dispose of the asset only in the long run. Also, the investor could be acquiring the asset to further diversify an existing portfolio.

Personal Financial Objectives That Require Investment Instruments

Many clients have personal financial objectives that require the accumulation of funds. These objectives were reviewed in earlier chapters of this book. For various reasons such as age, family size, income level, or amount of accumulated wealth, these objectives have different degrees of importance to clients. Objectives that have a high priority with many clients include the desire to be able to

- meet emergency expenditures (for example, due to serious illness)
- acquire expensive personal assets (for example, a new home or automobile)
- pay the education expenses of children
- provide a sufficient retirement income
- accumulate wealth

Clients also possess different views as to the importance of the various outcomes achievable from owning investment instruments. For some clients, high current income received in cash that is spendable now is a paramount consideration, whereas current cash income ranks very low in importance for other clients who have a different time perspective and prefer long-term growth in value of the investment. Some clients may require stability of the asset's value so that they can withdraw monies from the investment at any time without any loss. Others may emphasize the need for stability of the yearly income from the investment. Some clients may opt for investments that provide some tax advantages, while others believe this to be a low priority.

Thus, in addition to having different objectives for acquiring investment instruments, clients expect different outcomes from their investment portfolios. The successful financial planner must know each client's personal financial objectives and investment expectations so that he or she can advise whether investments already owned or being considered by a client are appropriate.

CATEGORIES OF INVESTMENT ASSETS

Before one can fully understand investment risks and the measurement of returns (discussed later in this chapter) some basic knowledge concerning different types of investment instruments and their distinguishing characteristics is essential. This section divides these alternatives into four broad categories—cash equivalents, long-term debt instruments, equity securities, and real estate and other investments—and describes some critical characteristics in each category.

Cash Equivalents

To satisfy the need to make transactions and to have readily accessible money in case of an emergency, many individuals use instruments that are known as cash equivalents. Typically cash equivalents either have no specified maturity date or have one that is one year or less in the future. The first major purpose for using cash equivalents is ready access to the investment principal, considering the investor's overriding concern for safety of principal. A second purpose for using cash equivalents is that they serve as a receptacle for accumulating funds to purchase other investment assets in an amount that meets the minimum purchase requirement (such as $500 or $1,000 with some mutual funds or CDs) or minimizes the per unit transaction acquisition cost (such as buying a round lot of 100 shares of a publicly traded stock or 5 bonds to avoid higher per share or bond prices). Finally, a third use of cash equivalents is when investors, uncertain about the direction of the economy or prices of investment alternatives, place monies in these instruments until such time as they can determine the direction of the economy or prices of potential investments. However, investments in this category often provide only a modest current income and typically have little or no potential for capital appreciation.

Bank Deposits

The most widely known and used types of cash-equivalent investments are savings accounts and certificates of deposit (CDs) at banks, savings and loans, and credit unions. Since these investments are usually insured to a limit of $100,000 by the Federal Deposit Insurance Corporation (FDIC), they have minimal risk. In addition, few restrictions are placed on withdrawals of deposits in savings accounts.

CDs, which are deposits for a specified period of time such as 3, 6, or 12 months (although maturities of up to 10 years are available), generally impose a loss of a portion of the interest earnings as a penalty for a withdrawal before maturity, although some banks have reduced this to a minimal or zero amount. Because of the time commitment made by the investor, the interest rate earned on CDs exceeds that earned on savings accounts.

Another characteristic of savings accounts and CDs is their ease of acquisition and disposal. Both can be opened or closed at any office of the issuer with little delay and at no cost. Savings accounts can be increased or decreased in virtually any desired sum. CDs can be acquired in sufficiently varied dollar amounts and with staggered maturities that make subsequent conversion to cash relatively easy and virtually penalty-free. At maturity CDs can be automatically reinvested for an equivalent time period without any action taken by the investor.

Money Market Instruments

Money market deposit accounts (MMDAs) and money market mutual funds (MMMFs) are other popular cash equivalents. For both types of investments, minimum initial dollar amounts are typically required to open the account. In the case of MMDAs offered by banks, virtually any amount can be added to the account. MMDAs typically are insured like savings accounts and CDs. MMDAs allow withdrawals at the bank window or by check. However, a limit is imposed on the number of checks that are allowed at little or no cost per month, and additional checks can be costly. The earnings rate obtained from these instruments often increases depending on the size of the investor's account.

In contrast, MMMFs frequently require minimum dollar deposits, and they are not FDIC insured. MMMFs provide access by check, by wire transfer, and, in some cases, by phone. MMMFs are technically mutual funds, and investments therein are technically used to buy shares in the fund. Since MMMFs often belong to a commonly managed family of funds, these MMMF shares can be readily redeemed for shares in other funds within the family with little or no delay or transaction cost.

Both MMDAs and MMMFs hold portfolios of short-term obligations of the federal government and its agencies, of state and local governments, and of businesses. The securities usually have maturity dates averaging under 30 days.

Another popular cash-equivalent investment is U.S. Treasury bills (T-bills). These obligations of the U.S. government have maturity dates when issued of 90 or 180 days, or one year, and are backed by the full taxing authority of the government. With this backing, T-bills are the safest investment available and thus pay investors the lowest interest rate of the various money market instruments. When the term *risk-free* investment is used, it refers to T-bills. In this context, risk free means no possible risk of default on paying interest or principal when due. These instruments, sold on a discount basis, require a minimum purchase of $10,000, making them difficult to acquire for clients of modest means. They can be readily sold and converted to cash at a modest cost to meet client needs and can be acquired directly from a Federal Reserve bank.

Many other investments have the characteristics of cash equivalents, such as the short-term obligations of state and local governments and of businesses and the long-term debt obligations of governments, businesses, and nonprofit institutions that are to mature within one year. Some of the characteristics of these types of securities are described below.

Long-Term Debt Instruments

Owners of long-term debt instruments are creditors of the issuing institution, whether it is a government, business, or nonprofit organization. This status grants the investors the legal right to enforce their claims to interest income and principal repayment as contained in the indenture (agreement) that specifies the terms and conditions of the debt issue. In the case of business debt instruments, debt claims have priority over any claims of its owners.

Bond issues of state and local governments (both of which are referred to as municipals) and of businesses typically are quality rated by Standard and Poor's Corporation (S&P) and/or Moody's Investors Service as to the likelihood that the issuer will default on the timely payment of interest or principal. Based on a financial analysis of the issuer, a letter grade is assigned to each bond issue. Bonds rated at the top of the B grade (BBB for S&P, Baa for Moody's) or higher are considered to be "investment quality." Lower ratings are assigned for bonds assessed as "speculative." These rating organizations evaluate the bond when it is issued and continue to monitor the issuer during the bond's life. The lower the quality rating, the greater is the risk of default and the higher will be the interest rate (return) that the investor will expect to earn.

Governmental Debt Securities

Governmental debt includes securities of the federal, state, and local governments, and their agencies. Some federal bonds are backed by the full faith and credit of the U.S. government. For example, all U.S. Treasury obligations have such backing. Other U.S. government bonds issued by federal agencies or organizations, such as the Tennessee Valley Authority, are not direct obligations of the U.S. Treasury. These bonds, known collectively as *agency bonds,* provide investors with a return greater than that available on U.S. Treasury bonds. A few of these agency bonds have guarantees that effectively place the full faith and credit of the U.S. Treasury behind the bonds.

Some state and local government bonds, known as *general obligations,* are backed by the taxing power of the state or local government. Others, usually issued by agencies of a state or local government, are known as *revenue bonds.* They are backed by the revenues earned from such ventures as turnpikes, airports, and sewer and water systems. Without the taxing authority behind them, these revenue bonds are viewed as riskier and pay investors a somewhat higher interest rate than do general obligation bonds.

Typically interest earned on debt issues of the federal government, although subject to federal income taxation, is exempt from income taxation by state and local governments. Exceptions to the exemption from state and local income taxation include mortgage-backed securities issued by federal agencies such as the Government National Mortgage Association (Ginnie Mae) or the Federal National Mortgage Association (Fannie Mae). Interest earned on most, but not all, municipal bonds is exempt from federal income taxation and income taxation by the state in which the bond originates. States generally tax interest earned on municipal bonds issued in other states.

Maturities of governmental debt instruments vary from more than one year to 30 years. Bonds with maturities of 10 years or less are often referred to as being of intermediate-term duration and have somewhat less risk than longer term bonds. If such a risk difference does exist, intermediate-term obligations would pay a slightly lower rate than would a longer duration bond.

Corporate Debt Securities

Businesses are major contributors to the supply of debt securities available in the marketplace. These securities, either notes if intermediate term or bonds if long term, have various characteristics, which are detailed in the indenture. Some of the more frequently encountered characteristics include the following:

- *secured*—a promise backed by specific assets as further protection to the bondholder should the corporation default on payment of interest or principal
- *debenture*—an unsecured promise, based only on the issuer's general credit status, to pay interest and principal
- *callable*—an option exercisable at the discretion of the issuer to redeem the bond prior to its maturity date at a specified price
- *convertible*—an option exercisable by the bondholder to exchange the bond for a predetermined number of common or preferred shares

For bonds of the same quality rating, these features affect the interest rate available to the investor. If the feature provides a benefit to the bondholder, such as being secured or convertible, a lower interest rate is paid. If the feature provides a benefit to the issuer, such as the flexibility of not having specific assets pledged as collateral (debenture) or the presence of a call feature, the interest rate is higher.

The market often assigns labels to securities. One label frequently heard in the news is *junk bonds,* now more commonly called *high yield bonds*. These bonds have low quality ratings from S&P or Moody's and are risky because the firm either has a very large amount of debt outstanding relative to its equity base or has suffered financial reverses and may be headed for serious trouble or bankruptcy. Because the risk is high, the return on junk bonds also is high.

Note: The term *junk bonds* can also apply to certain municipal bonds if the government or agency tax or revenue base sharply deteriorates.

Equity Securities

Equity investments represent an ownership position in a business. As such, they represent a higher risk for the investor than do the debt investments. Although an equity interest can be as the sole owner of a proprietorship or as one of several partners in a partnership, this discussion will focus on equity as evidenced by shares of stock issued by a corporation.

Corporations acquire equity funds by selling ownership shares to either a very few individuals or to the public. In the former case the individuals often agree not to sell the shares to others, hence keeping the firm closely held and the shares not marketable. When equity shares are sold to the public, a market for their resale emerges, and the ownership interest can be readily sold or purchased. Corporations can and often do offer different types of ownership interests of which the two most popular are common and preferred stock.

Common Stock

Investors in common stock have the ultimate ownership rights in the corporation. They elect the board of directors that oversees the management of the firm. Each common share receives an equal portion of the dividends distributed as well as any liquidation proceeds. If the firm is unsuccessful, losses will occur that can lead to a cessation of any dividend payments and, if losses continue, to an eradication of the common equity ownership and eventual bankruptcy.

The current income distributed as dividends to the shareholder is at the sole discretion of the board of directors. The board is under no legal obligation to make dividend payments and may instead retain the profits within the business. Only by threatening to or actually electing a new board can the common shareholders be in the position to force a dividend payment, regardless of the profitability of the business.

The owners of common stock also vote on major issues such as mergers, name change, sale of a major part of the business, or liquidation. Lastly, common stockholders usually have a *preemptive right,* which is the right to maintain their relative voting power by purchasing shares of any new issues of common stock of the corporation.

Preferred Stock

Preferred stockholders usually have two privileges that provide them with a preferential position relative to common stockholders. The first privilege is the right to receive dividends before any dividends are paid to the common shareholders. This preference is usually limited to a specified amount per share each year. As previously stated, dividends are payable only if declared by the board. If the preferred shares are noncumulative and no dividend is paid to the preferred shares in any one year, the dividend is skipped and doesn't ever have to be paid. In the next year the corporation can pay the specified annual preferred dividend and then pay a large dividend to the common shareholders. To prevent this from happening, many preferred stocks have a cumulative provision associated with the issue. This provision requires the corporation to pay all the skipped preferred dividends as well as the current year's preferred dividend before any dividends can be paid to the common shareholders.

The second privilege of preferred stockholders is the right to receive up to a specified amount for each share (plus current or cumulative dividends) at time of liquidation. This liquidation value must be paid to the preferred stockholders in full before anything can be paid to the common stockholder.

In exchange for these two preferences, preferred stockholders surrender the basic rights of common shareholders, which were previously described. Occasionally preferred stocks may have callable or convertible provisions such as those for bonds. The effect of these features on the amount of the preferred dividend is the same as on the bond interest rate. The preferred's stated dividend is higher if the feature favors the corporation or lower if it benefits the shareholder. In some cases preferred stockholders elect some or all members of the board of directors if dividends have not been paid to them for a specified number of years.

American Depositary Receipts (ADRs)

Many investors desire to own shares in foreign corporations. These shares can be purchased abroad in the same way that domestic corporation shares are purchased in the United States. However, problems, such as fluctuating foreign exchange rates and inconvenient trading hours due to time differences, make these transactions somewhat complex. To overcome these problems, some U.S. banks have acquired shares in foreign corporations and hold these shares in trust in one of their foreign branches. Then they sell negotiable instruments, called American Depositary Receipts (ADRs), that represent a specified number of shares in a foreign company. ADRs are the equivalent of ownership of the stock, trade as such in domestic markets, and have rights and privileges as are accorded common shareholders in the country of issue.

Investment Companies

Investment companies can be distinguished in several ways. For example, there is a distinction between closed-end and open-end investment companies. At formation a *closed-end* investment company issues a given number of shares. Rarely, if ever, are additional shares issued. These shares are traded in the stock markets in exactly the same manner as those of operating corporations, such as General Motors. That is, the forces of demand and supply for the stock determine the share price.

The closed-end investment company uses the proceeds from the initial sale of its stock to acquire a portfolio of securities. The market value of this portfolio influences, but does not directly determine, the market price of the closed-end company's shares. Theoretically the value of a share in a closed-end investment company should equal the net asset value of the portfolio. The net asset value (NAV) is calculated as follows:

$$\text{Net asset value} = \frac{\text{Total assets} - \text{total liabilities}}{\text{Number of shares outstanding}}$$

However, the shares of most closed-end investment companies sell at a discount of about 5 to 15 percent below their net asset values. When stock market prices in general are buoyant, the discount, as a percentage of net asset value, typically declines. The reverse occurs during periods when general stock market prices decline. Occasionally these shares trade at a premium, that is, a market price that is higher than the NAV.

An *open-end* investment company, popularly called a mutual fund, continually sells and redeems its shares at net asset value. Hence the shares are not sold on the stock market. Similar to closed-end companies, mutual funds acquire a portfolio of securities in which each of the fund's shares owns a proportionate interest. As sales and redemptions of the fund's shares take place, the size of the fund's total portfolio changes, increasing when additional shares are sold and decreasing when shares are redeemed.

The nature of the acquisition fees is another distinguishing characteristic among investment companies. Buyers of closed-end shares, since the shares are traded on securities markets, are subject to normal stock-brokerage commissions for both purchase and sale transactions. Some mutual funds charge a sales fee and are called *load* funds. The loading is regulated, and it can be as high as 8.5 percent of the value of the investment. If no sales fee is levied, the fund is called a *no-load* fund.

Technically this load-no-load distinction should refer not only to an initial sales fee but also to other fees that carry different names but are used to compensate individuals for selling and marketing efforts. One of these fees is the 12-b(1) fee, which is an annual charge against the net assets of the fund that typically ranges from 0.1 to 1.6 percent. A second type of marketing fee is called an exit fee, deferred-sales charge, or back-end load. This is not a modest charge simply to cover the expenses of processing a redemption. Rather, the exit fee is sometimes as high as 4 or 5 percent of the dollar value of the shares being redeemed and is used to pay the marketing and selling costs. Some individuals believe that a true no-load fund assesses investors neither a front-end, a 12-b(1), nor a deferred sales fee, since these are all forms of marketing and selling costs.

Regardless of whether the fund is load or no-load, the shareholders must pay the administrative, transactions, and investment advising expenses incurred by the fund. These expenses are deducted from the interest, dividend, and capital-gain fund income prior to distributing fund income to the shareholders.

Under the federal laws that regulate security transactions, a prospectus (a document that gives a potential buyer the relevant information about a newly issued security) must be delivered to security buyers before a purchase takes place. The initial material of the prospectus includes required tables showing the amount of all loads and other expenses associated with the purchase, holding, and sale of the fund's shares. Therefore the magnitude of these additional fees can be determined by the investor. In addition, the National Association of Securities Dealers is now seeking comments on a proposal: when open-end load funds are bought through a stockbroker, the confirmation sent to the customer must explicitly state the amount, if any, of exit fees that will be charged when the shares are redeemed. Unfortunately this is a notification *after* the investor has already bought the shares.

Investment companies can also be differentiated on the basis of their portfolio objectives. Although more than 9,000 investment companies exist, they can be segregated into several broad categories based on their portfolio objective. For most of the portfolio categories, subcategories exist. Except for two categories, money market and index funds, the investment company can be either open-end or closed-end. These major categories are as follows:

- *money market mutual funds*—These funds own a portfolio of short-term interest-bearing securities. As mentioned earlier, they are used by investors as an alternative to cash. They operate only as open-end funds. Subcategories include funds that focus mainly on nontaxable securities or federal securities only or on diversified portfolios.
- *index funds*—These funds own a portfolio of common stock that replicates a major market index such as the S&P 500. They operate only as open-end funds.
- *bond companies*—These companies own a portfolio of bonds. Subcategories include some that invest only in U.S. government issues, municipal issues, corporate issues, or low-quality (junk) bonds. Further subcategories can be short-term (up to 4 or 5 years), intermediate-term (5 to 10 years), or long-term (10 or more years duration) bond funds.
- *common stock companies*—These companies hold a portfolio of common stocks and perhaps a small number of preferred stocks. Subcategories include those that invest primarily in conservative (defensive) stocks, growth stocks, aggressive growth stocks, or foreign stocks.
- *mixed portfolio companies*—These companies own a portfolio of bonds, stocks, and other investment instruments. Subcategories include balanced companies and income companies.

- *specialty companies*—These companies have very specialized portfolios designed for investors who seek special investment opportunities. One such company might invest in precious metals, a second might focus on commodities or commodity trading, and a third might engage in option trading.

In some cases, an investment company is a totally separate organization that has no links to any other business venture. More often, to enable the fund sponsors to meet a wide range of client preferences, a fund is a part of a family of funds representing several of the above categories or subcategories of portfolio objectives. This feature permits investors to move their investments from stocks to bonds to money market instruments as conditions change. Small fees are sometimes charged when a switch is made within the family of funds. Every time a switch is made, there is an income tax consequence since a sale and then a purchase transaction occurred.

Several reasons have been advanced as to the current popularity of investment companies. The first is that each share in an investment company benefits from the pooled diversification of the portfolio. In addition, the professional management that selects and continuously monitors the securities and the appropriate securities markets should provide better overall portfolio performance than can the typical individual investor. A third reason is that many investors lack the time to properly select securities and can better delegate this responsibility to others. A fourth reason is that the wide diversity of investment companies allows an investor to select the diversified portfolio that best suits his or her investment objective. The tax and record keeping provided by the fund management is another reason for the popularity of investment companies. Last, as more companies institute 401(k) plans for their employees, shares of different mutual funds frequently are some of the permitted choices suitable for participants.

Real Estate and Other Investments

Real Estate

Many forms of real estate ownership are available to investors. One such form is the purchase of property directly, either as an individual or as a managing partner in a partnership. One way that requires less active management by the investor is owning shares in a real estate investment trust (which is similar to an investment company but the trust either owns property it manages or owns a portfolio of real estate mortgages). A second way is by owning a limited-partnership interest in a general partnership. This limited-partnership interest has no active role in the firm's management. Real estate investments usually involve more complexities than the previous investment categories because of

- the uniqueness of each property

- the differing rights associated with ownership of each property
- the absence of organized markets for the ready sale and purchase of the property or ownership interest
- the complexity of the federal taxation of the income and appreciation from real estate (other than the investor's primary residence) since the passage of the Tax Reform Act of 1986

Most individuals do not purchase their homes primarily for the purpose of realizing a current return or an appreciation in its value. Rather, the main purpose has been to provide shelter for oneself and family. However, ownership of one's home, with few exceptions, has over the past 40 years been one of the most secure and most rapidly rising investment opportunities. As with all investments, market conditions can change. If expenditures for the primary residence are being made because the major objective is to achieve the benefits from an investment, then the property must be examined from that perspective.

Other Investments

Virtually any asset can be used for investment purposes. Over the years, such activities as cattle feeding (usually a farming or feed lot operation) or oil-and-gas drilling and exploration activities have been used as limited-partnership tax-advantaged investments. The growth of the options, futures, and commodities markets has spawned investment instruments that offer different objectives. The Cold War whetted investor preferences for ownership of precious metals that might rise sharply in value if relations between countries deteriorated. These markets collapsed with the recent détente between Russia and the United States. The federal government's granting permission for U.S. citizens to own gold was instrumental in expanding markets for investment instruments such as gold bullion, gold coins, gold futures, and gold mining stocks. Although coins and stamps have long been collectibles, other types of collectibles have become popular because of the strong economic performance of stamps and coins. Art, ceramics, and china have captured the fancy of many individuals due to the appreciation of selected items. For most collectibles the spread between the current purchase price and the amount of the sales proceeds an investor receives from a dealer is sizable.

Similar to real estate, each of these investments is a specialty field unto itself. Any technical treatment of the characteristics of these investments is beyond the scope of this introductory discussion.

Summary

This overview described the investment instruments that most clients use. The markets offer other alternatives that appeal to some investors. However, these alternatives either are very risky, require specialized knowledge, or require a minimum expenditure that is beyond the means of most clients.

INVESTMENT RISK AND RETURN

Susan and Bob keenly desire to purchase a home 3 years hence and expect to need $25,000 for the down payment and closing costs. They visited the local savings and loan association (S&L) and were informed that, ignoring taxes, they would need to begin now by depositing $645 monthly for the next 36 months into the S&L's savings account to meet their objective. They went to a mutual fund representative who recommended a fund that invests solely in obligations of the U.S. Treasury. This strategy would require Susan and Bob to invest about $620 per month which, if current rates were maintained over their 3-year planning horizon, would have a terminal value of $25,000. However, even this amount exceeded their ability to save. Then the representative inquired how much they could save each month. When they replied that $560 would be the absolute maximum, the representative recommended a high-income corporate bond fund that would enable their monthly savings to accumulate to the target amount within the 3-year period.

What returns are being offered to Susan and Bob? The following table shows the interest rate represented by each of the investment alternatives.

Investment	Monthly Investment	Interest Rate
Savings and loan	$645	4.75 percent
U.S. Treasuries	$620	7.25 percent
High-income corporate bond fund	$560	13.60 percent

Why does such a variation in rates of return for different types of investments exist? One reason centers on differences in the risk, either real or perceived, associated with different types of investments. If no such differences exist, earnings on investments will not vary. Once risk becomes a distinguishing feature among alternative investments, the investor must consider the potential effect of that risk. To induce investors to purchase assets possessing some degree of risk, sellers must pay a *risk premium* or a return adequate to compensate for the asset's actual or perceived risk.

Meaning of Investment Risk

In the field of insurance, risk typically is viewed as the potential for loss. However, investment assets are acquired with the expectation of receiving some type of gain, thereby causing the insurance-oriented definition to be inadequate for the purpose of explaining investment risk.

Since gain can result from owning investment assets, a more useful definition of investment risk must include positive, zero, and negative gains (losses). Further, the magnitude of positive and negative gains can vary rather sizably from one period to the next. If both elements (positive-negative gains and variation in magnitude) are considered, investment risk can be defined as the variability in the expected return to be obtained from an investment. The greater the expected potential variation in the return, the greater is the risk of the investment.

Causes of Investment Risk

Variation in an investment's return is the result of one or more distinct forces affecting the particular asset. These forces have an unequal impact on the variation in the return on different investments. In addition, some of these forces affect investment return on an almost daily basis, whereas others do so only infrequently. Their combined effect constitutes the total investment risk for a particular real or intangible asset.

These forces, or causes of investment risks, can be divided into three categories that reflect their relative scope and frequency. The first category is called The Big Three. These forces tend to affect most investments and occur with the greatest frequency. They may have the greatest impact on the variation in investment returns. In the short run, less common forces, called The Modest Three and The Minor Three, contain the potential to create very large changes in an investment's return.

The Big Three

The first of The Big Three causes of investment risk is *purchasing power risk,* sometimes called inflation risk. Inflation is the increase in the general level of prices. Purchasing power risk also includes the variation in return that can be caused by deflation, which is the decline in the general level of prices. With rising prices, the value of an investment asset or of the income earned thereon, or both, must increase at a rate equal to or greater than the inflation rate. Otherwise the purchasing power of the dollars invested or earned on the asset will decline.

Investment assets that are most susceptible to this risk include the full range of fixed-dollar investments such as savings accounts, certificates of deposit, bonds, bond funds, other debt instruments, life insurance cash values, and fixed annuities. During a time of rapid inflation the potential of these investments for an increase either in the real value of the assets or in the return earned from them varies from slight to none. On the other hand, when deflation occurs (twice in the last 50 years), these same investments have the potential for positive returns in value. This occurs because the annual income typically does not vary with economic conditions (such as the interest on a bond) and the purchasing power of that income stream rises.

For other investment assets the effect of purchasing power risk is quite different. Some assets increase in value or pay higher current income, or both, during periods of inflation. Such assets include real estate, precious metals, and business ownership interests such as common stock. Not all these assets move up in value with inflation in the short run, but over long periods of time the direction of the prices these assets command in the marketplace tends to parallel that of the general price level. Therefore these assets tend to provide greater protection against the inflation risk than the fixed-dollar investments, but they are more susceptible to the risk of deflation.

The second of The Big Three is *interest-rate risk.* Due to many forces at work in the economy, such as the actions of the Federal Reserve System to control the money supply, the changes in the demand for borrowed funds for consumption or investment purposes, or the movement of foreign exchange rates, the interest rate for any level and duration of risk will change over time. The result is a change in either the value of securities, the income earned on securities, or both. This effect, known as the interest-rate risk, has two segments: capital and reinvestment.

In the *capital segment,* any change in market interest rates typically leads to an opposite change in the value of investments. When interest rates rise (fall), the value of an investment declines (increases). This inverse relationship is most pronounced for financial instruments, such as bonds, mortgages, and U.S. Treasury bills, that have a contractually specified rate of interest or return and a specified time to maturity. Any change in interest rates for these investments will generate some opposite change in their market value (price). The longer the time until maturity, the greater will be the resulting change in market price. For other instruments, such as common stock or real estate, the relationship is not as pronounced. For example, a small increase (decrease) in interest rates may have little effect on stock market prices. However, a series of small changes or one sizable change in interest rates can cause many stock market prices to move sharply in the opposite direction.

The following example will illustrate why the value of an investment changes when interest rates change. Suppose that an investor purchased a bond when the market interest rate for the bond's risk was 8 percent and that this $1,000 face-amount bond has a maturity date one year hence and pays interest of $80 annually. Next assume that on the following day the market interest rate for bonds of this same risk and duration rises to 9 percent. Of course this investor would now like to sell this bond for $1,000. However, the investor will not be able to do so because a potential buyer can obtain $90 interest (instead of $80) by purchasing a newly issued, one-year maturity bond. However, a price can be determined that would make the total return, interest income, and appreciation in the market price of the 8 percent bond such that a potential buyer would be virtually indifferent to either the existing 8 percent or a newly issued 9 percent bond. This price would have to be somewhat less than $1,000 so that the buyer's total return would be about 9 percent. Alternatively, if the market interest rate had fallen to 7 percent, for example, the value of the 8 percent bond would rise above its $1,000 face amount so that the total return to the buyer would be equal to 7 percent.

Rather than the one-year maturity used in the previous example, suppose the security had a 10-year maturity. With a 9 percent market interest rate, a buyer would have $10 less interest each year for 10 years if he or she buys the 8 percent debt instrument. Therefore the resulting market price change for this 8 percent security with a 10-year maturity date must be greater than for the one-year maturity in the previous example. This potential change in the market price of debt securities takes on importance if a sale of the security is anticipated prior to its stated maturity date. The longer the time remaining until maturity, the greater will be the resulting market price change. If no sale is planned, the market price's ups and downs are of little consequence to the investor unless an unexpected event creates the need to sell.

How can a financial planner make use of this relationship between the interest rate and the market price of debt securities? If it is anticipated that the forces affecting interest rates are working to increase interest rates, the planner should advise the investor to sell the debt instruments in his or her portfolio. If interest rates do in fact rise, securities similar to those that were disposed of can be repurchased at lower prices. If interest rates are expected to decrease, the investor should be advised to purchase debt securities that, after interest rates decrease, can be sold at a gain.

The *reinvestment segment,* which is the second segment of the interest-rate risk, comes into play when debt securities mature. At this point the investor must reinvest the principal in new securities. Of course, if then-current interest rates exceed those earned on the matured security, the investor realizes higher future income. What is the result if current interest rates are below those on the matured instrument? The reinvestment element of the interest-rate risk is present because the investor will now realize less income from the reinvested money. The way to minimize the reinvestment element is to stagger the maturities of the securities held in the portfolio so that only a small percentage will mature in any one year. Thus only a long year-to-year downward trend of interest rates would be significantly detrimental to the investor's income stream.

The last of The Big Three causes of investment risk is *market risk.* Participants in the market for investments should continuously monitor and assess events occurring in the total environment that affect the particular investment asset. These events could be political, economic, demographic, or social in nature and are important because they can affect the expected returns from an investment. The inferences drawn from this monitoring form the basis for decisions to buy, hold, or sell selected or all investment assets. When a sufficient number of market participants act in a similar fashion, market prices for a particular investment (or investment assets in general) can react rather sharply, as the stock market did in October 1987 and 1989 and August 1998.

Although stock market events capture the attention of the news media, similar declines can occur in markets for other investment assets. For example, at the time of this writing, the markets are experiencing rather sharp price declines for certain types of hotels and department stores. Some analysts are forecasting a long-term decline in residential real estate prices due to changing demographic patterns in the population. Since not all investment sectors are affected to the same degree at the same time, a strategy that spreads an investor's assets over numerous investment markets can mitigate the effect of market events occurring in one or two investment sectors.

The Modest Three

The next broad category of causes of investment risk, here labeled as The Modest Three, has less overall effect than The Big Three on the value of investment assets in general. When present, however, they can drastically affect the value of certain investment assets. For some types of investments, however, The Modest Three do not apply at all.

The first of The Modest Three is *business (default) risk.* For whatever reason, such as a change in consumer preference away from a particular good or service, ineffective management, law change, or foreign competition, some enterprises will experience financial difficulties and eventually fail. Frequently debt principal or interest payments will not be made on a timely basis, and the organization will be in default. This result can occur in both profit-seeking businesses and nonprofit institutions such as colleges or municipalities. In addition to loss of current and future interest payments, investors in these bonds often lose some or all of the initial sum invested. Because all debts must be paid in full before any funds can flow to the stockholders, rarely is anything left to the owners of profit-seeking firms that have failed. (There is no equity ownership in nonprofit or governmental organizations.) Of course, this risk is not associated with debt instruments of the U.S. Treasury because they are backed by the full faith, credit, and taxing power of the federal government.

Investment tactics to minimize the business (default) risk include the purchase of investments only issued by organizations having a high credit rating. As mentioned earlier, both Moody's and Standard & Poor's provide assessments of the issuing organization for securities such as bonds. Obtaining the information for other forms of investments, such as limited partnerships, requires a more diligent investigation by the financial planner and the investor.

The second of The Modest Three is *liquidity risk.* An investment asset is deemed to be liquid (that is, there is no liquidity risk) if the asset can be converted to cash (sold) quickly at any time and without any loss of principal. Generally funds can be withdrawn from a savings account any time the bank is open, and some funds can be withdrawn through automatic tellers any time of the day or night. Thus this asset is liquid. However, the requirement of a 30-day wait to withdraw from a savings account would make the account less liquid. The ability to sell an asset quickly but only at a market price substantially below investor cost is also a characteristic of a nonliquid investment.

Liquidity, as defined above, is a critical concept when evaluating the appropriateness of investment assets for a client's emergency reserve. These funds may be needed quickly, and the client may not want to suffer a loss. In these situations only highly safe, highly liquid assets such as savings accounts, some CDs, life insurance cash values, Treasury bills, and similar investments are recommended.

The next cause of investment risk is called *marketability risk.* Somewhat similar to liquidity risk, this risk occurs when an investment asset cannot be sold quickly at its current market price. This situation arises if, for example, a large block of a thinly traded security comes to the market and significantly depresses its market price. If a more leisurely sale spread out over a period of time had been feasible, the market price might not have dropped at all. For example, at almost any time 100 shares of a Fortune 500 firm's stock can be sold without affecting the market price; however, selling 20 million of the firm's shares might depress the price substantially.

Some investments, such as homes and other real estate, are affected by marketability risk to a greater degree than are standardized financial assets traded on some form of organized market. Admittedly real estate or other assets can always be sold, but a price other than one associated with a distress sale probably cannot be realized.

Because of the existence of marketability risk for some types of investment assets, it does not follow that investors should be advised to completely avoid assets that are not readily marketable. Rather, only a portion of a client's total portfolio should be so positioned.

The Minor Three

The effect of the last three causes of investment risk, called The Minor Three, can be just as severe as those described above, but the relative infrequency of their occurring causes them to be assigned to this category.

The first of The Minor Three is *tax risk.* Virtually all investments have some tax consequences. Income and appreciation in value will at some time be subject to income taxation. In addition, investment assets may be subject to estate and inheritance taxation and gift taxation when ownership is transferred.

In some instances the tax code provides specific incentives to encourage certain types of investments as desirable public policy. However, what the government granteth, the government canst remove. In 1986 the favorable federal income tax treatment of capital gains was removed, and restrictions were placed on the exclusion of certain municipal bond interest from federal income taxation. Although some revision in capital-gains taxation has since been made, it is not as favorable as that which was removed. Other provisions within the tax code still favor certain investments, but these provisions could be removed by subsequent legislation. New laws could also penalize certain investments by imposing special tax consequences on income or appreciation derived therefrom.

When the tax laws remove some favorable, or add some unfavorable, tax consequences, the value of the affected investment assets falls. To cope with the effects of this type of investment risk, financial planners and investors must monitor events occurring in the national tax arena and make investment decisions accordingly. Investments should be based primarily on their economic value and contribution to investor's goals and should *not* be based solely on their tax advantages.

The second of The Minor Three is called *event risk,* which refers to a variety of possible occurrences that can significantly affect the riskiness of a specific investment asset. One example of such an event is a takeover move.

During the 1980s some individuals and corporations went on a buying spree and acquired some of the largest corporations in the United States. For example, a corporation would perhaps purchase less than 5 percent of the targeted corporation's common stock and then announce its intention to complete the acquisition, using borrowed funds to finance the purchase of the remaining shares. Investors may view this as a decline in the quality of the targeted corporation's previously issued bonds. Why does this occur? Typically a new, nonoperating corporation is created as the mechanism to arrange the financing of the acquisition. The acquirer will generally buy the total equity interest with about 90 or more percent of debt and the remainder with his or her own funds. This tactic is known as a leveraged buyout (LBO). Shortly after the acquisition takes place, the acquired firm is usually merged into the newly formed corporation. As a result of this merger, the bonds from the acquired corporation have the same status as the bonds recently issued by the acquiring corporation. A business that has a high ratio of debt to equity can encounter financial difficulties if it does not have sufficient earnings to meet the interest obligations of the debt. Because this situation could occur, the previously issued bonds (particularly if they are debentures) are perceived to have higher risk, thus requiring a higher return. Since the interest rate is fixed for the life of the bond issue, the only way for these bonds to provide a higher return is for their price to fall. Thus, when a corporation becomes the target of a takeover attempt, its bonds tend to fall sharply in value.

The last cause of investment risk is called *additional commitment risk.* Some investments may require the buyer to put additional money into his or her investment when certain conditions occur. This additional funding requirement may arise at an inopportune time for the investor. If funds are not available, the investor might be forced to sell the asset at an unfavorable market price. Investments such as certain limited partnerships that can require additional contributions are viewed as being more risky than those that require no further investment.

Summary

As we have seen, investment risk arises for many reasons. Each of these reasons may not be as totally independent of each other as these descriptions make it seem. For example, investors may view inflation as a major forthcoming issue and begin to sell bonds, thus driving down bond prices. Should the monetary authorities seek to mitigate the potential inflation by raising interest rates, bond prices will tumble even further. In addition, if the firm is an announced target for an LBO, the bonds of the targeted firm could then plummet in value.

Investment Return

While most investments do not guarantee that an investor will obtain a return, the expectation of obtaining a return is a primary reason why individuals invest. As was suggested in the definition of an investment, total investment return has two major components: current income and capital appreciation. Not all investments produce both forms of return. Some investments, such as savings accounts, can produce only current (interest) income. Others, such as undeveloped land, can produce only capital appreciation (unless the land can be farmed or rented). Still others, such as borrowing to purchase corporate common stock, can produce negative current income if the interest expense is greater than the dividends, but could provide capital appreciation.

Regardless of the possible combination of returns, a method for comparing the investment returns from different investment assets is an absolute necessity. Over the years and before computers or calculators, three methods for performing quick calculations of investment return acquired widespread acceptance within the investment community. These three measures are still widely used and are (1) the current yield, (2) the holding-period return (HPR), and (3) the approximate yield.

Current Yield

The current yield is perhaps the most widely used measure of financial return. This measure relates the current annual income from an investment to its market price today. The calculation is as follows:

$$\begin{array}{c}\text{before-tax}\\ \text{current yield}\end{array} = \frac{\text{current annual income}}{\text{current market price}}$$

For example, assume that an investor plans to purchase a corporate bond currently selling at $1,050. The bond will pay the investor an annual interest income of $98. If the bond is purchased, its before-tax current yield to the investor would be

$$\begin{array}{c}\text{before-tax}\\ \text{current yield}\end{array} = \frac{\$98}{\$1{,}050}$$

$$= .0933 \text{ or } 9.33\%$$

One advantage of the current yield is that it provides a quick way to compare different investments being considered for purchase, retention, or sale. Its major shortcoming is that it fails to look beyond the present moment. The investments being compared may have different potentials for future increases or decreases in their income streams or market prices. This element is not considered when calculating the current yield. A second shortcoming is that the calculation is made on a before-tax basis. To calculate the after-tax current yield, the above formula must be modified so that the current annual income is reduced by the investor's marginal income tax rate (MRT). The following formula makes this adjustment:

$$\text{after-tax current yield} = \frac{\text{current annual income} \times (1 - \text{MRT})}{\text{current market price}}$$

$$\text{where MRT} = \text{investor's combined federal and state marginal income tax rate}$$

If a 40 percent marginal tax rate (income) applies to this investor, the after-tax return would be

$$\text{after-tax current yield} = \frac{\$98 \times (1-.40)}{\$1{,}050}$$

$$= .056 \text{ or } 5.6\%$$

Alternatively, the before-tax current yield as shown above can be multiplied by one minus the investor's marginal tax rate to adjust for taxes to obtain 5.6 percent [9.33% x (1 – .40)].

Holding-Period Return (HPR)

Although its name may imply that the holding-period return is a measure of the return over *any* holding period, it is only appropriate for investment periods of one year or less. This is because no consideration of the timing of the investment returns, and therefore of the time value of money, is made. The holding-period return relates the total amount of current income plus the total amount of capital appreciation to the beginning dollar value of the investment. The following formula will determine the before-tax HPR for a one-year period:

$$\text{before-tax HPR} = \frac{\text{total current income} + \text{total capital appreciation}}{\text{total initial investment}}$$

For example, assume that Charles purchased an investment on January 1, 1997, for $800. It is now January 1, 1998, and he wants to know what has been the return on his investment. During his one-year holding period, he has received $50 of current income. In addition, the market price of the investment has increased to $840. Based on this information, the before-tax HPR for this investment would be as follows:

$$\frac{\text{before-tax}}{\text{HPR}} = \frac{\$50 + (\$840 - \$800)}{\$800}$$

$$= \frac{\$90}{\$800}$$

$$= .1125 \text{ or } 11.25\%$$

If an after-tax basis is desired, then the HPR formula becomes

$$\frac{\text{after-tax}}{\text{HPR}} = \frac{\text{total current income} \times (1 - \text{MRT}) + \text{total capital appreciation} \times (1 - \text{MRT})}{\text{total initial investment}}$$

If Charles is in a combined federal and state income tax bracket of 30 percent, then his after-tax return would be

$$\frac{\text{after-tax}}{\text{HPR}} = \frac{\$50\,(1-.30) + [(\$840 - \$800)\,(1-.30)]}{\$800}$$

$$= \frac{\$35 + \$28}{\$800}$$

$$= .07875 \text{ or } 7.88\%$$

At the current time, the federal income tax rules apply different tax rates to current investment income, such as dividends or interest, and to capital appreciation. The maximum tax rate for individuals is 39.6 percent for interest and dividend income and 28 percent for capital appreciation (gain). If in the previous illustration Charles was in the 31 percent federal income tax bracket for interest and dividends and paid an additional 2 percent in state income taxes on *all* his income, his after-tax HPR would be as follows:

$$\frac{\text{after-tax}}{\text{HPR}} = \frac{\$50\,(1 - .33) + (\$840 - \$800)\,(1 - .30)}{\$800}$$

$$= \frac{\$33.5 + \$28}{\$800}$$

$$= .07687 \text{ or } 7.69\%$$

For holding periods shorter than one year, the HPR as calculated above requires modification. If, for example, Charles held the investment for only one-half of a year and achieved the same results, his 7.69 after-tax HPR should be multiplied by 2. This results in an annualized after-tax HPR of 15.38 percent

(7.69 x 2). Or, if Charles had achieved his gains in 3 months or in 2 weeks, his annualized HPR would be found by multiplying the after-tax HPR by 4 or 26, respectively.

Approximate Yield

The true yield on an investment can be described as the rate of interest or discount rate (called the internal rate of return) that makes the present value of the benefits derived from an investment exactly equal to the present value of the cost to purchase the investment. The approximation of the interest or discount rate can be found by using the following formula:

$$\begin{matrix}\text{before-tax}\\ \text{approximate}\\ \text{yield}\end{matrix} = \frac{\text{annual income} + \dfrac{\text{future price} - \text{current price}}{\text{number of years}}}{\dfrac{\text{future price} + \text{current price}}{2}}$$

Suppose Elly has been advised that a particular stock that is currently selling for \$50 a share is expected to increase in value to \$68 by the end of 3 years. The annual dividends are expected to be \$3 for each of the next 3 years. Based on this information, Elly's approximate yield for the holding period would be

$$\begin{matrix}\text{before-tax}\\ \text{approximate}\\ \text{yield}\end{matrix} = \frac{\$3 + \dfrac{\$68 - \$50}{3}}{\dfrac{\$68 + \$50}{2}}$$

$$= \frac{\$3 + \$6}{\$59}$$

$$= .1525 \text{ or } 15.25\%$$

With no difference in tax rates between the two types of income, multiplying the approximate yield by one minus the investor's marginal tax rate (1 - MRT) will provide the after-tax approximate yield. If the earned income tax rate and the capital appreciation tax rate differ, then each segment of the numerator must be multiplied by one minus the investor's marginal tax rate (as shown in the after-tax HPR formula).

The approximate-yield concept can provide a meaningful estimate of an investment's yield over both short and long holding periods. Applications of this approach include (1) estimating the yield over a planned investment horizon, as shown in the previous illustration, (2) determining the yield from the date of acquisition to the present on a currently owned investment, or (3) determining what the yield was for an investment that has been sold. Only the purpose of the calculation changes; the formula remains unchanged.

REAL AFTER-TAX RATE OF RETURN

Earlier it was noted that inflation has been almost continual over the last 50 years. Therefore any analysis or recommendation to a client concerning particular investments should include inflation as a factor. One useful method adjusts the annual after-tax rate of return for inflation. If the holding-period return is used, for example, the real after-tax rate of return can be calculated using the following formula:

$$\text{real after-tax rate of return} = \frac{(1 + \text{after-tax HPR})}{(1 + \text{current rate of inflation})} - 1$$

Both the after-tax HPR and the rate of inflation must be expressed as decimals in this formula.

For example, if an investor earned an after-tax HPR of .08 (8 percent) during a year when the inflation rate was .04 (4 percent), the investor's real after-tax rate of return would be

$$\begin{aligned}\text{real after-tax rate of return} &= \frac{(1 + .08)}{(1+.04)} - 1\\ &= 1.038 - 1\\ &= .038 \text{ or } 3.8\%\end{aligned}$$

Whenever the rate of inflation exceeds the after-tax rate of return obtained over a holding period, the investor will realize a negative real after-tax rate of return. This was the result for many investments during the late 1970s and early 1980s, when inflation rates in the United States neared and even exceeded 10 percent and the before-tax return on some investments was 5 percent. Today savings accounts often pay about a 4 percent before-tax rate of return. If the investor is in the 28 percent income tax bracket, the real after-tax return sinks to zero if the inflation rate is 2.88 percent.

TAXABLE INCOME COMPARED TO TAX-EXEMPT INCOME

Some municipal bonds provide their owners with interest income that is exempt from federal income taxation. Often clients desire to know what would be the equivalent taxable rate for the purpose of making comparisons between these municipals and corporate or Treasury bonds. The following formula converts a tax-exempt yield to an equivalent taxable yield as follows:

$$\text{equivalent fully taxable yield} = \frac{\text{tax-exempt yield}}{(1 - \text{MRT})}$$

A fully taxable yield can be converted to an equivalent tax-exempt yield as follows:

$$\text{equivalent tax-exempt yield} = \text{fully taxable yield} \times (1 - \text{MRT})$$

To use these formulas, the tax-exempt yield or the fully taxable yield must be expressed as a percentage, whereas the marginal tax rate must be expressed as a decimal.

For example, assume that Bruce inherited some municipal bonds that have a current yield of 6.5 percent. Recently it was recommended that he purchase taxable corporate bonds as a means of increasing his income. He wonders if it would be worthwhile to sell these municipals and purchase corporate bonds with the proceeds. His marginal income tax rate is 28 percent. Bruce does not have any capital appreciation in the municipal bonds and does not expect any such appreciation in the corporate bonds. Based on this information, the equivalent fully taxable yield would be

$$= \frac{6.5\%}{(1 - .28)}$$

$$= 9.03\%$$

If one ignores transactions costs, Bruce would be no better or worse off if he continues to hold the municipal bonds or if he sells them and purchases corporate bonds paying 9.03 percent. His after-tax income would increase only if he can earn a fully taxable return in excess of 9.03 percent.

To verify this, suppose that the corporate bonds paid 9.04 percent. Use of the equivalent tax-exempt yield formula would produce

$$= 9.04\% \times (1 - .28)$$

$$= 6.509\%$$

This yield is slightly more than the 6.5 percent currently being earned. If transactions costs (usually $10 per bond for the first five bonds and less as more bonds are purchased or sold) are taken into consideration, an increase this small cannot justify the sale and purchase.

HISTORICAL PATTERNS OF BEFORE-TAX RETURNS

At this point, the question might arise as to what size returns can be expected from different investments. This depends on the time frame used in the analysis and the particular events occurring during the time frame. One might, for example, examine the returns of different types of assets in the 1970s and 1980s and the early 1990s and compare these returns to the consumer price index (CPI). The 1970s were a decade for tangibles, such as collectibles, commodities, and real estate. These assets had compound annual rates of growth ranging from 12 to 35 percent and outperformed both the CPI and financial assets such as stocks, bonds, and Treasury bills. However, the 1980s tell a different story. During that decade stocks, bonds, and Treasury bills outperformed the CPI and the tangibles. The first few years of the 1990s have been turbulent. Foreign stocks due to the sluggish domestic economy and domestic bonds due to falling interest rates have been the best performers. Also most financial assets experienced returns in excess of the inflation rate.

Table 12-1 (see below) displays several asset categories and includes those assets most likely to be part of client portfolios. The most sophisticated types of investments, such as master limited partnerships, commodity mutual funds, and equipment-leasing partnerships, appeal only to a very small percentage of clients and are purposely omitted. The total return includes both current income

TABLE 12-1
Historical Investment Returns for Periods Ending December 31, 1997

	Total Annual Return (in Percent)			
Asset	5-Year	10-Year	15-Year	20-Year
Large company stocks	20.24	18.05	17.52	16.65
Small company stocks	19.34	16.46	14.09	17.71
Long-term corporate bonds	9.22	10.85	11.91	10.29
Long-term government bonds	10.51	11.32	11.88	10.39
Intermediate government bonds	6.40	8.33	9.47	9.51
Treasury bills	4.57	5.44	6.15	7.29
Inflation	2.60	3.41	3.41	4.89

(dividends or interest) and capital appreciation when appropriate. The data for municipal bonds, however, include only the current yield since trading before maturity is relatively unusual for municipal bonds. For the various categories, the data shown represent a before-tax return. Consequently, the data are not exactly comparable since the municipal-bond yield should be adjusted to an equivalent fully taxable yield.

In general, the longer the time to maturity for debt instruments, the larger will be the total return. This relationship between duration and return is not perfect. The 15-year returns for U.S. Treasury, corporate, and municipal bonds exceeded the 20-year return due to the abnormally high interest rates during the years 1979-1982. When risk rises, such as corporate debt rather than U. S. Treasuries, the before-tax return rises.

As the data in table 12-2 suggest, when a longer holding period is examined, common stock investments provide the higher return. However, as shown in table 12-2, the return for all assets is much lower over the 70-year period than has been experienced in the last 10 to 20 years.

TABLE 12-2
Average Annual Pretax Return (Geometric Mean), 1926–1997

Large company stocks	11.0%
Small company stocks	12.7%
Long-term corporate bonds	5.7%
Long-term government bonds	5.2%
Intermediate-term government bonds	5.3%
Treasury bills	3.8%
Inflation	3.1%

INVESTMENT PRINCIPLES, STRATEGIES, AND TACTICS

Now that the types of investments frequently used and various investment risks and returns have been examined, this section will describe some of the policy recommendations and techniques that are recommended by successful financial planners and used by many successful investors. Not all are appropriate to all situations, but collectively they provide the planner with some guidelines so that clients will receive prudent advice concerning investment strategies and tactics.

Meet Emergency and Protection Needs First

No investment should be undertaken unless the investor has first accomplished two highly important personal objectives: emergency needs and protection needs. The consequences of not having satisfied these objectives are too great, as are the risks associated with investments. Obviously some of the client's emergency funds could be placed in investments that will provide some current return. However, the choices should be limited to the first category of investments (cash equivalents), as previously described.

Match Investment Instrument with Investment Objective

Any investment must be appropriate for the personal financial objective that is being sought. For example, individual retirement accounts (IRAs) accumulate interest on a tax-free basis until the monies are withdrawn. Therefore using tax-free municipal bonds as the funding instrument in an IRA is not a prudent course of action, since the IRA provides the benefit of tax deferral and similarly municipal bonds are exempt from current income taxation. Seeking the higher rate of taxable return commensurate with the client's risk preferences would be a better course of action due to the tax-free buildup.

When funds are being accumulated for purposes that are not deferable, it is essential to have virtually the precise amount available at the needed time. For example, investments whose market price fluctuates sharply or investments that are not readily salable would not be appropriate for funding a child's expected education expenses. For this type of objective, the proper approach should include matching the investment's maturity with the date the funds will be needed.

As another example, a young client's funding for retirement should not use short-term investments, since these usually are at the low end of the structure of returns and offer little opportunity for appreciation over the planning horizon. Instead, investments that have as their objective long-term capital growth are more effective in offsetting the inflation that is likely to occur over the next 10, 20, or 30 years.

Equity Investments Require Extended Holding Horizon

Investments in common stocks that are owned individually or through investment companies should generally have a planned holding period of at least 3 years. Any period shorter than this subjects the investment to increased risk. The problem of market timing, or when to buy or sell, and the transactions costs of the purchase and sale work to make success quite difficult with shorter-term holding horizons.

In addition, the behavior of the stock market favors at least a 3-year planning horizon. Combined with the dividend income earned on a portfolio of common stocks, the ups and downs of the market typically are such that only a few 3-year holding periods fail to provide a positive return. For a horizon of 5 years, even fewer periods fail to provide a positive return. Many shorter periods, however, for example one year or less, have produced a negative total return.

Other equity investments, such as real estate, require even longer planned holding periods due to their relatively larger transactions costs and their general lack of marketability. Indeed, for some limited partnerships that invest in real estate, financial advisers often advocate at least a 10-year planned holding period.

Change with the Times

Grandpa said, "Never sell the XYZ stock"; but Grandpa has died and conditions have changed. Wise investors monitor the economic, financial, and security markets and continually utilize the new information to restructure their portfolios as conditions dictate. All too often individuals are wedded to a particular investment for emotional, rather than rational, reasons. Other individuals do not sell a particular asset because of the income tax consequences associated with the transaction. However, the time comes when the best course of action is to sell, take the gain, and pay the tax. Perhaps even more difficult is the decision to sell at a loss. No one likes to see a personal decision turn sour, but future conditions might only increase the loss if the asset is not sold.

Beware of Tax-Saving Rationale

Investment analysis and decision making should focus on the underlying economic facts. Sometimes planners who recommend investments focus on the tax benefits that will accrue to the client rather than on the economic soundness of the venture. The Tax Reform Act of 1986 stands as a monument to the fact that the government can drastically change the tax rules. Many investments previously made solely on the basis of tax considerations have generated problems and losses for their owners. Certainly tax considerations influence investment decisions, and their effect must be analyzed. However, tax considerations are only one of many factors that determine the economic soundness of an investment.

Understand the Investment

A financial planner should never recommend to a client any investment that is not fully understood by both the planner and the client. Both ethical and legal factors make this imperative. The hidden consequences arising out of the investment can be significant. For example, purchasing a real estate or oil-and-gas limited-partnership interest results in the need to file at least six additional tax forms each year. Other examples include understanding the consequences of purchasing taxable zero coupon bonds or the risks of investing in newly formed businesses. Remember that some large corporations lost hundreds of millions of dollars by holding investment instruments whose risk and price volatility were not understood.

Diversify the Portfolio

Diversification of an investment portfolio is a matter of degree. The old adage, "Don't put all your eggs in one basket," never provided the answer to the question, "In how many baskets should the eggs be put?"

Effective portfolio diversification can be viewed as a hierarchy. The narrowest perspective at the bottom of the hierarchy is based on modern portfolio theory. Under this view a security is selected on the basis of how its return varies as compared to the variation in the return on other securities in the portfolio. Ideally the return for each security should vary with respect to the other securities in the portfolio so that the only risk remaining for the portfolio as a whole is market risk. Other risks, such as business risk, are virtually eliminated through diversification. Experts suggest that approximately 20 carefully selected securities will largely achieve this result.

Further up the hierarchy, a somewhat broader view of diversification would expand the scope of this process to include investments other than securities that are owned by the client. This wider spectrum could include the client's home, other real estate investments, collectibles, and precious metals. Investing in both gold as a precious metal and in gold-mining stocks as a security would not provide additional diversification and, unless compelling reasons existed, one of these two investments should be sold.

The apex of the hierarchy represents the broadest view of diversification and recognizes the client's occupation, the nature and stability of his or her employer, and the investments used in such employment-related benefits as pension and 401(k) plans. For example, a client who is employed as a commission sales representative by a firm whose sales move up and down with the business cycle and who has selected the employer's stock as the investment instrument for contributions to the 401(k) plan has little diversification should the economy enter a recession. Sage advice might be to reduce the dependence on the employer by using some different investments for the 401(k) plan if such choices are permitted. In addition, the client should place other funds into investments whose performance varies in a manner markedly different from that associated with his or her employment-related income sources.

Recognize the Role of Intuition

Hard financial and economic analysis by itself is not always sufficient to determine what is an appropriate investment. Some other element, perhaps neither quantifiable nor ascertainable from sophisticated analysis, can provide the hunch that a particular investment will be successful. A recently related story concerns a financial planner who, after purchasing a particular brand of running shoes, noticed that many acquaintances were wearing the same product. Intuition said to recommend a purchase, and investigation confirmed the producer to be a healthy, profitable corporation. The result was a most successful investment for some clients who benefited from a period of rapid growth in the firm's sales and profits.

Expect Mistakes

Not all investments will perform as expected. The planner and client must recognize that mistakes will occur and then dispose of the asset, take the loss, and move on to other (hopefully more successful) investments. However, every mistake should provide some insight or information that will benefit future investment analysis and decision making.

Use a Consistent Pattern of Investing

Attempts to outguess the market or to predict the start of the next downturn or upturn and thus achieve superior returns through market timing for each and every investment may not be worth the effort. For example, $5,000 was invested every year in a particular stock mutual fund beginning in 1975. If an investment was made on the first business day of each year, the twenty $5,000 investments along with the reinvestment of all dividends and capital gains would have grown to a value of $484,521 in twenty years for an average annual total return of 13.5 percent. Suppose this investor had perfect knowledge (or with perfect hindsight) and the purchases were made each year at the lowest net asset value per share of this fund. How much better would the return have been? The accumulated value would have been $500,249 and the average annual total return would have been 14.1 percent over the 20-year period. Either the 13.5 or the 14.1 percent returns are both quite acceptable. And how many individuals can accurately predict the lowest point of the market in any one year, let alone in every year for 20 years?

Another study, using the Standard and Poor's index for the years 1968 to 1988, returned 18.5 percent per year if the purchases were made at the lowest point and 16.6 percent if the purchases were at the peak of the market for the year. A disciplined pattern of investing, made at consistent periodic intervals, would have earned a return somewhere between these two percentages. The technique of dollar-cost averaging, which is based on such a pattern of investing, usually achieves satisfactory results.

Take Advantage of the Power of Compounding

Compound interest, or interest earned on interest, is a powerful force in determining the size, at some future time, of an accumulation of funds. The importance of this concept should not be ignored in a client's investment program. Many investments provide easy reinvestment of current income that results in the benefit of compounding. Some of the more frequently encountered examples are as follows:

- *passbook savings accounts*—The interest is automatically added to the account, and the investor must take specific action by withdrawing the interest to prevent compounding from occurring.
- *certificates of deposit*—Small CDs typically do not distribute interest during the life of the instrument. Rather, the interest is automatically reinvested, most often at the same rate being earned on the principal amount invested in the CD.
- *mutual funds*—Most mutual funds allow for the automatic purchase of additional shares whenever current income or capital gains are credited to a shareholder's account.
- *common stocks*—Many large corporations permit the investor to reinvest dividends in additional shares of that corporation's common stock. Often no brokerage charges are levied, and in rare cases the corporation subsidizes the purchase by providing up to a 5 percent discount from the average market price of its stock over the past 3 months.
- *zero coupon bonds*—Bonds that do not make an annual interest payment to the bondholder, such as U.S. Government Series EE bonds and selected issues of corporate, government, and municipal bonds, have a built-in automatic compounding of interest over their life.

Work with Professionals

The appropriateness of an investment to the client's objectives and the degree of diligence used to verify that an investment is, in fact, appropriate are forces that are imposing a higher standard today on those providing investment advice than was true in the past. Working with investment professionals, particularly those who specialize in specific investments, helps to ensure that the recommended investments are appropriate for the achievement of client objectives. Therefore the abilities of investment counselors, brokers, and bankers should be drawn upon by financial planners.

Beware of High-Pressure Sales Tactics

Most marketers possess persuasive skills, which sometimes border on pressure selling. Unfortunately marketers of investment products are no exception. Frequently tales of high-pressure, boiler-room, telephone solicitations receive widespread coverage in the news media. These are the blatant examples. Although caution on the part of the financial planner and the client might lead to a missed opportunity, the frequency of that occurring is far less than implied by the solicitations and does not outweigh the benefits of careful investigation.

Expect Markets to Overreact

Investment markets are not perfect, or perhaps the players lack perfection. Since perfect knowledge does not exist, when either good or bad news reaches the marketplace, the market often overreacts. Good news may produce too much euphoria that initially drives prices up disproportionately. Conversely, bad news may bring out high degrees of pessimism that drive prices below what are justifiably based on the information. Within a few days the market tends to assess the news more rationally and prices adjust to reflect the reality of the information. Therefore a financial planner's knee-jerk reaction to market behavior fails to provide clients with the advice needed to make proper decisions. Of course, when either upward or downward *trends* emerge in the market, appropriate action must be taken.

Avoid Discretionary Power

Many clients prefer to have others perform the necessary work of managing their portfolios and grant broad managerial powers to accomplish this end. Although this may be an indication of trust in the judgment of the person receiving this power, conflict is likely to develop. Portfolio performance that does not meet a client's expectations, such as a sharp decline in market prices that generates portfolio losses, can precipitate this conflict. To avoid this problem financial planners may want to suggest that approval from the client must be obtained before any action is taken. Exceptions to receiving this prior approval might include times when the client cannot be readily reached or when surgery or other medical treatment precludes the client from taking an active role.

Apply the Control Process

Up to this point, emphasis has been on the need for selecting investments that match a client's objectives. To select these investments there must be performance standards. These performance standards are the first step of the control process. Monitoring performance, the second step, provides the data for the third step, the comparison of performance with standards. If targeted results (the standards) are being met, there may be no need for a change within the portfolio. However, if economic forecasts make certain investments questionable, then, despite having achieved the targeted results, the investments should be sold.

If the targeted results are not being met, the client has a problem investment. A problem investment is any investment that is not achieving its expected level of performance. When faced with a problem investment, the client has two choices—retain or sell. The actual choice will depend on the estimate of the investment's *future* performance. If a new acceptable standard, revised due to changed economic or financial conditions, is achievable, then the client should be advised to retain the problem investment. Otherwise, disposal of the problem investment should be recommended.

FOCUS ON ETHICS
Understanding Investment Risk

In the 1980s many headlines were written concerning *junk* bonds. Both the yields and the name of these securities implied high risk. Many families suffered financial loss directly or indirectly through investments in securities bearing a level of risk well above what their portfolios warranted.

In the early 1990s, the same thing happened with derivatives, hybrid securities that few really understand. Although derivatives have valid uses in hedging and speculation, their high level of risk makes them a poor choice for all but the most sophisticated investors.

It is the financial planner's responsibility to comprehend and effectively communicate the risk associated with alternative investments. To do otherwise is an ethical, professional, and potentially legal error that can lead to disastrous results.

ECONOMIC ENVIRONMENT AND INVESTMENT TACTICS

Business cycles resemble roller coasters. Both have a long, slow ride up to the top (peak) and then a short, fast trip down to the bottom (trough) before starting the long upward ride again. In economic terms, the long ride up is called the *expansionary phase* of the cycle. Economic events that typically occur during this phase include the following:

- increases in demand for goods and services leading to increases in output and employment
- widespread optimism among consumers and business firms concerning future economic conditions
- increases in incomes, profits, and dividends
- rising prices for stocks and tangible assets
- inflationary pressures due to productive capacity limitations
- increasing interest rates due to demand for borrowing to finance the expansion, followed by Federal Reserve restrictive monetary actions to reduce inflationary pressures

During the downward phase of the cycle, often called a *recession,* the reverse of the activities in the expansionary stage takes place.

When investors believe that either of these two phases represents the current situation, then the critical question is, "Will this condition continue into the future?" If analysis provides a positive answer, the investment decision is easy: Buy those investments that will perform well under those conditions. In the early expansionary stages, the recommendations would include, for example, convertible bonds, common stocks, real estate, and commodities. In the early stages of a recession, bonds and other debt instruments are more appropriate.

Those periods at or near the peak or trough of the business cycle are the most difficult to assess. How long will this expansion or contraction continue? If analysis provides no clear signal, this is not a time to either dispose of or acquire new investments except cash equivalents, such as money market mutual funds or short-term CDs. When conditions become clearer, the investor should be advised to dispose of those investments that are not suitable and to acquire those that are appropriate for the forthcoming conditions.

INVESTMENT MARKETS AND REGULATION

Many types of markets exist for investments. This section will first describe major types of markets where investments trading occurs on a regular basis. These markets are (1) true-auction markets, (2) negotiated markets, (3) dealer markets, and (4) organized-securities markets. Following this material, the purpose and thrust of the major federal laws and regulations affecting investments will be covered.

Investment Markets

True-Auction Markets

In true-auction markets, investment assets such as artwork, collectibles, or real estate are offered for sale to the highest bidder. The bidding continues until no one exceeds the last bid price. When this occurs, the sale is consummated. Since the advent of telecommunications, potential buyers need not attend these trading sessions. Normally only a small number of potential buyers participate in true-auction markets for several reasons. First, buyers might not be aware that such an auction is being held. Second, buyers often prefer first-hand evaluation of the asset, and the cost of attending these auctions can be high. Third, for some of these assets (such as a particular painter's artwork) only a relatively few potential purchasers exist either regionally, nationally, or internationally. Lastly, the unit price of some of these investments dictates that only a handful of bidders will have the financial resources.

A variant of this form of auction market is used by the Federal Reserve System in its marketing of U.S. Treasury T-bills. Although competitive bidding from financial institutions takes place on a regular basis (every Monday for delivery on Thursday), small investors can submit noncompetitive bids specifying the amount (subject to a minimum face value of $10,000) and the desired maturity. These bids are accepted at the average price (interest return) for all competitive bids accepted in that day's auction. In this manner the small investor has the opportunity to acquire T-bills directly from the issuer and earn a rate competitive with that being earned by financial institutions.

Negotiated Markets

Negotiated markets predominate for the trading of real estate and similar investment assets. In these markets, sellers list their offerings with brokers who then seek to attract buyers through various advertising and other marketing methods. After a buyer has been located, negotiations determine the price.

Large institutional investors such as pension funds and mutual funds often employ brokers to locate buyers or sellers of large blocks of bonds or stocks. When these transactions involve listed securities (see subsequent treatment of organized-securities market), this negotiated market is called the third market because the transaction does *not* take place on the floor of an organized exchange. This market has many of the same characteristics as the true-auction market such as the lack of general awareness that the asset is available for purchase and sale. Also, as in auction markets, there is often a need for physical examination of the asset, especially a piece of real estate. Lastly, the high unit cost that restricts the number of participants in auction markets may have the same effect in negotiated markets.

Dealer Markets

For many securities, one or more dealers make an active market by offering to buy (at a bid price) and sell (at an ask price) as much of a particular security as desired by investors. The difference between the bid and ask price is the dealer's spread, or compensation, for making the market and bearing the risk of holding an inventory of the security. The dealer makes the market. When demand for the security rises, the dealer raises its bid and ask prices; when demand falls, the dealer lowers these prices. Similar adjustments are made for changes in supply.

The over-the-counter market, which is a network of securities dealers, includes over 30,000 different securities issues. A numerical majority, but not the dollar-value majority, of all stocks are traded on this market. In addition to the stocks of operating corporations, this market also includes shares of some closed-end investment companies and most government and corporate bonds.

Organized Securities Markets

Formal trading locations and markets exist for securities listed on one or more of the national or regional exchanges. The most noted, the New York Stock Exchange, lists the securities of approximately 1,500 firms and actively maintains trading in these corporations' common and preferred stocks and their bonds. Each security is assigned a trading post on the floor of the exchange where commission brokers, employed by the various stock-brokerage firms, meet to engage in auction trading for the buy and sell orders transmitted to them. Each listed security is assigned to a specialist who makes a continuous, fair, and orderly market for the issue. The specialist performs this job by buying or selling the particular issue to offset any imbalance that develops in the number of buy and sell orders coming to the security's trading post from the commission brokers. The specialist maintains records of special orders brought to the market and accommodates members of the exchange for transactions that are less than the standard amount, which for stocks is 100 shares.

All exchanges have membership requirements for individuals trading on the floor of the exchange. Also exchanges maintain listing requirements that must be met by a corporation before any trading of its securities can take place on the exchange. The New York Stock Exchange has the most stringent requirements, including a national rather than local interest in the security, a minimum number of shareholders and publicly traded shares, and a minimum dollar amount of profits, assets, and market value of the corporation's common stock. Other exchanges, such as the American Stock Exchange, the Pacific Stock Exchange, and the Philadelphia Stock Exchange, tend to pattern their membership and listing requirements after those of the New York Stock Exchange except that their requirements are not as stringent.

Regulation of the Markets

Both state and federal regulations govern trading terms, conditions, and practices in all four markets. Federal laws dominate the organized securities and dealer markets whereas state laws are of greater importance in the true-auction and negotiated markets. The focus of this discussion centers on the most important federal laws and briefly describes the main purpose of each.

Securities Act of 1933

The Securities Act of 1933 requires issuers of new securities to file a registration statement with the Securities and Exchange Commission (SEC). The issuing corporation may *not* sell the security until the SEC verifies that the information contained in the registration statement is complete and is not false or misleading. Once approval is obtained, a prospectus is prepared that contains a summary of information from the registration statement. Then the securities can be sold to the public if a copy of the prospectus is made available to all interested buyers.

No attempt to evaluate the investment merits of the proposal is made by the SEC. Rather, the SEC merely seeks to verify that the statements are true.

Securities Exchange Act of 1934

As the name implies, the emphasis of the Securities Exchange Act of 1934 is to regulate the various securities markets. Its scope includes the organized securities exchanges, the over-the-counter markets, all stockbrokers and dealers, and the securities traded in these markets. In addition to requiring registration with the SEC, this act requires these institutions, individuals, and issuing corporations to file periodic updated data with the SEC.

Further, this regulation extends to many practices that occur in the market which the SEC believes are detrimental or misleading. When this occurs, the SEC develops and promulgates, after public hearings and comments, rules and procedures that must be followed. Examples of such include methods of calculating and comparing mutual fund performance between funds, advertising of returns earned on funds, and trading practices of dealers who purchase for their own account.

The Maloney Act of 1938

The Maloney Act of 1938 permits the establishment of trade associations for the purpose of self-regulation of a segment of the securities industry. The only self-regulating organization (SRO) that has formed is the National Association of Securities Dealers (NASD). This SRO regulates the securities firms, their owners, and stockbrokers, and establishes rules of practice to which members must adhere. Securities firms that are not members of NASD are regulated by the SEC.

The Investment Company Act of 1940

The Investment Company Act of 1940 established rules and regulations that apply to all investment companies with respect to their dealings with and on behalf of their shareholders. This act is designed to require investment companies (1) to provide adequate disclosure to shareholders and (2) to refrain from paying excessive advisory, management, or brokerage fees. Significant amendments to this act, which were passed in the 1970s, regulate fees associated with contractual purchase plans entered into by individual investors.

Investment Advisers Act of 1940

The Investment Advisers Act of 1940 as amended requires that advisers register with either the SEC or state regulatory authorities, depending on the circumstances. (A full discussion of this act is in chapter 2 of this text.) Registration does not guarantee the competence of any adviser; rather, it provides a modest degree of protection from fraudulent or unethical practices, principally by requiring that the adviser provide full disclosure to clients.

SOURCES OF INVESTMENT INFORMATION AND ADVICE

Investment recommendations and decisions typically are made on the basis of either *security analysis* or *technical analysis*. Security analysis starts with an analysis of the economy and its direction, the industry under consideration and its direction, and the firm and the characteristics of its security under consideration. This three-tiered approach also applies to other investments such as real estate. Technical analysis, on the other hand, involves the examination of current market prices, trading volume and direction, and other trends occurring in the marketplace as a means of predicting the future direction of security prices. Regardless of which approach a planner or investor uses, information is an essential ingredient. This section of the chapter will describe various sources of published information and advice that are readily available.

Investment Information

General Information

Many books, written either for the general public or for college courses, provide technically accurate information concerning the field of investment. The scope and depth of their coverage far surpass this brief overview. Both public libraries and bookstores have wide selections. Due to the fact that many new investment instruments keep appearing in the marketplace and that Congress seems to tinker with the tax laws affecting investments on an almost yearly basis, books published even a very few years ago will not provide the most up-to-date information. However, the basic information contained in older books will certainly be reliable.

Descriptive Information

This information includes data from which analysis can occur. For security analysis, data published by the Federal Reserve System, the Department of Commerce, or the Department of Labor about the overall economic environment often are available without charge. Industry trade associations, general business and specialized magazines, and the daily and financial newspapers have information on specific industries. A corporation's annual report or the financial statements for a real estate or tax-advantaged investment are sources of data. Corporations must submit to the SEC a special form, Form 10-K, that contains additional information about the corporation and is available by request. If a new security is under consideration, the prospectus becomes a major source of information. Even if an investor is considering the purchase of a corporation's existing securities, a recent prospectus for the corporation will provide insight into the firm beyond that obtainable from other sources.

Data describing the patterns of behavior in securities markets are reported in major newspapers and in the specialized financial press. The latter category includes the *Wall Street Journal*, *Investor's Daily*, and *Barron's* and provides more complete information than do general newspapers. Information concerning the amount and direction of stock price changes, interest rates, volume of trading, and other similar data is available on a daily basis. In addition, on-line news retrieval systems and Internet instantaneously make information about past and up-to-the-minute events available.

Overall there appears to be no scarcity of descriptive information. Financial planners and investors must ascertain which sources and types of descriptive information are best suited to their purposes.

Analytical Information

The process of analysis involves breaking problems and information into smaller pieces so that they can be more readily examined and understood. Then the pieces must be synthesized (that is, put back into the whole) to reach an integrated conclusion. Many of the sources referred to in the previous section also provide analytical information. In addition, many financial subscription services perform analyses and sell the results to subscribers. Summary information is also available from full-service brokerage firm reports.

Investment Advice

Investment Newsletters

Numerous investment newsletters, available on a subscription basis, make evaluations as to the attractiveness or unattractiveness of the markets as a whole or of specific industries or firms. These newsletters advise subscribers as to whether a buy, hold, or sell strategy is most appropriate.

Sales Personnel

Regardless of the type of investment under consideration, individuals involved in its marketing offer recommendations for its purchase or sale. Many of these individuals suggest prudent courses of action; however, others place personal gain ahead of customer needs or objectives.

Bankers and Specialized Money Management Firms

Individuals within this group provide single-purpose planning and advice with respect to a client's investment needs. Some overlap within this group exists, such as bankers recommending the use of the bank's specialized money management unit, the trust department, for managing a customer's portfolio. Portfolio management is now also being offered by some stock-brokerage firms.

Financial Consultants

A relatively new field emerged and began to gain acceptance during the 1970s and 1980s. This field, comprehensive financial planning, focuses on the total set of client needs, objectives, and means of achievement. One important element in the comprehensive financial planning process is the use of investments to accumulate funds for education, retirement (financial independence), and other objectives. The financial consultants have a legal and ethical responsibility to their clients to recommend only those investments whose risk-return characteristics match the client's risk-taking profile and financial objectives.

A FINAL WORD

The intent of this chapter has been to provide basic information on many dimensions of the knowledge needed for effective investing. The reader should recognize that no simple solution is appropriate for all client situations. We shall end with the late financier Bernard Baruch's response to the question of how to become rich through investing: "If you have the tenacity of the barnacle, the strength of the elephant, and the courage of a lion, then you have a chance!" And you thought investment involved only bulls and bears.

NOTE

1. The reader might ask: "Wouldn't money in such a checking account experience an increase in its value during a period of deflation and therefore qualify as an investment?" Indeed it would, but in only 2 of the last 50 years has the year-end consumer price index (CPI) been lower than the beginning-of-the-year CPI. Even in those 2 years the decrease was very slight.

13

Planning the Client's Estate

Ted Kurlowicz

Chapter Outline

THE GOALS OF ESTATE PLANNING

Planning the client's estate is an essential step in the ongoing process of lifetime financial planning. The narrow view of estate planning is that the process merely involves the conservation and distribution of a client's estate. The broader role of the estate planner, however, is to maximize the distributable wealth of a client and transfer the wealth to the client's beneficiaries in an appropriate fashion. The estate plan reflects lifetime financial planning strategies that lead to increases in the client's distributable wealth, in addition to planning for the disposition of such wealth. Thus the estate plan is not independent from lifetime planning with respect to income taxes, investments, insurance, and retirement planning.

Since the lifetime financial planning steps are thoroughly covered in other chapters, this discussion will focus on planning for the conservation and distribution of a client's estate. However, it is essential for the estate planner to bear in mind that the estate plan should be part of a cohesive financial plan for the client.

Selecting the appropriate alternatives in estate planning involves answering the "who," "how," and "when" questions. The client must determine who will be the recipients of his or her property. The "who" question is generally the easiest for the client to answer and will often be determined without significant professional advice.

The client must also determine how the transferees will receive the client's property. For example, the property can be distributed outright to the transferees. Otherwise property could be left to the transferees in trust with various restrictions on the transferee's enjoyment rights. Finally, a transferee could receive a partial interest in property. One example of a partial interest is a life estate.

The client can generally only answer the "how" question with significant professional advice. The estate planner should be able to determine the client's goals and design a transfer mechanism that both meets these goals and complies with state property law.

The transfer taxes imposed on a specific transfer of property often depend on the form of the property transfer. Planning for the resolution of the "how" question will often focus on the minimization of these transfer taxes within the framework of the client's objectives.

Finally, it must be determined "when" a client's estate will be distributed. Typically distributions will not be made from the client's property until his or her death. However, it may be appropriate to transfer specific items of a client's wealth during his or her lifetime. The reasons for lifetime gifts are numerous, but the primary estate planning purpose of lifetime giving is the reduction of the client's estate tax base. Systematic, planned lifetime giving is often recommended to wealthy clients to reduce the amount of death taxes payable upon testamentary dispositions.

STARTING THE PROCESS

The estate planning process begins with gathering data from the client. This is usually accomplished by interviewing the client and completing a fact finder, similar to (or in conjunction with) the fact-finding interviews. Although the estate plan is a subset of the client's lifetime financial plan, estate planning concerns generally gain prominence later in the client's life. Generally the client should be well on the way toward reaching his or her wealth accumulation and retirement planning goals. Since the primary concern of the estate planner is to determine the appropriate responses to the "who," "how," and "when" questions, the process should begin with the fact finder to ensure that both the estate planner and the client have a full understanding of the client's asset inventory. An accurate asset inventory will indicate the composition and magnitude of the wealth available for distribution. This data will help the client and planner determine whether the assets are in the appropriate form for distribution and whether their total value is adequate to provide the desired distributions to the client's heirs. Planning to convert the assets into the appropriate form or to accumulate additional wealth could follow.

Three Primary Questions in Estate Planning

1. *Who* should receive the client's property?
2. *How* should transferees receive the property?
3. *When* should transferees receive the property?

Once the client and the estate planner are aware of the assets available for distribution, the dispositive goals of the client must be ascertained. In many cases this is a simple question. For example, a married individual may want to leave all of his or her wealth to a surviving spouse. In other cases the "who" decision is more difficult and will require some soul-searching by the client. The estate planner should be aware that the client may not be able to answer the "who" question immediately. For example, the client may want to disinherit some children or to ensure that children from a prior marriage are provided for.

Finally, the client must determine how the property will be distributed. The client might be aware that some heirs do not have the acumen to handle outright distributions of property. The client may wish to restrict the ultimate right of an heir to dispose of the property received from the client. This is why the estate planner must have an in-depth interview to determine client objectives. It is prudent for the estate planner to make the client aware of the alternative forms of property transfers and the benefits and risks associated with each. This will assist the client in providing the estate planner with the basic objectives and will permit the estate planner to draft a more complete proposal to recommend to the client.

The interview process between the estate planner and the client is often an uncomfortable event. Many clients feel uneasy talking about issues associated with their death and personal family matters. It is not unusual for the client to modify his or her initial intentions during the estate planning process. The alternative distribution choices discussed with the planner will often raise issues that the client had failed to contemplate initially. It may be necessary to interview spouses separately if an estate plan is drawn up for a marital unit. This is particularly true if the goals of the spouses are not congruent. However, a thorough interview with appropriate follow-up will result in the greatest probability that the estate planner will receive an accurate picture of the client's objectives and thus design a plan that will satisfy the client.

OWNERSHIP OF PROPERTY

The asset inventory of the client as indicated in the fact finder may or may not provide the complete picture to the estate planner. The manner in which the client owns the property may also be a factor. It is important for the estate planner to determine the form of property ownership and inquire about any additional property rights held by the client that are not indicated on the asset inventory form. Some forms of property interest provide less than full use and enjoyment rights and may have been ignored by the client in completing the fact finder. Knowledge of the forms of property interest is essential to the estate planner to determine all of the possible property rights held by the client and the possible forms of dispositions the client can ultimately make to his or her heirs.

Forms of Property Interest

Individual Ownership of Property

Fee Simple Ownership. The most complete interest in property is a *fee simple estate* (outright ownership of property). The individual who holds such an unlimited interest in property owns all the rights associated with the property, including the current possessory rights and the ability to transfer the property at any point during his or her lifetime or at death. In planning the estate of a client a property held outright by the client is an obvious asset to be considered in the dispositive scheme. If the estate of a married couple is being planned, it is possible that either spouse might own substantial property individually.

Life Estates. The life estate is a common form of property ownership and provides the life tenant with the right to possess and enjoy the property for a time period measured by the life of an individual (typically the life tenant). The life estate gives the owner the absolute right to possess, enjoy, and receive current income from the property until the life interest terminates.

Term Interests. A term interest provides the current tenant with the right to possess, enjoy, and receive income from the property during a specified term. The interest of the current tenant terminates at the end of the specified term.

Future Interests. A future interest in property is the current right to future enjoyment of the property. A future interest in property could either be vested or contingent on the occurrence of some future event. The future interest holder has no immediate right to use and enjoy the property. One type of future interest is a remainder interest, which is an interest that takes effect immediately upon the expiration of another interest in the same property. For example, a remainder interest might take effect upon the termination of a life estate or a term of years. A remainder interest is often held by one individual, the remainderperson, on property contained in a trust that currently benefits another individual—for example, a life income beneficiary.

Another type of future interest is a reversionary interest. The reversionary interest occurs when the current property owner transfers current possessory rights to another. The reversionary interest gives the transferor the right to the return of the property at the end of the possessory term of the transferee. For example, a parent could create a trust for a child for a term of years and retain a reversionary interest in the trust corpus following the child's interest.

Forms of Property Interest

- Individual ownership
  - Fee simple estate
  - Life estate
  - Term interest
  - Future interest
- Joint concurrent ownership
  - Tenancy in common
  - Joint tenancy with right of survivorship
  - Tenancy by the entireties
  - Community property

Joint Concurrent Ownership of Property

Current possessory rights to property may be held by more than one individual. Such a partial current interest in property is often generically referred to as joint ownership of property.

Tenancy in Common. Two or more individuals may hold current possessory rights to property without survivorship rights. Such individuals, known as tenants in common, each hold an undivided interest in the property and may transfer their interest during their lifetime or at their death. Both related and unrelated individuals may hold property by tenancy in common.

Joint Tenancy with Right of Survivorship. Two or more individuals may hold property jointly with their survivors ultimately receiving the entire interest in the property. Both related and unrelated individuals may hold property jointly with rights of survivorship. Since this property interest transfers automatically at the death of a joint tenant to his or her surviving tenants, the property is not subject to disposition by a decedent at his or her death. Usually a joint tenant may transfer his or her interest during life without consent of the other joint tenants. Such a transfer will generally sever the joint tenancy and destroy the survivorship rights of the joint tenants.

Tenancy by the Entireties. A tenancy by the entirety is a property interest restricted solely to spouses. It is joint ownership of the property by the spouses with rights of survivorship. A tenancy by the entirety creates a unique situation with respect to disposition of the property. Property is transferred automatically to the surviving spouse at the death of a joint tenant. Thus the property is not subject to disposition by will of a deceased spouse. In addition, the property cannot be transferred during the lifetime of the spouses unless both tenants consent. Tenancy by the entirety is severed automatically upon divorce. An estate planner must know the laws within his or her state jurisdiction with respect to joint property since property held jointly by spouses may or may not be presumed to be held with such rights of survivorship.

Community Property. Nine states—Arizona, California, Idaho, Louisiana, Nevada, New Mexico, Texas, Washington, and Wisconsin—have some form of community-property laws with respect to spousal property. Property in such states is treated as either separate or community property. Generally speaking, property acquired during marriage is treated as community property and is equally owned by the spouses. Although community property is not technically jointly held, the law limits the ability of each spouse to transfer community property to individuals other than his or her spouse.

Other Property Rights

Other property interests may be held by a client and used as a vehicle for the transfer of a client's wealth. These other rights generally provide varying restrictions on the ability of the holder to enjoy or transfer the property. These forms of property ownership should be used when the restrictions are appropriate for the objectives of the client.

Nonownership Property Rights

- Beneficial interest
- Powers
    - Power of appointment
        - General power
        - Special power
    - Power of attorney

Beneficial Interest in Property. Certain property interests may provide one individual with a beneficial interest in property, such as the right to current income or principal distributions. An example of a beneficial interest is the interest owned by the beneficiary of a trust. The trust is created by a grantor who transfers title to the trust property (corpus) to a trustee. The trustee's function is to hold legal title to and administer the trust property for the benefit of the beneficiary. The trustee's ability to make distributions to the beneficiary is determined by the terms of the trust. The trustee may be required to make specific distributions or may be given broad discretion as to the size or timing and to the identity of the beneficiaries. Thus the trustee could possibly be left with substantial dispositive decisions. Trust beneficiaries themselves are generally limited in their ability to transfer their interests until trust distributions are actually received.

Powers. Certain powers to make property decisions may be held by (or transferred by) the client. A *power of appointment* provides the holder of a power with the ability to transfer the property subject to the power. The holder may have a broad power to transfer the property to virtually any recipient. This is known as a *general power*. Or the holder may have a *special power,* which typically provides the holder with a limited class of potential recipients of the property. Any powers of appointment held by a client should be considered in his or her dispositive plans. In addition, a client may wish to grant a power of appointment to another to delegate the ability to transfer the client's property.

Another power that can be held or granted by a client is a *power of attorney.* A power of attorney gives the holder of the power (the attorney-in-fact) the ability to stand in the place of or represent the grantor of the power (the principal) in various transactions. Among the possible transactions is the ability of the attorney-in-fact to transfer property for the principal. The advantages of using a power of attorney will be discussed below.

ESTATE PLANNING DOCUMENTS

The estate plan is a roadmap directing how the client's wealth will be assembled and disposed of during the client's life or at his or her death. The plan itself is useless unless the documents of the plan have been drafted appropriately. The documents must be drafted carefully to avoid hidden traps and to provide direction to the appropriate personal representatives, fiduciaries, and beneficiaries of the client. These directions must be drafted according to the principles of state law and should unambiguously state the intent of the client. Since these documents necessarily involve compliance with state law, they should be prepared by an attorney who specializes in estate planning in the local jurisdiction.

The Client's Will

Despite the importance of the will in a client's estate plan, it is estimated that seven out of ten Americans die without a valid will. Unfortunately these individuals have left the disposition of their estates to the provisions of state intestacy law. In addition, the estates of these individuals will be handled by a court-appointed administrator. In many cases the estate will be subject to unnecessary taxes and administration expenses. In any event, a valid will is necessary for the implementation of a cohesive estate plan.

Requirements for a Valid Will

Although the requirements for wills are provided by the laws of the various states, several items are universal. With some minor exceptions for rare circumstances the following are required for a valid will:

- The will must be in writing.
- The testator, or creator of the will, must sign the will at the end of the document, usually in the presence of witnesses.
- A number of witnesses (generally two or three) must sign the will after the testator's signature. The witnesses are attesting that the signature of the testator is in fact his or her signature.

What Can a Valid Will Accomplish?

The client's will is the centerpiece of the estate plan. Although its primary function is to direct the disposition of the client's wealth, it serves other purposes as well. A properly drafted will can accomplish the following objectives:

- Direct the disposition of the client's probate assets.
- Nominate the personal representative of the testator, known as the executor, who will handle the administration of the client's estate.
- Nominate the guardians of any minor children of the testator.
- Create testamentary trusts that will take effect at the testator's death to hold the property of the testator for the benefit of named beneficiaries.
- Name the trustee of any trust created under the will.
- Provide directions to the executor and/or trustees named in the will indicating how these fiduciaries will manage assets contained in the estate or testamentary trust. (The directions could be quite specific or provide broad powers to the fiduciaries.)
- Provide directions for payment of the estate's taxes and expenses. (Care should be taken in naming the components of the estate that will be responsible for taxes and expenses. Incorrect designation of the component obligated to pay such expenses could result in increased death taxes or inappropriately diminished shares of specific beneficiaries.)
- Establish the compensation of executors and/or trustees named in the will.

FOCUS ON ETHICS
Trusts, "Don't Trusts," and Loss of Trust

Financial planning often includes the use of trusts to save taxes. An equally important goal is to control wealth distribution. Because of the desire of clients to retain control, even from the grave, trusts might more appropriately be called "don't trusts."

Estate planning is fraught with moral and ethical pitfalls. For example, a divorced and remarried person may elect to leave his or her entire estate to the second spouse with no provision for the children of the first marriage. Another example is a client who, anticipating an irrevocable life insurance trust, applies for coverage before establishing the trust. Informed that this premature application invalidates gift tax advantages of the trust, the client may want to redate legal documents or simply to claim the tax benefit anyway, hoping never to be audited. Financial planners must not succumb to this pressure.

To decline business because of moral, ethical, or legal objections may be financially painful in the short run. However, in the long run, the financial professional with an unquestioned reputation attracts more and higher quality business. That same professional also has a clear conscience and the knowledge that the likelihood of legal, ethical, and malpractice problems is dramatically reduced.

Trusts

A trust is a relationship (generally in the form of a written document) that divides the ownership of property. Legal title to the trust is held by one party, known as a trustee. The beneficial or equitable interest in the trust property is owned by the beneficiaries of the trust. The trustee has the duty to manage the trust property provided by the grantor of the trust for the benefit of the beneficiaries. The trust is used to provide for beneficiaries when, for one reason or another, they are unable to administer the trust assets for themselves. For example, a trust may be created to provide for minor beneficiaries. Minor beneficiaries are incapable under state law of holding property in their own name and perhaps lack the necessary experience and financial acumen to manage the trust property. The trust is an excellent tool for handling and/or consolidating accumulations of wealth.

The trustee manages the trust property under the terms of the trust. The trust terms are the directions and intentions of the grantor with respect to the management of the trust. For example, there may be directions with respect to the investment of trust assets. More importantly, there are directions with respect to providing for the beneficiaries of the trust. The trust terms may be restrictive and provide the trustee with very little discretion. For example, the terms may provide for specified distributions of income and/or principal to designated beneficiaries at various points in time. Or the trustee may be provided with "sprinkle" powers permitting the trustee to determine when distributions of either income or principal are appropriate for the various beneficiaries. The trustee has the legal obligation to manage the trust prudently and, to the extent the trustee has discretionary powers, to act impartially with respect to the beneficiaries.

Since the trust terms describe the intentions of the grantor, a trust should be drafted carefully under the direction of an attorney who specializes in such matters. In addition, the grantor should select the trustee, whether a private individual or a corporate trustee, with great care.

Living (Inter Vivos) Trust

A trust can be created during the lifetime of a grantor. It could be created for several reasons. The trust could hold property and operate prior to the death of the grantor. Or a trust could be created during the lifetime of the grantor simply to receive assets at the grantor's death. Such a trust is known as a *pour-over* trust.

A trust could be either revocable or irrevocable. A revocable trust is created when the grantor transfers trust property to the trust but reserves the power to alter or revoke the agreement. Since the revocable trust is an incomplete transfer, the creation of a revocable trust has no effect on the client's income, estate, or gift tax situation. The revocable trust gives the grantor the ability to observe the management of the trust assets without relinquishing ultimate control of the assets. Thus the grantor can reclaim the trust assets at any time. The revocable trust becomes irrevocable only when the grantor modifies the trust to become irrevocable or dies and therefore is no longer able to modify the trust.

The revocable trust has gained popularity in recent times as an estate plan in itself. It is drafted to provide the dispositive directions normally contained in a client's will. The client will then transfer all appropriate assets to the trustee to be retitled in the trustee's name. At the grantor's death the trust becomes irrevocable and all property contained in the trust is managed or disposed of under the terms of the trust. The revocable trust is popular as an estate plan since property disposed of by the revocable trust avoids the publicity, delay, and some expenses associated with the probate process.

A living trust can also be designated as irrevocable by the grantor. Since the irrevocable trust is a completed gift, it is effective for gift and estate tax purposes. A properly designed irrevocable trust can receive property from the grantor which, as a completed gift, will avoid the gross estate of the grantor at his or her death. In addition, funds placed in the irrevocable trust become the property of the trustee and are exempt from the claims of the grantor's creditors. The irrevocable trust is an effective estate planning tool for older grantors who face substantial estate tax burdens.

Testamentary Trust

A testamentary trust is created under the will of the testator. Since the will can be changed as long as the testator retains legal capacity, the testamentary trust is never irrevocable until the client's death (or permanent legal disability). A testamentary trust does not receive property until the client dies and the proceeds are transferred to the trust by the executor. Since the trust is contained in the client's will, it is subject to probate. In a simple will testamentary trusts are often drafted to provide for the testator's children should the spouses die in a common disaster. In a more complex estate plan testamentary trusts are often the vehicles for the marital and family trusts described earlier in this chapter.

Estate Planning Documents

- Will
- Trusts
- Durable powers of attorney (including health care power of attorney)
- Living will

Durable Power of Attorney

A power of attorney is a written document that enables the client, known as the *principal,* to designate a holder of the power, known as the *attorney-in-fact,* to act on the principal's behalf. The attorney has the power to act in behalf of the principal only with respect to powers specifically enumerated in the document. A *durable* power of attorney is an estate planning document that is not terminated by the legal disability of the principal. Since this document provides the attorney-in-fact with the potential to abuse the privileges granted by the document, these documents are construed very narrowly in transactions with third parties. Thus any powers that the principal wishes to grant to the attorney-in-fact should be specifically enumerated. The document should also clearly specify whether or not the legal disability of the principal has any effect on the power of attorney.

A power of attorney should be drafted prudently for the specific circumstances of the client. Care should be taken as to the choice of the attorney-in-fact, the powers granted to him or her, and when the powers take effect. The advantages of a durable power of attorney include these:

- An older client can execute a durable power of attorney and avoid the necessity of having a guardian or a conservator appointed should the client lose legal capacity.

- The attorney-in-fact can be given the power to manage the principal's assets should the principal suffer a permanent or temporary loss of legal capacity. This is particularly important for owners of a closely held business.
- The durable power can replace or complement a revocable trust. The attorney-in-fact can manage the client's assets subsequent to a client's legal disability and, if empowered, continue the client's dispositive scheme. For example, the attorney-in-fact could continue to make annual exclusion gifts or contributions after the legal disability but prior to the death of the principal.
- Most states allow a *health care power of attorney* in which the attorney-in-fact can make medical care decisions on behalf of the principal.

Living Wills

A living will is a document indicating the client's intentions should the client become disabled and lack the legal capacity to make decisions for himself or herself. Generally speaking, the living will deals with the health care measures that the client wants imposed should he or she become legally disabled. If a living will is desired, the document should carefully spell out whether or not the client desires that heroic measures be taken should he or she experience a life-threatening accident or illness. Living wills are not valid in all states, and local counsel should be obtained if the client wishes to state his or her intentions in this regard.

TRANSFERS AT DEATH—AN OVERVIEW

Knowledge of how property is transferred at death under the laws of the jurisdictional state is necessary to plan an estate. A common misconception is that the decedent's will determines the distribution of the estate. Under most circumstances the will actually affects the distribution of only a small portion of the decedent's property. This fact does not minimize the importance of a carefully drafted will, but merely emphasizes the importance of coordinating all of the client's testamentary transfers, including the client's will, in the estate planning process.

Probate Property

Transfers through Will Provisions

Many misconceptions exist with respect to the various terms associated with the estate planning process. Popular opinion of estate planning is that a primary goal is to reduce the size of the probate estate. The probate estate includes all assets passing by will or intestacy. Probate property is owned outright by the decedent and is not transferred by operation of law or contract, as discussed below. For married individuals probate property is generally limited to the individually owned property of a deceased spouse. Thus the probate estate is often minimized by the usual form of property ownership between spouses—tenancy by the entirety.

Probate (which technically means the process of proving the validity of the will) begins when the original will is deposited in the court with jurisdiction over the decedent's estate. The probate court oversees matters involving the settlement of the estate, distribution of probate property, appointment and supervision of fiduciaries, and disputes concerning the decedent's will. If a valid will exists, the probate court will ensure that the probate property is distributed according to the terms of the will after all estate settlement costs are paid. Although the court has jurisdiction solely over probate property, the state and federal taxing authorities may have the statutory authority to collect any unpaid taxes from nonprobate property if probate assets are insufficient.

Transfers by Intestacy

If a decedent dies without a valid will, all probate property passes under the laws of intestate succession of the jurisdiction state. The intestate laws are deemed to replace the intent of a decedent in the distribution of his or her

The Probate Estate

Items included in the probate estate:

- Fee simple ownership
- Nonterminating ownership interests (certain life estates, term interests, future interests, beneficial interests, and powers that do not terminate at the decedent's death)
- Tenancy in common

Items excluded from the probate estate:

- Transfers by operation of law
  - Joint tenancy with right of survivorship
  - Tenancy by the entireties
  - Community property (in community property states)
  - Living trusts
  - Totten trusts
- Transfers by operation of contract
  - Life insurance proceeds payable to a named beneficiary rather than the estate or the executor
  - Retirement plan death benefits payable to a named beneficiary
  - Payable at death investment accounts

probate property. The default mechanism provided by the intestacy laws may be of little significance since the probate assets are not substantial in the typical estate.

States vary with respect to intestate laws. Distribution under the intestate laws will depend upon the related individuals who survive the decedent. A decedent's spouse receives primary consideration and will receive the decedent's entire probate estate if the decedent is not also survived by children or parents. If the decedent is survived by children, the surviving spouse and children will generally receive 50 percent each of the estate. The parents of a married decedent will generally get a share only if the decedent is not also survived by children. If the decedent is not survived by any of these related individuals, the next closest related survivors will inherit.

State intestacy laws also apply to a transfer under a will or contract that is deemed invalid.

Transfers of Nonprobate Property

Transfers by Operation of Law

The nature of certain ownership interests in property causes the property to pass automatically at the death of a decedent. Such property is not subject to the laws of probate and does not pass under the will or intestacy rules. The most significant example of property that is transferred by operation of law is property held jointly with rights of survivorship. The survivorship provisions cause such property to automatically pass to the surviving joint tenant at the death of the joint tenant. As discussed earlier, property held as tenants by the entirety is also an example of an operation-of-law transfer. Many married individuals own property acquired during their marriage in this fashion. For example, the family home, automobile, and significant investments are often held jointly by spouses. At the death of one spouse the property passes automatically to the survivor outside the jurisdiction of the probate court.

As noted earlier, living trusts can be effective tools in estate planning. Recall that only irrevocable living trusts affect the grantor's income, estate, and gift taxation. However, both revocable and irrevocable living trusts are methods of transferring property by operation of law, thus avoiding some of the expense, publicity, and delay of probate.

In addition, it is quite common for elderly parents to reduce their probate estate by creating operation-of-law transfers to their descendants. One such transfer is the establishment of joint bank or securities accounts with their children or grandchildren with survivorship rights. A similar vehicle for transfer by operation of law is the *Totten trust.* A Totten trust occurs when an individual (generally a parent or grandparent) opens up a bank account in trust for a named individual. At the death of the account holder this property passes automatically by operation of law to the named beneficiary. It should be noted that both such transactions are incomplete gifts and, while effective in reducing probate, have no impact on the taxable estate.

Transfers by Operation of Contract

Another form of nonprobate transfer is transfer by contract. The most common form of transfer by contract involves the transfer of life insurance or employment benefit proceeds to a named beneficiary. The policy proceeds of a life insurance policy will be distributed to the beneficiary designated by the owner of the policy. The same result occurs if an employee has named individuals as beneficiaries of various employment benefits, such as death benefits from retirement plans. These benefits will pass by operation of contract and will not become part of probate unless they are made payable to the executor (or the estate) in lieu of a named beneficiary.

OVERVIEW OF TAXES IMPOSED ON TRANSFERS OF WEALTH

The most significant costs of transferring wealth are the various transfer taxes imposed at the federal and state levels. The tax rates applicable to affected transfers can be quite high (the marginal rate can exceed 100 percent under certain circumstances). The relatively large impact of these transfer taxes makes tax reduction a primary focus in the estate plan with respect to the conservation of a client's wealth. By optimizing the solutions to the "who," "how," and "when" questions the client may be able to implement a plan that approximates his or her stated objectives and holds the transfer-tax reduction of his or her estate to a minimum. The primary focus of this discussion will be the federal estate and gift transfer taxes, but the federal generation-skipping transfer tax (GSTT) and state death taxes will also be discussed.

The Federal Transfer Tax System

The federal tax system consists of three components—gift taxes, estate taxes, and generation-skipping taxes. The federal estate and gift taxes are separate tax systems imposed on different types of transfers, but the systems are unified with respect to tax brackets and tax base. The generation-skipping transfer taxes are separate taxes applied under different rules in addition to any applicable estate or gift taxes.

Federal Gift Taxes

Federal gift taxes will apply only if the following two elements are present:

- There is a completed transfer and acceptance of *property*.
- The transfer is for less than full and adequate consideration.

These two essential elements of a taxable gift reveal some noteworthy facts. First, only property transfers are subject to gift taxation. Thus the transfer of services by an individual is not a taxable gift. In addition, all completed transfers including direct and indirect gifts of property are taxable. Finally, the less than full and adequate consideration requirement does not contain an element of intent. Therefore it is not necessary that the grantor intends to make a gift. It is merely required that the transfer be for less than full consideration. Generally speaking, transfers between unrelated individuals in a business setting are treated as "bad bargains" and are not treated as taxable transfers.

Exempt Transfers. Certain transfers are exempt from the gift tax base by statute. First, a transfer of property pursuant to a divorce or property settlement agreement is deemed to be for full and adequate consideration under some circumstances. Second, transfers directly to the provider of education or medical services on behalf of an individual are not taxable gifts to the recipient of the services. Finally, gifts that are disclaimed by the donee in a qualified disclaimer are not treated as taxable gifts.

The Annual Exclusion. Much of the design and complexity involved in gift tax planning involves the annual exclusion. Qualifying gifts of $10,000 (to be indexed for inflation beginning in 1999) or less may be made annually by a donor to each of any number of donees without gift tax. The exempt amount can be increased to $20,000 (also indexed) if the donor is married and the donor's spouse elects to join in making the gifts on a timely filed gift tax return.

To qualify for an annual exclusion the gift must provide the donee with a present interest. Outright interests or current income interests in a trust will provide the beneficiary with a present interest. Trust provisions giving the beneficiaries current withdrawal powers can be used to qualify gifts to a trust for an annual exclusion even if the trust provides for deferred benefits. Use of the annual exclusion in the estate planning process will be discussed below.

Deductions from the Gift Tax Base. Two types of gifts are fully deductible from the transfer tax base. First, the *marital deduction* provides that unlimited qualifying transfers made by a donor to his or her spouse are fully deductible from the gift tax base. The marital deduction will prove quite useful if it is necessary to rearrange ownership of marital assets in the implementation of the estate plan. This deduction is similar to the marital deduction against federal estate taxes discussed below.

The *charitable deduction* provides that qualifying transfers to a legitimate charity will be deductible against the gift tax base. Thus all qualifying transfers made to charity will avoid transfer tax.

The Applicable Credit. A cumulative credit is currently available against federal gift tax due on taxable transfers. For 1999 the *applicable credit amount* is

TABLE 13-1
Scheduled Increases in Credit and Exclusion Amounts for Estate and Gift Taxes

Year	Applicable Exclusion Amount	Applicable Credit Amount
1999	$650,000	$211,300
2000 & 2001	$675,000	$220,550
2002 & 2003	$700,000	$229,800
2004	$850,000	$287,300
2005	$950,000	$326,300
2006 & Later	$1,000,000	$345,800

$211,300 and scheduled increases are shown in table 13-1. Under the unified nature of the federal estate and gift taxes this credit provides a dollar-for-dollar reduction of transfer tax otherwise payable against taxable transfers either during lifetime or at death or both. The credit can be used against each dollar of transfer tax until it is exhausted. The 1999 tax credit of $211,300 is equivalent to an exemption of $650,000 of taxable transfers from the federal estate or gift tax. Scheduled increases in this exemption, called the *applicable exclusion amount,* are shown in table 13-1. Since no taxes are due on transfers until aggregate transfers by the donor have exceeded $650,000, the first tax rate bracket applicable to a transfer actually subject to tax is 37 percent. The applicable credit amount is discussed further below.

The Federal Transfer Tax System

- Federal Gift Tax
- Federal Estate Tax
- Generation-Skipping Transfer Tax (GSTT)

The Federal Estate Tax

Often the most difficult task in calculating the estate tax is determining the assets that are included in the decedent's estate tax base. Some of the included assets are obvious, such as individually owned property. However, the estate tax rules often cause the inclusion of property in surprising circumstances. For example, property previously transferred by a decedent can be brought back to the estate tax base by provisions of the statute.

The Gross Estate. The starting point in the estate tax calculation is determining the property included in the gross estate for federal tax purposes. The gross estate includes the property included in the probate estate, but it also includes property transferable by the decedent at death by other means. The decedent's gross estate includes

- property individually owned by the decedent at the time of death
- (some portion of) property held jointly by the decedent at the time of death
- insurance on the decedent's life if either (1) incidents of ownership are held by the decedent within 3 years of death or (2) the proceeds are deemed payable to the estate
- pension or IRA payments left to survivors
- property subject to general powers of appointment held by the decedent at the time of death
- property transferred by the decedent during his or her lifetime if the decedent retained (1) a life interest in the property, (2) a reversionary interest valued greater than 5 percent of the property at the time of death, or (3) rights to revoke the transfer at the time of death

As the list above indicates, the gross estate of the decedent is defined much more broadly than the probate estate, and a reduction of the probate estate will often have little effect on the size of the federal estate tax paid.

Items Deductible from the Gross Estate. Analogous to the federal gift tax rules, certain items are deductible from the gross estate for estate tax calculation purposes. First, legitimate debts of the decedent are deductible from the gross estate if these debts are obligations of the gross estate. Second, reasonable funeral and other death costs of the decedent are deductible from the gross estate. Third, the costs of estate settlement, such as the executor's commission and attorney fees, are deductible to the extent such fees are reasonable.

Marital Deduction. As with the gift tax, qualifying transfers to a surviving spouse are deductible under the marital-deduction rules. Since the marital deduction is unlimited, the usual dispositive scheme (100 percent to the surviving spouse) will result in no federal death taxes for a married couple until the death of the survivor of the two spouses. As a client's wealth increases, sophisticated planning is needed to make optimal use of the marital deduction. Planning for the marital deduction will be discussed below.

Charitable Deduction. The federal estate tax charitable deduction provides that transfers at death to qualifying charities will be fully deductible from the estate tax base. The charitable deduction is an excellent device to reduce the gross estate of a wealthy individual. As we will discuss below, the transfer of a remainder of current term interest to charity can substantially reduce the estate tax burden of a wealthy client without significantly disrupting his or her dispositive goals.

Credits against the Estate Tax. The applicable credit amount discussed above with respect to gift taxes is similarly applicable to transfers occurring at death. If the applicable credit has not been exhausted by sheltering lifetime gifts, it is available against transfers made at the death of a decedent. The optimal use of the applicable credit in conjunction with the marital deduction will be discussed below.

The state death tax credit provides a dollar-for-dollar reduction (within certain limits) against the federal estate tax due for any state death taxes paid by the estate. The state death tax credit is limited, and the maximum state death tax credit available to a particular estate is provided for by a progressive rate schedule in the federal tax code. The size of the credit against the federal estate tax is equal to the lesser of the state death tax actually paid or the maximum state death tax allowable under the progressive credit schedule. State death taxes are usually equal to at least the maximum state death tax allowable under the federal estate tax rules.

Generation-Skipping Transfer Tax (GSTT)

The GSTT was created by the Tax Reform Act of 1986 to prevent the federal government from losing transfer tax if a transferor attempts to skip one generation's level of transfer tax by transferring property to a generation more than one generation below the level of the transferor (for example, when a grandparent makes a gift of property to a grandchild). Although the GSTT is designed to prevent a transferor from finding a transfer tax loophole in the federal estate/gift tax system, it is different from the unified estate and gift tax system in many ways. The GSTT is applied at a flat rate equal to the highest current estate or gift tax bracket on every taxable generation-skipping transfer. Thus any taxable transfers will be currently subject to a 55 percent rate if the GSTT applies. This GSTT is applicable in addition to any estate or gift tax that might otherwise be applicable to the transfer. Thus if the GSTT applies, a transfer could easily be subject to a tax rate in excess of 100 percent of the value of the asset transfer. Obviously, planning to avoid the GSTT is of paramount importance for wealthy individuals.

The GSTT applies to three different types of transfers. First, the GSTT applies to a *direct skip,* which is an outright transfer during life or at death to an individual who is more than one generation below the transferor. The direct skip gift tax applies only if the parents of the skip beneficiary are alive at the time of the direct skip.

The GSTT is also applicable to a *taxable distribution.* A taxable distribution is a distribution of either income or principal from a trust to a person more than one generation below the level of the trust grantor. The recipient of the taxable distribution is a skip beneficiary of the trust. Thus a taxable distribution can occur when a trustee makes a distribution to a skip beneficiary even if a nonskip beneficiary still holds a current beneficial interest in the trust.

Finally, a *taxable termination* is also subject to a GSTT. The taxable termination occurs when there is a termination of a property interest held in trust as a result of death, lapse of time, or otherwise and a skip beneficiary receives the remainder interest outright in the trust.

A $1 million exemption (indexed for inflation beginning in 1999) is available to each taxpayer to be applied against GSTT for all potential generation-skipping transfers. The exemption can be applied against transfers during life or at death. Thus a married couple can split gifts and make up to $2 million (also indexed) of generation-skipping transfers without incurring the GSTT. The exemption must be affirmatively allocated to specific transfers in the transferor's appropriate tax return. If this GSTT exemption is not allocated on a gift tax return during the life of a transferor or in the transferor's will, the taxing authorities will allocate the exemption by default. A client would be making a substantial mistake by failing to appropriately allocate the GSTT exemption.

State Death Taxes

Most material on estate planning minimizes the discussion of state death taxes. Although state death taxes are generally applied at a lower rate than the federal estate tax, these taxes should not be ignored for many reasons. First, the majority of estates will not be subject to federal death taxes due to the applicable exclusion amount ($650,000 for 1999). The average estate will, however, be subject to state death taxes. In large estates the federal estate death tax is admittedly the largest expense. However, the state death taxes will also be quite significant. Finally, the state death tax base is defined differently from the federal estate tax bases in many states. Planning for state death taxes should not be ignored since the taxable transfers for state purposes can often be avoided by simple planning that might otherwise be ineffective (and thus disregarded) for purposes of federal estate tax planning. For example, many states exempt life insurance benefits paid to a named beneficiary.

State Death Taxes

- State Inheritance Tax
- State Estate Tax
- Credit Estate Tax (sponge tax)

State Inheritance Taxes

Some states impose a tax on the right of a beneficiary to receive the property from the estate of the decedent. The tax rate is based on the amount of property received by each beneficiary and is often based on the relationship of the beneficiary to the decedent. An inheritance received by a close relative is generally subject to a lower rate than an inheritance received by a more distant relation. In many cases the inheritance tax on property received by relatives outside the decedent's immediate family (surviving spouse or children) is subject to a tax that exceeds the federal state death tax credit. In many circumstances the state inheritance tax could be more significant than any federal estate tax due. Despite the fact that inheritance taxes are imposed on the right to receive property, payment of these inheritance taxes is usually the responsibility of the estate.

State Estate Tax

A state with an estate tax is similar to the federal system in that both taxes are imposed on the privilege of transferring property by the decedent. These taxes are generally imposed at progressive rates and apply to a tax base similar to the federal system.

Credit Estate Tax

All states currently impose a credit estate tax (also known as a sponge tax) to bring the total state death tax liability up to the maximum federal death tax credit. In many states this sponge tax is the sole form of state death tax. Thus the state death taxes paid will generally be at least as great as any federal death tax credit allowable.

Factors to Consider in Planning for State Death Taxes

A detailed analysis of each state's inheritance or estate tax is beyond the scope of this discussion. However, there are some peculiarities in the state death tax base that an estate planner should be aware of in the state where his or her clients are located. First, it is important to note that some states will not tax property held jointly by a decedent at the time of his or her death. As we have discussed above, jointly held property is included in the federal estate tax base. Quite often a decedent can avoid state death taxes without affecting federal taxes by transferring property to joint ownership prior to his or her death.

In addition, some states provide for no marital deduction for individually owned property transferred to a surviving spouse. Therefore severing a joint ownership of property with a surviving spouse may create state death taxes even if that property is transferred to the surviving spouse in a transfer deductible from the federal estate tax base.

Finally, life insurance is often not taxable at the state level if payable to a named beneficiary. It is important to note that life insurance can often avoid state death taxes even if owned individually by an insured at the time of his or her death provided the estate is not the named beneficiary.

PRESERVING THE CLIENT'S WEALTH

There are many techniques that can be used to reduce the tax associated with transferring a client's wealth to his or her heirs. The appropriate answer to the "who" question may be used to reduce tax. For example, qualifying transfers to a surviving spouse are fully deductible from the gross estate. The optimal resolution of the "how" question could also reduce estate taxes. For example, transferring assets to a family trust takes advantage of the applicable credit against federal estate taxes. Finally, if the "when" question is answered appropriately, the gross estate of a grantor can be substantially reduced through a systematic lifetime gifting program, and substantial wealth can be transferred free of all transfer taxes.

The Advantages of Lifetime Gifts

Nontax Advantages of Lifetime Gifts

Clients give away property during their lifetime for many reasons. The advantages of making lifetime gifts are as follows:

- The donor can provide for the support, education, and welfare of the donee.
- The donor gets the pleasure of seeing the donee enjoy the gift.
- The donor avoids the publicity and administrative costs associated with a probate transfer at death.
- The donated property is protected from the claims of the donor's creditors.

Tax Advantages of Lifetime Gifts

Although the federal gift and estate taxes are unified for tax purposes, there are some distinctions that make lifetime gifts favorable from a tax standpoint. The tax advantages of lifetime gifts include these:

- The annual gift tax exclusion for gifts of $10,000 or less (adjusted for inflation beginning in 1999) provides a complete loophole from federal gift and estate taxes. Each year any number of $10,000 gifts ($20,000, also adjusted for inflation, if the spouse joins in them) can be made to reduce the ultimate transfer tax base of a donor.

- The gift tax is imposed on the value of the gift at the time a completed transfer is made. Thus any posttransfer appreciation on the property avoids all transfer tax.
- The gift tax payable on gifts made more than 3 years prior to the donor's death is excluded from the donor's estate tax base.
- The income produced by gifted property is shifted to the donee for income tax purposes. Lifetime gifting may be used to move taxable income from a high-bracket donor to a lower-bracket donee. (This advantage is somewhat limited by special tax rules related to unearned income of children under age 14.)
- Unlimited qualifying transfers can be made between spouses without incurring gift taxes. Spouses can advantageously shift assets between themselves to meet the needs of the estate plan of each spouse.

The Opportunities Created by the Annual Gift Tax Exclusion

As discussed above the annual exclusion allows the donor to make up to $10,000 worth of gifts (adjusted for inflation) tax free to any number of donees each year. If the donor's spouse elects to split gifts with the donor for the tax year, the annual exclusion is increased to $20,000 (also adjusted) per donee. If the client has a substantial estate and several individuals to benefit, the systematic use of annual exclusion gifts can cause the transfer of substantial wealth free of transfer tax.

> *Example:* Tom Taxplanner, a 65-year-old widower, has two children and four grandchildren. Tom can make up to $60,000 of qualifying transfers annually to his heirs without ever subjecting the transfers to federal gift or estate taxes. If Tom lives an additional 16 years (his actual life expectancy), he can give away $960,000 and save up to $528,000 of estate tax (assuming a maximum 55 percent bracket). The actual tax savings are even greater since the appreciation on the property transferred also escapes gift and estate taxes.

The annual exclusion is available only for gifts that provide the donee with a present interest. For example, an outright transfer of property provides a present interest. Since the outright transfer is often unfavorable (for example, the donee is a minor), significant planning is often necessary to design gifts that restrict the donee's current access to the funds while qualifying for the annual exclusion.

Gifts to Minors

Quite often annual exclusion gifts will be made to minor children or grandchildren as part of the estate plan of a wealthy client. This creates problems

Transferring Assets to Minors: Techniques That Restrict Access

- Uniform Gifts to Minors Act (UGMA)
- Uniform Transfers to Minors Act (UTMA)
- Sec. 2503(b) Trust
- Sec. 2503(c) Trust
- Irrevocable Trust with Current Withdrawal Powers

for the donor and donee. First, there are restrictions on a minor's ability to hold or otherwise deal with property under state law. In addition, the donor will naturally be concerned about the safety of the funds if the minor has significant access rights. Fortunately there are several methods for making annual exclusion gifts to minors with restrictions on the minor's access to the property.

Uniform Gifts to Minors Act (UGMA) or Uniform Transfers to Minors Act (UTMA). The UGMA and UTMA statutes are model laws that have been adopted in various forms in individual states. They permit the transfer of funds to a custodial account for the benefit of a minor. The custodian of the UGMA or UTMA account manages the property under the rules provided by state law. There are restrictions on the type of property permissible as an investment for these purposes. The original model act, UGMA, has been expanded in many states to increase the types of permissible investments. In a majority of states the newer model act, UTMA, has been adopted, and relatively few restrictions exist in these states on the permissible investments. A UGMA or UTMA transfer is particularly favorable for smaller gifts because it provides for the protection of the assets without the expense of the administration of the trust. The provisions for distribution from the UGMA are provided under the various state laws. Generally speaking, the UGMA funds can be accumulated during the minority of the donee, but the custodial assets must be distributed to the beneficiary upon majority.

Sec. 2503(b) Trust. A Sec. 2503(b) trust is an irrevocable trust created by a donor during his or her lifetime to receive annual exclusion gifts. The trust requires that income be distributed at least annually to (or for the benefit of) the minor donee. The minor would receive distribution of the trust principal whenever the trust agreement specifies. A distribution of principal does not have to be made at the majority of the donee. The annual gift tax exclusion is limited to the value of the income interest provided by the trust. The Sec. 2503(b) trust should be invested in income-producing property and is less favorable in some respects than the UGMA gift because income cannot be accumulated.

Sec. 2503(c) Trust. A Sec. 2503(c) trust is another type of irrevocable trust designed to receive annual exclusion gifts for a minor. This type of trust requires that income and principal be distributed to the minor at age 21. However, the trust is allowed to accumulate current income prior to the termination of the trust.

Irrevocable Trust with Current Withdrawal Powers. A client often wishes to make gifts to a trust with the purpose of accumulation. If the trust provides for accumulation and does not currently benefit the donee, the annual gift tax exclusion would normally be forfeited. Provisions of the law, however, permit the annual exclusion if current beneficial rights are given to the donee. An annual exclusion is permitted if the donee is granted at least temporary withdrawal rights to the deposits to the trust. Under these rules a gift to a trust will qualify for the annual exclusion if the donee has the noncumulative, temporary (for example, 30 days) right to demand up to the annual exclusion amount from his or her share of the amount contributed to the trust by the donor. These provisions are frequently called *Crummey powers,* named after the taxpayer who litigated the landmark decision authorizing an annual gift tax exclusion for gifts and trusts subject to these powers.

Irrevocable trusts with withdrawal powers are often used for the purposes of holding life insurance on the life of the grantor. Since the life insurance will be paid with annual premium additions to the trust, it is intended that these premiums will accumulate in the policy and no distributions will be made until the death of the grantor. If each beneficiary is provided with the ability to withdraw a pro rata share of the annual premium addition to the trust, the annual premium will qualify as an annual exclusion gift to the beneficiaries. Thus a life insurance trust can be created without gift tax costs. The estate tax advantage of the life insurance trust will be discussed below.

Federal Estate Tax Planning

Despite the advantages of systematic annual gifting most individuals will desire to retain a significant portion of their wealth until death. To the extent this wealth is included in the gross estate of the decedent, it will be included in the estate tax calculations. Due to the deduction and credits provided by the estate tax laws, a properly designed estate can distribute significant wealth to the decedent's heirs while minimizing or deferring federal estate taxes.

Planning for the Marital Deduction

The marital deduction provides that certain transfers at death from a deceased spouse to a surviving spouse are fully deductible from the gross estate for estate tax purposes. This deduction is unlimited as long as the property is included in the gross estate of a deceased spouse and is transferred to a surviving spouse in a qualifying manner.

Through *maximum* use of the marital deduction a married couple can, at their option, eliminate all federal estate taxes due at the first death of the two spouses. The estate plan of a marital unit making full use of this marital deduction merely defers the estate taxes until the second spouse dies. The marital deduction will be available at the second death only if the surviving spouse remarries and transfers the property to his or her new spouse. Thus a decedent can avoid all federal estate taxes on his or her estate by making a qualifying transfer of all property included in his or her gross estate (both probate and nonprobate property) to the surviving spouse.

Simply answering the "who" question in favor of the surviving spouse will not necessarily qualify such transfers for the marital deduction. Tax laws provide that only qualifying transfers will be eligible for this deduction. Thus the "how" question must also be answered appropriately.

Outright Transfers. The simplest and most common method of transferring property to a surviving spouse—the unrestricted transfer—is eligible for an unlimited marital deduction. This includes all property included in the gross estate of the decedent that passes directly to the surviving spouse. Therefore outright transfers of probate assets by will or intestacy qualify for the marital deduction. In addition, transfers by operation of law or contract that pass outright to the surviving spouse at death similarly qualify. Thus life insurance proceeds payable to the surviving spouse or jointly held property received from survivorship by the deceased spouse qualify for the marital deduction.

Property transfers that place restrictions on the surviving spouse's use or enjoyment of the property may or may not qualify for the marital deduction. The marital deduction was envisioned to prevent a substantial first-death tax to a married couple if the usual dispositive scheme (100 percent to the spouse) is followed. However, Congress intended that the estate taxes would be payable at the second death of the two spouses. Thus a general rule of thumb is that the marital deduction is available only for transfers to a surviving spouse that would cause the ultimate inclusion of the property in the surviving spouse's gross estate. Property transferred to a surviving spouse will not qualify for the marital deduction if the interest is terminable at the death of the surviving spouse.

An interest in property left to a surviving spouse will be nondeductible if

- it terminates upon the occurrence of an event or a contingency, such as death, and
- a third party gains possession of the property after the surviving spouse's interest terminates.

A common example of a nondeductible terminable interest is the transfer of a life estate to the surviving spouse with the remainder interest being paid to the couple's children under the terms of the deceased spouse's will. Such a transfer would not create a second-death tax since the surviving spouse's interest terminates and therefore would not be included in his or her estate. However, a first-death tax would be payable since the life estate transferred to the surviving spouse would not qualify for the marital deduction.

Congress recognized that many married individuals prefer leaving property in trust for the surviving spouse. The transferor may be concerned that the spouse may be unable to properly manage the trust property. Or the transferor-spouse might want to limit the invasion rights of the surviving spouse. In addition, it is generally the intent of individuals to ultimately leave their property to their children. The transferor-spouse may want to control the ultimate disposition of the property to preserve the rights of his or her children. This is particularly true if the transferor-spouse has children from a prior marriage. Fortunately the marital-deduction rules have created several opportunities that meet many of these objectives.

Estate Trust. A transfer to a surviving spouse through an estate trust qualifies for a marital deduction. Under this arrangement a deceased spouse leaves a life estate in trust to the surviving spouse. The surviving spouse's estate is the remainderperson of this trust. Income from the estate trust can either accumulate or be paid to the surviving spouse at the discretion of the trustee. Since the remainder interest is transferred to the surviving spouse's estate, the property will be included in his or her gross estate, and a second-death estate tax may be payable at that time.

Power-of-Appointment Trust. Another common marital-deduction trust is the power-of-appointment trust. This trust is designed to distribute income to the surviving spouse during his or her life and provides the surviving spouse with a general power of appointment over the trust property. The general power of appointment may be exercisable by the surviving spouse in all events, or may be exercisable only at the death of the surviving spouse. Since the surviving spouse has a general power of appointment over the trust principal, the principal is included in his or her gross estate for federal tax purposes.

QTIP Marital-Deduction Trust. A special provision of the tax law provides for a marital deduction if qualifying terminable interest property (QTIP) is left to a surviving spouse. Under these rules a terminable property interest can be transferred to a surviving spouse and such interest will qualify for the marital deduction. The QTIP deduction is available if the executor of the deceased spouse elects for QTIP treatment on the estate tax return. The QTIP trust can be funded by probate assets or other types of testamentary dispositions. The surviving spouse must have the right to all income annually from the QTIP for life. At the death of the surviving spouse the QTIP election provides that the property will be included in the surviving spouse's gross estate.

The primary advantage of the QTIP is the ability of the transferor-spouse to control the transfer of his or her assets. The ultimate disposition of the QTIP

Transfers Qualifying for the Marital Deduction

- Outright transfers
  - By will or intestacy
  - By operation of law
  - By operation of contract
- Estate Trust
- Power-of-appointment trust
- QTIP trust

property would be predetermined by the terms of the trust created by the original transferor-spouse. Thus the QTIP trust permits a transferor-spouse to provide for his or her surviving spouse but still preserve the ultimate interests of his or her children.

Planning for the Lifetime Estate and Gift Tax Exclusion

The applicable credit against estate or gift tax is designed to prevent the imposition of these transfer taxes on moderate-sized estates. As noted earlier, the credit ($211,300 for 1999) is applied dollar-for-dollar against any estate or gift tax due, and provides a shelter against approximately $650,000 of taxable transfers during a transferor's lifetime or at death.

For the lifetime exclusion amount to be applicable to a transfer, the transferor must first create estate or gift tax. Thus the lifetime exclusion amount is not applicable to a transfer that is exempt or deductible from the tax base as a result of other provisions of the federal transfer tax rules. For example, if a transfer is exempt from estate or gift tax as a result of the marital deduction or annual exclusion, the transferor's exclusion amount will not be applicable.

Coordination of the Marital Deduction and Lifetime Exclusion

The maximum use of a marital deduction is the typical dispositive scheme for most married individuals. All property is generally left either outright to the surviving spouse or in other manners qualifying for the marital deduction at the first spouse's death. Since no estate tax will be payable under these circumstances, the lifetime exclusion available at the death of the first spouse to die will be wasted.

With appropriate planning each spouse can make maximum use of the applicable credit, and the marital unit as a whole can shelter up to $1.3 million in marital wealth from federal estate taxes. This shelter can only be accomplished if each spouse makes maximum use of the $650,000 exclusion. As discussed above the usual marital dispositive scheme does not take advantage of the $650,000 exclusion available to the first spouse at his or her death. Thus all assets transferred to the surviving spouse under the marital deduction will be sheltered by only one applicable credit available at the second spouse's death.

The usual dispositive scheme can be altered to make maximum use of each spouse's applicable credit and optimal use of the marital deduction. Again, this requires appropriate answers to the "who" and "how" questions. With some restrictions, all the objectives of the usual dispositive scheme can be accomplished without wasting the applicable credit of either spouse. This maximum estate tax shelter is accomplished by designing each spouse's estate plan to transfer property to both a marital and applicable credit trust. This arrangement is commonly referred to as an AB trust arrangement. The AB trust arrangement is designed to operate as follows:

- The A trust is some form of marital-deduction trust. This trust receives assets in a manner qualifying for the marital deduction and provides for maximum use of these assets by the surviving spouse. The remainder of the assets transferred by the decedent are placed into the B trust.
- The B trust is designed *not* to qualify for the marital deduction. Instead the B trust, funded with approximately $650,000, will be part of the taxable estate since it will not be deductible under the marital deduction. However, the $650,000 transferred to the B trust qualifies for the $650,000 applicable credit equivalent.

The "how" question must be answered by designing the transfer to the B trust in a nonqualifying manner for the marital deduction. Therefore the surviving spouse's interest in the B trust must be limited to a life estate, perhaps with some limited invasion rights. Since the B trust is designed as a nonqualifying terminable interest, the assets in the B trust will not be included in the surviving spouse's gross estate and the remainder interest can be reserved for the children.

The "who" question must be answered with respect to the B trust, often referred to either as the *family trust, credit-shelter trust,* or *bypass trust.* The B trust can be used to provide substantial rights to the surviving spouse but must fail to qualify for the marital deduction. If the client is extremely wealthy, the B trust could entirely avoid benefiting the surviving spouse, and is an excellent way to provide for other heirs at the first death.

The AB trust arrangement makes maximum use of each spouse's applicable credit, and since the A trust qualifies for the marital deduction and the B trust is sheltered by the applicable credit, no estate tax will be paid at the first spouse's death. Thus the AB trust arrangement does not change the usual first-death tax results. However, the second-death taxes are reduced since an additional $650,000 exclusion amount applicable credit equivalent was used at the time of the first death. Thus the surviving spouse's estate is reduced in size by the amount of property transferred to the B trust at the first death of the two spouses.

AB Trust Arrangement

Client creates two testamentary trusts

A Trust	B Trust
• Spouse is beneficiary • Receives assets not placed in B trust • Qualifies for marital deduction • Subject to estate taxation at death of spouse	• Spouse receives no more than life income interest and limited invasion powers; children may receive current and/or remainder interest. • Receives $650,000 of assets • Does not qualify for marital deduction; makes use of applicable credit • Escapes estate taxation at death of spouse

Planning Charitable Contributions

Qualifying gifts of property to charities may generate deductions against federal income, gift, and estate taxes. Although some limitations exist for the charitable deduction for income tax purposes, qualifying gifts of property are deductible in full against either the federal gift or estate tax base.

Charitable contributions are deductible for federal income, estate, and gift tax purposes only if made to qualified organizations. Generally speaking, an organization is qualified if it is operated exclusively for religious, charitable, scientific, literary, or educational purposes. In addition, the charity must hold such qualified status under the rules of the Internal Revenue Service. A list of qualified charities is published by the IRS and may be inspected by any individuals interested in making a charitable contribution.

Advantages of Gifts to Charity. The value of property gifted to a qualified charity is fully deductible from the federal gift or estate tax base. In addition, the value of property gifted to charity will be deductible from the federal income tax base of the donor. (Some limitations exist on the size of the income tax deduction, but they are not discussed here.) Thus a donor can reduce current income taxes and the eventual size of his or her taxable estate. Quite simply, any property gifted to charity will remove the property (including any postcontribution appreciation) from the transfer-tax base of the donor. Since the charitable gift tax deduction is unlimited, charitable contributions can be even more effective than gifts to noncharitable donees in reducing the size of the gross estate of a wealthy client. The charitable deduction is similarly unlimited for testamentary bequests to charities. Through the techniques discussed below, charitable contributions can significantly reduce the decedent's estate tax liability without completely divesting other heirs of the donated property.

Gifts of Remainder Interests to Charity. One disadvantage of an outright lifetime contribution of property to charity is that the donor loses the current enjoyment of the property. Fortunately there are methods to take advantage of the tax benefits provided to charitable contributions while retaining the donor's use or enjoyment of the property. Certain types of trust arrangements, known as *charitable remainder trusts*, can be employed to retain the current enjoyment of the property for the life of the donor (or lives of the donor's family members) while providing gift, estate, and income tax advantages. The charitable remainder trust can be established during the donor's lifetime or at his or her death. The charitable remainder trust permits the donor to retain the current income for the donor or his or her family. The income from the trust corpus will be retained for a time period (usually measured by the life of the donor or lives of selected family members) with the charitable institution holding the remainder interest. The current tax deduction is measured by the present value of the remainder interest held by charity. Thus the donor (or possibly members of the donor's family) receives current benefit of the trust property and current tax advantages, while the charity receives the benefit of the property outright when the remainder interest is distributed. To prevent abuses of the transfer tax system, tax rules carefully specify the types of charitable remainder trusts eligible for such tax benefits.

Donating Income Interests to Charity. Under some circumstances a client may donate a current income interest to charity as opposed to a remainder interest. Under this arrangement, known as a *charitable lead trust*, a trust is established to provide a charity with a current term income interest. The remainder interest in the trust is retained by the grantor (or for his or her family). The donor gets an upfront income and gift or estate tax deduction for the present value of the lead income interest donated to charity. However, the grantor remains taxable annually on the actual trust income.

The charitable lead trust is generally used for testamentary dispositions. If the current income interest bequested to the charity is substantial, the estate will receive a deduction in an amount equal to a large portion of the value of the property placed in the trust. Thus the taxable estate is significantly reduced while the family retains the ultimate control of the trust property through its remainder interest. The charitable lead trust is an excellent tool for extremely wealthy individuals who have other substantial assets to leave to their heirs currently, since the assets placed in the charitable lead trust may not be available for several years.

The Role of Life Insurance in the Estate Plan

Life insurance can serve either as an estate liquidity or estate enhancement tool. The most appropriate use of life insurance in the estate plan depends upon the age, family circumstances, and financial status of the particular client.

Life Insurance for Estate Enhancement

Life insurance is generally used for estate enhancement for (1) younger clients, (2) clients with dependent family members, and (3) clients with small to moderate-sized estates. Clients in these categories generally have protection as the primary need for their life insurance coverage. These individuals need to protect their families from the loss of future earnings with which to support the family members. These clients are either in or are headed toward their peak earning years, and their families rely on these future earnings for such things as the educational and medical needs of the children, the support needs of the client and his or her spouse, and the eventual retirement needs of the client and his or her spouse.

The death taxes facing a younger client with a small to moderate-sized estate are relatively minor. The applicable credit and marital deduction will generally remove the danger of federal estate taxes for these individuals. Thus estate liquidity is not the primary concern. It is highly improbable, however, that these individuals have accumulated enough wealth to replace future income and support of a prematurely deceased breadwinner. Life insurance is the perfect estate enhancement tool to replace some or all of the financial loss created by the premature death. The use of life insurance coverage to provide for such a loss is discussed in chapters 10 and 11.

Life Insurance for Estate Liquidity Purposes

For older clients with larger estates estate liquidity becomes a primary focus in the use of life insurance. Older clients have generally completed or nearly completed the heaviest support and educational expense years for dependent children. These individuals are usually well along in the funding of their retirement plans and have fewer years of employment ahead of them.

Since these clients may have accumulated substantial wealth, the protection offered by the marital deduction and lifetime exclusion may be inadequate to shelter their estates. Although the marital deduction will generally shelter all of the estate from tax at the death of the first spouse, the second death creates a substantial tax problem in the foreseeable future (if the spouse is of similar age). As noted earlier, with optimal planning the lifetime exclusion and marital deduction can shelter only $1.3 million of total family wealth from taxes in 1999, increasing to $2 million in 2006.

In addition, an affluent client may have accumulated substantial wealth that is not liquid. For example, an interest in a closely held family business is often assigned a high value for the purposes of the federal estate tax. However, the business interest may be unmarketable to purchasers outside the family group. If the heirs are to remain in the business, they must discover a method to pay any estate taxes due.

Under the circumstances described above, life insurance is quite useful in providing for estate liquidity. Life insurance can be secured by a client to provide death proceeds equal to the size of the wealth lost in the form of the substantial state death taxes and federal estate tax. In addition, the life insurance proceeds provide cash, which, as opposed to illiquid estate assets, is more readily available to provide for the liquidity needs of settling the estate.

The estate tax treatment of the life insurance selected by these individuals is critical. Since affluent clients are hoping to solve liquidity problems rather than add to a tax burden, life insurance should be purchased and owned in a manner that keeps the death proceeds out of the gross estate if at all possible. Thus these individuals often have ownership arrangements for the life insurance that provide the insured with no incidents of ownership. This can be accomplished by having either the spouse or children of the insured apply for and own the life insurance policy. Or, as discussed below, a trust can be designed to own the life insurance policy. However, the estate or the executor should never be the beneficiary of the proceeds since this beneficiary designation would place the proceeds in the gross estate for tax purposes.

Life Insurance Trusts

Revocable Trusts. A revocable life insurance trust is designed to own and/or be the designated beneficiary of life insurance coverage on the grantor's life. The revocable life insurance trust serves no estate tax planning purposes. Since the trust is revocable, the insured is treated as the owner of the policy and the death proceeds will be included in the insured's gross estate. The revocable trust is ordinarily used when a specific, perhaps temporary, protection need exists.

The revocable trust is an excellent method for providing life insurance benefits for the protection of young children. If the insured dies, the trust becomes irrevocable and the children can be provided for by the beneficial terms of the trust. The revocable life insurance trust is also an excellent method of providing protection for children following a divorce.

Irrevocable Life Insurance Trusts. An irrevocable life insurance trust is generally used by older clients who have a more stable family and financial situation. The irrevocable trust can be designed to provide for heirs life insurance benefits that will be excluded from the client's gross estate. In addition, contributions to the trust can be designed to avoid gift or generation-skipping taxes. Thus the irrevocable life insurance trust is a perfect tool for the estate liquidity needs of older wealthy clients without adding to the tax burden. Since the trust is irrevocable, the client should be certain of his or her beneficial intent at the time the trust is drafted.

CONCLUSION

Although the estate planning process suggests a certain finality, the process should be ongoing. The estate planner should never be satisfied that the client has approved a plan and executed the necessary documents. The estate planner and the client should take the necessary steps to coordinate the estate plan with the client's other personal and financial considerations. For example, property transfers may be necessary to convert the client's property into the appropriate form. Since a will disposes only of probate property, it may frustrate the intent of the plan if the client's property is not converted into a form passing through probate.

In addition, all appointed individuals, such as executors, trustees, and attorneys-in-fact, should be informed of their roles and the intentions of the client. In many cases members of the family will be relied upon to make responsible decisions with respect to the estate plan. These family members should be informed, to the extent necessary, of the client's dispositive intentions.

Finally, periodic follow-up is necessary in a successfully planned estate. Many aspects of the estate plan will be revocable. Such flexibility may provide additional opportunities for the estate planner and the client. Changes in the tax law should be monitored and may necessitate new estate planning steps as a result. The failure to follow up will probably result in client dissatisfaction and perhaps malpractice claims against the estate planner.

14

Retirement Planning

Kenn Tacchino and David A. Littell

Chapter Outline

Not too long ago retirement meant being given a gold watch and then quietly living out one's remaining few years with family. But changing lifestyles, increased longevity, and improved expectations have drastically altered the nature of retirement. Today, people anticipate active, vibrant retirements in which they enjoy life and economic self-sufficiency. They see retirement not as the short final phase of life but as the reward phase of life—the icing on the cake. What's more, a significant percentage of the population has become increasingly interested in achieving the financial independence currently associated with retirement. Put another way, the so-called graying of America has resulted in a maturing retirement planning movement.

Retirement planning is no easy process, however. Financial services professionals who engage in retirement planning must be prepared to answer some tough questions. Several of these questions concern their role as a retirement planner, the amount of income their clients will need for retirement, the sources of retirement income available from employers and Uncle Sam and strategies for maximizing retirement income. This chapter will explore these questions with the intent of providing financial services professionals with the knowledge and tools they need to properly serve their clients' retirement needs.

WHAT IS THE ROLE OF THE RETIREMENT PLANNER?

Holistic Retirement Planning

Retirement planning is a multidimensional field. As such it requires that the planner be schooled in the nuances of many financial planning specialties as well as other areas. Unfortunately, many so-called planners approach retirement planning from only one point of view, investments, for example. This perspective, the perspective offered by specializing in just one field, is too limited for dealing with the diversified needs of the would-be retiree. A client is better served by a team of planners who have specialized but complementary backgrounds or by a single planner who is experienced in a variety of important retirement topics.

Whether the retirement team or the multitalented individual is the vehicle, the holistic approach to retirement planning is the only means by which a client's needs can be fully and adequately met. Under the holistic approach to retirement planning the planner is required to communicate with clients concerning such topics as

- employer-provided retirement plans
- social security
- income tax issues
- insurance coverage
- investments
- long-term care options
- retirement communities
- relocation possibilities
- wellness
- nutrition
- lifestyle choices

Some examples will help to give the flavor of the variety of topics that may be discussed while retirement planning.

Example 1: Adam (aged 65) is retired and he and his wife receive $30,000 in pension income and $10,000 in social security income. Adam would like to know how he will be taxed for federal tax purposes. Adam and his wife file jointly.

The general rule that applies to all retirees, including Adam, is that pension income is fully taxable. However, a taxpayer filing a joint return can exclude all social security benefits from income for tax purposes if provisional income is $32,000 or less. (Provisional income is defined as adjusted gross income plus tax-exempt interest plus half of social security benefits.) For provisional income between $32,000 and $44,000, as much as 50 percent of social security income is taxable. If provisional income exceeds $44,000, as much as 85 percent of social security income is taxable.

In this case, Adam's combined income is calculated by adding his $30,000 pension to one-half of his $10,000 social security benefit ($5,000). Since $35,000 ($30,000 + $5,000) exceeds the base amount of $32,000 by $3,000, Adam will be taxed on one-half of this amount or $1,500. Thus Adam must pay federal taxes on his $30,000 pension and on $1,500 of his social security benefit. Adam can take heart, however, in the fact that married taxpayers 65 or over are each entitled to an increase of $750 in their standard deduction ($950 for single taxpayers).

Example 2: Barbara (aged 58) has questions about investing for retirement. Barbara is currently heavily concentrated in aggressive growth equities. Barbara's planner should advise her that she should become less growth oriented and begin to be more concerned with a portfolio that provides enough income for retirement needs. This change in emphasis from aggressive growth to more conservative income stocks is needed for two important reasons. First, since Barbara has only a few years until retirement, she has less time to recover losses should the higher-risk growth stocks suffer reverses. Second, Barbara should become increasingly concerned about having sufficient income in the retirement years.

Barbara's planner should not, however, just offer her one-time advice to change portfolio strategies, but should help Barbara to implement his or her suggestions and continue to offer investment advice. A change to income-oriented stocks combined with the downward risk profile of the portfolio will have the effect of generating more *current annual income* for Barbara but less *total return* each year from the portfolio. As a consequence, until retirement actually takes place, the reinvestment of the portfolio's annual income stream becomes an ever increasing segment of total portfolio management for Barbara.

Example 3: Charlie and his wife, Ann, have heard about long-term care insurance from a friend and wonder if it would be right for them. Charlie, aged 65, has recently retired and his personal disability income policy has just expired. Ann, also retired with no personal disability income policy, is slightly older than Charlie and has a family history of poor health. Charlie and Ann have a retirement income of $35,000 per year and are not in a position to spend down (that is, shed income and qualify for medicaid to pay for nursing home care). Charlie and Ann are covered by medicare but their planner informs Charlie that nursing home stays are not covered by medicare to any significant degree.

Charlie and Ann are good candidates for long-term care insurance. Long-term care insurance pays cash benefits of a stipulated amount for every day that the insured utilizes nursing home facilities. Without a long-term care policy the costs of a nursing home would quickly deplete Charlie's and Ann's assets.

Charlie and Ann are uncertain about what level of benefits to purchase. The average cost for a nursing home stay is $22,000 annually, but the facilities that Charlie and Ann would be comfortable with cost $30,000 to $40,000 per year. Charlie's retirement planner advises him that premiums for, say, a $100 a day policy ($36,500 annually) would be approximately $1,800 per year each ($3,600 total). Charlie and Ann can then decide at the appropriate time whether they would prefer to take the $30,000 nursing home and use the extra income ($6,500 per year) for annual living expenses or choose the more expensive home and supplement the difference from their other sources of income.

Applying Knowledge to Client Objectives: The Art of Retirement Planning

The successful retirement planner must not only have a working knowledge of a large variety of financial planning and retirement-related topics but also know how to apply the knowledge to a client's particular situation. This requires understanding a client's objectives, attitudes, and personal preferences. For example, retirement planners should be prepared to help clients to meet the important general objectives of maintaining their preretirement standard of living during retirement, becoming economically self-sufficient, minimizing taxes on retirement distributions, adapting to the retirement lifestyle, and the client's individual objectives, such as taking care of a dependent parent or dealing with special health needs (see table 14-1, which is based on an American College study). In addition, planners should be prepared to deal with a variety of attitudes on how long the client wants to work, what the client's prospects are for health and longevity, whether the client can be disciplined enough to save for retirement and to what extent the client accepts investment risk. It is this application of a broad range of knowledge to a diverse group of clients that makes retirement planning more art than science.

TABLE 14-1
Ranking of Client Retirement Objectives in Order of Priority by Financial Services Professionals

1. Maintaining preretirement standard of living
2. Maintaining economic self-sufficiency
3. Minimizing taxes
4. Retiring early
5. Adapting to noneconomic aspects of retirement
6. Passing on wealth to others
7. Improving lifestyle in retirement
8. Caring for dependents

For the retirement planner the primary responsibility in the "art of retirement planning" is to make clients aware that they are making choices about their retirement every day. For example, should the client take an expensive vacation or take a moderately priced vacation and save the difference for retirement? The planner cannot force the client to make lifestyle choices that will provide an adequate source of retirement funds. The planner can, however, make the client aware of the large amount of funds needed for retirement and point out that a spendthrift lifestyle (one that uses the full after-tax income to support the current standard of living) hurts a retiree in two ways.

First, a spendthrift lifestyle minimizes the retiree's ability to accumulate savings that will produce an adequate income stream to complement his or her employer pension and social security. These three elements—private savings, employer pensions, and social security—are considered essential for a secure retirement. If any leg on this "three-legged stool" is missing, the client is in danger of falling short of an economically secure retirement. Second, the retiree becomes accustomed to an unnaturally high standard of living. By living below their means before retirement, clients will establish a lifestyle that is more easily maintained in the retirement years.

Forcing clients to think about retirement planning and their lifestyle choices is a primary responsibility of the retirement planner. However, two other important facets to retirement planning exist. The planner must devise different retirement strategies for clients who are prepared for retirement and for those who are not and the planner must overcome roadblocks to retirement saving.

Clients Are Never Too Young or Too Old

Planners must deal with clients of all ages and retirement planning takes on different characteristics for different age groups. Those new to the retirement planning field soon find out that clients are never too old or too young to plan for retirement. Starting early, however, can mean all the difference in the world. (See table 14-2.)

TABLE 14-2
Funding an IRA: The Advantages of Starting Young*

IRA One		IRA Two	
Age start	18	Age start	35
Age end	21	Age end	65
Amount per year	$2,000	Amount per year	$2,000
Rate of return	8%	Rate of return	8%
Value at age 65	$266,360	Value at age 65	$244,692
Total amount contributed	$8,000	Total amount contributed	$60,000

Age	Amount	Value	Age	Amount	Value
18	$2,000	$2,160	18	$ 0	$ 0
19	2,000	4,493	19	0	0
20	2,000	7,012	20	0	0
21	2,000	9,733	21	0	0
22	0	10,512	22	0	0
23	0	11,353	23	0	0
24	0	12,261	24	0	0
25	0	13,242	25	0	0
26	0	14,301	26	0	0
27	0	15,445	35	2,000	2,160
28	0	16,681	36	2,000	4,493
29	0	18,015	37	2,000	7,012
30	0	19,456	38	2,000	9,733
.	.	.	.	.	.
.	.	.	.	.	.
.	.	.	.	.	.
.	.	.	.	.	.
61	0	211,445	61	2,000	188,678
62	0	228,360	62	2,000	205,932
63	0	246,629	63	2,000	224,566
64	0	266,360	64	2,000	244,692

*This comparison dramatically illustrates the value of saving for retirement while young. Note that at age 65 IRA One will have accumulated more funds than IRA Two even though the capital contribution for IRA Two is $52,000 more than IRA One.

Unfortunately, some clients don't save for retirement until the time to retire is upon them. But even though clients who start thinking about retirement when it is imminent have lost the ability to set aside savings on a systematic basis and to let compound interest work for them, planning can still be conducted for these clients. Important decisions must be made about distributions from qualified plans, liquidation of personal assets, and investment of any private savings. Developing a retirement plan for the client who has procrastinated also includes determining what funds are available for retirement and creating strategies, even if the funds are inadequate.

One such strategy calls for the planner to suggest that the client postpone retirement. The combined effect of lengthening the accumulation period and shortening the retirement period is financially desirable. If delaying retirement from his or her current job is not feasible, the client can achieve similar results by working for another employer after forced retirement. A second strategy is to recommend that the client move to an area with a lower cost of living. This move will enable the client to stretch his or her retirement dollars. What's more, by freeing up some of the equity in the home the client can make assets available for investment purposes.

After recommending these strategies, the planner needs to help the client change his or her expectations about retirement. By forcing the client to look realistically at the lifestyle he or she will be able to afford, the planner can save the client from overspending during the early retirement years and avoid becoming financially destitute in the later retirement years.

Overcoming Roadblocks to Retirement Saving

Perhaps the biggest roadblock to retirement planning is the tendency of many working people to use their full after-tax income to support their current standard of living. For this reason clients must be taught when they are young to follow a budget that allows them to live within their means and that also provides for retirement savings. Planners should make their clients aware that a spending ratio of no higher than 90/10 is generally desired. Under a 90/10 spending ratio, 90 percent of the client's earnings are directed toward the current standard of living, and 10 percent is directed toward other long-term financial objectives, such as the children's education and the client's own retirement. For example, a family with a gross annual income of $50,000 should allocate no more than $45,000 (including taxes) of its total income to standard-of-living and lifestyle items, leaving $5,000 or more for the long-term objectives. Furthermore, planners should recommend that as income rises, the percentage spent on the current standard of living should decline.

A second impediment to retirement saving is unexpected expenses (including expenses arising from inadequate insurance or the cost of major repairs to a home) and unexpected decreases in income (for example, due to unemployment). The client should set up an emergency fund to handle these inevitable problems. Usually about 3 to 6 months' income should be set aside for this objective. In addition, agents should conduct a thorough review of their clients' insurance needs to make sure they are adequately covered. Two often overlooked areas are long-term disability insurance and umbrella liability insurance.

Roadblocks to Retirement Saving

1. Tendency to spend all income
2. Unexpected expenses
3. Divorce
4. Frequent employment changes
5. Other accumulation needs

A third roadblock to saving for retirement occurs in the case of a divorced client. Divorce often leaves one or both parties with little or no accumulation of pension benefits or other private sources of retirement income. These clients may have only a short time to accumulate any retirement income and may not be able to earn significant pension or social security benefits. If the marriage lasted 10 years or longer, however, divorced persons are eligible for social security based on their former spouse's earnings record.

Another common retirement planning problem concerns workers who have frequently changed employers. Generally these people will not accumulate vested pension benefits because they never stayed with an employer long enough to become vested. Even if they did become vested, they may have received a distribution of their accumulated pension fund upon leaving the job and probably spent this money rather than investing it or rolling it over for retirement. Planners should advise clients who change jobs to roll over vested benefits into an IRA or into their new qualified plan to preserve the tax-deferred growth of their retirement funds. They should also advise clients who have recently changed jobs that if they have not met the participation requirements of their new employer's plan, then annual tax-deductible contributions can be made to an IRA until they do, regardless of salary.

A final impediment to acquiring adequate retirement savings is the long-term accumulation objectives that clients must meet before retirement. The down payment on a primary residence and/or vacation home and the education of children can consume any long-term savings that people have managed to accumulate. Since these objectives have a greater urgency for completion than retirement, they supplant retirement as a saving priority. Although these objectives are worthy, it is important to remind clients that savings must be carved out for retirement purposes in addition to other long-term objectives.

HOW MUCH WILL YOUR CLIENTS NEED?

Another important task in retirement planning is determining how much the client will need to save in order to achieve his or her retirement goals. Estimating a client's financial needs during retirement is like trying to predict the future: Such estimates are fraught with complicating factors and clouded by unknown variables. For example, the planner and client must establish what standard of living is desired during retirement, when retirement will begin, what inflation assumptions should be made before and after retirement, and what interest can be earned on invested funds. In addition, for clients who are forced by economic necessity to liquidate their retirement nest egg the client and planner must estimate the life expectancy over which liquidation will occur. Many of these variables can dramatically change overnight and without warning. The following are examples of how variables could change.

- The client may be planning to retire at age 65 but health considerations, or perhaps a plant shutdown, force retirement at age 62.
- A younger client may be planning on a relatively moderate retirement lifestyle but business success may lead to a higher retirement income expectation.
- Forecasters may predict that long-term inflation will result in an annual 4 percent increase in the cost of living when in reality 6 percent increases occur. (Even a one percentage point disparity can make a significant difference.)
- Clients may hope for an after-tax rate of return of 7 percent when in fact investment returns are adversely affected by a bear market, or the real after-tax rate of return is suppressed by rising tax rates.
- Clients may plan on a short life expectancy and have the "misfortune" of living longer.

While it is important to understand that planning is, at best, an educated guess, it still beats the alternative. What's more, changing variables can be overcome if the retirement plan is revised and adjusted annually. Once the planner has explained to his or her client the tentative nature of the plan and the need for hands-on monitoring, then the task of setting out a plan for the client begins.

Creating a Retirement Plan

There are three basic facets to any retirement plan. The planner must first determine where the client stands financially for retirement purposes. Then the planner must assess where the client wants to be financially during retirement and the client's ability to reach this goal. Finally, the planner must road map the way for a client to achieve his or her goals.

Stage 1: Where Are We?

In order to calculate a client's retirement needs, the planner must first add up the client's existing resources. These may include the amount of any social security benefits due, the amount of any pension benefits due, any private savings the client has accumulated to date, including IRAs and personally owned life insurance, and any other sources of retirement income, such as the proceeds from the sale of a home.

Stage 2: Where Do We Want to Go?

Once a financial inventory of possible sources of retirement income has been taken, the next step is to determine how much annual income will be needed in the first year of retirement to achieve the client's goals. There are two common ways of determining this, the replacement ratio method and the expense method.

Replacement Ratio Method. The replacement ratio method of retirement planning assumes that the standard of living enjoyed during the years just prior to retirement will be the determining factor for the standard of living during retirement. For clients at or near retirement it is much easier to define the target. For example, if the 64-year-old near-retiree is earning $50,000, then the retirement income for that retiree should maintain most of the current purchasing power that that person has. If, however, a younger client is involved, growth estimates should be made to approximate what the salary will be at retirement.

Note that the entire final salary is not needed for determining the proper amount of purchasing power. In general, a 70 to 90 percent replacement ratio of a client's final average salary is typically used for individual retirement planning purposes. Support for this range rests upon the elimination of some employment-related taxes and some expected changes in spending patterns that reduce the retiree's need for income (see figure 14-1).

Reduced Taxes. Retirees can assume that a lower percentage of their income will go toward paying taxes in the retirement years because, in many cases, there is an elimination or a reduction of certain taxes that they previously had to pay. Tax advantages for the retiree include the elimination of the social security tax, an increased standard deduction depending on the retiree's age and filing status, the exclusion of all or part of the amount of the social security benefit from gross income, reductions in state and local income taxes, and an increased ability to use deductible medical expenses.

Reduced Living Expenses. Retirees face a variety of changes in spending patterns after retirement, and some of these changes will reduce a retiree's living expenses. These reductions include elimination of work-related expenses; elimination of home-mortgage expenses; elimination of dependent care, that is, child-rearing expenses; elimination of long-term savings obligations; and reduction in automotive expenditures.

FIGURE 14-1
Justification of a 70 to 90 Percent Replacement Ratio

Joe Jones (aged 64) has fixed salary of $100,000 and would like to maintain his current purchasing power when he retires next year. If joe has no increased retirement-related expenses, Joe can do this by having a retirement income of 70 percent of his final salary as illustrated below. If Joe has increased retirement-related expenses, a somewhat higher figure should be used. (Note that postretirement inflation will be accounted for later.)

Working salary			$100,000
less annual retirement savings		$18,000	
less social security taxes		4,891	
less reduction in federal taxes	(extra $750 deduction for being 65)	210	
	(no tax on portion of social security received)	1,650	
less annual commuting expenses to work		450	
less mortgage expenses	(mortgage expires on retirement date)	4,799	
Reductions subtotal			30,000
Total purchasing power needed at 65			$ 70,000
Percentage of final salary needed			70%

Additional Factors. It is not all good news for the retiree, however. Retirees also face several factors that tend to increase the amount of income they will need during the retirement period. These include possible increases in long-term inflation, increased medical expenses, increased travel expenses, and other retirement-related expenses.

Expense Method. The expense method of retirement planning focuses on the projected expenses that the retiree will have. As with the replacement ratio method it is much easier to define the potential expenses for those clients who are at or near retirement. For example, if the 64-year-old near-retiree expects to have $3,000 in monthly bills ($36,000 annually), then the retirement income for that retiree should maintain $36,000 worth of purchasing power in today's dollars. If, however, a younger client is involved, more speculative estimates of retirement expenses must be made (and periodically revised).

A list of expenses that should be considered includes expenses that may be unique to the particular client as well as other more general expenses.

Some expenses that tend to increase for retirees include the following:

- utilities and telephone
- medical/dental/drugs/health insurance
- house upkeep/repairs/maintenance/property insurance
- recreation/entertainment/travel/dining
- contributions/gifts

On the other hand, some expenses tend to decrease for the retiree:

- mortgage payments
- food
- clothing
- income taxes
- property taxes
- transportation costs (car maintenance/insurance/other)
- debt repayment (charge accounts/personal loans)
- child support/alimony
- household furnishings

Stage 3: The Retirement Road Map

Both the replacement ratio method and the expense method can be used to determine the income level a retiree will need at age 65. They do not, however, calculate the amount of savings that the client must accumulate in order to achieve a consistent level of financial security throughout retirement. The amount that the client needs to save to achieve his or her goals is a function of two opposing factors: the savings that the client currently has (stage 1) and the income that the client will need (stage 2), both factors are influenced by inflation. In order to better understand the effect of inflation over time, consider the loss of purchasing power that occurs in the following example.

> *Example:* Al Edwards (aged 65) is retiring this year and needs $50,000 of retirement income to maintain his current standard of living. If the inflation rate is 4 percent per year over Al's retirement period, Al will need to have an increasing amount of retirement income each year of retirement. Table 14-3 illustrates the amount of annual income Al will need at specified intervals to maintain a consistent amount of purchasing power.

To calculate the true retirement income needed the planner must provide inflation protection both before and after retirement for all the client's resources.

In order to accomplish this, the planner must decide which of the client's resources are subject to a decline in purchasing power due to the effects of inflation.

TABLE 14-3
Retirement Income for Al Edwards

Al's Age	Income
65	$50,000
70	60,833
75	74,012
80	90,047
90	133,292
100	197,304

Any social security that the client might receive will *not* be subject to a decline in purchasing power, because social security is indexed each year to reflect inflation. Therefore the planner will not have to provide inflation protection for a client's social security benefit. The planner cannot, however, generally assume any inflation protection for pension benefits. For this reason the client will need to fund for an amount that can be used to bolster a non-inflation-protected benefit during retirement.

Another item that will be affected by inflation is the retirement income deficit itself. The retirement income deficit is any shortfall that exists between what the client has (stage 1) and what the client needs (stage 2). This is not inflation-proof before or after retirement. The planner will therefore need to calculate an inflation factor that protects the client's purchasing power for this amount.

The final step in mapping a client's retirement needs is to calculate the target amount of savings needed. In order to do this, work sheets, such as those in figures 14-2 and 14-3, are helpful. The first work sheet, based on the replacement ratio method, produces the estimated income gap between the desired retirement income and the available retirement benefits. That gap is then adjusted for inflation. The amount of additional capital needed to fill the gap and to supplement the pension benefit (inflation-unprotected) is then computed. Finally, the funding pattern that will be used to generate the needed new capital is calculated.

The second work sheet, based on the expense method, calls for an estimate of the client's current monthly and annual living expenses. The total of these expenses (line 10) is then adjusted inflation to reflect the expected total at retirement date. Next, a capital sum is calculated (lines 15-19) that will be sufficient, together with interest earnings, to provide an inflation-adjusted income during the estimated number of years in the retirement period.

FIGURE 14-2
Replacement Ratio Method Work Sheet

1.	Current annual gross salary	$__________
2.	Retirement-income target (multiply line 1 by 0.8) (80 percent target)	$__________
3.	Estimated annual benefit from pension plan, not including IRAs, 401(k)s, or profit-sharing plans[1]	$__________
4.	Estimated annual social security benefits[1]	$__________
5.	Total retirement benefits (add lines 3 and 4)	$__________
6.	Income gap (subtract line 5 from line 2)[2]	$__________
7.	Adjust gap to reflect inflation (multiply line 6 by factor A, below)	$__________
8.	Capital needed to generate additional income and close gap (multiply line 7 by 16.3)[3]	$__________
9.	Extra capital needed to offset inflation's impact on pension (multiply line 3 by factor B, below)	$__________
10.	Total capital needed (add lines 8 and 9)	$__________
11.	Total current retirement savings (includes balances in IRAs, 401(k)s, profit-sharing plans, mutual funds, CDs)	$__________
12.	Value of savings at retirement (multiply line 11 by factor C, below)	$__________
13.	Net capital gap (subtract line 12 from line 10)	$__________
14.	Annual amount in current dollars to start saving now to cover the gap (divide line 13 by factor D, below)[4]	$__________
15.	Percentage of salary to be saved each year (divide line 14 by line 1)[5]	__________%

(continued)

Figure14-2—Continued

Capital Calculation Factors
(Assume 4 percent inflation before and after retirement and 8 percent annual return before and after retirement.)

Years to Retirement	Factor A	Factor B	Factor C	Factor D
10	1.5	7.0	2.2	17.5
15	1.8	8.5	3.2	35.3
20	2.2	10.3	4.7	63.3
25	2.7	12.6	6.9	107.0
30	3.2	15.3	10.1	174.0

[1]Lines 3 and 4: Employers can provide annual estimates of your projected retirement pay; estimates of social security benefits are available from the Social Security Administration at (800) 234-5772. Both figures will be stated in current dollars, not in the higher amounts that you will receive if your wages keep up with inflation. The work sheet takes this into consideration.

[2]Line 6: Even if a large pension lets you avoid an income gap, proceed to line 9 to determine the assets you may need to make up for the erosion of a fixed pension payment by inflation.

[3]Line 8: This calculation includes a determination of how much capital you will need to keep up with inflation after retirement and assumes that you will *deplete the capital over a 25-year period.*

[4]Line 14: Amount includes investments earmarked for retirement and payments by employee and employer to defined-contribution retirement plans such as 401(k)s. The formula assumes you will increase annual savings at the same rate as inflation.

[5]Line 15: Assuming earnings rise with inflation, you can save a set percentage of gross pay each year, and the actual amount you stash away will increase annually.

Source: Reprinted with permission of *U.S. News & World Report,* August 14, 1989, issue. Copyright 1989.

WHAT SOURCES OF RETIREMENT INCOME ARE AVAILABLE?

Understanding how much a client will need for retirement is only one part of sound retirement planning. In addition, understanding the potential sources of retirement income is another crucial function with which the retirement planner must be familiar. There are many types of investment vehicles that a client may use for investing retirement assets, many of which are described in

FIGURE 14-3
Expense Method Work Sheet

Estimated Retirement Living Expenses and Required Capital (in current dollars)

	Monthly	x 12 =	Annual
1. Food	______		______
2. Housing:			
a. Rent/mortgage payment	______		______
b. Insurance (if not included in a.)	______		______
c. Property taxes (if not included in a.)	______		______
d. Utilities	______		______
e. Maintenance (if you own)	______		______
f. Management fee (if a condominium)	______		______
3. Clothing and Personal Care:			
a. Wife	______		______
b. Husband	______		______
c. Dependents	______		______
4. Medical Expenses:			
a. Doctor	______		______
b. Dentist	______		______
c. Medicines	______		______
d. Medical insurance to supplement medicare	______		______
5. Transportation:			
a. Car payments	______		______
b. Gas	______		______
c. Insurance	______		______
d. License	______		______
e. Car maintenance (tires and repairs)	______		______
f. Other transportation	______		______
6. Miscellaneous Expenses:			
a. Entertainment	______		______
b. Travel	______		______
c. Hobbies	______		______
d. Club fees and dues	______		______
e. Other	______		______
7. Insurance	______		______
8. Gifts and Contributions	______		______
9. Income Taxes (if any)	______		______
10. Total Annual Expenses (current dollars)	______		$______
11. Inflation Rate until Retirement (I)	______		
12. Total Years until Retirement (N)	______		
13. Inflation Adjustment Factor $(1 + I)^N$		x	______
14. Total Annual Expenses (future dollars)		=	______
15. Inflation Rate Postretirement (i)	______		

(continued)

FIGURE 14-3—Continued

	Monthly x 12 = Annual
16. After-tax Rate of Return (r)	________
17. Anticipated Duration of Retirement (n)	________
18. Inflation-Adjusted Discount Factor $a = \frac{1 + i}{1 + r}$	________
19. Capital Required at Retirement to Fund Retirement Living Expenses line 14 x $\frac{1 - a^n}{1 - a}$	$ ________
20. One-Time Expenses	+$ ________
21. Total Capital Need at Retirement	=$ ________

chapter 12 of this book. In addition, there are several sources of retirement income that bear close examination in this chapter. These include

- qualified plans
- nonqualified plans
- IRAs
- social security benefits

Qualified Plans

Perhaps the most valuable way to save for retirement is through a qualified plan. The advantageous nature of a qualified plan stems from the fact that, even though the employer is able to take a tax deduction when contributions are made, contributions to the plan are made on a before-tax basis. In other words, the employee does not have to pay income tax on those contributions when they are made. Instead, the employee pays income tax when funds are distributed from the plan some years later. In addition, investment earnings on plan assets are also tax-deferred. This combination of tax-deferred contributions and tax-deferred earnings is like receiving an interest-free loan from the government. In other words, Uncle Sam allows the client to invest funds for retirement that otherwise would be lost to taxation.

A final tax advantage applicable to qualified plans is that distributions from these plans—although taxed at retirement—are subject to special tax treatment. For example, clients might be able either to reduce the taxes they pay out on a lump-sum distribution by using forward averaging or to delay paying taxes on a distribution by rolling over the funds into an IRA.

Figure 14-4 demonstrates the income tax advantages of a qualified plan.

FIGURE 14-4
Tax Advantages of a Qualified Plan

Assume that a client is a professional who is aged 50, is married, and wants to retire at 65. Assume the professional's total earnings after business expenses are $200,000, his or her personal deductions and exemptions are $30,000, and his or her needs for living expenses are $110,000.

	Without Plan	With Plan
Gross earnings	$200,000	$200,000
Pension contributions	0	46,275
Current compensation	$200,000	$153,725
Income tax (federal only)	66,400	43,725
Net "take-home pay"	$133,600	110,000
Living expenses	110,000	110,000
Personal savings	$ 23,600	$ 0
At Age 65		
	Without Plan	With Plan
Pension accumulation at 10%	$ 0	$1,470,272
Savings accumulation at net 7%	593,045	0
Taxes on lump-sum distribution	0	625,986
Net cash after taxes	$593,045	$ 844,286
Gain for Qualified Plan: $251,241		

Qualified plans can be categorized in several ways. One way they can be categorized is by focusing on what the employer provides. For one category of plans the employer promises to pay an annual retirement benefit (defined-benefit plans). For another category, the employer pays a specified amount of deferred compensation into an employee's individual account (defined-contribution plans). A second way to categorize qualified plans is to distinguish plans that are typically geared to employer profits (profit-sharing plans) from those that are not (pension plans). A third way to categorize qualified plans is to focus on the business entity that is adopting the plan. If a corporate entity qualifies a retirement plan, the plan is simply known as a qualified plan; if a partnership or self-employed person sponsors a qualified plan, the plan is known as a Keogh plan. Over the years the rules for Keogh and corporate plans have evolved so that only a few minor distinctions exist between the two plans. Therefore only the defined-benefit/defined-contribution and pension/profit-sharing differences are examined in the following paragraphs.

Defined-Benefit versus Defined-Contribution Plans

Under a defined-benefit plan the required employer contributions vary depending on what is needed to pay the promised benefits. The maximum annual benefit that can be provided in a defined-benefit plan is 100 percent of the employee's average compensation (limited to $160,000 of compensation) for the employee's 3 consecutive years of highest pay up to a maximum of $130,000 per year (as indexed in 1999). A defined-benefit plan usually uses a benefit formula to stipulate a promised retirement benefit. This promised benefit is typically a percentage of the employee's final salary (for example, 50 percent of final salary).

Defined-contribution plans, on the other hand, specify the contribution the employer makes annually and provide an unknown benefit to the employee. The maximum annual contribution that can be provided in a defined-contribution plan is the lesser of $30,000 or 25 percent of the first $160,000 (as indexed in 1999) of the employee's salary. By their nature defined-contribution plans base an employee's benefit on the employee's entire career earnings and *not* the employee's final salary. Defined-contribution plans are sometimes called *individual account plans* because they provide an individual account similar to a bank account for each employee.

Retirement Planning Considerations. Clients covered by defined-contribution plans may find themselves short of retirement income if investment results are unfavorable. This is because, unlike a defined-benefit plan, the employer's obligation begins and ends with making the annual contribution. If plan investments are poor in a defined-contribution plan, the employee suffers the loss and may have inadequate retirement resources. For example, a person who had planned to retire in November 1987—one month after the October stock market crash—might have seen his or her plan assets decline by one-third. Therefore, this client had to delay retirement for several years. In a defined-benefit plan the employer suffers the loss.

A second problem is that contributions in a defined-contribution plan are based on participants' salaries for each year of their career, rather than on their salary at retirement as in most defined-benefit plans. For example, if inflation increases sharply in the years just prior to retirement, the chances of achieving an adequate income-replacement ratio are diminished because most of the annual contributions were based on deflated salaries that occurred before the inflationary spiral. By contrast, if the participant had been covered by a final-average defined-benefit plan, the *employer* would have had to make significant contributions to account for the increased final-average salary due to higher inflation.

Another instance where either a defined-benefit plan or a defined-contribution plan may provide inadequate retirement income occurs if the client joins the plan late in his or her career. Under this circumstance, since years to retirement are growing short, a defined-contribution plan may not provide enough time to accumulate an acceptable amount of assets. A defined-benefit plan, where the benefit is based in part on length of service, would also provide a relatively small benefit since these plans are geared to provide adequate replacement ratios for long-service employees only.

Pension versus Profit-Sharing Plans

Under a pension plan the organization is committed to making annual payments to the retirement plan, since the main purpose of the plan is to provide a pension benefit. Under a profit-sharing plan, however, an organization can retain the flexibility necessary to avoid funding the plan annually. What's more, a profit-sharing plan isn't necessarily intended to provide a retirement benefit as much as to provide tax deferral of present compensation. To this end, under certain profit-sharing plans employees are permitted to withdraw funds after they have been in the profit-sharing account for 2 years.

Retirement Planning Considerations. Two important factors should be kept in mind if a client has a profit-sharing plan: First, retirement planners should closely monitor the funding of the plan. It would be an easy mistake to assume that the employer is making scheduled payments when in actuality the employer isn't contributing as expected because employer contributions to the profit-sharing plan are discretionary. It would also be an easy mistake to assume that the employee is allowing the funds to accumulate for retirement when in actuality the employee is depleting the account by taking withdrawals.

Another important factor concerning profit-sharing plans is that the ability to withdraw funds prior to retirement under some profit-sharing plans opens up some interesting planning possibilities for the client and his or her planner. For example, the client may want to gradually take money out while employed (starting after age 59½ to avoid a 10 percent tax penalty) in order to reposition assets or take advantage of an excellent investment opportunity. In addition, the client may want to prepay any debt that would carry over into retirement, such as prepaying a mortgage or reducing interest expenses on a major capital purchase.

Types of Qualified Plans

Once the planner understands the basic characteristics of each category of qualified plans, the planner is well on the way to understanding the specific type of plan that a client has. For example, if a client has a plan that falls into the defined-contribution and pension categories, the planner knows that employer contributions are mandatory but that the employee takes the risks associated with investment performance and preretirement inflation.

The final component that the planner needs to understand is the plan's benefit or contribution formula. These formulas are unique to the specific type of plan involved.

Defined-Benefit Pension Plans. As its name implies, a defined-benefit pension plan falls within both the defined-benefit and pension categories. In a defined-benefit pension plan the employer's contributions under the plan are determined actuarially on the basis of the benefits expected to become payable. These benefits are determined under a benefit formula. There are a number of types of defined-benefit formulas. The most common type, the *unit-benefit formula,* accounts for both service and salary in determining the participant's pension benefit. For example, a unit-benefit formula might read

> Each plan participant will receive a monthly pension commencing at normal retirement date and paid in the form of a life annuity equal to 2 percent of final-average annual salary multiplied by the participant's years of service. Normal retirement age is the later of age 65 or 5 years of plan participation.

Under this formula an employee with 20 years of service and a $50,000 final-average salary will receive $20,000 a year in the form of life annuity payments (.02 x $50,000 x 20). There are a number of less common formulas that are also used. In a *flat-percentage-of-earnings formula* the benefit is tied to salary but not to length of service. For example, a formula might read

> Each plan participant will receive a monthly pension benefit payable for life, commencing at normal retirement date and paid in the form of a life annuity equal to 40 percent of the final-average monthly salary the participant was paid.

Two other types of formulas are commonly found in union plans. First is the *flat-amount-per-year-of-service formula,* which relates the pension benefit solely to the participant's length of service and does not reflect the participant's salary. For example, all participants receive a monthly benefit of $10 per month times the number of years of service worked. The second is a *flat-amount formula.* A flat-amount formula provides the same monthly benefit for each participant. For example, each plan participant will receive a pension benefit of $200 a month.

Understanding the basic benefit structure is just the beginning of understanding how much a client will receive from a defined-benefit plan. Every element of the formula affects the ultimate benefit. In the unit-benefit formula shown above, the benefit is tied to four factors: years of service, final-average salary, the form of benefit, and the timing that benefits begin. In a defined-benefit plan salary can be defined inclusively, to cover all wages paid, or be limited to only base salary, excluding bonuses, overtime or other extraordinary pay. Final-average salary is usually defined to include the highest 3-to-5 years of salary, although this also can vary.

The definition of years of service can also vary from plan to plan. Some plans exclude years prior to plan participation, and some exclude part-time service or give only partial credit for part-time service. For an early retiree, the timing that payments begin is a key element. A plan for example may provide a retirement age of 65, but allow early retirement at 62. However, the benefit will generally be reduced to reflect the longer payout period. What this should point out is that helping a client determine what he or she is eligible for can be tricky, especially if the person is going to retire early, late, or has an unusual employment history with the company.

Money-Purchase Pension Plans. A money-purchase pension plan is a form of defined-contribution plan. It is also, as the name states, a pension plan. Under a money-purchase pension plan the company's annual contributions are mandatory and are specified in this plan. For example, the money-purchase contribution formula may provide that annual contributions will equal 10 percent of compensation for each participant. The definition of compensation will vary from plan to plan. In some cases it will include overtime, bonuses, and the like; in other cases it will be restricted to base salary. In order to correctly estimate the amount of retirement savings that clients will have, the planner must accurately forecast the approximate compensation that is involved in each case.

Profit-Sharing Plans. A profit-sharing plan falls into both the profit-sharing and defined-contribution categories. There are two parts to the contribution formula in a profit-sharing plan. One relates to how much the company contributes to the plan and the other relates to how the contribution is allocated among the participants.

In most profit-sharing plans employer contributions are made on a discretionary basis. The employer decides whether a contribution will be made and how much that contribution will be. Typically, contributions are geared to profits, although the employer can make contributions even if there are no profits. However, a profit-sharing plan can also be written to require a specified contribution. One way to do this is to state the required contribution as a specified percentage of profits or some other objective formula stated in the plan. This approach is appropriate when the employer wants employees to feel that they have a clear and determinable stake in the performance of the company.

The heart of a profit-sharing plan is the method of allocating the employer contribution among the participants. This formula must be definite and predetermined. Historically, the most common allocation formula has been one that allocates the total contribution so that each participant receives a contribution that is the same percentage of compensation, for example, 3 percent or 5 percent. This allocation formula has been popular in part because it satisfies the requirement that contributions or benefits cannot discriminate in favor of highly compensated employees. Another way to allocate contributions is to integrate the formula with social security so that employees who earn more than the taxable wage base receive a higher portion of the company's contribution. Newer, more exotic ways to allocate even a larger portion of the contribution to the older, more highly compensated employees include the age-weighted and cross-tested allocations methods.

401(k) Plans. One of the most popular types of qualified plans is the 401(k) defined-contribution profit-sharing plan. A 401(k) plan allows employees to elect to defer current salary, which is contributed to the plan on a pretax basis. In today's market, many employers, even those with defined-benefit, or money-purchase plans, opt for a complementary 401(k) plan.

From a retirement planning perspective, 401(k) plans are an excellent way for employees to save for retirement, and in most cases clients should be encouraged to take full advantage of them. In addition to the tax deferral, most employers make additional matching contributions, meaning that if the employee contributes the employer will match some portion of the contribution. It's not uncommon for an employer to contribute, for example, fifty cents to the plan for each dollar that the employee contributes, up to the first 6 percent of compensation that the participant saves. The law allows a maximum salary deferral each year of up to $10,000 (indexed for 1999). However, certain nondiscrimination rules, and other plan limits could reduce the overall allowable salary deferral.

In addition to encouraging participation in the plan, retirement planners must also be aware of the following factors concerning 401(k) plans.

- 401(k) salary reductions in some cases could reduce benefits available under a group life or health insurance plan.
- 401(k) salary reductions are immediately 100 percent vested and cannot be forfeited, but matching contributions can be subject to a vesting schedule.
- Participants will have limited access to salary deferral contributions while still employed. The law only allows in-service withdrawals upon a severe financial hardship or attainment of age 59 ½. However some plans allow limited access through loans.

403(b) Plans. A 403(b) plan (sometimes referred to as a tax-sheltered annuity [TSA] or tax-deferred annuity [TDA]) is similar to a 401(k) plan in many respects. Both plans permit an employee to defer taxes on income by allowing before-tax contributions to the employee's individual account and by allowing deferrals in the form of salary reduction. However, 403(b) plans are distinguishable from 401(k) plans in several ways.

- The 403(b) market is comprised of public schools and certain types of tax-exempt organizations only. These are the so-called 501(c)(3) tax-exempt organizations.
- The 403(b) plans are not viewed as qualified plans, but they contain many of the benefits of a qualified plan (for example, before-tax

contributions). Note, however, that lump-sum distributions from a 403(b) plan are not entitled to the special tax treatment of forward averaging.

A summary of the main kinds of qualified plans is given in figure 14-5.

FIGURE 14-5
Principal Types of Qualified Plans: A Recap

Pension	Profit-Sharing	Specialty
Defined-benefit Money-purchase	Profit-sharing 401(k)	403(b)

Defined-Contribution	Defined-Benefit
Money-purchase Profit-sharing 401(k) 403(b)	Defined-benefit

Keogh	Corporate
Defined-benefit Money-purchase Profit-sharing 401(k)	Defined-benefit Money-purchase Profit-sharing 401(k)

IRAs

One of the most important sources of retirement income that retirement planners can counsel their clients about is an individual retirement account (IRA). There are three types of IRAs: traditional IRAs, Roth IRAs, and education IRAs. Since education IRAs are not really intended as retirement savings vehicles, they are not discussed here. Traditional IRAs are similar to qualified plans in many respects. Both encourage retirement savings by allowing contributions to be made with pretax dollars (if the taxpayer is eligible) and earnings to be tax deferred until retirement, at which time all withdrawals are taxable. In contrast Roth IRA contributions are not deductible, but qualifying withdrawals are not subject to income tax.

The Ground Rules

IRA Contributions. Traditional IRAs and Roth IRAs are subject to certain limitations, including the following:

- Total contributions to IRAs may not exceed $2,000 a year or 100 percent of compensation, whichever is smaller.
- Traditional IRA contributions may not be made during or after the year in which the client reaches age 70 ½, but Roth IRA contributions may continue during and after that year.
- IRA funds may not be commingled with the client's other assets; the funds may contain only IRA contributions and rollover contributions.
- IRA funds may *not* be used to buy a life insurance policy.
- Funds contributed to an IRA may not be invested in collectibles.
- No loans may be taken from IRA accounts.

Traditional IRAs

Eligibility for Deductible IRAs. Any person under age 70½ who receives $2,000 in compensation (either salary or self-employment earned income) may make a $2,000 contribution to a traditional IRA. In addition, if a person is married, even if he or she doesn't work, that person can contribute $2,000 as long as the spouse's salary is at least $4,000 (then each spouse can make a $2,000 contribution).

The contribution, however, is only deductible if certain eligibility requirements are satisfied. The contribution will be deductible if neither the taxpayer nor the taxpayer's spouse is an active participant in an employer-maintained retirement plan. If the taxpayer is an active participant, then the contribution is deductible only if his or her adjusted gross income falls below prescribed limits (designed to approximate a middle-class income). If an individual is not an active participant, but his or her spouse is, then the contribution is deductible (for the nonparticipant) if the couple's income is less than a different higher income threshold.

Active Participant. The first eligibility issue concerns whether the client is an active participant in an employer-maintained plan. Employer-maintained plans include every type of qualified plan, as well as all federal, state, and local government plans. Not included, however, are nonqualified retirement arrangements.

The term *active participant* has a special meaning that depends on the type of plan involved. Generally a person is an active participant in a defined-benefit plan unless excluded under the eligibility provision in the plan. In general, if the person is an active participant in any type of defined-contribution plan and the plan specifies that employer contributions must be allocated to the individual's account, then the person is an active participant.

Monetary Limits. The second issue of IRA deductibility is the taxpayer's income. If a taxpayer is an active participant, fully deductible contributions are allowed only if the taxpayer has an adjusted gross income that falls below a specified level (see table 14-4). The level for unreduced contributions depends on the taxpayer's filing status. For 1999, married couples filing a joint return will get a full IRA deduction if their adjusted gross income is $51,000 or less. Married persons filing separately cannot get a full IRA deduction. Single taxpayers and taxpayers filing as heads of households will get a full IRA deduction if their adjusted gross income is $31,000 or less. For taxpayers whose adjusted gross income falls between the no-deduction level and the full-deduction level, their reduced deduction is determined on a prorata basis. For example, in 1999, a single taxpayer who is an active participant and has AGI of $36,000 can only make a $1,000 deductible contribution.

TABLE 14-4
1999 Adjusted Gross Income Limits for Deductible IRA Contributions

Filing Status	Full IRA Deduction	Reduced IRA Deduction	No IRA Deduction
Individual or head of household	$31,000 or less	$31,000.01–$40,999.99	$41,000 or more
Married filing jointly	$51,000 or less	$51,000.01–$60,999.99	$61,000 or more
Married filing separately	Not available	$0.01–$9,999.99	$10,000 or more

Special Spousal Rule. If a married taxpayer and his or her spouse are both active participants, then the deduction rules just described apply to both IRAs. However, the rules are different when only one spouse is an active participant. In this case a $2,000 deductible IRA contribution is allowed for the nonactive participant spouse as long as the couple's AGI does not exceed $150,000. The deduction is phased out if the couple's joint AGI exceeds $150,000 and will be gone entirely if their AGI is $160,000 or more. A deductible contribution is not available for the nonactive participant spouse if the couple files separate tax returns.

> *Example:* Joe and Jane Morgan are considering establishing IRAs for themselves and ask you whether contributions are deductible. Joe earns $80,000 and Jane does not have any income because she stays home with the children. Joe is an active participant in a retirement plan and Jane, of course, is not. Joe cannot make a deductible IRA contribution on his own behalf because their income exceeds $60,000. However, he can make a $2,000 deductible IRA contribution for Jane because their joint income is less than $150,000.

Roth IRAs

Beginning with 1998, most individuals have a choice between contributing to the traditional IRA or to the new Roth IRA each year. The newer Roth IRA is tied to the old rules in that total contributions for the year (to either type of IRA) cannot exceed $2,000 (and spousal IRAs are allowed). Contributions to a Roth IRA are not deductible, but distributions are tax free as long as certain eligibility requirements are satisfied. The maximum contribution to a Roth IRA is phased out for single taxpayers with an AGI between $95,000 and $110,000 (pro rata reduction over $15,000 income spread) and for married joint filers with an AGI between $150,000 and $160,000 (pro rata reduction over $10,000 income spread). For purposes of this calculation, the AGI is modified in the same way as for traditional IRAs.

Unlike traditional IRAs, contributions can even be made after attainment of age 70 ½ and the minimum distribution rules that require distributions from IRAs beginning at age 70 ½ do not apply. However, the IRA minimum distribution requirement that applies to payments after the death of the participant does not apply to Roth IRAs.

For distributions to be "qualified distributions" that are entirely tax free they have to meet two requirements. First, the distribution must be made after the 5-tax-year period beginning with the first tax year for which a contribution was made to an individual's Roth IRA. Second, the distribution must be made after one of the four following events has occurred:

- The participant has attained age 59 ½.
- The distribution is paid to a beneficiary because of the participant's death.
- The participant has become disabled.
- The withdrawal is made to pay qualified first-time homebuyer expenses.

Qualified first-time homebuyer expenses include acquisition costs of a first home (paid within 120 days of the distribution) for the participant, spouse, or any child, grandchild, or ancestor of the participant or spouse. This exception, however, has a $10,000 lifetime limit per IRA (or Roth IRA) participant. If a distribution does not meet these requirements, it is referred to as a nonqualifying distribution. Even nonqualifying distributions receive somewhat favorable tax treatement. Contributions can be withdrawn first, without having to pay any taxes. Any amounts withdrawn above total contributions would then be subject to income tax and the 10 percent penalty on early withdrawals.

Nonqualified Plans

Another tax-advantaged way to save for retirement is to use a nonqualified retirement plan. In the case of nonqualified plans, the tax savings are not attributable to Uncle Sam but instead stem from the fact that, in most cases, the employer defers his or her business deduction so that specifically chosen employees won't be deemed to be in constructive receipt of deferred compensation promised them.

A nonqualified deferred-compensation plan is an employer-provided retirement benefit that is typically given to highly compensated executives and managers. There are three basic types of nonqualified plans. Under a so-called top-hat plan the executive defers part of his or her salary for retirement purposes. For this reason top-hat plans are sometimes referred to as pure deferred-compensation arrangements. Under an excess-benefit plan the employer provides benefits beyond the dollar restrictions imposed on qualified plans. And under a supplemental executive retirement plan the employer provides a second tier of retirement benefits in addition to any qualified benefits. In this case, however, qualified benefits are not at their maximum legal limits.

Retirement Planning Considerations

Even though all three of these plans can provide for abundant retirement savings, planners must be wary of certain potential problems for clients covered by them. One trap awaiting clients covered by nonqualified deferred-compensation plans is that they have somewhat inflexible withdrawal provisions. In qualified plans distributions can generally be rolled over into an IRA, with taxable withdrawals occurring as needed. Nonqualified benefits cannot be rolled over to an IRA. Also the participant generally cannot be given a choice of distribution options at retirement time. The distribution options are generally quite limited and are often required (to avoid tax problems) at the time participation begins.

A second trap awaiting clients covered by nonqualified deferred-compensation plans is that promised benefits are typically subject to loss for a variety of reasons. For example, the nonqualified plan may contain a forfeiture provision stipulating that benefits will be forfeited if certain conditions are not met. In many circumstances the client may be either unwilling or unable to meet his or her part of the commitment. A second way nonqualified benefits can be lost is if the employer sponsoring the plan goes bankrupt. Nonqualified plan funds are typically held as corporate assets that are subject to the claims of corporate creditors in bankruptcy. By contrast, funds in a qualified plan are held in a trust or insurance contract separate from business assets and are not subject to forfeiture in case of bankruptcy.

A final insecurity associated with nonqualified plans is the threat of immediate taxation to the employee that would result in a lower overall retirement accumulation. For example, despite employer contentions to the contrary some plans are construed by the IRS as providing an immediate economic benefit to the employee, or the employee may be deemed to be in constructive receipt of the income. In either case the prefunded benefit will be taxable while the client is still employed and the advantages of tax deferral will be lost.

Despite all these problems, nonqualified plans have an important role in retirement planning for upscale clients. The major reason is that the qualified plan rules limit plan benefits and a second tier nonqualified plan is necessary to ensure the executive with an adequate replacement ratio.

Social Security

Another important source of retirement income is social security. When people use the term *social security*, they are actually referring to the Old-Age, Survivor's, Disability, and Health Insurance program of the federal government. For retirement planning purposes planners should be familiar with the entire social security system, particularly the old-age and health insurance programs.

Eligibility

A client is eligible for social security retirement benefits if he or she is covered by social security and has credit for a stipulated amount of work that is based on quarters of coverage. A worker receives credit for one quarter of coverage for earning a specified dollar amount on which social security taxes are paid. For example, in 1999 this dollar amount was $740. A worker earning $700 would receive a quarter of coverage. The maximum credit for a calendar year is four quarters. Therefore the worker paying social security taxes on as little as $2,960 during 1999, regardless of when it was earned during the year, would receive credit for the maximum four quarters. A person is fully insured for purposes of receiving social security retirement benefits if he or she has 40 quarters of coverage. *Normal retirement age* is 65 for clients born before 1938 and increases to age 67 for those born after 1959.

Retirement Benefits

Old-age insurance benefits are based on a worker's *primary insurance amount* (PIA). The PIA, in turn, is a function of the worker's *average indexed monthly earnings* (AIME) on which social security taxes have been paid. For retirement planning purposes the planner need not know how to calculate the AIME and PIA. Instead, the best method to estimate a client's expected social security benefits is to request the employee's data from the Social Security Administration. To obtain this information the client can mail in either Form SSA-7050-F3 or Form SSA-7004-PC-0P1. The social security office will provide data relating to the client's earnings history and estimated primary insurance amount. Another way to request information is through the Internet. The Social Security Administration's website is www.ssa.gov.

Retirement Planning Considerations. Planners should make their clients aware that social security is geared toward providing benefits for those with a lower income and cannot be relied on as a proportionally large source of retirement income for affluent clients. For example, a person with a $10,000 salary prior to retirement will receive approximately a 50 percent income replacement ratio from social security whereas a person with a $100,000 salary will only receive a 10 percent income replacement ratio.

Early and Deferred Retirement. A worker who is fully insured is eligible to receive monthly retirement benefits as early as age 62. Electing to receive benefits prior to normal retirement age, however, results in a permanently reduced retirement benefit. If a worker born before 1938 elects to receive retirement benefits prior to age 65, benefits are permanently reduced by five-ninths of one percent for every month that the early retirement precedes age 65. For example, if a worker retires at age 62, the monthly benefit will be only 80 percent of what the worker would have received had he or she waited until age 65.

Workers who delay applying for retirement benefits until after age 65 are eligible for an increased benefit for each year retirement is delayed beyond age 65 and up to age 70. There are no additional increases for delaying beyond age 70. The increase depends on the year of birth. For those born after 1942 the increase is 8% for each year benefits are delayed. For persons born before that date the increase is somewhat less.

Medicare

In addition to understanding the amount of retirement benefits provided by social security and the people who are covered by social security, retirement planners need to understand the medicare system.

Eligibility for Medicare. Part A, the hospital portion of medicare, is available at no monthly cost to any person aged 65 or older as long as the person is entitled to monthly retirement benefits under social security or the railroad retirement program. If a person is 65 and not eligible they can buy into the program as long as they pay a $309 (for 1999) monthly premium for part A and enroll in part B as well.

Any person eligible for part A of medicare is also eligible for part B. However, a monthly premium must be paid for part B. This monthly premium $45.50 in 1999, is adjusted annually and represents only about 25 percent of the cost of the benefits provided. The remaining cost of the program is financed from the federal government's general revenues.

Persons receiving social security or railroad retirement benefits are automatically enrolled in medicare if they are eligible. If they do not want part B, they must elect out in writing. Other persons eligible for medicare must apply for part B benefits. Anyone who elects out of part B or who does not enroll when initially eligible may later apply for benefits during the general enrollment period between January 1 and March 31 of each year. However, the monthly premium will be increased by 10 percent for each 12-month period during which the person was eligible but failed to enroll.

Medicare: Part A Benefits. Part A of medicare provides benefits for expenses incurred in hospitals (for stays up to 90 days in each benefit period), skilled nursing facilities (if a physician certifies that skilled nursing or therapeutic care is needed for a condition that was treated in a hospital within the last 30 days), and hospices (for terminally ill persons who have a life expectancy of 6 months or less). In addition, home-health-care benefits are covered if a patient needs further care at home for a condition treated in a hospital or skilled nursing facility. Up to 100 post-hospitalization home-care visits are covered by part A. Even more comprehensive home-care coverage is provided by part B. In order for benefits to be paid, the facility or agency providing benefits must participate in the medicare program. Virtually all hospitals are participants, as are most other facilities or agencies that meet the requirements of medicare.

Medicare: Part B Benefits. Part B, the supplementary medical insurance portion of medicare, provides benefits for the following medical expenses not covered under part A:

- physicians' and surgeons' fees that result from house calls, office visits, or services provided in a hospital or other institution (Under certain circumstances benefits are also provided for the services of chiropractors, podiatrists, and optometrists.)
- diagnostic tests in a hospital or in a physician's office
- physical therapy in a physician's office, or as an outpatient of a hospital, skilled nursing facility, or an approved clinic, agency, or public-health agency
- drugs and biologicals that cannot be self-administered
- radiation therapy
- medical supplies, such as surgical dressings, splints, and casts
- rental of medical equipment, such as oxygen tents, hospital beds, and wheelchairs
- prosthetic devices, such as artificial heart valves or contact lenses after a cataract operation
- ambulance service if a patient's condition does not permit the use of other methods of transportation
- pneumococcal vaccine and its administration
- home health services as described for part A when prior hospitalization has not occurred
- mammograms

With some exceptions, part B pays 80 percent of the approved charges for covered medical expenses after the satisfaction of a $100 annual deductible.

Retirement Planning Considerations. Although the preceding list for part B of medicare may appear to be comprehensive, planners need to make their clients aware that numerous medical products and services are not covered by part B. Some of these products and services that represent significant expenses for the elderly include the following:

- drugs and biologicals that can be self-administered
- routine physical, eye, and hearing examinations (except mammograms)
- routine foot care
- immunizations, except pneumococcal vaccinations or immunization required because of an injury or immediate risk of infection
- cosmetic surgery unless it is needed because of an accidental injury or to improve the function of a malformed part of the body
- dental care unless it involves jaw or facial bone surgery or the setting of fractures
- custodial care
- eyeglasses, hearing aids, and orthopedic shoes

In addition, benefits are not provided to persons who are eligible for workers' compensation or treated in government hospitals. Benefits are provided only for services received in the United States, except for physicians' services and ambulance services rendered for a covered hospitalization in Mexico or Canada under part A.

HOW TO HELP CLIENTS OVERCOME INADEQUATE RETIREMENT RESOURCES

In addition to determining how much income a client will need to retire and understanding the various sources of retirement income, the planner must also help clients produce as much retirement income as possible from their existing resources. The final part of this chapter will address four strategies that the planner can recommend to accomplish this goal:

- trading down to a less expensive home
- reverse annuity mortgages
- postretirement employment
- maximizing pension benefits

Trading Down: Relocation to a Less Expensive Home

If your client can be persuaded to sell his or her home and relocate to a smaller, less expensive residence, the money made available from the transaction can be a valuable source of retirement income. For example, if your client can sell his or her house for $200,000 and buy a new residence for $100,000, the $100,000 gain can be used to produce an extra $10,000 a year in income (assuming a 10 percent interest rate). This can be very desirable from a financial perspective, because retirees can capitalize on what for many is their single most important financial asset—their home. In addition, this can be very desirable from a tax standpoint because the internal revenue code allows a taxpayer to exclude up to $250,000 of gain from the sale or exchange of property if the following restrictions are met.

- During the prior 5 years, the property must have been owned and used by the taxpayer as the taxpayer's principal residence for periods aggregating 2 years or more.
- The taxpayer may not have excluded a gain from sale of a principal residence in the prior 2 years.

Married taxpayers can exclude up to $500,000 if certain restrictions are met.

Cashing in While Staying at Home—The Reverse Annuity Mortgage

If your client would like to take some equity out of his or her house, but is reluctant to leave the home, an alternative that is available is a reverse annuity mortgage (RAM). Under one type of reverse annuity mortgage the client sells a remainder interest in the home but retains the right to occupy the house until death. The purchaser of the remainder interest acquires the right to take possession of the property after the homeowner's death (or the death of the homeowner and the spouse). The consideration for acquiring the remainder interest in the house is that the purchaser agrees to make periodic payments to the seller during the seller's life. These payments can significantly enhance a client's retirement income.

Under another type of reverse annuity mortgage the annuity payments plus interest are held as a series of loans against the value of the home. In this case, the amount paid out in an income stream plus interest will be recovered by the lender from eventual sale proceeds after the death of the retiree.

Postretirement Employment

A third alternative that can be used to provide the retiree with extra cash is a part-time job during the retirement years. Many retirees find that working on a scaled-back basis not only meets their financial needs but also helps them adapt psychologically to the changes that retirement brings. This is especially true for clients whose self-esteem and sense of self-worth were tied to their careers.

Working after retirement poses a potential problem for retirees, however. They can lose social security income benefits if their earnings exceed specified limits, called annual-exempt amounts. In general, social security benefits will be reduced by $1.00 for each $3.00 earned in excess of the limit for retirees aged 65 through 69 (or by $1.00 for each $2.00 earned in excess of the limit [$9,600 in

1999] for retirement benefit recipients under age 65). The earnings limit for those over age 65 is $15,500 in 1999 but is scheduled to rise to $30,000 in 2002. For clients aged 70 or above, there is no reduction in social security income benefits regardless of the amount of their earnings.

FOCUS ON ETHICS
Who Is the Client?

One of retirement planning's unique challenges is focusing on who the client is. This needs further explanation.

Current law requires married retirees to accept a joint and survivor annuity rather than a single-life annuity (in the absence of a spousal waiver). Obviously the monthly check is lower for the joint and survivor payout.

What should the financial counselor do if the client wants the higher single-life benefit and tries to talk the spouse into signing a waiver. Should the pension holder die first, this could leave the spouse with little or no income. The ethical issue is defending the welfare of the vulnerable spouse. This is more easily done when the client is viewed as the couple as opposed to the pension-receiving spouse.

Pension Maximization

The final strategy that we will discuss is so-called pension maximization. Qualified plans typically stipulate the type of distribution that your client will receive. The normal form of benefit for a married individual is a joint and survivor benefit of not less than 50 percent or greater than 100 percent. One strategy available for your married clients is to have your client elect a different payment option by electing out of the normal benefit form with the spouse's written consent. If a married individual who would otherwise be locked into a joint and survivor annuity elects to have his or her benefit paid in the form of a life annuity, he or she can increase retirement income significantly. If at the same time life insurance is purchased (or kept in force) on the life annuitant, the spouse's future also remains secure.

> *Example:* Joe Jones (aged 65) and his wife Sally (aged 62) are eligible to receive a $1,500 joint and survivor benefit from the $200,000 they have in Joe's retirement plan (qualified joint and survivor 100 percent). If they elect to receive a life annuity based on Joe's life, they will receive $325 more each month ($1,825). The extra $3,900 a year represents a 22 percent increase in annual income for them. If they can purchase (or keep in force) life insurance on Joe that would provide for Sally for anything less than the $3,900 a year, they will stretch their retirement savings and take a big step toward their financial security goals.

15

Sample Planning Case

Dale S. Johnson and Jai P. Sawhney

Chapter Outline

INTRODUCTION

In this sample planning case we make recommendations only for generic types of investment vehicles, insurance products, and other planning techniques. We give hypothetical names to recommended instruments and techniques for purposes of identification in planning reports. Although we secured specialist advice in developing our recommendations for the case, in an actual planning practice we would involve these advisers directly with the client in developing more specific recommendations.

Our emphasis in this chapter is on the process of planning rather than specific planning strategies and techniques. Professional financial planners who read this case may think of numerous alternatives for accomplishing the client's financial objectives. Some may work even better than our recommendations. Whatever the alternatives, adherence to the planning process, the integrity of the planning information provided, and the client's objectives is essential.

Limitations of space preclude printing complete before-and-after financial profiles. In practice, you should prepare a Current Financial Profile (base case) for each client that reflects financial information as of the end of the year preceding the current planning year. Then, project these numbers through the agreed-on planning time frame to show the client the future consequences of maintaining this position. Finally, prepare a second Financial Profile that incorporates your planning recommendations, including projections. The two profiles demonstrate the consequences of your recommendations and permit both you and the client to evaluate them.

Limitations of space also diminish our demonstrations of alternative planning scenarios. For example, we could illustrate a client's Financial Profile under the following hypothetical conditions: the client becomes disabled in any year of the planning time frame; the client dies in any year of the planning time frame; the client dies 2 years after transferring ownership of life insurance policies to a trust, and the proceeds are included in the estate; the client retires in any year other than the one projected; the client inherits $1 million in any year of the planning time frame, etc. We could also vary any assumption, the balance in any account or asset item, the inflation factor, anticipated income levels, and all other variables associated with data-entry items to illustrate reconsolidated amounts represented in planning report schedules. There is really no limit to the number of what-if scenarios that could be illustrated.

This planning case is for a hypothetical client. Family member names, business entities, and other names are hypothetical. The planning firm—Financial Planning Associates—is fictitious.

CASE NARRATIVE AND PERSONAL PROFILE

Personal Planning Information

Gloria Darsteller is a 36-year-old, single, marketing account executive with Brentwood Broadcasting Corporation, a privately held radio broadcasting network located in New York City. Until 2 years ago, Gloria had worked for 4 years in administrative positions at the same company. At that time she moved into marketing and writing public relations and lobbying materials for major corporations and nonprofit organizations for this broadcast network.

Her income has increased dramatically over the past 2 years, with prospects of continuing increases over the next few years. Gloria expects her $71,000 salary and bonus in 1996 to exceed $100,000 by 1998, with a 10 percent annual increase over the next 10 years. She enjoys her work and the increased income her success in this new activity has brought her; however, she now confronts tax and personal financial management problems that she had not previously anticipated.

Gloria has conflicting feelings about her new affluence: on the one hand, she wants to enjoy it in moderation; on the other hand, she wants to create a capital base that, within 10 years, will enable her to radically change her mode of employment and living if she chooses. In current dollars, she would like to have an annual after-tax income of a least $40,000 after 10 more years of working.

Gloria believes that she pays a high price for affluence with the stresses of her job and living in the city. She has little time to pursue her personal interests. (She is a frustrated dramatist who has had one of her plays produced in a small off-Broadway setting.) She has a strong attachment to a house she purchased last year near Woodstock, New York. In 10 years, she might want to relocate to Woodstock and become a part-time real estate broker and a full-time writer. Meanwhile, she wants to explore further real estate investment opportunities in the Catskills.

Gloria seeks ongoing financial counseling to further her basic objectives and define them more precisely. She realizes that her investment experience has been tentative and limited. She must now manage an increasing income, complicated tax considerations, and the temptation to expand her consumer lifestyle—a temptation all the more enticing because until 2 years ago she had lived modestly on an administrative salary.

Financial Objectives and Assumptions

Gloria's major financial objectives are as follows:

- Establish and maintain an adequate level of liquid reserves through a disciplined cash-management program.
- Increase investment net worth on a systematic basis through a diversified investment program.
- Accumulate enough capital to maintain her lifestyle and be economically independent before the age of 50.
- Provide for adequate income in case of her disability.
- Minimize taxes while investing for long-range objectives and tax-sheltered income.
- Distribute estate assets (with minimal shrinkage) to her parents (if they survive her) and to her sister and sister's children if her parents do not survive her.

Gloria's Risk Profile indicates that she has a fairly high tolerance for risk. She has a strong preference for growth mutual funds, growth-oriented common stock, and directly owned real estate to build her investment capital base. On the other hand, she expresses a strong concern to preserve her capital, provide for future income, reduce her federal tax burden, and provide inflation protection. In counseling, we determined that, once she was fully aware of the risks associated with her expected return levels (initially 15+ percent), her risk tolerance level falls between 2 and 3 on a 0 to 4 scale. She now understands the need to maintain an appropriate level of liquidity, flexibility, and balance between growth investments and fixed income returns, especially in tax-exempt bonds.

In consultations, we agreed to use an inflation factor of 4 percent throughout the initial 10-year planning time frame. Other planning assumptions are as follows:

- We will seek current returns on municipal bond fund investments of about 6.0 percent and monitor these yields closely for reinvestment purposes.
- We will aim for a growth rate of 9–12 percent annually in common stock-based investments.
- In rental real estate, we will aim for a 10 percent annual growth rate by focusing on investments in the Catskill resort area near Woodstock or in New York City.
- Reinvestment will be in similar vehicles at similar rates of return.
- We will plan for a 4-year horizon initially and use projected checkpoints in 2000 and 2006 for longer-term adjustments to the continuing planning process.
- We will phase in several elements of Gloria's cash management and investment program over the first 4 years of the initial 10-year planning time frame.

Inventory of Assets

Until October 1995, Gloria had done little to bring her personal finances under control or reduce her increasing taxes except contribute to IRA accounts. At the advice of her accountant, in April 1996 she purchased the two-bedroom residential rental property in Woodstock. In October 1996, Gloria invested an additional $12,000 in the property to add a bathroom and laundry room, so that she can rent it year-round.

Gloria actively manages this property. She sets rents, advertises, interviews prospective lessees, collects monthly rental payments, and lets construction and repair contracts. Under a one-year lease, she rents the house for $9,600. She expects to increase annual rent by 10 percent over the foreseeable future.

The purchase price of the house was $95,000. After a $10,000 down payment, she financed the balance with a 30-year fixed-rate mortgage at 7.5 percent. Its depreciable basis, on the 27.5-year MACRS schedule, is $107,000. She has a homeowner's policy with coverage on the dwelling of $98,000 with no inflation rider and on the replacement cost of contents of $10,000. The annual insurance premium is $261.

In March 1996, Gloria purchased a Honda Accord for $17,500. She allocates it 100 percent to business use, both at Brentwood and for overseeing her rental property. She depreciates the car on the MACRS schedule. She paid $2,500 down and financed $15,000 on a 4-year loan at 9 percent, with monthly payments of $373 beginning April 1, 1996. She pays $1,500 per year for garage space in the city plus $60 per month for gasoline and maintenance. In addition, at a premium of $680 per year (the car is registered in the county where her rental property is located) she carries $100,000/$300,000 liability limits, $150,000 no-fault medical benefits, and $200 deductible comprehensive and collision insurance.

In June 1999, Gloria expects to replace the Honda with a new Ford Explorer that she believes will cost $33,000. She plans to pay $10,000 down and finance $23,000 on a 4-year loan at 9 percent. She will continue to allocate the car to 100 percent business use. She also expects total annual operating expenses of this car to be $3,500 beginning in 1999.

Until 2 years ago, Gloria saved about 20 percent of her gross income, using a savings account and certificates of deposit. In this way, she accumulated about $30,000 before she made her first stock investment. Last year, she established a cash management account with full check-writing privileges at her securities broker-dealer. This account is invested in a tax-exempt municipal bond fund now valued at $19,132. It currently yields 6 percent, which is automatically reinvested.

Gloria deposits her monthly salary check and year-end commission-based bonus in the cash management account and writes checks on it to cover her major monthly expenses. She maintains a small checking account at Citibank for odds and ends, with an average balance of $500. In addition, she leaves on deposit with her broker the certificates of common stock in RCI and Flintstone corporations. Neither of these stocks has been a satisfactory investment; RCI (a telecommunications company) has been a disaster. She also owns 200 shares in

Brentwood Broadcasting, which she purchased early in August 1996 for $49 per share. She holds these certificates herself.

Over the past 3 years, Gloria has occasionally traded stocks for small short-term gains (or losses) on the recommendation of her account representative. Initially, she thought that as her income rose she would systematically invest in the stock market. She now believes that this type of investing may expose her to unwonted risks and continuing oversight.

She came to this conclusion early last year after considering several investment offerings in both private and public limited partnership real estate syndications. She decided that, if she was going to be serious about real estate, she wanted to choose her own investments and take an active role in managing them. She also decided that she would limit her subsequent direct investments in common stock to no more than 20 percent of her investable funds in any given year. With that decision, she bought the rental house in Woodstock.

Gloria's personal assets are minimal. She has a modest collection of personal jewelry items (to which she adds about $500 worth annually), likes lithographs (she spends about $500 annually to add to her collection), and expects to spend about $1,000 annually to add to and replace household furnishings. Her hobby is photography. She spends about $250 annually on photographic supplies and expects to purchase an enlarger in 1998 for about $1,000.

Gloria's assets include the following:

Cash		$ 500
RCI (300 shares @ 7.25)		2,175
Flintstone (200 shares @ 29.00)		5,800
Brentwood (200 shares @ 54.00)		10,800
TF Cash Mgmt. Acct.		19,132
IRA 1 (9%)		2,818
IRA 2 (10%)		2,928
IRA 3 (11%)		4,684
IRA 4 (8.5%)		2,085
Rental real estate (15%)		121,250
Business automobile		10,000
Personal assets		
Household furniture	$15,000	
Jewelry	5,000	
Lithographs	4,000	
Photo equipment	4,000	28,000
Total assets		$210,172

Gloria pays all credit card balances within 2 or 3 months of billing and incurs occasional interest charges on department store charge cards. Her liabilities consist of only the following two longer-term items:

Rental real estate mortgage	$84,717
Business auto loan	8,429
Total liabilities	$93,146

Cash Inflows and Outflows

In 1996, Gloria earned $71,000 in salary and bonus. In 1997, she expects a gross income of more than $90,000, including at least $85,000 in salary and bonus. After that, her earnings will be limited only by the time she puts into her work and by account assignments at the company. These assignments are designed to encourage account executives to aim for incomes of $100,000-$130,000 annually. Gloria expects her compensation to exceed $100,000 in 1998 and grow at about a 10 percent average annual rate over the next 10 years.

Gloria's current financial position includes these specific and estimated items:

Salary	$60,000
Bonus	25,000
Rental real estate	9,600
Dividends (Brentwood)	312
State tax refund	700
Est. gross income	$95,612

Sources of Income

Most of Gloria's income derives from her employment at Brentwood Broadcasting. Each year her salary is scaled to 85 percent of the previous year's gross compensation; bonus compensation above salary is determined at the end of October and paid before the end of each year.

Tax-Deductible Uses of Cash

A financial planning fee of $2,000 for 1997 will decrease to a $750 retainer for 1998. It is aggregated with other employee business expenses (including a $175 income tax return preparation fee) as miscellaneous deductions (subject to the 2 percent floor). Tax-deductible uses of cash (except N.Y. state tax and interest expense) are expected to increase by our assumed inflation factor of 4 percent.

Therapy and counseling	$ 1,500
Medicine and drugs	700
IRA contribution (?)	2,000
New York State tax (estimate)	6,000
Interest expense (credit cards)	175
Charitable contributions (50%)	1,000
Miscellaneous deductions	8,500
Gross deductions	$19,875

In addition to these personal deductible expenses, there will be other expenses in 1997 and subsequent years directly attributable to the rental real estate investment. They are estimated as follows:

Advertising	$ 200
Insurance	813
Car and travel	500
Cleaning and maintenance	400
Repairs	500
Supplies	580
Taxes	967
Total expenses (except interest and depreciation)	$3,960

In addition, Gloria estimates that expenses for the Honda in 1997 will total $2,781 (garage in the city, gas, oil, maintenance, and insurance); for the Explorer beginning in 1999, she estimates annual expenses will total $3,500.

We will use our software to compute mortgage interest and depreciation after information is entered for the rental real estate property and the business cars.

Nondeductible Uses of Cash

General living expenses are assumed to increase at 4 percent annually (except furnishings, jewelry, and lithographs, which will remain level). They are estimated as follows:

Food	$ 5,000
Clothing and cleaning	1,500
Entertainment	2,000
Vacations	3,000
Gifts, etc.	1,000
Transportation	900
Repair/maintenance furniture	200
Interior furnishings (annual)	1,000
Photo supplies	250
Rent (NYC apt.)	6,600
Jewelry (annual)	500
Lithographs (annual)	500
Utilities and phone	2,000
Total	$24,450

Risk Coverages, Employee Benefits, and Retirement Assets

At Brentwood, a group-term life insurance contract provides coverage to one and one-half times the nearest $1,000 of her annual compensation; her parents are primary beneficiaries. She is also covered with a group disability income contract for up to $2,500 per month, coordinated with social security benefits for total and permanent disability. This policy pays a maximum of $400 per week for short-term disability of 6 months (with a 7-day waiting period). It will also pay the same for long-term disability if it is certified by a licensed physician that she cannot work. She is also covered by a group health insurance policy to which she makes no premium contributions. This contract provides a stop/loss limit of $250,000 and an overall maximum benefit of $500,000, with a $200 deductible for medical and $50 deductible for dental expenses.

Gloria has no company-sponsored retirement program at Brentwood. Management has discussed a profit-sharing plan, but none has been put into effect. At this point, her only formal retirement plan consists of four individual retirement accounts she opened in 1992, 1993, 1995, and 1996. In 1994, she made a second contribution of $2,000 to the account opened in 1993. She wonders whether it makes sense for her to continue annual contributions to this type of program now that her annual income will soon exceed $100,000.

Estate Conservation and Distribution

Gloria has no dependents. Her retired parents live in Florida and are financially secure. An older sister, Eileen Brennan, is in a second marriage with two children, plus an older child from a previous marriage. At this point, Gloria wants her estate to pass to her parents if they are still living at her death; if not, to her sister and sister's children. She has no will and wonders how it should be drawn, particularly to leave something to her two nieces and her nephew if she should die prematurely. At the death of the second of her parents, she expects an inheritance of approximately $50,000.

PLANNERS' NOTES

General Design of the Financial Plan

In designing Gloria's financial planning for the next 10 years, we conclude that her strong interest in directly owned real estate, with capital growth and tax-reducing advantages coupled with her active participation in managing them, argues for a systematic investment program ultimately involving approximately 40 percent of her surplus cash. We begin this type of investment only in 2000 and will continue it through the initial planning horizon of 10 years and perhaps beyond. We defer further real estate investment in order to (1) maintain a relatively high level of liquidity in the first 4 years of her plan, (2) increase her holding of stock in Brentwood Broadcasting, and (3) buy a condominium in New York City for her personal residence. If interest rates and growth prospects still look good in the Catskills in 2000, she can look seriously for further investment rental property. By that point, her annual cash flow should permit this additional investment. She should also be more diversified in her total investment capital structure by that date.

Until 2000, the 40 percent allocation of surplus cash will be made to tax-exempt municipal bond funds (instead of real estate), one of which will be used as a cash management account. This will provide tax-free accumulation through reinvestment and the liquidity to move to other investments before 2000 should that seem appropriate. It will also provide her with tax-equivalent yields comparable to those of aggressive growth stock and mutual funds. We also suggest that she allocate up to 40 percent of her surplus cash to Orion Shares, beginning in 2000. This is an aggressive growth mutual fund that has averaged 28 percent appreciation over the past 5 years. We recommend that she invest the remaining 20 percent of surplus cash in selected issues of growth common stock, also beginning in 2000. Through installing an automatic cash management feature in her financial plan, each year's surplus cash is allocated to these investments in this order.

Our assessment of this strategy is based partly on the fact that Gloria is not interested in directly overseeing broad-based stock market investments, but wants to put money occasionally into an aggressive or speculative stock. On the other hand, she is interested in managing her own real estate investments. Because she is bright and a quick learner (having already obtained her real estate license), we recommend that she build on her own interests.

Before fully installing the rental real estate segment of her investment program, we believe that Gloria should purchase a condominium in the city for her personal residence. She agrees that this purchase should take precedence over further rental real estate investment until her cash flow improves and she has acquired other substantial equity investments. She has already looked over possibilities and determined price ranges. We recommend that she close by the end of June 1997 and pay $15,000 down on a one-bedroom condominium priced at about $195,000. She should be able to finance the balance on a 30-year mortgage at about 7.5 percent.

By giving up her apartment (it is rent-stabilized and, like most New Yorkers, she considers that an asset) and applying its annual rental to loan amortization, she will secure strong investment potential and several tax advantages of home ownership. In addition, we recommend that Gloria purchase 50 additional shares in Brentwood Broadcasting this year and in each of the next 3 years. This additional stock ownership will permit her to participate more fully in the expected growth of that company.

Planning Objectives

By 2006, if Gloria follows our recommendations, our forecasts indicate that her investment and personal net worth will be sufficient to provide considerably more annual income than the $40,000 minimum she would like. Her assets will support an even higher annual income at that time if she sells the condo or converts it to a rental income unit when she moves to the Catskills. At that point, she should be sufficiently independent to sell and invest further in real estate at her own pace—or to write the plays that may bring her back to New York City for as much time as she would want to spend there in any case.

The Format of the Planning Case

In 3 hours of consultation and information clarification with Gloria, we determined that she expects a comprehensive 10-year planning report confined to essential information, basic financial reports and analyses, and specific recommendations based on this information. We are providing reports for the following years: 1997, 1998, 1999, 2000, and 2006. These reports include current federal tax law and New York State and New York City tax law as of June 1997. This means that our active planning is for only 4 years. The year 2000 and the final year provide sextant readings for the direction of her planning decisions and permit us to foresee (however speculatively) any problem areas that may develop. We could produce a report for each of these 10 years. Doing so, however, would double the number of pages in the report schedules to allow for 10 columns instead of 5.

For help in understanding these reports, Gloria specifically requested that the verbal text our firm provides be included. We agreed that her age, single status, and plans for a major change in her mode of living after the 10-year initial planning horizon nullify most of the value of estate and retirement planning reports. On this basis, we prepared planning reports for Gloria Darsteller as illustrated in her *Personal Financial Plan*, which follows.

Editor's note: Special thanks to ExecPlan, Inc., and Jay S. Edley, CPA, Manager of Tax and Technical Services, for providing updated output for this case.

PERSONAL FINANCIAL PLAN
for
Gloria Darsteller

Start 1997, 10 yrs., Infl. = 4.0%

Financial Planning Associates
1997

Contents

PREFACE

We at Financial Planning Associates are pleased to participate with you in your financial and tax planning. The reports that follow comprise your *Personal Financial Plan* as of this date and are based on information you provided. These reports include our forecasts of changes in your financial and tax positions through the years ahead; they assume that you will implement the recommendations we have made.

Please be assured that we will continue to work with you, and with your other advisers and service representatives, to provide ongoing consultation and oversight as you take the necessary steps to implement your financial decisions. For you, the most significant advantages in our professional relationship will come from your continuing access to our financial management experience and counsel. We therefore urge you to use this aspect of our service.

Financial planning is not a specific, one-time event. Rather, it is the continuing application of the same dynamic and interactive process of decision making that brought you to this point in our professional association. Changing conditions and circumstances in your personal life, the financial services marketplace, and tax law are a compelling reality. Charting your financial future through these changes requires that you be flexible and adaptable to ongoing decision making. We have designed our recommendations for your Financial Plan with this need in mind.

As in any planning process, the analyses and reports that follow look necessarily to the future and use a number of forecasting techniques. A variety of assumptions and judgmental elements are inherent in any attempt to forecast future results. You should therefore understand that these forecasts are no more than tentative projections from your current position. Differences in tax law, investment climates, interest rates, personal circumstances, and the like will have profound effects on both the accuracy of our forecasts and the continuing suitability of our recommendations for your evolving circumstances.

For these reasons, all of us will need to be sensitive and alert to these changes. Their impact on your ongoing Financial Profile will require us to reexamine and alter as necessary the strategic course charted from this point. Only thus can you realistically expect to attain the financial objectives toward which we have helped you aim in the process of planning.

As you review our recommendations and supporting reports, remember that the planning process is complete only if financial strategies and tactics are implemented as they are developed. Our recommendations for decisive action are structured around our understanding of your needs, objectives, and resources. You may want to modify some of these recommendations or assign them different priorities. Any changes you make will alter the forecasts and projections and, create a different Financial Plan. That is your prerogative. It is *your* Financial Plan.

After you have determined just what you want and are willing to do, you must then implement your financial decisions to close your decision-making loop. Then you will begin to move from where you are now to where you want to be. Only through decisive action can you experience the peace of mind that comes from knowing that your financial affairs are under control through your own management. Timely implementation of the decisions you make now and in the future will be the basis for achieving your financial goals and objectives.

While you are reading and evaluating the reports contained in your Financial Profile, you may find it helpful to keep in mind the following description of the essential elements of comprehensive personal financial planning—the process in which you have participated with us so that we can help you chart your own financial directions.

Note: Throughout the verbal text of these reports we purposefully print basic terminology and concepts with initial capital letters to draw them to your attention and disclose their relationships. These items are referred to repeatedly in numerical schedules and analytical reports as either headings or "bottom-line" categories. In fact, these concepts constitute the design and strategy of your Financial Plan. For that reason, they are the most important concepts and terms for fully understanding the significance of these reports. They will likely be the points on which you may have questions and further comments.

Comprehensive Personal Financial Planning

When you fully implement comprehensive personal financial planning decisions you create your own personal financial management system. This system focuses on managing and controlling all financial allocation decisions that affect your Tax Liabilities, Cash Flows, and Net Worth. Its aim is to integrate fully and simultaneously the three distinct specialist areas of Tax Planning, Risk Management, and Investment Planning in a comprehensive planning process. By adhering to this process we can measure the consequences of each financial decision through its effects on your Tax Liabilities, Cash Flows, and Net Worth. In addition, comprehensive planning integrates all of your personal planning concerns and considerations with your financial objectives, so that these will be realistic and congruent with who you are and what you want to do with your financial resources.

The comprehensive financial planning method enables you to make appropriate personal financial decisions by allocating your Cash Flows and Investment Capital Assets toward the achievement of your overall personal financial objectives. To make this method succeed, you must provide the complete factual information that any good decision-making process requires. From Financial Planning Associates and other advisers, you need support for your decisions through their knowledge of current tax law and the suitable alternatives in the financial services marketplace. You also need analyses of your financial information such as we provide. In this sense, you make the decisions; we facilitate your decision making.

In this role, we act solely in your best interests and help you determine and acquire the financial services and products you need on an ongoing basis in order to have a fully developed personal financial management system. In our consultations and in the reports and recommendations included here for your Financial Plan, we provide you with this support.

To help clarify the main sections of these reports and analyses, the essential elements of personal financial planning will provide useful guidance. Two simple explanatory approaches have proved to be particularly helpful. The first is the Allocational Principle of Cash Flows, for spending controls. The second is the Production Principle of Investment Capital, for structuring spending for investment to produce Cash Flows for specific purposes on an ongoing basis.

The Allocational Principle of Cash Flows

The Allocational Principle of Cash Flows assumes that all of your personal Cash Inflows are spent in three categories: 1) Personal Spending, 2) Taxes, and 3) Saving and Investment. Personal spending encompasses everything you purchase for use and consumption, including housing, food, clothing, transportation, vacations, hobbies, entertainment, gifts, and premiums for risk management contracts (such as life insurance policies). Spending for taxes includes federal, state, and local income taxes and social security tax. Spending for saving and investment includes every dollar from current Cash Inflows that you set aside to fund specific shorter term and lifetime objectives, income maintenance during retirement, and distributions to heirs and beneficiaries through estate transfers. In other words, your spending for saving and investment is deferred spending since it will actually be expensed at some future date(s).

All Cash Inflows are finally spent. This means that they must be matched and balanced by the sum of all of your Cash Outflows and outlays. The total Cash Inflow allocated to acquiring assets creates the basis of total Net Worth, which is the difference in dollar value between Total Assets and Total Liabilities. In other words, your assets are created through saving (not spending now for consumption and taxes) and investing any annual Cash Surplus basic living expenses and tax obligations have been paid.

Among the assets that you acquire, successful Investment Assets (explained below) create an increasing capital base that produces additional Cash Flows, either in the form of current income or as future growth in value, or both. Reinvesting Cash Inflows created by investments compounds the growth rate of your Investment Capital base, thus increasing both your Personal and your Investment Net Worth over time. Holding constant or reducing liabilities accelerates this increase of Investment Net Worth.

Your personal financial management system attempts to create additional Cash Surplus for investment by employing legal and suitable tax-reduction techniques that convert some of the dollars that you would otherwise spend for taxes into additional dollars that you can spend for investment. This effect is also accelerated if spending for lifestyle maintenance is held constant or reduced as your personal income, income from investments, and other Cash Inflows increase.

Effective personal financial planning begins with an analysis of how your Cash Flows (both inflows and outflows) are being generated and allocated. Once this analysis is available, we can begin to focus on managing and controlling all Cash Outflows related to living expenses, taxes, and investment—the three parts of the allocational principle in which all of your Cash Inflows are ultimately spent.

Your comprehensive personal financial management system permits you to use this Cash Flow Management principle in every area of your financial life. By using it in all your financial decisions, you can direct the appropriate allocations of Cash Surplus and Investment Capital to each of your funding objectives in each area of your primary planning concerns during lifetime employment and retirement. In addition, you can also control the distribution of these Cash Flows and Investment Assets in your estate. Your financial planning reports are structured around cash flow management.

Let's look now at how the Allocational Principle of Cash Flows relates to the second principle we mentioned above: the Production Principle of Investment Capital.

The Production Principle of Investment Capital

Your Investment Capital Asset structure can be compared to that of any business entity. We can usefully think of this business entity as a money factory that consists of all the financial resources that work together to produce a desired amount of money each year. Any organized business consists of several departments that require investment in time or capital to fund their expected production of Cash Flows. For most persons, these "departments" would include Job, Investments, Social Security, Pension, and Insurance.

In a sense, it does not matter which department of the business entity produces the Cash Flows as long as they are adequate to take care of annual spending requirements, which include the three parts of the allocational principle: 1) Personal Spending, 2) Spending for Taxes, and 3) Spending for Saving and Investment. However, without planning and proper funding, one or more of these departments may not actually produce the desired level of Cash Flows as needs arise.

Like any capital enterprise, if this entity is to succeed in producing income over the long term, it must accomplish two goals: (1) generate enough output of cash each year to cover your personal spending and taxes payable, and (2) produce enough to reinvest in itself for capital growth. Reinvestment in yourself assures that there will be enough Cash Inflow, at every projectible point, to fund your specifically determined financial objectives at a level consistent with your determined needs. If one department of your business shuts down, the other departments must increase their production to maintain the levels of Cash Inflow you need.

When you retire, for example, your Job department closes and your Pension, Social Security, and Investment departments must fill the cash-inflow gap up to the level of spendable dollars you require or desire. Similarly, if you die or become disabled, your Insurance department joins the other still-functioning departments to replace the Cash Inflows of capital production that you lost (or your survivors lost) when your Job department closed down. Your ability to earn money through employment is a capital-producing asset.

Your Personal Assets—such as your personal residence and automobiles—factor into your Total Asset structure and therefore into your Personal Net Worth. However, they are not included in your Investment Capital Asset structure if you acquire them for use and consumption rather than for the production of Cash Flows. If your Personal Assets have market value—that is, if they have a ready buyer at a price you accept—you can of course liquidate them for cash. One of the aims of personal financial planning, however, is to ensure that you will not have to resort to this extreme measure to produce the dollars you will need to spend now or later for living, taxes, and investment. On the other hand, at some point in your life, such as in retirement or at your death, you may want to liquidate some of your Personal Assets or convert them to Investment Capital Assets.

Allocating Cash Flows and Investment Capital

To sum up, the relationship between the Allocational and Production Principles of Cash Flows and Investment Capital is central to the basic thrust of comprehensive personal financial planning. To see yourself—your life circumstances and all of your financial resources—as a business entity assumes that your business is an ongoing Capital Investment Structure designed to produce Cash Flows.

As an individual economic entity, you are initially funded toward the future by the Cash Surplus from your Cash Inflows that you allocate to saving and investment. All of your further investments, plus the reinvestment of the Cash Inflows and realized Capital Appreciation that your current investments produce, are allocated to new departments of your business or to increased funding of currently active departments. In turn, these departments are assigned specific cash-flow-production objectives to meet your lifetime financial needs as well as the financial needs of your survivors.

Comprehensive personal financial planning is actually a method for creating and spending cash flows. We can sum it up as follows:

> Personal financial planning is the comprehensive, systematic method for establishing, maintaining, nourishing, and eventually liquidating or otherwise disposing of your capital assets to produce desired levels of cash flow for attaining specific financial objectives during your lifetime and within your desires and intentions for distributing your estate.

This comprehensive personal spending method is employed systematically in the following areas of special planning focus:

1. **Tax Planning**: planning for the reduction of tax liabilities to increase cash flows for personal spending and for investment allocation
2. **Cash Flow and Liability Management**: maintaining and enhancing personal cash flows through employment, professional practice, or

business ownership, and controlling allocations of expenditure for lifestyle maintenance, taxes, and investment; efficiently controlling personal debt levels

3. **Risk Management and Insurance Planning**: planning for the protection of cash flows through sound financial management and through cost-effective insuring against risks to income and assets
4. **Investment Planning and Management**: planning for and managing the building of a capital base for generating future cash flows by spending current annual surpluses of cash for investment assets; managing investment programs and maintaining appropriate levels of liability associated with investment net worth
5. **Business Interests and Employee Benefits**: planning and managing the integration of personal financial planning objectives, the assets and cash flows of business ownership interests, and the various employee benefits typically associated with corporate executives and other salaried employees
6. **Retirement and Economic Independence**: planning the allocation of specific investment dollars (in conjunction with social security benefits and pension and other retirement plans) to provide adequate capital to generate the cash flows deemed necessary for economic independence
7. **Estate Conservation and Distribution**: planning for the lifetime accumulation and appropriate titling of assets and their distribution according to dispositive intentions at death

To these areas of special emphasis your own personal concerns, your particular objectives, and your particular circumstances are integrated to create your personal financial management system.

Most of your personal financial transactions generate tax payable now, next year, or at some deferred taxable event that your capital production structure creates. For this reason, comprehensive financial planning integrates tax planning strategies and tactics so as to foresee and control these Tax Liabilities. As we noted above, comprehensive planning also tries to convert some of what you would otherwise pay as taxes into additional Surplus Cash for investment. Our analyses of both your current and your future financial position carefully track the tax consequences of your financial transactions.

The function of Risk Management in comprehensive financial planning is essentially to provide a hedge against the events (such as death, disability, liability judgments, and major illness) that could threaten the success of your management of Cash Flows and Investment Capital Assets. In this light, we recommend life insurance to replace the Investment Capital that you would not be able to accumulate within your financial planning strategies were you to die prematurely. In some instances, because of the tax-favored accumulation of Investment Capital within life insurance contracts, we may recommend them for investment purposes. Generally, if your Investment Capital program succeeds, the time may come when your only need for pure life insurance protection would be to provide liquidity for settling your estate.

Similarly, all other insurance contracts are used to protect the continuity and conservation of your Cash Inflows and accumulated Investment and Personal Assets. Unless you are a formally organized ongoing business (in which case premiums for insurance contracts would be a tax-deductible business expense), the premiums you pay for contracts of insurance are a nondeductible personal capital expense item. In other words, your spending for insurance premiums is to protect the income-producing potential of your life, and of your accumulated Investment Capital, for the benefit of yourself and your survivors.

Concluding Remarks

If you arrange and managed your financial life in a comprehensive strategy as outlined above, you will have a systematic method for establishing, maintaining, nourishing, and eventually liquidating or otherwise disposing of your Investment Capital Assets and their associated Cash Flows. You will have, in effect, a Personal Financial Plan.

Your current Financial Profile reflects your present financial and tax position. The reports that follow are designed to provide you with the systematic method and information support you need for moving your Profile toward your personal financial objectives in the years ahead. We urge you to carefully read and evaluate these reports. Our specific recommendations are included in the section entitled "Our Summary and Recommendations."

You are assured of our availability for further consultation, information support, and help with implementing these recommendations to convert them to your personal financial decisions. As you complete that still unfinished task, your Financial Profile will become your *Personal Financial Plan.*

GOALS AND OBJECTIVES

GOALS AND OBJECTIVES

This section recapitulates your financial objectives as we understand them. We made a distinction between your objectives for creating and increasing Investment Capital Assets and your objectives for conserving and distributing these assets from your estate. Your investment growth objectives are taken fully into account throughout the reports covering the next ten years. Your estate conservation and distribution objectives are taken into account in the Estate Planning recommendations so as to help you realize your dispositive intentions towards heirs and beneficiaries with the least amount of estate shrinkage through taxation and settlement costs.

Lifetime Planning

In our consultations, we refined your short-term and long-range financial objectives. The total horizon in which we are planning consists of only 10 years, or until you reach a level of Investment Net Worth that will support your economic independence.

Following is a summary of your financial objectives as of this date.

1. Establish and maintain an adequate level of liquid reserves through a disciplined cash-management program.
2. Increase your Investment Net Worth on a systematic basis through a diversified investment program focused on real estate.
3. Accumulate enough capital to maintain your lifestyle and be economically independent.
4. Maintain your current standard of living in the event of your long-term disability.
5. Minimize taxes while meeting Investment Capital accumulation objectives in the most efficient manner; reduce income tax liabilities, if possible, with creative sheltering of investment income.

Estate Planning

Your desires and objectives for conserving and distributing your estate are summarized below.

1. Avoid unnecessary taxes and estate shrinkage at your death.
2. Leave the assets in your estate at death to either or both of your parents if they survive you; if not, to your sister, Eileen Brennan, if she survives you; if not, to the children of Eileen in a manner that preserves the capital for their education or for the distribution to them equitably after they reach the age of 23.

SUMMARY AND RECOMMENDATIONS

In our discussions and in the analysis of your current financial profile, there are several clearly indicated steps you now need to take to start moving more directly toward your overall financial objectives. In our planning time frame for 1997 and beyond, we have included our specific recommendations in the computations and forecasts to illustrate their consequences on your financial and tax position if you implement them. Because of the limited scope (number of years presented) of this plan, we have not provided any estate planning reports. However, specific recommendations for conserving and distributing your estate have been summarized in the Estate Planning section.

We summarize below our specific recommendations for your overall financial planning. After this summary, we include an Action Checklist to indicate by priority ranking the steps you now need to take to fully implement your personal financial management decisions and provide ongoing oversight.

Specific Recommendations

- Use the Tax-Free Cash Management Account as your investment control account. From its cash surpluses each year, allocate investment funds as indicated in our investment recommendations below.
- Establish an investment program designed to provide an investment portfolio by 2006 that is balanced between real estate investment properties, selected issues of growth common stock, growth mutual funds, and municipal bonds. To achieve this aim, allocate your surplus cash as follows:

  - 25 percent annually to the Tax-Free Cash Management Account, beginning in the current year, at yields of 6.0 percent or better
  - 15 percent annually to a Tax-Free Municipal Bond Fund beginning in 2000, at yields of 6.0 percent or better.
  - 40 percent to an aggressive growth mutual fund, such as Orion Shares, beginning in 2000, at an annual yield of at least 9 percent
  - 20 percent to nondividend Selected Aggressive Stock with anticipated returns of about 12 percent annually, beginning in 2000
  - an additional 50 shares during each of the next 4 years in Brentwood Corporation common stock, for both dividend income and projected appreciation of about 10 percent annually.

  This means that during the next 4 years, we will increase your holdings of Brentwood to 400 shares and build the Tax-Free Cash Management Account to a substantial balance. Beginning in late 2000 or early 2001, we can use this balance as a down payment on further rental real estate investment opportunities—or do so earlier if your evolving circumstances support that plan.

  In any case, by 2001 we will need to rearrange the percentage allocations above to position you to start a concerted real estate investment program, so that by 2006 your investment in this category will be significantly larger than your reports now project. This modification will also diminish your projected holdings in growth common stock, mutual fund shares, tax-free municipal bond funds in 2006.

- Buy the condominium in the city for your personal residence; use $15,000 from your current balance in the Tax-Free Cash Management Account as a down payment and secure 30-year mortgage financing at 7.5 percent for $180,000 of the $195,000 purchase price of the unit you have looked at.
- Initiate contributions to IRAs. These provide a tax deferred method to save towards retirement. The return on these accounts should equal or exceed the tax free cash management account. However, if Brentwood installs a retirement plan; pension, profit sharing or 401k; we will need to reevaluate these contributions since they will no longer provide a tax deduction based your income level and the current phase-out rules for IRA deductibility.
- Continue to actively manage your rental property in Woodstock. After 2000, as positive and fully taxable cash flows begin to be generated by this property, we can evaluate several options for liquidating or exchanging it for similar property to continue the tax-reducing advantages of this form of investment in the light of tax law at that time.
- Liquidate your holdings in RCI and Flintstone common stock. The net capital loss from these two transactions will provide a deduction this year. Neither stock is likely to recover significantly enough to permit a gain over the opportunity cost of having your capital tied up there. The proceeds will add to cash available this year to apply $15,000 to the purchase price of the condo and maintain an appropriate balance in the Tax-Free Cash Management Account.
- Purchase a disability income insurance contract that will provide you $18,000 per year of income in addition to the Brentwood coverage, for a total of $48,000 of replacement income coverage in the event of your disability. Buy only a guaranteed renewable contract with the most liberal definition of disability. The annual premium should be approximately $680.
- Increase your homeowner's insurance coverage on the Woodstock rental property to 100 percent of its replacement value, and have the coverage adjusted each year for approximate appreciation in value. Purchase homeowner's coverage on the condo in the city for at least 80 percent of its replacement value and have the coverage adjusted annually for appreciated value. The premium for $220,000 of initial coverage on the condo should be approximately $980.

- In 1998, drop comprehensive and collision coverage on the Honda and self-insure; this will save you approximately $275 annually in cash outflow.
- In the early years of your plan, we recommend that you slightly reduce or defer some of your planned expenditures for jewelry, lithographs, photography equipment, and household furnishings to direct more cash to investment.
- Have your attorney draft a simple will expressing your estate distribution wishes—specifically, that your entire estate should pass to either or both of your parents jointly if they survive; if they do not survive you, that your entire estate should pass to your married sister, Eileen Brennan, after bequests to each of your sister's living children (three as of this date) of $25,000; if neither your parents nor your sister survives you, that your entire estate should pass in equal shares to the surviving children of your sister, Eileen Brennan, and that a trust be established for these children from which income and principal can be distributed to them in equitable amounts until they reach the age of 23, after which the remaining trust principal will be distributed to each surviving child equally.

Implementation Schedule

We share with you the responsibility of following through with your decisions and implementing our suggestions and recommendations. We will arrange appointments and be present, as needed, to coordinate activities and provide relevant information for other professionals.

To implement our recommendations, you should take the steps indicated in the checklist below. When you have completed steps scheduled for the current year, your *Personal Financial Plan* will begin.

Action Checklist for Implementation

Recommen-dation	Action Required	Time Frame	Party Responsible	Date Completed
(1)	Change cash management/ investment practices	Now	Client	
(2)	Arrange purchase of 50 shrs. Bentwood stock over each of next 4 years	Now	Client/co.	
(3)	Close on condo	Now	Client/agent	
(4)	Start IRA contributions	Now	Client	
(5)	Ongoing mgmt.		Client	
(6)	Sell RCI and Flintstone	Now	Client/broker	
(7)	Purchase disability income policy	Now	Client/agent	
(8)	Acquire/increase home-owners insurance	Now	Client/agent	
(9)	Reduce/defer personal purchases	1997	Client	
(10)	Have attorney draft will	Now	Client/attorney	
(11)	Drop comp/collision coverage	1998	Client	

CURRENT FINANCIAL PROFILE OVERVIEW

CURRENT FINANCIAL PROFILE OVERVIEW

This section consists of summaries of your current Financial Profile between the beginning and ending dates of our planning horizon. The purpose of these summaries is to provide you a comparative analysis and evaluation of your present financial position. The summaries include the overall effects of your current financial transactions and assumes that you will implement the specific recommendations we have developed for your endorsement.

The information included in this overview is derived from the more detailed tax and financial analyses included in subsequent sections of this document (or in your case file, from which we can provide copies at your request). These summaries outline your interrelated financial and tax transactions over a period of ten years, starting with 1997.

Your Net Worth

A conservative valuation of your present assets and liabilities reveals that your Net Worth is $151,439.

Based upon the information you provided and the assumptions we made in projecting your Profile for the next ten years, your Net Worth increases at a rate higher than the anticipated inflation rate.

Your Taxes, Cash Flows, and Purchasing Power

For the first year of the planning time frame, your income is taxed at a Marginal Bracket Rate of twenty-eight percent. Your tax profile is typical for your income level.

This analysis indicates that the overall growth in your Cash Inflows will be sufficient to offset the effects of inflation. Inflation has the effect of progressively reducing the real value or purchasing power of the dollar. In 2006 each current dollar will be worth sixty-six cents, assuming an average inflation rate of four percent. In 1997 you will receive a Gross Real Income of $94,912. From this amount you will pay an Income Tax of $21,777. Your Net Real Income will therefore be $73,136. This Net Real Income excludes the cash you will receive from liquidating assets as well as the tax losses that will be generated by your direct participation investments. Real Income represents your current spendable income or purchasing power. Your purchasing power is estimated to increase steadily throughout the ten-year span covered in your Financial Profile. In order to maintain your current level of purchasing power in the last year of our planning time frame, you must produce a Net Real Income of $104,095 in 2006 to neutralize the combined impact of taxes and inflation (taxflation) on your Cash Inflows. Your projected Net Real Income of $149,023 in 2006 is derived from $219,773 of Gross Real Income less $70,750 of projected Income Tax. Therefore, your purchasing power will not be adversely affected over the next ten years.

In the first year of the plan you are in a sound Cash Flow position. During 1997 you will spend about 23 percent of your total pretax Cash Inflows for living expenses. Your future spendable income will grow faster than your future living expenses. Therefore, the amount of Surplus Cash available for saving and investment will be increasing each year.

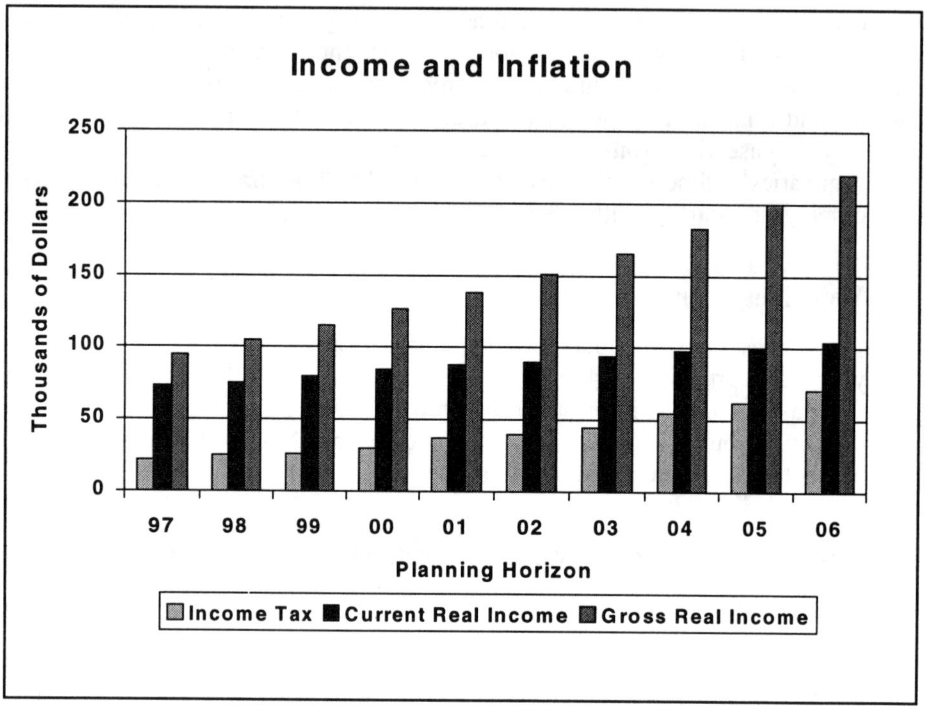

INCOME TAX MANAGEMENT

INCOME TAX MANAGEMENT

Your Income

You earn a total of $85,000 in Personal Service Income (salaries, wages, bonuses) in 1997. In addition, you earn $312 in interest and dividends, your rental real estate produces $9,600 and the sale of stocks generates $7,975. The total of your Cash Inflows for this year is $103,587 after considering the loss of $8,301 from your direct participation or other investments and before considering any other adjustments or deductions for tax purposes.

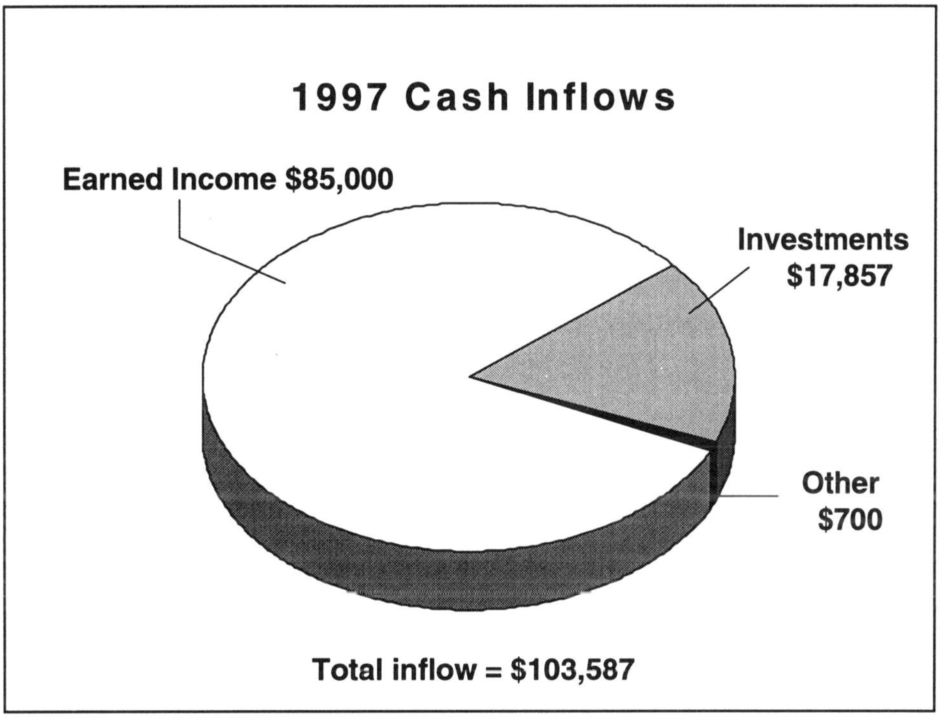

In 2006 you are projected to earn a total of $200,426 in Personal Service Income (salaries, wages, bonuses). Your interest and dividend earnings are projected to be $3,128. The adjusted investment earnings for tax purposes is computed to be $199,778; this computation takes into consideration the loss of $3,775 from your direct participation in tax-favored investments.

Your Tax-Favored/Direct Participation Investments

The total value of your tax-favored or direct participation investments changes from $128,700 in 1997 to $277,530 in 2006. These investments produce a gross positive pretax Cash Flow of $9,600 in the first year of your Financial Profile, while pretax Cash Flow from your investments will be $16,219 in 2006. Your investments also produce a taxable loss of $8,301 in the first year of this Profile. In 2006, your taxable loss from investment will be $3,775. Your Tax Preferences amount to $1,217 in 1997. All of your Investment Interest expense is fully deductible. Your Tax Preferences will amount to $1,216 in 2006. All of your Investment Interest expense will be fully deductible that year. For financial details on each tax-favored or direct participation investment, please review the Investment Analysis schedule.

Your Retirement Plans

As of the end of 1997, you have accumulated $15,974 in your Retirement Plans. Your contributions to these plans this year result in a tax deduction of $2,000.

You will have accumulated $69,402 in your Retirement Plans as of the end of 2006. The tax deduction resulting from your contributions to these plans will be $2,000 that year.

Your Income Taxes

We compute your 1997 Income Tax as $21,777. This tax consists of $10,764 in Federal Regular Tax and $5,027 in social security tax. In addition, your Total Tax Liability includes $5,986 in state and local income taxes.

The federal income taxes computed above are based upon your 1997 Single Status while claiming one Exemption. In addition to the Exemption, a total of $21,851 is applied against your Adjusted Gross Income as Itemized Deductions. After adjusting your Itemized Deductions for the required phase-outs (reductions because of your income level), your Taxable Income is $50,085.

Your Marginal Federal Tax Bracket is twenty-eight percent in 1997. This tax rate is applied to $25,085 of your current Taxable Income of $50,085. An increase of Taxable Income of $10,415 or more will move you into the thirty-one percent bracket. In such a case, the higher rate is applicable only to the amount of income that falls in the higher bracket. If you decrease your federal Taxable Income by $25,085 or more you will fall into the fifteen percent bracket. Your federal income taxes in this year were computed after the application of a 70.28% indexing factor to the base year 1988, as required under current income tax law.

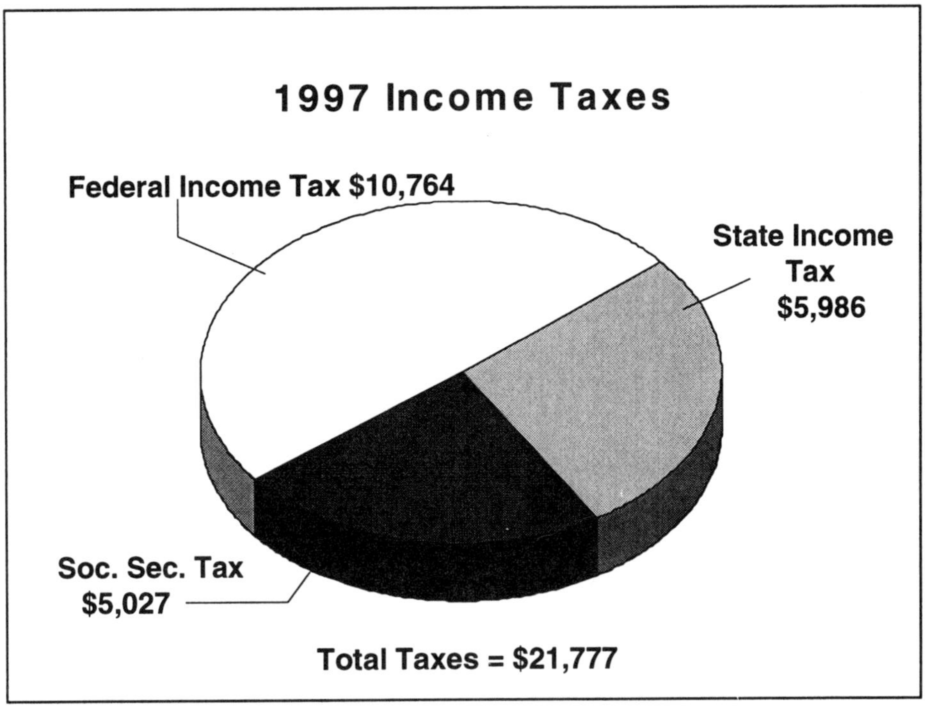
1997 Income Taxes
Federal Income Tax $10,764
State Income Tax $5,986
Soc. Sec. Tax $5,027
Total Taxes = $21,777

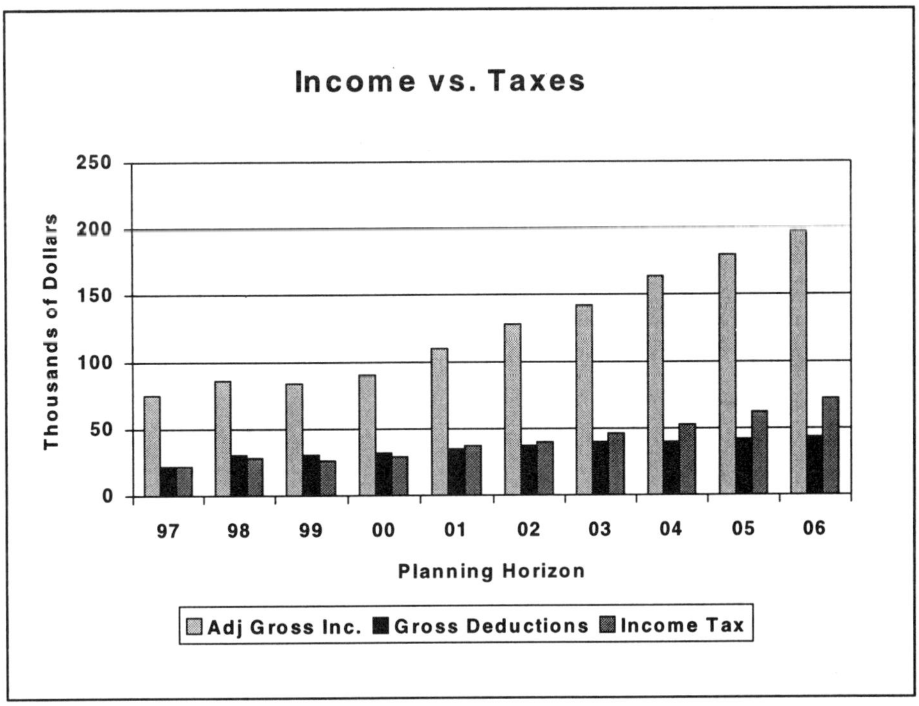
Income vs. Taxes
Thousands of Dollars
250
200
150
100
50
0
97
98
99
00
01
02
03
04
05
06
Planning Horizon
Adj Gross Inc.
Gross Deductions
Income Tax

CASH FLOW MANAGEMENT

CASH FLOW MANAGEMENT

An Analysis of Your Cash Flows

Your Cash Inflow of $103,587 in the first year of your Profile changes to $217,303 in 2006. During this period of ten years you will receive a total of $1,495,123 in cash. Cash Inflow includes all cash received in a year before your spending for investment resulting from our installation of Automatic Cash Management, as explained below. Your highest annual Cash Inflow amounts to $217,303 and is received in 2006, whereas your lowest annual Cash Inflow of $103,587 occurs in 1997. If all the varying amounts of cash you receive over the years are discounted by a factor of five percent, the Net Present Value of this stream is $1,142,466. In other words, $1,142,466 today will produce all of the cash you will receive in the next ten years if it yields a net return of five percent.

Similarly, your annual Cash Outflow of $102,974 in the first year of your Profile changes to $152,545 in 2006. The total of all your cash expenditure items in the ten-year period adds up to $1,199,675. The highest level of your annual spending of $152,545 occurs in 2006; your smallest annual Cash Outflow amounting to $95,019 occurs in 1998. Your annual Cash Outflow includes all of your non-investment spending, such as for household expenses, education, cash purchases, donations, paydown of debt, and taxes. Discounted by the factor of five percent, the Net Present Value of your total cash expenditures over our planning horizon is $932,444. This means that $932,444 today, yielding five percent, will take care of all your projected noninvestment cash spending for the next ten years.

The total of your Nondeductible Living Expenses changes from $21,710 in the first year of your Profile to $28,386 in 2006. Over the ten-year span, your Nondeductible Living Expenses total $241,476 with a Net Present Value of $188,397 if we use five percent as the discounting factor. In relation to your Gross Real Income, the total of your Nondeductible Living Expenses decreases from 23 percent in 1997 to 13 percent in 2006.

The total of your Income Tax changes from $21,777 in the first year of your Profile to $70,750 in 2006. Over the ten-year span, your Income Tax totals $395,290 with a Net Present Value of $295,348 if we use five percent as the discounting factor. Incidentally, you pay the highest amount of Income Tax in 2006 of $70,750. You pay the lowest amount of Income Tax in 1997 of $21,777.

Your Net Cash Flow in 1997, after spending for taxes, living expenses, paydown of debts, and purchases is $614. Your Net Cash Flow after spending for taxes, purchases, and living expenses will be $64,758 in 2006.

Managing Your Cash Flows for Investment

To reflect as possible your financial position as realistically in the years ahead, we created simulation models of your expected Cash Flows, Income Taxes, Investment Net Worth, and the effects of each on the other in view of

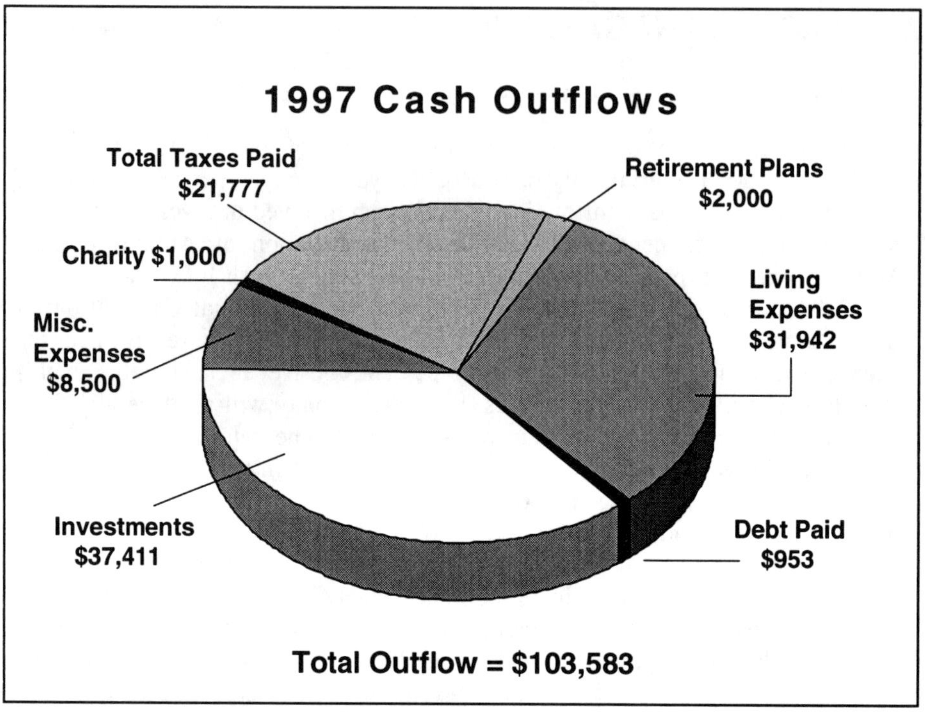

your specific objectives and cash allocations for investment. We performed this simulation with proper consideration for all of your interrelated and dynamic financial activities that may not actually occur simultaneously, but should be assumed to do so in order to disclose the consequences of their interrelationships when they do happen.

In your Automatic Cash Management simulations we employ an automatic control to limit the amount of your noninvested cash to an average of $500. This noninvested cash can be considered as cash on hand or in a nonincome-producing checking account. Your Citibank checking account serves this purpose.

We employ an additional allocational tactic in the Automatic Cash Management simulation. Surplus Cash available for investment is directed to mutual funds in each applicable year of your Profile. This investment is projected to yield six percent.

Based on the saving and investment criteria defined in your Automatic Cash Management simulations, a total of $297,186 will be invested over the ten years of your planning horizon. Your annual Cash Surplus for investment peaks at $64,759 in 2006. The lowest Cash Surplus for investment takes place in 1999, when your Net Cash Flow does not provide an investable Cash Surplus. The Net Present Value of all the Surplus Cash you will spend for investment during these years is $211,562, discounted at five percent.

ASSET AND LIABILITY MANAGEMENT

ASSET AND LIABILITY MANAGEMENT

Your Assets

For purposes of analysis as well as planning, we have separated your Total Assets into two categories according to their potential for producing current or future Cash Flows. These categories are conventionally defined as follows:

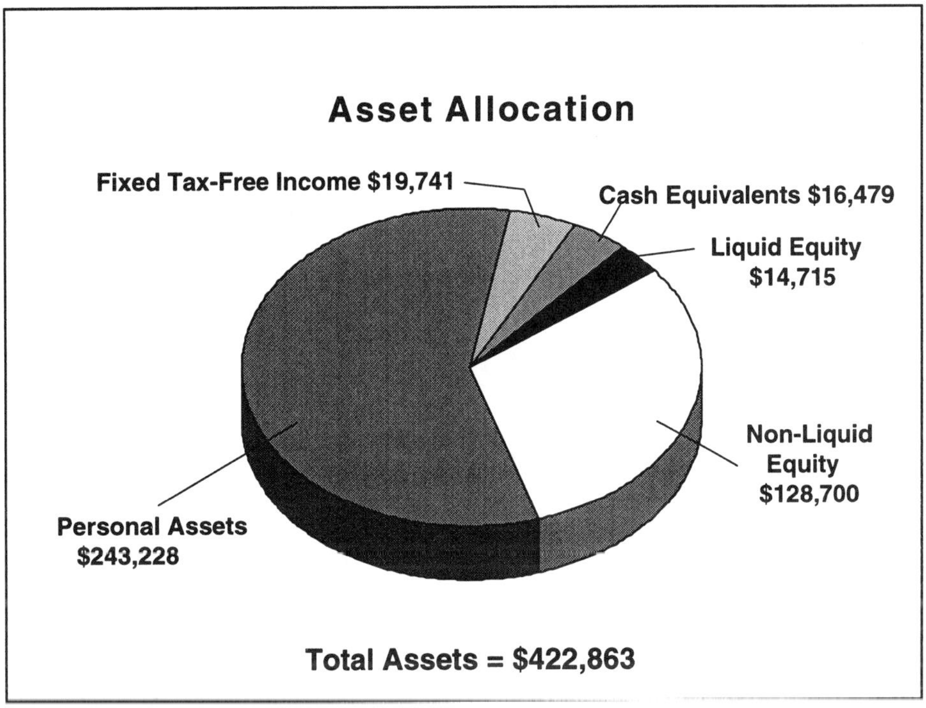

Personal Assets. These assets are normally not allocated for conversion to investment capital for the production of income in the event of premature death or retirement; they are acquired and held for use and consumption.

Investment Assets. These assets are normally acquired to produce income and/or future capital growth; they are available to you in retirement or if you become disabled, and are available to your survivors in the event of your premature death.

The value of your Personal Assets in 1997 totals $259,707. With the exception of $505 in cash All of this amount is considered nonliquid. These Personal Assets, when netted against your Personal Liabilities of $179,047, yield a Personal Net Worth of $80,660.

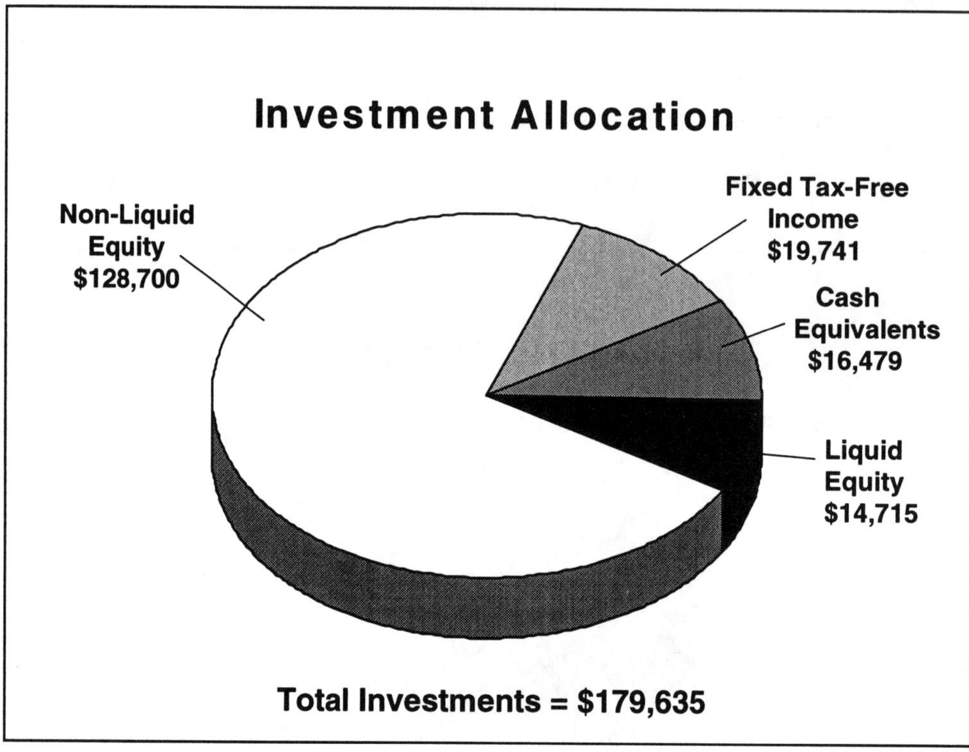

The value of all your Investment Assets in 1997 is $163,156. Your Investment Liabilities amount to $92,377. Therefore, your Investment Net Worth is $70,779.

We compute your Net Worth at the end of 1997 as $151,439. This consists of $422,863 in assets and $271,424 in liabilities. Your Total Assets at that time will include $34,961 of Liquid Assets and $387,902 of Nonliquid Assets.

At the end of 2006 your Net Worth is projected to be $1,078,614, consisting of $1,308,776 in assets and $230,162 in liabilities. Your Total Assets at that time will include $421,525 of Liquid and $887,251 of Nonliquid Assets.

The growth of your total Investment Net Worth is the more reliable gauge by which you can evaluate the effectiveness of your Investment Capital Production structure and thus your progress towards the achievement of your strategic financial objectives. At some point in your personal financial future it may become necessary to move assets from the Personal category to the Investment category in order to meet your objectives and needs.

Your Liabilities

The total amount of your outstanding debt at the end of 1997 is $271,424. The amount of $179,047 is considered personal debt and $92,377 is considered investment-related liabilities. You have $179,047 of outstanding mortgage loans on your residence. For these and other personal loans you are making payments in 1997 totaling $8,985. Of this amount, $953 reduces the outstanding principal balance of your personal debt. The remaining amount of $8,032 is the interest you pay on this debt. As shown on the Income Statement, the interest paid on home mortgages is deducted in computing your income taxes.

The total amount of your outstanding debt at the end of 2006 will be $230,162. The amount of $157,616 is personal debt and $72,546 is investment-related liabilities. You will have $157,616 as outstanding personal amortized loans at the end of this period. In 2006 you will be making payments on these loans totaling $15,278. Of this amount, $3,152 reduces the outstanding principal balance. The remaining amount of $12,126 is deductible interest to the extent that it is allocable to residential mortgages.

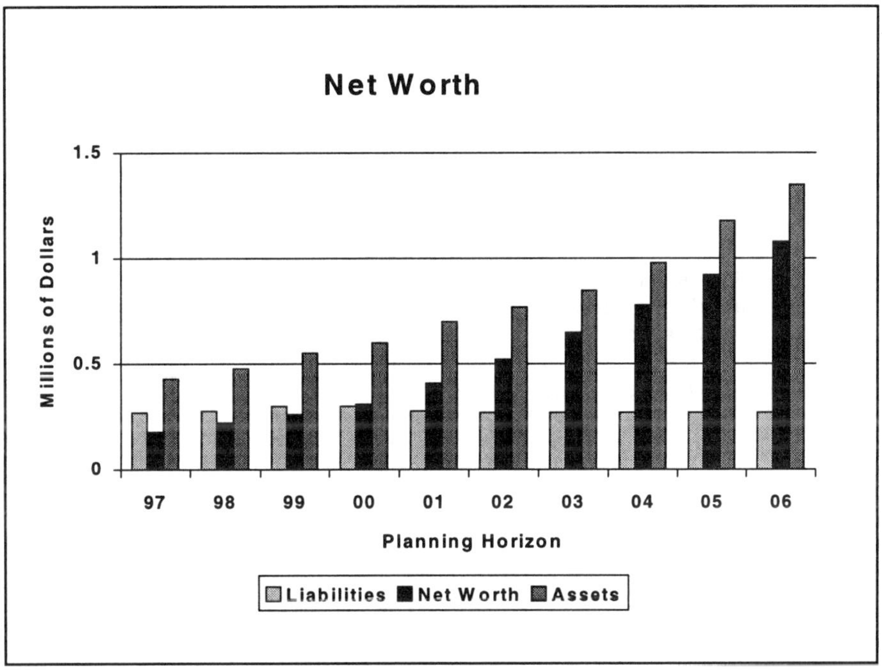

An Analysis of Your Real Estate Investment

Your rental real estate property in Woodstock represents a significant beginning in your desire to focus your investment program in this type of asset. As we plan for future investments, it is important for you to become accustomed to analyzing them for their net effects as investments.

The following analysis gives a breakdown of how this investment produces various economic and tax consequences.

Financial Planning Associates
INVESTMENT ANALYSIS

	1997	1998	1999	2000	2006
	Age: 37	38	39	40	46
Rental Real Est					
Asset Value	117,700	129,470	142,417	156,659	277,530
Liability	83,589	82,696	81,734	80,696	72,546
Cash Contributed	11,092	11,290	11,498	11,716	13,275
Cash Received	9,600	10,176	10,787	11,434	16,219
Ordinary Income	9,600	10,176	10,787	11,434	16,219
Depreciation	3,892	3,891	3,892	3,891	3,891
Inv Int Sch E	6,303	6,239	6,170	6,094	5,507
Cash Expenses	3,960	4,158	4,366	4,584	6,143
Net Inv Inc-Ncsh	–4,555	–4,112	–3,641	–3,135	678
Passive Loss C/O	0	0	0	0	–829
Disallowed	0	0	0	0	151
Inv Exp Tax Prefs	1,217	1,216	1,217	1,216	1,216
Psv Loss C/O-AMT	0	0	0	0	0
Disallowed	0	0	0	0	0

Comprehensive Analysis (1997–2006)

	Cur Value	% of Tot	PV @ 5%
Total amount contributed	121,128	84.29%	95,077
Initial net asset value	22,582	15.71%	22,582
Total contribution	143,710	100.00%	117,659
Projected change in value	182,402	57.88%	111,979
Total cash received	126,536	40.15%	97,805
Accumulated tax savings	6,197	1.97%	5,404
Total benefit	315,135	100.00%	215,189

Current after-tax yield:	–0.96%
Internal rate of return:	26.03%

CONSERVING AND DISTRIBUTING YOUR ESTATE

CONSERVING AND DISTRIBUTING YOUR ESTATE

The financial and tax consequences of your untimely death are described in this section of your Financial Profile. In fact, of course, none of us knows when this event will happen. The importance of seeing its consequences, however, is the opportunity it affords to notice the difference between those consequences when they flow from decisions made within a lifetime personal financial management system that anticipates this event and the consequences of the event when it is not planned for.

The differences can be measured in very substantial dollars. They can also be measured in the profound negative emotions and frustrations that survivors and beneficiaries often experience when the decedent makes no intentional plans to distribute estate assets.

The shrinkage of your estate values will result primarily from the need to pay any personal debt, administration expenses, and federal, state, and local death and estate taxes. Before death occurs, there are many alternatives for arranging these matters to the greatest advantage of all interested parties, especially your estate tax liabilities (if any).

Estate Analysis

The reports, analyses, and computations of your estate settlement costs and taxes would be drawn from the integrated information and forecasts of your overall financial position for a year selected as the hypothetical date of your death. As we agreed, however, a complete analysis of your estate conservation and distribution objectives would be of little value to you at this time.

Right now, our primary concern is to build a living estate. The objectives associated with that aim are reflected elsewhere in these reports and in our recommendations. To assure that your accumulated assets pass with a minimum of shrinkage to beneficiaries you wish to designate, you should consult with your attorney for drafting a simple will and explore means to reduce the New York State inheritance taxes that might be imposed.

As of 1997 and thereafter, current federal estate tax law passes $600,000 free of tax. Through the early years of your living plan, your total Net Worth should be well within this figure. However, as forecasts show, your Net Worth is expected to increase substantially over the next ten years.

To fully realize your desires for distributing your estate assets, you should carefully monitor your taxable estate as your Net Worth rises. As your estate values increase and become subject to taxation, you may want to consider certain bequests or testamentary trusts in your will, such as for your sister, Eileen, or for her children.

Your Current Will

As of this date, you have no formal will. This is a serious deficiency of your current financial profile. Without a valid will, your estate would be distributed under the intestacy laws of the state of New York. This would not satisfy your estate distribution intentions. You should execute a simple will as a priority item. (See "Summary and Recommendations" section above.)

OTHER FINANCIAL ANALYSES

Financial Planning Associates
INCOME STATEMENT

	1997	1998	1999	2000	2006
	Age: 37	38	39	40	46
Earned Income					
Compensation	85,000	93,500	102,850	113,135	200,426
IRA 3	–2,000	–2,000	–2,000	–2,000	–2,000
	83,000	91,500	100,850	111,135	198,426
Interest/Dividends					
Brentwood	312	375	438	520	658
Orion Shares	0	0	0	71	2,470
	312	375	438	591	3,128
Investments					
Rental Real Est	–4,555	–4,112	–3,641	–3,135	678
Business Auto 1	–3,746	–3,512	–3,253	–9	0
Business Auto 2	0	0	–11,243	–15,780	–4,453
Rental Real Est	0	0	0	0	–829
Disallowed	0	0	0	0	151
	–8,301	–7,624	–18,137	–18,925	–4,453
Other					
State Tax Refund	700	0	0	0	0
	700	0	0	0	0
Net Capital Gain	–1,125	0	–163	0	0
Adj Gross Income	74,586	84,251	82,987	92,801	197,101
Deductions					
Charitable 50%	1,000	1,040	1,082	1,125	1,423
State Tax Paid	3,875	4,208	4,097	4,792	12,893
Local Tax Paid	2,111	2,293	2,232	2,613	6,917
Condominium	7,857	13,370	13,235	13,090	11,951
Misc Expense Ded	7,008	7,155	7,534	7,705	8,156
Reductn For High Inc	0	0	0	0	–675
Gross Deductions	21,851	28,066	28,180	29,325	40,665
Standard Deduction	4,150	4,300	4,450	4,650	5,900
Allowed Deductions	21,851	28,066	28,180	29,325	40,665
Pers Exemptions	2,650	2,750	2,850	2,950	3,150
Taxable Income	50,085	53,435	51,958	60,526	153,285
Fed Income Tax	10,764	11,572	11,036	13,287	44,239
Fed Tax Bracket	28.0	28.0	28.0	28.0	31.0

Financial Planning Associates
BALANCE SHEET

	1997	1998	1999	2000	2006
	Age: 37	38	39	40	46
LIQUID ASSETS					
Cash Balance	505	501	500	500	501
Stocks & Bonds					
Brentwood	14,715	19,247	24,476	30,490	51,135
Orion Shares	0	0	0	7,390	147,558
Sel Aggressive Stk	0	0	0	3,748	80,276
TF Cash Mgmt Acct	19,741	28,776	27,037	31,457	98,923
TF Muni Fund	0	0	0	2,652	43,132
	34,456	48,023	51,513	75,737	421,024
Liquid Assets	34,961	48,524	52,013	76,237	421,525
NONLIQUID ASSETS					
Retirement Plans					
IRA 1	3,072	3,348	3,649	3,977	6,670
IRA 2	3,221	3,543	3,897	4,287	7,597
IRA 3	7,419	10,455	13,825	17,566	50,422
IRA 4	2,262	2,454	2,663	2,889	4,713
	15,974	19,800	24,034	28,719	69,402
Investments					
Business Auto 1	11,000	7,000	0	0	0
Business Auto 2	0	0	33,000	27,000	0
Rental Real Est	117,700	129,470	142,417	156,659	277,530
	128,700	136,470	175,417	183,659	277,530
Personal Property					
Condominium	214,500	235,950	259,545	285,500	505,780
Furniture/Fixture	15,000	15,000	15,000	15,000	15,000
Jewelry	5,200	5,408	5,624	5,849	7,401
Lithographs	4,160	4,326	4,499	4,679	5,921
Photo Equipment	4,368	4,543	4,724	4,913	6,217
	243,228	265,227	289,393	315,942	540,319
Nonliquid Assets	387,902	421,497	488,843	528,319	887,251
Total Assets	422,863	470,021	540,856	604,556	1,308,776
LIABILITIES					
Mortgage Loans					
Condominium	179,047	177,314	175,446	173,433	157,616
	179,047	177,314	175,446	173,433	157,616
Investments					
Rental Real Est	83,589	82,696	81,734	80,696	72,546
Business Auto 1	8,788	4,943	738	0	0
Business Auto 2	0	0	20,137	14,867	0
	92,377	87,639	102,609	95,563	72,546
Total Liabilities	271,424	264,953	278,055	268,996	230,162
Net Worth	151,439	205,068	262,801	335,560	1,078,614

Financial Planning Associates
CASH FLOW STATEMENT

	1997	1998	1999	2000	2006
	Age: 37	38	39	40	46
BEGINNING OF YEAR					
Idle Cash On Hand	500	505	501	500	502
SOURCES OF CASH					
Cash Income					
Compensation–CI	85,000	93,500	102,850	113,135	200,426
Interest + Dividends	312	375	438	520	658
	85,312	93,875	103,288	113,655	201,084
Investments					
Rental Real Est	9,600	10,176	10,787	11,434	16,219
	9,600	10,176	10,787	11,434	16,219
Sale/Withdrawals					
RCI Corp	2,175	0	0	0	0
Flintstone	5,800	0	0	0	0
TF Cash Mgmt Acct	0	0	1,739	0	0
	7,975	0	1,739	0	0
Tax Refund					
State Tax Refund	700	0	0	0	0
	700	0	0	0	0
Total Cash Inflow	103,587	104,051	115,813	125,089	217,303
Tot Cash Available	104,087	104,556	116,314	125,589	217,805
USES OF CASH					
Fully Tax Deductible					
IRA 3	2,000	2,000	2,000	2,000	2,000
Condominium	7,857	13,370	13,235	13,090	11,951
	9,857	15,370	15,235	15,090	13,951
Partly Deductible					
Medicine & Drugs	700	728	757	787	996
Therapy/Counseling	1,500	1,560	1,622	1,687	2,135
Charity Contrb–50%	1,000	1,040	1,082	1,125	1,423
Misc Ded–2% Limit	8,500	8,840	9,194	9,561	12,098
	11,700	12,168	12,655	13,161	16,653

Financial Planning Associates
CASH FLOW STATEMENT (cont.)

Not Tax Deductible					
Credit Card Int	175	175	175	175	175
Food	5,000	5,200	5,408	5,624	7,117
Clothing	1,500	1,560	1,622	1,687	2,135
Entertainment	2,000	2,080	2,163	2,250	2,847
Vacations	3,000	3,120	3,245	3,375	4,270
Gifts/Celebrations	1,000	1,040	1,082	1,125	1,423
Transportation	900	936	973	1,012	1,281
Condo Ins Premium	980	1,019	1,060	1,102	1,395
Disability Ins	680	707	735	765	968
Rent	3,300	0	0	0	0
Repair/Maint Furn	200	208	216	225	285
Condo Repair/Maint	900	1,800	1,872	1,947	2,463
Utility/Phone	2,000	2,080	2,163	2,250	2,847
Household Frnshg	0	0	1,000	1,000	1,000
Photo Supplies	250	260	270	281	356
	21,885	20,185	21,986	22,818	28,561
Taxes Paid					
Fed Tax Paid	10,764	11,572	11,036	13,287	44,239
State Tax Paid	3,875	4,208	4,097	4,792	12,893
Local Tax Paid	2,111	2,293	2,232	2,613	6,917
FICA/Soc Sec Tax	5,027	5,150	5,286	5,435	6,701
	21,777	23,223	22,651	26,127	70,750
Purchase/Deposits					
Brentwood	2,700	2,943	3,208	3,497	0
TF Cash Mgmt Acct	609	9,035	0	4,420	16,190
TF Muni Fund	0	0	0	2,652	9,714
Orion Shares	0	0	0	7,072	25,903
Sel Aggressive Stk	0	0	0	3,536	12,952
Furniture/Fixture	0	0	0	1,000	1,000
Jewelry	250	250	250	250	250
Lithographs	500	500	500	500	500
Photo Equipment	0	0	1,000	0	0
Condominium	15,000	0	0	0	0
	19,059	12,728	4,958	22,927	66,509
Investments					
Rental Real Est	11,092	11,290	11,498	11,716	13,275
Business Auto 1	7,260	7,357	7,458	747	0
Business Auto 2	0	0	17,506	10,491	4,453
	18,352	18,647	36,462	22,954	17,728
Liability Liquidation					
Condominium	953	1,733	1,868	2,013	3,152
	953	1,733	1,868	2,013	3,152
Total Cash Outflow	103,583	104,054	115,814	125,089	217,304
END OF YEAR					
Cash Balance	505	501	500	500	501

Financial Planning Associates
SUPPORTING SCHEDULE

	SINGLE 1997 Age: 37	SINGLE 1998 38	SINGLE 1999 39	SINGLE 2000 40	SINGLE 2006 46
Income					
Earned Income	83,000	91,500	100,850	111,135	198,426
Adj Gross Income	74,586	84,251	82,987	92,801	197,101
Allowed Deductions	21,851	28,066	28,180	29,325	40,665
Pers Exemptions	2,650	2,750	2,850	2,950	3,150
Taxable Income	50,085	53,435	51,958	60,526	153,285
Capital Gains					
RCI Corp	–1,800	0	0	0	0
Flintstone	675	0	0	0	0
Net Capital Gain	–1,125	0	–163	0	0
LTCG Txd At Max Rt	–1,125	0	0	0	0
Capital Gains–AMT	–1,125	0	0	0	0
Investments					
Ordinary Income	9,600	10,176	10,787	11,434	16,219
Depreciation	3,892	3,891	10,492	14,451	3,891
Invstmt Interest	7,268	6,873	7,587	7,701	5,507
Other Expenses	6,741	7,036	10,845	8,207	10,596
Alt Min Tax Adjs	1,217	1,216	2,867	3,361	1,216
Investment Income	–8,301	–7,624	–18,137	–18,925	–3,775
Passive Losses					
Rental Real Est	0	0	0	0	–829
Psv Ls Ald–Rental	4,555	4,112	3,641	3,135	0
Disallowed	0	0	0	0	151
Psv Ls Ald–AMT Rnt	3,338	2,896	774	0	0
Investment Interest					
Inv Int Sch E	7,268	6,873	7,587	7,701	5,507
Tax Preferences					
Rental Real Est	1,217	1,216	1,217	1,216	1,216
Business Auto 2	0	0	1,650	2,145	0
Tot Tax Prefs	1,217	1,216	2,867	3,361	1,216
Federal Tax Liab					
Regular Tax	10,764	11,572	11,036	13,287	40,306
Gross Fed Inc Tax	10,764	11,572	11,036	13,287	40,306
Alt Minimum Tax	0	0	0	0	3,933
Alt Min Tx Credit	0	0	0	0	615
AMT Credit C/Over	0	0	0	0	245
Disallowed	0	0	0	0	–860
Fed Income Tax	10,764	11,572	11,036	13,287	44,239

Financial Planning Associates
SUPPORTING SCHEDULE (cont.)

Fed Tax Analysis					
Indexing Factor	70	77	84	92	142
Fed Tax Bracket	28.0	28.0	28.0	28.0	31.0
$ To Next Bracket	10,415	9,465	13,492	7,524	26,315
Net Bracket	31.0	31.0	31.0	31.0	36.0
Previous Bracket	15.0	15.0	15.0	15.0	28.0
$ To Prev Bracket	25,085	27,435	24,958	32,426	67,185
Alt Minimum Tax					
Adj Gross Income	74,586	84,251	82,987	92,801	197,101
State Tax Refund	–700	0	0	0	0
Contributions	–1,000	–1,040	–1,082	–1,125	–1,423
Condominium	–7,857	–13,370	–13,235	–13,090	–11,951
Adjusted AMTI	65,029	69,841	68,670	78,586	183,727
Rental Real Est	0	0	0	0	829
Disallowed	0	0	0	0	–151
Net Capital Gain	1,125	0	163	0	0
Capital Gains-AMT	–1,125	0	0	0	0
Rental Real Est	1,217	1,216	1,217	1,216	1,216
Business Auto 2	0	0	1,650	2,145	0
AMT Exemptions	–33,750	–33,750	–33,750	–33,750	–15,470
AMT Taxable Inc	32,496	37,307	37,950	48,197	170,150
Gross Alt Min Tx	8,449	9,700	9,867	12,531	44,239
Fed Tax Less FTC	–10,763	–11,571	–11,035	–13,286	–40,306
Alt Minimum Tax	0	0	0	0	3,933
Other Tax Liabs					
FICA/Soc Sec Tax	5,027	5,150	5,286	5,435	6,701
NYS Pers Serv Inc	83,000	91,500	100,850	111,135	198,426
NYS Capital Gain	–1,125	0	0	0	0
NYS Unearned Inc	–7,989	–7,249	–17,863	–18,334	–1,325
NYS Aj Gross Inc	73,886	84,251	82,987	92,801	197,101
NYS It Deductns	–15,865	–21,565	–21,851	–21,920	–16,148
NYS Taxable Inc	58,021	62,686	61,136	70,881	180,953
NYS Tax Prefs	1,217	1,216	2,867	3,361	1,216
NYS Calculated Tax	3,875	4,208	4,097	4,792	12,634
NYS Supplemental Tx	0	0	0	0	259
NYS Net Tax	3,875	4,208	4,097	4,792	12,893
NYS Allocated Tax	3,875	4,208	4,097	4,792	12,893
NYC Income Tax	2,111	2,293	2,232	2,613	6,917
New York City Tax	2,111	2,293	2,232	2,613	6,917
New York State Tax	3,875	4,208	4,097	4,792	12,893
Tot State/Local Tx	5,986	6,501	6,329	7,405	19,810
Total Inc Tax	21,777	23,223	22,651	26,127	70,750

Financial Planning Associates
FINANCIAL SUMMARY

	1997	1998	1999	2000	2006
	Age: 37	38	39	40	46
Gross Real Income					
Personal Earnings	85,000	93,500	102,850	113,135	200,426
Dividends Rcvd	312	375	438	591	3,128
Rental Real Est	9,600	10,176	10,787	11,434	16,219
	94,912	104,051	114,074	125,160	219,773
Income & Inflation					
Gross Real Inc	94,912	104,051	114,074	125,160	219,773
Total Inc Tax	–21,776	–23,222	–22,650	–26,126	–70,750
Net Real Income	73,136	80,829	91,424	99,033	149,023
Cur Real Inc =	73,136	76,061	79,103	82,267	104,095
At Infltn Rate Of	4	4	4	4	4
Cash Flow					
Idle Cash On Hand	500	505	501	500	502
Norml Cash Inflow	103,587	104,051	114,074	125,089	217,303
Assets Sold	0	0	1,739	0	0
Norml Cash Outflw	102,974	95,019	115,814	107,409	152,545
Cash Invested	609	9,035	0	17,680	64,759
Cash Balance	505	501	500	500	501
Net Worth					
Personal Assets	243,733	265,728	289,894	316,442	540,820
Investment Assets	179,130	204,293	250,964	288,115	767,957
Personal Liabilities	–179,047	–177,314	–175,446	–173,433	–157,616
Investmt Liabilities	–92,377	–87,639	–102,609	–95,563	–72,546
Personal Net Worth	64,686	88,414	114,448	143,009	383,204
Investment Net Worth	86,753	116,654	148,355	192,552	695,411
Net Worth	151,439	205,068	262,801	335,560	1,078,614

CAPITAL NEEDS ANALYSIS

CAPITAL NEEDS ANALYSIS

In this section we describe your needs for capital in the event of your premature death or disability. At death, current life insurance proceeds are included in the computation of Cash Flow to provide for current expenses and set up investments for future cash needs of survivors and beneficiaries. In the case of disability the amount of annual payments provided by your disability income insurance will be included in the computation of Cash Flow and the analysis of possible need for additional capital.

If your capital needs are in excess of available income and liquid assets, the shortfall may be offset by increasing your life and/or disability income insurance coverages. The amount of risk you feel comfortable assuming yourself can reduce the additional insurance coverage you might otherwise need. Keep in mind that the analysis shown on the following page includes all of your current assets and the growth expectations we discussed during consultation.

The Cash Flow report in this section is designed to reflect your detailed cash needs for the next 10 years. The Capital Needs report is less detailed; it shows the overall capital you need compared with the income and investments available. Both reports provide important information for evaluating the consequences of losing your income and capital production through disability and/or death.

Financial Planning Associates
CAPITAL NEEDS ANALYSIS

CAPITAL NEEDS			
Funds Needed in Next 10 Years			
Mortgage Payments	144,737		
Household Costs	60,664		
Medical Expenses	26,413		
Food Clothing Transportation	112,857		
Other Living Expenses	67,955		
Nonliquid Assets Purchased	243,604		
Income Taxes Paid	395,290		
Other Needs	115,808		
Total Funds Needed		1,167,328	
Funds Available in Next 10 Years			
Personal Service Income	1,354,681		
Liquid Capital Int & Divs	46,957		
Other Investment Income	126,536		
Additional Taxable Income	700		
Total Funds Available		1,528,873	
Funds Available in Excess of Needs			361,545
INVESTMENT NEEDS			
Desired Capital Reserve		0	
Capital Reserve Available			
Investment Beg Balance	38,407		
Investment Growth	41,573		
Client's IRA Beg Balance	12,515		
Client's IRA Growth	36,887		
Total Investment Capital Available		129,382	
Excess Investment Capital Available			129,382
EXCESS FUNDS AVAILABLE			490,927

You have adequate sources of capital to meet your needs.

Appendix A

Preparing Financial Statements

David M. Cordell and Stephan R. Leimberg

The preparation of organized financial information is an important but often-ignored aspect of personal financial planning. Like businesses, individuals must often prepare financial information for external use. Banks and other lending institutions rarely make loans to individuals without first analyzing their current financial position and future ability to repay the loan. However, the primary use of financial information in personal financial planning is for internal purposes.

Financial analysis, planning, and control are important planning techniques, whether conducted by the individual alone or by the individual assisted by a professional. The focus of this appendix is on financial statements useful for such internal purposes. It is difficult, if not impossible, to identify financial objectives and formulate strategies for their achievement without knowing a client's current financial situation and resources. In addition, the ongoing analysis of personal financial information is crucial in monitoring whether financial objectives are being achieved.

Two primary pieces of client information used by planners are the current financial position (represented by the *financial position statement,* or *balance sheet*) and the cash-flow status (represented by the *cash-flow statement*). Before each is discussed in greater detail, a few general comments introduce this topic.

While it is common to see personal financial statements that have been prepared only at the end of a calendar or fiscal year, both the timing and frequency of financial statements often vary. When a lending institution needs personal financial information for loan purposes, it usually requires that the information be prepared as of the date of the loan application. Similarly, a financial planner needs financial information at the time the planning process begins and at the time of each subsequent review of a client's financial plan. If reviews take place every 6 months, it is necessary to update personal financial statements at these same intervals. In other words, personal financial statements are not prepared at arbitrary times, but rather when the information is needed for the financial planning process.

The financial position and cash-flow status relate to what has occurred in the past. For financial planning, it is necessary to prepare pro forma (or projected) balance sheets and cash-flow statements. These pro formas illustrate future financial statements if certain activities are implemented under specified assumptions. Finally actual financial statements can be compared with past projections to see if the client's financial plan was realized.

FINANCIAL POSITION STATEMENT

The financial position statement shows an individual's (or family's) wealth at a specified time. It reflects the results of the individual's past financial activities and contains three basic classifications: assets, liabilities, and net worth. These three categories make up the basic accounting equation:

ASSETS = LIABILITIES + NET WORTH

Financial planners can choose from many different formats for the financial position statement since there is no standard. Usually, statements group the items that make up assets and liabilities into subclassifications that better enable the planner to analyze the components of the client's total financial situation and to evaluate the mix of assets in relation to the client's objectives. Table A-1 shows John and Mary Sample's financial position in a typical format.

TABLE A-1
Financial Position Statement—John and Mary Sample

ASSETS		LIABILITIES AND NET WORTH	
Cash and Cash Equivalents		LIABILITIES	
Cash	$ 12,000	Credit card balances	$ 2,000
Money market fund	50,000	Consumer loans	4,000
Life insurance cash value	18,000	Automobile loans	12,000
	$ 80,000	Mortgage loans	220,000
		TOTAL LIABILITIES	$238,000
Other Financial Assets			
Stock	$150,000	NET WORTH	$692,000
Bonds, taxable	90,000		
Bonds, tax-exempt	80,000		
Vested pension and 401(k)	120,000		
	$440,000		
Personal Assets			
Residence	$300,000		
Automobiles	30,000		
Household furnishings, possessions, jewelry, art	80,000		
	$410,000		
TOTAL ASSETS	$930,000	TOTAL LIABILITIES AND NET WORTH	$930,000

Assets

Assets are items the client owns. It is immaterial whether the item was purchased for cash, financed by borrowing, or received as a gift or inheritance. Items that the client possesses but does not own, such as rented apartments or leased automobiles, are not shown as assets.

It is common practice for personal financial position statements to show assets at their current fair market values. These values may vary considerably from the original purchase prices. In contrast, business financial statements must list many assets on the basis of adjusted historical costs, net of depreciation.

At a minimum, assets should be subdivided into two categories: financial assets and personal (or nonfinancial) assets. Many statement formats include other categories such as use assets, nonuse assets, personal assets, investment assets, and retirement assets, among others. The financial position statement in table A-1 uses three major categories of assets by separating total assets into (1) cash and cash equivalents, (2) other financial assets, and (3) personal assets. Other financial assets are sometimes further subdivided, according to their relative liquidity, income characteristics, tax status, or growth characteristics.

Liabilities

Liabilities are the debts of the client. While the financial position statement in table A-1 does not separate liabilities into major subcategories, it is not unusual to see liabilities grouped by the time period in which they must be repaid. For example, the statement might show subtotals for short-term liabilities (due in one year or less), intermediate-term liabilities (due in one to 5 years), and long-term liabilities (due in more than 5 years).

In theory, the liabilities section of the financial position statement should show all liabilities as of the date of the statement—even if the client has not received a formal bill. This process may require the client to make estimates for such items as taxes due, utility charges owed, and credit-card obligations. In practice, clients and planners often ignore relatively small accruals for unaudited statements.

Net Worth

Net worth measures the client's wealth or equity at the date of the financial position statement. It is calculated by restating the basic accounting equation as follows:

NET WORTH = TOTAL ASSETS – TOTAL LIABILITIES

In other words, net worth is what remains if all the client's assets are sold at their fair market values and all debts are paid. If a client has a negative net worth, the client is considered to be bankrupt. However, such clients can avoid formal bankruptcy proceedings if cash flow is sufficient to service all financial obligations.

By itself, net worth reveals little about the nature of the assets or liabilities. A client with considerable net worth may have all his or her assets tied up in nonincome-producing assets, such as homes, automobiles, and other personal possessions. Conversely, a client with a modest net worth may hold most assets in the form of financial assets that may be generating income, capital appreciation, or both. Further, it is possible for a client to have a positive cash balance with a negative net worth or to have a zero cash balance with a very high net worth. The key to understanding net worth is to recognize that it is simply a residual—the difference between total assets and total liabilities.

A client's net worth may increase or decrease during a period of time. Other things being equal, a client's net worth will increase as a result of any one of the following:

- appreciation in the value of assets
- addition to assets through retaining income
- addition of assets through gifts or inheritances
- decrease in liabilities through forgiveness

The following are examples of actions that have no effect on net worth:

- paying off a debt. The cash account declines by the same amount that the liability declines, leaving the difference between total assets and total liabilities unchanged.
- buying an asset with cash. Total assets remain unchanged because cash declines by the same amount that the other asset category increases. However, commissions and other transaction costs cause net worth to decline because the cash that pays these costs is not reflected in the value of the purchased asset.

The Format of the Financial Position Statement

Obviously, any financial statement should be in a format that is understandable, and uniformity is desirable. However, the actual format is really secondary to the quality of the information. It should be noted that the format of a financial position statement (and a cash-flow statement) is often determined by the software system used by the financial planner for analyzing data and producing reports.

Financial position statements have traditionally been presented in two columns—one containing assets, the other containing liabilities and net worth. The term *balance sheet* is derived from the fact that these two sides must balance according to the accounting equation (total assets = total liabilities + net worth).

It is now more common in personal financial planning to present financial position statements in a single-column format. The major advantage of the single-column format is that it facilitates the preparation of pro forma financial position statements and the comparison of consecutive statements over time.

CASH-FLOW MANAGEMENT

Cash-flow management is one of the most basic tools in financial planning. Ironically, practitioners frequently find that clients resist the management process more than any other technique even though it is critical to reaching a goal. Communicating the importance of cash-flow management and talking the client through the process are among the practitioner's greatest services.

Although the well-heeled client sometimes considers cash-flow management as an activity for the less fortunate, the advantages cut across income levels. Cash-flow management is always beneficial and is especially useful when the client needs to accomplish any of the following objectives:

- measure periodic progress toward the achievement of specific goals (a) within a defined time frame and (b) within the confines of limited resources
- monitor especially complex elements of economic activity
- provide guidelines for evaluating the economic performance of elements constituting the client's cash flow
- communicate a planning strategy to those affected by the budget
- provide incentive (goals) for the performance of individuals involved
- control household expenses
- achieve desired wealth accumulation/savings goals, such as retirement or children's education
- monitor the performance of a specific investment, such as a securities portfolio, rental property, or a closely held business
- reposition assets to improve the likelihood of accomplishing goals

What Is Cash-Flow Management?

Cash-flow management is essentially a euphemism for the budget planning and control process. Financial planners adopted the change in terminology partly because cash-flow management is more inclusive than budgeting. More importantly, the word *budget* carries negative connotations for many clients, making them less likely to participate in the process.

Cash-flow management consists of three basic components: cash-flow analysis, cash-flow planning, and budgeting. In practice, many planners mix aspects of each of the three and consider them as a single process.

Cash-Flow Analysis

Cash-flow analysis, or revenue and expense analysis, is the process of gathering data concerning the client's cash-flow situation, presenting the data in an organized format (the cash-flow statement), and identifying strengths, weaknesses, and important patterns. Cash-flow analysis is the starting point for the client and the financial counseling team to develop objectives. It also reveals inefficient, ineffective, or unusual utilization of resources, highlights alternative courses of action, motivates the client, and makes family members aware of the need to conserve resources.

Cash-Flow Planning

Cash-flow planning involves identifying courses of action that will help optimize *net discretionary cash flow.* Net discretionary cash flow is defined as the difference between income and expenses. Positive cash flow is available for any use, whether for consumption, investment, or gifting. However, in most financial planning situations, the primary benefit of net discretionary cash flow is to provide a source of investable funds.

Note that the goal is to optimize rather than to maximize. Maximizing net discretionary cash flow means to make it as large as possible. Pursuit of this goal suggests increasing income in any way possible. Presumably this mandate includes working longer hours, finding a second job, or seeking employment for the non-earning spouse. On the expense side, maximization implies having a less expensive home and automobile, quitting the club, and discontinuing vacations and eating out. Clearly these approaches represent changes in lifestyle and standard of living, not to mention family relationships. In contrast, optimization means seeking the best, not necessarily the largest, net discretionary income.

Optimal net discretionary income implies a balance between investing for the future and maintaining and/or improving the current lifestyle. While the distinction between maximizing and optimizing may seem arcane, the difference is important not only in substance, but also in style. Optimization holds greater appeal to clients because it puts wealth accumulation in perspective. It also gives clients greater control since they ultimately decide their own funds allocation according to their own personal preferences.

Cash-flow planning is interwoven through almost all aspects of personal financial planning. At the extreme, each of the following is a factor or a tool in cash-flow planning:

- income tax planning
- investment planning
- insurance planning
- estate planning
- retirement planning

- employee benefits
- saving/investment vehicles

Some practitioners believe that cash-flow planning includes each of the six steps in financial planning (see chapter 1) in a sort of microcosm of the larger process. Some even view cash management as the framework within which other planning functions are employed.

The more common approach is simply to use cash-flow planning as an extension of cash-flow analysis in an iterative process that involves other planning areas. For example cash-flow analysis reveals opportunities for increasing net discretionary income by addressing income and expense factors. Cash-flow planning then considers what to do with the increase in discretionary net income. The result may include an insurance or investment alternative that represents a financial commitment. Typically, the commitment raises expenses, thus lowering net discretionary income calculated in the cash-flow analysis. Based on this new level, the client may consider another alternative for the remaining net discretionary income.

Budgeting

Budgeting is the process of creating and following an explicit plan for spending and investing the resources available to the client. In simplest terms, the process works via the establishment of a working budget model followed by a comparison of actual and expected results. By constantly monitoring the budget, the practitioner and client can recognize problems as they occur and even anticipate problems. Budgeting provides both a means of financial self-evaluation and a guideline to measure actual performance.

Budgeting does have some disadvantages, however. For example, many individuals have a psychological aversion to the record keeping required and may not maintain sufficient information for the budget to be useful. Obviously, to the extent the data utilized are inaccurate, the conclusions drawn from the budget may be misleading. For some clients a rote dependence on budgeting numbers inhibits creativity, stifles risk taking, and encourages mechanical thinking. Such clients may forfeit investment opportunities or fail to minimize losses.

Here are some guidelines for establishing a budget:

- Make the budget flexible enough to deal with emergencies, unexpected opportunities, or other unforeseen circumstances.
- Keep the budget period long enough to utilize an investment strategy and a workable series of investment procedures—typically one calendar year.
- Make the budget simple and brief.
- Follow the form and content of the budget consistently.

- Eliminate extraneous information.
- Estimate especially with insignificant items.
- Tailor the budget to specific goals and objectives.
- Remember that a budget is also a guideline against which actual results are to be measured. Unexpected results should be analyzed: they may be the norm and deserve to be incorporated in a revised budget.
- Pinpoint, in advance, variables that may influence the amounts of income and expenditures. Income items include expected annual raises and increases or decreases in interest or dividend rates. Expenditures include costs, changing tastes or preferences, or changes in family circumstances.

Creating the Cash-Flow Statement and Budget

Budgeting requires looking to the future, but for most clients the best place to start is the past. The basic sources of budget information are personal financial statements, prior years' tax returns, canceled checks, and projections of income and expenditures for the target period. Once initial estimates have been made, they must be adjusted in light of special circumstances or considerations. Usually, practitioners use a cash-flow worksheet in assembling the data and input the data in a computer program to create the cash-flow statement.

A family budget should project income and expenditures for any planning period that is convenient or appropriate for a specific purpose. Most planners budget for 12 months at a time, usually coinciding with a calendar year. Generally, the budget is calculated on a month-by-month basis since some cash flows occur only in specific months.

It is often appropriate to budget for longer periods of time, such as a 4-year period of college education. However, for long-range budgeting, keep in mind that the budget's accuracy decreases as the length of the period covered increases.

Constructing a cash-flow statement or a cash budget is largely a mechanical process involving very specific steps. Although some clients present unusual situations, the majority fit into the following framework.

STEP 1—Estimate the Family's Annual Income

Identify fixed amounts of income expected from each of the following:

- salary
- bonus
- self-employment
- real estate
- dividends—close corporations
- dividends—publicly traded corporations

- interest—savings accounts
- interest—taxable bonds
- interest—tax-free bonds
- trust income
- other fixed-payment income
- variable sources of income

The client's income can be affected by salary increases, bonuses, dividend or interest-rate changes, proceeds from the sale of stocks or other assets, inheritances, and many other events.

If a family experiences an irregular income flow or extreme variations of income, two income estimates should be developed. One estimate should be based on the lowest amount of income that might be received, while the other should be based on a higher but still reasonable estimated figure.

STEP 2—Develop Estimates for Both Fixed and Discretionary Expenses

Annual expenditures can be classified as either fixed or discretionary. However, "fixed" applies only in the short run and can often be changed without imposing a radical shift in the client's lifestyle. Even the most fixed of all expenditures, housing, can be changed if necessary.

Discretionary expenditures, by definition, can be prevented or timed through proper budgeting so that sufficient income is available.

Canceled checks and charge account receipts serve as a good basis for developing the following expenditure estimates:

- fixed expenses
  –housing (mortgage or rental payments)
  –utilities
  –food, groceries, etc.
  –clothing and cleaning
  –income taxes
  –social security
  –property taxes
  –transportation
  –medical and dental
  –debt repayments
  –household supplies and maintenance
  –life and disability insurance
  –property and liability insurance
  –current school expenses
- discretionary expenses
  –vacations, travel, etc.
  –gifts and contributions

–household furnishings
–education fund
–savings
–investments
–other

Note that a client's expenditures can vary as a result of increased costs of living, unexpected business expenses, financial catastrophes (such as uninsured theft or fire losses), changes in tastes or preferences, and large-scale expenses (such as college or retirement).

STEP 3—Determine the Excess or Shortfall of Income within the Budget Period

Subtracting total expenses from total income reveals the client's net cash flow. Discretionary expenses already include listings for savings, investments, and an education fund. If projected net cash flow is positive, the client can allocate even more to these categories (although most clients are more adept at finding ways to spend the money).

Individuals, like businesses, commonly project some months with positive net income and others with negative. In practice, cash or cash-equivalent balances simply grow in positive months and shrink in negative months.

STEP 4—Consider Available Methods of Increasing Income or Decreasing Expenses

If net cash flow is negative, either income must increase or expenses must decrease. This is bad news for the client, but it is better to recognize the situation early.

Clients should be realistic in identifying categories for revision—blind optimism is counterproductive. Practitioners should encourage clients to avoid lowering the savings, investment, and education-planning figures, unless there is no alternative.

STEP 5—Calculate Income and Expenses as a Percentage of the Total to Determine a Better Allocation of Resources

Many clients benefit from a comparison of their spending patterns to those of the general population. However, practitioners must recognize that the ratios can vary dramatically according to age, income, family structure, geography, and other factors.

As noted earlier, an organized cash-flow planning approach is useful in evaluating the potential of major adjustments in cash flows and portfolio characteristics.

Other Considerations

Families who experience difficulty in predicting income or who have highly variable cash outflows should consider two budgets—one based on the lowest income and highest expenditures expected (worst-case budget), and the second based on the client's reasonable expectations of income and expenses (average-case budget).

In some cases it also makes sense to prepare a budget based on the highest possible income and lowest possible expenditures (best-case budget). This third alternative budget is often used to ascertain whether the cost of a "hoped for" expenditure, such as a new car, is within reach if everything falls into place.

Another conservative approach is to base the budget on only fixed and certain income. Limiting expenditures to this conservative estimate ensures that fixed and expected costs will be covered. Any excess income can then be used for investment or discretionary spending, or placed in a *contingency fund.*

Budgeting should allocate cash reserves for such contingencies as (a) liquidity needs, (b) emergencies, (c) scheduled expenditures, and (d) investment opportunities. These cash reserves should be invested according to the speed at which they will be needed. In other words, funds should be placed in investments suitable for the needs to be satisfied.

Short-term reserves to meet liquidity needs—day-to-day transactions—should be placed in an interest-bearing checking account. Clients should maintain balances that are large enough to qualify for payment of interest and, if available, waiver-of-service fees. However, they should not allow excessive amounts to accumulate in the checking account since the interest rate is very low. The optimal size depends on numerous factors, such as monthly cash flow, timing of receipts and payments, and the client's comfort level. Practitioners often advise retaining intermediate reserves equal to 3 to 6 months of expenses in a money market account as an emergency fund. Some families, rather than building emergency funds, have lines of credit through various banks or credit cards. This enables them to invest any excess income, or use it to increase their standard of living. There are two drawbacks to using this technique. First, the interest charged on credit-card borrowing is usually high. Second, the client must have sufficient income to repay the loan. If the emergency is a lost job, for example, payment becomes problematic.

Sample Pro Forma Cash-Flow Statement

Table A-2 is an illustration of the Sample family's budget, or pro forma cash-flow statement, reflecting $5,800 excess of income over expenditures for the year. With this estimate of the year's expected financial results available early in the year, the Sample family can then plan its investment or spending of the projected excess.

However, as the illustration in table A-3 indicates, if Mr. Sample does not receive his expected bonus of $15,000, the family will experience a budgeted shortfall of $4,500. This is so even after projected reductions in income taxes of $4,500 (from $28,000 to $23,500) and in medicare taxes of $200 (from $7,700 to $7,500) as a result of not receiving the bonus. On this basis, the Sample family must modify its spending and investing plans for the year. This example illustrates the importance of preparing budgets that reflect conservative as well as optimistic results.

TABLE A-2
Pro Forma Cash-Flow Statement—John and Mary Sample (With Bonus)

Annual Income	Amount	% of Total Income
Salary/Bonus—John	$125,000	74.4%
Salary/Bonus—Mary	30,000	17.9
Self-Employment (Business)	0	0.0
Dividends—Close Corporation Stock	0	0.0
Dividends—Investments	3,000	1.8
Interest on Savings Accounts	2,000	1.2
Interest on Bonds, Taxable	5,000	3.0
Interest on Bonds, Exempt	3,000	1.8
Trust Income	0	0.0
Rental Income	0	0.0
Other	0	0.0
Total Annual Income	$ 168,000	100.1%*
Fixed Expenses		
Housing (Mortgage/Rent)	$ 15,500	9.2%
Utilities & Telephone	7,000	4.2
Food, Groceries, Etc.	10,500	6.3
Clothing and Cleaning	7,000	4.2
Income Taxes	28,000	16.7
Social Security and Medicare Taxes	7,700	4.6
Real Estate Taxes	5,000	3.0
Transportation	8,000	4.8
Medical/Dental Expenses	8,000	4.8
Debt Repayment	5,000	3.0
Housing Supplies/Maint.	6,000	3.6
Life Insurance	8,000	4.8
Prop. & Liability Ins.	5,000	3.0
Current School Exp.	4,500	2.7
Total Fixed Expenses	$ 125,200	74.9%
Variable Expenses		
Vacations, Travel, Etc.	$ 4,000	2.4%
Recreation/Entertainment	5,000	3.0
Contributions, Gifts	7,500	4.5
Household Furnishings	5,000	3.0
Education Fund	5,000	3.0
Savings	3,000	1.8
Investment	2,500	1.5
Other	5,000	3.0
Total Variable Expenses	$ 37,000	22.2%
Total Expenses	$ 162,200	97.1%
Net Cash Flow	$ 5,800	3.0%

*Discrepancies in totals are due to rounding.

Adapted with permission from *Financial Planning* TOOLKIT, Financial Data Center (610-527-5216).

TABLE A-3
Pro Forma Cash-Flow Statement—John and Mary Sample (No Bonus)

Annual Income	Amount	% of Total Income
Salary/Bonus—John	$110,000	71.9%
Salary/Bonus—Mary	30,000	19.6
Self-Employment (Business)	0	0.0
Dividends—Close Corporation Stock	0	0.0
Dividends—Investments	3,000	2.0
Interest on Savings Accounts	2,000	1.3
Interest on Bonds, Taxable	5,000	3.3
Interest on Bonds, Exempt	3,000	2.0
Trust Income	0	0.0
Rental Income	0	0.0
Other	0	0.0
Total Annual Income	$153,000	100.1%
Fixed Expenses		
Housing (Mortgage/Rent)	$ 15,500	10.1%
Utilities & Telephone	7,000	4.6
Food, Groceries, Etc.	10,500	6.9
Clothing and Cleaning	7,000	4.6
Income Taxes	23,500	15.4
Social Security and Medicare Taxes	7,500	4.9
Real Estate Taxes	5,000	3.3
Transportation	8,000	5.2
Medical/Dental Expenses	8,000	5.2
Debt Repayment	5,000	3.3
Housing Supplies/Maint.	6,000	3.9
Life Insurance	8,000	5.2
Prop. & Liability Ins.	5,000	3.3
Current School Exp.	4,500	2.9
Total Fixed Expenses	$120,500	78.8%
Variable Expenses		
Vacations, Travel, Etc.	$ 4,000	2.6%
Recreation/Entertainment	5,000	3.3
Contributions, Gifts	7,500	4.9
Household Furnishings	5,000	3.3
Education Fund	5,000	3.3
Savings	3,000	2.0
Investments	2,500	1.6
Other	5,000	3.3
Total Variable Expenses	$ 37,000	24.3%
Total Expenses	$ 157,500	103.1%
Net Cash Flow	$ –4,500	–3.0%

Adapted with permission from *Financial Planning* TOOLKIT, Financial Data Center (610-527-5216).

APPENDIX B

Time Value of Money Tables

Appendix B
Time Value of Money Tables

TABLE B.1
FUTURE VALUE OF A SINGLE SUM FACTORS
FVSS Factor = $(1 + i)^n$ where i = rate and n = periods

i =	0.5%	1%	1.5%	2%	2.5%	3%	3.5%	4%	4.5%	5%
n = 1	1.0050	1.0100	1.0150	1.0200	1.0250	1.0300	1.0350	1.0400	1.0450	1.0500
2	1.0100	1.0201	1.0302	1.0404	1.0506	1.0609	1.0712	1.0816	1.0920	1.1025
3	1.0151	1.0303	1.0457	1.0612	1.0769	1.0927	1.1087	1.1249	1.1412	1.1576
4	1.0202	1.0406	1.0614	1.0824	1.1038	1.1255	1.1475	1.1699	1.1925	1.2155
5	1.0253	1.0510	1.0773	1.1041	1.1314	1.1593	1.1877	1.2167	1.2462	1.2763
6	1.0304	1.0615	1.0934	1.1262	1.1597	1.1941	1.2293	1.2653	1.3023	1.3401
7	1.0355	1.0721	1.1098	1.1487	1.1887	1.2299	1.2723	1.3159	1.3609	1.4071
8	1.0407	1.0829	1.1265	1.1717	1.2184	1.2668	1.3168	1.3686	1.4221	1.4775
9	1.0459	1.0937	1.1434	1.1951	1.2489	1.3048	1.3629	1.4233	1.4861	1.5513
10	1.0511	1.1046	1.1605	1.2190	1.2801	1.3439	1.4106	1.4802	1.5530	1.6289
11	1.0564	1.1157	1.1779	1.2434	1.3121	1.3842	1.4600	1.5395	1.6229	1.7103
12	1.0617	1.1268	1.1956	1.2682	1.3449	1.4258	1.5111	1.6010	1.6959	1.7959
13	1.0670	1.1381	1.2136	1.2936	1.3785	1.4685	1.5640	1.6651	1.7722	1.8856
14	1.0723	1.1495	1.2318	1.3195	1.4130	1.5126	1.6187	1.7317	1.8519	1.9799
15	1.0777	1.1610	1.2502	1.3459	1.4483	1.5580	1.6753	1.8009	1.9353	2.0789
16	1.0831	1.1726	1.2690	1.3728	1.4845	1.6047	1.7340	1.8730	2.0224	2.1829
17	1.0885	1.1843	1.2880	1.4002	1.5216	1.6528	1.7947	1.9479	2.1134	2.2920
18	1.0939	1.1961	1.3073	1.4282	1.5597	1.7024	1.8575	2.0258	2.2085	2.4066
19	1.0994	1.2081	1.3270	1.4568	1.5987	1.7535	1.9225	2.1068	2.3079	2.5270
20	1.1049	1.2202	1.3469	1.4859	1.6386	1.8061	1.9898	2.1911	2.4117	2.6533
21	1.1104	1.2324	1.3671	1.5157	1.6796	1.8603	2.0594	2.2788	2.5202	2.7860
22	1.1160	1.2447	1.3876	1.5460	1.7216	1.9161	2.1315	2.3699	2.6337	2.9253
23	1.1216	1.2572	1.4084	1.5769	1.7646	1.9736	2.2061	2.4647	2.7522	3.0715
24	1.1272	1.2697	1.4295	1.6084	1.8087	2.0328	2.2833	2.5633	2.8760	3.2251
25	1.1328	1.2824	1.4509	1.6406	1.8539	2.0938	2.3632	2.6658	3.0054	3.3864
26	1.1385	1.2953	1.4727	1.6734	1.9003	2.1566	2.4460	2.7725	3.1407	3.5557
27	1.1442	1.3082	1.4948	1.7069	1.9478	2.2213	2.5316	2.8834	3.2820	3.7335
28	1.1499	1.3213	1.5172	1.7410	1.9965	2.2879	2.6202	2.9987	3.4297	3.9201
29	1.1556	1.3345	1.5400	1.7758	2.0464	2.3566	2.7119	3.1187	3.5840	4.1161
30	1.1614	1.3478	1.5631	1.8114	2.0976	2.4273	2.8068	3.2434	3.7453	4.3219
35	1.1907	1.4166	1.6839	1.9999	2.3732	2.8139	3.3336	3.9461	4.6673	5.5160
40	1.2208	1.4889	1.8140	2.2080	2.6851	3.2620	3.9593	4.8010	5.8164	7.0400
45	1.2516	1.5648	1.9542	2.4379	3.0379	3.7816	4.7024	5.8412	7.2482	8.9850
50	1.2832	1.6446	2.1052	2.6916	3.4371	4.3839	5.5849	7.1067	9.0326	11.4674

TABLE B.1 (CONTINUED)
FUTURE VALUE OF A SINGLE SUM FACTORS
FVSS Factor = $(1 + i)^n$ where i = rate and n = periods

i =	5.5%	6%	6.5%	7%	7.5%	8%	8.5%	9%	9.5%	10%
n = 1	1.0550	1.0600	1.0650	1.0700	1.0750	1.0800	1.0850	1.0900	1.0950	1.1000
2	1.1130	1.1236	1.1342	1.1449	1.1556	1.1664	1.1772	1.1881	1.1990	1.2100
3	1.1742	1.1910	1.2079	1.2250	1.2423	1.2597	1.2773	1.2950	1.3129	1.3310
4	1.2388	1.2625	1.2865	1.3108	1.3355	1.3605	1.3859	1.4116	1.4377	1.4641
5	1.3070	1.3382	1.3701	1.4026	1.4356	1.4693	1.5037	1.5386	1.5742	1.6105
6	1.3788	1.4185	1.4591	1.5007	1.5433	1.5869	1.6315	1.6771	1.7238	1.7716
7	1.4547	1.5036	1.5540	1.6058	1.6590	1.7138	1.7701	1.8280	1.8876	1.9487
8	1.5347	1.5938	1.6550	1.7182	1.7835	1.8509	1.9206	1.9926	2.0669	2.1436
9	1.6191	1.6895	1.7626	1.8385	1.9172	1.9990	2.0839	2.1719	2.2632	2.3579
10	1.7081	1.7908	1.8771	1.9672	2.0610	2.1589	2.2610	2.3674	2.4782	2.5937
11	1.8021	1.8983	1.9992	2.1049	2.2156	2.3316	2.4532	2.5804	2.7137	2.8531
12	1.9012	2.0122	2.1291	2.2522	2.3818	2.5182	2.6617	2.8127	2.9715	3.1384
13	2.0058	2.1329	2.2675	2.4098	2.5604	2.7196	2.8879	3.0658	3.2537	3.4523
14	2.1161	2.2609	2.4149	2.5785	2.7524	2.9372	3.1334	3.3417	3.5629	3.7975
15	2.2325	2.3966	2.5718	2.7590	2.9589	3.1722	3.3997	3.6425	3.9013	4.1772
16	2.3553	2.5404	2.7390	2.9522	3.1808	3.4259	3.6887	3.9703	4.2719	4.5950
17	2.4848	2.6928	2.9170	3.1588	3.4194	3.7000	4.0023	4.3276	4.6778	5.0545
18	2.6215	2.8543	3.1067	3.3799	3.6758	3.9960	4.3425	4.7171	5.1222	5.5599
19	2.7656	3.0256	3.3086	3.6165	3.9515	4.3157	4.7116	5.1417	5.6088	6.1159
20	2.9178	3.2071	3.5236	3.8697	4.2479	4.6610	5.1120	5.6044	6.1416	6.7275
21	3.0782	3.3996	3.7527	4.1406	4.5664	5.0338	5.5466	6.1088	6.7251	7.4002
22	3.2475	3.6035	3.9966	4.4304	4.9089	5.4365	6.0180	6.6586	7.3639	8.1403
23	3.4262	3.8197	4.2564	4.7405	5.2771	5.8715	6.5296	7.2579	8.0635	8.9543
24	3.6146	4.0489	4.5331	5.0724	5.6729	6.3412	7.0846	7.9111	8.8296	9.8497
25	3.8134	4.2919	4.8277	5.4274	6.0983	6.8485	7.6868	8.6231	9.6684	10.8347
26	4.0231	4.5494	5.1415	5.8074	6.5557	7.3964	8.3401	9.3992	10.5869	11.9182
27	4.2444	4.8223	5.4757	6.2139	7.0474	7.9881	9.0490	10.2451	11.5926	13.1100
28	4.4778	5.1117	5.8316	6.6488	7.5759	8.6271	9.8182	11.1671	12.6939	14.4210
29	4.7241	5.4184	6.2107	7.1143	8.1441	9.3173	10.6528	12.1722	13.8998	15.8631
30	4.9840	5.7435	6.6144	7.6123	8.7550	10.0627	11.5583	13.2677	15.2203	17.4494
35	6.5138	7.6861	9.0623	10.6766	12.5689	14.7853	17.3796	20.4140	23.9604	28.1024
40	8.5133	10.2857	12.4161	14.9745	18.0442	21.7245	26.1330	31.4094	37.7194	45.2593
45	11.1266	13.7646	17.0111	21.0025	25.9048	31.9204	39.2951	48.3273	59.3793	72.8905
50	14.5420	18.4202	23.3067	29.4570	37.1897	46.9016	59.0863	74.3575	93.4773	117.391

TABLE B.1 (CONTINUED)
FUTURE VALUE OF A SINGLE SUM FACTORS
FVSS Factor = $(1 + i)^n$ where i = rate and n = periods

i =	10.5%	11%	11.5%	12%	12.5%	13%	13.5%	14%	14.5%	15%
n = 1	1.1050	1.1100	1.1150	1.1200	1.1250	1.1300	1.1350	1.1400	1.1450	1.1500
2	1.2210	1.2321	1.2432	1.2544	1.2656	1.2769	1.2882	1.2996	1.3110	1.3225
3	1.3492	1.3676	1.3862	1.4049	1.4238	1.4429	1.4621	1.4815	1.5011	1.5209
4	1.4909	1.5181	1.5456	1.5735	1.6018	1.6305	1.6595	1.6890	1.7188	1.7490
5	1.6474	1.6851	1.7234	1.7623	1.8020	1.8424	1.8836	1.9254	1.9680	2.0114
6	1.8204	1.8704	1.9215	1.9738	2.0273	2.0820	2.1378	2.1950	2.2534	2.3131
7	2.0116	2.0762	2.1425	2.2107	2.2807	2.3526	2.4264	2.5023	2.5801	2.6600
8	2.2228	2.3045	2.3889	2.4760	2.5658	2.6584	2.7540	2.8526	2.9542	3.0590
9	2.4562	2.5580	2.6636	2.7731	2.8865	3.0040	3.1258	3.2519	3.3826	3.5179
10	2.7141	2.8394	2.9699	3.1058	3.2473	3.3946	3.5478	3.7072	3.8731	4.0456
11	2.9991	3.1518	3.3115	3.4785	3.6532	3.8359	4.0267	4.2262	4.4347	4.6524
12	3.3140	3.4985	3.6923	3.8960	4.1099	4.3345	4.5704	4.8179	5.0777	5.3503
13	3.6619	3.8833	4.1169	4.3635	4.6236	4.8980	5.1874	5.4924	5.8140	6.1528
14	4.0464	4.3104	4.5904	4.8871	5.2016	5.5348	5.8877	6.2613	6.6570	7.0757
15	4.4713	4.7846	5.1183	5.4736	5.8518	6.2543	6.6825	7.1379	7.6222	8.1371
16	4.9408	5.3109	5.7069	6.1304	6.5833	7.0673	7.5846	8.1372	8.7275	9.3576
17	5.4596	5.8951	6.3632	6.8660	7.4062	7.9861	8.6085	9.2765	9.9929	10.7613
18	6.0328	6.5436	7.0949	7.6900	8.3319	9.0243	9.7707	10.5752	11.4419	12.3755
19	6.6663	7.2633	7.9108	8.6128	9.3734	10.1974	11.0897	12.0557	13.1010	14.2318
20	7.3662	8.0623	8.8206	9.6463	10.5451	11.5231	12.5869	13.7435	15.0006	16.3665
21	8.1397	8.9492	9.8350	10.8038	11.8632	13.0211	14.2861	15.6676	17.1757	18.8215
22	8.9944	9.9336	10.9660	12.1003	13.3461	14.7138	16.2147	17.8610	19.6662	21.6447
23	9.9388	11.0263	12.2271	13.5523	15.0144	16.6266	18.4037	20.3616	22.5178	24.8915
24	10.9823	12.2392	13.6332	15.1786	16.8912	18.7881	20.8882	23.2122	25.7829	28.6252
25	12.1355	13.5855	15.2010	17.0001	19.0026	21.2305	23.7081	26.4619	29.5214	32.9190
26	13.4097	15.0799	16.9491	19.0401	21.3779	23.9905	26.9087	30.1666	33.8020	37.8568
27	14.8177	16.7386	18.8982	21.3249	24.0502	27.1093	30.5414	34.3899	38.7033	43.5353
28	16.3736	18.5799	21.0715	23.8839	27.0564	30.6335	34.6644	39.2045	44.3153	50.0656
29	18.0928	20.6237	23.4948	26.7499	30.4385	34.6158	39.3441	44.6931	50.7410	57.5755
30	19.9926	22.8923	26.1967	29.9599	34.2433	39.1159	44.6556	50.9502	58.0985	66.2118
35	32.9367	38.5749	45.1461	52.7996	61.7075	72.0685	84.1115	98.1002	114.338	133.176
40	54.2614	65.0009	77.8027	93.0510	111.199	132.782	158.429	188.884	225.019	267.864
45	89.3928	109.530	134.082	163.988	200.384	244.641	298.410	363.679	442.840	538.769
50	147.270	184.565	231.070	289.002	361.099	450.736	562.073	700.233	871.514	1083.66

TABLE B.1 (CONTINUED)
FUTURE VALUE OF A SINGLE SUM FACTORS
FVSS Factor = $(1 + i)^n$ where i = rate and n = periods

i =	16%	17%	18%	19%	20%	22%	24%	26%	28%	30%
n = 1	1.1600	1.1700	1.1800	1.1900	1.2000	1.2200	1.2400	1.2600	1.2800	1.3000
2	1.3456	1.3689	1.3924	1.4161	1.4400	1.4884	1.5376	1.5876	1.6384	1.6900
3	1.5609	1.6016	1.6430	1.6852	1.7280	1.8158	1.9066	2.0004	2.0972	2.1970
4	1.8106	1.8739	1.9388	2.0053	2.0736	2.2153	2.3642	2.5205	2.6844	2.8561
5	2.1003	2.1924	2.2878	2.3864	2.4883	2.7027	2.9316	3.1758	3.4360	3.7129
6	2.4364	2.5652	2.6996	2.8398	2.9860	3.2973	3.6352	4.0015	4.3980	4.8268
7	2.8262	3.0012	3.1855	3.3793	3.5832	4.0227	4.5077	5.0419	5.6295	6.2749
8	3.2784	3.5115	3.7589	4.0214	4.2998	4.9077	5.5895	6.3528	7.2058	8.1573
9	3.8030	4.1084	4.4355	4.7854	5.1598	5.9874	6.9310	8.0045	9.2234	10.6045
10	4.4114	4.8068	5.2338	5.6947	6.1917	7.3046	8.5944	10.0857	11.8059	13.7858
11	5.1173	5.6240	6.1759	6.7767	7.4301	8.9117	10.6571	12.7080	15.1116	17.9216
12	5.9360	6.5801	7.2876	8.0642	8.9161	10.8722	13.2148	16.0120	19.3428	23.2981
13	6.8858	7.6987	8.5994	9.5964	10.6993	13.2641	16.3863	20.1752	24.7588	30.2875
14	7.9875	9.0075	10.1472	11.4198	12.8392	16.1822	20.3191	25.4207	31.6913	39.3738
15	9.2655	10.5387	11.9737	13.5895	15.4070	19.7423	25.1956	32.0301	40.5648	51.1859
16	10.7480	12.3303	14.1290	16.1715	18.4884	24.0856	31.2426	40.3579	51.9230	66.5417
17	12.4677	14.4265	16.6722	19.2441	22.1861	29.3844	38.7408	50.8510	66.4614	86.5042
18	14.4625	16.8790	19.6733	22.9005	26.6233	35.8490	48.0386	64.0722	85.0706	112.455
19	16.7765	19.7484	23.2144	27.2516	31.9480	43.7358	59.5679	80.7310	108.890	146.192
20	19.4608	23.1056	27.3930	32.4294	38.3376	53.3576	73.8641	101.721	139.380	190.050
21	22.5745	27.0336	32.3238	38.5910	46.0051	65.0963	91.5915	128.169	178.406	247.065
22	26.1864	31.6293	38.1421	45.9233	55.2061	79.4175	113.574	161.492	228.360	321.184
23	30.3762	37.0062	45.0076	54.6487	66.2474	96.8894	140.831	203.480	292.300	417.539
24	35.2364	43.2973	53.1090	65.0320	79.4968	118.205	174.631	256.385	374.144	542.801
25	40.8742	50.6578	62.6686	77.3881	95.3962	144.210	216.542	323.045	478.905	705.641
26	47.4141	59.2697	73.9490	92.0918	114.475	175.936	268.512	407.037	612.998	917.333
27	55.0004	69.3455	87.2598	109.589	137.371	214.642	332.955	512.867	784.638	1192.53
28	63.8004	81.1342	102.967	130.411	164.845	261.864	412.864	646.212	1004.34	1550.29
29	74.0085	94.9271	121.501	155.189	197.814	319.474	511.952	814.228	1285.55	2015.38
30	85.8499	111.065	143.371	184.675	237.376	389.758	634.820	1025.93	1645.50	2620.00
35	180.314	243.503	327.997	440.701	590.668	1053.40	1861.05	3258.14	5653.91	9727.86
40	378.721	533.869	750.378	1051.67	1469.77	2847.04	5455.91	10347.2	19426.7	36118.9
45	795.444	1170.48	1716.68	2509.65	3657.26	7694.71	15994.7	32860.5	66749.6	134106.8
50	1670.70	2566.22	3927.36	5988.91	9100.44	20796.6	46890.4	104358.4	229349.9	497929.2

TABLE B.2
PRESENT VALUE OF A SINGLE SUM FACTORS
PVSS FACTOR = $1/(1+i)^n$ where i = rate and n = periods

i =	0.5%	1%	1.5%	2%	2.5%	3%	3.5%	4%	4.5%	5%
n = 1	0.9950	0.9901	0.9852	0.9804	0.9756	0.9709	0.9662	0.9615	0.9569	0.9524
2	0.9901	0.9803	0.9707	0.9612	0.9518	0.9426	0.9335	0.9246	0.9157	0.9070
3	0.9851	0.9706	0.9563	0.9423	0.9286	0.9151	0.9019	0.8890	0.8763	0.8638
4	0.9802	0.9610	0.9422	0.9238	0.9060	0.8885	0.8714	0.8548	0.8386	0.8227
5	0.9754	0.9515	0.9283	0.9057	0.8839	0.8626	0.8420	0.8219	0.8025	0.7835
6	0.9705	0.9420	0.9145	0.8880	0.8623	0.8375	0.8135	0.7903	0.7679	0.7462
7	0.9657	0.9327	0.9010	0.8706	0.8413	0.8131	0.7860	0.7599	0.7348	0.7107
8	0.9609	0.9235	0.8877	0.8535	0.8207	0.7894	0.7594	0.7307	0.7032	0.6768
9	0.9561	0.9143	0.8746	0.8368	0.8007	0.7664	0.7337	0.7026	0.6729	0.6446
10	0.9513	0.9053	0.8617	0.8203	0.7812	0.7441	0.7089	0.6756	0.6439	0.6139
11	0.9466	0.8963	0.8489	0.8043	0.7621	0.7224	0.6849	0.6496	0.6162	0.5847
12	0.9419	0.8874	0.8364	0.7885	0.7436	0.7014	0.6618	0.6246	0.5897	0.5568
13	0.9372	0.8787	0.8240	0.7730	0.7254	0.6810	0.6394	0.6006	0.5643	0.5303
14	0.9326	0.8700	0.8118	0.7579	0.7077	0.6611	0.6178	0.5775	0.5400	0.5051
15	0.9279	0.8613	0.7999	0.7430	0.6905	0.6419	0.5969	0.5553	0.5167	0.4810
16	0.9233	0.8528	0.7880	0.7284	0.6736	0.6232	0.5767	0.5339	0.4945	0.4581
17	0.9187	0.8444	0.7764	0.7142	0.6572	0.6050	0.5572	0.5134	0.4732	0.4363
18	0.9141	0.8360	0.7649	0.7002	0.6412	0.5874	0.5384	0.4936	0.4528	0.4155
19	0.9096	0.8277	0.7536	0.6864	0.6255	0.5703	0.5202	0.4746	0.4333	0.3957
20	0.9051	0.8195	0.7425	0.6730	0.6103	0.5537	0.5026	0.4564	0.4146	0.3769
21	0.9006	0.8114	0.7315	0.6598	0.5954	0.5375	0.4856	0.4388	0.3968	0.3589
22	0.8961	0.8034	0.7207	0.6468	0.5809	0.5219	0.4692	0.4220	0.3797	0.3418
23	0.8916	0.7954	0.7100	0.6342	0.5667	0.5067	0.4533	0.4057	0.3634	0.3256
24	0.8872	0.7876	0.6995	0.6217	0.5529	0.4919	0.4380	0.3901	0.3477	0.3101
25	0.8828	0.7798	0.6892	0.6095	0.5394	0.4776	0.4231	0.3751	0.3327	0.2953
26	0.8784	0.7720	0.6790	0.5976	0.5262	0.4637	0.4088	0.3607	0.3184	0.2812
27	0.8740	0.7644	0.6690	0.5859	0.5134	0.4502	0.3950	0.3468	0.3047	0.2678
28	0.8697	0.7568	0.6591	0.5744	0.5009	0.4371	0.3817	0.3335	0.2916	0.2551
29	0.8653	0.7493	0.6494	0.5631	0.4887	0.4243	0.3687	0.3207	0.2790	0.2429
30	0.8610	0.7419	0.6398	0.5521	0.4767	0.4120	0.3563	0.3083	0.2670	0.2314
35	0.8398	0.7059	0.5939	0.5000	0.4214	0.3554	0.3000	0.2534	0.2143	0.1813
40	0.8191	0.6717	0.5513	0.4529	0.3724	0.3066	0.2526	0.2083	0.1719	0.1420
45	0.7990	0.6391	0.5117	0.4102	0.3292	0.2644	0.2127	0.1712	0.1380	0.1113
50	0.7793	0.6080	0.4750	0.3715	0.2909	0.2281	0.1791	0.1407	0.1107	0.0872

TABLE B.2 (CONTINUED)
PRESENT VALUE OF A SINGLE SUM FACTORS
PVSS FACTOR = $1/(1 + i)^n$ where i = rate and n = periods

i =	5.5%	6%	6.5%	7%	7.5%	8%	8.5%	9%	9.5%	10%
n = 1	0.9479	0.9434	0.9390	0.9346	0.9302	0.9259	0.9217	0.9174	0.9132	0.9091
2	0.8985	0.8900	0.8817	0.8734	0.8653	0.8573	0.8495	0.8417	0.8340	0.8264
3	0.8516	0.8396	0.8278	0.8163	0.8050	0.7938	0.7829	0.7722	0.7617	0.7513
4	0.8072	0.7921	0.7773	0.7629	0.7488	0.7350	0.7216	0.7084	0.6956	0.6830
5	0.7651	0.7473	0.7299	0.7130	0.6966	0.6806	0.6650	0.6499	0.6352	0.6209
6	0.7252	0.7050	0.6853	0.6663	0.6480	0.6302	0.6129	0.5963	0.5801	0.5645
7	0.6874	0.6651	0.6435	0.6227	0.6028	0.5835	0.5649	0.5470	0.5298	0.5132
8	0.6516	0.6274	0.6042	0.5820	0.5607	0.5403	0.5207	0.5019	0.4838	0.4665
9	0.6176	0.5919	0.5674	0.5439	0.5216	0.5002	0.4799	0.4604	0.4418	0.4241
10	0.5854	0.5584	0.5327	0.5083	0.4852	0.4632	0.4423	0.4224	0.4035	0.3855
11	0.5549	0.5268	0.5002	0.4751	0.4513	0.4289	0.4076	0.3875	0.3685	0.3505
12	0.5260	0.4970	0.4697	0.4440	0.4199	0.3971	0.3757	0.3555	0.3365	0.3186
13	0.4986	0.4688	0.4410	0.4150	0.3906	0.3677	0.3463	0.3262	0.3073	0.2897
14	0.4726	0.4423	0.4141	0.3878	0.3633	0.3405	0.3191	0.2992	0.2807	0.2633
15	0.4479	0.4173	0.3888	0.3624	0.3380	0.3152	0.2941	0.2745	0.2563	0.2394
16	0.4246	0.3936	0.3651	0.3387	0.3144	0.2919	0.2711	0.2519	0.2341	0.2176
17	0.4024	0.3714	0.3428	0.3166	0.2925	0.2703	0.2499	0.2311	0.2138	0.1978
18	0.3815	0.3503	0.3219	0.2959	0.2720	0.2502	0.2303	0.2120	0.1952	0.1799
19	0.3616	0.3305	0.3022	0.2765	0.2531	0.2317	0.2122	0.1945	0.1783	0.1635
20	0.3427	0.3118	0.2838	0.2584	0.2354	0.2145	0.1956	0.1784	0.1628	0.1486
21	0.3249	0.2942	0.2665	0.2415	0.2190	0.1987	0.1803	0.1637	0.1487	0.1351
22	0.3079	0.2775	0.2502	0.2257	0.2037	0.1839	0.1662	0.1502	0.1358	0.1228
23	0.2919	0.2618	0.2349	0.2109	0.1895	0.1703	0.1531	0.1378	0.1240	0.1117
24	0.2767	0.2470	0.2206	0.1971	0.1763	0.1577	0.1412	0.1264	0.1133	0.1015
25	0.2622	0.2330	0.2071	0.1842	0.1640	0.1460	0.1301	0.1160	0.1034	0.0923
26	0.2486	0.2198	0.1945	0.1722	0.1525	0.1352	0.1199	0.1064	0.0945	0.0839
27	0.2356	0.2074	0.1826	0.1609	0.1419	0.1252	0.1105	0.0976	0.0863	0.0763
28	0.2233	0.1956	0.1715	0.1504	0.1320	0.1159	0.1019	0.0895	0.0788	0.0693
29	0.2117	0.1846	0.1610	0.1406	0.1228	0.1073	0.0939	0.0822	0.0719	0.0630
30	0.2006	0.1741	0.1512	0.1314	0.1142	0.0994	0.0865	0.0754	0.0657	0.0573
35	0.1535	0.1301	0.1103	0.0937	0.0796	0.0676	0.0575	0.0490	0.0417	0.0356
40	0.1175	0.0972	0.0805	0.0668	0.0554	0.0460	0.0383	0.0318	0.0265	0.0221
45	0.0899	0.0727	0.0588	0.0476	0.0386	0.0313	0.0254	0.0207	0.0168	0.0137
50	0.0688	0.0543	0.0429	0.0339	0.0269	0.0213	0.0169	0.0134	0.0107	0.0085

TABLE B.2 (CONTINUED)
PRESENT VALUE OF A SINGLE SUM FACTORS
PVSS FACTOR = $1/(1 + i)^n$ where i = rate and n = periods

i =	10.5%	11%	11.5%	12%	12.5%	13%	13.5%	14%	14.5%	15%
n = 1	0.9050	0.9009	0.8969	0.8929	0.8889	0.8850	0.8811	0.8772	0.8734	0.8696
2	0.8190	0.8116	0.8044	0.7972	0.7901	0.7831	0.7763	0.7695	0.7628	0.7561
3	0.7412	0.7312	0.7214	0.7118	0.7023	0.6931	0.6839	0.6750	0.6662	0.6575
4	0.6707	0.6587	0.6470	0.6355	0.6243	0.6133	0.6026	0.5921	0.5818	0.5718
5	0.6070	0.5935	0.5803	0.5674	0.5549	0.5428	0.5309	0.5194	0.5081	0.4972
6	0.5493	0.5346	0.5204	0.5066	0.4933	0.4803	0.4678	0.4556	0.4438	0.4323
7	0.4971	0.4817	0.4667	0.4523	0.4385	0.4251	0.4121	0.3996	0.3876	0.3759
8	0.4499	0.4339	0.4186	0.4039	0.3897	0.3762	0.3631	0.3506	0.3385	0.3269
9	0.4071	0.3909	0.3754	0.3606	0.3464	0.3329	0.3199	0.3075	0.2956	0.2843
10	0.3684	0.3522	0.3367	0.3220	0.3079	0.2946	0.2819	0.2697	0.2582	0.2472
11	0.3334	0.3173	0.3020	0.2875	0.2737	0.2607	0.2483	0.2366	0.2255	0.2149
12	0.3018	0.2858	0.2708	0.2567	0.2433	0.2307	0.2188	0.2076	0.1969	0.1869
13	0.2731	0.2575	0.2429	0.2292	0.2163	0.2042	0.1928	0.1821	0.1720	0.1625
14	0.2471	0.2320	0.2178	0.2046	0.1922	0.1807	0.1698	0.1597	0.1502	0.1413
15	0.2236	0.2090	0.1954	0.1827	0.1709	0.1599	0.1496	0.1401	0.1312	0.1229
16	0.2024	0.1883	0.1752	0.1631	0.1519	0.1415	0.1318	0.1229	0.1146	0.1069
17	0.1832	0.1696	0.1572	0.1456	0.1350	0.1252	0.1162	0.1078	0.1001	0.0929
18	0.1658	0.1528	0.1409	0.1300	0.1200	0.1108	0.1023	0.0946	0.0874	0.0808
19	0.1500	0.1377	0.1264	0.1161	0.1067	0.0981	0.0902	0.0829	0.0763	0.0703
20	0.1358	0.1240	0.1134	0.1037	0.0948	0.0868	0.0794	0.0728	0.0667	0.0611
21	0.1229	0.1117	0.1017	0.0926	0.0843	0.0768	0.0700	0.0638	0.0582	0.0531
22	0.1112	0.1007	0.0912	0.0826	0.0749	0.0680	0.0617	0.0560	0.0508	0.0462
23	0.1006	0.0907	0.0818	0.0738	0.0666	0.0601	0.0543	0.0491	0.0444	0.0402
24	0.0911	0.0817	0.0734	0.0659	0.0592	0.0532	0.0479	0.0431	0.0388	0.0349
25	0.0824	0.0736	0.0658	0.0588	0.0526	0.0471	0.0422	0.0378	0.0339	0.0304
26	0.0746	0.0663	0.0590	0.0525	0.0468	0.0417	0.0372	0.0331	0.0296	0.0264
27	0.0675	0.0597	0.0529	0.0469	0.0416	0.0369	0.0327	0.0291	0.0258	0.0230
28	0.0611	0.0538	0.0475	0.0419	0.0370	0.0326	0.0288	0.0255	0.0226	0.0200
29	0.0553	0.0485	0.0426	0.0374	0.0329	0.0289	0.0254	0.0224	0.0197	0.0174
30	0.0500	0.0437	0.0382	0.0334	0.0292	0.0256	0.0224	0.0196	0.0172	0.0151
35	0.0304	0.0259	0.0222	0.0189	0.0162	0.0139	0.0119	0.0102	0.0087	0.0075
40	0.0184	0.0154	0.0129	0.0107	0.0090	0.0075	0.0063	0.0053	0.0044	0.0037
45	0.0112	0.0091	0.0075	0.0061	0.0050	0.0041	0.0034	0.0027	0.0023	0.0019
50	0.0068	0.0054	0.0043	0.0035	0.0028	0.0022	0.0018	0.0014	0.0011	0.0009

HALF PRICE BOOKS®

Half Price Books
1835 Forms Drive
Carrollton, TX 75006
OFS OrderID 39492562

Thank you for your order, Main Address!

Thank you for shopping with Half Price Books! Please contact Support@hpb.com. if you have any questions, comments or concerns about your order (113-5969133-7103407)

Visit our stores to sell your books, music, movies games for cash.

SKU	ISBN/UPC	Title & Author/Artist	Shelf ID	Qty	OrderSKU
S437012637	9781579960131	Fundamentals of Financial Planning	26--03--3	1	

SHIPPED STANDARD TO:
Main Address
800 Avondale Ave
1033837-1-0123
Grandview Heights OH 43212
j1gg094j97htty5@marketplace.amazon.com

ORDER# **113-5969133-7103407**
AmazonMarketplaceUS

TABLE B.2 (CONTINUED)
PRESENT VALUE OF A SINGLE SUM FACTORS
PVSS FACTOR = $1/(1 + i)^n$ where i = rate and n = periods

i =	16%	17%	18%	19%	20%	22%	24%	26%	28%	30%
n = 1	0.8621	0.8547	0.8475	0.8403	0.8333	0.8197	0.8065	0.7937	0.7813	0.7692
2	0.7432	0.7305	0.7182	0.7062	0.6944	0.6719	0.6504	0.6299	0.6104	0.5917
3	0.6407	0.6244	0.6086	0.5934	0.5787	0.5507	0.5245	0.4999	0.4768	0.4552
4	0.5523	0.5337	0.5158	0.4987	0.4823	0.4514	0.4230	0.3968	0.3725	0.3501
5	0.4761	0.4561	0.4371	0.4190	0.4019	0.3700	0.3411	0.3149	0.2910	0.2693
6	0.4104	0.3898	0.3704	0.3521	0.3349	0.3033	0.2751	0.2499	0.2274	0.2072
7	0.3538	0.3332	0.3139	0.2959	0.2791	0.2486	0.2218	0.1983	0.1776	0.1594
8	0.3050	0.2848	0.2660	0.2487	0.2326	0.2038	0.1789	0.1574	0.1388	0.1226
9	0.2630	0.2434	0.2255	0.2090	0.1938	0.1670	0.1443	0.1249	0.1084	0.0943
10	0.2267	0.2080	0.1911	0.1756	0.1615	0.1369	0.1164	0.0992	0.0847	0.0725
11	0.1954	0.1778	0.1619	0.1476	0.1346	0.1122	0.0938	0.0787	0.0662	0.0558
12	0.1685	0.1520	0.1372	0.1240	0.1122	0.0920	0.0757	0.0625	0.0517	0.0429
13	0.1452	0.1299	0.1163	0.1042	0.0935	0.0754	0.0610	0.0496	0.0404	0.0330
14	0.1252	0.1110	0.0985	0.0876	0.0779	0.0618	0.0492	0.0393	0.0316	0.0254
15	0.1079	0.0949	0.0835	0.0736	0.0649	0.0507	0.0397	0.0312	0.0247	0.0195
16	0.0930	0.0811	0.0708	0.0618	0.0541	0.0415	0.0320	0.0248	0.0193	0.0150
17	0.0802	0.0693	0.0600	0.0520	0.0451	0.0340	0.0258	0.0197	0.0150	0.0116
18	0.0691	0.0592	0.0508	0.0437	0.0376	0.0279	0.0208	0.0156	0.0118	0.0089
19	0.0596	0.0506	0.0431	0.0367	0.0313	0.0229	0.0168	0.0124	0.0092	0.0068
20	0.0514	0.0433	0.0365	0.0308	0.0261	0.0187	0.0135	0.0098	0.0072	0.0053
21	0.0443	0.0370	0.0309	0.0259	0.0217	0.0154	0.0109	0.0078	0.0056	0.0040
22	0.0382	0.0316	0.0262	0.0218	0.0181	0.0126	0.0088	0.0062	0.0044	0.0031
23	0.0329	0.0270	0.0222	0.0183	0.0151	0.0103	0.0071	0.0049	0.0034	0.0024
24	0.0284	0.0231	0.0188	0.0154	0.0126	0.0085	0.0057	0.0039	0.0027	0.0018
25	0.0245	0.0197	0.0160	0.0129	0.0105	0.0069	0.0046	0.0031	0.0021	0.0014
26	0.0211	0.0169	0.0135	0.0109	0.0087	0.0057	0.0037	0.0025	0.0016	0.0011
27	0.0182	0.0144	0.0115	0.0091	0.0073	0.0047	0.0030	0.0019	0.0013	0.0008
28	0.0157	0.0123	0.0097	0.0077	0.0061	0.0038	0.0024	0.0015	0.0010	0.0006
29	0.0135	0.0105	0.0082	0.0064	0.0051	0.0031	0.0020	0.0012	0.0008	0.0005
30	0.0116	0.0090	0.0070	0.0054	0.0042	0.0026	0.0016	0.0010	0.0006	0.0004
35	0.0055	0.0041	0.0030	0.0023	0.0017	0.0009	0.0005	0.0003	0.0002	0.0001
40	0.0026	0.0019	0.0013	0.0010	0.0007	0.0004	0.0002	0.0001	<0.0001	<0.0001
45	0.0013	0.0009	0.0006	0.0004	0.0003	0.0001	0.0001	<0.0001	<0.0001	<0.0001
50	0.0006	0.0004	0.0003	0.0002	0.0001	<0.0001	<0.0001	<0.0001	<0.0001	<0.0001

TABLE B.3
FUTURE VALUE OF AN ANNUITY FACTORS
FVA Factor = $((1 + i)^n\text{-}1)/i$ where i = rate and n = periods

i =	0.5%	1%	1.5%	2%	2.5%	3%	3.5%	4%	4.5%	5%
n = 1	1.0000	1.0000	1.0000	1.0000	1.0000	1.0000	1.0000	1.0000	1.0000	1.0000
2	2.0050	2.0100	2.0150	2.0200	2.0250	2.0300	2.0350	2.0400	2.0450	2.0500
3	3.0150	3.0301	3.0452	3.0604	3.0756	3.0909	3.1062	3.1216	3.1370	3.1525
4	4.0301	4.0604	4.0909	4.1216	4.1525	4.1836	4.2149	4.2465	4.2782	4.3101
5	5.0503	5.1010	5.1523	5.2040	5.2563	5.3091	5.3625	5.4163	5.4707	5.5256
6	6.0755	6.1520	6.2296	6.3081	6.3877	6.4684	6.5502	6.6330	6.7169	6.8019
7	7.1059	7.2135	7.3230	7.4343	7.5474	7.6625	7.7794	7.8983	8.0192	8.1420
8	8.1414	8.2857	8.4328	8.5830	8.7361	8.8923	9.0517	9.2142	9.3800	9.5491
9	9.1821	9.3685	9.5593	9.7546	9.9545	10.1591	10.3685	10.5828	10.8021	11.0266
10	10.2280	10.4622	10.7027	10.9497	11.2034	11.4639	11.7314	12.0061	12.2882	12.5779
11	11.2792	11.5668	11.8633	12.1687	12.4835	12.8078	13.1420	13.4864	13.8412	14.2068
12	12.3356	12.6825	13.0412	13.4121	13.7956	14.1920	14.6020	15.0258	15.4640	15.9171
13	13.3972	13.8093	14.2368	14.6803	15.1404	15.6178	16.1130	16.6268	17.1599	17.7130
14	14.4642	14.9474	15.4504	15.9739	16.5190	17.0863	17.6770	18.2919	18.9321	19.5986
15	15.5365	16.0969	16.6821	17.2934	17.9319	18.5989	19.2957	20.0236	20.7841	21.5786
16	16.6142	17.2579	17.9324	18.6393	19.3802	20.1569	20.9710	21.8245	22.7193	23.6575
17	17.6973	18.4304	19.2014	20.0121	20.8647	21.7616	22.7050	23.6975	24.7417	25.8404
18	18.7858	19.6147	20.4894	21.4123	22.3863	23.4144	24.4997	25.6454	26.8551	28.1324
19	19.8797	20.8109	21.7967	22.8406	23.9460	25.1169	26.3572	27.6712	29.0636	30.5390
20	20.9791	22.0190	23.1237	24.2974	25.5447	26.8704	28.2797	29.7781	31.3714	33.0660
21	22.0840	23.2392	24.4705	25.7833	27.1833	28.6765	30.2695	31.9692	33.7831	35.7193
22	23.1944	24.4716	25.8376	27.2990	28.8629	30.5368	32.3289	34.2480	36.3034	38.5052
23	24.3104	25.7163	27.2251	28.8450	30.5844	32.4529	34.4604	36.6179	38.9370	41.4305
24	25.4320	26.9735	28.6335	30.4219	32.3490	34.4265	36.6665	39.0826	41.6892	44.5020
25	26.5591	28.2432	30.0630	32.0303	34.1578	36.4593	38.9499	41.6459	44.5652	47.7271
26	27.6919	29.5256	31.5140	33.6709	36.0117	38.5530	41.3131	44.3117	47.5706	51.1135
27	28.8304	30.8209	32.9867	35.3443	37.9120	40.7096	43.7591	47.0842	50.7113	54.6691
28	29.9745	32.1291	34.4815	37.0512	39.8598	42.9309	46.2906	49.9676	53.9933	58.4026
29	31.1244	33.4504	35.9987	38.7922	41.8563	45.2189	48.9108	52.9663	57.4230	62.3227
30	32.2800	34.7849	37.5387	40.5681	43.9027	47.5754	51.6227	56.0849	61.0071	66.4388
35	38.1454	41.6603	45.5921	49.9945	54.9282	60.4621	66.6740	73.6522	81.4966	90.3203
40	44.1588	48.8864	54.2679	60.4020	67.4026	75.4013	84.5503	95.0255	107.030	120.800
45	50.3242	56.4811	63.6142	71.8927	81.5161	92.7199	105.782	121.029	138.850	159.700
50	56.6452	64.4632	73.6828	84.5794	97.4843	112.797	130.998	152.667	178.503	209.348

TABLE B.3 (CONTINUED)
FUTURE VALUE OF AN ANNUITY FACTORS
FVA Factor = $((1 + i)^n-1)/i$ where i = rate and n = periods

i =	5.5%	6%	6.5%	7%	7.5%	8%	8.5%	9%	9.5%	10%
n = 1	1.0000	1.0000	1.0000	1.0000	1.0000	1.0000	1.0000	1.0000	1.0000	1.0000
2	2.0550	2.0600	2.0650	2.0700	2.0750	2.0800	2.0850	2.0900	2.0950	2.1000
3	3.1680	3.1836	3.1992	3.2149	3.2306	3.2464	3.2622	3.2781	3.2940	3.3100
4	4.3423	4.3746	4.4072	4.4399	4.4729	4.5061	4.5395	4.5731	4.6070	4.6410
5	5.5811	5.6371	5.6936	5.7507	5.8084	5.8666	5.9254	5.9847	6.0446	6.1051
6	6.8881	6.9753	7.0637	7.1533	7.2440	7.3359	7.4290	7.5233	7.6189	7.7156
7	8.2669	8.3938	8.5229	8.6540	8.7873	8.9228	9.0605	9.2004	9.3426	9.4872
8	9.7216	9.8975	10.0769	10.2598	10.4464	10.6366	10.8306	11.0285	11.2302	11.4359
9	11.2563	11.4913	11.7319	11.9780	12.2298	12.4876	12.7512	13.0210	13.2971	13.5795
10	12.8754	13.1808	13.4944	13.8164	14.1471	14.4866	14.8351	15.1929	15.5603	15.9374
11	14.5835	14.9716	15.3716	15.7836	16.2081	16.6455	17.0961	17.5603	18.0385	18.5312
12	16.3856	16.8699	17.3707	17.8885	18.4237	18.9771	19.5492	20.1407	20.7522	21.3843
13	18.2868	18.8821	19.4998	20.1406	20.8055	21.4953	22.2109	22.9534	23.7236	24.5227
14	20.2926	21.0151	21.7673	22.5505	23.3659	24.2149	25.0989	26.0192	26.9774	27.9750
15	22.4087	23.2760	24.1822	25.1290	26.1184	27.1521	28.2323	29.3609	30.5402	31.7725
16	24.6411	25.6725	26.7540	27.8881	29.0772	30.3243	31.6320	33.0034	34.4416	35.9497
17	26.9964	28.2129	29.4930	30.8402	32.2580	33.7502	35.3207	36.9737	38.7135	40.5447
18	29.4812	30.9057	32.4101	33.9990	35.6774	37.4502	39.3230	41.3013	43.3913	45.5992
19	32.1027	33.7600	35.5167	37.3790	39.3532	41.4463	43.6654	46.0185	48.5135	51.1591
20	34.8683	36.7856	38.8253	40.9955	43.3047	45.7620	48.3770	51.1601	54.1222	57.2750
21	37.7861	39.9927	42.3490	44.8652	47.5525	50.4229	53.4891	56.7645	60.2638	64.0025
22	40.8643	43.3923	46.1016	49.0057	52.1190	55.4568	59.0356	62.8733	66.9009	71.4027
23	44.1118	46.9958	50.0982	53.4361	57.0279	60.8933	65.0537	69.5319	74.3529	79.5430
24	47.5380	50.8156	54.3546	58.1767	62.3050	66.7648	71.5832	76.7898	82.4164	88.4973
25	51.1526	54.8645	58.8877	63.2490	67.9779	73.1059	78.6678	84.7009	91.2459	98.3471
26	54.9660	59.1564	63.7154	68.6765	74.0762	79.9544	86.3546	93.3240	100.914	109.182
27	58.9891	63.7058	68.8569	74.4838	80.6319	87.3508	94.6947	102.723	111.501	121.100
28	63.2335	68.5281	74.3326	80.6977	87.6793	95.3388	103.744	112.968	123.094	134.210
29	67.7114	73.6398	80.1642	87.3465	95.2553	103.966	113.562	124.135	135.788	148.631
30	72.4355	79.0582	86.3749	94.4608	103.399	113.283	124.215	136.308	149.688	164.494
35	100.251	111.435	124.035	138.237	154.252	172.317	192.702	215.711	241.688	271.024
40	136.606	154.762	175.632	199.635	227.257	259.057	295.683	337.882	386.520	442.593
45	184.119	212.744	246.325	285.749	332.065	386.506	450.530	525.859	614.519	718.905
50	246.217	290.336	343.180	406.529	482.530	573.770	683.368	815.084	973.445	1163.91

TABLE B.3 (CONTINUED)
FUTURE VALUE OF AN ANNUITY FACTORS
FVA Factor = $((1 + i)^n - 1)/i$ where i = rate and n = periods

i =	10.5%	11%	11.5%	12%	12.5%	13%	13.5%	14%	14.5%	15%
n = 1	1.0000	1.0000	1.0000	1.0000	1.0000	1.0000	1.0000	1.0000	1.0000	1.0000
2	2.1050	2.1100	2.1150	2.1200	2.1250	2.1300	2.1350	2.1400	2.1450	2.1500
3	3.3260	3.3421	3.3582	3.3744	3.3906	3.4069	3.4232	3.4396	3.4560	3.4725
4	4.6753	4.7097	4.7444	4.7793	4.8145	4.8498	4.8854	4.9211	4.9571	4.9934
5	6.1662	6.2278	6.2900	6.3528	6.4163	6.4803	6.5449	6.6101	6.6759	6.7424
6	7.8136	7.9129	8.0134	8.1152	8.2183	8.3227	8.4284	8.5355	8.6439	8.7537
7	9.6340	9.7833	9.9349	10.0890	10.2456	10.4047	10.5663	10.7305	10.8973	11.0668
8	11.6456	11.8594	12.0774	12.2997	12.5263	12.7573	12.9927	13.2328	13.4774	13.7268
9	13.8684	14.1640	14.4663	14.7757	15.0921	15.4157	15.7468	16.0853	16.4317	16.7858
10	16.3246	16.7220	17.1300	17.5487	17.9786	18.4197	18.8726	19.3373	19.8142	20.3037
11	19.0387	19.5614	20.0999	20.6546	21.2259	21.8143	22.4204	23.0445	23.6873	24.3493
12	22.0377	22.7132	23.4114	24.1331	24.8791	25.6502	26.4471	27.2707	28.1220	29.0017
13	25.3517	26.2116	27.1037	28.0291	28.9890	29.9847	31.0175	32.0887	33.1997	34.3519
14	29.0136	30.0949	31.2207	32.3926	33.6126	34.8827	36.2048	37.5811	39.0136	40.5047
15	33.0600	34.4054	35.8110	37.2797	38.8142	40.4175	42.0925	43.8424	45.6706	47.5804
16	37.5313	39.1899	40.9293	42.7533	44.6660	46.6717	48.7750	50.9804	53.2928	55.7175
17	42.4721	44.5008	46.6362	48.8837	51.2493	53.7391	56.3596	59.1176	62.0203	65.0751
18	47.9317	50.3959	52.9993	55.7497	58.6554	61.7251	64.9681	68.3941	72.0132	75.8364
19	53.9645	56.9395	60.0942	63.4397	66.9873	70.7494	74.7388	78.9692	83.4551	88.2118
20	60.6308	64.2028	68.0051	72.0524	76.3608	80.9468	85.8286	91.0249	96.5561	102.444
21	67.9970	72.2651	76.8257	81.6987	86.9058	92.4699	98.4154	104.768	111.557	118.810
22	76.1367	81.2143	86.6606	92.5026	98.7691	105.491	112.701	120.436	128.732	137.632
23	85.1311	91.1479	97.6266	104.603	112.115	120.205	128.916	138.297	148.399	159.276
24	95.0699	102.174	109.854	118.155	127.130	136.831	147.320	158.659	170.917	184.168
25	106.052	114.413	123.487	133.334	144.021	155.620	168.208	181.871	196.699	212.793
26	118.188	127.999	138.688	150.334	163.023	176.850	191.916	208.333	226.221	245.712
27	131.597	143.079	155.637	169.374	184.401	200.841	218.825	238.499	260.023	283.569
28	146.415	159.817	174.535	190.699	208.452	227.950	249.366	272.889	298.726	327.104
29	162.789	178.397	195.607	214.583	235.508	258.583	284.031	312.094	343.041	377.170
30	180.881	199.021	219.101	241.333	265.946	293.199	323.375	356.787	393.782	434.745
35	304.159	341.590	383.879	431.663	485.660	546.681	615.640	693.573	781.644	881.170
40	507.252	581.826	667.850	767.091	881.592	1013.70	1166.14	1342.03	1544.96	1779.09
45	841.836	986.639	1157.23	1358.23	1595.07	1874.16	2203.04	2590.56	3047.17	3585.13
50	1393.05	1668.77	2000.61	2400.02	2880.79	3459.51	4156.10	4994.52	6003.54	7217.72

TABLE B.3 (CONTINUED)
FUTURE VALUE OF AN ANNUITY FACTORS
FVA Factor = $((1 + i)^n - 1)/i$ where i = rate and n = periods

i =	16%	17%	18%	19%	20%	22%	24%	26%	28%	30%
n = 1	1.0000	1.0000	1.0000	1.0000	1.0000	1.0000	1.0000	1.0000	1.0000	1.0000
2	2.1600	2.1700	2.1800	2.1900	2.2000	2.2200	2.2400	2.2600	2.2800	2.3000
3	3.5056	3.5389	3.5724	3.6061	3.6400	3.7084	3.7776	3.8476	3.9184	3.9900
4	5.0665	5.1405	5.2154	5.2913	5.3680	5.5242	5.6842	5.8480	6.0156	6.1870
5	6.8771	7.0144	7.1542	7.2966	7.4416	7.7396	8.0484	8.3684	8.6999	9.0431
6	8.9775	9.2068	9.4420	9.6830	9.9299	10.4423	10.9801	11.5442	12.1359	12.7560
7	11.4139	11.7720	12.1415	12.5227	12.9159	13.7396	14.6153	15.5458	16.5339	17.5828
8	14.2401	14.7733	15.3270	15.9020	16.4991	17.7623	19.1229	20.5876	22.1634	23.8577
9	17.5185	18.2847	19.0859	19.9234	20.7989	22.6700	24.7125	26.9404	29.3692	32.0150
10	21.3215	22.3931	23.5213	24.7089	25.9587	28.6574	31.6434	34.9449	38.5926	42.6195
11	25.7329	27.1999	28.7551	30.4035	32.1504	35.9620	40.2379	45.0306	50.3985	56.4053
12	30.8502	32.8239	34.9311	37.1802	39.5805	44.8737	50.8950	57.7386	65.5100	74.3270
13	36.7862	39.4040	42.2187	45.2445	48.4966	55.7459	64.1097	73.7506	84.8529	97.6250
14	43.6720	47.1027	50.8180	54.8409	59.1959	69.0100	80.4961	93.9258	109.612	127.913
15	51.6595	56.1101	60.9653	66.2607	72.0351	85.1922	100.815	119.347	141.303	167.286
16	60.9250	66.6488	72.9390	79.8502	87.4421	104.935	126.011	151.377	181.868	218.472
17	71.6730	78.9792	87.0680	96.0218	105.931	129.020	157.253	191.735	233.791	285.014
18	84.1407	93.4056	103.740	115.266	128.117	158.405	195.994	242.585	300.252	371.518
19	98.6032	110.285	123.414	138.166	154.740	194.254	244.033	306.658	385.323	483.973
20	115.380	130.033	146.628	165.418	186.688	237.989	303.601	387.389	494.213	630.165
21	134.841	153.139	174.021	197.847	225.026	291.347	377.465	489.110	633.593	820.215
22	157.415	180.172	206.345	236.438	271.031	356.443	469.056	617.278	811.999	1067.28
23	183.601	211.801	244.487	282.362	326.237	435.861	582.630	778.771	1040.36	1388.46
24	213.978	248.808	289.494	337.010	392.484	532.750	723.461	982.251	1332.66	1806.00
25	249.214	292.105	342.603	402.042	471.981	650.955	898.092	1238.64	1706.80	2348.80
26	290.088	342.763	405.272	479.431	567.377	795.165	1114.63	1561.68	2185.71	3054.44
27	337.502	402.032	479.221	571.522	681.853	971.102	1383.15	1968.72	2798.71	3971.78
28	392.503	471.378	566.481	681.112	819.223	1185.74	1716.10	2481.59	3583.34	5164.31
29	456.303	552.512	669.447	811.523	984.068	1447.61	2128.96	3127.80	4587.68	6714.60
30	530.312	647.439	790.948	966.712	1181.88	1767.08	2640.92	3942.03	5873.23	8729.99
35	1120.71	1426.49	1816.65	2314.21	2948.34	4783.64	7750.23	12527.4	20189.0	32422.9
40	2360.76	3134.52	4163.21	5529.83	7343.86	12936.5	22728.8	39793.0	69377.5	120393
45	4965.27	6879.29	9531.58	13203.4	18281.3	34971.4	66640.4	126383	238388	447019
50	10435.6	15089.5	21813.1	31515.3	45497.2	94525.3	195373	401374	819103	1659761

TABLE B.4
PRESENT VALUE OF AN ANNUITY FACTORS
PVA Factor = $(1 - (1/(1 + i)^n))/i$ where i = rate and n = periods

i =	0.5%	1%	1.5%	2%	2.5%	3%	3.5%	4%	4.5%	5%
n = 1	0.9950	0.9901	0.9852	0.9804	0.9756	0.9709	0.9662	0.9615	0.9569	0.9524
2	1.9851	1.9704	1.9559	1.9416	1.9274	1.9135	1.8997	1.8861	1.8727	1.8594
3	2.9702	2.9410	2.9122	2.8839	2.8560	2.8286	2.8016	2.7751	2.7490	2.7232
4	3.9505	3.9020	3.8544	3.8077	3.7620	3.7171	3.6731	3.6299	3.5875	3.5460
5	4.9259	4.8534	4.7826	4.7135	4.6458	4.5797	4.5151	4.4518	4.3900	4.3295
6	5.8964	5.7955	5.6972	5.6014	5.5081	5.4172	5.3286	5.2421	5.1579	5.0757
7	6.8621	6.7282	6.5982	6.4720	6.3494	6.2303	6.1145	6.0021	5.8927	5.7864
8	7.8230	7.6517	7.4859	7.3255	7.1701	7.0197	6.8740	6.7327	6.5959	6.4632
9	8.7791	8.5660	8.3605	8.1622	7.9709	7.7861	7.6077	7.4353	7.2688	7.1078
10	9.7304	9.4713	9.2222	8.9826	8.7521	8.5302	8.3166	8.1109	7.9127	7.7217
11	10.6770	10.3676	10.0711	9.7868	9.5142	9.2526	9.0016	8.7605	8.5289	8.3064
12	11.6189	11.2551	10.9075	10.5753	10.2578	9.9540	9.6633	9.3851	9.1186	8.8633
13	12.5562	12.1337	11.7315	11.3484	10.9832	10.6350	10.3027	9.9856	9.6829	9.3936
14	13.4887	13.0037	12.5434	12.1062	11.6909	11.2961	10.9205	10.5631	10.2228	9.8986
15	14.4166	13.8651	13.3432	12.8493	12.3814	11.9379	11.5174	11.1184	10.7395	10.3797
16	15.3399	14.7179	14.1313	13.5777	13.0550	12.5611	12.0941	11.6523	11.2340	10.8378
17	16.2586	15.5623	14.9076	14.2919	13.7122	13.1661	12.6513	12.1657	11.7072	11.2741
18	17.1728	16.3983	15.6726	14.9920	14.3534	13.7535	13.1897	12.6593	12.1600	11.6896
19	18.0824	17.2260	16.4262	15.6785	14.9789	14.3238	13.7098	13.1339	12.5933	12.0853
20	18.9874	18.0456	17.1686	16.3514	15.5892	14.8775	14.2124	13.5903	13.0079	12.4622
21	19.8880	18.8570	17.9001	17.0112	16.1845	15.4150	14.6980	14.0292	13.4047	12.8212
22	20.7841	19.6604	18.6208	17.6580	16.7654	15.9369	15.1671	14.4511	13.7844	13.1630
23	21.6757	20.4558	19.3309	18.2922	17.3321	16.4436	15.6204	14.8568	14.1478	13.4886
24	22.5629	21.2434	20.0304	18.9139	17.8850	16.9355	16.0584	15.2470	14.4955	13.7986
25	23.4456	22.0232	20.7196	19.5235	18.4244	17.4131	16.4815	15.6221	14.8282	14.0939
26	24.3240	22.7952	21.3986	20.1210	18.9506	17.8768	16.8904	15.9828	15.1466	14.3752
27	25.1980	23.5596	22.0676	20.7069	19.4640	18.3270	17.2854	16.3296	15.4513	14.6430
28	26.0677	24.3164	22.7267	21.2813	19.9649	18.7641	17.6670	16.6631	15.7429	14.8981
29	26.9330	25.0658	23.3761	21.8444	20.4535	19.1885	18.0358	16.9837	16.0219	15.1411
30	27.7941	25.8077	24.0158	22.3965	20.9303	19.6004	18.3920	17.2920	16.2889	15.3725
35	32.0354	29.4086	27.0756	24.9986	23.1452	21.4872	20.0007	18.6646	17.4610	16.3742
40	36.1722	32.8347	29.9158	27.3555	25.1028	23.1148	21.3551	19.7928	18.4016	17.1591
45	40.2072	36.0945	32.5523	29.4902	26.8330	24.5187	22.4955	20.7200	19.1563	17.7741
50	44.1428	39.1961	34.9997	31.4236	28.3623	25.7298	23.4556	21.4822	19.7620	18.2559

TABLE B.4 (CONTINUED)
PRESENT VALUE OF AN ANNUITY FACTORS
PVA Factor = $(1 - (1/(1 + i)^n))/i$ where i = rate and n = periods

i =	5.5%	6%	6.5%	7%	7.5%	8%	8.5%	9%	9.5%	10%
n = 1	0.9479	0.9434	0.9390	0.9346	0.9302	0.9259	0.9217	0.9174	0.9132	0.9091
2	1.8463	1.8334	1.8206	1.8080	1.7956	1.7833	1.7711	1.7591	1.7473	1.7355
3	2.6979	2.6730	2.6485	2.6243	2.6005	2.5771	2.5540	2.5313	2.5089	2.4869
4	3.5052	3.4651	3.4258	3.3872	3.3493	3.3121	3.2756	3.2397	3.2045	3.1699
5	4.2703	4.2124	4.1557	4.1002	4.0459	3.9927	3.9406	3.8897	3.8397	3.7908
6	4.9955	4.9173	4.8410	4.7665	4.6938	4.6229	4.5536	4.4859	4.4198	4.3553
7	5.6830	5.5824	5.4845	5.3893	5.2966	5.2064	5.1185	5.0330	4.9496	4.8684
8	6.3346	6.2098	6.0888	5.9713	5.8573	5.7466	5.6392	5.5348	5.4334	5.3349
9	6.9522	6.8017	6.6561	6.5152	6.3789	6.2469	6.1191	5.9952	5.8753	5.7590
10	7.5376	7.3601	7.1888	7.0236	6.8641	6.7101	6.5613	6.4177	6.2788	6.1446
11	8.0925	7.8869	7.6890	7.4987	7.3154	7.1390	6.9690	6.8052	6.6473	6.4951
12	8.6185	8.3838	8.1587	7.9427	7.7353	7.5361	7.3447	7.1607	6.9838	6.8137
13	9.1171	8.8527	8.5997	8.3577	8.1258	7.9038	7.6910	7.4869	7.2912	7.1034
14	9.5896	9.2950	9.0138	8.7455	8.4892	8.2442	8.0101	7.7862	7.5719	7.3667
15	10.0376	9.7122	9.4027	9.1079	8.8271	8.5595	8.3042	8.0607	7.8282	7.6061
16	10.4622	10.1059	9.7678	9.4466	9.1415	8.8514	8.5753	8.3126	8.0623	7.8237
17	10.8646	10.4773	10.1106	9.7632	9.4340	9.1216	8.8252	8.5436	8.2760	8.0216
18	11.2461	10.8276	10.4325	10.0591	9.7060	9.3719	9.0555	8.7556	8.4713	8.2014
19	11.6077	11.1581	10.7347	10.3356	9.9591	9.6036	9.2677	8.9501	8.6496	8.3649
20	11.9504	11.4699	11.0185	10.5940	10.1945	9.8181	9.4633	9.1285	8.8124	8.5136
21	12.2752	11.7641	11.2850	10.8355	10.4135	10.0168	9.6436	9.2922	8.9611	8.6487
22	12.5832	12.0416	11.5352	11.0612	10.6172	10.2007	9.8098	9.4424	9.0969	8.7715
23	12.8750	12.3034	11.7701	11.2722	10.8067	10.3711	9.9629	9.5802	9.2209	8.8832
24	13.1517	12.5504	11.9907	11.4693	10.9830	10.5288	10.1041	9.7066	9.3341	8.9847
25	13.4139	12.7834	12.1979	11.6536	11.1469	10.6748	10.2342	9.8226	9.4376	9.0770
26	13.6625	13.0032	12.3924	11.8258	11.2995	10.8100	10.3541	9.9290	9.5320	9.1609
27	13.8981	13.2105	12.5750	11.9867	11.4414	10.9352	10.4646	10.0266	9.6183	9.2372
28	14.1214	13.4062	12.7465	12.1371	11.5734	11.0511	10.5665	10.1161	9.6971	9.3066
29	14.3331	13.5907	12.9075	12.2777	11.6962	11.1584	10.6603	10.1983	9.7690	9.3696
30	14.5337	13.7648	13.0587	12.4090	11.8104	11.2578	10.7468	10.2737	9.8347	9.4269
35	15.3906	14.4982	13.6870	12.9477	12.2725	11.6546	11.0878	10.5668	10.0870	9.6442
40	16.0461	15.0463	14.1455	13.3317	12.5944	11.9246	11.3145	10.7574	10.2472	9.7791
45	16.5477	15.4558	14.4802	13.6055	12.8186	12.1084	11.4653	10.8812	10.3490	9.8628
50	16.9315	15.7619	14.7245	13.8007	12.9748	12.2335	11.5656	10.9617	10.4137	9.9148

TABLE B.4 (CONTINUED)
PRESENT VALUE OF AN ANNUITY FACTORS
PVA Factor = $(1 - (1/(1 + i)^n))/i$ where i = rate and n = periods

i =	10.5%	11%	11.5%	12%	12.5%	13%	13.5%	14%	14.5%	15%
n = 1	0.9050	0.9009	0.8969	0.8929	0.8889	0.8850	0.8811	0.8772	0.8734	0.8696
2	1.7240	1.7125	1.7012	1.6901	1.6790	1.6681	1.6573	1.6467	1.6361	1.6257
3	2.4651	2.4437	2.4226	2.4018	2.3813	2.3612	2.3413	2.3216	2.3023	2.2832
4	3.1359	3.1024	3.0696	3.0373	3.0056	2.9745	2.9438	2.9137	2.8841	2.8550
5	3.7429	3.6959	3.6499	3.6048	3.5606	3.5172	3.4747	3.4331	3.3922	3.3522
6	4.2922	4.2305	4.1703	4.1114	4.0538	3.9975	3.9425	3.8887	3.8360	3.7845
7	4.7893	4.7122	4.6370	4.5638	4.4923	4.4226	4.3546	4.2883	4.2236	4.1604
8	5.2392	5.1461	5.0556	4.9676	4.8820	4.7988	4.7177	4.6389	4.5621	4.4873
9	5.6463	5.5370	5.4311	5.3282	5.2285	5.1317	5.0377	4.9464	4.8577	4.7716
10	6.0148	5.8892	5.7678	5.6502	5.5364	5.4262	5.3195	5.2161	5.1159	5.0188
11	6.3482	6.2065	6.0697	5.9377	5.8102	5.6869	5.5679	5.4527	5.3414	5.2337
12	6.6500	6.4924	6.3406	6.1944	6.0535	5.9176	5.7867	5.6603	5.5383	5.4206
13	6.9230	6.7499	6.5835	6.4235	6.2698	6.1218	5.9794	5.8424	5.7103	5.5831
14	7.1702	6.9819	6.8013	6.6282	6.4620	6.3025	6.1493	6.0021	5.8606	5.7245
15	7.3938	7.1909	6.9967	6.8109	6.6329	6.4624	6.2989	6.1422	5.9918	5.8474
16	7.5962	7.3792	7.1719	6.9740	6.7848	6.6039	6.4308	6.2651	6.1063	5.9542
17	7.7794	7.5488	7.3291	7.1196	6.9198	6.7291	6.5469	6.3729	6.2064	6.0472
18	7.9451	7.7016	7.4700	7.2497	7.0398	6.8399	6.6493	6.4674	6.2938	6.1280
19	8.0952	7.8393	7.5964	7.3658	7.1465	6.9380	6.7395	6.5504	6.3701	6.1982
20	8.2309	7.9633	7.7098	7.4694	7.2414	7.0248	6.8189	6.6231	6.4368	6.2593
21	8.3538	8.0751	7.8115	7.5620	7.3256	7.1016	6.8889	6.6870	6.4950	6.3125
22	8.4649	8.1757	7.9027	7.6446	7.4006	7.1695	6.9506	6.7429	6.5459	6.3587
23	8.5656	8.2664	7.9845	7.7184	7.4672	7.2297	7.0049	6.7921	6.5903	6.3988
24	8.6566	8.3481	8.0578	7.7843	7.5264	7.2829	7.0528	6.8351	6.6291	6.4338
25	8.7390	8.4217	8.1236	7.8431	7.5790	7.3300	7.0950	6.8729	6.6629	6.4641
26	8.8136	8.4881	8.1826	7.8957	7.6258	7.3717	7.1321	6.9061	6.6925	6.4906
27	8.8811	8.5478	8.2355	7.9426	7.6674	7.4086	7.1649	6.9352	6.7184	6.5135
28	8.9422	8.6016	8.2830	7.9844	7.7043	7.4412	7.1937	6.9607	6.7409	6.5335
29	8.9974	8.6501	8.3255	8.0218	7.7372	7.4701	7.2191	6.9830	6.7606	6.5509
30	9.0474	8.6938	8.3637	8.0552	7.7664	7.4957	7.2415	7.0027	6.7778	6.5660
35	9.2347	8.8552	8.5030	8.1755	7.8704	7.5856	7.3193	7.0700	6.8362	6.6166
40	9.3483	8.9511	8.5839	8.2438	7.9281	7.6344	7.3607	7.1050	6.8659	6.6418
45	9.4173	9.0079	8.6308	8.2825	7.9601	7.6609	7.3826	7.1232	6.8810	6.6543
50	9.4591	9.0417	8.6580	8.3045	7.9778	7.6752	7.3942	7.1327	6.8886	6.6605

TABLE B.4 (CONTINUED)
PRESENT VALUE OF AN ANNUITY FACTORS
PVA Factor = $(1 - (1/(1 + i)^n))/i$ where i = rate and n = periods

i =	16%	17%	18%	19%	20%	22%	24%	26%	28%	30%
n = 1	0.8621	0.8547	0.8475	0.8403	0.8333	0.8197	0.8065	0.7937	0.7813	0.7692
2	1.6052	1.5852	1.5656	1.5465	1.5278	1.4915	1.4568	1.4235	1.3916	1.3609
3	2.2459	2.2096	2.1743	2.1399	2.1065	2.0422	1.9813	1.9234	1.8684	1.8161
4	2.7982	2.7432	2.6901	2.6386	2.5887	2.4936	2.4043	2.3202	2.2410	2.1662
5	3.2743	3.1993	3.1272	3.0576	2.9906	2.8636	2.7454	2.6351	2.5320	2.4356
6	3.6847	3.5892	3.4976	3.4098	3.3255	3.1669	3.0205	2.8850	2.7594	2.6427
7	4.0386	3.9224	3.8115	3.7057	3.6046	3.4155	3.2423	3.0833	2.9370	2.8021
8	4.3436	4.2072	4.0776	3.9544	3.8372	3.6193	3.4212	3.2407	3.0758	2.9247
9	4.6065	4.4506	4.3030	4.1633	4.0310	3.7863	3.5655	3.3657	3.1842	3.0190
10	4.8332	4.6586	4.4941	4.3389	4.1925	3.9232	3.6819	3.4648	3.2689	3.0915
11	5.0286	4.8364	4.6560	4.4865	4.3271	4.0354	3.7757	3.5435	3.3351	3.1473
12	5.1971	4.9884	4.7932	4.6105	4.4392	4.1274	3.8514	3.6059	3.3868	3.1903
13	5.3423	5.1183	4.9095	4.7147	4.5327	4.2028	3.9124	3.6555	3.4272	3.2233
14	5.4675	5.2293	5.0081	4.8023	4.6106	4.2646	3.9616	3.6949	3.4587	3.2487
15	5.5755	5.3242	5.0916	4.8759	4.6755	4.3152	4.0013	3.7261	3.4834	3.2682
16	5.6685	5.4053	5.1624	4.9377	4.7296	4.3567	4.0333	3.7509	3.5026	3.2832
17	5.7487	5.4746	5.2223	4.9897	4.7746	4.3908	4.0591	3.7705	3.5177	3.2948
18	5.8178	5.5339	5.2732	5.0333	4.8122	4.4187	4.0799	3.7861	3.5294	3.3037
19	5.8775	5.5845	5.3162	5.0700	4.8435	4.4415	4.0967	3.7985	3.5386	3.3105
20	5.9288	5.6278	5.3527	5.1009	4.8696	4.4603	4.1103	3.8083	3.5458	3.3158
21	5.9731	5.6648	5.3837	5.1268	4.8913	4.4756	4.1212	3.8161	3.5514	3.3198
22	6.0113	5.6964	5.4099	5.1486	4.9094	4.4882	4.1300	3.8223	3.5558	3.3230
23	6.0442	5.7234	5.4321	5.1668	4.9245	4.4985	4.1371	3.8273	3.5592	3.3254
24	6.0726	5.7465	5.4509	5.1822	4.9371	4.5070	4.1428	3.8312	3.5619	3.3272
25	6.0971	5.7662	5.4669	5.1951	4.9476	4.5139	4.1474	3.8342	3.5640	3.3286
26	6.1182	5.7831	5.4804	5.2060	4.9563	4.5196	4.1511	3.8367	3.5656	3.3297
27	6.1364	5.7975	5.4919	5.2151	4.9636	4.5243	4.1542	3.8387	3.5669	3.3305
28	6.1520	5.8099	5.5016	5.2228	4.9697	4.5281	4.1566	3.8402	3.5679	3.3312
29	6.1656	5.8204	5.5098	5.2292	4.9747	4.5312	4.1585	3.8414	3.5687	3.3317
30	6.1772	5.8294	5.5168	5.2347	4.9789	4.5338	4.1601	3.8424	3.5693	3.3321
35	6.2153	5.8582	5.5386	5.2512	4.9915	4.5411	4.1644	3.8450	3.5708	3.3330
40	6.2335	5.8713	5.5482	5.2582	4.9966	4.5439	4.1659	3.8458	3.5712	3.3332
45	6.2421	5.8773	5.5523	5.2611	4.9986	4.5449	4.1664	3.8460	3.5714	3.3333
50	6.2463	5.8801	5.5541	5.2623	4.9995	4.5452	4.1666	3.8461	3.5714	3.3333

Appendix C

Keystrokes for Solving Selected TVM Problems Using the HP-12C Calculator

Robert M. Crowe

Note: The individual keystrokes in this appendix are separated by commas.

1. Preliminary "housekeeping" and miscellaneous chores
   a. Clearing memory
      yellow f, REG or
      yellow f, FIN
   b. Setting number of decimal places displayed
      yellow f and desired number
   c. Clearing display or eliminating last keystroke
      CLX
   d. Raising a number to a power
      base number, ENTER, exponent, y^x
2. Future value of a single sum problems
   a. Finding FVSS
      amount of present value, CHS, PV, number of periods, n, interest rate, i, FV
   b. Finding approximate n
      amount of present value, CHS, PV, amount of future value, FV, interest rate, i, n
   c. Finding i
      amount of present value, CHS, PV, amount of future value, FV, number of periods, n, i
3. Present value of a single sum problems
   a. Finding PVSS
      amount of future value, FV, number of periods, n, interest rate, i, PV
   b. Finding approximate n
      see 2b above
   c. Finding i
      see 2c above

4. Future value of an annuity problems
   a. Finding FVA
      amount of one payment, CHS, PMT, interest rate, i, number of payments, n, blue g, END, FV
   b. Finding approximate n
      future value of the annuity, FV, amount of one payment, CHS, PMT, blue g, END, interest rate, i, n
   c. Finding i
      future value of the annuity, FV, amount of one payment, CHS, PMT, number of payments, n, blue g, END, i
5. Future value of an annuity due problems
   a. Finding FVAD
      amount of one payment, CHS, PMT, interest rate, i, number of payments, n, blue g, BEG, FV
   b. Finding approximate n
      future value of the annuity due, FV, amount of one payment, CHS, PMT, blue g, BEG, interest rate, i, n
   c. Finding i
      future value of the annuity due, FV, amount of one payment, CHS, PMT, number of payments, n, blue g, BEG, i
6. Sinking fund problems
   a. Finding sinking fund payment
      target amount of sinking fund, FV, interest rate, i, number of payments, n, blue g, BEG (or END), PMT
   b. Finding approximate n
      target amount of sinking fund, FV, interest rate, i, amount of one payment, CHS, PMT, blue g, BEG (or END), n
   c. Finding i
      target amount of sinking fund, FV, amount of one payment, CHS, PMT, number of payments, n, blue g, BEG (or END), i
7. Present value of an annuity problems
   a. Finding PVA
      amount of one payment, CHS, PMT, interest rate, i, number of payments, n, blue g, END, PV
   b. Finding approximate n
      present value of the annuity, CHS, PV, amount of one payment, PMT, blue g, END, interest rate, i, n
   c. Finding i
      present value of the annuity, CHS, PV, amount of one payment, PMT, number of payments, n, blue g, END, i
8. Present value of an annuity due problems
   a. Finding PVAD
      amount of one payment, CHS, PMT, interest rate, i, number of payments, n, blue g, BEG, PV

   b. Finding approximate n

      present value of the annuity due, CHS, PV, amount of one payment, PMT, blue g, BEG, interest rate, i, n

   c. Finding i

      present value of the annuity due, CHS, PV, amount of one payment, PMT, number of payments, n, blue g, BEG, i

9. Debt service/capital sum liquidation problems

   a. Finding the payment

      beginning amount of loan or capital sum, CHS, PV, interest rate, i, number of payments, n, blue g, BEG (or END), PMT

   b. Finding the approximate n

      beginning amount of loan or capital sum, CHS, PV, interest rate, i, amount of one payment, PMT, blue g, BEG (or END), n

   c. Finding i

      beginning amount of loan or capital sum, CHS, PV, amount of one payment, PMT, number of payments, n, blue g, BEG (or END), i

   d. Creating an amortization schedule

      annual interest rate, i (or blue g, 12 ÷ if loan payments are to be made monthly), blue g, END (normally), beginning amount of loan, PV, amount of one loan payment, CHS, PMT, 1 (or 12 if loan payments are to be made monthly), yellow f, AMORT (to show total interest payments in first year), $x \gtrless y$, (to show total principal payments in first year), RCL, PV (to show unpaid loan balance at end of first year); repeat 1 (or 12), yellow f, AMORT $x \gtrless y$, RCL, PV to show the total interest payments, principal payments, and unpaid loan balance for each successive year of the loan's duration

10. Present value of uneven cash flows problems

   a. Cash flows at end of year: ungrouped data (see text for grouped data) amount of first cash flow, blue g, CFj, second cash flow, blue g, CFj, etc. through entire sequence; then interest rate, i, yellow f, NPV

   b. Cash flows at beginning of year: ungrouped data (see text for grouped data)

      amount of first cash flow, blue g, CFo, second cash flow, blue g, CFj, third cash flow, blue g, CFj, etc. through entire sequence; then interest rate, i, yellow f, NPV

   c. Cash flows that grow by a constant percentage, with first payment made immediately

      blue g, BEG, amount of first cash flow, PMT, 1 plus interest rate, ENTER, 1 plus growth rate, ÷, 1, –, 100, x, i, number of payments, n, PV

d. Cash flows that grow by a constant percentage, with first payment made after one year

   divide answer found in 10c by (1 plus interest rate)

11. Future value of uneven cash flows problems

    a. Generally

       Compute present value as in 10a or 10b above; then ENTER, CHS PV, interest rate, i, number of years, n, FV

    b. Special case: deposits growing by a constant percentage

       Compute present value as in 10c or 10d above; then STO, 1, yellow f, FIN, RCL, 1, PV, interest rate, i, number of years, n, FV

12. Net present value problems

    a. Ungrouped data

       amount of initial outflow, CHS, blue g, CFo; then amount of each succeeding inflow or outflow, including zeros, pressing blue g and CFj after each (CHS, blue g, and CFj for outflows); then interest rate, i, yellow f, NPV

    b. Grouped data

       amount of initial outflow, CHS, blue g, CFo; then amount of first inflow or outflow, including zeros, blue g, CFj (CHS, blue g, CFj for outflows); then number of times that amount occurs in succession, blue g, Nj; repeat the process for each subsequent inflow, outflow, or zero flow or group of same; then interest rate, i, yellow f, NPV

13. Internal rate of return problems

    Same as NPV problems except for last four keystrokes; instead of interest rate, i, yellow f, and NPV, press yellow f, IRR

14. Conversion of nominal interest rate to effective interest rate problems

    a. Discrete compounding or discounting

       nominal interest rate, ENTER, number of compounding periods per year, n, ÷, i, 100, CHS, ENTER, PV, FV, +

    b. Continuous compounding or discounting during 360-day year

       1, ENTER, nominal interest rate, %, blue g, e^x, Δ %

Appendix D

Keystrokes for Solving Selected TVM Problems Using the HP-17B II Calculator

Robert M. Crowe

Note: The individual keystrokes in this appendix are separated by commas. They reflect use of the Algebraic system of entry logic, rather than the Reverse Polish Notation system.

1. Preliminary "housekeeping" and miscellaneous chores
   a. Turning the machine on or off
      CLR or colored shift key, OFF
   b. Adjusting contrast on display screen
      Hold down CLR, + or –
   c. Selecting the Algebraic system of entry logic
      Shift, MODES, ALG menu key, EXIT
   d. Returning to main menu
      Shift, MAIN or EXIT one or more times
   e. Clearing a problem or data from memory
      Menu key for menu to be cleared of problem
      or data, shift, CLEAR DATA
   f. Setting number of decimal places to be displayed
      DSP, FIX menu key, desired number, INPUT
   g. clearing display screen
      CLR
   h. Eliminating last keystroke
      ←
   i. Setting number of payment periods/compounding periods per year to one, if both are the same
      Shift, MAIN, FIN menu key, TVM menu key,
      OTHER menu key, 1, P/YR menu key, shift,
      MAIN, CLR
   j. Setting the calculator for payments at beginning or end of each period
      Shift, MAIN, FIN menu key, TVM menu key, OTHER menu key, BEG or END menu key, shift, MAIN
   k. Raising a number to a power
      Base number, shift, y^x, exponent, =

2. Future value of a single sum problems
   a. Finding FVSS

      Shift, MAIN, FIN menu key, TVM menu key, number of periods, N menu key, periodic interest rate, I%YR menu key, amount of present value, +/–, PV menu key, FV menu key

   b. Finding n (number of periods)

      Shift, MAIN, FIN menu key, TVM menu key, periodic interest rate, I%YR menu key, amount of present value, +/–, PV menu key, amount of future value, FV menu key, N menu key

   c. Finding i (periodic interest rate)

      Shift, MAIN, FIN menu key, TVM menu key, number of periods, N menu key, amount of present value, +/–, PV menu key, amount of future value, FV menu key, I%YR menu key

3. Present value of a single sum problems
   a. Finding PVSS

      Shift, MAIN, FIN menu key, TVM menu key, number of periods, N menu key, periodic interest rate, I%YR menu key, amount of future value, FV menu key, PV menu key

   b. Finding n (number of periods)

      See 2.b. above

   c. Finding i (periodic interest rate)

      See 2.c. above

4. Future value of an annuity problems
   a. Finding FVA

      Set the calculator for end-of-period payments (see 1.j. above); set the calculator for one payment/compounding period per year, if both are the same (see, 1.i. above); shift, MAIN, FIN menu key, TVM menu key, number of payments, N menu key, periodic interest rate, I%YR menu key, amount of one payment, +/, PMT menu key, FV menu key

   b. Finding n (number of payments)

      Set the calculator for end-of-period payments (see 1.j. above); set the calculator for one payment/compounding period per year, if both are the same (see 1.i. above); shift, MAIN, FIN menu key, TVM menu key, periodic interest rate, I%YR menu key, amount of one payment, +/–, PMT menu key, future value of the annuity, FV menu key, N menu key

   c. Finding i (periodic interest rate)

      Set the calculator for end-of-period payments (see 1.j. above); set the calculator for one payment/compounding period per year, if both are the same (see 1.i. above); shift, MAIN, FIN menu key, TVM menu key, number of payments, N menu key, amount of payment, +/–, PMT menu key, future value of the annuity, FV menu key, I% YR menu key

5. Future value of an annuity due problems
   a. Finding FVAD

      Set the calculator for beginning-of-period payments (see 1.j. above); set the calculator for one payment/compounding period per year, if both are the same (see 1.i. above); shift, MAIN, FIN menu key, TVM menu key, number of payments, N menu key, periodic interest rate, I%YR menu key, amount of one payment, +/, PMT menu key, FV menu key

   b. Finding n (number of payments)

      Set the calculator for beginning-of-period payments (see 1.j. above); set the calculator for one payment/compounding period per year, if both are the same (see 1.i. above); shift, MAIN, FIN menu key, TVM menu key, periodic interest rate, 1%YR menu key, amount of one payment, +/–, PMT menu key, future value of the annuity, FV menu key, N menu key

   c. Finding i (periodic interest rate)

      Set the calculator for beginning-of-period payments (see 1.j. above); set the calculator for one payment/compounding period per year, if both are the same (see 1.i. above); shift, MAIN, FIN menu key TVM menu key, number of payments, N menu key, amount of one payment, +/–, PMT menu key, future value of the annuity, FV menu key, I%YR menu key

6. Sinking fund problems
   a. Finding sinking fund payment

      Set the calculator for beginning-of-period or end-of-period payments, as appropriate (see 1.j. above); set the calculator for one payment/compounding period per year, if both are the same (see 1.i. above); shift, MAIN, FIN menu key, TVM menu key, target amount of sinking fund, FV menu key, periodic interest rate, I%YR menu key, number of payments, N menu key, PMT menu key

   b. Finding n (number of payments)

      Set the calculator for beginning-of-period or end-of-period payments as appropriate (see 1.j. above); set the calculator for one payment/compounding period per year, if both are the same (see 1.i. above); target amount of sinking fund, FV menu key, periodic interest rate, I%YR menu key, amount of one payment, +/–, PMT menu key, N menu key

   c. Finding i (periodic interest rate)

      Set the calculator for beginning-of-period or end-of-period payments, as appropriate (see 1.j. above); set the calculator for one payment/compounding period per year, if both are the same (see 1.i. above); target amount of sinking fund, FV menu key, number of payments, N menu key, amount of one payment, +/–, PMT menu key, I%YR menu key

7. Present value of an annuity problems
   a. Finding PVA
      Set the calculator for end-of-period payments (see 1.j. above); set the calculator for one payment/compounding period per year, if both are the same (see 1.i. above); shift, MAIN, FIN menu key, TVM menu key, number of payments, N menu key, periodic interest rate, 1%YR menu key, amount of one payment, PMT menu key, PV menu key
   b. Finding n (number of payments)
      Set the calculator for end-of-period payments (see 1.j. above); set the calculator for one payment/compounding period per year, if both are the same (see 1.i. above); shift, MAIN, FIN menu key, TVM menu key, periodic interest rate, I%YR menu key, present value of the annuity, +/–, PV menu key, amount of one payment, PMT menu key, N menu key
   c. Finding i (periodic interest rate)
      Set the calculator for end-of-period payments (see 1.j. above); set the calculator for one payment/compounding period per year, if both are the same (see 1.i. above); shift, MAIN, FIN menu key, TVM menu key, number of payments, N menu key, present value of the annuity, +/–, PV menu key, amount of one payment, PMT menu key, I%YR menu key

8. Present value of an annuity due problems
   a. Finding PVAD
      Set the calculator for beginning-of-period payments (see 1.j. above); set the calculator for one payment/compounding period per year, if both are the same (see 1.i. above); shift, MAIN, FIN menu key, TVM menu key, number of payments, N menu key, periodic interest rate, I%YR menu key, amount of one payment, PMT menu key, PV menu key
   b. Finding n (number of payments)
      Set the calculator for beginning-of-period payments (see 1.j. above); set the calculator for one payment/compounding period per year, if both are the same (see 1.i. above); shift, MAIN, FIN menu key, TVM menu key, periodic interest rate, I%YR menu key, amount of one payment, PMT menu key, present value of the annuity, +/–, PV menu key, N menu key

c. Finding i (periodic interest rate)

Set the calculator for beginning-of-period payments (see 1.j. above); set the calculator for one payment/compounding period per year, if both are the same (see 1.i. above); shift, MAIN, FIN menu key, TVM menu key, number of payments, N menu key, amount of one payment, PMT menu key, present value of the annuity, +/–, PV menu key, I%YR menu key

9. Debt service/capital sum liquidation problems

a. Finding the payment

Set the calculator for beginning-of-period or end-of-period payments, as appropriate (see 1.j. above); set the calculator for one payment/compounding period per year, if both are the same (see 1.i. above); shift, MAIN, FIN menu key, TVM menu key, beginning amount of loan or capital sum, +/–, PV menu key, periodic interest rate, I%YR menu key, number of payments, N menu key, PMT menu key

b. Finding n (number of payments)

Set the calculator for beginning-of-period or end-of-period payments, as appropriate (see 1.j. above); set the calculator for one payment/compounding period per year, if both are the same (see 1.i. above); shift, MAIN, FIN menu key, TVM menu key, beginning amount of loan or capital sum, +/–, PV menu key, periodic interest rate, I%YR menu key, amount of one payment, PMT menu key, N menu key

c. Finding i (periodic interest rate)

Set the calculator for beginning-of-period or end-of-period payments, as appropriate (see 1.j. above); set the calculator for one payment/compounding period per year, if both are the same (see 1.i. above); shift, MAIN, FIN menu key, TVM menu key, beginning amount of loan or capital sum, +/–, PV menu key, amount of one payment, PMT menu key, number of payments, N menu key, I%YR menu key

d. Creating an amortization schedule

Set the calculator for end-of-period payments (see 1.j. above); set the calculator for one payment/compounding period per year, if both are the same (see 1.i. above); FIN menu key, TVM menu key, total number of payments, N menu key, periodic interest rate, I%YR menu key, original loan amount, +/–, PV menu key, amount of one payment, PMT menu key, OTHER menu key, AMRT menu key, 1, #P menu key, INT menu key to see total interest paid during first amortization period, PRIN menu key to show total principal repaid during first amortization period, BAL menu key to show unpaid balance at end of first amortization period, NEXT menu key to perform calculations applicable to next amortization period, INT menu key to see total interest paid during second amortization period, PRIN menu key to see total principal paid during second amortization period, BAL menu key to show unpaid balance at end of second amortization period, NEXT, etc. to end of loan period

10. Present value of uneven cash flows problems (**Editor's Note:** Each cash flow should be entered as a positive or negative amount, as appropriate.)
    a. Cash flows at end of year
       Shift, MAIN, FIN menu key, CFLO menu key, #T? menu key to ON, shift, CLEAR DATA, YES menu key, 0, INPUT, amount of first cash flow, INPUT, number of times it occurs, INPUT, amount of second cash flow, INPUT, number of times it occurs, INPUT, amount of third cash flow, INPUT, number of times it occurs, INPUT, etc. through entire sequence; then EXIT, CALC menu key, periodic interest rate, I% menu key, NPV menu key
    b. Cash flows at beginning of year
       Shift, MAIN, FIN menu key, CFLO menu key, #T? menu key to ON, shift, CLEAR DATA, YES menu key, amount of first cash flow, INPUT, amount of second cash flow (or amount of first cash flow if it is grouped data), INPUT, number of times it occurs (minus 1 if it is a continuation of the grouped data in the first cash flow), INPUT, amount of next cash flow, INPUT, number of times it occurs, INPUT, etc. through the entire sequence; then EXIT, CALC menu key, periodic interest rate, I% menu key, NPV menu key
    c. Cash flows that grow by a constant percentage, with first payment made immediately
       Set the calculator for beginning-of-period payments (see 1.j. above); set the calculator for one payment/compounding period per year, if both are the same (see 1.i. above); shift, MAIN, FIN menu key, TVM menu key, amount of first cash flow, PMT menu key, 1 plus periodic interest rate, +, 1 plus growth rate, —, 1, x, 100, =, I%YR menu key, number of payments, N menu key, PV menu key
    d. Cash flows that grow by a constant percentage, with first payment made after one period
       Divide answer found in 10.c. by (1 plus periodic interest rate)

11. Future value of uneven cash flows problems
    a. Cash flows at end of year
       Use procedure in 10.a. except for the final keystroke, which should be the NFV menu key, rather than the NPV menu key
    b. Cash flows at beginning of year
       Multiply answer found in 11.a. by (1 plus periodic interest rate)

c. Deposits growing by a constant percentage

Compute present value as in 10.c. or d. above; then STO, 1, shift, CLEAR DATA, RCL, 1, PV menu key, periodic interest rate, I%YR menu key, number of deposits, N menu key, FV menu key

12. Net present value problems

Use procedure in 10.a. or b. above, but press +/– key after any cash flows that are outflows

13. Internal rate of return problems

Same as NPV except for last three keystrokes; instead of (or in addition to) periodic interest rate, I% menu key, and NPV menu key, press IRR menu key

14. Conversion of nominal interest rate to effective interest rate problems

Shift, MAIN, ICNV menu key, PER or CONT menu key, depending on whether compounding is periodic or continuous, nominal interest rate, NOM% menu key, number of compounding periods per year, P menu key, EFF% menu key

Appendix E

Keystrokes for Solving Selected TVM Problems Using the BA-II Plus Calculator

Robert M. Crowe

Note: The individual keystrokes in this appendix are separated by commas.

1. Preliminary "housekeeping" and miscellaneous chores
   a. Clearing memory
      2nd, MEM, 2nd, CLR Work
   b. Entering and clearing the standard-calculator mode
      2nd, QUIT, 2nd, CLR TVM
   c. Entering and clearing the prompted-worksheet mode
      CF, 2nd, CLR Work (to compute NPV or IRR in uneven cash flow problems)
      OR
      2nd, Amort, 2nd, CLR Work (to solve amortization problems)
   d. Setting number of decimal places to be displayed
      2nd, Format, desired number of decimal places, ENTER
   e. Clearing display of an incorrect or unwanted number or an error message
      CE/C (one or more times)
   f. Eliminating last keystroke before entering
      →
   g. Clearing a problem from the calculator
      (1) Clearing a problem while in the standard-calculator mode
          2nd, CLR, TVM, CE/C
      (2) Clearing a problem while in the prompted-worksheet mode
          CF, 2nd, CLR Work
          or
          2nd, Amort, 2nd, CLR Work
   h. Setting number of payment periods per year and number of compounding periods per year
      2nd, P/Y, 2nd, SET, desired number of payment periods per year, ENTER, ↓, desired number of compounding periods per year, ENTER

   i. Setting the calculator for payments at beginning of period or end of period
      2nd, BGN; if current setting is acceptable, 2nd, QUIT; if not, 2nd, SET, 2nd, QUIT
   j. Raising a number to a power
      base number, y^x, exponent, =
2. Future value of a single sum problems
   a. Finding FVSS
      amount of present value, +/–, PV, number of periods, N, interest rate, I/Y, CPT, FV
   b. Finding n
      amount of present value, +/–, PV, amount of future value, FV, interest rate, I/Y, CPT, N
   c. Finding i
      amount of present value, +/–, PV, amount of future value, FV, number of periods, N, CPT, I/Y
3. Present value of a single sum problems
   a. Finding PVSS
      amount of future value, FV, number of periods, N, interest rate, I/Y, CPT, PV
   b. Finding n
      see 2b above
   c. Finding i
      see 2c above
4. Future value of an annuity problems
   a. Finding FVA
      Set the calculator for end-of-period payments (see 1i above).
      amount of one payment, +/–, PMT, interest rate, I/Y, number of payments, N, CPT, FV
   b. Finding n
      Set the calculator for end-of-period payments (see 1i above).
      future value of the annuity, FV, amount of one payment, +/–, PMT, interest rate, I/Y, CPT, N
   c. Finding i
      Set the calculator for end-of-period payments (see 1i above).
      future value of the annuity, FV, amount of one payment, +/–, PMT, number of payments, N, CPT, I/Y
5. Future value of an annuity due problems
   a. Finding FVAD
      Set the calculator for beginning-of-period payments (see 1i above).
      amount of one payment, +/–, PMT, interest rate, I/Y, number of payments, N, CPT, FV

b. Finding n

Set the calculator for beginning-of-period payments (see 1i above).
future value of the annuity due, FV, amount of one payment, +/–, PMT, interest rate, I/Y, CPT, N

c. Finding i

Set the calculator for beginning-of-period payments (see 1i above).
future value of the annuity due, FV, amount of one payment, +/–, PMT, number of payments, N, CPT, I/Y

6. Sinking fund problems

a. Finding sinking fund payment

Set the calculator for beginning-of-period payments or end-of-period payments, as appropriate (see 1i above).
target amount of sinking fund, FV, interest rate, I/Y, number of payments, N, CPT, PMT

b. Finding n

Set the calculator for beginning-of-period payments or end-of-period payments as appropriate (see 1i above).
target amount of sinking fund, FV, interest rate, I/Y, amount of one payment, +/–, PMT, CPT, N

c. Finding i

Set the calculator for beginning-of-period payments or end-of-period payments, as appropriate (see 1i above).
target amount of sinking fund, FV, amount of one payment, +/–, PMT, number of payments, N, CPT, I/Y

7. Present value of an annuity problems

a. Finding PVA

Set the calculator for end-of-period payments (see 1i above).
amount of one payment, +/–, PMT, interest rate, I/Y, number of payments, N, CPT, PV

b. Finding n

Set the calculator for end-of-period payments (see 1i above).
present value of the annuity, +/–, PV, amount of one payment, PMT, interest rate, I/Y, CPT, N

c. Finding i

Set the calculator for end-of-period payments (see 1i above).
present value of the annuity, +/–, PV, amount of one payment, PMT, number of payments, N, CPT, I/Y

8. Present value of an annuity due problems

a. Finding PVAD

Set the calculator for beginning-of-period payments (see 1i above).
amount of one payment, +/–, PMT, interest rate, I/Y, number of payments, N, CPT, PV

b. Finding n

Set the calculator for beginning-of-period payments (see 1i above).
present value of the annuity, +/–, PV, amount of one payment, PMT, interest rate, I/Y, CPT, N

c. Finding i

Set the calculator for beginning-of-period payments (see 1i above).
present value of the annuity, +/–, PV, amount of one payment, PMT, number of payments, N, CPT, I/Y

9. Debt service/capital sum liquidation problems

a. Finding the payment

Set the calculator for beginning-of-period payments or end-of-period payments, as appropriate (see 1i above).
beginning amount of loan or capital sum, +/–, PV, interest rate, I/Y, number of payments, N, CPT, PMT

b. Finding n

Set the calculator for beginning-of-period payments or end-of-period payments, as appropriate (see 1i above).
beginning amount of loan or capital sum, +/–, PV, interest rate, I/Y, amount of one payment, PMT, CPT, N

c. Finding i

Set the calculator for beginning-of-period payments or end-of-period payments, as appropriate (see 1i above).
beginning amount of loan or capital sum, +/–, PV, amount of one payment, PMT, number of payments, N, CPT, I/Y

d. Creating an amortization schedule

Set the calculator for end-of-period payments (see 1i above).
Set the calculator for the appropriate number of payments per year and number of compounding periods per year (see 1h above).
2nd, QUIT, beginning amount of loan, +/–, PV, interest rate, I/Y, number of payments, N, CPT, PMT, 2nd, Amort, 2nd, CLR Work, 1, ENTER, ↓, 1, ENTER, ↓ (shows unpaid loan principal after first year), ↓ (shows amount paid on principal in first year), ↓ (shows amount paid as interest in first year), ↓, ↓, 2, ENTER, ↓ (shows unpaid loan principal after second year), ↓ (shows total amount paid on principal during first two years), ↓, ↓, 3, ENTER, etc. Repeat this process throughout the loan's duration to show the gradually declining loan balance at the end of each year, the total amount applied on the principal to that point, and the total amount paid as interest to that point.

10. Present value of uneven cash flows problems (Note: Each cash flow should be entered as a positive or negative amount, as appropriate.)
    a. Cash flows at end of period: ungrouped data (see text for grouped data)
        CF, 2nd, CLR Work, ENTER, ↓, amount of first cash flow, ENTER, ↓, ENTER, ↓, amount of second cash flow, ENTER, ↓, ENTER, ↓, amount of third cash flow, ENTER, ↓, ENTER, ↓, etc. through entire sequence; then NPV, interest rate, ENTER, ↓,CPT
    b. Cash flows at beginning of period: ungrouped data (see text for grouped data)
        CF, 2nd, CLR Work, amount of first cash flow, ENTER, ↓, amount of second cash flow, ENTER, ↓, ENTER, ↓, amount of third cash flow, ENTER, ↓, ENTER, ↓, etc. through entire sequence; then NPV, interest rate, ENTER, ↓, CPT
    c. Cash flows that grow by a constant percentage, with first payment made immediately
        Set the calculator for beginning-of-period payments (see 1i above). amount of first cash flow, PMT, 1 plus interest rate, ÷, 1 plus growth rate, –, 1, x, 100, =, I/Y, number of payments, N, CPT, PV
    d. Cash flows that grow by a constant percentage, with first payment made after one period
        divide answer found in 10c by (1 plus interest rate)
11. Future value of uneven cash flows problems
    a. Generally
        Compute present value as in 10a or 10b above; then STO, 1, CF, 2nd, CLR Work, 2nd, QUIT, RCL, 1, +/–, PV, interest rate, I/Y, number of payments, N, CPT, FV; clear memory when completed as in 1a above.
    b. Special case: deposits growing by a constant percentage
        Compute present value as in 10c or 10d above; then STO, 1, 2nd, CLR TVM, RCL, 1, PV, interest rate, I/Y, number of payments, N, CPT, FV; clear memory when completed as in 1a above.
12. Net present value problems (Note: Typically the first cash flow is an outflow and thus is entered as a negative. In some problems one or more of the subsequent cash flows also are outflows. They too should be entered as negatives, though this is not shown in the keystroke sequences below.)
    a. Ungrouped data
        CF, 2nd, CLR Work, amount of initial outflow, +/–, ENTER, ↓, amount of second cash flow, ENTER, ↓, ENTER, ↓, amount of third cash flow, ENTER, ↓, ENTER, ↓, etc. through the entire sequence, including zeros; then NPV, interest rate, ENTER, ↓, CPT

b. Grouped data

CF, 2nd, CLR Work, amount of initial outflow, +/–, ENTER, ↓, amount of second cash flow, ENTER, ↓, number of times it occurs in succession, ENTER, ↓, amount of third cash flow, ENTER, ↓, number of times it occurs in succession, ENTER, ↓, etc. through the entire sequence, including zeros; then NPV, interest rate, ENTER, ↓, CPT

13. Internal rate of return problems

    Same as NPV except for (or in addition to) last five keystrokes; instead of (or after) pressing NPV, interest rate, ENTER, ↓, and CPT, press IRR, CPT

14. Conversion of nominal interest rate to effective interest rate problems

    2nd, I Conv, 2nd, CLR Work, nominal interest rate, ENTER, ↓, ↓, number of compounding periods per year, ENTER, ↑, CPT

APPENDIX F

Table of Effective Interest Rates

TABLE F
Effective Annual Interest Rates

Nominal Rate	Compounding Frequency					
	Semi-Annually	Quarterly	Monthly	Weekly	Daily (365 days)	Continuous
0.25%	0.2502%	0.2502%	0.2503%	0.2503%	0.2503%	0.2503%
0.50%	0.5006%	0.5009%	0.5011%	0.5012%	0.5012%	0.5013%
0.75%	0.7514%	0.7521%	0.7526%	0.7528%	0.7528%	0.7528%
1.00%	1.0025%	1.0038%	1.0046%	1.0049%	1.0050%	1.0050%
1.25%	1.2539%	1.2559%	1.2572%	1.2577%	1.2578%	1.2578%
1.50%	1.5056%	1.5085%	1.5104%	1.5111%	1.5113%	1.5113%
1.75%	1.7577%	1.7615%	1.7641%	1.7651%	1.7654%	1.7654%
2.00%	2.0100%	2.0151%	2.0184%	2.0197%	2.0201%	2.0201%
2.25%	2.2627%	2.2691%	2.2733%	2.2750%	2.2754%	2.2755%
2.50%	2.5156%	2.5235%	2.5288%	2.5309%	2.5314%	2.5315%
2.75%	2.7689%	2.7785%	2.7849%	2.7874%	2.7881%	2.7882%
3.00%	3.0225%	3.0339%	3.0416%	3.0446%	3.0453%	3.0455%
3.25%	3.2764%	3.2898%	3.2989%	3.3023%	3.3032%	3.3034%
3.50%	3.5306%	3.5462%	3.5567%	3.5608%	3.5618%	3.5620%
3.75%	3.7852%	3.8031%	3.8151%	3.8198%	3.8210%	3.8212%
4.00%	4.0400%	4.0604%	4.0742%	4.0795%	4.0808%	4.0811%
4.25%	4.2952%	4.3182%	4.3338%	4.3398%	4.3413%	4.3416%
4.50%	4.5506%	4.5765%	4.5940%	4.6008%	4.6025%	4.6028%
4.75%	4.8064%	4.8353%	4.8548%	4.8623%	4.8643%	4.8646%
5.00%	5.0625%	5.0945%	5.1162%	5.1246%	5.1267%	5.1271%
5.25%	5.3189%	5.3543%	5.3782%	5.3875%	5.3899%	5.3903%
5.50%	5.5756%	5.6145%	5.6408%	5.6510%	5.6536%	5.6541%
5.75%	5.8327%	5.8752%	5.9040%	5.9152%	5.9180%	5.9185%
6.00%	6.0900%	6.1364%	6.1678%	6.1800%	6.1831%	6.1837%
6.25%	6.3477%	6.3980%	6.4322%	6.4455%	6.4489%	6.4494%
6.50%	6.6056%	6.6602%	6.6972%	6.7116%	6.7153%	6.7159%
6.75%	6.8639%	6.9228%	6.9628%	6.9783%	6.9824%	6.9830%
7.00%	7.1225%	7.1859%	7.2290%	7.2458%	7.2501%	7.2508%
7.25%	7.3814%	7.4495%	7.4958%	7.5139%	7.5185%	7.5193%
7.50%	7.6406%	7.7136%	7.7633%	7.7826%	7.7876%	7.7884%
7.75%	7.9002%	7.9782%	8.0313%	8.0520%	8.0573%	8.0582%
8.00%	8.1600%	8.2432%	8.3000%	8.3220%	8.3278%	8.3287%
8.25%	8.4202%	8.5088%	8.5692%	8.5928%	8.5989%	8.5999%
8.50%	8.6806%	8.7748%	8.8391%	8.8642%	8.8706%	8.8717%
8.75%	8.9414%	9.0413%	9.1096%	9.1362%	9.1431%	9.1442%
9.00%	9.2025%	9.3083%	9.3807%	9.4089%	9.4162%	9.4174%
9.25%	9.4639%	9.5758%	9.6524%	9.6823%	9.6900%	9.6913%
9.50%	9.7256%	9.8438%	9.9248%	9.9564%	9.9645%	9.9659%
9.75%	9.9877%	10.1123%	10.1977%	10.2311%	10.2397%	10.2411%
10.00%	10.2500%	10.3813%	10.4713%	10.5065%	10.5156%	10.5171%

TABLE F (CONTINUED)
Effective Annual Interest Rates

Nominal Rate	Compounding Frequency					
	Semi-Annually	Quarterly	Monthly	Weekly	Daily (365 days)	Continuous
10.25%	10.5127%	10.6508%	10.7455%	10.7826%	10.7921%	10.7937%
10.50%	10.7756%	10.9207%	11.0203%	11.0593%	11.0694%	11.0711%
10.75%	11.0389%	11.1912%	11.2958%	11.3367%	11.3473%	11.3491%
11.00%	11.3025%	11.4621%	11.5719%	11.6148%	11.6260%	11.6278%
11.25%	11.5664%	11.7336%	11.8486%	11.8936%	11.9053%	11.9072%
11.50%	11.8306%	12.0055%	12.1259%	12.1731%	12.1853%	12.1873%
11.75%	12.0952%	12.2779%	12.4039%	12.4533%	12.4660%	12.4682%
12.00%	12.3600%	12.5509%	12.6825%	12.7341%	12.7475%	12.7497%
12.25%	12.6252%	12.8243%	12.9617%	13.0156%	13.0296%	13.0319%
12.50%	12.8906%	13.0982%	13.2416%	13.2978%	13.3124%	13.3148%
12.75%	13.1564%	13.3727%	13.5221%	13.5808%	13.5960%	13.5985%
13.00%	13.4225%	13.6476%	13.8032%	13.8644%	13.8802%	13.8828%
13.25%	13.6889%	13.9230%	14.0850%	14.1487%	14.1652%	14.1679%
13.50%	13.9556%	14.1989%	14.3674%	14.4337%	14.4508%	14.4537%
13.75%	14.2227%	14.4754%	14.6505%	14.7194%	14.7372%	14.7402%
14.00%	14.4900%	14.7523%	14.9342%	15.0057%	15.0243%	15.0274%
14.25%	14.7577%	15.0297%	15.2185%	15.2928%	15.3121%	15.3153%
14.50%	15.0256%	15.3077%	15.5035%	15.5806%	15.6006%	15.6040%
14.75%	15.2939%	15.5861%	15.7892%	15.8691%	15.8899%	15.8933%
15.00%	15.5625%	15.8650%	16.0755%	16.1583%	16.1798%	16.1834%
15.25%	15.8314%	16.1445%	16.3624%	16.4483%	16.4705%	16.4742%
15.50%	16.1006%	16.4244%	16.6500%	16.7389%	16.7620%	16.7658%
15.75%	16.3702%	16.7049%	16.9382%	17.0302%	17.0541%	17.0581%
16.00%	16.6400%	16.9859%	17.2271%	17.3223%	17.3470%	17.3511%
16.25%	16.9102%	17.2673%	17.5166%	17.6150%	17.6406%	17.6448%
16.50%	17.1806%	17.5493%	17.8068%	17.9085%	17.9349%	17.9393%
16.75%	17.4514%	17.8318%	18.0977%	18.2027%	18.2300%	18.2345%
17.00%	17.7225%	18.1148%	18.3892%	18.4976%	18.5258%	18.5305%
17.25%	17.9939%	18.3983%	18.6813%	18.7933%	18.8223%	18.8272%
17.50%	18.2656%	18.6823%	18.9742%	19.0896%	19.1196%	19.1246%
17.75%	18.5377%	18.9668%	19.2677%	19.3867%	19.4177%	19.4228%
18.00%	18.8100%	19.2519%	19.5618%	19.6845%	19.7164%	19.7217%
18.25%	19.0827%	19.5374%	19.8566%	19.9831%	20.0159%	20.0214%
18.50%	19.3556%	19.8235%	20.1521%	20.2823%	20.3162%	20.3218%
18.75%	19.6289%	20.1100%	20.4483%	20.5824%	20.6172%	20.6230%
19.00%	19.9025%	20.3971%	20.7451%	20.8831%	20.9190%	20.9250%
19.25%	20.1764%	20.6847%	21.0426%	21.1846%	21.2215%	21.2277%
19.50%	20.4506%	20.9728%	21.3408%	21.4868%	21.5248%	21.5311%
19.75%	20.7252%	21.2615%	21.6396%	21.7897%	21.8288%	21.8353%
20.00%	21.0000%	21.5506%	21.9391%	22.0934%	22.1336%	22.1403%

About the Authors

Ken Cooper, PhD, is professor of management and finance at Ohio Northern University. He is a former holder of the Charles Lamont Post Chair of Ethics and the Professions at The American College.

Robert M. Crowe, PhD, CLU, ChFC, CFP, is a financial consultant and author, as well as adjunct professor of finance and insurance at The American College. Previous positions he has held include the deanship of the College of Business Administration at Memphis State University and the University of Tulsa. He also served as an economic affairs officer for the United Nations in Switzerland. He earned his doctorate as a fellow of the S.S. Huebner Foundation for Insurance Education at the University of Pennsylvania.

Robbin Derry, PhD, is senior lecturer at the University of Pennsylvania's Wharton School. She is a former holder of the Charles Lamont Post Chair of Ethics and the Professions at The American College.

Ronald F. Duska, PhD, is professor of ethics and chairholder of the Charles Lamont Post Chair of Ethics and Professions at The American College. The Post Chair supports research and studies of the social responsibilities and ethical challenges facing business. Duska received his PhD. in philosophy from Northwestern University. Most recently, he was professor of philosophy at Rosemont College, and he has taught at Villanova University, St. Joseph's University, Pennsylvania State University, and the University of Pennsylvania's Wharton School.

Edmund W. Fitzpatrick, MA, PhD, is professor of systems management at the National Defense University. He is a former faculty member at The American College who developed and taught computer-related courses for the College's designation and graduate programs. Dr. Fitzpatrick received his MA from the University of Minnesota and his PhD from the Catholic University of America in Washington, DC.

Charles E. Hughes, DBA, CLU, CPCU, is retired associate professor of insurance from The American College. He was assistant dean for graduate programs at the University of Connecticut and was in the insurance business for several years. He earned his PhD at Georgia State University.

James F. Ivers III, JD, LLM, ChFC, is professor of taxation at The American College. He developed the College's course in income taxation. Mr. Ivers is the coauthor of *Planning for Business Owners and Professionals* and *Stanley and Kilcullen's Federal Income Tax Law,* published by Warren, Gorham & Lamont. A member of the bar in Pennsylvania and Florida, he is a consultant and frequent speaker on taxation and financial planning. Mr. Ivers is a graduate of Villanova University. He received his JD and his LLM from the Boston University School of Law.

Dale S. Johnson, a consultant, provides services to many financial planning organizations. He holds a PhD from the University of Michigan, an MA from Tulane University, and a BA from Rhodes College. A former faculty member at The American College, Dr. Johnson has published numerous articles on financial planning in professional journals.

Jeffrey B. Kelvin, JD, LLM, CLU, ChFC, is a former faculty member at The American College and received his BA at Temple University and his JD and LLM from the Temple University School of Law.

Ted Kurlowicz, JD, LLM, CLU, ChFC, is professor of taxation at The American College. His responsibilities include preparation of courses in estate planning and planning for business owners and professionals. He received his BA from the University of Connecticut, his law degrees from Widener University School of Law and Villanova University School of Law, and his MA from the University of Pennsylvania.

Stephan R. Leimberg, JD, CLU, is former professor of taxation and estate planning at The American College and is adjunct professor in the masters of taxation program of Temple University School of Law and Villanova University School of Law. He is author of more than forty books in estate planning, financial planning, and employee benefits.

David A. Littell, JD, is associate professor of taxation at The American College. A native of Chicago, David holds a BA in psychology from Northwestern University and a JD from the Boston University School of Law. At The American College he is responsible for course development in pension and retirement planning. He is a member of the Delaware County Bar Association. He was previously an attorney with Saul, Ewing, Remick & Saul, and Paul Tanker & Associates, both Philadelphia-based firms.

Lewis B. Morgan, PhD, is professor of counseling and human services at Villanova University. He received his EdM from Rutgers University and his PhD from the University of Connecticut.

Michael J. Roszkowski, PhD, is associate professor of psychology and director of marketing research at The American College. Dr. Roszkowski earned his BS at St. Joseph's University and his MEd, and PhD at Temple University.

William J. Ruckstuhl, MBA, CLU, ChFC, is adjunct professor of finance at The American College. He received his BS from Grove City College and his MBA from the University of Pennsylvania.

Jai P. Sawhney, MBA, MS, is founder of ExecPlan, Inc., a financial planning software firm, in Princeton, New Jersey. Mr. Sawhney holds an MBA degree from New York University and an MS in Operations Research from Delhi University.

Kenn B. Tacchino, JD, LLM, is director of the Tax Institute at Widener University in Chester, Pennsylvania. He is also adjunct professor of taxation at The American College. Mr. Tacchino received his BA from Muhlenberg College, his JD from Western New England School of Law, and his LLM from Widener University School of Law.

Glossary

AB trust arrangement • an arrangement of two trusts designed to maximize the use of two spouse's applicable credit amounts. The A trust is some form of marital deduction trust; the B trust does not qualify for the marital deduction but receives a sum that will qualify for the applicable credit amount.

accurate empathy • this occurs when the financial planner's sense of the client's world fits the client's self-image; it gives clients the sense that the planner is in touch with them.

active listening • the act of putting together a speaker's words and nonverbal behaviors to get the essence of the communication being sent. With active listening, one becomes involved in the inner world of another person while, at the same time, maintaining one's own identity and responding meaningfully to the person's messages.

actual cash value • a term used in many property insurance contracts. Actual cash value typically is defined as replacement cost minus a reduction for depreciation or obsolescence.

additional commitment risk • the risk that an investor may be required to put additional money into an investment asset at an inopportune time, which may force the investor to sell the asset at an unfavorable market price.

additional living expenses • the increased costs necessary to maintain normal living standards when the insured's dwelling is uninhabitable because of damage caused by a covered peril.

adjusted gross income (AGI) • an intermediate calculation made while determining an individual's income tax liability for a given year. The AGI is used as a base amount to determine how the taxpayer must treat certain other items for tax purposes; for example, the maximum amount of charitable contributions that may be deducted by an individual in a given year is generally 50 percent of the individual's AGI.

advising • a type of structured communication in which an expert provides knowledge to a client, who in turn uses this knowledge to reach a decision.

agency bond • a type of bond issued by a federal agency or organization that is not a direct obligation of the U.S. Treasury. Such bonds provide investors with a return greater than that available on U.S. Treasury bonds; a few of these agency bonds have guarantees that effectively place the full faith and credit of the U.S. Treasury behind them.

"all risks" coverage • a type of coverage provided by the special form of the homeowners insurance policy. It does not mean that all losses are covered; rather, a loss is covered unless it is specifically excluded from coverage in a list specific to the special form or in a list common to all homeowners policies.

alternative minimum tax (AMT) • a separate and parallel system of income taxation to the regular system, with completely different rules and tax rates. It applies to any taxpayer whose tax liability under this parallel system is greater for that year than the liability under the regular income tax system. This system ensures that taxpayers who enjoy certain tax benefits cannot reduce their tax liability below a minimum amount by claiming certain tax deductions.

altruism • an unselfish regard for the welfare of others.

American Depository Receipts (ADRs) • a type of negotiable instrument that represents a specified number of shares in a foreign company. They are sold by U.S. banks that have acquired shares in foreign corporations and hold these shares in trust in one of their foreign branches. ADRs are the equivalent of ownership of the stock, trade as such in domestic markets, and have rights and privileges as are accorded common shareholders in the country of issue.

amortization schedule • a tool used in connection with installment loans. It shows how much of a debt service payment is used to pay interest and how much is being applied to reduce the principal of the loan.

annuity • (1) a series of payments of equal amounts made at the end of each of a number of consecutive periods. (2) in insurance, a contract that provides for the systematic liquidation of a principal sum over a period of time, usually the lifetime of the person receiving the payments (annuitant). Annuities can be purchased by a single premium or on an installment premium basis; payments may cease upon the death of the annuitant, or arrangements can be made to guarantee payments to the annuitant's survivors on some basis.

annuity due • a series of payments of equal amounts made at the beginning of each of a number of consecutive periods.

applicable credit amount • a cumulative credit of $211,300 (for 1999) that is currently available against federal estate and gift tax due on taxable transfers. This credit is equivalent to an exemption on $650,000 (for 1999) worth of property. Formerly called *unified credit.*

approximate yield • an estimate of the internal rate of return on an investment; it was commonly used to estimate bond yields to maturity because it is easy to calculate, but financial calculators can now compute actual yields to maturity almost as quickly.

assets under management • defined in Section 203(A) as the securities portfolios with respect to which an investment adviser provides continuous and regular supervisory or management services.

assignment of income doctrine • a tax doctrine which holds that income is taxed to the person who earns it, or to the person who owns the asset that produces it.

availability bias • a bias that alters people's perception of risk. Events that are easy to imagine or recall (such as those that receive heavy media coverage) tend to be judged as more probable than they actually are; events that are dull or abstract are judged as less probable than they actually are.

"baby boom" generation • those born from the mid-1940s to mid-1960s. Also called *baby boomers.*

balance sheet • see *financial position statement.*

basic form of homeowners policy • an old type of homeowners insurance policy that covers losses from fire, wind, hail, explosion, riot, smoke, and a few other perils.

basic hospital expense policy • a basic type of medical expense insurance that provides benefits for expenses associated with hospital confinement. Such a policy would reimburse the insured for room-and-board charges up to a specified number of dollars per day for a specified number of days. As an additional benefit, the policy might pay for general nursing, medicines, and other miscellaneous hospital charges.

beneficial interest in property • a type of property right that provides an individual with a beneficial interest, such as the right to current income or principal distributions. One example of this is the interest owned by the beneficiary of a trust.

benefit period • in disability income insurance, the length of time during which income benefits are paid. This period can range from 2 years to when the insured reaches age 65 to the insured's entire lifetime.

bounded rationality • the manner in which human beings behave, that is, with limits on their rationality. People's choices in financial matters are shaped not only by knowledge and rational thinking but by values and emotions.

broad form of homeowners policy • a type of homeowners insurance policy that is essentially the basic form with the addition of several perils (such as the weight of ice, snow, or sleet and the accidental discharge or overflow of water or steam) and an expansion of coverage for other perils. Also called *Form HO-2*.

brochure rule (SEC Rule 204-3) • an SEC rule requiring all registered investment advisers to deliver a written disclosure statement to each client, both existing and prospective.

budgeting • the process of creating and following an explicit plan for spending and investing the resources available to the client, which works via the establishment of a working budget model followed by a comparison of actual and expected results. It provides a means of financial self-evaluation and a guideline to measure actual performance.

business activity • in homeowners insurance policies, this consists of any activity carried out with an expectation of profit or gain, with evidence of continuity of the activity.

business risk (default risk) • the risk that for some reason—such as a change in consumer preference away from a particular good or service, ineffective management, law change, or foreign competition—an enterprise will experience financial difficulties and eventually fail. As a result, an investor loses not only the current and future interest or dividend payments but some or all of the initial amount invested as well.

business standard • test set forth by SEC Release No. IA-770 to determine if the Investment Advisers Act of 1940 applies to a financial services professional; it concerns whether the practitioner is presented to the public as being "in the business" of providing advice about securities.

callable bond • a type of corporate debt security that has an option exercisable at the discretion of the issuer to redeem the bond before its maturity date at a specified price.

capital asset • any property held by the taxpayer that is not property held for sale by the taxpayer or is not intellectual or artistic property created by the taxpayer.

capital gain • income realized through the sale or exchange of a capital asset. Special tax rules apply to capital gains.

capital loss • a loss resulting from the sale of a capital asset. Special tax rules apply to capital losses; basically, they can be deducted only against the taxpayer's capital gains and not against ordinary income, such as wages. However, an individual taxpayer may deduct $3,000 of capital losses in excess of capital gains against the taxpayer's other income; any remaining capital losses must be carried over to future tax years.

cash equivalents • financial instruments that satisfy the need to make transactions, to have readily accessible money in case of emergencies, and to serve as a receptacle for accumulating funds to purchase other investment assets. Cash equivalents typically have no specified maturity date or have one that is 1 year or less in the future; they often provide only a modest current income and typically have little or no potential for capital appreciation.

cash-flow analysis • the process of gathering cash-flow information, presenting the data in an organized format, and identifying strengths, weaknesses, and important patterns. Also called *revenue and expense analysis.*

cash-flow management • the budget planning and control process. It consists of three components: cash-flow analysis, cash-flow planning, and budgeting.

cash-flow statement • an organized list of a client's cash inflows and outflows. Also see *budgeting.*

CD-ROM (compact disk, read-only memory) • identical in appearance to an audio compact disk, but capable of holding over 600 megabytes of data. This form of hardware is particularly attractive for delivering multimedia programs, which incorporate sound and graphical and photographic images.

CDW • see *collision damage waiver.*

cell • a place on a computer program's spreadsheet where a column and row intersects. Cells contain math formulae, data, or label names.

charitable lead trust • a type of trust arrangement designed to provide a charitable institution with a current term income interest. The remainder interest in the trust is retained by the grantor or the grantor's family. The donor gets an upfront income and gift or estate tax deduction for the present value of the lead income interest donated to charity; however, the grantor remains taxable annually on the actual trust income. The charitable lead trust is generally used for testamentary dispositions, permitting a large deduction in the taxable estate.

charitable remainder trust • a type of trust arrangement used to retain the current enjoyment of property for the life of the donor (or the life of the donor's family members) while providing gift, estate, and income tax advantages. A charitable institution holds the remainder interest and receives the property when the trust's assets are distributed. A charitable remainder trust can be established during a donor's lifetime or at his or her death.

chip (semiconductor) • the microprocessor in a computer. This component allows software to manipulate data.

choice shift (risky shift) • a phenomenon seen when studying the difference between individual and group reactions to risk. A group decision is usually more extreme than a decision favored by most members of the group when they are polled individually, before group discussion. The shift is typically toward more risky action, although it may sometimes be toward a more cautious one.

churning • the process of generating brokerage commissions through unnecessary securities transactions; advising a client to make unnecessary transactions is also considered churning.

clarifying response • a type of response during active listening that enhances communication. There are two forms of clarifying response. In the first, one attempts to restate or clarify what the speaker has had difficulty in expressing clearly. In the second, one asks the speaker to clarify what he or she means.

closed-end investment company • a type of investment company that issues a given number of shares at its formation, rarely issuing additional shares. These shares are traded in stock markets like shares of operating corporations. The company uses the proceeds from the initial sale of shares to acquire a portfolio of securities. The market value of this portfolio influences the market price of the closed-end company's shares, but the market price is normally lower than the per share value of the portfolio. Normal brokerage sales commissions apply for both the purchase and sale of the shares.

closed-ended question • a type of question that solicits singular facts or one-word replies.

coinsurance • a feature in several types of insurance policies. In major medical health insurance policies, coinsurance refers to a sharing of the costs—for example, 80 percent paid by the insurer and 20 percent by the insured—typically between the deductible and the maximum dollar limit in the policy. In property insurance policies, coinsurance is a provision that penalizes an insured who does not carry a sufficient amount of insurance in relation to the value of the insured property.

coinsurance (percentage participation) clause • found in major medical expense insurance policies, this provision requires the insured to pay part of eligible medical expenses in excess of the deductible. A typical provision requires the insured to pay 20 percent (or 25 percent) of the expenses eligible for payment by the insurer. Some policies also have a stop-loss limit, which modifies the coinsurance provision when an insured's out-of-pocket eligible expenses reach a designated level; at that point, the insured's payment participation ceases and the insurer starts paying 100 percent.

collision • under the PAP, upset of the covered auto or its impact with an object or another vehicle.

collision damage waiver (CDW) • insurance offered by auto rental companies on vehicles rented from them. The PAP does not provide the specialized coverages found in the CDW, such as the loss-of-use benefit; therefore, purchase of the CDW is usually recommended.

community property • found in some states, property acquired during marriage is considered to be equally owned by the spouses. Community property is not technically jointly held, but the law limits the right of each spouse to transfer community property to individuals other than his or her spouse.

compensation test • test set forth by SEC Release No. IA-770 to determine if the Investment Advisers Act of 1940 applies to a financial services professional. A practitioner who charges a fee for investment advice or receives a commission on the sale of a securities product meets this test; in fact, it is almost impossible for a financial services professional not to meet this test in today's environment.

compound interest • interest computed by applying an interest rate to the sum of the original amount and the interest credited to it in earlier time periods.

compounding • the process by which money today (present value) grows over time to a larger amount (future value).

comprehensive major medical expense coverage • a type of medical expense coverage that is a combination of basic hospital expense and major medical expense coverage.

comprehensive view of financial planning • the position that financial planning must consider all aspects of a client's financial situation (including financial needs and objectives) and must use several integrated and coordinated planning strategies.

constructive receipt doctrine • a tax doctrine which holds that a taxpayer is deemed to have received income for tax purposes when it is either credited to the taxpayer's account, set apart for the taxpayer, or otherwise made available to be taken into the taxpayer's possession. If a condition or restriction limits the taxpayer's right to receive the income, however, this doctrine does not apply.

consultative (client-focused) planning or selling • an approach to financial planning that requires the practitioner to gather as much information as possible from the client about needs, goals, interest, and assets in order to put together an insurance or investment package that best meets the client's needs.

contingency fund • a cash reserve allocated for such situations as liquidity needs, emergencies, scheduled expenditures, and investment opportunities; it should be invested according to how quickly the funds would be needed.

continuous compounding • the process of compounding interest an infinite number of times per year rather than at discrete time intervals. It represents the upper limit of the total interest credited to a sum for a particular stated or nominal annual interest rate.

conversion of interest to principal • occurs when interest is credited to a sum and begins to earn interest on itself.

convertible bond • a type of corporate debt security; it has an option exercisable by the bondholder to exchange the bond for a predetermined number of common or preferred shares.

corridor deductible • a type of deductible sometimes used in medical expense insurance. It is typically a small deductible ($100 to $250) for a major medical expense policy that has been superimposed over a basic hospital expense policy; the deductible applies after basic benefits are exhausted and before major medical benefits begin.

counseling • this type of structured communication consists of providing assistance to clients as they explore their present situations, begin to understand where they are in relation to where they want to be, and act to get from where they are to where they want to be; it takes place over a period of time, and an interpersonal relationship often develops between counselor and client.

covered auto • under the PAP, any vehicle shown in the declarations of the policy. It also includes any trailer the named insured owns.

credit estate (sponge) tax • a tax imposed by all states that brings the total state death tax liability up to the maximum federal death tax credit. In many states, this is the sole form of state death tax.

current yield • a widely used measure of financial return. The before-tax current yield equals the current annual income from an investment divided by the investment's current market price.

dealer market • a market in which dealers offer to buy (at a bid price) and sell (at an ask price) as much of a particular security as desired by investors.

debenture • a type of corporate debt security; it is an unsecured promise to pay interest and principal backed only by the issuer's general credit status, not by the backing of specific assets.

debt service payment • for an installment loan, a level periodic payment of interest on the remaining unpaid principal and some repayment of the principal.

deductible • the amount of money that must be paid by the insured before the insurance company becomes liable for the loss.

deduction • an item of expense that reduces the amount of income that is subject to tax.

deferred annuity • a series of consecutive, equal, periodic payments that will begin more than one period from the present.

defined-benefit plan • a type of qualified retirement plan in which the required employer contributions vary depending on what is needed to pay the promised benefits. These plans usually use a benefit formula to stipulate a promised benefit, which is typically a percentage of the employee's final salary.

defined-contribution plan • a type of qualified retirement plan in which the required annual employer contributions are specified and the eventual employee benefit is unknown. With these plans, the retirement benefit is based on an employee's entire career earnings, not just on the employee's final salary.

depreciation • (1) in property insurance, a reduction in the value of an asset resulting from the asset's age, its use, its condition, and any other factor causing deterioration. (2) in income taxation, a deduction that allows a taxpayer to recover the cost of certain property for tax purposes by allowing the taxpayer to deduct a specified portion of the cost of the property each year against income.

directive interview • this type of structured communication is an interview in which the interviewer directs and controls the pace and content to be covered; it is a formalized, structured form of interaction. Its advantages are that it can be brief and that it provides measurable data; its disadvantages are that it is often inflexible and does not allow the interviewee to choose topics for discussion.

disability income insurance • a type of health insurance that helps reimburse a person for earnings lost because of long-term illness or injury.

disclosure • the financial planner's presentation to the client of all material facts regarding potential conflicts of interest; the client can then make an informed decision about entering into or continuing an advisory relationship with the planner.

discounting • the process by which money due in the future (future value) is reduced over time to a smaller amount today (present value). This concept acknowledges the fact that a dollar received in the future is not as valuable as a dollar received today.

durable power of attorney • a type of power-of-attorney that serves as an estate planning document; it is not terminated by the legal disability of the principal unless specifically enumerated.

dwelling program • a series of insurance forms that provide coverage for dwellings, other structures, personal property, additional living expenses, and rental value to persons in dwellings that do not meet the eligibility requirements for homeowners insurance. Coverage provided under the dwelling program is narrower than that provided by the homeowners program.

economic benefit doctrine • a tax doctrine which holds that a taxpayer must pay tax whenever an economic benefit has been conferred on the taxpayer regardless of whether the taxpayer has actually received any cash or property. For example, if an employer pays life insurance premiums covering the life of an employee who has the right to name the beneficiary under the policy, the life insurance coverage is an economic benefit subject to income tax.

effective interest rate • the annual interest rate that produces in one compounding the same amount of interest as does the nominal annual rate with its compounding frequency.

either/or question • a relatively ineffective type of question, in which the client's answer is limited to only two options.

elimination period • in disability income insurance, the number of days that must elapse between the start of a disability and the start of benefit payments. This avoids coverage of short-term illness or injury that temporarily disables an insured and for which risk retention is more economical that insurance. The elimination period typically ranges from 30 days to 1 year. Also called *waiting period.*

equivalent fully taxable yield • for a given tax rate, the pre-tax yield that a fully taxable bond would have to earn to provide the same yield after taxation as that offered by a tax-exempt bond.

estate trust • a type of trust that qualifies for the federal estate tax marital deduction. A deceased spouse leaves a life estate in trust to the surviving spouse, whose estate is the remainder person. Income from the estate trust can either accumulate or be paid to the surviving spouse at the discretion of the trustee; the trust's assets are included in the surviving spouse's estate.

event risk • the risk that one of a variety of possible occurrences that can significantly affect the riskiness of a specific investment asset—for example, a takeover attempt—will happen.

excess-benefit plan • a type of nonqualified retirement plan in which the employer provides benefits beyond the dollar restrictions imposed by qualified plans.

exclusions from gross income • certain items of money or other property received by the taxpayer that are excluded from gross income by the Internal Revenue Code.

These items include gifts, income from tax-exempt bonds, workers compensation benefits, and many other items.

expected family contribution (EFC) • the total amount a student and student's family are expected to contribute annually for college education before becoming eligible for financial aid. The amount is calculated by adding together the expected student contribution and the expected family contribution.

expense method • a method of determining how much annual income an individual will need in the first year of retirement. This method focuses on the retiree's projected expenses; therefore, it is easier to use with those who are near retirement. Some expenses tend to increase after retirement, including utility and phone bills, medical expenses and health insurance, house repairs and maintenance, entertainment and traveling expenses, and gifts and contributions. Others tend to decrease, including mortgage payments, food and clothing expenses, income and property taxes, transportation costs, debt repayment, child support and alimony, and household furnishing expenses.

familiarity bias • a bias that alters people's perception of risk. Risks that are familiar are feared less than those that are unfamiliar; this helps explain why people overreact to unexpected news.

family member • under the PAP, anyone who is related to the named insured by blood, marriage, or adoption and who resides in the named insured's household.

Federal Supplemental Education Opportunity grant • a federal grant available in amounts of up to $4,000 per year for college students who show exceptional need.

fee simple ownership • the most complete type of individual ownership interest in property; the individual owns all the rights associated with the property, including the current possessor rights and the ability to transfer the property at any point during his or her lifetime or at death.

fiduciary • one who holds another's trust or confidence; in financial planning, the investment adviser is a fiduciary who owes the client an affirmative duty of utmost good faith and full and fair disclosure of all the material facts.

filing status • a set of categories used to classify individuals when paying federal income tax. The four categories are single, married filing jointly, married filing separately, and unmarried head of household. The amount of taxable income that will fall into each tax bracket depends on the individual's filing status.

financial position statement • an organized list of the components of an individual's or family's wealth at a specified time. It reflects the results of past financial activities and covers three basic classifications (assets, liabilities, and net worth), which can be grouped in subclassifications to permit better analysis of the total financial situation.

Form ADV • the SEC form a financial planner must complete and file to become a registered investment adviser.

Form HO-4 • a type of homeowners insurance policy designed primarily for tenants who occupy residential rental property. It is similar to the HO-2 (broad form) except that it provides no coverage on the dwelling or other structures.

Form HO-6 • a type of homeowners insurance policy used by condominium unit owners and cooperative apartment occupants. The building itself is not covered, but the form does provide some coverage for additions and alterations. Additional coverage may be needed, however, if the building owner's insurance is "bare walls" coverage; the unit owner must then insure the entire interior, including all fixtures, interior partitions, and paint or wallpaper.

Form HO-8 • a type of homeowners insurance policy that is useful when a dwelling's replacement cost is considerably higher than its market value. The HO-8 provides insurance on the basis of the cost of repairing or replacing the property using common construction materials and methods, eliminating the replacement-cost provision in other homeowners policies; thus a homeowner can purchase a lesser amount of coverage without being exposed to the penalty for underinsuring.

401(k) plan • a type of qualified retirement plan that allows employees to elect deferral of taxation on current salaries or bonuses simply by placing the money in the plan. Participants sign a salary reduction agreement so that employee contributions to the plan can be made with before-tax contributions. Matching contributions from the employer are often found in these plans.

403(b) plan • a type of retirement plan with many of the features of qualified plans, such as before-tax contributions in the form of salary deferrals. These plans are similar to 401(k) plans, but they can only be used public schools and certain types of tax-exempt organizations (501(c)(3) tax-exempt organizations). Also called *tax-deferred annuity (TDA)*.

future interest • a type of individual property ownership consisting of the current right to future enjoyment of the property; there is no right to immediate use of the property. One type of future interest, a remainder interest, takes effect immediately upon the expiration of another interest in the same property. Another type of future interest, a reversionary interest, occurs when the current property owner transfers current possessory rights to another but keeps the right to the return of the property at the end of the possessory term of the transferee.

future value of a single sum • an amount determined by compounding a present value at a particular interest rate for a particular length or time. The basic formula is

FVSS = *PVSS* × $(1 + i)^n$, where *PVSS* is the present value of a single sum, *i* is the periodic interest rate expressed as a decimal, and *n* is the number of periods during which compounding occurs.

FVSS factor • when determining the future value of a single sum, the FVSS factor is $(1 + i)^n$, where *i* is the periodic interest rate expressed as a decimal and *n* is the number of periods during which compounding occurs.

FVSS • see *future value of a single sum.*

general power of appointment • a broad right to make property decisions; the holder of such a right can transfer the property subject to the power to virtually any recipient.

generation-skipping transfer tax (GSTT) • a tax on property transferred to an individual more than one generation below the level of the transferor (a *skip beneficiary*), such as a grandchild. It is applied at a flat rate equal to the highest current estate or gift tax bracket (currently 55 percent) in addition to any estate or gift tax; thus the total tax could exceed 100 percent of the transferred asset's total value. The GSTT can apply to direct skips (outright transfers during life or at death to a skip beneficiary), taxable distributions (income or principal distributed from a trust to a skip beneficiary), and taxable terminations (termination of property interests held in trust as a result of death, lapse of time, or otherwise and a skip beneficiary receives the remainder interest outright in the trust).

genuineness • a quality necessary to be an effective counselor. Genuine counselors are aware of themselves and their feelings, thoughts, values, and attitudes; always express themselves openly and honestly; and do not play roles; they communicate expressively without concealing anything; and they are consistent (do not think or feel one thing but say another).

gross estate • used as the starting point in the calculation of federal estate tax, the gross estate includes the property included in the probate estate as well as property transferable by other means at the time of death. This means the gross estate includes property individually owned by the decedent; some portion of property held jointly; insurance on the decedent's life if incidents of ownership were held by the decedent within 3 years of death or if the proceeds are payable to the estate; pension or IRA payments left to survivors; property subject to general powers of appointment held by the decedent; and property transferred by the decedent during his or her lifetime if the decedent retained a life interest in the property, a reversionary interest valued at greater than 5 percent of the property's value at the time of death, or rights to revoke the transfer.

gross income • the sum of every item of value, whether consisting of money or other property, that is either made available to or comes into the possession of the taxpayer. Certain particular items of value are specifically excluded from gross income by the Internal Revenue Code.

grouped cash flows • a cash-flow sequence that has some consecutive payments of the same amount and arithmetic sign (positive or negative).

GSTT • see *generation-skipping transfer tax.*

guaranteed renewable contract • for disability income insurance, a type of policy in which the insurer reserves the right to change premium rates for all insured of the same class but cannot cancel or refuse to renew the policy.

hardware • any part of a computer that can be seen or touched, such as the monitor, floppy drive, and printer.

hold harmless agreement • an agreement in which one party assumes the liability of another for bodily injury or property damage as an incidental obligation in contracts dealing with services, premises, or products. One example of such agreements is commonly found in leases of dwellings or apartments, in which the landlord may transfer to the tenant financial responsibility for damage to the property and for bodily injuries to third parties that, in the absence of the lease, would be borne by the landlord.

holding-period return (HPR) • a measure of financial return. The before-tax HPR for a 1-year period equals total current income from an investment plus the investment's total capital appreciation divided by the total initial investment.

holistic retirement planning • an all-inclusive appoach that requires the retirement planner or planning team to cover such topics as employer-provided retirement plans, social security, income tax issues, insurance coverage, investments, long-term care, retirement communities, relocation, wellness, nutrition, and lifestyle.

Hope Scholarship Tax Credit • an education tax credit of up to $1,500 per student per year for tuition and related expenses incurred during the first 2 years of post-secondary education; the credit equals 100 percent of the first $1,000 of tuition and fees, and 50 percent of the next $1,000 of tuition and fees. This credit will be indexed for inflation for years beginning after 2000; it cannot be used in the same year as the Lifetime Learning Tax Credit.

HPR • see *holding-period return.*

illusion of control bias • a bias that alters people's perception of risk. People tend to underestimate the risk involved in events under their control, such as driving a car, relative to activities in which control is given to someone else, such as flying as a passenger in a plane.

income-shifting technique • the reduction of income tax liability by transferring taxable income to a taxpayer in a lower marginal tax bracket than the taxpayer who would otherwise have to report the income. An outright gift of property is the simplest income-shifting technique; however, the gift tax consequences of giving away property must be considered.

index fund • a mutual fund that owns a portfolio of common stock that replicates a major market index, such as the S&P 500.

individual retirement account (IRA) • a type of retirement savings plan similar in many ways to a qualified plan. Traditional IRAs allow the accumulation of contributions made with before-tax dollars (if the individual is eligible) and deferral of tax on earnings until retirement. Such plans are subject to various restrictions on contributions and eligibility.

information technology • the application of science to solving the problems of collecting, classifying, storing, retrieving, and disseminating knowledge.

inheritance tax • a tax some states impose on the right of a beneficiary to receive property from the estate of a decedent. The tax rate is based on the amount of property received by each beneficiary and is often based on the relationship of the beneficiary to the decedent. This tax can often be higher than any estate tax due; payment is usually the responsibility of the estate.

Insider Trading Sanction Act • a 1984 law that, among other things, gives the SEC the authority to seek the imposition of civil penalties against insider-trading violations for as much as three times the profit gained (or loss avoided) as a result of the unlawful purchase or sale of securities.

insurable interest • a relationship to the person or thing insured that the law requires so that the insurance contract is not merely a wager. The basis for insurable interest in property and liability contracts includes a property right, a contract right, and legal liability. In life insurance contracts, an individual has an unrestricted insurable interest in his or her own life; beyond this, the basis for the existence of an insurable interest is a close family relationship or a financial relationship.

insurance • the business of transferring pure risks by means of a two-party contract. As a risk-financing method, insurance involves a transfer of the financial burden of risk through a contract for a price (premium); it is also a loss-sharing device and a system for reducing risk.

interest-rate risk • the risk that interest rates associated with an investment will change, leading to a change in the value of securities, the income earned on securities, or both. There are two segments of this effect, the capital segment and the reinvestment segment. In the capital segment, a change in market interest rates typically leads to an opposite change in the value on investments; this inverse relationship is most pronounced for financial instruments that have a contractually specified rate of interest or return and a specified time frame, such as bonds and mortgages. In the reinvestment segment, the risk relates to the fact that if interest rates fall (rise) after the security is purchased, the value of the reinvested cash flows will be lower (higher) than projected when the asset was purchased.

internal limit • a dollar limit on the coverage provided by homeowners insurance on certain types of personal property. For example, there is a $1,000 limit for loss by theft of jewelry, watches, and furs.

internal rate of return • the interest rate that equates the present value of the stream of cash inflows to the present value of the stream of cash outflows.

interpretive response • a type of leading response in which the counselor cuts to the heart of the matter, "translating" what the client has said.

intestate • having died without a valid will. When a decedent dies intestate, all probate property passes under the laws of intestate succession of the jurisdiction state.

intrastate exemption • an exemption to the Investment Advisers Act of 1940; it applies to investment advisers whose clients are all residents of the state in which the adviser maintains the principle office and place of business and who does not furnish advice or issue analyses or reports with respect to listed securities or securities admitted to unlisted trading privileges on any national securities exchange. Such investment advisers need not register with the SEC, but must still comply with the act's antifraud provisions.

investment • in financial planning, an asset purchased by an individual or an institution with the expectation that the asset acquired will increase (or hold) its value and/or generate a current income flow commensurate with the associated risk. The asset may be tangible (land, buildings, artworks, jewels, and the like) or intangible (shares of stock, bonds, money in a savings account, and other financial assets).

investment adviser representative • defined in the SEC's Rule 203-3(a) as a supervised person of an investment adviser if clients who are natural persons represent more than 10 percent of the clients of the supervised person. In 1998, SEC Release No. IA-1733 changed this, specifying that a supervised person can have the greater of five natural-person clients or the number of natural-person clients permitted under the 10 percent allowance without being subject to state qualification requirements.

Investment Advisers Act of 1940 • the statutory body of law that controls the regulation of financial planners.

Investment Advisers Supervision Coordination Act • a 1996 law primarily concerning the regulation of investment advisers by the SEC or state authorities based on the level of assets under an adviser's management; as a result, investment advisers need to register with either the SEC or state authorities, but not both.

IRA • see *individual retirement account.*

irrevocable life insurance trust • a type of trust designed to provide to heirs life insurance benefits that are excluded from the insured's gross estate. In addition, contributions to the trust can be designed to avoid gift or generation-skipping taxes. Therefore the irrevocable life insurance trust provides for the liquidity needs of older wealthy clients without adding to the tax burden.

itemized deductions • income tax deductions, listed on Schedule A of Form 1040, that can be taken in lieu of the standard deduction. Itemized deductions include charitable contributions, deductions for interest payments, taxes, casualty losses, certain business expenses of employees, and other items.

joint tenancy with right of survivorship • a type of joint concurrent ownership of property, in which two or more individuals hold property jointly and in which, upon the death of a tenant, the surviving tenants receive the entire interest in the property. The individuals may be related or unrelated. Because this property interest transfers automatically at the death of a joint tenant to the surviving tenants, the property is not subject to disposition by a decedent at his or her death. A joint tenant usually may transfer his or her interest during life without consent of the other joint tenants; such a transfer generally severs the joint tenancy and destroys the survivorship rights of the joint tenants.

junk bond • a bond with a low quality rating that is risky because the issuing firm either has a large amount of debt outstanding relative to its equity base, or has suffered financial reverses and may be headed for serious trouble or bankruptcy. Because the risk is high, junk bonds have high yields, so they are also called *high-yield bonds.*

large-loss principle • a theory that suggests that in the purchase of insurance, first priority should be given to exposures that might cause significant financial loss. The definition of a large loss differs among individuals, but risks listed as serious during the risk-evaluation process should, by implication, be large losses and should receive first priority in the use of insurance.

leading question • a type of question that leads the client toward a conclusion which the counselor, not the client, has already formulated. This type of question is considered ineffective, dishonest, and manipulative.

leading response • a type of response in which the financial counselor takes the lead (to a certain extent) and deviates somewhat from the client's preceding responses.

liability loss • a loss resulting from damage to or destruction of others' property or personal injuries to others.

life estate • a common type of individual property ownership in which the life tenant has the right to possess and enjoy the property for a time period measured by the life of an individual (typically the life tenant).

Lifetime Learning Tax Credit • an education tax credit of up to $1,000 calculated as 20 percent of the first $5,000 of tuition and related expenses, increasing to 20 percent of the first $10,000 in expenses for years beginning after 2002. It cannot be used in the same year as the Hope Scholarship Tax Credit.

limited-payment policy • a type of whole life insurance policy, in which the premium-payment policy lasts only for a specified number of years.

liquidity risk • the risk that an investment asset cannot be converted to cash (sold) quickly at any time without any loss of principal.

living (*inter vivos*) trust • a trust created during the lifetime of the grantor. Such a trust can hold property and operate before the death of the grantor or simply receive assets at the grantor's death. The trust may be revocable (with the grantor transferring property to the trust but reserving the power to alter or revoke the agreement) or irrevocable.

living will • a document indicating an individual's intentions should he the individual become disabled and lack the legal capacity to make decisions for himself or herself. Living wills generally deal with the health care measures an individual wants imposed should he or she become legally disabled, such as whether heroic measures should be taken in the event of a life-threatening accident or illness.

load fund • a type of mutual fund that charges a sales fee, which can be up to 8.5 percent of the value of the investment.

loss control (risk control) • the use of certain techniques to reduce the probability that events resulting in financial loss will occur and to minimize the magnitude of losses that do occur. These techniques include risk avoidance, loss prevention, and loss reduction.

loss prevention • a loss-control technique, which consists of the attempt to control inescapable risks and forestall losses. Loss prevention must precede the occurrence of a loss and is directed at reducing the frequency of loss. Loss-prevention actions tend to be directed at hazards or conditions that increase the likelihood of a loss occurring; they can be positive or negative in nature.

loss reduction • a loss-control technique, which is directed at reducing loss severity. Loss-reduction actions are designed to minimize the magnitude of a loss and its financial effects; these actions can be used before, during, or after a loss has occurred.

loss settlement provision • a feature in homeowners policies, similar to coinsurance in property insurance policies. This provision requires that at the time of loss, the amount of insurance carried on the damaged dwelling must be 80 percent or more of the full replacement value of the dwelling at the time the loss occurs. If it is less than 80 percent, the insurer agrees to pay the greater of the actual cash value of the loss or a proportion of the cost to repair or replace the dwelling determined by the ratio of the amount of insurance carried to the amount of insurance required.

major medical expense policy • a type of medical expense insurance that, unlike a basic hospital expense policy, provides a broad range of coverage for virtually all kinds of expenses associated with illness or injury. These policies have several common characteristics: a high aggregate maximum limit on benefits, a deductible, and a coinsurance provision.

marginal tax rate • the income tax rate applicable to each income bracket.

market risk • the risk that political, economic, demographic, or social events will have widespread effects that change the expected return from an investment.

marketability risk • the risk that an investment asset cannot be sold quickly at its current market price.

medical expense insurance • a type of health insurance that provides coverage for hospital bills, physicians' costs, and various other expenses related to periods of sickness or injury. It is often provided through an employer-sponsored benefit program.

medical payments coverage in the PAP • coverage for reasonable expenses incurred for necessary medical and funeral services because of bodily injury sustained by an insured. Subject to certain exclusions, benefits are payable to the named insured and family members if injured while occupying any motor vehicle designed for public roads or if struck by a motor vehicle.

mental accounts • subjective standards that are employed as yardsticks to gauge value. Financial services professionals must recognize that because of mental accounts, clients may have different risk tolerance levels for different funds, depending on how they acquired the money and what they intend to do with it. Also, a client is likely to be more upset about a given loss than pleased about an equivalent gain.

MHz (megahertz) • the measure of how fast a computer chip can process data; often referred to as a computer's *clock speed.*

money market mutual fund • a type of mutual fund that owns a portfolio of short-term interest-bearing securities. Such funds are typically used by investors as an alternative to cash. Some of these funds have specialized portfolios, focusing only on nontaxable securities or federal securities or featuring a diversified portfolio.

money-purchase pension plan • a type of defined-contribution plan in which the employer's annual contributions are mandatory and are based on the employee's compensation (for example, 10 percent of the employee's compensation). The definition of *compensation* varies between plans; it might be restricted to base salary, or it might include overtime, bonuses, and the like.

multiple purpose view of financial planning • the position that financial planning must deal with at least a large part of one basic category of client financial needs (for example, insurance planning, tax planning, and retirement planning), and some aspects of one or more other categories.

multitasking • running more than one computer program, or application, at a time.

mutual fund • an open-end investment company.

national de minimis standard • a part of the Investment Advisers Supervision Coordination Act that relieves some financial advisers from some regulatory burden; investment advisers may not be required to register in any state unless the adviser has a place of business in the state or, during the preceding 12-month period, has had more than five clients who are residents of the state.

negotiated market • a market in which sellers list their offerings with brokers, who then seek to attract buyers through advertising and other marketing methods. After a buyer is located, negotiations determine the price. The trading of real estate is an example of a negotiated market.

net discretionary cash flow • the difference between income and expenses.

net present value • the present value of a stream of cash inflows minus the present value of the stream of cash outflows, with both present values calculated on the basis of an appropriate rate of interest.

no-fault benefits • under a no-fault automobile insurance plan, benefits paid to the insured by his or her insurance company for losses below a certain dollar limit or below some verbalized statement regarding the severity of the injury. These benefits typically include some combination of medical expenses, lost wages, replacement of services, survivors' benefits, and funeral expenses.

no-load fund • a type of mutual fund that does not charge a sales fee.

noncancelable contract • a type of disability income insurance policy in which the insurer can neither change premium rates nor cancel the policy.

nondirective interview • this type of structured communication is an interview that affords both the interviewer and interviewee a wide range of subject matters to discussed; the interviewee usually controls the pacing and purpose of the interview. Its advantages are that there is greater flexibility and more in-depth responses than with a directive interview, and a closer relationship between the interviewer and interviewee is established; its disadvantages are that it consumes more time than a directive interview, and it often provides data that are difficult to measure objectively.

noninsurance transfer • a method of transferring risk without the use of insurance. This type of transfer is more often initiated by businesses, whereas individuals are more often the recipient of such transfers. An example is shipping goods F.O.B. point of origin, in which the merchandise supplier transfers to the purchaser responsibility for damage to the goods while in transit.

nonowned auto • under the PAP, any private passenger auto, pickup, van, or trailer not owned by or furnished or available for the regular use of the insured. This includes a temporary substitute auto.

nonqualified retirement (deferred-compensation) plan • a type of employer-sponsored retirement plan typically given to highly compensated executives and managers; it provides the employees with tax savings because, in most cases, the employer defers the business deduction so that the employees are not deemed to be in constructive receipt of deferred compensation promised to them. Nonqualified plans come in three basic types: the *top-hat plan,* the *excess benefit plan,* and the *supplemental executive retirement plan.*

nonrecognition transaction • a transaction that produces a monetary benefit for the taxpayer in which taxation is deferred. Such a transaction typically involves the sale or exchange of property at a realized gain that is not currently recognizable (reportable on Form 1040).

nonverbal behaviors • nonlinguistic actions that make up a large part of communication. From the two main sources of nonverbal behaviors, the body and the voice, come seven important types of nonverbal signs of meaning: body position, body movement, gestures, facial expressions, eye contact, voice tone, and voice pitch.

open-end investment company • a type of investment company that continually sells and redeems its shares at net asset value; shares are not sold in stock markets. The company acquires a portfolio of securities in which each of the fund's shares owns a proportionate interest. As sales and redemptions of the fund's shares take place, the size of the total portfolio changes, increasing when additional shares are sold and decreasing when shares are redeemed. An open-end investment company may charge a sales fee when shares are purchased. Also called a *mutual fund.*

open-ended question • a type of question that encourages expansive responses, especially when soliciting opinions, thoughts, ideas, values, and feelings.

opportunity cost • the implied cost of undertaking a financial action. It is usually represented as the rate that could have been earned by investing in the best alternative activity with the same resource(s).

organized securities market • a market for securities listed on the national or a regional exchange. Such markets have formal trading posts and specialized brokers, membership requirements for individuals trading there, and listing requirements for corporations that wish to have their securities traded there.

other structures • other structures on the premises that are not attached to the house. These include garages, toolsheds, and such things as fences, driveways, and retaining walls.

PAP • see *Personal Auto Policy.*

paper deduction • an income tax deduction that represents or is related to some entry on the books of a taxpayer's business or investment activity, but is not a cash-flow item. The most important paper deduction is for depreciation.

Parent Loan for Undergraduate Students (PLUS loan) • a loan available through the Direct Loan Program and the Family Federal Education Loan Program. This type of loan is not based on need, but the borrower cannot have a bad credit record; it must be repaid within 10 years.

partial disability • condition representing a partial recovery from total disability. In disability income insurance policies, the typical definition states that although the insured has returned to work, he or she is unable to perform all the major duties of his or her occupation or is unable to work on more than a half-time basis. Also see *residual disability.*

passive loss • a tax loss typically generated by activities in which the taxpayer has an ownership interest but does not participate in the activity of the business.

pass-through entity • an entity that is not subject to income tax at the entity level; instead, the responsibility for paying income tax is shifted to the owners of the entity. Partnerships and S corporations are pass-through entities.

Pell grant • a federal grant for undergraduate students who qualify under the needs-analysis formula; available in amounts of up to $2,700 per year (1997–1998).

pension maximization • a retirement planning strategy sometimes used by married individuals. By electing a single-life annuity payment from a qualified plan instead of a joint and survivor annuity, an individual can significantly increase the annual retirement benefit and use some of the extra money on life insurance to provide for the surviving spouse.

perceived risk • one's interpretation of the riskiness of a situation, which is not necessarily the same as the objective riskiness. A person's experiences and inclinations toward risk taking as well as the circumstances of a particular situation affect the interpretation of riskiness.

performance fee • a fee charged by an investment adviser based on capital appreciation of all or any portion of a client's funds; it is permitted only in certain situations. Also called *incentive fee.*

peril • a cause of loss.

Perkins loan • a loan of up to $3,000 per year ($15,000 cumulative) for students who show exceptional need. The program is administered by colleges but uses federal funds; interest is only 5 percent, and payments can be spread over 10 years after the student leaves school.

Personal Auto Policy (PAP) • a common type of automobile insurance. It contains coverage for four perils: liability, medical payments, uninsured motorists, and damage to your auto. For the most part, the insured may choose the coverages he or she desires and an amount of insurance for each coverage.

personal liability coverage • coverage provided by a homeowners insurance policy that provides protection for activities and conditions at the residence where the insured maintains a covered residence and for personal activities of the named insured and members of the insured's family anywhere in the world. It includes legal liability involving bodily injury or property damage and medical benefits for persons (other than residents of the insured household) who suffer bodily injury at an insured location or who are injured because of an insured's activities away from the insured location; there are also some significant exclusions, such as the one for bodily injury and property damage arising from business pursuits.

personal loss • a loss of earning power because of premature death, disability, periods of unemployment, or superannuation as well as the extra expenses associated with injuries or periods of sickness.

personal property • any item normally contained in a dwelling, such as furniture, appliances, and clothing, and items stored in a garage, other structure, or outdoors.

physical attending • using one's body to communicate. The five basic attributes associated with physical attending are (1) face the other person *squarely,* (2) adopt an *open* posture, (3) *lean* toward the other person, (4) maintain good *eye* contact, and (5) be *relaxed* while attending (SOLER).

pitch • a measurement of how close together the dots of a computer monitor screen are. These dots are used to form the images seen on the screen.

PLUS loan • see *Parent Loan for Undergraduate Students.*

power of appointment trust • a type of trust that qualifies for the federal estate tax marital deduction. It is designed to distribute income to the surviving spouse during his or her lifetime and provides the surviving spouse with a general power of appointment over the trust property. The general power of appointment may by exercisable in all events or only at the death of the surviving spouse; the trust's assets are included in the surviving spouse's estate.

power of attorney • a right giving the holder of the power (the attorney-in-fact) the ability to represent the grantor of the power (the principal) in specifically enumerated transactions; among the possible transactions is the ability of the attorney-in-fact to transfer property for the principal.

preemptive right • a right typically held by common stockholders that allows them to maintain their relative voting power by purchasing shares of any new issues of common stock of the corporation.

present value of a single sum • an amount determined by discounting a future value at a particular rate for a particular length of time. The basic formula is $PVSS = FVSS/(1 + i)^n$, where $FVSS$ is the future value of a single sum, i is the periodic rate expressed as a decimal, and n is the number of periods during which discounting occurs.

principle of indemnity • the cardinal principle of insurance, which states that a person may not collect more than his or her actual loss in the event of the occurrence of an insured peril.

pro forma • projected. Pro forma financial statements represent the planner's best estimate of what those statements will look like at a future point in time.

probate estate • the estate of a deceased individuals, containing all assets passing by will or intestacy.

problem investment • an investment that is not reaching its expected level of performance. The investor must decide whether to retain or sell a problem investment, depending on the estimate of the investment's future performance.

product/policy replacement • the process of terminating a life insurance policy and buying another. Although it can be beneficial for a client, *replacement* often refers to situations in which the salesperson generates commissions by actions that work to the client's detriment.

professional • a person engaged in a field that requires specialized knowledge not generally understood by the public, a threshold entrance requirement, a sense of altruism, and a code of ethics.

property loss • a type of loss resulting from damage to one's own property. Property losses include direct losses, which are associated with the need to replace or repair damaged or missing property, and indirect losses, which are consequences from direct losses (such as additional living expenses caused by a direct loss).

prospectus • a document that gives a potential buyer the relevant information about a newly issued security. Under the federal laws that regulate security transactions, it must be delivered to security buyers before a purchase takes place; it must include tables showing the amount of all loads and other expenses associated with the purchase, holding, and sale of a mutual fund's shares.

purchasing-power (inflation) risk • the risk that the value of an investment asset or the income earned from it will not increase at a rate greater than or equal to the rate of inflation, which would lead to a decrease in the purchasing power of the dollars invested in or earned on the asset. Investments most susceptible to this risk include all fixed-dollar investments, such as savings accounts, certificates of deposit, bonds and other debt instruments, life insurance cash values, and fixed annuities; assets that tend to provide greater protection against this risk include real estate and business ownership interests, such as common stock.

pure risk • the chance of loss, for example, the chance that fire will destroy one's home. This is different than the term *risk* used in investments, which involves the chance of gain or loss.

PVSS factor • when determining the future value of a single sum, the PVSS factor is $1/(1 + i)^n$, where i is the periodic interest rate expressed as a decimal and n is the number of periods during which compounding occurs.

PVSS • see *present value of a single sum.*

QTIP marital deduction trust • a type of trust in which qualifying terminable interest property (QTIP) willed to a surviving spouse qualifies for the marital deduction; the executor of the deceased spouse's estate must elect QTIP treatment on the estate tax return. The trust can be funded by probate assets or other types of testamentary dispositions. The surviving spouse must have the right to all income annually from the QTIP for life; the property is included in the surviving spouse's estate.

qualified retirement plan • a type of employer-sponsored retirement plan, in which the contributions are made on a before-tax basis and the employer can take a current tax deduction. The employee pays no income tax on the funds until they are distributed from the plan; investment earnings on plan assets are also tax-deferred. In addition, the distributions from such plans may qualify for special tax treatment.

question bombardment • a faulty questioning technique in which the counselor asks two or more questions without giving the client a chance to respond.

RAM (random access memory) • the main memory of the computer, where the computer temporarily stores programs and data while it is working with them.

rapport • a relationship marked by harmony or accord. Rapport between a financial planner and client can be aided by the planner's friendly, interested concern; an unhurried, leisurely pace; an accepting, nonjudgmental attitude; attentive, active listening; and an egalitarian relationship.

real after-tax rate of return • the rate of return on an investment when both taxes and inflation are factored in. If the rate of inflation exceeds the after-tax rate of return obtained over a holding period, the investor realizes a negative real after-tax rate of return.

reflection of feeling • a type of response during active listening that enhances communication. One shows understanding of the speaker's experience by responding to the speaker's feelings, which may be stated directly or only implied (nonverbalized). By paraphrasing the speaker's feelings, one enables the speaker to get in closer touch with those feelings and facilitates working through the problem.

replacement cost • a term used in many property insurance contracts, referring to the cost of repairing or replacing a damaged asset. For personal property, *replacement* means replacement with a comparable asset at the current price.

replacement ratio method • a method of determining how much annual income an individual will need in the first year of retirement. This method assumes that the standard of living during the years just before retirement should be the determining factor for the standard of living during retirement; therefore, it is easier to use with those who are near retirement. In general, a 70 to 90 percent replacement ratio of an individual's preretirement income is used for retirement planning purposes because of lowered taxes and changes in spending after retirement.

residual disability • condition representing a partial recovery from total disability. Under disability income insurance policies, a typical definition might state that an insured with residual disability can engage in his or her regular occupation or another occupation, but because of the accident or sickness, the insured's income has been reduced by at least 20 percent. Also see *partial disability.*

restatement of content • a type of response during active listening that enhances communication. By paraphrasing what the speaker has just said, one encourages the speaker to delve more deeply into the situation by showing they are "on the same wavelength."

retirement income deficit • any shortfall between the amount an individual planning for retirement has and the amount needed to achieve the individual's goals.

reverse annuity mortgage • a mortgage that allows an individual to take some equity out of his or her house without having to leave the home. In one type of reverse annuity mortgage, the individual sells a remainder interest in the house but retains the right to occupy the home until death, at which time the purchaser of the remainder interest takes possession; the purchaser must make periodic payments to the seller during his or her life. In the second type, the annuity payments plus interest are held as a series of loans against the value of the house; the amount paid out plus interest is recovered by the lender from eventual sale proceeds after the death of the retiree.

revocable life insurance trust • a type of trust designed to own and/or be the designated beneficiary of life insurance coverage on the grantor's life. Because the trust is revocable, the insured is treated as the owner of the policy and the death proceeds are included in the insured's gross estate. The revocable life insurance trust is an excellent method for providing life insurance benefits for the protection of young children or for young children following a divorce.

risk analysis • the first step in the risk management process. It consists of three parts: the identification of risks, the measurement of losses associated with identified risks, and evaluation of the potential financial effects such losses would have.

risk avoidance • a loss-control technique, consisting of the elimination of a given activity or condition that gives rise to a risk. This method makes the possibility of a loss nonexistent, but it can be extremely difficult to achieve.

risk management • the systematic process of risk analysis and control. This process was originally developed for business applications, but it has been modified for use in the discovery and treatment of risks facing individuals and families. The process includes three steps: risk analysis, risk-treatment planning, and risk-treatment plan implementation.

risk retention • the process of financing or paying for one's own losses. It may be financed formally, with funds set aside and earmarked for a particular risk, or informally, with funds taken from a savings account or simply out of pocket. Retention is also practiced with the use of insurance, because deductibles, exposure to loss by causes excluded under an insurance contract, and exclusions on losses to certain types of property or coverage on certain types of loss all result in the retention of some risk.

Roth IRA • a type of individual retirement account in which after-tax contributions are required, but earnings and distributions after age 59½ are not taxed. Roth IRAs also have other characteristics that make them more beneficial that traditional IRAs for many people.

rule of 72 • a quick method of estimating how long it will take for an amount to double in value at various compound interest rates. In this method, the number 72 is divided by the applicable interest rate expressed as a whole number. The quotient is the approximate number of periods until the amount doubles.

SEC Release No. IA-770 • a 1981 pronouncement from the Securities and Exchange Commission that set forth three separate tests (advice or analyses about securities, business standard, and compensation test) to determine whether the Investment Advisers Act of 1940 applies to a financial services professional's activities.

SEC Release No. IA-1092 • a 1987 pronouncement from the Securities and Exchange Commission that reaffirmed the three-prong approach set forth in IA-770 and clarified certain antifraud and full disclosure provisions of the Investment Advisers Act of 1940.

Sec. 1231 asset • a type of asset that receives different tax treatment depending on whether the asset is sold at a gain or at a loss. If sold at a gain, the gain is treated as a capital gain; if sold at a loss, the loss is treated as an ordinary loss, not a capital loss, and can be deducted against the taxpayer's ordinary income. The assets that receive this tax treatment include all depreciable property as well as land used in the taxpayer's business.

Sec. 2503(b) trust • a type of irrevocable trust created by a donor during his or her lifetime to receive gifts to a minor that qualify for the annual gift tax exclusion. The trust income must be distributed at least annually to or for the benefit of the minor donee; trust principle is distributed to the minor whenever the trust agreement specifies.

Sec. 2503(c) trust • a type of irrevocable trust created by a donor during his or her lifetime to receive gifts to a minor that qualify for the annual gift tax exclusion. The trust income and principal must be distributed to the minor at age 21; however, the trust can accumulate current income until the trust terminates.

security • as used in interpreting the Investment Advisors Act of 1940, one of many financial instruments, including stocks, bonds, certificates of deposit, commercial paper, limited partnerships, variable annuity products, investment contracts, and numerous others.

security analysis • the process of evaluating securities in order to make investment recommendations and decisions. It typically includes an analysis of the economy and its direction, the industry under consideration and its direction, and the characteristics of the firm under consideration.

simple annuity or annuity due • an annuity or annuity due in which the frequency of payments and the frequency of compounding or discounting are identical.

simple interest • interest computed by applying an interest rate to only an original principal sum.

single-premium whole life insurance • this is the most extreme form of limited-payment life insurance, in which one premium payment is made at the inception of the contract.

single-purpose view of financial planning • the position that the selling of a single financial product or service to a client in order to solve a single financial problem constitutes financial planning.

sinking fund payment • a type of financial problem in a future sum is achieved by contributing a series of equal payments. The future sum, the number of payments, and the compound interest rate are known and the size of the payments must be determined.

small adviser exception • an exemption to the Investment Advisers Act of 1940; it applies to investment advisers who, during the preceding 12 months, have had fewer than 15 clients and who neither present themselves to the public as investment advisers nor act as investment advisers to any investment company registered under the Investment Company Act of 1940. Such investment advisers need not register with the SEC, but must still comply with the Investment Advisers Act's antifraud provisions.

social security • the Old-Age, Survivor's, Disability, and Health Insurance program of the federal government; an important source of retirement income.

software • any part of a computer that cannot be seen or touched. The most important software consists of computer programs. A computer program may be stored on a floppy disk, in the computer memory, or on magnetic tape; the medium that holds the program (software) is hardware.

special form of homeowners policy • a type of homeowners insurance policy that provides the broadest possible coverage available on dwellings. It is written on what is called an "all-risk" basis, meaning that a loss is covered unless it is specifically excluded from coverage in a list specific to the special form or in an additional list common to all homeowners policy forms. Also called *Form HO-3*.

special power of appointment • a limited right to make property decisions; the holder of such a right can transfer the property subject to the power to a limited class of potential recipients.

specialist view of financial planning • see *single-purpose view of financial planning*.

speculation • an effort to obtain a high return in a short period of time by purposely buying and selling tangible or intangible assets whose value is very uncertain over the next few days, weeks, or months.

spousal IRA • a type of individual retirement account that allows up to an additional $2,000 in annual savings and the opportunity to split contributions to meet retirement needs and to receive tax-favorable distribution. It can be set up even if the spouse has received no compensation during the tax year.

Stafford loan • this type of loan is the major source of education borrowing from the federal government; such loans are available directly from the federal government through the Direct Loan Program, or through the Family Federal Education Loan Program from participating banks, credit unions, and other lenders. This type of loan may be subsidized (for students with financial need) or unsubsidized (available even to those with no need under the aid formula), and must be repaid within 10 years.

standard deduction • a fixed amount that may be claimed as an income tax deduction instead of itemizing deductions. The amount of the standard deduction depends on the individual's filing status.

straight life (ordinary life/continuous premium) policy • a type of whole life insurance policy, in which the premium-payment period is the entire length of the contract (that is, as long as the insured is alive.)

subchapter S election • an election certain corporations can make in which corporate income is "passed through" to the shareholders for taxation purposes. With this election, shareholders are taxed on their proportional interest in the corporation's taxable income and the corporation is treated for tax purposes very much like a partnership (that is, not subject to income tax at the entity level).

subrogation • a process in insurance whereby the insurer is substituted for the insured for the purpose of claiming indemnity from a third person for a covered loss. Once the insurance company pays a loss to an insured, the insurer takes over the rights of that insured to recover from a third party for the loss.

summarization • a type of response during active listening that enhances communication. Summaries can focus and capsulize a series of scattered ideas to present a clear perspective. Summarization permits both the speaker and listener to gauge the accuracy with which messages have been sent and received.

supervised person • defined in Section 202(a)(25) as a partner, officer, director (or other person occupying a similar status or performing similar functions), or employee of an investment adviser, or other person who provides investment advice on behalf of the investment adviser and is subject to the supervision and control of the investment adviser.

supplemental executive retirement plan • a type of nonqualified retirement plan in which the employer provides a second tier of retirement benefits in addition to any qualified benefits (which are not at their maximum legal limits).

tax avoidance • the reduction of tax liability through reasonable interpretation of the tax laws.

tax basis in an asset • the amount that the taxpayer has invested in the property. It generally equals the amount the taxpayer paid for the property, plus the cost of improvements to the property, if any. This basis is subtracted from the amount realized when the asset is sold to determine how much of the sales proceeds is taxable.

tax credit • a dollar-for-dollar reduction, authorized in the Internal Revenue Code, of the actual tax payable. It is of more value to the taxpayer than a deduction of an equal amount.

tax evasion • the reduction of tax liability by ignoring or flouting the tax laws.

tax risk • the risk of adverse changes in tax law relating to income from and appreciation in value of an investment asset or the transfer of asset ownership.

taxable entity • a taxpayer under the federal income tax system that is not an individual person, such as a trust, estate, or corporation. (However, a corporation that makes the subchapter S election is not a taxable entity.) Special tax rules and tax rates apply to each of these types of entities that do not apply to individual taxpayers.

taxable income • the amount of income that is actually subject to tax in a given year.

tax-exempt transaction • a transaction that produces a monetary benefit for the taxpayer with no taxation for the taxpayer. One example of a tax-exempt transaction is the receipt of income from a public purpose municipal bond, which is excludible from the taxpayer's gross income for federal income tax purposes.

tax-preference item • an item that is deductible under the regular tax system but is not deductible under the alternative minimum tax (AMT) system.

technical analysis • a type of analysis involving the examination of current market prices, trading volume and direction, and other trends in the marketplace as a means of predicting the future direction of security prices; typically used as a basis for making investment recommendations and decisions.

temporary substitute auto • under the PAP, an auto used by the insured when a covered auto is out of normal use because of breakdown, repair, servicing, loss, or destruction.

tenancy by the entireties • a type of joint concurrent ownership of property restricted solely to spouses; it is a joint ownership of property by the spouses with rights of survivorship. The property is transferred automatically to the surviving spouse at the time of death of a joint tenant. The property is therefore not subject to disposition by will of a deceased spouse; in addition, the property cannot be transferred during the lifetime of the spouses unless both tenants consent. Tenancy by the entireties is severed automatically upon divorce.

tenancy in common • a type of joint concurrent ownership of property, in which two or more individuals (tenants in common) each hold an undivided interest in the property and may transfer their interest during their lifetime or at their death. There are no survivorship rights; both related and unrelated individuals may hold property by tenancy in common.

term interest • a type individual of property ownership that provides the current tenant with the right to possess, enjoy, and receive income from the property during a specified term; the interest of the current tenant ends at the end of the specified term.

term life insurance • a type of life insurance that provides coverage for a limited period or time. If the insured dies during that period, the specified amount is paid to the designated beneficiary; if not, the policy expires and all obligations of the insurance company terminate. The premium rate increases as the insured's age rises. This type of life insurance is well suited to situations where there is a temporary need for protection.

testamentary trust • a trust created under the will of the testator. It does not receive property until the grantor dies and property is transferred to the trust by the executor. Because a testamentary trust is contained in the grantor's will, it is subject to probate.

thrill seeker • the personality type most likely to be consistently risk seeking in all aspects of life, including financial matters.

top-hat plan • a type of nonqualified retirement plan in which the employee defers part of his or her salary for retirement purposes. Also called a *pure deferred-compensation arrangement.*

total disability • the meaning of this varies among different disability income insurance policies. Under the *any occupation* definition, insureds are considered totally disabled when they cannot perform the major duties of any gainful occupation for which their education, training, or experience makes them reasonably suited. Under the *your occupation* definition (which is less restrictive), insureds are considered totally disabled when they cannot perform the major duties of their regular occupations.

Totten trust • a bank account set up by an individual (generally a parent or grandparent) in trust for a named individual; at the death of the account holder, this property passes automatically by operation of law to the named beneficiary.

true-auction market • a market in which investment assets—such as artwork, collectibles, or real estate—are offered for sale to the highest bidder. The bidding continues until no one exceeds the last bid price; then the sale is consummated.

tuition account program • a state-sponsored college funding program. Approaches vary, but a typical one might allow purchase of college tuition hours at current prices, locking in the cost years in advance; the implied investment return is not taxed as income until the tuition benefit is claimed or funds are otherwise distributed.

UGMA/UTMA gifts • gifts made under the Uniform Gifts to Minors Act (UGMA) or Uniform Transfers to Minors Act (UTMA), which permit the transfer of funds to a custodial account for the benefit of a minor. Such transfers are particularly favorable for smaller gifts because assets are protected without the expense of administration of a trust.

umbrella liability policy • insurance policy that provides excess liability limits over underlying liability coverage limits and, in most cases, broader coverage than the underlying policies. Agreed-upon limits of the underlying coverages must be maintained. The umbrella policy also covers situations not covered by underlying insurance policies, such as personal injury in the form of libel, slander, and invasion of privacy. It does contain some exclusions, such as those for intentional acts and damage to the insured's own property.

unconditional positive regard • an attitude of valuing the client, or being able to express appreciation of the client as a unique and worthwhile person.

underinsured motorists coverage • under the PAP, coverage that provides payment to the insured when the at-fault driver or owner has liability insurance at least equal to the financial responsibility limit but less than the limit carried by the insured. This benefit becomes an excess amount over the at-fault party's liability insurance up to the amount of the loss or maximum limit carried by the insured.

ungrouped cash flow • a cash-flow sequence that includes no consecutive payments of the same amount and arithmetic sign (positive or negative).

uninsured motorists coverage • under the PAP, this coverage provides that if an insured sustains bodily injury (and in some states, property damage) in an auto accident in which the other driver was at fault but was uninsured, the insured may recover from his or her own insurance company those sums to which he or she is legally entitled.

unit-benefit formula • the most popular way of specifying employee retirement benefits for a defined-benefit pension plan. This type of formula takes both length of service and salary into account.

universal life insurance • a type of flexible-premium life insurance. The policy requires a stipulated premium payment during the first year of coverage; afterward, the policyowner may pay whatever amounts at whatever times he or she wishes, or even skip payments, as long as the cash value is large enough to cover required policy charges. Two death-benefit designs are available; the policyowner may also change the face amount of the policy.

variable annuity • a type of annuity that provides a variable periodic payment to the annuitant; the size of the payment depends on the performance of an underlying investment portfolio, typically common stocks.

voice pitch • highness or lowness of a voice on a musical scale; a nonverbal behavior. A high-pitched voice may indicate anxiety, fear, or anger; a low-pitched voice may indicate comfort or control of strong emotions.

voice tone • loudness or softness of voice; a nonverbal behavior. Talking loudly or shouting may indicate anger or hostility; talking very softly may indicate fear or shyness.

whole life insurance • a type of life insurance that provides for payment of the policy's face amount upon the death of the insured regardless of when death occurs. The premium remains constant throughout the premium-payment period of the contract, leading to a buildup of the policy's cash value.

"why" question • a type of question that should generally be avoided, because asking "why" tends to question the client's motivation, or lack of it, and thus creates a certain defensiveness. "Why" questions carry with them a connotation of implied disapproval, forcing the client to justify or defend his or her thoughts, ideas, or actions.

yield to maturity • the internal rate of return for a bond, that is, the rate that would discount the coupons and par value to equal the price of the bond.

zero coupon bond • a bond that does not make an annual interest payment to the bondholder but has a built-in automatic compounding of interest over its life. Examples include U.S. Government Series EE bonds and selected issues of corporate, government, and municipal bonds.

Index

Editor's note: A lowercase *n.* following a page number refers the reader to a note on said page. Thus "249 n. 15" refers to note 15 on page 249.